# LEGAL COUNSELING, NEGOTIATING, AND MEDIATING: A PRACTICAL APPROACH

# LEGAL COUNSELING, NEGOTIATING, AND MEDIATING: A PRACTICAL APPROACH

## Second Edition

G. Nicholas Herman
*Adjunct Professor of Law, NCCU School of Law*
*Senior Lecturer in Law, Duke Law School*
*Adjunct Professor, Elon University*

Jean M. Cary
*Professor of Law, Campbell University School of Law*

2009

ISBN: 978-1-4224-2262-5

| **Library of Congress Cataloging-in-Publication Data** |
| --- |
| Herman, G. Nicholas. |
| Legal counseling, negotiating, and mediating : a practical approach / G. Nicholas Herman, Jean M. Cary. |
| p. cm. |
| Includes index. |
| ISBN 978-1-4224-2262-5 (casebound) |
| 1. Attorney and client--United States. 2. Negotiation in business--United States. 3. Dispute resolution (Law)--United States. I. Cary, Jean M. II. Title. |
| KF311.H4654 2009 |
| 340.023'73--dc22 |
| 2009021369 |

Editorial Offices
121 Chanlon Rd., New Providence, NJ 07974 (908) 464-6800
201 Mission St., San Francisco, CA 94105-1831 (415) 908-3200
www.lexisnexis.com

MATTHEW ◆ BENDER

(2009–Pub.1154)

# DEDICATIONS

This book is dedicated to:

Mrs. Bette Bower

— GNH

George W. Danser

— JMC

# PREFACE

Most of the literature on legal counseling, negotiating and mediating falls into one of three categories: the academic literature, the practice literature, or the lay literature. The academic literature, largely drawn from the disciplines of psychology, economics, and sociology, is often highly conceptual and theoretical. The practice literature is largely based on professional experience and thus is usually too anecdotal and devoid of pertinent ethical and legal ramifications. The lay literature, particularly on negotiating, is typically aimed at providing general advice about how to improve one's interpersonal relationships and negotiate in everyday affairs. Within all three categories, albeit to varying degrees, there are many works that are insightful, thought provoking, and useful.

However, a common criticism of much of the literature is that, upon close reading, what often sounds good and even may be quite interesting, frequently is not very helpful in terms of teaching one *how* to engage in effective legal counseling, negotiating, and mediating. For example, notable exceptions aside, a good bit of the academic literature is quite difficult to understand and tends to supplant reality with heuristic simulations of limited utility. Similarly, the practice literature often places too much reliance on personal "war stories" that are not representative of the most common situations encountered in practice, and the lay literature tends to be dominated by general shibboleths and postulates that are often too abstract to apply in a meaningful way. Thus, there is a need to heed these criticisms to take a more understandable, realistic, and practical approach in writing about legal counseling, negotiating, and mediating.

This book tries to do that. In writing it, we have kept in mind two obvious facts. First, the topics at hand are, at bottom, "practical skills" that are integral to effective legal representation. Second, while most law students will become practicing lawyers, some will become judges, academicians, or use their law degree in business or other professions. Therefore, in writing about legal counseling and negotiating (including negotiating during mediation and plea bargaining), we have, first and foremost, sought to be eminently practical in our descriptive and prescriptive treatment of these skills, including their ethical and legal ramifications. At the same time, we have sought to encourage broader and more creative thinking about these subjects by discussing some of the more important theoretical approaches to them. That is, notwithstanding the difficulty of achieving the best balance among theory, practice, ethics, and law, this book addresses all to try to close the gaps in between. In treating these matters, however, the overall effort has been to emphasize that blend of theory, practice, ethics, and law that is most *meaningful* in the sense of having real-life application to effective client representation.

— GNH
— JMC

# ACKNOWLEDGMENTS

The authors gratefully acknowledge the following persons for their review of various portions of this book: Jane Wettach; Mark W. Morris; Walter Nunnallee; Dickson Phillips; Richard J. Snider; and Caroline Thatcher.

The authors also acknowledge the permissions granted to reproduce excerpts from the following:

ABA Model Rules of Professional Conduct, 2008 Edition. Copyright © 2009 by the American Bar Association. Reprinted with permission. Copies of ABA Model Rules of Professional Conduct, 2008 Edition are available from Service Center, American Bar Association, 321 North Clark Street, Chicago, IL 60654, 1-800-285-2221.

# Table of Contents

# Table of Contents

# Table of Contents

# Table of Contents

# Table of Contents

# Table of Contents

# Table of Contents

# Table of Contents

# Table of Contents

# Table of Contents

# Table of Contents

# Table of Contents

# Table of Contents

# Table of Contents

# INTRODUCTION

# Chapter 1

## LEARNING LEGAL COUNSELING AND NEGOTIATING

**SYNOPSIS**

**§ 1.01 THE IMPORTANCE OF LEGAL COUNSELING AND NEGOTIATING**

**§ 1.02 "LEARNING BY DOING" AND THE ROLE OF THIS BOOK**

## § 1.01 THE IMPORTANCE OF LEGAL COUNSELING AND NEGOTIATING

Courses in legal counseling and negotiating, sometimes called "Interviewing, Counseling and Negotiating" (ICN), are viewed by some law professors as "soft" courses in contrast to harder courses in doctrinal or statutory law such as constitutional law, torts, property, civil procedure, criminal law, contracts, and the like. This may be true in the sense that, while courses in substantive law require you to learn complex legal rules whose proper application to myriad factual situations often depends upon rigorous legal analysis and an appreciation of nuances in the law and the facts, courses in legal counseling and negotiating generally do not focus on these matters. Instead, the focus is on learning and applying the processes and techniques (including pertinent ethical and legal considerations) that effective lawyers use in advising their clients and helping them to resolve their legal problems or disputes without litigation. As such, legal counseling and negotiating courses are sometimes thought of as being heavy on "how to" mechanics and light on intellectual substance.

However, it is a mistake to think that legal counseling and negotiating involve purely mechanical skills that are separable from knowledge of the substantive law and intellectual legal skills. This is because your knowledge of the law and ability to engage in legal analysis largely shape the content of your advice to a client and your representation in negotiations. Legal counseling and negotiating courses thus do not intend to downplay knowledge of the law and legal-reasoning skills, but are taught with the assumption that you will actively use the intellectual skills you are acquiring in substantive-law courses as you learn legal counseling and negotiating. In this way, a legal counseling and negotiating course brings the practical application of these intellectual skills to the actual practice setting. The intent is, as it is often said, to help "bridge the gap between theory and practice."

The importance of legal counseling and negotiating is underscored by the fact that most lawyers spend more time on these matters than on any other single category of legal work. It is estimated that of the total time that lawyers spend in handling disputes for individual clients, approximately 43.9% is devoted to matters directly related to legal counseling and negotiating (with 16.0% being devoted to conferring with the client, 12.8% devoted to factual investigation, and 15.1% devoted to settlement discussions). In contrast, the remaining 56.1% of lawyers' time is typically spent on wholly separate categories of legal work, such as conducting legal research (10.1%), drafting pleadings (14.3%), engaging in discovery (16.7%), attending trials or hearings (8.6%), engaging in appeals (0.9%), and performing miscellaneous legal work (5.5%).[1] Thus, for most lawyers, legal counseling and negotiating constitute the most prevalent aspects of client representation.

## § 1.02 "LEARNING BY DOING" AND THE ROLE OF THIS BOOK

In broad terms, "counseling" involves establishing a counseling relationship with your client, interviewing and obtaining information relevant to the decision to be made by your client, analyzing the decision to be made, advising your client about the decision, and implementing the decision. "Negotiating" involves the processes and techniques used in trying to resolve your client's disputes or common problems with another party in order to reach a satisfactory agreement. The counseling function is, of course, integral to representing your client in negotiations.

The best way to learn the skills, concepts, and processes of counseling and negotiating (including plea bargaining, which is covered in this book) is to "just do it," under the guidance and critique of your professor and fellow students. This "learning by doing" approach, also used in teaching trial practice and other practical skills such as taking depositions, has achieved wide-spread recognition, particularly from the success of programs sponsored by the National Institute for Trial Advocacy,[2] a non-profit educational organization that conducts continuing legal education programs in practical skills for lawyers throughout the country.

This book is designed for use in connection with this "learning by doing" approach. The main text will provide you with the processes, concepts, and techniques involved in counseling and negotiating, along with illustrations of how various concepts and techniques may be applied. The Appendices contain role plays that may be used in conducting simulated counseling and negotiating sessions from which you can develop your own effectiveness in these practical skills.

---

[1] *American Bar Association Section of Legal Education and Admissions to the Bar, Report of The Task Force on Law Schools and the Profession: Narrowing the Gap, Legal Education and Professional Development — An Educational Continuum,* 40 (1992).

[2] National Institute for Trial Advocacy (NITA), Notre Dame Law School, Post Office Box 6500, Notre Dame, Indiana 46556-9974; 800-225-6482; Fax 219-282-1263; nita.1@nd.edu; Web site: www.nita.org

# PART I
## COUNSELING

# Chapter 2

# OVERVIEW OF THE COUNSELING PROCESS AND DECISION-MAKING MODELS

## § 2.01   WHAT IS "COUNSELING"?

Clients come to lawyers for all sorts of reasons. A client might want you to prepare a will, handle a closing on the purchase of a home, or incorporate a new business. A client might ask you to draft a piece of legislation, a contract, or an employee handbook. A client might be in trouble, as when she has been charged with a crime, has been fired from her job, or faces a bitter divorce. A client might seek your services because she has been sued, or because she wants to file a lawsuit to seek redress for personal injuries or some other damages she has sustained. A client might want to hire you to serve as her agent in a transaction, negotiator in a business deal, or spokesperson before a city council or other public body. Or a client might simply want to talk with you about the potential legal ramifications of a particular situation or plan of action. In short, a client might call upon you to serve in any number of roles — as draftsman, advocate, litigator, agent, dealmaker, negotiator, spokesperson, or general advisor.

Regardless of the particular services you are called upon to render for a client, you will always also serve as a "counselor" to your client. That is, in the course of every representation, you will engage in an ongoing process of advising and consulting with your client to the end of helping her understand and deal with her legal situation or problem. This is what is meant by "counseling" and by the designation used on the letterhead of many attorneys that identifies them not only as "Attorneys" but also as "Counselors At Law."

## § 2.02  AN OVERVIEW OF THE COUNSELING PROCESS

Generally speaking, the process of counseling is a five-step process of decision-making. It also includes the process of orally gathering information from your client through interviewing. The overall process involves five interrelated functions that culminate in taking a course of action on behalf of your client. In outline form, these functions call upon you to:

(1) Establish a Professional and Interpersonal Relationship with Your Client by:

- Establishing rapport with your client through a relationship of trust, confidence, and comfort;
- Establishing the nature and scope of the representation;
- Understanding the division of authority between you and your client in making decisions affecting the representation;
- Establishing attorney's fees for the representation, or financial eligibility for unpaid legal services.

(2) Obtain Information Relevant to Your Client's Situation and Potential Courses of Action by:

- Interviewing your client about the facts of the situation and her underlying interests, needs, concerns, and feelings;
- Understanding your client's views about the issues involved;
- Exploring your client's objectives, and potential legal theories;
- Conducting any necessary factual investigation;
- Conducting any necessary legal research.

(3) Analyze Potential Courses of Action by:

- Identifying potential courses of action for achieving your client's objectives;
- Evaluating the legal and non-legal pros and cons of each potential course of action;
- Comparing the various courses of action and your client's objectives in light of the risks and costs involved.

(4) Advise Your Client about Potential Courses of Action by:

- Explaining your client's legal rights and the legal ramifications of each potential course of action;
- Advising your client about the relative benefits, risks, and costs of each potential course of action;
- Discussing with your client the probabilities of the various outcomes and the legal and non-legal consequences of each potential course of action.

(5) Decide Upon the Course of Action to be Taken and Implement the Course of Action by:

- Arriving at a decision with your client about what course of action will be taken;
- Explaining the means and process by which you will implement the course of action;
- Explaining your client's responsibilities and role in implementing the course of action;
- Consulting with and advising your client throughout the process of implementing the course of action.

It is important to bear in mind that this counseling process continues throughout the entire representation. Although, in some situations, all of the five functions outlined above might be covered in a single meeting with a client (*e.g.*, where a client hires you merely to prepare a boilerplate instrument in a routine transaction), in the majority of cases you will be counseling your client over a period of time. Counseling often occurs through numerous meetings and phone conversations with your client, and through opinion letters, other correspondence, or e-mail.

In most cases, and particularly where litigation is involved, there will be numerous decisions that will have to be made during the representation. Changes in circumstances will present additional courses of action to be explored, analyzed, explained, decided upon, and implemented. Decisions or courses of action that were previously agreed upon may have to be modified or abandoned altogether. In sum, your role as counselor to your client spans the entirety of the representation — from the time of the initial client meeting to the conclusion of the representation.

## § 2.03   DECISION-MAKING MODELS

Studies have shown that clients give the highest ratings to lawyers who have a high level of interpersonal skills.[1] Clients consistently rate lawyers who have excellent relational skills as being more competent, effective, and worthy of recommendation to future clients than lawyers who have poor interpersonal skills. Indeed, clients consider the interpersonal skills of a lawyer as being a more important measure of lawyer effectiveness than knowledge of the law, advocacy skills, or even the results of the representation.[2]

In part, the extent of your interaction with your client and the interpersonal skills you employ with your client in counseling and interviewing are shaped by how you strike the balance between your client's control over the legal representation and your control over it. In other words, who should be in charge of the representation? Who should be responsible for making which decisions? Who should control the objectives of the representation? Who should control the means? To what extent should control over the representation be shared between you and your client? The answers to these questions turn upon what decision-making model of counseling the lawyer chooses to adopt.

In his 1974 book, *Lawyer and Client: Who's in Charge?*, Douglas Rosenthal sets forth two models about the distribution of control in legal representation. One model, which he calls the "traditional" model, vests primary control with the lawyer. The other model contemplates a sharing of control between lawyer and client over most decisions affecting the representation. Since the publication of Rosenthal's book, academicians have variously identified and debated different models of lawyer counseling from the standpoint of legal ethics and practical-skills instruction. Out of this discourse, essentially three models or approaches have emerged. For purposes of clarity, these approaches may be called the "Lawyer-Centered Model," the "Client-Centered Model," and the "Collaborative Model."[3]

---

[1] *See* Stephen Feldman & Kent Wilson, The Value of Interpersonal Skills in Lawyering, 5 Law & Hum. Behav. 311 (1981).

[2] Id. *See also* Robert F. Cochran Jr. et. al., *The Counselor-At-Law: A Collaborative Approach to Client Interviewing and Counseling* 2, 58–59 (1999).

[3] For other general discussions about counseling models, *see* Robert F. Cochran, Jr. et. al., *The*

## [1] The Lawyer-Centered Model

Under the "lawyer-centered model" of counseling, the client essentially delegates to the lawyer primary responsibility for problem solving and decision-making in the representation.[4] The lawyer has broad autonomy and authoritarian control over the professional relationship, and the client's role in the representation is largely passive.[5] Some scholars have likened the lawyer's role under this model to that of "Guru," where the client is a disciple of the lawyer-master, or to that of "Godfather," where the lawyer parentally shoulders the entire burden of the client's legal situation.[6] The somewhat dogmatic nature of this approach to counseling is exemplified by the remarks of Judge Clement Haynsworth who told a law school graduating class:

> [The lawyer] serves his clients without being their servant. He serves to further the lawful and proper objective of the client, but the lawyer must never forget that he is the master. He is not there to do the client's bidding. It is for the lawyer to decide what is morally and legally right, and, as a professional, he cannot give in to a client's attempt to persuade him to take some other stand . . . . During my years of practice, . . . I told [my clients] what would be done and firmly rejected suggestions that I do something else which I felt improper . . .[7]

The lawyer-centered model has been widely criticized as being inconsistent with client dignity and the intrinsic value of client self-determination. It has also been criticized as being inconsistent with studies that have shown that active client participation in the representation may lead to results more satisfying to clients.[8] In addition, a rigid application of the lawyer-centered model may run afoul of Rule 1.2(a) of the American Bar Association's Model Rules of Professional Conduct, which mandates that "[a] lawyer shall abide by a client's decisions concerning the objectives of the representation . . . and shall consult with the client as to the means by which they are to be pursued." (*See* § 6.03). Finally, from the standpoint of interpersonal relations, lawyers who adopt an inflexible lawyer-centered approach to counseling may be viewed by many clients as being dogmatic, paternalistic, condescending, and overbearing. In addition, interpersonal interaction between the lawyer and client is often circumscribed because of the lawyer's largely unfettered control over decision-making.

---

*Counselor-At-Law: A Collaborative Approach to Client Interviewing and Counseling*, Chapters 1 and 9 (1999); Paul J. Zwier & Anthony J. Bocchino, *Fact Investigation: A Practical Guide to Interviewing, Counseling, and Case Theory Development*, Chapter 6 (2000); Thomas L. Shaffer & Robert F. Cochran, Jr., *Lawyers, Clients, and Moral Responsibility*, 3-54 (1994); David A. Binder, et. al., *Lawyers as Counselors: A Client-Centered Approach*, Chapter 2 (1991); Judith L. Maute, Allocation of Decision-making Authority Under the Model Rules of Professional Conduct, 17 U.C. Davis L. Rev. 1049 (1984); John Basten, Control and the Lawyer-Client Relationship, 6 J. Legal Prof. 10 (1981).

[4] *See* Paul J. Zwier & Anthony J. Bocchino, *Fact Investigation: A Practical Guide to Interviewing, Counseling, and Case Theory Development* 143 (2000).

[5] Douglas E. Rosenthal, *Lawyer and Client: Who's in Charge?* 2 (1974).

[6] *See* Thomas L. Shaffer & Robert F. Cochran, Jr., Lawyers as Strangers and Friends: A Reply to Professor Sammons, 18 U. Ark. Little Rock L. J. 30-39, 5-14 (1995); Thomas L. Shaffer & Robert F. Cochran, Jr., *Lawyers, Clients, and Moral Responsibility* 3-54 (1994).

[7] Clement F. Haynsworth, Professionalism in Lawyering, 27 S.C.L. Rev. 627, 628 (1976).

[8] *See* Douglas E. Rosenthal, *Lawyer and Client: Who's in Charge?* 36–46 (study showed that plaintiffs who were actively involved in their cases obtained higher settlements and verdicts than plaintiffs who allowed their lawyers to control the representation).

On the other hand, in many circumstances, the lawyer-centered model is entirely consistent with the expectations that clients place upon lawyers. After all, clients seek out lawyers for their expertise in the law and their objective professional judgment about what legal rights and remedies are available in a particular situation. If a legal course of action is available, many clients expect — and will even direct — that their lawyers "take charge of the case" and assume responsibility for critical decision-making during the representation. In short, it is as common for clients to grant to their lawyers broad control over the representation, as it is common for patients to grant to their physicians broad control over the most appropriate course of medical treatment. When this allocation of decision-making control over the professional relationship is made with the informed consent of the client, whether out of the client's deference to the lawyer's expertise or by virtue of the client's express directive to the lawyer, there is nothing wrong with taking a *limited* lawyer-centered approach to counseling, so long as that approach is not taken to extremes and does not violate the Rules of Professional Conduct.

## [2]    The Client-Centered Model

The "client-centered model" may be viewed as being at the opposite end of the theoretical spectrum from the lawyer-centered model. According to the leading proponents of this model, "the client-centered conception 'fills in' the traditional [lawyer-centered] approach by stressing that problems have non-legal as well as legal aspects, and by emphasizing the importance of clients' expertise, thoughts and feelings in resolving problems. In a client-centered world, [the lawyer's] role involves having clients actively participate in identifying their problems, formulating potential solutions, and making decisions."[9]

Accordingly, under this model, the lawyer (1) helps identify problems from the client's perspective, (2) actively involves the client in the process of exploring potential solutions, (3) encourages the client to make those decisions which are likely to have a substantial legal or non-legal impact, (4) provides advice based on the client's values, (5) acknowledges the client's feelings and recognizes their importance, and (6) repeatedly conveys a desire to help.[10] The approach expressly requires that the lawyer develop and employ a high level of interpersonal skills and interpersonal interaction with the client.

Because the client-centered model places a premium on "the autonomy, intelligence, dignity and basic morality of the individual client,"[11] the model espouses a professional relationship that is distinctly client dominant and aimed at providing the client with "maximum satisfaction."[12] The client is given primary decision-making power throughout the representation, and the lawyer is obligated to make every reasonable effort to accede to the client's decisions about the ends and means of the representation. Some scholars have likened the lawyer's role in this relationship to that of a "hired gun," where the lawyer's primary job is to

---

[9] David A. Binder, et. al., *Lawyers as Counselors: A Client-Centered Approach* 18 (1991).

[10] Id. at 19–22.

[11] Id. at 18.

[12] Id. at 261.

achieve the autonomous wishes of the client regardless of the effects of the representation upon third persons.[13]

In terms of how legal advice should be given, although the client-centered model does not eschew giving legal advice, it discourages lawyers from "taking the lead" in rendering opinions about the proper decision the client should make.[14] Instead, the model calls upon the lawyer to engage the client, somewhat like a psychotherapist, in an advice-giving dialogue, through which the client is psychologically encouraged to "find herself" in the representation and arrive at decisions that she feels and comes to believe are her own. For example, the leading text on the client-centered model illustrates this approach in the following counseling dialogue:

| | |
|---|---|
| Lawyer: | Next Diana, why don't we turn to the question I asked you to think about, whether to insist on a personal [financial] guarantee from the officers [of the company]? |
| Client: | I've been thinking about it a lot, and I'm still not sure what to do. What do you suggest? |
| Lawyer: | I hate to sound like a lawyer, but there's not one right answer. A lot depends on the unique circumstances of your situation. What I suggest is this. Let's discuss the likely pros and cons both of having and not having personal guarantees. We'll even prepare a chart of the likely consequences. If you still want my opinion after we've done that, I'll certainly give it to you. But by postponing my view, I'll be able to take what you say into account in giving you my opinion. Does that sound all right? |
| Client: | That sounds like it'll take some time, and frankly I don't want to devote the time or money to it. You're a lawyer, and I'm sure you've come across these situations lots of times. I'll go along with what you think is best. |
| Lawyer: | I'm not sure that I know what's best. But you tell me if I'm wrong. My sense is that your primary objective is for this deal to go through and that you feel the company itself is pretty solid. If I'm right about those things, probably you're better off not insisting on personal guarantees. Is that a decision you're comfortable with? |
| Client: | [I don't know.] I know we've gone round and round on this, but I just can't decide. What do you think I ought to do? |

---

[13] *See* Thomas L. Shaffer & Robert F. Cochran, Jr., *Lawyers, Clients, and Moral Responsibility* 15-29 (1994).

[14] *See* David A. Binder, et. al., *Lawyers as Counselors: A Client-Centered Approach,* Chapters 15 and 20 (1991).

Lawyer: Well, I agree that it's time to cut bait on this one. In the abstract, either decision might be proper, so primarily my advice grows out of what you've said as we've talked. I know your accountant has advised you to get personal guarantees, and I don't want to come between you and her. You can tell me if I'm wrong, but what you've indicated is that your primary objective is for this deal to go through, and that you feel the company itself is pretty solid. Also, you have some fear that insisting on guarantees might sour this deal and soil future business opportunities. Based on these feelings, I think you'd be best off not insisting on personal guarantees. Does that seem sound? . . . .[15]

The principal features of the client-centered model — considering problems from the client's perspective, involving the client in exploring potential solutions, encouraging the client to participate in the decision-making process, and recognizing the importance of the client's views, values, and feelings — are certainly essential to effective counseling and effective representation. On the other hand, if the client-dominant *process* of the client-centered approach is taken to an extreme, it may deprive the client of the very *substance* she seeks from her lawyer: an objective and candid assessment of her situation, uninhibited advice as to what she can do about it, and — consistent with her expectations and informed consent — an appropriate level of attorney control over the representation.

## [3] The Collaborative Model

The "collaborative model" of counseling represents a middle ground between the lawyer-centered model and the client-centered model but still leaves primary decision-making control with the client. The leading proponents of this model explain its features and benefits as follows:

We believe that the authoritarian [lawyer-centered] model provides too small a role for clients, the client-centered approach provides too small a role for lawyers, and that clients will be best served when lawyers and clients resolve problems in the law office through collaborative decision making. Under this model, the client would control decisions, but the lawyer would structure the process and provide advice in a manner that is likely to yield wise decisions.

This model would be likely to avoid the problems of the authoritarian [lawyer-centered] model. The client's control of the decisions would ensure client dignity. It would also be likely to yield superior results to the authoritarian [lawyer-centered] model. [Douglas] Rosenthal found that the more varied forms of client participation and the more persistently the client employed them, "the better his chances of protecting his emotional and economic interests in the case outcome." We share Rosenthal's call for lawyers and clients to engage in "mutual participation in a cooperative relationship in which the cooperating parties have relatively equal status,

---

[15] Id. at 348–349. *See also* David A. Binder, et al., *Lawyers as Counselors: A Client-Centered Approach* at 368–371 (2d ed. 2004).

are equally dependent, and are engaged in activity 'that will be in some ways satisfying to both [parties].' "

A collaborative client counseling model would also avoid the weaknesses of the client-centered counselors. It would provide the lawyer and client with an opportunity to consider the effects of their decisions on other people. It would provide the flexibility to counsel the client in a wide variety of ways. Finally it would enable the client and lawyer to engage in a collaborative deliberation that would be likely to yield practical wisdom.[16]

Some scholars have analogized the lawyer's role under the collaborative model to that of being a "friend" to the client, where the lawyer acts as a listener, sounding board, clarifier, evaluator, and caring advisor.[17] Through these attributes, the lawyer employs and imparts "practical wisdom" for his client and helps her to exercise "practical reason" in decision-making.[18] Of course, the collaborative model of counseling and the role of the lawyer as a professional "friend" require that the lawyer employ a high level of interpersonal skills. In general, in the view of the authors of this book, the collaborative model is descriptive of the most balanced decision-making approach in most cases.

## [4]    Using Different Decision-Making Models

It should be apparent from the foregoing discussion that to use any single counseling model in all situations would be inappropriate. There is simply no "one-size-fits-all" approach to legal counseling. Insofar as counseling is essentially a process of decision-making, the most appropriate model to employ in a particular situation will depend largely upon the type of decision to be made, taking into account (1) the particular needs and expectations of your client, (2) the particular subject matter of the representation, and (3) your particular role in the representation — whether as draftsman, advocate, litigator, agent, dealmaker, negotiator, spokesperson, or general advisor. Moreover, different models may be appropriate to employ at different stages of a particular representation because there will usually be different kinds of decisions to be made and different functions that you will have to perform during the representation.

For example, from the standpoint of *decision-making control*, the lawyer-centered approach may be appropriate when your client expressly requests that you take unilateral action in the representation, when an emergency arises that requires you to preserve your client's rights and there is no time for consultation, when your client is under a disability and it is necessary to take some action to protect her interests (*see also* § 6.06), or when the decisions to be made are technical or tactical in nature, such as decisions relating to drafting, procedure,

---

[16] Robert F. Cochran, Jr., et. al., *The Counselor-At-Law: A Collaborative Approach to Client Interviewing and Counseling* 6–7 (1999).

[17] *See* Paul J. Zwier & Anthony J. Bocchino, *Fact Investigation: A Practical Guide to Interviewing, Counseling, and Case Theory Development* 145–152 (2000); Thomas L. Shaffer & Robert F. Cochran, Jr., *Lawyers, Clients, and Moral Responsibility* 40–54, 113–134 (1994); Anthony T. Kronman, *The Lost Lawyer: Finding Ideals of the Legal Profession* 131 (1993); Thomas D. Morgan, Thinking About Lawyers as Counselors, 42 Fla. L. Rev. 439, 453 (1990).

[18] *See* Robert F. Cochran, Jr. et. al., *The Counselor-At-Law: A Collaborative Approach to Client Interviewing and Counseling* 7, 176–182 (1999); Anthony T. Kronman, *The Lost Lawyer: Failing Ideals of the Legal Profession* 14–17 (1993).

trial tactics or trial strategy (*see also* § 6.03). On the other hand, collaborative or client-centered counseling would be essential when making decisions such as whether to file a lawsuit, whether to accept a settlement offer (*see also* § 9.02), or whether your client in a criminal case should plead guilty, waive her privilege against self-incrimination and testify at trial, or appeal a conviction. As a matter of ethics, your client is the only person who can make final decisions on these types of matters (*see* §§ 6.03 and 19.06). A collaborative or client-centered approach may also be most appropriate when deciding what offers or counteroffers to make in negotiations, when you are called upon to serve as an intermediary between clients who consult you on a matter that affects both of them (*see also* § 6.08), when deciding what claims or defenses to raise in a lawsuit, or when deciding how to structure a new business enterprise. In short, different counseling approaches are warranted in different situations.

## § 2.04   COUNSELING TO PREVENT HARM TO THE CLIENT AND OTHERS

The preceding discussion has focused on how you strike the balance between your client's control over the representation and your control over it. Closely intertwined with this question is an even more controversial question: the extent to which you should assert power over your client to protect her from herself, or to protect others from her. For example, if your client insists on a course of action that you believe will seriously harm her personal or legal interests or will do serious injury to the legitimate rights of a third person, to what extent should you try to intervene and prevent the harm?

Guidance in answering this question is, in some circumstances, addressed by obligations imposed upon you by the Rules of Professional Conduct discussed in Chapter 6 of this book. For example, if your client insists on pursuing a course of action that would be unlawful or would cause you to violate a rule of professional conduct, you may have to withdraw from the representation (*see* § 6.11). If your client becomes afflicted by a disability such that you reasonably believe she cannot adequately act in her own interests, the ethical rules allow you to seek the appointment of a legal guardian or take other unilateral protective action on behalf of your client (*see* § 6.06). Generally, however, these types of circumstances are rare.

The more common situation occurs when your client wants to pursue a course of action, which, though not unlawful or unethical, is contrary to your best judgment and is likely to pose grave consequences for her or otherwise cause serious harm to the legitimate rights or interests of others. For example, if you represent a mother in a custody case who, without *any* rational or arguable legal basis, is determined to deprive the father of all visitation rights with their young child, the mother's attitude and position are not only likely to undermine her chances of being awarded sole custody in the eyes of a judge, but may also cause serious harm to the child. In situations such as these, short of seeking your client's permission to withdraw from the representation, what should you do?

One scholar has posited three different roles that are worthy of consideration in this regard: the lawyer as "Guide," "Governor," or "Guardian":

> The guide's role is to take the client wherever the client wants to go. This
> role is not limited to that of a technician; it includes also those of explorer,

strategist, and counselor. The guide maps out options and assists the client to clarify the client's thinking and feeling about the options. When asked, he gives advice as to which option he believes to be most consistent with the client's expressed objectives, simply clarified. The guide has no will apart from the client's will except to serve the client's will.

The governor's role is to limit where the client may go, in order to prevent the client from trespassing on the legitimate interests of others. The governor respects the client's wishes completely, unless and until they lead the client to choose a course of action that the governor believes will violate some standard of justice or fairness that is owing to third parties or to the body politic. Then, the governor restrains the client from acting on the choice.

The guardian's role is to promote the client's best interest. Unlike the governor, the guardian is unconcerned with protecting the interests of other people insofar as they conflict with the client's. Unlike the guide, the guardian exercises independent judgment in determining what the client's interests are. He considers the client's choices as a relevant factor, but overrules them if he thinks that they are wrong.[19]

In situations where your client's decision to pursue a particular course of action would be injurious to her or cause unjust injury to others, the Guide-Governor-Guardian roles basically indicate two options. First, you could adopt the role of Guide, in which case you would support and advance your client's decision regardless of the injurious consequences. Second, you could adopt the role of Governor or Guardian, in which case, as Governor, you would overrule any decision that would unjustly injure the rights or interests of third persons, or, as Guardian, you would overrule any decision that would be injurious to your client's best interests.

The problem with the first option is that, by simply acquiescing to your client's undesirable decision, your representation may result in harming her rather than helping her, and you might compound the overall damage by senselessly harming others as well. The problem with the second option is that, by simply overruling your client's undesirable decision, you will effectively supplant your proper roles as representative and advisor to your client with the roles of master and dictator over her.

The obvious third option is that you could engage in collaborative counseling and seek to persuade your client not to pursue the injurious decision. This is the most appropriate approach. It avoids dictatorial decision-making by you, preserves client dignity and client self-determination, and enhances the prospect that your client will recognize that your advice to pursue an alternative course of action is genuinely being given to advance her best interests based upon your objective professional judgment and expertise. As a practical matter, in the vast majority of situations, you will find that such efforts at persuasion will be successful, particularly if undertaken patiently and persistently.

In the end, if your efforts at persuasion are unsuccessful, you will have to decide whether to (1) nevertheless accede to your client's harmful course of action, or (2)

---

[19] Anthony G. Amsterdam, "Handling a Problem Situation," in Materials for NYU School of Law's Lawyering Course 26 (1988).

withdraw from the representation under the Rules of Professional Conduct, which permit withdrawal if your client "insists upon pursuing an objective that [you] consider repugnant, imprudent, or contrary to [your] advice and judgment" (*see* § 6.03). As between these choices, your decision will no doubt be largely governed by the severity of the harm you believe will occur if you proceed to advance your client's undesirable course of action. If the harm is likely to be substantial, withdrawal from the representation may be appropriate, so long as your withdrawal would not create an even greater harm to your client. After all, your fundamental role is to help your client, not to harm her. If your client is unwilling to benefit from your independent professional judgment, your ability to effectively represent her will become extremely difficult, if not impossible.

It is essential to emphasize, however, that withdrawal from representation is a drastic option that should only be considered in the most serious situations. From the standpoint of professional ethics, you are generally required to abide by your client's decisions concerning the objectives of the representation (*see* § 6.03). While this obligation applies regardless of the subject matter of the representation, it is particularly acute in criminal cases where, for example, a lawyer may never overrule a criminal defendant's knowing, intelligent, and voluntary decisions about matters affecting "fundamental" constitutional rights such as whether to plead guilty, waive a trial by jury, testify at trial, or appeal a conviction (*see* Id.). Thus, whenever your client decides upon a course of action that you believe will be substantially injurious, and you are unsuccessful in persuading her to adopt an alternative course of action, you generally should only seek to withdraw from the representation if doing so would not work a greater injury to her than would occur if you proceeded to implement her undesirable decision (*see also* § 6.11).

## § 2.05   A CARING PERSPECTIVE ON COUNSELING

Caring about your clients can make you a better lawyer. Clients typically need your guidance and counsel on matters affecting critical rights and interests that have a significant impact on their personal well-being. A client who believes that her lawyer actually cares about what happens to her often feels more comfortable with and confident in her lawyer, and that comfort and confidence will help lawyer and client work together more effectively. For all the celebration in the popular media of the lawyer as "hired gun," most clients would prefer to have their matters handled by someone who cares.

Adopting a caring perspective does not mean that you become enmeshed in all of a client's personal issues. You are not trained in psychotherapy, and you are not being paid for that service. A caring perspective does mean, however, that you see yourself as trying to help others, in part because you want to make their lives a little better. Such a perspective entails a degree of personal involvement. While not all lawyers can care about all clients in all contexts, the more you can care about your clients the more satisfied they are likely to be with your services. In addition, caring about your clients is likely to leave you more satisfied with yourself over the course of your career.

## § 2.06  PATIENCE IN COUNSELING

Finally, consistent with the interpersonal nature of the counseling process and the importance to your client of the decisions to be made and actions to be taken, you must be patient in your role as counselor. This means that you must not only take the time to be thorough in the counsel you give, but you must also take the time to be thorough in obtaining and considering all information that may be pertinent to your counsel. As proponents of the client-centered approach emphasize, you should make a deliberate effort to understand your client's situation from her perspective, involve her in exploring potential solutions, and encourage her to appropriately participate in the decision-making process. After all, as between you and your client, your client is always the ultimate owner of her legal situation or problem. What you own is the unique professional capacity to help her deal with it, and this helping role can be most effectively accomplished if your client is integrally involved in the representation.

# Chapter 3

# THE INITIAL CLIENT MEETING

## § 3.01  OBJECTIVES OF THE INITIAL CLIENT MEETING

For a new client, the initial client meeting marks the beginning of the attorney-client relationship. At this meeting, your objectives include:

(1)  Putting your client at ease and developing rapport;

(2)  Interviewing your client to get a basic factual picture of his situation;

(3)  Explaining the attorney-client privilege, if appropriate;

(4)  Obtaining a sense of your client's objectives;

(5)  Determining whether representing your client would constitute a conflict of interest;

(6)  Making a decision about representing your client and establishing the nature and scope of the representation;

(7)  Giving your client appropriate preliminary advice;

(8)  Establishing an initial course of action;

(9)  Establishing attorney's fees and other financial obligations for the representation; and

(10)  Making arrangements for follow-up conferences and communication with your client.

19

It is important to keep in mind that the first meeting with a new client is only an *initial* meeting that will be followed by further client conferences. You and your client may have to meet a number of times before a final decision can be made about whether you will represent him and what that representation will entail. Moreover, even if it is decided at the initial meeting that you will represent your client, it is not uncommon for the scope of the representation to be initially limited to obtaining additional information or conducting further investigation before you and your client will be in a position to fully analyze and decide upon a course of action. Final decisions about the ultimate nature and scope of the representation may not be made until the second or third meeting with your client. Thus, in most cases, the initial client meeting is only the starting point of your representation and role as counselor to your client.

This chapter provides an overview of how you go about accomplishing the principal objectives of the initial client meeting in the context of the counseling functions outlined in § 2.02, in which you "Establish a Professional and Interpersonal Relationship with Your Client" and "Obtain Information Relevant to Your Client's Situation and Potential Courses of Action." Chapter 4 provides specific techniques for client interviewing, which is a major component of the initial meeting and subsequent client conferences, and concludes with an illustration of an attorney-client dialogue during an initial client meeting and interview. Chapter 5 discusses the three remaining functions of the overall counseling process outlined in § 2.02 that call upon you to: "Analyze Potential Courses of Action;" "Advise Your Client about Potential Courses of Action;" and "Decide Upon the Course of Action to be Taken and Implement the Course of Action." That chapter concludes with an illustration of an attorney-client dialogue during a decision-making meeting.

## § 3.02  HANDLING THE INITIAL PHONE CALL FROM YOUR CLIENT

New clients, or existing clients who have a new legal matter, rarely walk into your law office to see you unannounced. Typically, the client will initially contact your office by telephone to make an appointment. Lawyers usually handle this initial contact in one of two ways.

First, some lawyers use their secretary or a paralegal to "screen" all in-coming calls from prospective clients. The secretary or paralegal briefly talks with the client, determines the general nature of the client's situation or legal problem, and, if the particular matter falls within the lawyer's area of practice, advises the client about any consultation fee for the initial meeting and sets up an appointment for the client to see the lawyer. One drawback to this approach is that there is no personal contact between the lawyer and the client before the initial meeting. Simply "signing up" the prospective client for an appointment is impersonal and affords no opportunity for the lawyer to get any sense of the client's particular situation. In addition, in the absence of having some conversation with the client before the initial meeting, the lawyer cannot determine whether there is some immediate action that must be taken to protect the client, or whether it would be useful for the client to take some interim action or obtain certain information before coming to the initial meeting.

Consequently, under the second approach, the lawyer will either personally "screen" all phone calls from prospective clients, or, if an appointment for the client has already been set up by a secretary or paralegal, the lawyer will phone the client in advance of the meeting to briefly discuss the client's situation. In this way, the lawyer can obtain a general understanding of the nature of the client's matter in advance of the initial meeting, determine if a statute of limitations is about to run, provide the client with any emergency advice if necessary, and instruct the client about any information that he should obtain in the interim and bring with him to the meeting.

Having a short phone conversation with the prospective client before the initial meeting will help you and the client be better prepared for it and help to ensure that the status quo is preserved until the two of you are able to meet. In light of what the client tells you over the phone, you might also be able to conduct some preliminary legal research or review certain documents that the client sends you in advance of the meeting. Most importantly, this personalized phone contact will go a long way in helping to build rapport with the client.

It is important to remember, however, that an initial phone conversation with the prospective client is not the time to hear his entire story or to decide whether you will represent him. Your goal is simply to find out just enough information to confirm your willingness to meet with him, and to determine whether he needs any immediate advice to protect his interests before you are able to meet. At times, you will discover in the initial phone conversation that, for one reason or another, you will be unable to help the client with his particular situation. When that occurs, you can explain that you do not believe a meeting would be useful, and, if appropriate, refer him to another lawyer or some other person who might be able to help him. If you have determined that legal action on his behalf is time sensitive, explain to him the urgency of obtaining legal advice before the expiration of the critical time period.

## § 3.03   BEGINNING THE MEETING AND DEVELOPING RAPPORT

In representing any client, it is important to develop a relationship that is marked by close rapport. You want your client to trust you, have confidence in you, and be comfortable with you. You want him to see you as being honest, straightforward, dependable, competent, diligent in your legal services, and as being a person with whom he feels comfortable in interacting. Developing this rapport of trust, confidence, and comfort begins with the first impressions you create when you greet your client and sit down to begin the initial meeting.

In greeting a client, the most personable approach is to greet him in your law office's reception area and personally escort him to the office or conference room where you will hold the initial meeting. Introduce yourself by using your first name, shake hands, and address your client by first name if appropriate. Be on time for the appointment. Even if you are only a few minutes late, apologize for the delay.

If a friend or family member accompanies your client, remember that the attorney-client privilege generally does not extend to confidential communications between an attorney and client that are made in the presence of third persons. Therefore, exchange any pleasantries with your client's friend or family member in your reception area, but do not invite any third person to attend your private meeting with your client unless there is a special need for the third person's attendance.[1]

Every effort should be made to keep the meeting free from unnecessary interruptions or distractions. Accordingly, make sure your secretary holds all telephone calls, and do not permit other persons to enter the room during the meeting unless absolutely necessary. It is essential that your client have your undivided attention throughout the meeting.

At the outset of the meeting, it is sometimes appropriate to engage in some "small talk" to put your client at ease. Some clients will be anxious or nervous at the beginning of the meeting, and some friendly "chit chat" usually helps to start the meeting on easy ground. However, be careful not to get carried away with this type of "ice breaking." In most situations, after exchanging a few pleasantries, many clients are perfectly content to "get down to business" right away.

If there is a particular time constraint on the meeting (*e.g.*, the appointment is scheduled for only one hour), you might mention the time constraint at the outset so that your client is not caught by surprise when the allotted time draws to a close. Tell your client that your overall objective for the initial meeting is to get a basic understanding of his situation and to find out whether you might be able to help him.

## § 3.04  INTERVIEWING YOUR CLIENT TO GET A BASIC FACTUAL PICTURE OF YOUR CLIENT'S SITUATION

Once your client is at ease, you should open the meeting with a general question that invites him to tell his story and explain why he has come to see you. For example you might ask:

- *How can I help you?*
- *What can I help you with?*
- *What can I do for you?*
- *So, what brings you here today?*

Asking this type of opening question marks the beginning of your interview with your client. The process and techniques for client interviewing are detailed in Chapter 4. For present purposes, it is important to keep in mind that at this stage of the meeting your primary goal is get a basic factual picture of your client's situation. You want to find out: Why has the client come to see me? What are the basic facts and circumstances of his situation? Is his situation or problem something that I can help him with?

You will enhance your ability to obtain the factual information pertinent to answering these questions if you keep three points in mind. First, avoid interrupting your client at this stage. Let him talk, and let him vent if necessary. Second, encourage him to share his underlying interests, needs, feelings, and concerns about his situation. That is, let him share his story, situation or problem in his own way--from his own perspective. And third, hear what he has to say empathetically

---

[1] Confidentiality under the attorney-client privilege is not waived when communications with the lawyer are made in the presence of family or friends who are reasonably necessary to provide support to the client or who are otherwise necessary to facilitate communication with the attorney. McCormick, *Evidence* § 91 at 335 (4th ed. 1992).

and non-judgmentally. This is the time to patiently *listen* to your client, not to counsel him.

In addition, be sure to ask your client if he has brought any documents with him to the meeting. If so, you might briefly review them before your client talks about them. However, regardless of whether your client has brought with him a contract, a lawsuit, or an indictment, it is imperative that you take the time to listen to your client's situation in his own words. That is, resist any temptation to allow documents to inappropriately control the interview. At the outset, you want to know what your client has to *say* about the matter, not merely what some third person has written about it.

## § 3.05   EXPLAINING THE ATTORNEY-CLIENT PRIVILEGE, IF APPROPRIATE

In obtaining a basic factual picture of your client's situation, you of course want him to be honest with you and to confide in you. Frequently, as where your client has been sued or has been charged with a crime, his situation will be quite embarrassing and stressful. In these circumstances, it is sometimes useful to encourage him to speak freely with you by reminding him that what he tells you is protected by the attorney-client privilege. In particular, most clients do not know that the privilege applies even if you end up not representing the client. (*see* § 6.07).

In practice, many attorneys do not explain the privilege in the initial client meeting. They think clients understand that speaking to an attorney is a confidential communication, or they fear that discussing the privilege may signal that the lawyer believes the client has done something wrong. Other lawyers feel that when the nature of their legal services involves matters such as drafting transactional documents, there is no need for any special discussion of the privilege.

These views are understandable. Mentioning the privilege sometimes does not make sense in terms of the case or the client. On the other hand, it is usually a good practice to include some statement about the privilege at some point during the meeting. One never really knows what a client has to say or hide when he walks through the door. The failure to discuss the privilege at all may even constitute malpractice in some situations. In any event, you don't want your client to unintentionally waive the privilege by disclosing what happened at the meeting to others such that the waiver will come back to haunt you and your client.

If you decide to mention the privilege, be tactful. For example, at an appropriate time during the interview, you might simply allude to the privilege in an offhand way: "Well, as you probably know, everything we speak about in this room is confidential . . . " Expressed in this way, the privilege is mentioned in the context of general privacy concerns without implying that you feel your client is hiding information or is not being completely truthful with you.

## § 3.06   OBTAINING A SENSE OF YOUR CLIENT'S OBJECTIVES

When your client explains his situation, he will often indicate what objectives or goals he has in mind for dealing with his situation and how he thinks they may be accomplished. If he does not, probe his objectives or goals directly. This is important because obtaining a sense of your client's objectives will help you understand his initial expectations of you, and those expectations may be integral to deciding whether you will represent him and what the nature and scope of your representation will be. In probing your client's objectives or goals you might ask:

- *What are your goals?*
- *What do you want to happen?*
- *What do you want to do?*
- *Which of the things you mentioned is more important to you?*
- *What is the most important thing?*
- *How would you rank your concerns in the order of their importance?*
- *Do you have any ideas about how the situation might be resolved?*

Of course, in many instances, your client will be unsure about his objectives and will have little or no understanding about how you might be able to help him. After all, your client's primary purpose in meeting with you will often be to find out what, if anything, you might be able to do for him. Nevertheless, to the extent you are able to obtain at least some perspective from your client about what he would like to accomplish, that information will be useful to you when you engage in the counseling functions of advising him about his options, helping him decide on an appropriate course of action, and when implementing the course of action (*see* Chapter 5).

In addition, having a sense of your client's objectives and his thoughts about how they might be accomplished will often alert you to the importance of his *non-legal* as well as legal concerns. In many cases, you will find that your client's primary goals, interests, or needs relate to matters that the law either cannot resolve or can only partially resolve. For example, a client who has been sued for breach of contract may be far less concerned about the merits of the suit than with the impact that the suit may have on his reputation and business relationships with other customers. A spouse faced with a demand for alimony may be far more concerned about vindicating himself from accusations of marital misconduct than with being able to pay the particular amount of post-separation support sought by his wife. A truck driver who has been given a speeding ticket may be far less concerned with the amount of the fine he would have to pay if convicted than with the effect that a conviction may have on his continued employment. In short, knowing about your client's non-legal as well as legal concerns is critical to understanding the exact nature of your client's situation, which, in turn, may have a critical effect on the objectives and means of your representation.

## § 3.07  DETERMINING THE EXISTENCE OF A CONFLICT OF INTEREST

After you have listened to your client's description of his situation and have some understanding of his objectives, you will usually have enough information to determine whether representing him would create a conflict of interest. The most common conflict-of-interest situations are discussed in § 6.09.

If it becomes apparent that representing the client would be barred by an impermissible conflict-of-interest, you should cut the meeting short and explain to him the general nature of the conflict that disqualifies you from representing him. In explaining this conflict, you should, of course, be careful not to reveal any attorney-client privileged information that may form the basis for the conflict. You should also assure him that you will not disclose to others any information you learned from him up to this point. If your representation would not be automatically barred by a conflict-of-interest but would raise a potential conflict, the applicable ethical rules will only permit you to represent the client if you reasonably believe that your representation will not adversely affect your duties to another client or third person and if the new client consents to the representation after you have fully explained to him all pertinent implications of the potential conflict (*see* § 6.09).

## § 3.08   DECIDING WHETHER TO REPRESENT YOUR CLIENT AND ESTABLISHING THE NATURE AND SCOPE OF THE REPRESENTATION

After conducting a preliminary interview with the client, a decision will have to be made whether you will represent him and what the nature and scope of that representation will be. Establishing a formal attorney-client relationship does not depend on any formality such as a written agreement, but arises upon the client's express or implied request that you act on his behalf and your express or implied agreement to do so (*see* § 6.02). You and your client are generally free to limit the nature, scope, and objectives of the representation to certain legal services and not others. For example, you and the client may agree that you will represent him in the trial of the case but not on appeal, or that you will only represent him on a specific transaction but not on other transactions that may be related to your client's overall situation. Under the rules of professional ethics, whenever you establish the nature, scope, and objectives of the representation, you are required to consult with your client and obtain his consent (*see* § 6.03). In short, you cannot act as the legal representative of a client without having his authority to do so.

In the context of the initial client meeting, when relatively routine legal services are involved (*e.g.*, the preparation of a simple will or deed of trust, representation on a misdemeanor charge, or representation in an uncontested divorce case, etc.), the nature and scope of the representation will usually be easy to agree upon. On the other hand, in many situations, the information you obtain at the initial meeting will be insufficient to allow you and your client to decide upon the exact nature, scope, objectives, and means of the representation at that time. That is, the preliminary nature of the initial meeting often gives rise to the need to obtain additional information, conduct further investigation, and conduct legal research before you and your client can meaningfully discuss potential courses of action and decide upon a course of action that will define the ultimate nature and scope of the representation. For instance, before you agree to sue a doctor for medical malpractice on behalf of your client, you will need to examine your client's medical records and seek an expert opinion about the appropriateness of your client's course of treatment.

Consequently, at the time of the initial client meeting, you and your client may only be in a position to agree upon a limited form of representation, such as an agreement that you will research the applicable law, conduct further factual investigation, and perhaps take certain limited actions to protect or preserve your client's rights. After these tasks are performed, you will meet with your client again to counsel him about potential courses of action, collaborate with him in deciding upon a specific course of action, and begin to implement the course of action. Only then can the precise nature and scope of the representation be clearly established.

If you and your client decide you will represent your client on a limited basis pending further meetings, you should carefully define the scope of your representation by specifying the particular services you will render and confirm the scope of your representation in a follow-up letter. Similarly, if it is decided you will not represent your client at all, it is prudent for you to reiterate that decision in writing. Any ambiguity as to either the existence or scope of the representation will often be resolved in the layperson's favor (*see* § 6.02).

## § 3.09  GIVING PRELIMINARY ADVICE

If you undertake to represent your client for the limited purpose of conducting further investigation or research, it would of course be inappropriate for you to give him definitive legal advice about his situation before you have conducted that investigation or research. Nevertheless, a client will often press you for preliminary advice or a tentative assessment or prediction about the outcome of his situation. Receiving at least *some* preliminary advice is an understandable and legitimate client expectation.

There are essentially three ways in which you can, and should, provide your client with preliminary advice without rendering premature legal opinions about his situation. First, it will often be appropriate to provide your client with certain kinds of "protective" advice, such as advising him not to talk with other persons about the case, instructing him to refer any inquiries he receives about the case from other persons directly to you, or advising him to refrain from taking certain actions pending your next meeting with him.

Second, it may be appropriate to give your client a general overview of some of the legal considerations or legal processes that may affect his situation. For example, in a potential negligence case, you might briefly describe the elements of proof: the existence of a duty of care, breach of that duty, proximate cause of damage, and the types of damages recoverable. If litigation might be involved or your client has been charged with a crime, it may be appropriate to briefly outline the pretrial process, what happens at trial, and the process of taking an appeal. Similarly, it may be appropriate to provide your client with basic legal information about matters that may have to be considered in his situation, such as the statute of limitations for a particular cause of action, statutory guidelines for determining child support, or the maximum sentence for a particular offense.

Third, to the extent the information you obtain during the initial meeting at least indicates the types of options or courses of action that may be pertinent to your client's situation, these can be outlined in a noncommittal way. For example, if your client is interested in starting a new business venture, it may be appropriate to briefly outline the different options of establishing a corporation, a professional association, or a partnership. If your client is a defendant in a civil suit, you might outline various affirmative defenses that may be applicable to his situation. In doing so, however, you should emphasize that your preliminary advice or assessment of the situation is only tentative and is entirely dependent upon the further research and investigation into the situation.

## § 3.10   ESTABLISHING AN INITIAL COURSE OF ACTION

If you have decided to represent your client, before concluding the initial meeting, you should explain (1) what you will do next and when it will be done, and (2) what your client should do next and by when that should be done. As mentioned above, when the ultimate nature and scope of your representation have not yet been established, your tasks might involve researching the law or conducting additional fact investigation. Your client's tasks might include locating certain documents, obtaining other specified information, or even preparing a written account of key events. Appropriately involving your client at the outset of the representation sets the right tone for the attorney-client relationship and marks the beginning of a collaborative approach to the representation.

## § 3.11   ESTABLISHING ATTORNEY'S FEES

Rule 1.5(b) of the ABA Model Rules of Professional Conduct mandates that, except when charging a regularly represented client on the same fee basis or at the same rate, "[t]he scope of [your] representation and the basis or rate of [your] fee and expenses for which [your] client will be responsible shall be communicated to [your] client, preferably in writing, before or within a reasonable time after commencing the representation." (*See also* § 6.10). Your fee might:

(a)   be fixed;

(b)   be calculated on an hourly rate;

(c)   include a retainer in the form of an advance fee payment, where the outstanding balance of the advance is reduced as you perform your services and earn the fee;

(d)   include a nonrefundable retainer; or

(e)   constitute a contingent fee that is calculated as a percentage of the total monetary amount or interest in property recovered for the client (*see* § 9.04).

Regardless of the particular type of fee, you are obligated to inform your client about the rate of the fee or other basis on which it is calculated. With the exception of a contingent fee, which must be in writing (*see* § 9.04), you may communicate the rate or basis of the fee orally or by furnishing your client with a simple memorandum or copy of your customary fee schedule.

Because misunderstandings about fees are a common source of client complaints about lawyers to disciplinary authorities, the best practice is to explain your fee to your client at the initial meeting and then put it in writing. Your explanation and written fee agreement should specify:

(1)   the particular legal services you have agreed to provide your client;

(2)   any limits on the scope of those services, such as whether your representation includes an appeal;

(3)   how the fee will be computed and how your client will be billed;

(4)   any anticipated change in the fee rate in the future, and what different rates will be charged for paralegals or other lawyers who work on the case; and

(5)   what costs and expenses (*e.g.*, for court filings, expert witnesses, investigators, stenographers, transcriptions, photocopying, travel, computer-

assisted research, etc.) your client will be responsible for paying. (*See* § 6.10).

In addition, many clients will ask you at the initial meeting to estimate the total fees and costs you anticipate for the representation. Use your best judgment in providing an estimate, and perhaps provide your client with a range: "I would estimate that total fees and costs will be no less than $10,000 and may be as high as $20,000 depending upon how things go." Always emphasize to your client that your estimate is only a rough approximation that is subject to change depending on the circumstances.

## § 3.12  MAKING ARRANGEMENTS FOR FOLLOW-UP CONFERENCES

Before adjourning the initial meeting, be sure that you have (1) obtained all necessary information about how to contact your client, (2) discussed what tasks you and your client will perform until you confer again (*see* § 3.10), and (3) made at least tentative arrangements for the next conference with your client. In addition, explain to your client your office hours and how he can best contact you during the course of the representation (*e.g.*, by phone or e-mail). This includes explaining the roles of your secretary, paralegal, and any associate attorneys who will be assisting you in handling your client's matter. Emphasize, however, that even though other persons in your law office may be assisting you in the case, your client should not hesitate to contact you directly.

Most attorneys whose fees are based on an hourly rate charge their clients for phone conferences. If this is your practice, make sure your client understands it. At the same time, however, encourage your client to contact you whenever he feels it may be appropriate. Tell him that you are usually able to return your phone calls within 24 hours of receiving them, but that sometimes there may be an additional delay if you are involved in a protracted trial. *Keep your promise about promptly returning phone calls.* Failure to return client calls is one of the leading sources of complaints about lawyers to disciplinary authorities.

## § 3.13  DOCUMENTING THE INITIAL CLIENT MEETING

Your documentation of the initial client meeting should consist of (1) any pertinent documents you have obtained from your client, (2) your interview notes or post-interview memorandum to the client's file (*see* § 4.09), and (3) basic information for contacting the client, including notes about the initial course of action to be taken and any arrangements that have been made for the next client conference. The latter might be documented on a form like the following:

### *New Client Information Form*

Date: _____        File No.: _____

Client name: _____

(Nickname): _____

Legal matter: _____


Home address: _____

Work/business address: _____

E-mail address: _____

Facsimile No.: _____

Preferred address for receiving correspondence:

☐ Home ☐ Work/business ☐ E-mail ☐ Facsimile

Home phone: _____

Work/business phone: _____

Cellular phone/pager: _____

Preferred phone number:

☐ Home ☐ Work/business ☐ Cellular phone/pager

Best time to reach client: _____

Client's legal situation & objectives: _____

_____

_____

Attorney tasks: _____

_____

_____

_____

Client tasks: _____

_____

_____

_____

Deadlines/important dates:_____

_____

Other notes: _____

_____

_____

Next appointment date/contact with client: _____

# Chapter 4

## INTERVIEWING YOUR CLIENT

## § 4.01  INTRODUCTION

Interviewing your client is, of course, a major component of the initial client meeting. As mentioned previously, at the initial meeting, your interview will often be limited to getting only a basic factual picture of your client's situation. Even if an attorney-client relationship is established at the initial meeting, the ultimate nature and scope of your representation may not be decided upon until you have met with your client again and conducted a more in depth interview that is followed by counseling your client about potential courses of action and deciding upon an appropriate course of action.

This chapter discusses the process and techniques for interviewing your client at the initial meeting and during any follow-up meetings. The chapter begins with a brief discussion of certain commonly recognized facilitators and inhibitors of communication that are useful to keep in mind throughout the interviewing process and later when you counsel your client. The chapter concludes with an illustration of an attorney-client dialogue during an initial client meeting and interview.

## § 4.02  FACILITATORS OF COMMUNICATION

Psychologists have identified a number of factors or motivational circumstances that facilitate interpersonal communication.[1] For purposes of legal interviewing and counseling, the most important of these are (1) conveying empathetic understanding, (2) engaging in active listening, (3) encouraging communication through conveying expectations and recognition, and (4) keeping an open mind about what is relevant.

### [1]  Conveying Empathetic Understanding

"Empathy" means identifying with another person's experiences and feelings. It means putting yourself in another person's shoes. Conveying empathetic understanding for your client is important because his feelings about his situation are often just as important as, if not sometimes more important than, the specific events giving rise to his situation or legal problem. Regardless of whether your client expresses his feelings openly, subtly, or not at all, he will have feelings about matters such as how and why his situation occurred, about the people who are involved or affected by his situation, and about what may happen as a result of his situation or legal problem. Conveying empathy for your client will enhance communication because it tends to make him feel more open and comfortable in talking with you.

---

[1] For more expansive discussions about facilitators and inhibitors of communication, *see* G. Goodman, *The Talk Book* (1988); Raymond L. Gorden, *Interviewing, Strategy, Techniques, and Tactics* (4th ed. 1987); David A. Binder, et. al., *Lawyers as Counselors: A Client-Centered Approach,* Chapters 4–5 (1991); Robert M. Bastress & Joseph D. Harbaugh, *Interviewing, Counseling, and Negotiating,* Chapter 8 (1990); Gerard Egan, *You & Me: The Skills of Communicating and Relating to Others* (1977); Gerard Egan, *The Skilled Helper* (3d ed. 1986); Anthony G. Athos & John J. Gabarro, *Interpersonal Behavior: Communication and Understanding Relationships* (1978); Mathew McKay, et. al., *Messages: The Communication Book* (1983); Aron W. Siegman & Stanley Feldstein eds., *Non-Verbal Behavior and Communication* (1987); John L. Barkai, How to Develop the Skill of Active Listening, 30 Prac. Law 73 (1984).

There is no single way to convey empathetic understanding. However, you can show empathy for your client's feelings, personal perspectives, and points of view by, for example:

- Allowing your client to talk without unnecessary interruption;
- Maintaining appropriate eye contact;
- Being closely attentive to what your client is saying;
- Being closely attentive to your client's non-verbal expressions (*i.e.*, body language);
- Encouraging your client to express his feelings, thoughts, needs, interests, and concerns;
- Making responsive statements that acknowledge your client's feelings and concerns;
- Refraining from asking questions about sensitive matters until rapport has been established;
- Expressly stating a willingness to help your client in whatever way you can; and by
- Engaging in "active listening."

## [2]    Engaging in Active Listening

Many lawyers like to talk more than they like to listen. This is an understandable shortcoming. As advisors, lawyers are accustomed to giving advice; and as advocates, they are accustomed to performing and making presentations. Even lawyers who make a conscious effort to listen, often listen only partially and become distracted by thinking about what they want to say or ask next. In addition, many lawyers listen only passively, rarely making any verbal or non-verbal responses to indicate that they have actually heard and understood what the client has said.

"Active listening" is an enhanced method of communication by which the listener (1) is highly attentive to the complete context, content, and feelings expressed by the speaker's verbal and non-verbal behavior, and (2) accepts and acknowledges, in a non-judgmental way, the content and feelings expressed by the speaker by making reflective responses which mirror or capsulize what the speaker is saying and feeling. Active listening is a method of explicitly demonstrating not only comprehension, but also empathy and understanding.

There are five principal ways in which you can enhance communication with your client through active listening:

*(1) Allow your client to tell his story and avoid unnecessarily controlling the conversation.*

*(2) Be attentive to your client's non-verbal cues such as:*

- Tone of voice
- Volume of voice
- Pace of speech (pauses, accelerations, varying rates of speed)
- Body posture
- Eye contact
- Gestures
- Facial expressions

*(3) Be attentive to how your client structures his story by considering matters such as:*

- Where did he begin his story? Where did he end it?
- What parts of the story did your client develop in detail? Which did he gloss over?
- Which parts of the story did he treat as background and which parts did he consider "the main event"?
- How did your client sequence his story? Was it chronological, or in order of matters of importance? Which parts of the story seemed logically connected to one another?
- What parts of the story did he repeat"? Which parts did he omit?

Being attentive to these types of matters may provide you with clues about those things that your client deems most important, those things that he might be reluctant to reveal, and how he thinks and feels about his overall situation.

*(4) Acknowledge what your client is saying by occasionally using short prompts such as:*

"Yes" (or nodding your head, "Yes").

"Please, go on . . . "

"So, then what happened?"

"That's interesting"

"Can you tell me more about . . . ?"

"Uh-uh"; "Mm-hmm"; "I see . . . "

"Oh"; "Really"

*(5) Mirror what your client is saying or feeling by occasionally paraphrasing the essence of his remarks in a non-judgmental way:*

"It sounds like you feel . . . "

"That must have been hard for you."

"You must have been disappointed."

"I imagine that you are relieved by that."

"It seems like you're torn about what to do."

"I can see how that might be troubling . . . I think I can help; but first, can you tell me more about . . . ?"

In employing the techniques in *(4)* and *(5)* above, it is critical not to overuse them. A ritualistic singsong of "Mm-hmm," "I see," "That's interesting," "It sounds like you feel . . . ," "I imagine you were upset . . . ," etc., will come across as forced and fake. Focus on listening *intently*. If you do that, your active listening responses will be spontaneous and natural.

## [3]    Encouraging Communication Through Conveying Expectations and Recognition

Most people tend to act in accordance with the perceived expectations of those with whom they interact. In addition, most people have a strong need for attention and recognition from others. These desires to satisfy expectations and receive attention and recognition are strong motivators that often affect how people communicate.

Accordingly, when interviewing your client, if you explain your expectations about the types of information that would be useful to you in evaluating his situation or legal problem, he may be more forthcoming in providing that information than he would be had you not expressed those expectations. For example, if your client is reluctant to talk about a particular subject, after gently reminding him about the attorney-client privilege (*see* § 3.05), you might explain why that subject is important to talk about in order to fully understand his situation. Moreover, if you give your client "recognition" for his forthrightness in sharing information (*e.g.*, "I know this is difficult for you, but what you are saying is very helpful"), he is likely to continue to be responsive and cooperative in providing important information.

## [4]    Keeping an Open Mind about What is Relevant

For reasons of efficiency and simplicity of legal analysis, lawyers often routinize certain legal services and reduce the facts relevant to them into standard patterns or categories that match familiar types of legal cases. One scholar describes this process as follows:

> [T]he [client] tells a story of felt or perceived wrong to a third party (a lawyer) and the lawyer transforms the dispute by imposing "categories" on "events and relationships" which redefine the subject matter of dispute in ways "which make it amenable to conventional management procedures." This process of "narrowing" disputes occurs at various stages in lawyer-client interactions . . . . First, the lawyer may begin to narrow the dispute in the initial client interview. By asking questions which derive from the lawyer's repertoire of what is likely to be legally relevant, the lawyer defines the situation from the very beginning. Rather than permitting the client to tell a story freely to define what the dispute consists of, the lawyer begins to categorize the case as a "tort," "contract," or "property" dispute so that questions may be asked for legal saliency.[2]

This tendency to reflexively and prematurely categorize the client's legal situation before obtaining all the facts surrounding his story often causes a lawyer to make erroneous assumptions and jump to conclusions about what information from the interview is relevant and what information is mere surplusage. As a result, the lawyer may end up "hearing" only select portions of the client's overall situation and stifle complete communication by discouraging any discussion of facts that she

---

[2] Carrie Menkel-Meadow, The Transformation of Disputes by Lawyers: What the Dispute Paradigm Does and Does Not Tell Us, 1985 Mo. J. Disp. Res. 25, 31 (1985). *See also* Robert F. Cochran, Jr., et. al., *The Counselor-At-Law: A Collaborative Approach to Client Interviewing and Counseling* 39 (1999) (also quoting Professor Menkel-Meadow and calling this process the "hardening of the categories.").

perceives to be irrelevant. In turn, the danger is that the lawyer may end up largely misunderstanding the true nature of the client's legal and non-legal needs.

To guard against this danger, it is important to keep an open mind about what may or may not be relevant when interviewing your client. It is far better to hear your client's entire story than to abbreviate the interview at the risk that essential information (and particularly information that your client deems important) will not be obtained. This open-mindedness will not only enhance communication, but also will build rapport and likely result in more effective representation.

## § 4.03   INHIBITORS OF COMMUNICATION

Just as psychologists have identified various circumstances that facilitate communication, they have identified factors that tend to inhibit full and open communication. In lawyer-client interactions, the most important inhibitors are (1) fears of embarrassment or hurting the case, (2) anxiety, tension, or trauma, (3) etiquette barriers and prejudices, and (4) differing conceptions about relevant information.[3]

### [1]   Fears of Embarrassment or Hurting the Case

Clients often come to lawyers with situations or legal problems that are personally embarrassing or that sometimes cause strong feelings of guilt or shame. For example, a client may have committed a crime for which he has been charged, or neglected a business matter for which he has now been sued. In these types of situations, he may be understandably reluctant to provide complete information about what happened for fear that you will view him negatively.

Similarly, regardless of whether your client's particular situation may produce feelings of embarrassment or shame, he may be reluctant to disclose information that he perceives may somehow "hurt his case" in the sense of producing an adverse outcome. This reluctance to reveal damaging information may also be grounded in a fear that you will consider his case to be a "loser" and decide not to represent him.

Whether your client fears embarrassment or fears that he will hurt his case, complete disclosure of all pertinent facts is, of course, essential to effective representation. Knowing the full extent of your client's participation in the events giving rise to a criminal charge or lawsuit is critical to evaluate potential defenses. Information that may be damaging to your client's cause of action or legal right is important in assessing the merits of his claims and in preparing to counter anticipated defenses or other legal efforts to defeat his plan of action. Neither you nor your client can run or hide from adverse facts. The sooner you know the bad facts, the sooner you can prepare to counter them.

Accordingly, when faced with these communication inhibitors, you should draw upon the communication facilitators of (1) conveying empathetic understanding for your client's difficult situation, (2) engaging in active listening by non-judgmentally accepting and acknowledging his uncomfortable feelings, and (3) encouraging him to communicate by explaining the need for full information and by expressing

---

[3] *See also* David A. Binder, et. al., *Lawyers as Counselors: A Client-Centered Approach* 35–40 (1991); Robert M. Bastress & Joseph D. Harbaugh, *Interviewing, Counseling, and Negotiating* 176–184 (1990).

recognition for his forthright disclosures. In addition, in an appropriate situation, you might once again explain that his confidences are protected under the attorney-client privilege.

## [2] Anxiety, Tension, or Trauma

For the same reasons discussed in the preceding subsection, your client's willingness to communicate may be inhibited due to anxiety or tension. Alternatively, your client may be reluctant to talk about a traumatic event, such as the death of a loved one, a debilitating injury, or the circumstances surrounding the break up of a marriage. Apart from fears of embarrassment or hurting the case, your client may be angry, depressed, or humiliated. Here again, communication is likely to be enhanced if you draw upon the facilitators of empathetic understanding, active listening, and encouraging communication through expectations and recognition.

## [3] Etiquette Barriers and Prejudices

Sometimes your client will be uncomfortable in talking with you about certain matters due to "etiquette barriers"[4] grounded in social norms or conventions. For example, a client may have difficulty talking about intimate matters (such as sex or intimate medical problems with a lawyer who is of the opposite sex. Similarly, the age, social status, or economic status of a client may affect how comfortable he is in talking with a lawyer of a significantly different age or significantly different social or economic status. Depending on the extent of these differences, the client may feel inferior or subordinate to the lawyer or, alternatively, superior and dominant to the lawyer. In short, differences in gender, age, and socio-economic status may sometimes inhibit open communication between you and your client when talking about certain subjects.

In addition, various prejudices, biases, or cultural differences (*see also* § 18.02) may impede communication. Unfortunately, racial or sexual stereotyping may cause a client to be uncomfortable in trusting and interacting with a lawyer who is of a different race or of the opposite sex. A bias against public defenders may cause an indigent criminal defendant to lack initial confidence in his court-appointed lawyer. Even religious, moral, or philosophical differences between client and lawyer may inhibit open communication.

To deal with an etiquette barrier or prejudice that is impeding communication, you can use sensitivity and explanation. That is, tactfully acknowledge the barrier or prejudice and, if necessary, openly discuss the differences between yourself and your client. If the barrier or prejudice relates to the subject matter of the representation, acknowledge the delicacy of the matter and explain to your client that you are accustomed to handling such matters with the confidentiality, respect, and sensitivity they require. If your client still remains uncomfortable talking about the matter, you might consider calling upon an associate lawyer who does not have the same identity differences to interview the client on the particular subject.

---

[4] *See* Raymond. L. Gorden, *Interviewing, Strategy, Techniques, and Tactics* 76–78 (1969).

## [4]    Differing Conceptions about Relevant Information

Clients frequently approach lawyer interviews with preconceived notions about what information is legally relevant to their situations. Indeed, some clients even have strong preconceptions about the exact types of legal remedies or services that would be appropriate to resolve their problem. Consequently, it is not unusual for clients to have conceptions about relevant information that are markedly different from what their lawyers consider relevant. This may make it difficult for a client to see the connection between his lawyer's questions and the client's situation, and make it difficult for the lawyer to understand why the client persists in talking about certain matters that the lawyer thinks are essentially irrelevant to the problem at hand. Either way, communication is impeded.

In dealing with differing conceptions about what information is relevant, as discussed in § 4.02[4], you should always guard against prematurely categorizing your client's legal situation and keep an open mind about the potential relevance of any information that your client wants to impart. At the same time, because the information you begin to obtain during the interview will inevitably alert you to particular legal considerations, you should not hesitate to ask about specific, potentially relevant information that your client does not otherwise gratuitously volunteer to you. If your client appears to be irritated at your seemingly irrelevant questions, simply provide him with a brief explanation of why the requested information may be important to fully understand her legal situation.

## § 4.04   PURPOSES OF INTERVIEWING

As mentioned in § 3.04, your initial purpose in interviewing your client is to get a basic factual picture of his situation so that you can determine whether you can help him. In addition, you need to obtain a sense of his overall objectives — *i.e.*, what he wants to accomplish (*see* § 3.06). If you determine that you may be able to help him, the purposes of your interview become more expansive. Either at the initial meeting or at a subsequent meeting, you must obtain all information pertinent to his situation, objectives, and potential legal theories or courses of action that may be available to accomplish his objectives. Knowing how to ask different types of questions during the interview and how to use effective information gathering techniques can significantly facilitate these purposes.

## § 4.05   TYPES OF QUESTIONS

Knowing how to craft a question to obtain the desired information is one of your most important tools. Most questions can be categorized into five different types: (1) open questions, (2) follow up questions, (3) closed questions, (4) leading questions, and (5) summation questions. In a client interview, you will usually use all five types of questions. Choosing when to use which type depends on the exact information you need and where you are in the information gathering process. Regardless of the particular type of question you use in an interview, it is useful to always keep two rules in mind: first, make your questions as simple as possible; and second, ask only one question at a time.

## [1]   Open Questions

Open questions invite your client to answer with as much information as possible. When you ask your client an open question such as "How can I help you?" you are inviting him to explain in detail why he has sought help. An open question is a broad invitation to convey information. Open questions are not limited in scope or narrowly focused. Open questions are non-judgmental and do not suggest an answer. Instead, they permit your client to choose his own way of responding to and structuring the information requested.

Journalists are taught to ask open questions by beginning most questions in the early stages of an interview with one of the following words: "Who?", "What?", "When?", "Where?", "Why?", and "How?". As lawyers, we can learn much from journalists. They are trained questioners who make a living by efficiently gathering as much information as possible from the people whom they interview. In addition to the journalists' "five W's and an H", as these words are nicknamed, you can add three other phrases to the group: "Please tell me about . . . ," "Describe . . . ," and "Explain . . . ."

For example, assume a client has sought representation in a personal injury case involving a car accident. Contrast the amount of information the lawyer obtains by asking an open question as opposed to a leading question that suggests the answer:

- **Open Question:**

*Q:*          *How can I help you?*

*A:*          *I was injured in a bad car accident. The other driver's insurance company has refused to pay my hospital bills even though the other driver was at fault. My friends suggested that a lawyer might be able to help me get the money I'm owed.*

- **Leading Question:**

*Q:*          *You were in an automobile accident?*

*A:*          *Yes.*

The lawyer who asked the open question learned that (1) the client was injured; (2) the client thinks the other driver was at fault; (3) the other driver was insured; (4) the client's injuries required medical treatment; and (5) the client has discussed his case with friends. The lawyer who asked the leading question learned only one fact: the client was in an automobile accident. Consider another example:

- **Open Question:**

*Q:*          *What happened?*

*A:*          *Well, on December 28th I was driving from my home in North Carolina to visit my mother in Kentucky when a snowstorm came through the mountains of Western North Carolina. The road conditions were treacherous and I was driving really slow. There were all these ice patches on the road, and it was hard to stop without skidding. The car in front of me slowed to a crawl and I slowed down. The guy behind me was driving too fast and plowed into me. That set up a chain reaction. I hit the car in front of me and that car hit the one in front of him. My car was squashed like an accordion.*

- **Leading Question:**

*Q:*          *Your car was damaged in the accident?*

*A:*          *Yes.*

Again, contrast the amount of information the open question elicited as opposed to the single fact the lawyer learned from the leading question. Note that the open question began with one of the journalist's recommended words (*i.e.*, "what"), while the leading question suggested a specific answer. The open question resulted in a paragraph of information, while the leading question resulted in a monosyllabic response.

Open questions are particularly useful at the beginning of an interview because they encourage your client to talk and reveal those things that are most important to him. By allowing your client to control the initial flow of information through his answers to open questions, you are permitting him to vent his feelings as well as the facts relevant to his situation. The rest of the interview will go more smoothly if he has permission to express his feelings early in the interview. If your client is focused on his anger or frustration at what has happened to him and does not have permission to express his feelings, he may not be able to listen to any advice you give later in the interview. If you encourage him to tell you about his case by using open questions, and demonstrate that you are listening carefully to his feelings as well as the facts, he will believe that he has finally been "heard." Once he realizes you are focused on his case and are empathetic to his feelings as well as the facts, he will usually be able to respond to more detailed questions and listen to your advice.

Because your client has permission to choose which information to share in response to an open question, open questions also provide him "recognition" (*see* § 4.02[3]). Your client quickly perceives that you have confidence in his ability to decide what is important and how to structure his story, and this often motivates him to answer more forthrightly and thoroughly.

When asking open questions, avoid using phrases that communicate any limitation on information you seek. If there are no restrictions on the information requested, your client will recount not only what is important to him, but he will also provide more detailed information. Many lawyers unconsciously include limiting phrases such as "a little about," "generally," or "briefly" in their questions. These phrases tend to limit information gathering. They discourage a full recital of events and feelings. Contrast the following open questions with the following limiting questions:

- **Open Question:**

*Q:*          *Why were you traveling to Kentucky?*

*A:*          *My mother was having a difficult time. It was her first holiday after my Dad's death. I hoped my visit would cheer her up. Also, I needed to check on the administration of my Dad's estate before the end of the year.*

- **Limiting question:**

*Q:* Would you tell me a little about why you were traveling to Kentucky?

*A:* To visit my mother.

- **Open Question:**

*Q:* How long is the trip from Durham, NC to Louisville, Ky?

*A:* Well, it can take anywhere from ten to fourteen hours depending on the weather and traffic. In the winter there's the risk of snow and ice. In the summer, they're always tearing up the road somewhere, funneling the traffic to one lane and holding everyone up.

- **Limiting Question:**

*Q:* Briefly, how long is the trip from Durham, NC to Louisville, KY?

*A:* About twelve hours.

Although you may need to ask more pointed or narrow questions later in the interview, at the open-question stage you may want to avoid any limitations of obtaining information.

In addition to asking open questions, you should also use the active listening techniques discussed in § 4.02[2] to keep your client talking. Encourage your client to expansively recount his story by occasionally using the short prompts of "I see," "Mm-hmm," and "Can you tell me more about?" Avoid interrupting your client or seizing control of the interview when your client pauses in his story. In most instances, the unrestricted client will convey information more quickly and in greater depth if he has control over the flow of the story. Your silence at a pause in his story will encourage your client to keep talking. (*See* § 4.06[3].)

In addition to using open questions at the beginning of an interview, you will find that they are useful at the beginning of a new topic. An open question signals your client that you want to know everything about the topic and you trust him to give you that information. For instance, in the car accident case illustrated above, assume you now want to change the subject from how the accident occurred to the injuries your client suffered:

- **Open Question:**

*Q:* Now that we've covered how the accident happened, please tell me about your injuries.

*A:* When the guy behind me hit my car, my head was thrown forward. And then when I hit the car in front, my head was thrown back. I've had to wear this collar since the accident. Also, my right leg was broken when my car hit the car in front.

Although this question is technically not a "question," it acts as an open question by inviting a broad response with the phrase, "please tell me about." Similar phrases such as "please explain" and "please describe" make a sentence into an open question and encourage your client to give you the details on a new topic.

One danger of open questions is that they are not effective with a client who tends to ramble and cannot focus on a coherent story. When this is the case, you will get more information if you ask narrow questions to help your client focus on the subject of the interview. However, you need to guard against prematurely concluding that your client is rambling. Some lawyers who are anxious to "get to the bottom of the problem" assume too quickly that the client is rambling and attempt to seize control by jumping to closed questions before giving the client a chance to fully respond to open questions. This causes the client to edit and limit the information he is sharing.

## [2]    Follow Up Questions

Effective interviewers use pointed or directed follow up questions to clarify a client's series of responses to open questions. These follow up questions seek clarification of subjects raised in the client's initial story. They are more narrowly focused than open questions, but do not suggest an answer. They seek limited information and a short response. Such questions frequently incorporate phrases from the client's previous answer. For example, in the car accident case, the lawyer might ask a series of pointed or directed follow up questions to clarify the information obtained in the client's answers to the open questions asked above:

- **Pointed or Directed Follow Up Questions:**

*Q:*          *What time of day did the accident happen?*

*A:*          *It was late in the afternoon, a little before dark.*

*Q:*          *What lane were you in just before the car following you "plowed" into the rear of your car?*

*A:*          *I was in the far right lane designated for trucks and slow-moving vehicles.*

*Q:*          *Exactly what did you mean when you said the road conditions were "treacherous"?*

*A:*          *Icy, slippery, low visibility.*

Follow up questions build rapport with your client because they convey that you are listening closely to him. If you incorporate into your questions some of the phrases your client has used in his answers, you will communicate to your client that you are paying attention to his story and want to understand him completely. Such attention is comforting and flattering to your client.

The danger of follow up questions is that they tend to shut down your client's expansive answers to open questions. Thus, most effective interviewers stick with open questions until they have heard the basic story. Then they go back through the story with more pointed follow up questions to obtain clarification of important details.

## [3]    Closed Questions

The third type of question is the closed question. These questions are very narrow and seek one or two-word answers. They do not suggest the answer, but they do convey an expectation of brevity to the client. These questions often begin with a verb. They are used to clarify minute details. Examples of closed questions from our car accident case might be:

- **Closed Questions:**

*Q:*          *Were you wearing a seat belt at the time of the accident?*

*A:*         *Yes.*

*Q:*         *Were you alone in the car?*

*A:*         *No, my son was asleep in the back seat.*

*Q:*         *Was he injured?*

*A:*         *Not really. Just a few bruises.*

Although closed questions are extremely useful to clarify details, they will inhibit information-gathering if they are overused or used too early in the interview. They can turn the interview from an in-depth story told by the client into a back-and-forth exchange of short questions from the lawyer followed by short answers from the client.

If you find that your interview has degenerated into labored questioning followed by monosyllabic responses from your client, reflect on the types of questions you have been asking. If you want your client to do more of the talking, release control to him by starting your questions with the reporter words or phrases discussed in § 4.05[1]. That is, if you switch back to using open questions, your client will usually volunteer more information about his case.

## [4]   Leading Questions

Leading questions suggest an answer in the question. They are used to confirm facts that logically flow from the story your client has told. They are a shortcut to gathering information. Examples of leading questions from our car accident case might be:

- **Leading Questions:**

*Q:*         *You were traveling at less than twenty-five miles per hour at the time of the accident weren't you?*

*A:*         *That's right.*

*Q:*         *The car in front of you was also traveling at less than twenty-five miles per hour, isn't that right?*

*A:*         *Yes.*

      . . . . . .

*Q:*         *Your son was the only passenger in your car?*

*A:*         *Yes.*

*Q:*         *It was snowing at the time of the accident?*

*A:*         *Yes.*

Leading questions can be constructed in two ways. In the first method, the lawyer who wants to confirm a fact makes a statement of the fact and adds a tag line that indicates the statement is a question. In the first two examples of leading questions above, the statements occur at the beginning of the questions, and the tag lines of "weren't you?" and "isn't that right?" at the end of the sentence signal your client that he is expected to confirm or deny the stated fact. In the second method of constructing leading questions, the lawyer makes a statement of fact, but uses her voice to indicate that the statement is actually a question. For example, in the third and fourth questions above, the lawyer makes a statement but raises her voice in a questioning manner as indicated by the question mark at the end of the statement.

Either method of asking leading questions will work if the question is confirming a single fact. If you include multiple facts in your question, the answer will be confusing because it will be unclear which fact your client is confirming or denying. For example, if you ask, "Your son was the only passenger in the car, and it was snowing at the time of the accident?" your client's answer of "Yes" might be to the first fact, the second fact, or both facts. Therefore, when asking leading questions, it is essential to limit the inquiry to one fact per question in order to obtain accurate answers.

Occasionally, your leading question will elicit an unexpected response. When this occurs, you will need to pursue the topic with more open questions to understand the response. For example, if you ask the leading question, "You had your high beam headlights on didn't you?" and your client unexpectedly says, "No", you should then pursue the topic with a more open question such as, "Why not?" or "How did you make sure other drivers could see you in the snow?" Your client can then elaborate on his earlier response by explaining, "The visibility was so bad, and I found my high beams reflected off the snow as it fell. I turned on my hazard lights so the guy behind me could see me, but I left my headlights on low beam to minimize the reflection."

You can also use leading questions to give a client permission to admit facts that he may be embarrassed to disclose. For instance, you might recognize that a client does not want to admit that he had been drinking before driving home from a party. Thus you might ask, "Since it was New Year's Eve, I assume you might have had something to drink at the party?" This leading question has given your client an acceptable way to disclose a difficult fact.

In summary, leading questions are useful in an interview for two purposes. First, they are useful to confirm information. Second, they can be used to facilitate a client's admission of an embarrassing or difficult fact. If they are overused or used too early in the interview they may inhibit the free flow of information. Also, if you ask leading questions in a cold or hostile tone, they can also impair the rapport you are trying to establish with your client. Because leading questions are often associated with cross-examination, they should be used sparingly and gently in an interview. Your client will not take kindly to being cross-examined in an interview.

## [5]    Summary Questions

Summary questions list the facts and feelings you have learned from your client in the interview. They are useful to make sure you have understood everything your client has shared. They invite your client to elaborate or explain anything you may have misunderstood or omitted. For instance, in our car accident case, a lawyer might ask the following summary questions:

- **Summary Questions:**

**Q:**        *Now I want to make sure that I have all the facts that show the other driver was at fault. The road conditions were treacherous. You were in the far right lane traveling slowly behind a line of cars that were moving at less than twenty-five miles per hour. You were using your* *hazard lights and your low beam headlights so that you should have been visible to cars behind you. There were icy patches on the road that made driving any faster dangerous. The car that hit you was traveling at a much higher rate of speed when it plowed into you. Have I omitted anything?*

**A:**　　　*The only thing you didn't say is that it was snowing at the time of the accident.*

**Q:**　　　*Is there anything else I have left out?*

**A:**　　　*No, I think you got everything.*

　　　. . . . . .

**Q:**　　　*Let's go over how you felt when the other driver's insurance company denied coverage for the injuries you suffered. Initially you were angry. Then you felt that they didn't understand what had happened. When you tried to explain how fast their driver was going on the icy road, you felt they weren't listening to you. Have I understood what you said?*

**A:**　　　*Yes, I think that about covers it.*

Generally, summary questions should only be used for the more important topics in the interview. They should not be a verbatim playback, but a paraphrase of your client's story. They act as a probe of your client's memory to verify that he has completely and accurately recounted the important facts for each topic. If summary questions are overused, they can unnecessarily prolong the interview with boring recapitulations of every detail your client has shared.

## § 4.06　INFORMATION-GATHERING TECHNIQUES

There are a number of special techniques that can facilitate efficient and comprehensive information-gathering in an interview. Lawyers have come to rely on five particularly helpful techniques: (1) the funnel, (2) the time line, (3) the strategic use of silence, (4) the use of probes to rouse failed memories, and (5) the use of writings or demonstrations to re-create events. The funnel and the time line incorporate the five types of questions discussed in § 4.05 into a framework that maximizes the retrieval of information. The strategic use of silence often helps to facilitate the disclosure of delicate information from the client to the lawyer, particularly when combined with empathetic understanding, active listening, and recognition. The fourth technique, the use of probes to refresh failed memories, helps the client remember events he has temporarily forgotten or suppressed. The last technique, the use of writings or demonstrations to re-create events, may be helpful to understand matters that may be difficult to picture from purely verbal descriptions.

### [1]　The Funnel Technique

Gathering valuable information in an interview may be likened to searching for valuable items in a dark room. Suppose you enter a dark room with three things to help you find your way: a floodlight, a regular flashlight, and a penlight. Naturally, you would first orient yourself to the entire room by using the floodlight. As you identified particular areas where valuables might be stored, you would explore with your flashlight. When searching the smallest crevices or spaces, you would use your penlight. Similarly, in interviewing, skilled lawyers seek out valuable information by beginning with open questions (like a floodlight) to illuminate the client's overall story. They then use follow up and closed questions (like the flashlight) to explore and understand particular parts of the story. And finally, they use leading questions (the penlight) to pinpoint and clarify the finest details of the story. In interviewing, this method of obtaining valuable information is illustrated by a different metaphor, commonly referred to as the "funnel" technique.

When utilizing the funnel approach, a lawyer visualizes a common funnel as the structure of the questions she will ask on a particular topic. Each question corresponds to a place along the length of the funnel. The open questions, discussed in § 4.05[1], correspond to the open mouth of the funnel. The follow up questions, discussed in § 4.05[2], that pursue clarification of the answers given in response to the open questions, fit just below the mouth of the funnel. The narrower closed questions, discussed in § 4.05[3], correspond to a place one-half to two-thirds of the way further down the funnel. Leading questions, discussed in § 4.05[4], are toward the bottom of the funnel. Finally, summary questions that are asked at the end of a topic to make sure that all the information has been obtained, *see* § 4.05[5], fit at the bottom of the funnel. The summary questions correspond to a filter that strains and tests the information that has been winnowed down through the funnel. The diagram on the next page shows how these different types of questions fit along the length of the funnel.

## The Funnel

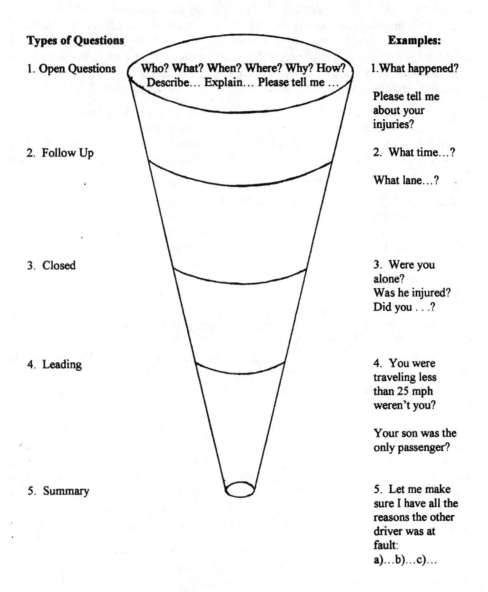

**Types of Questions**

1. Open Questions

2. Follow Up

3. Closed

4. Leading

5. Summary

Who? What? When? Where? Why? How?
Describe... Explain... Please tell me ...

**Examples:**

1. What happened?

Please tell me
about your
injuries?

2. What time...?

What lane...?

3. Were you
alone?
Was he injured?
Did you . . .?

4. You were
traveling less
than 25 mph
weren't you?

Your son was the
only passenger?

5. Let me make
sure I have all the
reasons the other
driver was at
fault:
a)...b)...c)...

As shown in this diagram, a lawyer will start with an open question to elicit a broad response. As the lawyer learns more about her client's situation, she will switch from open questions to follow up and then closed questions. When she thinks she has obtained a fairly clear picture of the situation, she then begins to ask a few leading questions to confirm that she has learned the necessary details. Finally, after she has a complete picture of her client's situation, she then asks some summary questions to verify that she does in fact have the complete picture and has not misunderstood or forgotten any of the important facts. By asking these five types of questions in an orderly pattern, she has "funneled" the information and ensured that she has gotten all the important details as well as the entire picture.

Each major topic of your client's situation may be "funneled." For example, if your client tells you he wants to discuss how he can recover for the personal injuries he suffered in the car accident as well as for the damages to his vehicle, he has presented two topics that should be funneled separately. Although many of the facts obtained by funneling the two topics will overlap because the personal injuries and the damages to the vehicle occurred in the same accident, each topic includes separate facts. Accordingly, you will need to conduct at least two separate funnels to exhaust the information your client has on these separate topics.

Many lawyers think of the first few open questions in the interview as a way to "get the list" of topics that will be funneled throughout the interview. Because you cannot effectively funnel two topics at the same time, it is usually a good idea to jot a note to yourself to return to the second topic after you have completed the first funnel.

The advantage of the funnel technique is that it presents an orderly framework for comprehensive information gathering. The disadvantage of the technique is that it is helpful only to the extent that the topic or topics you choose to funnel merit the time spent in inquiry. Therefore, efficient use of the technique requires that you choose which topics are sufficiently important to merit the time spent in funneling.

## [2]    The Time Line

Another technique for enhancing information-gathering is to construct a time line of your client's situation. Your client will often feel comfortable describing his situation with an opening sentence that begins with the phrase, "Well, the whole problem began with . . . ." You can then encourage your client to recount his story in chronological order by asking open questions that focus on what happened next.

When using the time line technique, most lawyers attempt to get an overview of the client's story by asking open questions that reveal the beginning, middle, and end of the situation. They then go back to fill in the details with follow up and closed questions. After they have a fairly good picture of the situation, they then ask a few leading questions to verify information that appears to logically follow from the sequence of events. Finally, they ask summary questions to make sure there are no gaps in the time line picture they have obtained.

When you use the time line technique, make sure you understand where the story appropriately begins and ends. Too often clients and lawyers start the time line too late or end it too early. They tend to think the time line should start with a legally significant event, instead of with a factually significant event. For instance, in a personal injury case, the car accident that resulted in the injuries to your client is not the beginning event of the time line. Instead, you will want to inquire about the road conditions before impact, the condition of the cars before impact, and the physical condition of the drivers before impact. Likewise, the time line should include not only the present medical condition of your client, but also his future treatment needs.

The advantages of using a time line are that gaps or omissions in the story are easy to spot, and the time line is easy to follow for both you and your client. The disadvantages are that some topics do not flow sequentially and therefore may be omitted, and some clients think more topically than chronologically. For instance, in a contract dispute, the events leading up to the signing of the contract and the subsequent breach may flow chronologically and be easy for your client to recount in a time line. However, the fact that the other party to the contract became insolvent may not occur to your client as part of the chronology of the overall story. Instead, that fact is more likely to be revealed in response to a topical question about the financial condition of the other party.

The time line method works particularly well when your client is trying to recall a specific sequence of events or when it would be useful to slow down what happened into a slow-motion description, as in a slow-motion movie. The time line can also aid a client who is reconstructing the important events in written form. If your client is having difficulty focusing on the time line during the interview, or if the interview time has drawn to a close before the client has finished recounting all of the key events to his story, you can ask your client to write out a time line at home. Most clients find the time line method easy to use on their own.

## [3]  The Strategic Use of Silence

As mentioned previously, lawyers often talk too much. They are accustomed to oral presentations. Words are their stock and trade. They forget that others are not as accustomed to verbalizing facts and feelings. Consequently, lawyers sometimes forget that a client may need time to think through an event in order to organize and formulate the words to completely describe it. To be an effective interviewer, you must be a patient listener; and one technique of patient listening involves the strategic use of silence.

Novices in the use of open questions sometimes mistake silence on the part of the client as a misunderstanding of the question. They then ask a second narrower question to clarify the first open question. The client then answers the second question. The broad initial question that invited expansive information remains unanswered.

In contrast, effective interviewers resist the temptation to prematurely ask a second narrower question. They patiently wait while the client organizes his thoughts to answer the broad question. They do not attempt to fill the silence. As a result, they are often rewarded with a detailed answer to the broad question.

In addition to using silence to permit your client to organize his thoughts to respond to a question, you may also use silence as a probe when no question is pending. Psychologists and psychiatrists have learned that people will often volunteer important information to fill an uncomfortable silence. This information might otherwise be withheld due to embarrassment or fear. Accordingly, just as a therapist uses silence to encourage her patient to reveal information, you can strategically use silence to encourage your client to reveal additional information.

## [4]  Failed Memory Probes

At times, a client may "shut down" during the interview. The client may say, "I don't remember" in response to a question; he may switch to another subject without finishing the particular story he was relating; or he may just sit back in uncomfortable silence. Before the interview can continue, you must diagnose what has caused this momentary interference or interruption in the dialogue. Clients usually shut down due to memory lapse, discomfort with the topic, or exhaustion.

If you conclude that your client has merely forgotten details that he once knew, you can use either a time line or visualization to refresh his memory. For instance, if your client says he can't remember whether he was wearing his seatbelt at the time of the collision, you might try the time line technique to jog his memory:

- **Time Line Probes:**

*Q:*     *Where was the last rest stop you took before the collision?*

*A:*     *We stopped for gas and a snack in Hickory, NC.*

*Q:*     *Describe each thing you did right before you got back onto the highway.*

*A:*     *Well, first I unlocked the car. Then, I opened the door and got into the driver's seat. I was carrying a cup of coffee that I placed in the drink holder between the two front seats.*

*Q:*     *What happened next?*

*A:*     *I guess, I put on my seatbelt and started the car, but I don't really remember.*

*Q:*     *Where was your son when you started the car?*

*A:*     *He was in the backseat. Oh, I remember now. He wanted me to put his half-finished can of Coke in the drink holder between the front seats because he wanted to take a nap. I had to unbuckle my seatbelt to reach the can. I took the can, placed it in the drink holder and buckled the seat belt back. I remember because we joked that he always waited until I had already buckled my seat belt before he asked me to take something from the backseat. That's the conversation we had as I was buckling my seatbelt for the second time.*

With some clients you can also try to use visualization to probe failed memory. When using this technique, you ask your client to visualize a certain event and describe the details as if he were experiencing the event in the present. For instance, if your client says he can't remember if he was wearing his seat belt at the time of the collision, you might try the following:

- **Visualization Probes:**

*Q:*     *Imagine yourself immediately after the collision. Visualize that time if you can. The guy behind you has just plowed into the rear of your car. I know this may be difficult for you, but try to go back in your mind to that time and tell me exactly how you feel.*

*A:*     *I'm stunned. Then the pain hits. I can't move. My right leg is bleeding and the pain seems unbearable. The entire weight of the front of the car seems to be on my leg.*

*Q:*     *What else do you feel?*

*A:*     *Well, I'm panicked about my son. I call out his name. He answers. He says he's scared. He wants to know what happened. Then he starts crying when he sees the blood on my leg. He gets real upset when he realizes I can't move.*

*Q:*     *Is he hurt?*

*A:*     *He says his knee hurts, but he'll be okay. He's scared about me.*

**Q:**          What else do you feel?

**A:**          My head and neck hurt from being thrown forward and then backward. My chest also hurts.

**Q:**          Why does your chest hurt?

**A:**          I don't know. I guess from hitting the steering wheel. No, wait a minute. I know why it hurts. It's from the seat belt. I remember now. I did have on my seat belt because the next day I had a big bruise across my chest where the seat belt was.

Sometimes when your client shuts down, it is not the result of a loss of memory, but from a feeling of awkwardness about the topic. Use your active listening skills to diagnose if the reason for the sudden change of topic or claimed lack of memory is truly from a memory lapse or from your client's discomfort with the topic. If you sense that your client is attempting to avoid the topic, you can either come back to it after you have established greater rapport with him, or you can pursue the topic by acknowledging the difficulty in discussing the issue. For instance, if your client is uncomfortable discussing what happened to his son after the accident, you might empathetically acknowledge the difficulty of the matter as follows:

- **Acknowledging the Difficulty of the Topic:**

**Q:**          It must have been hard to care for your son when you were in such pain. What happened to your son when the ambulance arrived?

**A:**          It was terrible. I didn't know what to do. They let him go with me to the hospital, but I was really in too much pain to think much about his needs.

**Q:**          Earlier, you said you were divorced. It must have been hard to call your ex-wife after the accident happened.

**A:**          You're not kidding. She was fit to be tied. She hadn't wanted me to take him on the visit to Kentucky. She had been worried about the weather conditions. I called her just before I went into surgery. She was furious. I felt terrible because our son had to stay with a social worker until his mother could get to the hospital to pick him up the next day. My ex blamed me for putting our son at risk.

Finally, a client may shut down during an interview from exhaustion. If your client has been recounting the facts of his case for a period of time, he may lose his focus and need a break. Suggest a break, or offer him a cup of coffee or water. If your client still has trouble focusing on your questions after the break, you might need to schedule a follow-up interview at a later time.

## [5]    Using Writings or Demonstrations to Re-create Events

Some events are difficult to understand from purely verbal descriptions. For example, in an automobile accident case, a diagram of the accident scene and the positions of the vehicles will often provide the best picture of what happened. When there are numerous heirs to a will, a diagram of a family tree may be helpful in understanding potential beneficiaries. A written time line of the phases of a construction project may be helpful in drafting a contract governing the parties' obligations in developing a residential subdivision. A physical demonstration may help explain a key event, such as how a person was injured or how a person acted.

Accordingly, when appropriate, you should not hesitate to have your client re-create an event on paper, whether a drawing, chart, or written summary. Similarly, having your client physically demonstrate an event will often help you better understand what happened.

## § 4.07   EXPLORING YOUR CLIENT'S OBJECTIVES

When your client first enters your office, he has at least one objective or goal in mind. He is seeking legal representation for a reason. Often he comes to the initial interview with several objectives. He may be able to articulate one or more of his objectives, but others may not yet be fully formed in his mind. As mentioned previously, one purpose of the initial interview is to begin the process of identifying your client's objectives. A second purpose is to begin the process of translating your client's objectives into a concrete plan of action.

Your client will often indicate his objective in the first few sentences of the initial interview. For example, he may say, "I need a will," or "I have been sued," or "I want help in recovering for my injuries." Each sentence articulates a reason why he scheduled the initial meeting with you. However, many times the reason initially expressed for seeking legal representation will be only the beginning of the process of identifying his objectives. For instance, when your client says he has been sued, you will realize that you have to analyze the lawsuit, explore possible defenses, investigate potential counterclaims, and discuss settlement prospects. In other words, your client's initial expression of his objective is only the first step in a lengthier process of clarifying objectives and arriving at potential solutions.

A good starting point for identifying your client's objectives is to focus on his actual needs. By using open questions to explore your client's feelings and concerns about his situation, you can begin to discern a picture of his overall needs. As you learn more about those needs, you can employ either the funnel method to explore specific topics or the time-line method to establish a framework for understanding important events. Once the factual picture becomes clearer, you can then ask more direct questions to find out what your client wants to accomplish.

It is also helpful to encourage your client to express his objectives in terms of factual results instead of legal remedies. For instance, if your client says he wants to declare bankruptcy, you should ask him to articulate his objective factually. What, exactly, does he want to protect? If he says he wants to protect his home from creditors, then protection of his home, not bankruptcy, is his factual objective.

By encouraging your client to define his objectives factually, you may be able to broaden the legal remedies that may be available to accomplish those objectives. For instance, you and your client may be able to explore several methods of protecting your client's home and not be limited to the single remedy of bankruptcy. That is, as an alternative to bankruptcy, it may be possible for you to draft a notice that the client claims his homestead exemption as a means of protecting his home, or you may be able to negotiate a debt repayment plan with your client's creditors that will both save his home and extinguish the need for bankruptcy. In sum, exploring your client's objectives in terms of his needs and what factual results he wants to obtain will help clarify his objectives and the most appropriate means that may be available for achieving them.

## § 4.08 EXPLORING LEGAL THEORIES

After you have a basic understanding of your client's overall objectives, you should begin exploring legal theories that may be relevant to accomplishing those objectives. As a result of your legal training, it is inevitable that even during the initial stages of the interview you will have already begun to spot potential legal issues and remedies in the case. In exploring legal theories, however, it is essential not to prematurely diagnose your client's legal situation. As the interview progresses, you may find it helpful to jot simple legal terms on a sheet of paper as you listen to your client's description of the situation. After you have a complete factual picture of the situation, you can refer back to your list to see if any of the legal theories you initially identified are applicable and should be more fully explored in connection with your client's factual objectives.

It will often be appropriate to ask closed questions when obtaining information relevant to potential legal theories because their viability depends upon specific factual showings. For example, a claim for intentional infliction of emotional distress typically requires a showing that the client's distress was severe or disabling in nature; a temporary restraining order requires a showing of irreparable harm; waiver may be a defense to conversion if the owner of the property accepted it back from the converter along with a sum of money for use of the chattel; a contract may not generally be rescinded based on unilateral mistake, but it may be avoided based on mutual mistake. Thus, to identify legal theories, you will have to ask specific questions that focus on the particular elements of potential claims, defenses, and legal remedies that may be applicable to your client's situation.

## § 4.09 TAKING NOTES DURING THE INTERVIEW

During the interview, it is difficult to convey empathetic understanding and engage in active listening if you are preoccupied with note taking. To maximize information-gathering and build rapport with your client, you should avoid doing anything that will distract him from telling his story and distract you from understanding it. On the other hand, you must have a method for remembering what you are told during the interview and documenting the matters decided at the meeting.

Lawyers usually use one of four methods to document the substance of the interview: (1) tape-record it, (2) have a paralegal or secretary sit in on the interview and take notes, (3) personally take detailed notes, or (4) personally take brief notes and write out or dictate a memorandum to the file shortly after the interview is over. No single method is best in all circumstances, and in some situations a lawyer may use more than one of these methods at the same time.

Generally, tape-recording the interview or having a third person take notes may inhibit or distract your client in sharing information. Many people feel more self-conscious when they are being tape-recorded, and many feel somewhat less relaxed when they are speaking to an audience of two people instead of one. However, these inhibitions are unlikely to exist if you are meeting with clients who are members of the board of directors of a corporation or city council. In these types of situations, using a tape recorder or using another person to take notes during the interview will be neither inhibiting nor distracting.

Many lawyers find that the handwritten notes they take during an interview are sufficient to adequately document it. This is particularly true when relatively simple or standard legal services are involved. Many other lawyers prefer to take only abbreviated notes during an interview; and, shortly after it is over, they use those notes to dictate or type a more detailed summary of what transpired in a memorandum to the file. As between these choices, most lawyers use the one that best fits their personal style and the relative complexity of the client's situation. You can employ either method effectively so long as your note taking does not become a distraction to your client or impede you from engaging in active listening. Finally, basic information about how to contact your client and short notes about preliminary objectives and initial tasks that will be undertaken in the representation might be documented on a simple form like the "New Client Information Form" shown at the end of § 3.13.

## § 4.10   ILLUSTRATION OF INITIAL CLIENT MEETING AND INTERVIEW[5]

Larry Odden is a partner in a general-practice law firm of eight lawyers. He received a phone call from a prospective client, Clara Miles, who told him she had been injured in a car accident approximately one year ago and wanted to talk with him about it (The statute of limitations in a personal injury action is three years). During the phone conversation, Clara said that a pickup truck ran a red light, broadsided her car, and that she sustained whiplash-type injuries to her neck and back. She said that her own insurance company paid the property damage to her car. She said she had a copy of her current medical bills and a copy of the accident report taken by the police officer who investigated the accident. She has not been contacted by anyone else about the accident, and she has not consulted with another lawyer.

Larry scheduled an appointment to meet with Clara at his office during her lunch break from her employment at a nearby clothing store. It was agreed the initial meeting would be limited to about an hour, and a follow-up appointment would be scheduled if necessary. Larry told her there would be no charge for the initial conference, and he asked her to bring the medical bills and accident report to the meeting.

At the time scheduled for the meeting, Larry greeted Clara in the firm's reception area and escorted her to a small conference room. After exchanging some pleasantries and small talk, the meeting proceeded as follows:

1.   L: Well, Clara, tell me how this accident happened.
2.   C: Let's see, where to begin . . . (pause). Last February, Saturday the 8th, my husband Dan and I, and our son Tommy, were driving up Franklin Street here in town. We were going to find a place to get some lunch and then go to the Carolina basketball game. Carolina was playing N.C. State that day. Anyway, as we were going through the intersection of Franklin

---

[5] This illustration is intended to show how a skilled attorney might handle an initial client meeting and interview. you might conduct the interview quite differently and may even disagree with some of the approaches taken by the lawyer. Bear in mind that the lawyer's approach is, in significant respects, affected by his personal style and interviewing philosophy. In addition, the lawyer's interaction with the client is significantly affected by the client's personality, demeanor, and body language — all of which are not readily apparent from a mere transcript.

and Estes Drive, a pickup truck ran a red light on Estes and hit our car from the right. That's basically how it happened.

3.  L: What happened after the collision?

4.  C: Well, I was really shaken up. It was a huge bang. After it happened, I remember turning around in my seat to see if Tommy was all right. He was in the back seat, had his seatbelt on thank God, and he was okay. My husband, Dan, he was driving; he seemed okay too. Our car was in the middle of the intersection, smashed in on my side, the passenger side, toward the front of the car. God, it was awful.

5.  L: I can imagine . . . (pause). You say you were shaken up. Were you hurt?

6.  C: Yes. Well, I went dizzy for a moment, didn't black out or anything, but was like in shock for a moment. When the truck hit us, like I said, it hit us on the passenger side toward the front of the car, not the passenger door itself. I was sitting in the front seat, had my seatbelt on, but was jerked left. And my head hit the side of the headrest of the driver's seat. I didn't have a concussion or anything. Then I felt myself thrown back into my own seat. Then, after a couple of seconds, that's when I looked to see if Tommy and my husband were all right.

7.  L: I see. What happened after you checked to see whether Tommy and your husband were okay?

8.  C: Dan got out of the car, and then I got out and got Tommy out. Dan told us to go over to the sidewalk to wait. The traffic was beginning to back up by now with our car and the pickup blocking the intersection. It was a mess.

9.  L: I know what you mean. Game day traffic is always bad. Was Tommy okay after you got him out of the car?

10. C: Yeah, like I said, he was all right. Maybe he was shaken up a bit, but he didn't have any injuries. He didn't complain about being hurt in any way.

11. L: How old is Tommy?

12. C: He's seven now; so, he was six at the time.

13. L: Since the accident, has this affected him in any way?

14. C: No, not really. I know he was frightened right when it all happened, but he got over it real quickly. He's had no nightmares or fears about riding in the car, which I was worried about at first. In fact, now and then, he still jokes about it all.

15. L: I'm glad to hear that. These kids really have a way of bouncing back, don't they? I have a son myself. He's a year older than Tommy.

16. C: Oh really?

17. L: Yes, and an eleven year-old daughter too. They keep my wife and me quite busy.

18. C: You're telling me . . . (chuckling).

19. L: Do you and Dan have any other children?

20. C: No, just Tommy.

21. L: So, tell me what was going on while you and Tommy were waiting at the sidewalk.

22. C: We just stood there, and it wasn't long before two, maybe three police cars showed up. I remember there were two officers starting to direct traffic, and the third officer started talking with Dan and the driver of the pickup truck. By the way, I brought the accident report you asked for.

23. L: Oh good; thanks. We can look at that in a minute. Were you involved in the conversation with the officer?

24. C: Not at that time. It was so cold outside that Tommy and I went into the Food Mart at the corner of the intersection to keep warm. I think we got hot chocolate or something. And I just watched what was going on outside from the window in the Food Mart. The officer was talking with my husband and the driver across the street. I never met the driver.

25. L: Did the officer ever talk with you?

26. C: At one point, it was later on, he came into the Food Mart, and he asked me what happened. I told him that we had a green light, that the light turned yellow when we were going through the intersection, and then the truck came out of nowhere and hit us.

27. L: You don't mind if I take a few notes, do you —

28. C: Oh, no, that's fine.

29. L: What did he say?

30. C: He said that's what my husband said, but that the other driver said he had the green light and was making a right-hand turn from Estes onto Franklin.

31. L: I see. So the driver of the pickup was not going through the intersection on Estes but was making a right-hand turn from Estes onto Franklin?

32. C: Yeah, apparently. But I didn't know that. All I knew was that he hit us. It happened so fast.

33. L: On Franklin Street, what lane were you traveling in?

34. C: We were in the far right lane, going straight on Franklin.

35. L: Did you have any further conversation with the officer?

36. C: No, not really.

37. L: Did he give a citation to anyone?

38. C: He told me he wasn't going to give anyone a ticket because he couldn't tell who was at fault. So nobody got a ticket.

39. L: Did he say anything else to you?

40. C: No, that's it. He was real nice.

41. L: Have you or Dan spoken to him since that day?

42. C: No.

43. L: Mm-hmm. So, the officer asked you what happened; you said your husband had the green light; that the light turned yellow when you got to the intersection; and then the truck came out of nowhere and hit your car.

44. C: Yes.

45. L: And the officer said that your husband basically said the same thing, but that the driver of the pickup said he had a green light.

46. C: Yeah.

47. L: And then the officer said he wasn't going to charge anyone because he didn't know who was at fault.

48. C: Right.

49. L: Did I leave anything out?

50. C: No, that's it. But sometime later, before everyone left, he gave my husband a sheet of paper with the other driver's insurance information; and I've brought that with me also.

51. L: Oh, thank you. Let me take a look at that for a moment, along with the accident report.

52. [Larry briefly reads the insurance information form and the accident report. He then goes over the accident report with Clara and verifies various details in the report, such as the date and time of the accident, the make and model of the vehicles, the name of the driver of the pickup truck (Ronald S. Smith), the description of the damage to each vehicle, the speed limit on Franklin Street and Estes Drive (25 mph for each), the accuracy of the officer's diagram of the accident scene and positions of the vehicles after impact, the fact that there were no independent eyewitnesses to the accident, the fact that no ambulance was called and no-one reported being injured, and the fact that the officer didn't charge either of the drivers.]

53.    L: Clara, this accident report is signed by Officer Boles. I know him. Do you remember if that's the name of the officer who spoke with you?

54.    C: Yes, that's him. I didn't talk with any other officer.

55.    L: The report notes that the "road conditions were icy." Do you remember that?

56.    C: Yes. There were small patches of snow and a bit of ice on the roads. We got a dusting of snow the night before and, like I said, it was very cold. But the roads weren't really covered with snow or ice, or anything like that.

57.    L: There were just patches of snow and ice here and there?

58.    C: Yes.

59.    L: Do you remember if your car skidded at all when it was going through the intersection?

60.    C: I don't believe so; I don't remember that.

61.    L: How about the pickup truck — did it skid at all?

62.    C: I can't remember that either. It all happened so fast.

63.    L: Was Dan driving a bit slower that day because of the road conditions?

64.    C: I would have to say that everyone was driving perhaps a little slower, but not much. It was a little slippery I guess, but it was no big deal.

65.    L: The report also notes that your car was not drivable and was towed from the scene.

66.    C: Yeah, they had to call a wrecker.

67.    L: Did you tell me over the phone that your insurance company paid for the property damage to your car?

68.    C: Yes, they did.

69.    L: How did that come about?

70.    C: Well, Dan handled all of that. First, I think he called Mr. Smith's insurance company, All-Good Insurance, but they said they wouldn't pay because they thought my husband was at fault. So our insurance company ended up paying to fix our car.

71.    L: Do you know if your insurance company paid for the damage to the pickup truck?

72.    C: I don't know.

73.    L: Do you know the name of the adjuster for your insurance company whom your husband spoke with?

74.    C: No, not off hand. But I can get that information for you.

75.    L: Okay. Let's see, the report also says that there was a passenger, a Jane Smith, in the pickup truck. Do you remember seeing her?

76.    C: No, I really don't. I saw the driver because he was talking with the officer and Dan across the street. But I don't remember a passenger.

77.    L: Okay. Clara, let's back up and talk a little more about how the accident happened. What I'd like to do is start about a minute or so just before the

accident, and like a slow-motion movie, frame by frame, get a picture in my mind about what happened. Can you help me with that?

78.  C: I'll try. But I'm not really sure where to start.

79.  L: That's all right. Let me try to help. Let's see, you were driving down Franklin, toward town; you were in the front seat, passenger side; Dan was driving; Tommy was in the back seat. You were in the right-hand lane, approaching the intersection at Estes Drive. Do you remember seeing the Hotel Sienna on the right-hand side of the road just before the intersection?

80.  C: Yes.

81.  L: Okay, tell me what happened from that point, in slow motion if you can.

82.  C: Well, okay, let's see . . . (pause). We're driving down Franklin; I did see the hotel . . . (pause).

83.  L: What's the very next thing you saw?

84.  C: I think there were two cars ahead of us . . . (pause). I'm having trouble remembering.

85.  L: You're doing just fine. There were two cars ahead of you —

86.  C: Yes, and we were one or two car lengths behind, going fairly slowly . . . (pause). I remember the light was green at that point. Then the car phone rang. I reached for it on the dash near the radio. Dan said something like, "I got it," and he picked up the phone. I looked up; the light was yellow. I then looked at Dan for a split second. Then we must have been in the intersection. And then, wham; we got hit . . . (pause).

87.  L: Anything else?

88.  C: No, I think that's all. That's the best I can remember.

89.  L: Okay, that's very helpful. Let me just rewind the tape back, so to speak, for a few seconds. You were one or two car lengths behind the car in front of you, and you saw the light was green at that point —

90.  C: Yes.

91.  L: Were any of the cars in front of you already in the intersection at that point?

92.  C: No. They were just about to go into the intersection. Just about to enter into it.

93.  L: All right. And your car was about one or two car lengths behind?

94.  C: Right.

95.  L: And then the car phone rang and you looked down and reached for it?

96.  C: Yes. It was mounted next to the radio on the dash, toward the driver's side.

97.  L: And then?

98.  C: Dan said, "I'll get it" and he reached over and picked up the phone from the dash.

99.  L: And did you see the traffic light at that point?

100.  C: I leaned back in my seat when he picked up the phone, and then I glanced up and saw the light was yellow.

101.  L: At this point, were you in the intersection?

102.  C: I'm not sure. After I glanced at the light, I turned and glanced at Dan who was holding the phone to his ear, and he answered it, "Hello," or something like that.

103.  L: And then?

104.  C: It happened so fast. All I remember then was that we got hit.

105.  L: Do you remember at what point you were actually in the intersection?

106.     C: I'm not sure. We were probably just entering it or into it when I looked at Dan when he was holding the phone.

107.     L: Did you ever see the light turn from yellow to red?

108.     C: No. I only saw it green and then yellow. I'm sure the light was yellow when we went into the intersection.

109.     L: Okay. That's helpful. Is there anything else you can remember in this slow motion sequence?

110.     C: No. That's the best I can remember.

111.     L: Did you ever find out who had been calling on the car phone?

112.     C: No, we never found out. I guess the phone went dead when the accident happened. Dan is self-employed as a plumber, so maybe some customer called. But we never did find out who called.

113.     L: Okay. Let's talk about the rest of that day. I believe you said that a wrecker came to tow your car —

114.     C: Yes. And there was another wrecker that came and towed away the pickup truck. Tommy and I just waited in the Food Mart the whole time.

115.     L: What happened after that?

116.     C: Well, not too long after Officer Boles talked with me, he left and my husband came into the Food Mart. We called his brother who lives in town, and he picked us up and drove us home. We missed the game, of course; but we still saw most of it on TV.

117.     L: What happened during the rest of the day?

118.     C: That afternoon we just lounged around the house. My husband was okay; and like I said, Tommy was okay. But I was still feeling shaken up, and I was beginning to feel sore in my neck and a little in my lower back.

119.     L: Mm-hmm.

120.     C: And toward evening it was starting to ache pretty badly, and Dan wanted me to call our doctor, I mean, Tommy's pediatrician. I don't really have a regular doctor, but Dr. Maria Partin is Tommy's doctor. Dan wanted me to call her. Anyway, I didn't at that time. But then I had a rough night. By morning, I could hardly get out of bed. I could hardly turn my head and my back was real stiff . . . (pause).

121.     L: Please go on . . .

122.     C: So, the next morning I called Dr. Partin, and she gave me the name of a doctor to call, but I've forgotten his name now. I ended up not calling him. Instead, the following day, Monday, I called Dr. Sally Byler, a chiropractor in town, whom my sister recommended and had once seen when she had a back problem. And then I saw Dr. Byler for about four months.

123.     L: Uh-uh. Did you see any other doctors for your injuries?

124.     C: No, just Dr. Byler.

125.     L: What was Dr. Byler's course of treatment?

126.     C: She gave me therapy, three times a week at first, and then two times a week. I had electrical muscle stimulation to my neck, shoulders and back; manipulation; and ultrasound therapy. I brought the bills for you [Clara hands the bills to Larry].

127.     L: Thanks. The last entry on these bills is for a visit on April 14. Have you seen Dr. Byler since then?

128.     C: No. The treatments helped me a lot at first, but then they were getting too expensive. Dan's insurance wouldn't cover the treatments, and we've had hard times money-wise over the past year with Dan's new plumbing

business. He used to have a partner in the business, but they broke up. So Dan was starting his own business, sort of starting all over again building up new customers. It's been hard making ends meet, so I stopped going to her. Anyway, my condition just sort of leveled off, not getting any worse, but not getting any better.

129.   L: I see. Tell me more about your injuries, Clara. You've talked about the night right after the accident. Can you give me a description of your injuries from that time up until now?

130.   C: Yeah. When I first started seeing Dr. Byler, I could hardly turn my head and I had difficulty walking and bending because of pain and spasms in my lower back. The mornings were the worst times. For the first two months, that would have been mid January to early March or so, the treatments helped me a lot and I did home exercises. Then, my neck and back sort of leveled off . . . (pause). I gained fifteen pounds, and I've still not lost that extra weight. I just can't make myself exercise. I used to walk every day, but I haven't since the accident. The constant pain saps my energy. My neck is still stiff in the mornings, but that usually goes away during the day. Like, I don't feel any neck pain right now. But my back, it aches, like a dull ache, almost all of the time, and mostly when I stand and sit for long periods of time. It's been an awful year, the stress and all — but I guess I'll just have to learn to live with it.

131.   L: This must be hard for you, day in and day out.

132.   C: Yes. [Clara becomes somewhat tearful].

133.   L: (Pause) . . . Did Dr. Byler recommend any medications?

134.   C: No. I guess I could take aspirin or something like that, but I've never really believed in taking a lot of medicines. I tried Tylenol for a while, but it didn't seem to do much good.

135.   L: It's been about eight months now since you last saw Dr. Byler. Have you thought about going back to see her or consulting with another doctor?

136.   C: No, not really. Our money situation is still real tight and, like I said before, I guess I've just resigned myself to having to learn to live with this and just make the best of things.

137.   L: Were you employed at the time of the accident?

138.   C: No. I first started working at Belk's as a sales clerk two weeks ago. I work five days a week, nine to three o'clock; with a lunch break in between. It's helping make ends meet, but it's hard on my back.

139.   L: I admire you for taking on work with all that you're going through. Do you think you can continue working those hours with your back as it is now?

140.   C: I think I can manage. I guess I'll just have to.

141.   L: I understand. When you mentioned your lunch break, Clara, that reminded me — when do you have to be back at Belk's?

142.   C: Oh, [looking at her watch], I still have some time. My supervisor said I could extend this lunch break a bit longer if I had to. But I'll have to get back after a while.

143.   L: All right. Let me ask you this, Clara: what are the things that concern you most about your situation — about all that you've been through?

144.   C: I'm worried about being a good mother and wife. I'm not my old self. I'm cranky when I'm aching all the time. It's been very stressful — our financial situation and all. It's been hard for me, very hard emotionally.

Dan works all the time he can, trying to re-establish his business, and I need to help make ends meet. But it's so hard to work and then take care of Tommy, rushing back after work to meet him at the bus stop after school, etc. And it's hard for me with the housework, with Dan doing more than his fair share. In fact, Dan did all the household chores for about three months. I could hardly do anything. For almost four months we couldn't even have intimate relations, if you know what I mean. It was awful. I just want my old self again, and I'm worried about my back in the long term — it's been nearly a year now.

145.    L: Again, I admire all you're doing.

146.    C: Thanks, that's nice of you to say. Do you think I have a good case? I mean, I'm not the kind of person who wants to take advantage, but my sister once made a claim in an accident case and received some compensation for all she went through. That's why I called your office to begin with. I know that All-Good, Mr. Smith's insurance company, thinks Dan was at fault; but that's not true. And my family and I have been through a lot.

147.    L: Yes, I think I can help you, Clara. If Mr. Smith made his turn against the red light, he would be considered "negligent." In other words, he would be considered at fault. And that would give you what's called a personal injury claim against him that would be paid by All-Good. Dan would also have a claim for what is called loss of consortium — the loss of your services to the family and loss of intimate relations for three or four months.

148.    C: How much do you think I could get?

149.    L: That's something I can't answer right now. There's some information that we will still need to get. As you know, there are two sides to this story. It's not unusual for there to be a dispute about the facts in a case —

150.    C: (Interposing), Will you represent me? And would you also represent Dan in his claim if he wanted you to?

151.    L: As I say, I think I can help you. But let me clear up an important but somewhat technical point first.

152.    C: Okay.

153.    L: I know that the facts, according to you and Dan, were that Mr. Smith ran the red light. On the other hand, if in fact the light had changed to green before Mr. Smith made his turn, then Dan may have been negligent and you may have a legal claim against him, which would be covered by the insurance company for your car under the law of our state. In saying this, please understand that I'm merely saying that it would be a conflict of interest for me to represent you and Dan in a claim against Mr. Smith, and at the same time represent you in any claim against your husband. The advice I give you and the discussions between us are protected by the attorney-client privilege. The same privilege exists for Dan if I represent him. But, if I represent you and Dan when you might pursue a claim against him, I would be put in a position that would violate those privileges.

154.    C: I see. But I would never make a claim against my husband or our insurance company because Dan did nothing wrong.

155.    L: Yes, and I understand. I know that what I just said was awkward, but I wanted you to know about this technical matter because, as you know,

there are two sides to the story about exactly what happened, even though your version and Dan's version are the same. And, as for representing Dan, I could only consider that if he decided he wanted to meet with me and after he and I had an opportunity to talk like we are doing here.

156. C: Thanks. I know what you mean. Like I said, I would only want to be compensated by Mr. Smith's insurance company. I think they are responsible because he was at fault. I know Dan is being supportive of me in all of this, and I'll leave it up to Dan whether he wants to meet with you about any claim. How would I pay you for representing me?

157. L: Our firm's fee in this kind of case is called a contingent fee. The fee is a one-third percentage of the gross amount we are able to recover for you, either from a settlement of the case or from a trial. If we have to file a lawsuit against Mr. Smith, you will have to pay for certain costs such as filing fees to the court, and certain other expenses incurred in preparing for trial. Those costs would be your responsibility regardless of the outcome of the case.

158. C: What if you are unable to recover any money for me?

159. L: Then there is no fee, because a third of zero is zero.

160. C: And these costs if a suit is filed — how much can they run?

161. L: Well, of course, it varies from case to case. But my best estimate is that, in a case such as yours, total costs would be $3,000 to $5,000 if there were a trial. [Larry briefly provides a further explanation of costs, such as deposition costs and fees charged by doctors for time spent while testifying].

162. C: Could I pay that over time, in installments to your firm?

163. L: Yes; we can make arrangements for that.

164. C: Do you think we will have to file a suit?

165. L: I really can't answer that right now, Clara. It's one of several options, which we need to discuss at some length. Because our time is getting short right now, I suggest we talk about that at our next meeting.

166. C: Okay. When should we meet again?

167. L: I think we should schedule our next appointment in about three weeks. That seems like a long time, but there are a number of things I need to look into in the meantime, and there are a few things I need you to get for me. Then we can meet again and discuss different options and decide on a game plan. Is that all right?

168. C: Sure. What do you need from me?

169. L: Do you have any photos of the damage to your car?

170. C: No, but I think the insurance adjuster for our insurance company had some photos taken.

171. L: You mentioned you could find out the name and phone number for that adjuster. Could you check on that for me and call me about it in a few days?

172. C: Sure.

173. [Larry then explains the procedure for obtaining Clara's medical records and has her sign a medical release form authorizing Dr. Byler to release a copy of Clara's medical records to the law firm. He also reviews with her a copy of the firm's standard contingent fee contract (*see* § 9.05), and tells her he will send an original contract to her in the mail for her signature. He also makes a copy of the accident report, insurance information sheet showing Mr. Smith's insurance information, and the medical bills from

Dr. Byler to keep in the file. Finally, he obtains from Clara pertinent contact information to fill out a "New Client Information Form" like that shown in § 3.13].

174.    L: All right, Clara, this is what I will do before our next meeting. As I mentioned, I'm going to get your medical records from Dr. Byler. After you get me the name and phone number of the adjuster for your insurance company, I will try to get from him or her a copy of the photos of your car and find out if the adjuster has any more information about the accident. Third, I'll also talk with Officer Boles to find out if he can tell me anything more about what Mr. and Ms. Smith said about the accident. At some point, I would also like to talk with your husband so I can hear his description of the accident first hand, but I think we can wait on that for now. Once I've done these things, and I think it will take about two weeks to get the medical records, I'll have my secretary call you so we can set up another appointment. Is that all right with you?

175.    C: Yes. I understand.

176.    L: Okay then. Finally, Clara, please do not hesitate to call me at any time. Our office hours are 8:30 a.m. to 5:00 p.m., Monday through Friday. If you have any concerns or some situation comes up that you need to call me about, please do. I'd rather know about it earlier than later. If I'm not in the office or available when you call, I'll be sure to call you back. I usually can do that the same day you call or the day after. But I will get back with you, okay?

177.    C: Yes.

178.    L: Also, Clara, if anyone from either insurance company calls you about the accident, tell them you can't talk with them, and just tell them to call me. Okay?

179.    C: Yes. Thank you so much. I enjoyed meeting you. And I'll call you in a day or so about the name and phone number of the adjuster for our insurance company. And if Dan wants to talk about making a claim also, I'll have him call you.

180.    L: Thank you, Clara. And I enjoyed meeting you too.

# Chapter 5

# DECISION-MAKING AND IMPLEMENTING THE DECISION

## § 5.01  INTRODUCTION

After you have thoroughly interviewed your client and obtained all factual and legal information pertinent to his situation, you must analyze potential courses of action, advise him about potential courses of action, collaborate with him in deciding upon the best course of action, and implement the course of action. This chapter discusses the process and techniques associated with these remaining functions of the overall counseling process.

## § 5.02  THE PROCESS OF LEGAL DECISION-MAKING

When counseling your client in decision-making, you and your client must address six, largely interrelated questions:

1.  *What is your client's factual and legal situation?*
2.  *What are your client's objectives or goals?*
3.  *What legal and non-legal options are available to your client for achieving his objectives?*
4.  *What are the pros and cons and likely outcomes of each option?*
5.  *Which option should your client choose? And,*
6.  *How will the option chosen be implemented?*

Usually you and your client will have answered the first two questions in the initial interview. Often the answers to questions 3 through 6 will be developed during a series of meetings with your client. You will learn some answers through independent research and investigation, and other answers will need to be developed during conferences throughout the course of the representation.

In the actual counseling session, addressing these questions involves six, corresponding tasks:

(1)    Summarizing your client's factual and legal situation;
(2)    Refining and clarifying your client's objectives;
(3)    Identifying potential options for achieving your client's objectives;
(4)    Discussing the pros and cons of each option;
(5)    Helping your client decide which option to choose; and
(6)    Implementing your client's decision.

As indicated above, these fundamental questions and tasks are largely interrelated. Although they may serve as a step-by-step agenda for the counseling session (which is the way they are treated in this chapter for instructive purposes), they are often addressed in a more loosely structured, free-flowing discussion between you and your client. During this discussion, there will be times when you will be advising your client, asking questions of him, and listening to him. Although most of the discussion should be "collaborative" in nature, there may be times when it will be appropriate for the discussion to be more "lawyer-centered" or "client-centered" (*see* § 2.03[4]).

In addition, you must keep in mind throughout this decision-making process that the Rules of Professional Conduct specifically require you to do three things: (1) abide by your client's decisions concerning the objectives of the representation and consult with him as to the means by which they are to be pursued (*see* § 6.03); (2) explain matters to your client to the extent reasonably necessary to permit him to make informed decisions regarding the representation (*see* § 6.04); and (3) exercise independent professional judgment and render candid advice (*see* § 6.05).

## § 5.03  SUMMARIZING YOUR CLIENT'S FACTUAL AND LEGAL SITUATION

Usually, a good starting point at a decision-making conference is to summarize your client's factual and legal situation. This helps to set the stage for clarifying your client's objectives. You have to completely understand your client's objectives before you and your client can meaningfully consider potential options for achieving those objectives.

In summarizing your client's factual situation, be brief and focus on the key facts. There is no need to rehash his entire story. The summary should be objective and balanced in the sense that you should include unfavorable as well as favorable facts, and not skew the facts either for or against your client. If your client has strong feelings about his situation, include your understanding of them in the summary. The primary purposes of the summary are to (1) confirm your understanding of your client's overall situation, and (2) set the stage for putting his situation into its applicable legal context. At the end of the factual summary you might ask your client, "Is what I've described a fair summary of your situation?"

In addition, and just as briefly, describe how your client's factual situation fits into the law or applicable legal process. This is important so that your client can get a general understanding for how the law may enable or constrain his objectives. At this stage, it will often be sufficient to identify the legal context in very general terms (*e.g.*, "In breach of contract cases, the law basically aims to put you in the same monetary position you would have been in had no breach occurred;" or "The lawsuit against you asks for money damages for the fair market value of the truck and physical and emotional injuries caused by the accident."). Remember that your main purpose at this point is to merely give your client a sense of the general area of the law or legal process that governs his situation. A more detailed explanation of the law may be appropriate when you and your client discuss the pros and cons of potential options for dealing with his situation.

## § 5.04   REFINING AND CLARIFYING YOUR CLIENT'S OBJECTIVES

After briefly summarizing your client's factual and legal situation, clarify your understanding of his overall objectives or goals. The question is, what does he want to accomplish? Although your client is likely to have given you at least a general sense of his objectives at the initial client meeting or during a more in-depth interview, he may have changed his objectives or refined them since you last saw him. Moreover, in the interim, additional events may have occurred to cause him to revise his objectives. In most cases, you will be able to confirm what you learned from him in the earlier interview (*e.g.*, "So, as I understand it, you would like to work out an agreement with your wife about child support — as in a 'separation agreement' that I just mentioned.").

The specificity of your client's objectives will, of course, depend upon the particular subject matter of the representation, the applicable law, and the number and types of decisions that need to be made. For example, while it is important to know that your client has the overall objective of working out an amicable agreement with his wife about child support, it will ultimately be necessary to be more specific about this objective in terms of the amount of child support he is willing to pay. The applicable law may largely shape this subsidiary objective (*e.g.*, a state-mandated child support guideline). Similarly, if your client has the overall objective of entering into a new business relationship with a supplier of goods, he will need to clarify his objectives about the basic elements of a deal (*e.g.*, quantity, price, and the time and method of delivery).

Thus, depending upon the particular nature of your client's situation and the decisions to be made, he may have multiple general objectives, and he may be unable to formulate more specific objectives until he has a greater understanding of the applicable law and his options. Accordingly, it will often be necessary for you to help your client refine and clarify his objectives throughout the decision-making process.

## § 5.05   IDENTIFYING POTENTIAL OPTIONS FOR ACHIEVING YOUR CLIENT'S OBJECTIVES

After your client's basic objectives have been confirmed or clarified, the next logical question is, what options are available to him for achieving these objectives? At this stage, the task is to identify all reasonably viable options that are (1) at least minimally consistent with your client's objectives, (2) personally acceptable to your client in the sense that he has not already ruled them out of bounds, and (3) not barred by law.[1] There is no reason to identify options that are merely "theoretically" possible but which are unrealistic under the circumstances. On the other hand, no realistic option should be overlooked, and it is important to identify all viable *non-legal* as well as legal options.

Unless your client has already identified potential options he has in mind (as might occur during the discussion about his objectives), you should take the lead in outlining the legal and non-legal options you believe may be viable. You should state these options briefly and in neutral terms. That is, reserve any discussion about the details of the options, their pros and cons, and their non-legal and legal ramifications until after all options have first been identified. In listing the options that have occurred to you, you might simply say, "As I see it, you have three options: first, you can . . . ; second, you could . . . ; and third, you might be able to . . . " After providing your list, particularly if your client's situation might be addressed by non-legal solutions, you might ask him, "Have any other options occurred to you?"

## § 5.06  DISCUSSING THE PROS AND CONS AND LIKELY OUTCOMES OF EACH OPTION

Once your client's options have been identified, you and your client should discuss the pros and cons of each option and the likely outcomes of each. "Pros" and "cons" are essentially consequences that are considered either "good" or "bad," or desirable or undesirable. These consequences may be tangible or intangible, and they may affect the client or other persons. Of course, the relative weight to be accorded to any consequence will depend upon the likelihood that the consequence will occur. Thus, discussing the pros and cons of different options often involves considering a wide variety of tangible and intangible consequences affecting your client and others under circumstances where making predictions about the likelihood of those consequences may be quite difficult.

In the overall process of discussing pros and cons, it is useful to keep four things in mind. First, you can focus the discussion by going over only one option at a time. In deciding which option to discuss first, you might choose one that your client came up with or one in which he has expressed particular interest. Otherwise, you might simply start with the first option you listed. In any event, try to discuss the various options separately rather than collectively.

Second, before getting into the pros and cons of an option, make sure that your client has an adequate understanding of what the option entails. For example, you will usually have to provide a more detailed explanation of a legal option than a non-legal one. If the option involves the filing of a lawsuit, you will need to explain matters such as the legal claims that would be raised, the remedies that would be sought, and an overview of the pretrial process. If your client is charged with a crime and the option under discussion is a potential plea bargain, you will need to explain matters such as the charges against your client, the prosecution's burden of proof, your client's right to a jury trial, the process of entering into a guilty plea, and the specific elements of a possible bargain. In short, there can be no meaningful

---

[1] *See* Robert F. Cochran, Jr. et. al., *The Counselor-At-Law: A Collaborative Approach to Client Interviewing and Counseling* 137–138 (1999) (referring to these factors as "minimal acceptance criteria").

discussion about the pros and cons of an option in the absence of having a good understanding of what it involves.

Third, once you move to a discussion of the pros and cons of each option, do not hesitate to directly ask your client what "upsides" or "downsides," or "advantages" or "disadvantages" he sees about each option. In addition, in a highly complex case, it may sometimes be useful to ask your client to prepare a written list of pros and cons about various options in advance of your meeting, or you might construct such a list with your client as you discuss each option at the meeting.[2] However, the utility of this exercise will depend upon whether your client is intellectually inclined to think about pros and cons in a balance-sheet type of format. For many clients, this approach is artificial and unnecessarily time consuming.

Fourth, just as your client's situation and objectives may present non-legal as well as legal options, there may be non-legal as well as legal pros and cons to those options. In general, non-legal pros and cons affect your client in a variety of personal ways outside of the law, whereas legal pros and cons relate to the potential outcomes of your client's legal rights or remedies. The distinction is important because your discussion of these different types of pros and cons involves somewhat different approaches.

## [1]　Discussing Non-Legal Pros and Cons

"Non-legal" pros and cons are consequences that tangibly or intangibly affect your client or others psychologically, socially, economically, and morally or ideologically. These consequences are usually highly personal and subjective, and they are frequently integral to a client's ultimate decision about which option to choose. For example, for various psychological, social, or moral reasons, a client charged with a serious crime may choose the option of going to trial rather than pleading guilty to a lesser charge under a plea bargain, even though the most likely outcome of the trial option is that he will be convicted on overwhelming evidence. Similarly, a client who has a strong case to recover substantial damages may choose to settle it for a much smaller sum rather than go to trial because of certain non-legal consequences he is unwilling to incur by taking the case to trial.

In discussing non-legal pros and cons, you and your client should consider, as appropriate, how each option may affect his:

(1)　*Psychological interests*:

- Level of anxiety or stress
- Self-esteem, self-respect, and self-image
- Need for recognition, status, power or authority
- Sense of personal satisfaction or well-being
- Willingness to take risks

(2)　*Social interests*:

- Family, friends, co-workers, and other third persons
- Personal reputation
- Good will

---

[2] *See* David A. Binder, et. al., *Lawyers As Counselors: A Client Centered Approach* 307–308 (1991); Robert F. Cochran, Jr., et. al., *The Counselor-At-Law: A Collaborative Approach to Client Interviewing and Counseling* 146–147, 163–164 (1999).

- Past, present, and future interpersonal relationships

(3) *Economic interests*:

- Financial obligations for attorney's fees and litigation costs
- Financial security or credit rating
- Short-term or long-term profits
- Business or institutional efficiency
- Past, present, or future business relationships

(4) *Moral or ideological interests*:

- Moral or philosophical principles
- Religious or political beliefs
- Sense of fairness or integrity
- Desire to promote or avoid precedent

Whether the effects of a particular option on any of these matters constitute a "pro" or a "con" is, of course, for your client to decide. In addition, he will often be in a better position than you to foresee the non-legal pros and cons that are likely to result from a particular option. Nevertheless, you can help your client identify these pros and cons by raising the ones that occur to you and by encouraging him to consider how each option may affect him in terms of the types of interests listed above.

## [2]   Discussing Legal Pros and Cons

"Legal" pros and cons are the most likely legal consequences of a particular option that affect your client or others. Generally speaking, a legal consequence that advances your client's objectives will fall within the "pro" column, and a legal consequence that undermines your client's objectives will fall within the "con" column. Here, unlike non-legal pros and cons, you are in a better position than your client to forecast the legal outcomes of an option and determine whether they will advance or undermine your client's objectives. After all, predicting legal consequences is a major part of giving "legal advice."

As mentioned previously, when a legal option is involved, you must first explain the legal process or legal principles pertinent to the option (*e.g.*, the general process of asserting a claim, defending a lawsuit, or incorporating a business; or the legal principles underlying a particular cause of action, defense, or provision in a contract, etc.). When discussing the legal pros and cons of an option, whether a legal option or a non-legal one, you must also explain (1) the legal ramifications of the option in terms of its legal advantages and disadvantages, and (2) your best prediction about the legal outcome of the option.

When discussing a legal option, these explanations will often involve providing your client with an analysis of the overall merits of his case — *i.e.*, how a jury, judge, administrative body, board commission, or licensing agency is most likely to view the evidence and what the outcome of the particular legal proceeding or process is most likely to be. When a non-legal option is being discussed, pertinent legal consequences should be pointed out as well. For example, if your client has been sued, the option of doing nothing in response to the suit (assuming that option might be viable under the circumstances) is likely to be that your client will incur a judgment by default; and, if the judgment is not paid, your client's property may be at risk and his credit rating may be impaired. Remember that regardless of whether you are discussing the legal pros and cons of a legal or non-legal option, you must explain the law in *plain English.*

When predicting the legal consequences of an option, you should never overstate or understate, or overestimate or underestimate, your prediction. Reasonably accurate predictions about legal outcomes, though often difficult to make, are critical to comparing options and arriving at a decision about the best option. Sometimes, a useful way to couch a prediction for your client, whether in litigation or transactional matters, is to state it in terms of a specific percentage (or range of percentages) of likelihood, rather than in vague terminology.

For example, if you couch your client's chances about a particular outcome as being "very good," "quite good," "pretty good," "either way," "not so good," "not very good," or "not good," your client may not understand what you really mean or may entirely misunderstand your assessment. On the other hand, some clients may have a better understanding of what you mean if you speak in terms of chances like "80%," "70%," "60%," "50-50," "40%," "30%," or "20%".

Along with expressing the likelihood of success in percentage terms, it may be useful to discuss a range of potential outcomes,[3] such as:

- *best possible*
- *best likely*
- *most likely*
- *worst likely*
- *worst possible*

For example, in a personal injury case, you might predict that the "most likely" outcome for your client at trial would be a verdict of approximately $100,000, that the "best likely" result would be twice that amount, and that the "worst likely" result would be $10,525.32 (representing the undisputed amount of his doctors' bills). Assuming that the case presents at least *plausible* "best possible" and "worst possible" outcomes, these might be mentioned as well; but there would be no need to mention them if those possibilities were purely theoretical. In predicting "best"-case or "worst"-case scenarios, these should also be described in percentage terms (*e.g.,* "I think the best we could hope for is a verdict of about $200,000, but I would put only a one-in-four chance on that happening; on the other hand, I would say that the chances of recovering only your doctors' bills are even smaller, less than 10%."). The same technique may be used when making predictions about non-litigation matters (*e.g.,* "I would say that the best likely result is that the City will just go ahead and grant your request to rezone to an R-1 district, but I would place only a 25% chance on that; the worst likely scenario is that the Council will prohibit your building altogether, but that's very unlikely — perhaps a 5% chance at most; and the most likely result is that they will allow you to build the building with a conditional use permit, which I would put at a 70% chance of happening.").

The legal outcomes of options are often difficult to predict because your bottom-line assessment depends upon making certain sub-predictions. For example, whether a jury is most likely to award $100,000 or $200,000 may largely depend upon whether the trial judge will admit or exclude certain evidence, or how the judge will rule on an unsettled question of law pertaining to damages. Similarly,

---

[3] *See also* David A. Binder, et. al., *Lawyers as Counselors: A Client-Centered Approach* 339–340 (1991).

whether a City will allow your client to build a day-care center in a particular zoning district may depend upon whether the State will first grant him a license to operate the proposed center. In these situations, you should *briefly* outline for your client the various factors and sub-predictions that relate to your overall assessment about the outcome of the option. After doing so, the best you might be able to say about the value of the case is that it is worth somewhere between $100,000 and $200,000, or that the chances of your client being able to build his day care center are a "toss up." In sum, when it is difficult for you to make a prediction about a legal consequence or outcome, you should not be afraid to explain why the prediction is difficult in light of the different factors, assumptions, and sub-predictions you have had to consider. Give your client the benefit of your best judgment, but, when applicable, don't hesitate to emphasize, "It all depends."

## § 5.07  HELPING YOUR CLIENT DECIDE WHICH OPTION TO CHOOSE

After you and your client have discussed the non-legal and legal pros and cons of each option, the question is, which option should your client choose? In theory, the best option is the one that is most likely to advance the greatest number of your client's objectives under circumstances where the non-legal and legal "pros" of the option outweigh the "cons." However, it is a mistake to suppose that choosing the best option is simply a process of tallying up the pros and cons of each option to identify the one that has the greatest number of advantages and least number of disadvantages. Different clients value and weigh pros and cons differently. Although most clients will consider the pros and cons of various options holistically and decide upon a best option in light of all the circumstances, many clients will choose one option over another solely because of some special value they place on one or more consequences of an option. Assuming your client fully understands his options and their pros and cons, you should respect the value preferences underlying his choice of a particular option.

On the other hand, if you believe your client is making a bad decision that is inconsistent with his values or objectives, don't hesitate to advise him against the decision and explain why. In this regard, it is entirely proper for you to discuss moral, economic, social and political considerations, as well as the law (*see* § 6.05). Your client's decision about his options must be knowing, intelligent, and voluntary; and, as mentioned previously, you have an ethical obligation to "exercise independent professional judgment and render candid advice" (*see also* § 6.05). Accordingly, if you believe your client is making a bad decision, you might go over his options and their pros and cons again to ensure that his decision is fully informed. In addition, if time is not of the essence, you might encourage your client to take some additional time to think through his options and meet with you again at a later time to make a final decision.

If your client is undecided about which option to choose, encourage him to "talk through" his options. Consider asking him questions such as:

- *Which option do you think will satisfy most of your objectives?*
- *Are there any particular upsides or downsides that you see about a particular option?*
- *All things considered, which option makes the most sense to you?*
- *Which option appears to be fairest to you?*

- *Which option do you think would be best for you in the short run, or in the long run?*
- *Is there anything about a particular option that concerns you most?*
- *Which option would most satisfy you personally?*
- *Is there any further information you would like to have before making a decision?*
- *Would you like to "sleep on the matter" for a while?*
- *Is there anyone else you would like to talk to before making a decision?*
- *Is there anything further that I can do to help you make your decision?*

The last of these questions will often prompt your client to ask, "If you were me, what would you do?" Indeed, clients often ask this question without any prompting at all. How you handle it will largely depend on the particular decision to be made and whether you believe it calls for a more lawyer-centered, client-centered, or collaborative approach to counseling.

For example, as discussed in § 2.03[4], if the decision relates to technical legal matters such as drafting, legal procedure, trial tactics or trial strategy, you might take a more lawyer-centered approach over the decision-making process and not hesitate to render an opinion about the best decision to make. On the other hand, if the decision involves matters such as whether to file a lawsuit, whether to accept a settlement offer, or whether your client should waive one or more of his "fundamental" rights in a criminal case, your response would have to be collaborative or client-centered in the sense that only your client can make the final decision on these matters. For example, if your client asks you what you would do when faced with the choice of pleading guilty or taking the case to trial, after fully discussing and advising him about the non-legal and legal pros and cons of the choices at hand, you might say:

> *I understand why you are asking me what I would do if I were in your shoes. But this is a decision that affects your fundamental legal rights, and therefore only you can make it. I can help you think through this important decision by going over again its upsides and downsides and the various options available to you. But I hope you will understand that it would be unfair to you for me to try to speculate on what decision I would make when I will not be personally affected by it. Only you have the right to make this decision.*

Then you might proceed by reviewing the pros and cons of the decision again or asking your client one or more of the questions listed above.

Lastly, if the decision relates to matters such as what offers or counteroffers to make in negotiations, what claims or defenses to raise in a lawsuit, or how to structure a transaction or new business enterprise, you might take a more middle-ground approach when responding to your client's question about what decision you would make. Here, you might strike a balance between making a directive and nondirective response by explaining which option you think would best satisfy your client's objectives and values, but at the same time pointing out that the final decision is for your client to make.

## § 5.08   IMPLEMENTING YOUR CLIENT'S DECISION

After your client has decided upon a course of action, you must continue to counsel him during the implementation of the representation. The Rules of Professional Conduct specifically require that you (1) "consult with [your] client as to the means by which [the objectives of the representation] are to be pursued" (*see* § 6.03), and (2) "keep [your] client reasonably informed about the status of a matter and promptly comply with reasonable requests for information" (*see* § 6.04).

For example, after your client has decided upon the substantive aspects of a will, contract, or other transactional matter, you will need to review with him all documents prepared in connection with the matter. If the representation involves litigation, you will need to counsel him throughout the discovery process, during settlement negotiations, when preparing for trial, throughout any trial of the case, and in connection with any appeal. In short, you have an obligation to keep your client reasonably informed about the status of the representation and appropriately counsel him about other decisions that need to be made in light of changed circumstances or new developments.

## § 5.09   CRISIS COUNSELING

A prospective or existing client will sometimes call you in a situation that he perceives to be a crisis. For example, the client may have just been arrested and put in jail, served with a lawsuit, lost his job, been seriously injured, or separated from his wife. Events like these often constitute "crises" for clients because the immediate situation overwhelms them with such a degree of anxiety, fear, or anger that they become panic stricken or rendered virtually dysfunctional. When counseling a client in these circumstances, it is useful to keep three things in mind.

First, after your client has told you the nature of the crisis, you should calmly and confidently assure him that you will help him get through the crisis. Along with this reassurance, give him any necessary immediate advice to preserve the status quo and arrange to meet with him as soon as possible. For example, if your client has been arrested and is phoning you from jail, you might say:

> . . . *Okay, John, I understand what's happened. We can deal with this, but I need you to be patient for a little bit. I will come see you at the jail at 4:00 this afternoon, and we will be able to talk then about what we need to do to get you released. Don't worry if I'm not there exactly at 4:00; the jail has only three meeting rooms and there is sometimes a delay in getting an available room. In the meantime, don't talk with anyone about this matter, and don't call your sister about the bond. She won't know what to do at this point, and I can call her later to explain everything after you and I have met. Are you clear about the present plan?* . . . . *Okay, just hang in there, and I'll see you this afternoon.*

Second, when you meet with your client, you must be especially calm, patient, and understanding about his situation. This is a critical time to convey empathetic understanding (*see* § 4.02[1]). Let your client vent his emotions, if necessary; and keep in mind that the stress of the situation may make it very difficult for him to rationally explain and understand what has happened. Along with reassuring your client about your ability to help him, it is usually best to set out a specific course of action about what you and your client will do to protect his rights in the short run.

For example, at the conclusion of the meeting with your client at the jail, you might say:

> . . . *So here's the plan, John. First, I will call your sister tonight to explain the situation and find out what she can do about helping with the bond. Second, I will call the U.S. Attorney tomorrow morning to discuss the bond situation and see if we can get your case before the magistrate first thing Monday morning. Third, I'll come see you again sometime tomorrow afternoon after I've talked with the U.S. Attorney. Finally, like I said before, I don't want you talking with anyone about this matter, and that includes talking about our plans for making bond. As for your sister, don't worry about her; I know what to say to her, and I think I will be able to calm her down before you see her. Do we have an agreement about the plan?*

Finally, in some crisis situations, your client's intellectual and emotional state may be impaired to the point that you believe he should be referred to a mental health professional or some other support agency or program. If this is the case, explain that his emotional affliction is not abnormal and that many people benefit from specialized counseling or support. If your client is amenable to a referral, advise him about a specific person or agency that he can call. Ideally, if your client consents, you should call the mental health professional or support agency yourself to make an appointment for your client. Often clients who are suffering from an emotional problem cannot find their way through a bureaucratic maze to schedule an appointment. Your help can facilitate the scheduling process.

## § 5.10   ILLUSTRATION OF DECISION-MAKING CONFERENCE[4]

As shown in § 4.10, Larry Odden held an initial meeting and interview with Clara Miles and agreed to represent her in a personal injury case. The day after the meeting, Clara called Larry and told him that John Jones was the name of the adjuster for her insurance company that paid for the property damage to her car. Larry obtained photos of the property damage to Clara's car from Jones and spoke with him about the company's investigation of the accident. Jones said that Ronald Smith, the driver of the pickup, called Jones a few weeks after the accident to say that he (Smith) had seen a doctor for neck strain following the accident. However, Jones said he has not heard anything further from Smith about his alleged injuries. Larry also met with Officer Boles and learned that Jane Smith, the passenger in the pickup truck, was Ronald Smith's wife, and that she corroborated Mr. Smith's story that he had a green light when he made his right-hand turn from Estes Drive onto Franklin Street. In addition, Larry has received a copy of Clara's chiropractic records from Dr. Byler.

Larry's secretary scheduled a follow-up appointment for Clara to meet with Larry. That office conference, after an exchange of greetings, proceeded as follows:

---

[4] This illustration is intended to show how a skilled attorney might handle a decision-making conference. You might conduct the conference quite differently and may even disagree with some of the approaches taken by the lawyer. Bear in mind that the lawyer's approach is, in significant respects, affected by his personal style and counseling philosophy. In addition, the lawyer's interaction with the client is significantly affected by the client's personality, demeanor, and body language — all of which are not readily apparent from a mere transcript.

1.  L: Clara, I have obtained a copy of your medical records from Dr. Byler; and I've spoken with Officer Boles and Mr. Jones, the adjuster for your insurance company.

2.  C: Okay.

3.  L: I learned from Officer Boles that there were no independent eyewitnesses to the accident. But, he said that Jane Smith, the passenger in the pickup truck, is Mr. Smith's wife; and she, like her husband, says that Mr. Smith had a green light when he was turning from Estes onto Franklin.

4.  C: She's just saying that because her husband is saying that. But that's not what happened.

5.  L: It just goes to show, once again, that there are two different stories about what happened.

6.  C: Will this hurt my case? Before, it was Dan's word and my word against Mr. Smith; now it's two against two, our word against theirs. Does this mean I don't have a case?

7.  L: No, it doesn't mean that. What Ms. Smith says really doesn't change matters much. From the beginning, there have been two versions about what happened — yours and Dan's on the one hand, and Mr. Smith's on the other. Mr. Smith either had a green light or he didn't. In any event, I'm beginning to develop a theory that Mr. Smith was at fault for the accident even if the light had just turned green before he started his turn.

8.  C: Oh, what's that?

9.  L: Well, I met with Officer Boles out at the accident scene. He showed me more exactly where each vehicle was positioned after the accident. What he told me was a little bit different from what was shown on his diagram in the accident report. So I took a photo of the intersection, and I had Officer Boles draw on it to show the positions of the vehicles as he saw them right after the accident. [Larry hands Clara the photo].

10. C: [Looking at the photo], What does this mean?

11. L: I'll explain; but first, what do you think about how he has drawn in the positions of the vehicles on the photo? Does that look right to you?

12. C: It looks right. But everything happened so fast that I didn't pay much attention to exactly where our car and the pickup were located in the road when the accident happened. Maybe Dan will know better.

13. L: Yes, I should talk with Dan at some point. But this is what Officer Boles would testify to [pointing to photo]. As you can see from his drawing on the photo, your car has basically cleared the intersection; it is actually through the intersection. If that's right, it means that even if the light on Franklin had turned from yellow to red at this point [indicating on photo], your car was almost completely through the intersection when the light was still yellow. It means that if your car were almost through the intersection when the light turned red on Franklin and green on Estes, Mr. Smith should have looked to see that he could make his turn safely and that your car had cleared the intersection. Do you see what I mean?

14. C: I think so . . . (pause).

15. L: Officer Boles also pointed out to me that, unlike many other traffic lights in town, when the light for traffic on Franklin turns to red, the light for traffic on Estes turns to green right away; there is no one or two-second delay. The bottom-line is that, if your car was almost all the way through the intersection when your light turned red, Mr. Smith should not have started his right-hand turn until he looked to see that he could do so safely.

At least, that's a good argument for us to a jury. Does that make sense?

16. C: Yes, now I see what you're saying. But, if what you are saying is right, why would we have to go to a jury?

17. L: Well, we may not have to. Having a jury decide the case will be necessary if the case can't be resolved by agreement, by a settlement that is satisfactory to you. In other words, if Mr. Smith's insurance company, All-Good Insurance, says they are unwilling to settle, or they make a final offer that you are unwilling to accept, then a jury will have to decide the case.

18. C: I really don't think I want to go through a trial, if at all possible.

19. L. Trial is certainly a last resort. It's very time consuming, and the costs can be expensive like I mentioned last time. It can also be stressful, and it can be risky . . . (pause). I do want to talk with you today about your various options so we can decide where to go from here. But, perhaps as a starting point, can we talk a bit more about some of the concerns you talked about last time?

20. C: Okay.

21. L: You mentioned last time that you want your life back, that all of this has been hard on you emotionally and financially, and that you're worried about your back in the long term. Is that a fair summary?

22. C: Yes, it is. I guess, also, I would like to resolve all of this quickly. It's been such a financial strain on us. And I think I've gone through a lot emotionally as well as physically, and I feel I should be compensated for all the stress. As for my back now, well, I don't think it's going to get any better. I guess I'll just have to manage to live with it. Do you think we might have a chance of settling this case quickly?

23. L: If All-Good Insurance is willing to discuss settlement right now — and that's an "if" — I think they would settle the case quickly only if they could settle it very cheaply.

24. C: Why is that?

25. L: If you settle the case, you will have to sign a document called a release, which is a promise that you will not sue Mr. Smith and make any further claim for your injuries. Once you sign a release, that's good for Mr. Smith's insurance company because then they won't have to pay for any future treatment for your back or future pain and suffering that you may incur after the release is signed. Dr. Byler's last medical report says you have chronic pain in your back, and the report recommends that you see an orthopedic surgeon for an evaluation of possible permanent injury. She goes on to say in her report that she "suspects permanent injury." When All-Good sees that report, the company might want to settle cheaply because they know that, once you sign a release, they will be off the hook for paying greater damages for possible permanent injury and future pain and suffering.

26. C: Why don't we just tell them that I will have future pain and probably have permanent injury? Can't we ask for that too?

27. L: Not unless a physician makes a formal diagnosis that you, in fact, have a permanent injury and that you will likely have future pain and suffering.

28. C: Why is that?

29. L: In your case, Clara, there are three types of damages that the law allows. First, you are entitled to the reasonable medical expenses you have incurred, which, according to Dr. Byler's bills are now $2,500. Second, you

are also entitled to reasonable compensation for past and present pain and suffering. There's no formula for that; it's thought of as an amount that a jury would reasonably award based on all of the circumstances. Finally, if you have a permanent injury, you are entitled to additional compensation for that permanency — depending upon the extent of the permanency — along with compensation for future pain and suffering and perhaps future medical expenses. But, the law says that all of these future damages cannot be speculative. There must be evidence, such as a formal diagnosis and prognosis from a doctor, that permanent injury exists and that you are most likely to incur future pain and suffering. Then, the future damages are not considered speculative and a person may be compensated for them.

30.  C: I don't know if I have permanent injury, but I do know that I still have a lot of pain in my back; and it's there almost all the time. Do you think it would help my case if I went to an orthopedic doctor?

31.  L: Well, if a doctor says you have permanent injury, then you would be entitled to compensation for that permanency. But, whether you go to another doctor, Clara, is a decision that I believe you should make based solely on your personal feelings about your health. I always tell my clients that this type of decision is so highly personal that it's not something that should be decided based on any legal case. If you have permanent injury, as Dr. Byler is worried about, that is something you will have to live with long after this case is over, regardless of whether you receive any compensation for future damages.

32.  C: Yeah, I recognize it's a personal decision. I'm very worried about my back. But I'm not sure what to do (pause . . . ). When you were talking about damages, can I get damages for all the stress I've been through? There have been a lot of times over the past year when I have been very depressed.

33.  L: That depends. Has your depression been chronic or disabling?

34.  C: No. I just get depressed now and then about not being a good enough mother and wife when my back is hurting real bad. I've just been generally stressed out, you know, by the whole situation.

35.  L: Yes. I know it's been hard on you. And then you have the added stress of trying to work —

36.  C: Yeah, this first month of working has been rough.

37.  L: I can imagine . . . (pause). Going back to your question about compensation for stress, the law in our State only allows compensation for emotional distress, as a separate type of damage, if the distress is very severe, such as chronic depression or a disabling emotional condition which may be generally diagnosed by a mental-health professional. So, I'm not really sure that what you've described to me fits into this rather narrow category of what our courts refer to as severe and disabling emotional distress. At the same time, however, all that you have gone through, not just the actual physical pain in your neck and back, generally falls within the overall category of pain and suffering, and I would want the other side to know about it.

38.  C: Right. Well, what are my options at this point?

39.  L: Well, as I see it, there are basically three options to consider. Without stating them in any particular order of preference, one option is to go ahead now and file a lawsuit to encourage settlement and get the ball rolling if the case can't be settled. A second option is not to file a lawsuit now, but instead

start negotiations with All-Good. A third option is to hold off on doing anything for now, to allow you some time to think about whether you want to see another doctor and to see whether your back condition changes over the next few months or so. There are certain pros and cons to each option.

40.   C: I'd really rather not sue and go to trial. Do we really have to do that?

41.   L: No, that's just one option to think about. And I'm just referring to filing a suit, not going to trial anytime soon. There are certain advantages to filing now, but there are disadvantages as well. What concerns you most about this option?

42.   C: Well, wouldn't filing a suit make them angry so they might not want to settle? And then, if we sued, my husband would be dragged into all of this. I don't want him to have to deal with all of this if we can avoid it. He's told me he'll be supportive of me, but he doesn't really want to be involved or make a claim for himself like we talked about last time.

43.   L: I really don't think that filing suit would hurt our chances of settling the case, and it might well encourage settlement by showing that we mean business. But, let's talk first about your concerns regarding Dan. How does he feel about you making a claim?

44.   C: As I say, he's supportive of me, but . . . (long pause). When he broke up with his former partner in the plumbing business, this former partner, Al, accused Dan of having stolen some money from the business, which isn't true. But I'm afraid the other side might find out about that and try to dig up dirt on Dan, to say he's just a thief and a bad person and that no one should believe him about how the accident happened.

45.   L: How long ago was this accusation made?

46.   C: About a year and a half ago.

47.   L: Did this partner, Al, take any legal action or seek any criminal charges against Dan?

48.   C: No. The whole thing has just fizzled away. Nothing has happened. But I wouldn't want to stir it all up again.

49.   L: I can understand that. If you filed a lawsuit, I think it is unlikely the other side would find out about this accusation by Al or care much about it unless Dan has some conviction for stealing money or some other conviction —

50.   C: Dan has no criminal record. And the accusation is just hogwash.

51.   L: Yes. Partnership breakups can sometimes be like marriage breakups —

52.   C: Yeah, it was ugly.

53.   L: Well, even though I don't think that any accusation by Dan's former partner would come up in your case, there is an important way in which Dan could become directly involved in your suit if we filed right away. If we filed suit, it's quite possible that Mr. Smith would immediately file a counter suit against your husband. When I spoke with Mr. Jones, he said Mr. Smith called him a few weeks after the accident because Smith had apparently gone to a doctor for treatment of strain in his neck. On the other hand, Jones says he has not heard anything further from Mr. Smith since that time. Even so, I think there is a good possibility that if we filed a suit, Mr. Smith would bring your husband into the case and make a cross claim against him for any injuries Smith sustained. Of course, even if we didn't file a lawsuit, Mr. Smith might still bring a suit against Dan at some point, although that suit, like any we file, would have to be filed within three years of the date of the accident.

54. C: If Dan were counter-sued, who would represent him?

55. L: Your insurance company would hire a lawyer to defend Dan and would pay for that defense.

56. C: Would they hire you?

57. L: No, they would get another lawyer.

58. C: I don't really see any advantages to filing a lawsuit right away.

59. L: The main advantage is that it would show All-Good from the get-go that we are very serious about your claim. If I merely contact All-Good and start negotiations, the adjuster for All-Good may well say that he or she is not interested in talking because Mr. Smith insists he had the green light and was not negligent. On the other hand, if we file a lawsuit, All-Good would know that we mean business and would have to hire a lawyer to defend Mr. Smith. After some initial discovery in the case — some initial sharing of information between both sides — All-Good might then become more interested in talking about a possible settlement before spending a whole lot of money in defending the suit at a trial . . .

60. C: (Interrupting), What if we first tried to negotiate with All-Good; and then, if they said they were not interested in talking, we go ahead and file a suit?

61. L: That's another option. It's the usual approach taken in a personal injury case, particularly when there is no dispute about who was at fault in the accident. I would prepare a document called a settlement brochure to send to All-Good. The brochure summarizes the facts of the case and your damages, such as your course of medical treatment, your pain and suffering, and any permanent injury and future pain and suffering. The brochure attaches a copy of the accident report along with your medical records and bills, and concludes with a demand — a specific offer of money — to settle the case. After the adjuster reviews the brochure, he or she will make a counteroffer. And then further offers and counteroffers are made until one side makes a final offer. When a final offer is on the table, the case is either settled or it's not. And if it's not, your option is to file a lawsuit to ask a jury to decide the case.

62. C: Why don't we just do a settlement brochure?

63. L: We could. But if we do that at this time, we would not be able to make a solid claim for any permanent injury because we don't yet know whether a doctor would diagnose you as having a permanent injury. If, after settlement negotiations are underway, we found out that you in fact have permanent injury, it would be difficult for us to say to All-Good, "Look, we misjudged our initial demand, and we are now making a new demand that is greater than our first one." In other words, good-faith negotiations on our part will require some compromise by gradually reducing our initial demand, not by increasing it. If we lose credibility with All-Good, they are likely to cut off negotiations altogether.

64. C: So, why would filing a lawsuit right now be better?

65. L: It might be better, but that depends on how you weigh its upsides and downsides. The downside, from what we've been talking about, is that it may well bring Dan into the lawsuit as a defendant, rather than as just a witness to the accident. The upside is that All-Good would know that we are real serious in taking this case to trial if necessary. In recent years, All-Good has tended to take a "low-ball" approach to settlement negotiations in non-catastrophic personal injury cases. They know that most

claimants don't have much money to pay for the costs of a trial, and that most people would rather get a smaller sum of money in their pockets than go through all the time, stress, and expense of getting a larger sum at trial. So, All-Good's perception about how serious we are about going to trial is critical to their decisions about how much to offer in settlement.

66.  C: I see. But if we file a lawsuit right now, we still wouldn't know if I have any permanent injury. Could we still ask for that in a suit?

67.  L: Yes; we could. We could allege in a suit that we believe you may have permanent injury in light of Dr. Byler's latest report, which raises that issue. But what she has said isn't, by itself, sufficient proof of permanent injury because no definitive diagnosis of permanency has been made. You see, if we file a lawsuit right away, I don't expect settlement discussions to start right away. Instead, over the next five months or so, the other side would want to take your deposition, your husband's deposition, and officer Boles's deposition. There would also be time for you to see a doctor about any permanent injury or need for further treatment, if you chose to do that. And if that doctor said you had permanent injury, he or she would be deposed as well —

68.  C: What's a deposition?

69.  L: A deposition is a way of finding out the testimony of a witness. For example, if they wanted to take Officer Boles's deposition, I and the lawyer for Mr. Smith would arrange a time when Boles would come to this office so that Smith's lawyer could ask him questions about his investigation of the accident. A stenographer would be present who would transcribe all of the questions and answers given in the deposition. That way, the other side will know what Boles's testimony will be.

70.  C: And, when would we start negotiations?

71.  L: Negotiations might start during the deposition phase, but most likely they would take place in earnest during mediation. Our courts require that all cases of this type go through non-binding mediation well before trial. Once the lawyers believe they have enough information to evaluate the case, a mediator is selected, and a time is arranged for the parties and their lawyers to meet to seriously discuss settlement. The mediator tries to bring the parties together. It's a required process, but it's informal and takes place in a conference room like this. If the case doesn't settle, it proceeds to trial.

72.  C: Do you think we would have good chance of settling this case at mediation?

73.  L: Statistically speaking, I would say yes, because the majority of lawsuits do settle that way. From what we know about your case now, Officer Boles's testimony about the position of the vehicles is important on the negligence question; and by the time of mediation, the other side would know his testimony from having taken his deposition. On the question of damages, once again, the issue of whether you have any permanent injury is quite important. This brings me to our third option —

74.  C: You mean seeing another doctor before we do anything —

75.  L: Yes. How do you feel about that?

76.  C: I don't know. I was hoping we could settle the case pretty quickly, which would help out Dan and me financially. And I don't know how I would pay to see another doctor . . . (pause).

77.  L: I thought you had some health insurance through Dan's plumbing business.

78.  C: We did. But we couldn't afford to keep up the payments on it, so we dropped it sometime last April. It wasn't any good anyway for my injury because it wouldn't cover the chiropractic bills. We still keep insurance for Tommy, but Dan and I don't have any health insurance at this time.

79.  L: I see . . . (pause). I am very sympathetic to your financial situation, Clara, but I don't think you can count on any guaranteed settlement of this case to help you out financially. It's a close case; and, at least at the beginning, there's a real chance that All-Good will decline to make any settlement offer at all for the simple reason that their insured, Mr. Smith, insists he had a green light. All-Good also knows, and it is important for you and me to keep in mind, that we are in a contributory negligence state. Under our law, that means that even if a jury were to believe that Mr. Smith was mostly at fault for the accident, if the jury also believes that Dan was somehow at fault, even in the slightest way, you would not be entitled to recover any damages at all from Mr. Smith. Most states don't have this harsh law, but we do.

80.  C: It sounds bad for us, doesn't it —

81.  L: Well, I don't want to create false hopes for you; and, at the same time I don't want to sound overly pessimistic. All I am saying is that, from what I know now, the case could go either way. We would have to prove by the greater weight of the evidence that Mr. Smith was negligent, and he would have to prove that Dan was contributorily negligent. Both sides would be taking a risk in front of a jury. And when there are risks for both sides, those risks tend to encourage compromise and settlement. I believe in your case, and I'll stand by you. Although there are no guarantees, my best judgment is that this case can be settled in the end, although it may take some time to get to that point.

82.  C: Do you think you might be able to get All-Good to make the payments for me to see another doctor?

83.  L: I'm quite sure they won't do that in your case. But if you decide to consult another doctor — and, again, this is a decision that I think you should make solely on a personal level — I can get you up to $1,500 to use to pay for another doctor.

84.  C: How's that?

85.  L: When I talked with Mr. Jones, I asked him whether you had a medical payments provision on your automobile insurance policy, and it turns out that you do. It has a limit of $2,000, which is available to you for medical bills for treatment of injuries in an auto accident regardless of how the accident happened. Dr. Byler's bills show that your unpaid balance to her is $500. So, you could use $500 of the $2,000 to pay off Dr. Byler, and that would leave you up to $1,500 to pay another doctor.

86.  C: Oh, I didn't know that! But wouldn't your firm take a one-third fee out of the $2,000?

87.  L: No, we wouldn't do that. This money is automatically available to you if you incur medical bills for an auto accident. Like a lot of other people, you just didn't know you had this benefit. So, no, we wouldn't take any fee out of the $2,000.

88.  C: I see. Thank you. But what doctor should I see?

89. L: I don't think it would be appropriate for me to recommend a particular doctor, because I'm not one. But, it seems to me that if you make a personal decision to see another doctor, perhaps you could call Tommy's pediatrician, Dr. Partin, and ask her whom she might recommend. Didn't she recommend someone before?

90. C: Yes, and I had forgotten the name of the person she had recommended. I do remember, though, that the doctor she mentioned was an orthopedic specialist.

91. L: Well, that's the kind of doctor that Dr. Byler recommends in her last medical report. She's another person you could ask for a possible referral.

92. C: Yeah, that's a good idea. And how would I arrange to have my new doctor's bills paid out of my medical payments policy?

93. L: You could have the doctor's office just send the bills to my office and I'll pass them on to Mr. Jones. Or you could do that yourself. Jones will then write a check directly to the doctor's office. And if you want to pay off Dr. Byler's remaining bill now, I can send the bill to Mr. Jones and he'll send her a check for the $500.

94. C: Would you do that?

95. L: Consider it done.

96. C: Larry, I'm basically feeling better about all of this. And I now think it makes sense for me to see if another doctor can help me. At least I will have some money to pay for that. But, can you tell me what you think I might be able to settle this case for, looking down the road?

97. L: Do you mean, as things stand right now?

98. C: Yes, not taking into account what another doctor would say, because we don't know anything about that now —

99. L: Well, as we sit here today, if there were no dispute about negligence, I would estimate the value of the case to be in the $12,000 to $15,000 range in terms of what a jury would award. But, because it's a close case on negligence and contributory negligence, I think it's basically a toss up about how a jury would decide who was at fault. In other words, there's a 50% chance you would get between $12,000 and $15,000, and a 50% chance you would get nothing. So I would discount the settlement value of the case by 50%, and that makes a settlement value of approximately $7,000. And that figure assumes you have not incurred any litigation costs.

100. C: Even $15,000 sounds somewhat low for what I've been through.

101. L: It is. But, generally, these cases don't result in high damage awards. Juries usually have difficulty sympathizing with neck and back pain unless it is very debilitating or the collision was very severe. It's hard for juries to put a value on an injury they can't see. It's hard for them to understand that, although you look healthy, you are in constant pain. Also, many juries are skeptical about medical treatment from chiropractors. On the other hand, I think a jury would like you, and they would listen carefully to all you've gone through. You must remember that my current evaluation of your case is based only what I know now. There are many other factors.

102. C: It still doesn't seem like much money. But, you said it might be different if my back turns out to be a long-term problem —

103. L: Yes. That can be a significant factor depending upon what a doctor says, particularly an orthopedic surgeon . . . (pause). You know, Clara, I've had many clients tell me that, in the end, they basically wouldn't trade

any amount of money for what they've gone through. That's hard for people to believe who haven't suffered through an injury, but it's what many clients say.

104.   C: Yeah, I sort of feel that way too.

105.   L: Well . . . (pause), do you think you might want to consult with another doctor?

106.   C: Yes; I'm pretty definite about that now. Do you think we should just wait on the results of that before we do anything else?

107.   L: Yes, that's my best judgment. After we know more about your back situation, we will be in a better position to factor that into your overall case. And, perhaps another doctor will be able to provide you with some further treatment to help you.

108.   C: After I see another doctor, what should we do?

109.   L: That will depend, of course, on what your doctor says. If your doctor recommends further treatment — physical therapy, for example — you will have to decide whether you want to go through that. If your doctor says that there's really nothing more he or she can do and makes a final diagnosis, then there's no reason to delay proceeding with your case. At that point, a decision would have to be made about whether it would be best to file a lawsuit right away or start negotiations by making a demand through a settlement brochure. Fortunately, from the standpoint of protecting your legal rights, we are not faced with any deadline on your case at this time. The latest we would have to file a lawsuit to preserve your claim would be three years from the date of the accident. That would be February 8, two years from now.

110.   C: If I end up having to go to physical therapy or get some other treatment, what about my time off from work?

111.   L: As part of personal injury damages, the law entitles you to be compensated for your gross wages lost during the times you have to take off from work to undergo treatment. This applies regardless of whether you use paid sick leave or vacation time from your work. Gross wages consist of your gross hourly pay rate, before taxes and other deductions. It's another element of damages, like expenses for medical treatment.

112.   C: I really don't want all of this to drag on too long. And I'm still sort of scared about filing a lawsuit, at least right away, because of how it might drag Dan into the suit . . . (pause).

113.   L: How we proceed and when we proceed is ultimately your decision, Clara. Your desire to move this case along and not drag Dan into it are completely legitimate concerns. I can try to help you by giving you the best advice I can about your options and their pros and cons. And I want you to know that I will support you in any decision you make. There is no right or wrong to these decisions.

114.   C: I know now that I want to call Dr. Partin to get a referral to another doctor. I'm going to do that. But, after that, I'm really not sure about what route to take.

115.   L: Perhaps this will help: I suggest that we don't have to decide that right now. If you call Dr. Partin and see another doctor, we will know more about your situation in the next two or three weeks. Then we can see where we are, discuss matters again, and plan a next step. At some point I will still need to talk with Dan about the details of the accident. And, if you want, I can also talk with him a bit about his concerns about Al and

any consequences about your filing a lawsuit if we end up taking that route later on. How does that sound?

116.   C: I'm comfortable with that. I think that's a good plan for now.

117.   L: Okay. So, why don't you give me a call after you've talked with Dr. Partin and decided on seeing another doctor. We can just keep in touch by phone for now. And, of course, please feel free to call me at any time if you have a question or want to discuss anything further in the meantime. Is that okay?

118.   C: Yes, that's a good plan. Thank you, Larry. I'll call you after I talk with Dr. Partin.

119.   L: You're welcome. It was nice to see you again. I'll look forward to hearing from you.

# Chapter 6

## ETHICAL CONSIDERATIONS IN COUNSELING

## § 6.01  INTRODUCTION

In 1983, the House of Delegates of the American Bar Association (ABA) adopted the Model Rules of Professional Conduct (Model Rules) to replace the Model Code of Professional Responsibility that had been adopted by the ABA in 1969. Most jurisdictions have adopted the Model Rules, in whole or in part, as professional standards for lawyers. The Rules are "partly obligatory and disciplinary and partly constructive and descriptive in that they define a lawyer's professional role."[1] If a lawyer fails to comply with an obligation or prohibition imposed by the Rules, he or she may be subject to discipline. In addition, even though a violation of the Rules does not, by itself, establish a cause of action for malpractice,[2] noncompliance with the Rules may well give rise to such a claim.[3]

As part of your professional role as an attorney, there are a number of Rules that are particularly pertinent to the overall attorney-client relationship and counseling function discussed in the preceding chapters. The Preamble to the Rules observes:

---

[1] Model Rules at *Scope*.

[2] Astarte, Inc. v. Pacific Indus. Systems, Inc., 865 F. Supp. 693 (D. Colo. 1994); Nagy v. Beckley, 578 N.E.2d 1134, *appeal denied*, 584 N.E.2d 131 (Ill. 1991); Lazy Seven Coal Sales, Inc. v. Stone & Hinds, P.C., 813 S.W.2d 400 (Tenn. 1991); McNair v. Rainsford, 499 S.E.2d 448 (S.C. App. 1998).

[3] *See generally*, Munneke & Davis, The Standard of Care in Legal Malpractice: Do the Model Rules of Professional Conduct Define It? 22 J. Legal. Prof. 233 (1998); Note, The Evidentiary Use of the Ethics Codes in Legal Malpractice: Erasing a Double Standard, 109 Harv. L. Rev. 1102 (1996); *Restatement (Third) of the Law Governing Lawyers* § 52(2) and cmt. f (2000).

As a representative of clients, a lawyer performs various functions. As advisor, a lawyer provides a client with an informed understanding of the client's legal rights and obligations and explains their practical implications. As advocate, a lawyer zealously asserts the client's position under the rules of the adversary system. As negotiator, a lawyer seeks a result advantageous to the client but consistent with requirements of honest dealing with others. As an evaluator, a lawyer acts by examining a client's legal affairs and reporting about them to the client or to others.

This Chapter discusses the most important Model Rules pertaining to your counseling role in establishing the attorney-client relationship, advising the client, representing clients who are under a disability, and serving as an intermediary between clients. Also discussed are other Rules that address some of the most common issues about client representation, such as preserving confidential information, determining conflicts of interest, setting attorney's fees, declining or terminating representation, and dealing with persons other than your client.[4] Ethical considerations in connection with counseling when negotiating are discussed in Chapter 9.

## § 6.02　ESTABLISHING THE ATTORNEY-CLIENT RELATIONSHIP

Because a lawyer not only represents clients but also is "an officer of the legal system and a public citizen having special responsibility for the quality of justice,"[5] many of the prescriptions and proscriptions contained in the Model Rules relate to a lawyer's responsibilities beyond the mere context of the attorney-client relationship.[6] Most of the ethical rules relating to counseling, however, presuppose the existence of an attorney-client relationship. Even so, it is essential to remember that your ethical responsibilities and fiduciary duties under the Rules will be triggered once a person consults you about a legal matter even if no employment relationship later arises. For example, if you give wholly gratuitous legal advice to another person, you will be held to the same standard of care as if you were formally employed.[7] In addition, your duty to preserve confidential communications (*see* § 6.07) generally extends to any initial consultation between you and a prospective client even if you do not end up representing the client.[8]

The existence and establishment of the attorney-client relationship is a question of fact that is primarily governed by principles of contract and agency law. Usually,

---

[4] The Model Rules contain numerous other ethical prescriptions and proscriptions regarding the lawyer's professional role that are beyond the scope of this book. For example, Rules 3.1–3.9 address the lawyer's role as "Advocate"; Rules 5.1–5.7 set out the responsibilities of "Law Firms and Associations"; Rules 6.1–6.5 address the lawyer's "Public Service" role; Rules 7.1–7.6 address "Information about Legal Services"; and Rules 8.1–8.5 deal with "Maintaining the Integrity of the Legal Profession."

[5] Model Rules at *Preamble [1]*.

[6] *See, e.g.*, Rules 4.1–4.4 (Transactions with Persons other than Clients); Rules 6.1–6.5 (Public Service); Rules 7.1–7.6 (Information about Legal Services); Rules 8.1–8.5 (Maintaining the Integrity of the Profession).

[7] *See* Franko v. Mitchell, 762 P.2d 1345 (Ariz. App. 1988).

[8] ABA Comm. on Ethics and Professional Responsibility, Formal Op. 90-358 (1990); Nolan v. Foreman, 65 F.2d 738, *reh'g denied*, 671 F.2d 1380 (5th Cir. 1982); Westinghouse Electric Corp. v. Kerr-McGee Corp., 580 F.2d 1311 (7th Cir. 1978).

the relationship arises upon the client's request that you act on his or her behalf and your agreement to do so.[9] That is, the relationship typically arises when you expressly agree to take the case or agree to advise the client.[10] However, the existence of the relationship does not depend upon any formality such as a written agreement or the payment of a retainer.[11] The relationship may be established based on conduct from which an agreement to represent may be reasonably inferred or implied, including consideration of all of the facts and circumstances bearing on the reasonableness of the client's subjective belief that the relationship was established.[12]

Given that the attorney-client relationship might be implied from the surrounding circumstances in the absence of an express agreement, lawyers have been particularly cautioned about rendering legal advice in informal settings. For example, it has been said that because "[i]t is quite possible that courts may predicate an attorney-client relationship on casually rendered advice, [a]ttorneys would therefore be wise to avoid giving advice at cocktail parties, in building corridors, over the backyard fence, and at civic organization meetings."[13] The establishment of an attorney-client relationship by implication may also arise when a prospective client meets with you at your office for an initial consultation or you give legal advice over the telephone. In these situations, if you perceive there may be any misunderstanding about your decision not to represent the prospective client, confirm your non-representation in a letter by registered or certified mail.[14] Even if you send a letter confirming your non-representation, information revealed to you in earlier conversations and the advice you gave still remain protected by the attorney-client relationship and may not be disclosed by you to anyone without the prospective client's permission.

## § 6.03   ESTABLISHING THE SCOPE OF REPRESENTATION

Model Rule 1.2 addresses your counseling responsibilities in conferring with your client about matters affecting the representation. In addition, the Rule speaks to your counseling responsibilities when your client is engaging in, or proposes to engage in, conduct that you know is criminal or fraudulent, or your client calls upon you to act in a way that would violate the Rules of Professional Conduct.

Rule 1.2 provides:

---

[9] Anderson v. Pryor, 537 F. Supp. 890 (W.D. Mo. 1982); Committee on Professional Ethics and Grievances v. Johnson, 447 F.2d 169 (3d Cir. 1971).

[10] *See* Hunt v. Disciplinary Board, 381 So. 2d 52 (Ala. 1980).

[11] *See* Hashemi v. Shack, 609 F. Supp. 391 (S.D. N.Y. 1984); United States v. Constanzo, 625 F.2d 465 (3d Cir. 1980); Guillebeau v. Jenkins, 355 S.E.2d 453 (Ga. App. 1987).

[12] *See* In re McGlothlen, 63 P.2d 1330 (Wash. 1983); United States v. Constanzo, 625 F.2d 465 (3d Cir. 1980); In re Petrie, 742 P.2d 796 (Ariz. 1987); Hashemi v. Shack, 609 F. Supp. 391 (S.D. N.Y. 1984); Kurtenbach v. Tekippe, 260 N.W.2d 53 (Iowa 1977). On the other hand, some courts insist that the attorney-client relationship does not exist in the absence of an express contract. *See, e.g.*, Pontiff v. Behrens, 518 So. 2d 23 (La. App. 1987); Holland v. Lawless, 623 P.2d 1004 (N.M. App. 1981).

[13] Friedman, The Creation of the Attorney-Client Relationship: An Emerging View, 22 Cal. W.L. Rev. 209, 220 (1986).

[14] *See* Mayo v. Engel, 733 F.2d 807 (11th Cir. 1984).

(a) Subject to paragraphs (c) and (d), a lawyer shall abide by a client's decisions concerning the objectives of representation and, as required by Rule 1.4, shall consult with the client as to the means by which they are to be pursued. A lawyer may take such action on behalf of the client as is impliedly authorized to carry out the representation. A lawyer shall abide by a client's decision whether to settle a matter. In a criminal case, the lawyer shall abide by the client's decision, after consultation with the lawyer, as to a plea to be entered, whether to waive jury trial and whether the client will testify.

(b) A lawyer's representation of a client, including representation by appointment, does not constitute an endorsement of the client's political, economic, social or moral views or activities.

(c) A lawyer may limit the scope of the representation if the limitation is reasonable under the circumstances and the client gives informed consent.

(d) A lawyer shall not counsel a client to engage, or assist a client, in conduct that the lawyer knows is criminal or fraudulent, but a lawyer may discuss the legal consequences of any proposed course of conduct with a client and may counsel or assist a client to make a good faith effort to determine the validity, scope, meaning or application of the law.

The relevant portions of the Comment to these provisions provides:

[1] Paragraph (a) confers upon the client the ultimate authority to determine the purposes to be served by legal representation, within the limits imposed by law and the lawyer's professional obligations. The decisions specified in paragraph (a), such as whether to settle a civil matter, must also be made by the client. *See* Rule 1.4(a)(1) for the lawyer's duty to communicate with the client about such decisions. With respect to the means by which the client's objectives are to be pursued, the lawyer shall consult with the client as required by Rule 1.4(a)(2) and may take such action as is impliedly authorized to carry out the representation.

[2] On occasion, however, a lawyer and a client may disagree about the means to be used to accomplish the client's objectives. Clients normally defer to the special knowledge and skill of their lawyer with respect to the means to be used to accomplish their objectives, particularly with respect to technical, legal and tactical matters. Conversely, lawyers usually defer to the client regarding such questions as the expense to be incurred and concern for third persons who might be adversely affected. Because of the varied nature of the matters about which a lawyer and client might disagree and because the actions in question may implicate the interests of a tribunal or other persons, this Rule does not prescribe how such disagreements are to be resolved. Other law, however, may be applicable and should be consulted by the lawyer. The lawyer should also consult with the client and seek a mutually acceptable resolution of the disagreement. If such efforts are unavailing and the lawyer has a fundamental disagreement with the client, the lawyer may withdraw from representation. *See* Rule 1.16(b)(4). Conversely, the client may resolve the disagreement by discharging the lawyer. *See* Rule 1.16(a)(3).

[3] At the outset of a representation, the client may authorize the lawyer to take specific action on the client's behalf without further consultation. Absent a material change in circumstances and subject to Rule 1.4, a lawyer may rely on such an advance authorization. The client may, however, revoke such authority at any time.

[4] In a case in which the client appears to be suffering diminished capacity, the lawyer's duty to abide by the client's decisions is to be guided by reference to Rule 1.4 . . . .

[6] The scope of services to be provided by a lawyer may be limited by agreement with the client or by the terms under which the lawyer's services are made available to the client. When a lawyer has been retained by an insurer to represent an insured, for example, the representation may be limited to matters related to the insurance coverage. A limited representation may be appropriate because the client has limited objectives for the representation. In addition, the terms upon which representation is undertaken may exclude specific means that might otherwise be used to accomplish the client's objectives. Such limitations may exclude actions that the client thinks are too costly or that the lawyer regards as repugnant or imprudent.

[7] Although this Rule affords the lawyer and client substantial latitude to limit the representation, the limitation must be reasonable under the circumstances. If, for example, a client's objective is limited to securing general information about the law the client needs in order to handle a common and typically uncomplicated legal problem, the lawyer and client may agree that the lawyer's services will be limited to a brief telephone consultation. Such a limitation, however, would not be reasonable if the time allotted was not sufficient to yield advice upon which the client could rely. Although an agreement for a limited representation does not exempt a lawyer from the duty to provide competent representation, the limitation is a factor to be considered when determining the legal knowledge, skill, thoroughness and preparation reasonably necessary for the representation. *See* Rule 1.1 . . . .

[9] Paragraph (d) prohibits a lawyer from knowingly counseling or assisting a client to commit a crime or fraud. This prohibition, however, does not preclude the lawyer from giving an honest opinion about the actual consequences that appear likely to result from a client's conduct. Nor does the fact that a client uses advice in a course of action that is criminal or fraudulent of itself make a lawyer a party to the course of action. There is a critical distinction between presenting an analysis of legal aspects of questionable conduct and recommending the means by which a crime or fraud might be committed with impunity.

[10] When the client's course of action has already begun and is continuing, the lawyer's responsibility is especially delicate. The lawyer is required to avoid assisting the client, for example, by drafting or delivering documents that the lawyer knows are fraudulent or by assisting a client in conduct that the lawyer originally supposed was legally proper but then discovers is criminal or fraudulent. The lawyer must, therefore, withdraw from the representation of the client in the matter. *See* Rule 1.16(a). In

some cases, withdrawal alone might be insufficient. It may be necessary for the lawyer to give notice of the fact of withdrawal and to disaffirm any opinion, document, affirmation or the like. *See* Rule 4.1 . . . .

[12] Paragraph (d) applies whether or not the defrauded party is a party to the transaction. Hence, a lawyer must not participate in a transaction to effectuate criminal or fraudulent avoidance of tax liability. Paragraph (d) does not preclude undertaking a criminal defense incident to a general retainer for legal services to a lawful enterprise. The last clause of paragraph (d) recognizes that determining the validity or interpretation of a statute or regulation may require a course of action involving disobedience of the statute or regulation or of the interpretation placed upon it by governmental authorities.

[13] If a lawyer comes to know or reasonably should know that a client expects assistance not permitted by the Rules of Professional Conduct or other law or if the lawyer intends to act contrary to the client's instructions, the lawyer must consult with the client regarding the limitations on the lawyer's conduct. *See* Rule 1.4(a)(5).

The mandate of Rule 1.2(a) that you must "abide" by your client's decisions concerning the objectives of the representation but only "consult" with him or her about the means by which they are to be pursued reflects a distinction between ends and means, whereby decisions about the ends are to be controlled by the client but decisions about the means may generally be controlled by you.[15] That is, decisions about the objectives of the representation, the ultimate resolution of the case, or matters affecting "substantive" or "fundamental" rights of the client are to be made by the client and pursued by you unless those objectives (1) fall outside the scope of the representation agreed upon between you and your client, (2) involve criminal or fraudulent conduct, or (3) call upon you to violate a rule of professional conduct. Consultation with your client is, of course, required to identify his or her objectives;[16] and you are also usually required to take all necessary actions consistent with those objectives even if not specifically requested by your client.[17] This obligation to abide by your client's objectives extends to adhering to his or her decision to cease pursuing a previously sought objective.[18]

The client's right to control decisions directly affecting his or her "substantive" or "fundamental" rights is particularly important in criminal cases due to constitutional prescriptions under the Fifth and Sixth Amendments to the United States Constitution. For example, the defendant has the right to decide whether to plead guilty, waive trial by jury, testify on his or her own behalf, represent himself or herself, assert a particular defense, or appeal a conviction.[19] Your duty is to fully

---

[15] *See* Blanton v. Womancare Clinic Inc., 696 P.2d 645 (Cal. 1985); Graves v. Taggares Co., 616 P.2d 1223 (Wash. 1980); Stricklan v. Koella, 546 S.W.2d 810 (Tenn. App. 1976).

[16] *See, e.g.*, In re Comstock, 664 N.E.2d 1165 (Ind. 1996) (failure to oppose motions to dismiss without consulting client).

[17] *See, e.g.*, In re Moore, 494 S.E.2d 804 (S.C. 1997) (duty to protect client's interests even though client did not specifically instruct lawyer to do so).

[18] *See, e.g.*, Red Dog v. State, 625 A.2d 245 (Del. 1993) (lawyer must respect client's decision to forego further appeals and accept death penalty); Burton v. Mottolese, 835 A.2d 998 (Conn. 2003) (lawyer cannot continue to litigate case after clients instructed her to stop).

[19] Jones v. Barnes, 463 U.S. 745 (1983); United States v. Boyd, 86 F.3d 719 (7th Cir. 1996); State v.

advise the defendant of all pertinent legal and practical ramifications affecting his or her decisions about these matters.[20] (*See also* § 19.06).

On the other hand, in contrast to decisions about the objectives of the representation or matters affecting constitutional rights of the client, you generally have the right to control the means of the representation such as tactics, trial strategy, and the procedural aspects of the case.[21] Nevertheless, under Rule 1.2(a) and Rule 1.4(a)(2), you still have a mandatory duty to consult with your client about these matters. In situations where you and your client disagree about the means for achieving the client's objectives, most courts will uphold your authority to make unilateral decisions about tactical or procedural matters even in the face of your client's objections[22] so long as those decisions do not affect a substantial right or interest of the client. For example, you generally may decide what witnesses to call at trial, what motions to file, how to cross-examine, and how to select the jury.[23] On the other hand, your client's consent is usually necessary when stipulating to facts that will foreclose an essential claim or defense,[24] when deciding what claims or defenses to assert,[25] or when deciding whether to appeal and the scope of the appeal.[26]

Rule 1.2(c) allows you to limit the scope of your representation to certain matters and not others. For example, you and your client might agree that you will handle the trial of the case but not an appeal,[27] or that you will only represent him or her on a specific transaction and not assume any duties beyond determining the legal sufficiency of documents involved in that transaction.[28] However, when limiting the scope of your representation, you are obligated to consult with and obtain the consent of your client; and your representation cannot be limited in a way that would materially impair the client's rights or diminish your other professional

---

Debler, 856 S.W.2d 641 (Mo. 1993); People v. Colon, 600 N.Y.S.2d 377 (App. Div. 1997). *But see* People v. Williams, 72 Cal. Rptr. 58, 62 (1998) ("Except for a handful of express constitutional rights that are deemed particularly 'fundamental' and personal, defense counsel is fully authorized to waive rights of constitutional dimension, directly by express waiver or indirectly by not raising an objection or making a particular motion.").

[20] *See* Strickland v. Washington, 46 U.S. 688 (1984); United States v. Teague, 953 F.2d 1525 (11th Cir. 1992); United States v. Goodwin, 531 F.2d 347 (6th Cir. 1976); Herring v. Estelle, 491 F.2d 125 (5th Cir. 1974); Caruso v. Zelinski, 689 F.2d 438 (3d Cir. 1982).

[21] Blanton v. Womancare Clinic Inc., 696 P.2d 645 (Cal. 1985); United States v. Boyd, 86 F.3d 719 (7th Cir. 1996); State v. Davis, 506 A.2d 86 (Conn. 1986).

[22] *See, e.g.,* Nahhas v. Pacific Greyhound Lines, 13 Cal. Rptr. 299 (Ct. App. 1961); United States v. Clayborne, 509 F.2d 473 (D.C. Cir. 1974); People v. Schultheis, 638 P.2d 8 (Colo. 1981); In re King, 336 A.2d 195 (Vt. 1975). *But see* State v. Ali, 407 S.E.2d 183 (N.C. 1991) (in the event of a disagreement about a tactical decision, the client's wishes must control in accordance with the principal-agent nature of the relationship).

[23] *See* Graves v. McKenzie, 68 P.2d 769 (Cal. 1983); State v. Davis, 506 A.2d 86 (Conn. 1986); In re King, 336 A.2d 195 (Vt. 1975).

[24] *See* Linsk v. Linsk, 449 P.2d 760 (Cal. 1969).

[25] *See* Boyd v. Brett-Major, 499 So. 2d 952 (Fla. App. 1984); Orr v. Knowles, 337 N.W.2d 699 (Neb. 1983).

[26] *See* Hawkeye-Security Insurance Co. v. Indemnity Insurance Co., 260 F.2d 361 (10th Cir. 1958); State v. Pence, 488 P.2d 1177 (Haw. 1971); In re Grubbs, 403 P.2d 260 (Okla. Crim. App. 1965).

[27] *See, e.g.,* Florida Bar v. Dingle, 220 So. 2d 9 (Fla. 1969); Young v. Bridwell, 437 P.2d 686 (Utah 1968).

[28] *See, e.g.,* Grand Isle Campsites, Inc. v. Cheek, 249 So. 2d 268 (La. App 1971), *modified,* 262 So. 2d 350 (La. 1972).

obligations, such as your duty to advise your client of important legal rights ancillary to the overall subject matter of the representation.[29]

The prohibition in Rule 1.2(d) against counseling the client to engage or assisting the client in conduct that you know is criminal or fraudulent may be violated if you fail to inquire into your client's objectives when it would be reasonable to do so.[30] That is, you will not be excused from assisting your client's unlawful or fraudulent conduct if you acted without appropriately investigating whether your advice or actions might aid him in perpetrating a fraud or in otherwise committing a crime.[31] If, after reasonable inquiry, you believe that your client expects assistance not permitted by the Rules of Professional Conduct, Rule 1.4(a)(15) requires you to advise your client regarding the relevant ethical limitations on your conduct so that he can make an informed decision about how to lawfully pursue his objectives.[32] If your client then continues to insist on pursuing an unlawful objective or a lawful objective by unlawful means, you should withdraw from the representation (*see* § 6.11).

Rule 1.2(d), however, expressly allows you to "counsel or assist a client to make a good faith effort to determine the validity, scope, meaning or application of the law." This means that you will not violate the prohibition against assisting your client in unlawful conduct by giving advice on a doubtful question concerning conduct later found to be criminal or fraudulent. It is not unethical to advise a client about a legal position that you believe can be supported by a good-faith argument for an extension, modification, or reversal of existing law, so long as there is at least some realistic possibility that the position will be successful.[33] For example, if your client seeks legal representation after having been told that a city ordinance prohibits certain parades or demonstrations on public property, if your investigation and legal research show that there is a good-faith argument that the ordinance is unconstitutional, you should first explain the prohibitions of the ordinance to your client, and then advise him why you believe the ordinance is unconstitutional and the chances of a successful challenge to the ordinance.

## § 6.04   THE DUTIES OF COMPETENCE, DILIGENCE, AND COMMUNICATION

It should be obvious that in representing a client, you must act competently and diligently, and adequately communicate with your client. These quintessential requirements of proper client representation are set out separately in the Model Rules. The Comments to these Rules aptly summarize their meaning and scope.

---

[29] *See, e.g.*, Greenwich v. Markhoff, 650 N.Y.S.2d 704 (App. Div. 1996) (even though retainer agreement purported to limit scope of representation to workers' compensation claim, lawyer had duty to advise client of potential personal injury action).

[30] *See, e.g.*, Harrell v. Crystal, 611 N.E.2d 908 (Ohio App. 1992) (lawyer failed to properly investigate clients' investments and individuals involved when advising clients on tax shelters); People v. Zelinger, 504 P.2d 68 (Colo. 1972) (lawyer failed to inquire whether car given to lawyer for fee was stolen).

[31] *See* ABA Com.on Ethics and Professional Responsibility, Informal Op. 1470 (1981).

[32] *See* People v. Doherty, 945 P.2d 1380 (Colo. 1997).

[33] *See* ABA Comm. on Ethics and Professional Responsibility, Formal Op. 85-352 (1985).

*[a] Competence*

Model Rule 1.1 provides: "A lawyer shall provide competent representation to a client. Competent representation requires the legal knowledge, skill, thoroughness and preparation reasonably necessary for the representation."

The Comment to Rule 1.4 explains:

[1] In determining whether a lawyer employs the requisite knowledge and skill in a particular matter, relevant factors include the relative complexity and specialized nature of the matter, the lawyer's general experience, the lawyer's training and experience in the field in question, the preparation and study the lawyer is able to give the matter and whether it is feasible to refer the matter to, or associate or consult with, a lawyer of established competence in the field in question. In many instances, the required proficiency is that of a general practitioner. Expertise in a particular field of law may be required in some circumstances.

[2] A lawyer need not necessarily have special training or prior experience to handle legal problems of a type with which the lawyer is unfamiliar. A newly admitted lawyer can be as competent as a practitioner with long experience. Some important legal skills, such as the analysis of precedent, the evaluation of the evidence and legal drafting, are required in all legal problems. Perhaps the most fundamental legal skill consists of determining what kind of legal problems a situation may involve, a skill that necessarily transcends any particular specialized knowledge. A lawyer can provide adequate representation in a wholly novel field through necessary study. Competent representation can also be provided through the association of a lawyer of established competence in the field in question.

[3] In an emergency a lawyer may give advice or assistance in a matter in which the lawyer does not have the skill ordinarily required where referral to or consultation or association with another lawyer would be impractical. Even in an emergency, however, assistance should be limited to that reasonably necessary in the circumstances, for ill-considered action under emergency conditions can jeopardize the client's interest.

[4] A lawyer may accept representation where the requisite level of competence can be achieved by reasonable preparation. This applies as well to a lawyer who is appointed as counsel for an unrepresented person . . .

[5] Competent handling of a particular matter includes inquiry into an analysis of the factual and legal elements of the problem, and use of methods and procedures meeting the standards of competent practitioners. It also includes adequate preparation. The required attention and preparation are determined in part by what is at stake; major litigation and complex transactions ordinarily require more elaborate treatment than matters of lesser consequence.

*[b] Diligence*

Model Rule 1.3 provides that "[a] lawyer shall act with reasonable diligence and promptness in representing a client." The Comment to the Rules provides in part:

[1] A lawyer should pursue a matter on behalf of a client despite opposition, obstruction or personal inconvenience to the lawyer, and take whatever lawful and ethical measures are required to vindicate a client's cause or endeavor. A lawyer must also act with commitment and dedication to the interests of the client and with zeal in advocacy upon the client's behalf. A lawyer is not bound, however, to press for every advantage that might be realized for a client. For example, a lawyer may have authority to exercise professional discretion in determining the means by which a matter should be pursued. *See* Rule 1.2. The lawyer's duty to act with reasonable diligence does not require the use of offensive tactics or preclude the treating of all persons involved in the legal process with courtesy and respect.

[2] A lawyer's work load must be controlled so that each matter can be handled competently.

[3] Perhaps no professional shortcoming is more widely resented than procrastination. A client's interests often can be adversely affected by the passage of time or the change of conditions; in extreme instances, as when a lawyer overlooks a statute of limitations, the client's legal position may be destroyed. Even when the client's interests are not affected in substance, however, unreasonable delay can cause a client needless anxiety and undermine confidence in the lawyer's trustworthiness. A lawyer's duty to act with reasonable promptness, however, does not preclude the lawyer from agreeing to a reasonable request for a postponement that will not prejudice the lawyer's client.

[4] Unless the relationship is terminated as provided in Rule 1.16, a lawyer should carry through to conclusion all matters undertaken for a client. If a lawyer's employment is limited to a specific matter, the relationship terminates when the matter has been resolved. If a lawyer has served a client over a substantial period in a variety of matters, the client sometimes may assume that the lawyer will continue to serve on a continuing basis unless the lawyer gives notice of withdrawal. Doubt about whether a client-lawyer relationship still exists should be clarified by the lawyer, preferably in writing, so that the client will not mistakenly suppose the lawyer is looking after the client's affairs when the lawyer has ceased to do so. For example, if a lawyer has handled a judicial or administrative proceeding that produced a result adverse to the client and the lawyer and the client have not agreed that the lawyer will handle the matter on appeal, the lawyer must consult with the client about the possibility of appeal before relinquishing responsibility for the matter. *See* Rule 1.4(a)(2). Whether the lawyer is obligated to prosecute the appeal for the client depends on the scope of the representation the lawyer has agreed to provide to the client. *See* Rule 1.2.

*[c] Communication*

Model Rule 1.4 provides:

(a) A lawyer shall:

(1) promptly inform the client of any decision or circumstance with respect to which the client's informed consent, as defined in Rule 1.0(e),

is required by these Rules;

(2) reasonably consult with the client about the means by which the client's objectives are to be accomplished;

(3) keep the client reasonably informed about the status of the matter;

(4) promptly comply with reasonable requests for information; and

(5) consult with the client about any relevant limitation on the lawyer's conduct when the lawyer knows that the client expects assistance not permitted by the Rules of Professional Conduct or other law.

(b) A lawyer shall explain a matter to the extent reasonably necessary to permit the client to make informed decisions regarding the representation.

The Comment to Rule 1.4 provides:

[1] Reasonable communication between the lawyer and the client is necessary for the client effectively to participate in the representation.

[2] If these Rules require that a particular decision about the representation be made by the client, paragraph (a)(1) requires that the lawyer promptly consult with and secure the client's consent prior to taking action unless prior discussions with the client have resolved what action the client wants the lawyer to take. For example, a lawyer who receives from opposing counsel an offer of settlement in a civil controversy or a proffered plea bargain in a criminal case must promptly inform the client of its substance unless the client has previously indicated that the proposal will be acceptable or unacceptable or has authorized the lawyer to accept or reject the offer. *See* Rule 1.2(a).

[3] Paragraph (a)(2) requires the lawyer to reasonably consult with the client about the means to be used to accomplish the client's objectives. In some situations — depending on both the importance of the action under consideration and the feasibility of consulting with the client — this duty will require consultation prior to taking action. In other circumstances, such as during a trial when an immediate decision must be made, the exigency of the situation may require the lawyer to act without prior consultation. In such cases the lawyer must nonetheless act reasonably to inform the client of actions the lawyer has taken on the client's behalf. Additionally, paragraph (a)(3) requires that the lawyer keep the client reasonably informed about the status of the matter, such as significant developments affecting the timing or the substance of the representation.

[4] A lawyer's regular communication with clients will minimize the occasions on which a client will need to request information concerning the representation. When a client makes a reasonable request for information, however, paragraph (a)(4) requires prompt compliance with the request, or if a prompt response is not feasible, that the lawyer, or a member of the lawyer's staff, acknowledge receipt of the request and advise the client when a response may be expected. Client telephone calls should be promptly returned or acknowledged.

[5] The client should have sufficient information to participate intelligently in decisions concerning the objectives of the representation and the

means by which they are to be pursued, to the extent the client is willing and able to do so. Adequacy of communication depends in part on the kind of advice or assistance that is involved. For example, when there is time to explain a proposal made in a negotiation, the lawyer should review all important provisions with the client before proceeding to an agreement. In litigation a lawyer should explain the general strategy and prospects of success and ordinarily should consult the client on tactics that are likely to result in significant expense or to injure or coerce others. On the other hand, a lawyer ordinarily will not be expected to describe trial or negotiation strategy in detail. The guiding principle is that the lawyer should fulfill reasonable client expectations for information consistent with the duty to act in the client's best interests, and the client's over-all requirements as to the character of representation. In certain circumstances, such as when a lawyer asks a client to consent to a representation affected by a conflict of interest, the client must give informed consent, as defined in Rule 1.0(e).

[6] Ordinarily, the information to be provided is that appropriate for a client who is a comprehending and responsible adult. However, fully informing the client according to this standard may be impracticable, for example, where the client is a child or suffers from diminished capacity. *See* Rule 1.14. When the client is an organization or group, it is often impossible or inappropriate to inform every one of its members about its legal affairs; ordinarily, the lawyer should address communications to the appropriate officials of the organization. *See* Rule 1.13. Where many routine matters are involved, a system of limited or occasional reporting may be arranged with the client.

[7] In some circumstances, a lawyer may be justified in delaying transmission of information when the client would be likely to react imprudently to an immediate communication. Thus, a lawyer might withhold a psychiatric diagnosis of a client when the examining psychiatrist indicates that disclosure would harm the client. A lawyer may not withhold information to serve the lawyer's own interest or convenience or the interests or convenience of another person. Rules or court orders governing litigation may provide that information supplied to a lawyer may not be disclosed to the client. Rule 3.4(c) directs compliance with such rules or orders.

The duty to communicate with your client is personal. Thus, the obligation is not satisfied by delegating responsibility for communicating to a subordinate, whether another lawyer, paralegal, or secretary.[34] Similarly, communicating with third parties instead of directly with the client does not fulfill the obligation.[35]

The duty of communication also extends to notifying your client about your failure to act, whether that failure was the result of incompetence, lack of diligence, or a disagreement with him or her about an appropriate course of action.[36] It has been held that if your failure to act would give rise to a legal malpractice claim, you

---

[34]  Mays v. Neal, 938 S.W.2d 830 (Ark. 1997); In re Galabasini, 786 P.2d 971 (Ariz. 1990).

[35]  In re Dreier, 671 A.2d 455 (D.C. 1996).

[36]  In re Hyde, 950 P.2d 806 (N.M. 1997); In re Brousseau, 697 A.2d 1079 (R.I. 1997); In re Glee, 472 S.E.2d 615 (S.C. 1996).

have a duty to promptly notify your client about the possibility of such a claim.[37] If the failure to act was due to your belief that continuing the representation would result in violating the Rules of Professional Conduct, you must appropriately notify your client of this fact and may not simply abandon the representation without following appropriate procedures for withdrawal.[38]

## § 6.05  ADVISING THE CLIENT

Adequately advising your client is, of course, central to your counseling function. In your role as advisor, Model Rule 2.1 provides that "[i]n representing a client, a lawyer shall exercise independent professional judgment and render candid advice. In rendering advice, a lawyer may refer not only to law but to other considerations such as moral, economic, social and political factors, that may be relevant to the client's situation."

The Comment to Rule 2.1 instructively provides:

[1] A client is entitled to straightforward advice expressing the lawyer's honest assessment. Legal advice often involves unpleasant facts and alternatives that a client may be disinclined to confront. In presenting advice, a lawyer endeavors to sustain the client's morale and may put advice in as acceptable a form as honesty permits. However, a lawyer should not be deterred from giving candid advice by the prospect that the advice will be unpalatable to the client.

[2] Advice couched in narrowly legal terms may be of little value to a client, especially where practical considerations, such as cost or effects on other people, are predominant. Purely technical legal advice, therefore, can sometimes be inadequate. It is proper for a lawyer to refer to relevant moral and ethical considerations in giving advice. Although a lawyer is not a moral advisor as such, moral and ethical considerations impinge upon most legal questions and may decisively influence how the law will be applied.

[3] A client may expressly or impliedly ask the lawyer for purely technical advice. When such a request is made by a client experienced in legal matters, the lawyer may accept it at face value. When such a request is made by a client inexperienced in legal matters, however, the lawyer's responsibility as advisor may include indicating that more may be involved than strictly legal considerations.

[4] Matters that go beyond strictly legal questions may also be in the domain of another profession. Family matters can involve problems within the professional competence of psychiatry, clinical psychology or social work; business matters can involve problems within the competence of the accounting profession or of financial specialists. Where consultation with a professional in another field is itself something a competent lawyer would recommend, the lawyer should make such a recommendation. At the same

---

[37] *See* Tallon v. Committee on Professional Standards, 447 N.Y.S.2d 50 (1982); In re Higginson, 64 N.E.2d 732 (Ind. 1996); Florida Bar v. Bazley, 597 So. 2d 796 (Fla. 1992).

[38] People v. Doherty, 945 P.2d 1380 (Colo. 1997); Florida Bar v. King, 664 So. 2d 925 (Fla. 1995); State v. Batista, 492 N.W.2d 354 (Wis. App. 1992).

time, a lawyer's advice at its best often consists of recommending a course of action in the face of conflicting recommendations of experts.

[5] In general a lawyer is not expected to give advice until asked by the client. However, when a lawyer knows that a client proposes a course of action that is likely to result in substantial adverse legal consequences to the client, duty to the client under Rule 1.4 [Communication] may require that the lawyer offer advice if the client's course of action is related to the representation. Similarly, when a matter is likely to involve litigation, it may be necessary under Rule 1.4 to inform the client of forms of dispute resolution that might constitute reasonable alternatives to litigation. A lawyer ordinarily has no duty to initiate investigation of a client's affairs or to give advice that the client has indicated is unwanted, but a lawyer may initiate advice to a client when doing so appears to be in the client's interest.

Like the duty to communicate, the duty to advise your client is personal and therefore may not be delegated to someone else. The obligation extends to personally interviewing your client.[39] Generally, you should apprise your client of the full implications of a proposed course of action, and this includes giving candid advice about whether it would be undesirable for him or her to pursue a particular course of action, even if it is not illegal or morally wrong.[40] In addition, you have a duty to advise your client of all potential courses of action that are reasonably pertinent to the subject matter of the representation.[41]

In exercising "independent professional judgment" under Rule 2.1, it has been said that "[e]motional detachment is essential to the lawyer's ability to render competent legal services."[42] Thus, a number of jurisdictions categorically prohibit a lawyer from having a sexual relationship with the client during the representation,[43] and the ABA has taken the position that a "lawyer shall not have sexual relations with a client unless a consensual sexual relationship existed between them when the client-lawyer relationship commenced."[44]

Apart from exercising independent professional judgment and rendering candid advice, Rule 2.1 encourages, but does not require, you to incorporate pertinent moral, economic, social, and political considerations in your advice. For example, in an appropriate case, your advice might include perspectives on how a course of

---

[39] *See* In re Pinkins, 213 B.R. 818 (Bankr. E.D. Mich. 1997) (unethical for lawyer to use legal assistant to screen clients to see whether they are eligible for bankruptcy protection); Michigan Informal Ethics Op. RI-128 (1992) (unethical for initial client interviews to be conducted by assistant with result that lawyer sometimes performed legal paperwork without ever having met client).

[40] *See* Summit, Rovins & Feldesman v. Fonar Corp., 623 N.Y.S.2d 245 (Sup. Ct. App. Div. 1995) (lawyer failed to predict and explain likelihood that corporate strategy would not succeed); Dobris, Ethical Problems for Lawyers upon Trust Terminations: Conflict of Interest, 38 U. Miami L. Rev. 1, 62–63 (1983) ("a lawyer has an affirmative duty to inform the client if she believes that the proposal is improper or unwise, even if it is not illegal or morally wrong.").

[41] *See* Nichols v. Keller, 19 Cal. Rptr. 601 (Ct. App. 1993) (even though attorney was hired to pursue workers' compensation claim, he had duty to advise client of potential damages claim against third parties).

[42] ABA Comm. on Ethics and Professional Responsibility, Formal Op. 92-364 (1992).

[43] *See, e.g.*, Bourdon's Case, 565 A.2d 1052 (N.H. 1989); Okla. Bar Ass'n. Legal Ethics Comm. Op. 308 (1994).

[44] Model Rule 1.8(j).

action might be sensitive to preserving racial harmony or gender equity,[45] or your advice might even include a discussion of moral considerations grounded in theology[46] so long as your religious beliefs are not forced upon the client.[47] A few courts have specially commented on the desirability of counseling a client about "fairness" considerations when entering into a prenuptial agreement,[48] and the unique opportunity that a lawyer may have in a drunk driving case to urge a problem drinker to receive treatment.[49]

## § 6.06   REPRESENTING A CLIENT WHO IS UNDER A DISABILITY

A client may be under a disability or suffer from a form of diminished capacity that seriously affects his or her decision-making capacity due to a variety of reasons such as alcohol or drug addiction, depression, minority, senility, retardation, or insanity. In representing a client afflicted by a disability or diminished capacity, Model Rule 1.14 provides:

> (a) When a client's capacity to make adequately considered decisions in connection with a representation is diminished, whether because of minority, mental impairment or for some other reason, the lawyer shall, as far as reasonably possible, maintain a normal client-lawyer relationship with the client.

> (b) When the lawyer reasonably believes that the client has diminished capacity, is at risk of substantial physical, financial or other harm unless action is taken and cannot adequately act in the client's own interest, the lawyer may take reasonably necessary protective action, including consulting with individuals or entities that have the ability to take action to protect the client and, in appropriate cases, seeking the appointment of a guardian ad litem, conservator or guardian.

> (c) Information relating to the representation of a client with diminished capacity is protected by Rule 1.6. When taking protective action pursuant to paragraph (b), the lawyer is impliedly authorized under Rule 1.6(a) to reveal information about the client, but only to the extent reasonably necessary to protect the client's interests.

The Comment to this Rule provides:

> [1] The normal client-lawyer relationship is based on the assumption that the client, when properly advised and assisted, is capable of making

---

[45] *See generally*, Hing, In the Interest of Racial Harmony: Revisiting the Lawyer's Duty to Work for the Common Good, 47 Stan. L. Rev. 901 (1995).

[46] *See generally*, Symposium, 27 Tex. Tech. L. Rev. 911 (1996) (essays by lawyers from diverse religious backgrounds describing how they reconcile their professional life with their faith); Beggs, Laboring Under the Sun: An Old Testament Perspective on the Legal Profession, 28 Pac. L. J. 257 (1996).

[47] *See* Tennessee Formal Ethics Op. 96-F-140 (1996) (lawyer opposed to abortion on religious grounds may not pressure client into foregoing right not to first discuss the abortion with her parents); Florida Bar v. Johnson, 511 So. 2d 295 (Fla. 1987) (lawyer disciplined for bullying client with threats that God would visit misfortunes on client).

[48] *See* In re Marriage of Foran, 834 P.2d 1081 (Wash. App. 1992).

[49] *See* Friedman v. Commissioner of Public Safety, 473 N.W.2d 828 (Minn. 1991).

decisions about important matters. When the client is a minor or suffers from a diminished mental capacity, however, maintaining the ordinary client-lawyer relationship may not be possible in all respects. In particular, a severely incapacitated person may have no power to make legally binding decisions. Nevertheless, a client with diminished capacity often has the ability to understand, deliberate upon, and reach conclusions about matters affecting the client's own well-being. For example, children as young as five or six years of age, and certainly those of ten or twelve, are regarded as having opinions that are entitled to weight in legal proceedings concerning their custody. So also, it is recognized that some persons of advanced age can be quite capable of handling routine financial matters while needing some special legal protection concerning major transactions.

[2] The fact that a client suffers a disability does not diminish the lawyer's obligation to treat the client with attention and respect. Even if the person has a legal representative, the lawyer should as far as possible accord the represented person the status of client, particularly in maintaining communication.

[3] The client may wish to have family members or other persons participate in discussions with the lawyer. When necessary to assist in the representation, the presence of such persons generally does not affect the applicability of the attorney-client evidentiary privilege. Nevertheless, the lawyer must keep the client's interests foremost and, except for protective action authorized under paragraph (b), must look to the client, and not family members, to make decisions on the client's behalf.

[4] If a legal representative has already been appointed for the client, the lawyer should ordinarily look to the representative for decisions on behalf of the client. In matters involving a minor, whether the lawyer should look to the parents as natural guardians may depend on the type of proceeding or matter in which the lawyer is representing the minor. If the lawyer represents the guardian as distinct from the ward, and is aware that the guardian is acting adversely to the ward's interest, the lawyer may have an obligation to prevent or rectify the guardian's misconduct. *See* Rule 1.2(d).

[5] If a lawyer reasonably believes that a client is at risk of substantial physical, financial or other harm unless action is taken, and that a normal client-lawyer relationship cannot be maintained as provided in paragraph (a) because the client lacks sufficient capacity to communicate or to make adequately considered decisions in connection with the representation, then paragraph (b) permits the lawyer to take protective measures deemed necessary. Such measures could include: consulting with family members, using a reconsideration period to permit clarification or improvement of circumstances, using voluntary surrogate decisionmaking tools such as durable powers of attorney or consulting with support groups, professional services, adult-protective agencies or other individuals or entities that have the ability to protect the client. In taking any protective action, the lawyer should be guided by such factors as the wishes and values of the client to the extent known, the client's best interests and the goals of intruding into the client's decisionmaking autonomy to the least extent feasible, maximiz-

ing client capacities and respecting the client's family and social connections.

[6] In determining the extent of the client's diminished capacity, the lawyer should consider and balance such factors as: the client's ability to articulate reasoning leading to a decision, variability of state of mind and ability to appreciate consequences of a decision; the substantive fairness of a decision; and the consistency of a decision with the known long-term commitments and values of the client. In appropriate circumstances, the lawyer may seek guidance from an appropriate diagnostician.

[7] If a legal representative has not been appointed, the lawyer should consider whether appointment of a guardian ad litem, conservator or guardian is necessary to protect the client's interests. Thus, if a client with diminished capacity has substantial property that should be sold for the client's benefit, effective completion of the transaction may require appointment of a legal representative. In addition, rules of procedure in litigation sometimes provide that minors or persons with diminished capacity must be represented by a guardian or next friend if they do not have a general guardian. In many circumstances, however, appointment of a legal representative may be more expensive or traumatic for the client than circumstances in fact require. Evaluation of such circumstances is a matter entrusted to the professional judgment of the lawyer. In considering alternatives, however, the lawyer should be aware of any law that requires the lawyer to advocate the least restrictive action on behalf of the client.

[8] Disclosure of the client's diminished capacity could adversely affect the client's interests. For example, raising the question of diminished capacity could, in some circumstances, lead to proceedings for involuntary commitment. Information relating to the representation is protected by Rule 1.6. Therefore, unless authorized to do so, the lawyer may not disclose such information. When taking protective action pursuant to paragraph (b), the lawyer is impliedly authorized to make the necessary disclosures, even when the client directs the lawyer to the contrary. Nevertheless, given the risks of disclosure, paragraph (c) limits what the lawyer may disclose in consulting with other individuals or entities or seeking the appointment of a legal representative. At the very least, the lawyer should determine whether it is likely that the person or entity consulted with will act adversely to the client's interests before discussing matters related to the client. The lawyer's position in such cases is an unavoidably difficult one.

[9] In an emergency where the health, safety or financial interest of a person with seriously diminished capacity is threatened with imminent and irreparable harm, a lawyer may take legal action on behalf of such a person even though the person is unable to establish a client-lawyer relationship or to make or express considered judgments about the matter, when the person or another acting in good faith on that person's behalf has consulted with the lawyer. Even in such an emergency, however, the lawyer should not act unless the lawyer reasonably believes that the person has no other lawyer, agency or other representative available. The lawyer should take legal action on behalf of the person only to the extent reasonably necessary to maintain the status quo or otherwise avoid imminent and irreparable harm. A lawyer who undertakes to represent a person in such an exigent

situation has the same duties under these Rules as the lawyer would with respect to a client.

[10] A lawyer who acts on behalf of a person with seriously diminished capacity in an emergency should keep the confidences of the person as if dealing with a client, disclosing them only to the extent necessary to accomplish the intended protective action. The lawyer should disclose to any tribunal involved and to any other counsel involved the nature of his or her relationship with the person. The lawyer should take steps to regularize the relationship or implement other protective solutions as soon as possible. Normally, a lawyer would not seek compensation for such emergency actions taken.

In representing a client who is under a form of diminished capacity, Rule 1.14(a) is largely uninstructive when it merely prescribes that "the lawyer shall, as far as reasonably possible, maintain a normal client-lawyer relationship with the client." The "normal client-lawyer relationship" referred to in the provision is defined by Rule 1.2(a) (*see* § 6.03) as one in which the lawyer "shall abide by a client's decisions concerning the objectives of representation."[50] The difficult questions faced by the lawyer are (1) how to determine whether and to what extent the client is under a disability;[51] and (2) if the client appears to be under a disability, whether the lawyer should act as an "advocate" and nevertheless try to abide by the client's decisions regarding the objectives of the representation, or seek the appointment of a guardian or take some other protective action under Rule 1.14(b) in the "best interest" of the client. The tension over your proper role in these circumstances — whether to serve as an advocate for your client or as a paternal protector of your client's best interests — has been hotly debated by scholars.[52]

When the client's capacity or competence is in serious question, it has been pointed out that there are six potential choices available to you: (1) presume the client's competence and honor his or her decisions about lawful objectives regardless of the consequences; (2) seek to persuade the client to make "better" choices about his or her objectives; (3) seek unofficial consent from a family member or close friend of the client to take protective action on the client's behalf; (4) proceed as a *de facto* guardian for the client; (5) seek the formal appointment of a guardian for the client; or (6) withdraw from the representation.[53] The choice that may be most appropriate in a particular situation will, of course, depend upon the nature and severity of your client's disability and the overall circumstances of the representation.

The choice of presuming your client's competence and honoring his or her decisions regardless of the consequences may run afoul of your duty as an advisor

---

[50] *See* In re M.R., 638 A.2d 1274 (N.J. 1994).

[51] *See generally*, Anderer, A Model for Determining Competency in Guardianship Proceedings, 7 Mental Health & Physical Disability L. Rep. 107 (1990); Luckasson & Ellis, Representing Institutionalized Mentally Retarded Persons, 7 Mental Disability L. Rep. (1983).

[52] *See, e.g.*, Devine, The Ethics of Representing the Disabled Client: Does Model Rule 1.14 Adequately Resolve the Best Interests/Advocacy Dilemma: 49 Mo. L. Rev. 493 (1984) (criticizing option of taking protective action as being inconsistent with advocacy model of representation); Luban, Paternalism and the Legal Profession, 1981 Wis. L. Rev. 454, 493 (lawyer's exercise of professional judgment for disabled client is "justified paternalism").

[53] Tremblay, On Persuasion and Paternalism: Lawyer Decisionmaking and the Questionably Competent Client, 1987 Utah L. Rev. 515, 519–520.

under Rule 2.1 to exercise "independent professional judgment" and render "candid" advice in connection with the representation (*see* § 6.05). In addition, this option may violate your duty under Rule 1.14(b) to protect your client's interests if you reasonably believe that he or she cannot adequately act in his or her own interests. For example, in a criminal case, a defendant's Sixth Amendment right to effective assistance of counsel may be violated if you blindly accede to his or her decisions affecting his or her "fundamental" rights in the face of a serious question about his or her competency.[54] In addition, if your client's disability is only temporary, you may easily be able to protect him or her from the adverse consequences of an ill-considered decision in accordance with Rule 1.14(b) by temporarily postponing action on the matter until he or she has regained the capacity to rationally reconsider his or her choices.[55]

In circumstances where the disability is not extreme, it would of course be a viable option to attempt to persuade your client that his or her decisions about the objectives of the representation are unwise.[56] If persuasion is unsuccessful or the nature of your client's disability makes rational communication with him or her impossible, short of seeking a formal appointment of a guardian, you might temporarily act as a *de facto* guardian, or seek the consent of a family member or close friend of the client to take protective action on his or her behalf. However, it has been argued that such "unilateral usurpation of client autonomy is never appropriate except in emergencies."[57] Consulting a family member or close friend about protective action is also controversial because it may constitute a violation of your duty to protect client confidences from disclosure (*see* § 6.07). Although a number of authorities take the view that limited consultation with a family member or close friend may be appropriate where the third person does not have an adverse interest in your client's affairs and your client has not expressly forbidden you to consult with the third person,[58] other authorities flatly prohibit such consultation when it would involve the disclosure of client confidences.[59] Rule 1.14(c) allows disclosure, "but only to the extent reasonably necessary to protect the client's interests."

---

[54] *See* Kilbert v. Peyton, 383 F.2d 56 (4th Cir. 1967) (ineffective assistance when lawyer, retained only 10 days earlier, allowed defendant to plead guilty on the basis of defendant's mere nod of the head despite serious doubts about defendant's mental condition); Red Dog v. State, 625 A.2d 245 (Del. 1993) (lawyer who doubted client's competence to forego further appeals had duty to timely inform the court and request judicial determination about competency); Speedy v. Wyrick, 702 F.2d 723 (8th Cir. 1983) (ineffective assistance not to entertain competency hearing when lawyer was aware of obvious indications of defendant's mental illness). *See also ABA Standards for Criminal Justice*, Standard 7-4.2 (1984) (defense counsel must raise competency issue whenever there is a good-faith doubt about competency, regardless of client's wishes).

[55] *See* N.Y. City Bar Ass'n. Op. 83-1 (lawyer's options properly include maintaining the *status quo* until client is capable of making a considered judgment); Iowa Ethics Op. 81-15 (lawyer unable to locate alcoholic client in personal injury action may not dismiss case, but should seek continuance and attempt to locate client, or seek appointment of guardian *ad litem* to make decisions in the case).

[56] *See* Genden, Separate Legal Representation for Protecting the Rights and Interests of Minors in Legal Proceedings, 11 Harv. C.R.-C.L.L. Rev. 565, 588–589 (1976).

[57] Tremblay, On Persuasion and Paternalism: Lawyer Decisionmaking and the Questionably Competent Client, 1987 Utah L. Rev. 515, 584.

[58] *See, e.g.*, Me. Bar Bd. of Overseers, Professional Ethics Comm. Op. 84 (1988); ABA Comm. on Ethics and Professional Responsibility, Informal Op. 89-1530 (1989); Neb. State Bar Ass'n, Advisory Comm. Op. 91-4 (1991).

[59] *See, e.g.*, Nassau County (N.Y.) Ethics Op. 90-17 (1990); California Ethics Op. 1989-112.

The option of seeking the formal appointment of a guardian is expressly authorized by Rule 1.14(b). If you reasonably believe your client cannot adequately act in his or her own interest, this option may be pursued even if your client objects.[60] In the litigation context, jurisdictions otherwise typically require the appointment of a guardian *ad litem* for minors and other persons suffering from certain mental disabilities.

Finally, while neither Rule 1.14 nor its Comment refer to the option of withdrawing from the representation, withdrawal may be permissible if you believe that your client's irrational behavior and incapacity to act in his or her own interests are making the representation "unreasonably difficult."[61] (*see also* § 6.11). However, it has been said that withdrawal is the least desirable option because it leaves the client without representation at a time when the protection of his or her interests is often most needed, and he or she is least able to hire other counsel.[62]

## § 6.07   PRESERVING CONFIDENTIALITY OF INFORMATION

Your duty to preserve confidential communications of your client is a central aspect of the attorney-client relationship.[63] The duty is given effect not only through the Rules of Professional Conduct, but also through the attorney-client privilege, the work product doctrine, and the law of evidence.[64] The obligation encourages people to seek early legal assistance, encourages them to communicate fully and frankly with a lawyer, and facilitates the full development of facts essential to proper client representation.[65]

Model Rule 1.6 provides:

(a) A lawyer shall not reveal information relating to the representation of a client unless the client gives informed consent, the disclosure is impliedly authorized in order to carry out the representation or the disclosure is permitted by paragraph (b).

(b) A lawyer may reveal information relating to the representation of a client to the extent the lawyer reasonably believes necessary:

(1) to prevent reasonably certain death or substantial bodily harm;

(2) to prevent the client from committing a crime or fraud that is reasonably certain to result in substantial injury to the financial interests or property of another and in furtherance of which the client has used or is using the lawyer's services;

(3) to prevent, mitigate or rectify substantial injury to the financial interests or property of another that is reasonably certain to result or has resulted from the client's commission of a crime or fraud in

---

[60] *See* Fla. Bar, Professional Ethics Comm. Op. 85-4 (1985); Ala. Bar, Op. 87-137 (1987).

[61] *See* Ill. Bar Ass'n Comm. on Professional Ethics, Op. 89-12 (1990).

[62] *See* Me. Bar Bd. of Overseers, Comm. on Professional and Judicial Ethics, Op. 84 (1988); N.Y. City Bar Ass'n, Comm. on Professional Ethics, Op. 83-1.

[63] AG GRO Servs. Co. v. Sophia Land C. Inc., 8 F. Supp. 2d 495 (D. Md. 1997).

[64] Comment to Rule 1.6 at paragraph [3].

[65] Comment to Rule 1.6 at paragraph [2].

furtherance of which the client has used the lawyer's services;

(4) to secure legal advice about the lawyer's compliance with these Rules;

(5) to establish a claim or defense on behalf of the lawyer in a controversy between the lawyer and the client, to establish a defense to a criminal charge or civil claim against the lawyer based upon conduct in which the client was involved, or to respond to allegations in any proceeding concerning the lawyer's representation of the client; or

(6) to comply with other law or a court order.

Because the duty of confidentiality embraces all information "relating to the representation," the duty covers not only information learned from your client, but also information obtained from others and even information which is available from public sources.[66] Disclosure is prohibited regardless of your motivation and regardless of whether a judicial proceeding is involved. For example, it is unethical for you to disclose a client's confidences without his or her consent when asking for assistance in the case from a lawyer outside your firm.[67]

The duty of confidentiality will usually be triggered once a prospective client consults you in good faith for the purpose of obtaining legal advice, even if you do not end up representing him or her.[68] The duty also continues after the attorney-client relationship is terminated.[69] If you practice in a law firm, you may disclose client confidences to other lawyers or employees in the firm unless your client has instructed you otherwise,[70] and the other employees of your firm also have a duty to protect your client's confidences from disclosure.[71]

Rule 1.6(a) recognizes that your disclosure of confidential information may be impliedly authorized to carry out the representation. For example, in a real estate transaction, information such as the purchase price of the property, the amount of an offer, the amount accepted, and the condition of the property would typically be matters that could be disclosed as being impliedly authorized by the representation.[72] When your client is under a disability, limited disclosure of confidential information may be appropriate when consulting with a family member or close friend of your client (see § 6.06), or when consulting with your client's physician

---

[66] Comment to Rule 1.6 at paragraph [3]. *See also* In re Anonymous, 654 N.E.2d 1128 (Ind. 1995).

[67] *See, e.g.,* In re Mandelman, 514 N.W.2d 11 (Wis. 1994). *See also* ABA Comm. on Ethics and Professional Responsibility, Op. 98-411 (1998) (encouraging consultation with other lawyers by means of hypotheticals when possible).

[68] Rule 1.18(b); ABA Comm. on Ethics and Professional Responsibility, Formal Op. 90-358 (1990). *See* Gilmore v. Goedecke, 954 F. Supp. 187 (E.D. Mo. 1996) (law firm could not represent defendant in age discrimination case because plaintiff had previously consulted another member of the firm by telephone).

[69] Comment to Rule 1.6 at paragraph [18]; United States v. Standard Oil Co., 136 F. Supp. 345 (S.D. N.Y. 1955).

[70] Comment to Rule 1.6 at paragraph [5].

[71] *See* Pennsylvania v. Mrozek, 657 A.2d 997 (Pa. 1995); State Bar of Mich. Comm. on Professional and Judicial Ethics, Op. RI-123 (1992) (information received by non-lawyer assistant is protected and may be basis for disqualification of lawyer even if assistant never conveyed the information to the lawyer). *See also* Me. Bar Bd. of Overseers Professional Ethics Comm. Op. 134 (1993) (lawyer must adequately train, monitor, and discipline non-lawyer employees to maintain confidentiality or be subject to discipline for disclosures).

[72] Ark. Bar Ass'n. Standing Comm. on Professional Ethics and Grievances, Op. 96-1 (1996).

concerning a medical condition that is interfering with your client's ability to communicate or make decisions.[73]

Although the Comment to Rule 1.6 recognizes that "other law may require that a lawyer disclose information about a client,"[74] there is no circumstance under the Rule that ever *mandates* the disclosure of a client's confidences.[75] Rather, Rule 1.6(b) authorizes *permissive* disclosure, in your discretion,[76] in only limited circumstances: (1) to prevent reasonably certain death or substantial bodily harm and (2) to prevent the client from committing (or to prevent, mitigate or rectify the results of) a crime or fraud that is reasonably certain to result (or has resulted) in substantial injury to the financial interests or property of another and in further-ance of which the client has used your services; (3) to defend yourself on a civil, criminal, or ethical charge, or to establish a claim that you may have in a controversy between you and your client; or (4) to secure legal advice about your compliance with your ethical obligations or to comply with other law or a court order. The first two of these exceptions are widely recognized.[77] The third exception is also well recognized, but you must scrupulously avoid revealing confidential information not necessary to your defense or claim and limit disclosure only to those having a need to know the information.[78]

With the widespread use of e-mail, it has been said that the use of encryption to protect the confidentiality of messages involving client communications is not necessary because the expectation of privacy for electronic mail is the same as that for ordinary telephone calls, and unauthorized interception of electronic messages is unlawful.[79] However, in unusual circumstances involving extraordinarily sensitive information, you should seriously consider employing security measures such as encryption, just as you would take other precautions in communicating highly

---

[73] ABA Comm. on Ethics and Professional Responsibility, Informal Op. 89-1530 (1989).

[74] Comment to Rule 1.6 at paragraph [12]. *See, e.g.*, United States v. Goldberger & Dubin, P.C., 935 F.2d 501 (2d Cir. 1991) (requirement in Internal Revenue Code, 26 U.S.C. § 6050 I, that every person who receives more than $10,000 in cash in connection with a trade or business must file a report with the IRS does not violate the federal constitution or the attorney-client privilege).

[75] *See* Utah State Bar Ethics Advisory Comm. Op. 97-12 (1998) (although lawyer who suspects client of committing child abuse may be legally obligated to report information pursuant to statute, lawyer is not ethically mandated to report such information).

[76] *See* Comment to Model Rule 1.6 at paragraph [7].

[77] *See, e.g.*, Purcell v. District Attorney for Suffolk County, 676 N.E.2d 436 (Mass. 1997) (lawyer could properly alert authorities when client stated intent to burn down a building); State v. Hansen, 862 P.2d 122 (Wash. 1993) (lawyer could advise judge that person who called lawyer to retain him had threatened to kill judge); ABA Comm. on Ethics and Professional Responsibility, Informal Op. 83-1500 (1983) (lawyer may disclose client's intent to commit suicide). As to whether a lawyer may reveal to a client's sexual partner that the client has Acquired Immune Deficiency Syndrome (AIDS), *see generally*, Isaacman, The Conflict Between Illinois Rule 1.6(b) and the AIDS Confidentiality Act, 25 J. Marshall L. Rev. 727 (1992).

[78] *See, e.g.*, Ohio Sup. Ct. Bd. of Comm'rs on Grievances and Discipline, Op. 91-16 (1991) (firm using collection agency to collect fee should reveal confidences only to degree necessary for that purpose); N.Y. County Lawyer's Ass'n Comm. on Professional Ethics, Op. 722 (1997) (lawyer may reveal confidences to rebut charges of actionable misconduct to extent reasonably necessary to defend against accusations); In re National Mortgage Equity Corp. Litig., 120 F.R.D. 687 (C.D. Cal. 1988) (law firm may disclose confidential information from client to establish firm was not aware that client issued misleading securities statement).

[79] ABA Comm. on Ethics and Professional Responsibility, Op. 99-413 (1999).

sensitive information such as not using a cellular telephone in certain circumstances.[80]

## § 6.08   SERVING AS AN INTERMEDIARY BETWEEN CLIENTS

Lawyers are sometimes asked to represent multiple clients who, despite potential conflicts of interest, desire to achieve a common or group objective. Generally, this type of multiple representation is permissible so long as the common representation will not adversely affect any one of the clients and all of them consent after full consultation. The following Comments to Model Rule 1.7 (otherwise discussed in § 6.09) explain:

> [29] In considering whether to represent multiple clients in the same matter, a lawyer should be mindful that if the common representation fails because the potentially adverse interests cannot be reconciled, the result can be additional cost, embarrassment and recrimination. Ordinarily, the lawyer will be forced to withdraw from representing all of the clients if the common representation fails. In some situations, the risk of failure is so great that multiple representation is plainly impossible. For example, a lawyer cannot undertake common representation of clients where contentious litigation or negotiations between them are imminent or contemplated. Moreover, because the lawyer is required to be impartial between commonly represented clients, representation of multiple clients is improper when it is unlikely that impartiality can be maintained. Generally, if the relationship between the parties has already assumed antagonism, the possibility that the clients' interests can be adequately served by common representation is not very good. Other relevant factors are whether the lawyer subsequently will represent both parties on a continuing basis and whether the situation involves creating or terminating a relationship between the parties.

> [30] A particularly important factor in determining the appropriateness of common representation is the effect on client-lawyer confidentiality and the attorney-client privilege. With regard to the attorney-client privilege, the prevailing rule is that, as between commonly represented clients, the privilege does not attach. Hence, it must be assumed that if litigation eventuates between the clients, the privilege will not protect any such communications, and the clients should be so advised.

> [31] As to the duty of confidentiality, continued common representation will almost certainly be inadequate if one client asks the lawyer not to disclose to the other client information relevant to the common representation. This is so because the lawyer has an equal duty of loyalty to each client, and each client has the right to be informed of anything bearing on the representation that might affect that client's interests and the right to expect that the lawyer will use that information to that client's benefit. *See*

---

[80] *See* Ariz. State Bar Comm. on Rules of Professional Responsibility, Op. 97-04 (1997) (lawyers should use e-mail cautiously, consider encryption, and include cautionary statement that information is confidential; S.C. Bar Ethics Advisory Comm. Op. 97-08 (1997) (lawyers may communicate with clients by e-mail but should discuss encryption options); Ark. Bar Ass'n Ethics Comm. Op. 98-2 (1998).

Rule 1.4. The lawyer should, at the outset of the common representation and as part of the process of obtaining each client's informed consent, advise each client that information will be shared and that the lawyer will have to withdraw if one client decides that some matter material to the representation should be kept from the other. In limited circumstances, it may be appropriate for the lawyer to proceed with the representation when the clients have agreed, after being properly informed, that the lawyer will keep certain information confidential. For example, the lawyer may reasonably conclude that failure to disclose one client's trade secrets to another client will not adversely affect representation involving a joint venture between the clients and agree to keep that information confidential with the informed consent of both clients.

[32] When seeking to establish or adjust a relationship between clients, the lawyer should make clear that the lawyer's role is not that of a partisanship normally expected in other circumstances and, thus, that the clients may be required to assume greater responsibility for decisions than when each client is separately represented. Any limitations on the scope of the representation made necessary as a result of the common representation should be fully explained to the clients at the outset of the representation. *See* Rule 12(c).

In what is often cited as the leading case in support of the lawyer's role as intermediary, the court in *Lessing v. Gibbons*, 45 P.2d 258, 261 (Cal. Ct. App. 1935) summarized some of the more common situations in which you may properly represent multiple clients in the same transaction even if they have potentially conflicting interests:

The position of an attorney who acts for both parties to the knowledge of each, in the preparation of papers needed to effect their purpose, and gives to each the advice necessary for his protection, is recognized by the law as a proper one. Were this not the rule, the common practice of attorneys in acting for both partners in drawing articles of copartnership or drawing agreements for the dissolution of copartnership, in acting for both the grantor and the grantee in the sale of real property, in acting for both the seller and purchaser in the sale of personal property, in acting for both the lessor and lessee in the leasing of property, and in acting for both the lender and the borrower in handling a loan transaction would be prohibited even though done in the utmost good faith and with the full consent of all parties concerned.

In addition to these situations, you may — albeit in more cautious circumstances — act as an intermediary between clients in uncontested family-law matters such as divorce, custody, child support, alimony or property division,[81] or in estate and probate matters.[82] On the other hand, although the Model Rules do not expressly prohibit you from serving as an intermediary between clients who are in litigation, it is essentially inconceivable that such representation would be permissible in light

---

[81] *See, e.g.*, Klemm v. Superior Court of Fresno County, 142 Cal. Rptr. 509 (Ct. App. 1977); Levine v. Levine, 436 N.E.2d 476 (N.Y. 1982); In re Eltzroth, 679 P.2d 1369 (Or. Ct. App. 1984).

[82] *See* Kidney Association of Oregon Inc. v. Ferguson, 843 P.2d 442 (Or. 1992); Alaska Ethics Op. 91-2 (1991). *See generally*, Collett, The Ethics of Intergenerational Representation, 62 Fordham L. Rev. 1453 (1994).

of the general conflict-of-interest Rule 1.7 (*see* § 6.09), which prohibits common representation of opposing parties in litigation.[83] Most authorities also prohibit common representation of clients in an adoption case even if they consent.[84]

Although many jurisdictions permit you to represent consenting spouses in an uncontested family-law matter (*e.g.*, in the preparation of a separation agreement),[85] some jurisdictions flatly prohibit such representation, notwithstanding full consultation and consent.[86] Even in jurisdictions where common representation of clients in a family-law matter is permitted, the dangers of such representation are often noted by the courts in language such as the following:

> Divorces are frequently uncontested; the parties may make their financial arrangements peaceably and honestly . . . . Even in that situation the attorney's professional obligations do not permit his descent to the level of a scrivener . . . . Representing the wife in an arm's length divorce, an attorney of ordinary professional skill would demand some verification of the husband's financial statement; or, at the minimum, inform the wife that the husband's statement was unconfirmed, that wives may be cheated, that prudence called for investigation and verification.[87]

Therefore, whenever you are considering representing both spouses in what appears to be an uncontested separation agreement, you should be especially alert to any obvious inequities on the face of their proposed agreement or other matters that may raise questions or conflicts about the substance of their agreement. If such inequities or potential conflicts are apparent, you should decline the common representation and advise the clients to obtain independent counsel.[88]

## § 6.09   CONFLICTS OF INTEREST

The Model Rules contain six separate rules dealing with conflict-of-interest situations in which you must decline to represent a client or withdraw from the representation if it has already been undertaken. Rules 1.7 and 1.9(a), discussed below, primarily address the circumstances under which you may represent a client whose interests are adverse to one of your existing or former clients. The four other rules, which are beyond the scope of this book, address conflict-of-interest situations where a lawyer engages in certain transactions respecting a client (Rule 1.8), where the disqualification of one lawyer in a firm will be imputed to other

---

[83] *See* Comment to Model Rule 1.7 at paragraph [17]; Pearce, Family Values and Legal Ethics: Competing Approaches to Representing Spouses, 62 Fordham L. Rev. 1253, 1265 (1994) (most commentators have determined that Rule 2.2 is limited by Rule 1.7).

[84] *See, e.g.*, In re Petrie, 742 P.2d 796 (Ariz. 1987); Rushing v. Bosse, 652 So. 2d 869 (Fla. 1995); ABA Informal Ethics Op. 87-1523 (1987); Indiana Ethics Op. 2 (1988); Pennsylvania Ethics Op. 95-59 (1995).

[85] *See* Levine v. Levine, 436 N.E.2d 467 (N.Y. 1982).

[86] *See, e.g.*, In re Breen, 552 A.2d 105 (N.J. 1989); Walden v. Hoke, 429 S.E.2d 504 (W. Va. 1993); Wisconsin Ethics Op. E-88-4 (1988); Alaska Rule of Professional Conduct 2.2(d); Iowa Code of Professional Responsibility for Lawyers DR 5-105(A). *See generally*, Gibbard & Hartmeister, Mediation and Wyoming Domestic Relations Cases — Practical Considerations, Ethical Concerns and Proposed Standards of Practice, 27 Land & Water L. Rev. 435, 454 (1992); Collett, And the Two Shall Become as One . . . Until the Lawyers Are Done, 7 Notre Dame J. Legal Ethics & Pub. Policy 101, 129 (1993).

[87] Ishmael v. Millington, 50 Cal. Rptr. 592, 596 (Ct. App. 1996).

[88] *See* In re Eltzroth, 679 P.2d 1369, 1373 n.7 (Or. App. 1984). *See also* Charles W. Wolfran, *Modern Legal Ethics* 730 (1996).

lawyers in the firm (Rule 1.10), where a lawyer engages in successive government and private employment (Rule 1.11), and where a lawyer formerly participated in a matter as a judge or arbitrator (Rule 1.12).

Rule 1.7, the "general" conflict-of-interest Rule, provides:

(a) Except as provided in paragraph (b), a lawyer shall not represent a client if the representation involves a concurrent conflict of interest. A concurrent conflict of interest exists if:

(1) the representation of one client will be directly adverse to another client; or

(2) there is a significant risk that representation of one or more clients will be materially limited by the lawyer's responsibilities to another client, a former client or a third person or by a personal interest of the lawyer.

(b) Notwithstanding the existence of a concurrent conflict of interest under paragraph (a), a lawyer may represent a client if:

(1) the lawyer reasonably believes that the lawyer will be able to provide competent and diligent representation to each affected client;

(2) the representation is not prohibited by law;

(3) the representation does not involve the assertion of a claim by one client against another client represented by the lawyer in the same litigation or other proceeding before a tribunal; and

(4) each affected client gives informed consent, confirmed in writing.

Under this Rule, you are prohibited from representing a client whose interests are directly adverse to those of a current client, or if there is a significant risk that your representation will be materially limited as a result of your other responsibilities or interests, even if the two representations are unrelated, unless you believe that you can provide competent and diligent representation to each client and both clients consent. The prohibition applies when an opponent of a current client retains you to represent him or her in a matter unrelated to your representation of the current client,[89] or when you accept representation that requires you to bring suit on behalf of the new client against an existing client.[90] The rationale for the Rule is to preserve your loyalty to your clients,[91] and to prevent you from diminishing the vigor of your representation of one client to avoid antagonizing the other client.[92]

Representation of dual clients is never permissible when the two clients oppose each other in the same litigation.[93] In contrast to this clear-cut situation, however, the Comment to the Rule states that an impermissible conflict does not exist when

---

[89] *See, e.g.,* In re Hansen, 586 P.2d 413 (Utah 1978).

[90] *See, e.g.,* Unified Sewerage Agency v. Jelco Inc., 646 F.2d 1339 (9th Cir. 1981).

[91] *See* Jeffry v. Pounds, 67 Cal. App. 3d 6, 136 Cal. Rptr. 373 (1977); ABA Informal Ethics Op. 1495 (1982); Comment to Rule 1.7 at paragraph [1].

[92] *See* Cinema 5 Ltd. v. Cinerama Inc., 528 F.2d 1384 (2d Cir. 1976); International Business Machines Corp. v. Levin, 579 F.2d 271 (3d Cir. 1978).

[93] Comment to Rule 1.7 at paragraph [17]. *See, e.g.,* GATX/Airlog Co. v. Evergreen Int'l Airlines, Inc.,

the simultaneous representation concerns an unrelated matter involving clients "whose interests are only economically adverse, such as representation of competing economic enterprises." In such a situation, the conflict is so diffused and general that client consent is not even required.[94]

Current ethics opinions are divided about whether a disqualifying conflict arises when you are called upon to advocate a legal position that would benefit one client but would have negative consequences for another client in a different case.[95] That is, a lawyer sometimes faces the situation of urging the court to interpret unsettled law in a way that would favor one client while representing another client who, in an unrelated matter, would benefit from a contrary interpretation of the law. The ABA has taken the position that you may not concurrently represent clients whose matters would require you to argue a directly contrary position in the same jurisdiction, unless neither case is likely to lead to precedent harmful to the other and each client consents. If the cases are pending in different jurisdictions, the concurrent representations are permitted if both clients consent and you reasonably believe that neither representation will be adversely affected by the other.[96] Other ethics opinions take the view that there is no conflict in arguing opposite sides of the same legal issue before the same judge when representing two different clients in separate cases,[97] or that a conflict only arises when the two cases are pending at the same time in an appellate court.[98]

Under subsection (a)(2) of Rule 1.7, you are prohibited from representing a client when the representation would be "materially limited" by your responsibilities to another client. This proscription often arises when representing multiple clients in a single matter, especially in criminal cases. Although single representation of codefendants in a criminal case is not a *per se* violation of the constitutional guarantee of effective assistance of counsel,[99] the Comment to Rule 1.7 states that "[t]he potential for conflict of interest in representing multiple defendants in a criminal case is so grave that ordinarily a lawyer should decline to represent more than one codefendant."[100] For example, a serious conflict arises from joint representation of codefendants when the prosecution offers a plea to one of the codefendants in exchange for his or her testimony against the other. Obviously, a lawyer who is representing the codefendants is then placed in the untenable position of giving advice to the codefendant who has been offered the plea while fighting against the anticipated testimony when representing the other codefendant. Most authorities agree with the general rule expressed in the Comment to Rule 1.7 that lawyers should ordinarily decline to represent more than one criminal codefendant.[101]

---

8 F. Supp. 2d 1182 (N.D. Cal. 1998); In re Ireland, 706 P.2d 352 (Ariz. 1985); Florida Bar v. Milin, 502 So.2d 900 (Fla. 1986).

[94] Comment to Rule 1.7 at paragraph [6].

[95] *See generally*, Dzienkowski, Positional Conflicts of Interest, 71 Tex. L. Rev. 457 (1993).

[96] ABA Comm. on Ethics and Professional Responsibility, Formal Op. 93-377 (1993).

[97] *See, e.g.*, State Bar of Cal. Standing Comm. on Professional Responsibility and Conduct, Op. 1989-108.

[98] *See* Philadelphia Bar Ass'n Professional Guidance Comm. Op. 89-27 (1990).

[99] Holloway v. Arkansas, 435 U.S. 475 (1978).

[100] Comment to Rule 1.7 at paragraph [23].

[101] *See, e.g.*, United States v. Hawkins, 139 F.3d 902 (7th Cir. 1998); Armstrong v. People, 701 P.2d 17 (Colo. 1985); Shongutsie v. State, 827 P.2d 361 (Wyo. 1992). *See generally*, Annotation, "Circum-

Multiple representations of clients by a single lawyer can also create impermissible conflicts of interest in civil cases. For example, a number of cases have held that it is generally impermissible for a lawyer to represent both the buyer and seller in a complex real estate transaction.[102] Numerous cases also hold that when an insurance company hires an attorney to represent the carrier and the insured in a personal injury case, the dual representation will be prohibited if the interests of the company become at odds with those of the insured,[103] as where a lawyer representing the insured under a reservation of rights brings a separate declaratory judgment action asserting that the plaintiff's claims fall outside the policy's coverage.[104] Similarly, when there is a non-frivolous dispute about liability in an automobile-accident personal injury case, it is generally considered to be improper for a lawyer to represent both the plaintiff-driver and his or her passenger in a suit against the driver of the of the adverse vehicle who claims that the plaintiff driver was at fault in causing the accident.[105] In addition, as pointed out in Section 6.08, impermissible conflicts of interest may arise when representing both spouses in a seemingly uncontested family-law matter.

Subsection (a)(2) of Rule 1.7 also prohibits you from representing a client if the representation may be materially limited by your own interests. Many of the most common situations in which the representation of a client may be compromised by a lawyer's personal interests are addressed by other specific rules. For example, lawyers may not enter into certain business transactions with clients except under certain circumstances (Rule 1.8(a)); lawyers are prohibited from preparing certain instruments giving them or their immediate relatives substantial gifts from clients (Rule 1.8(c)); lawyers are prohibited, during the representation of a client, from obtaining literary or media rights to a portrayal or account based in substantial part on information relating to the representation (Rule 1.8(d)); lawyers are prohibited from providing financial assistance to clients in connection with litigation except in limited circumstances (Rule 1.8(e)); payment of lawyers' fees by third parties is restricted to certain circumstances (Rule 1.8(f)); agreements with clients limiting lawyers' liability for malpractice are restricted (Rule 1.8(h)); lawyers may not acquire proprietary interests in the subject matter of litigation (Rule 1.8(i); lawyers are prohibited from having a sexual relationship with a client unless such a relationship existed between them when the client-lawyer relationship began (Rule 1.8(j)); and lawyers are prohibited from undertaking representation in certain cases where they have switched from government to private employment or vice versa (Rule 1.11), or when they have participated in certain cases as a former judge or arbitrator (Rule 1.12).

The general conflict-of-interest provisions in subsection (a) of Rule 1.7 are, however, subject to a significant exception. Even if the particular circumstances

---

stances Giving Rise to Prejudicial Conflict of Interests Between Criminal Defendants and Defense Counsel: State Cases," 18 A.L.R.4th 360 (1982).

[102] *See, e.g.*, Florida Bar v. Belleville, 591 So. 2d 170 (Fla. 1991); In re Pohlman, 604 N.Y.S.2d 61 (App. Div. 1993); Baldasarre v. Butler, 625 A.2d 458 (N.J. 1993).

[103] *See* Nelson Elec. Contracting Corp. v. Transcontinental Co., 660 N.Y.S.2d 220 (App. Div. 1997).

[104] State Farm v. Armstrong Extinguisher Serv., 791 F. Supp. 799 (D.S.D. 1992).

[105] *See, e.g.*, In re Thornton, 421 A.2d 1 (D.C. App. 1980); Fugnitto v. Fugnitto, 452 N.Y.S.2d 976 (Sup. Ct. App. Div. 1982). *Compare* Alabama Ethics Op. 82-662 (such representation of plaintiff-driver and passenger not prohibited if no possibility of liability on plaintiff-driver's part, and both driver and passenger consent to the common representation after disclosure of potential conflicts).

present a conflict of interest, the representation is not improper if (1) you reasonably believe that you will be able to provide competent and diligent representation to each affected client, and (2) your client gives informed consent to the other representation in writing. Under Model Rule 1.0(e), "informed consent" means that you have "communicated adequate information and explanation about the material risks of and reasonably available alternatives to the proposed course of conduct." As mentioned previously, the only circumstance in which consent cannot serve as an exception to Rule 1.7(a) is set out in subsection (b)(3) where "the representation [involves] the assertion of a claim by one client against another client represented by the lawyer in the same litigation or other proceeding before a tribunal."

While Rule 1.7 addresses the circumstances under which you may represent a client whose interests are adverse to one of your *existing* clients, Rule 1.9(a) addresses when you may properly represent a client whose interests are adverse to one of your *former* clients.[106] Rule 1.9(a) provides:

> A lawyer who has formerly represented a client in a matter shall not thereafter represent another person in the same or a substantially related matter in which that person's interests are materially adverse to the interests of the former client unless the former client gives informed consent, confirmed in writing.

Under this Rule, after your representation of a client is over, your continuing duty of loyalty to preserve his or her confidences prohibits you from representing another client in the "same or a substantially similar matter" in which the new client's interests are materially adverse to those of your former client, unless your former client consents in writing. That is, you have an obligation not to use confidential information about the former client to his or her disadvantage in the subsequent representation of another client.

The Rule may even be triggered to protect a former *prospective* client who you advised during an initial consultation but ended up not representing. For example, the Rule would be applicable if the prospective client disclosed confidential information to you during an initial office visit or phone conversation under circumstances where an attorney-client relationship would be implied.[107] (*See also* § 6.02). To guard against this disqualifying situation, it has been pointed out that you can warn the prospective client in the initial conference to reveal only enough information to enable you to determine whether you have a conflict of interest. Then, after you have determined that no conflict exists, the client would be allowed to discuss his or her confidential situation with you.[108]

In determining whether the representation of a new client involves the "same or substantially similar matter" (*i.e.*, subject matter, case, cause of action, or legal work) involved in the representation of the former client, courts variously consider the similarity of the legal issues, the similarity of the factual settings, the identity of the parties, and whether actual confidential information obtained from a former

---

[106] Rule 1.9 also contains subsections (b) and (c) which deal with the protection of client confidences gained by a lawyer in a prior affiliation with a law firm and after termination of the attorney-client relationship. These subsections are not discussed here.

[107] *See* Marshall v. State of New York Div. of State Police, 952 F. Supp. 103 (N.D. N.Y. 1997); Richardson v. Griffiths, 560 N.W.2d 430 (Neb. 1997).

[108] *See* ABA Formal Ethics Op. 90-358 (1990).

client could be used to his or her detriment in the representation of the new client.[109] For example, one court provided the following list of factors as being appropriate to consider:

> whether the liability issues presented are similar; whether any scientific issues presented are similar; whether the nature of the evidence is similar; whether the lawyer had interviewed a witness who was a key witness in both causes; the lawyer's knowledge of the former client's trial strategies, negotiation strategies, legal theories, business practices and secrets; the lapse of time between causes; the duration and intimacy of the lawyer's relationship with the clients; the functions being performed by the lawyer; the likelihood that actual conflict will arise; and the likely prejudice to the client if conflict a does arise.[110]

Many courts hold that "[o]nce the former client proves that the subject matters of the present and prior representations are 'substantially related,' the court will irrebutably presume that relevant confidential information was disclosed during the former period of representation."[111] Other courts engage in the circular reasoning of saying, "[i]f there is a reasonable probability that confidences were disclosed which could be used against the former client in the later adverse representation, . . . a substantial relationship between the two cases will be presumed."[112] These fictional and circular approaches to the "substantial relationship" test are the product of an effort to spare the former client from the self-defeating necessity of having to reveal the confidential information he or she imparted to his or her lawyer when seeking to disqualify the lawyer from representing another client, and it has the practical benefit of reducing the need for courts to hold *in camera* or *ex parte* proceedings every time a disqualification motion is filed. In essence, the test allows the courts to infer that, if there is a good deal of similarity between the matter handled for the former client and the matter on which the lawyer is now representing another client, then it is likely that the information learned by the lawyer from the former client would be useful to the new client and adverse to the former one, and therefore the lawyer should be disqualified from representing the new client.

Even the if the substantial relationship test is met and the representation of the new client would be materially adverse to the confidentiality interests or other interests of the former client, your representation of the new client is not prohibited if the former client consents in writing. Usually, you will not be permitted to treat the former client's bare knowledge of the new representation as consent to it.[113]

---

[109] *See generally*, Wolfran, Former Client Conflicts, 10 Geo. J. Legal Ethics 67 (1997).

[110] State ex rel. Wal-Mart Stores, Inc. v. Kortum, 559 N.W.2d 496, 501 (Neb. 1997).

[111] Duncan v. Merrill Lynch, Pierce, Fenner & Smith, Inc., 646 F.2d 1020, 1028 (5th Cir. 1981). *See also* Brotherhood Mut. Ins. Co. v. National Presto Indus. Inc, 846 F. Supp. 57 (M.N. Fla. 1994); Rogers v. Pittston Co., 800 F. Supp. 350 (W.D. Va. 1992); Sullivan County Reg'l Refuse Disposal v. Acworth, 686 A.2d 755 (N.H. 1996); Marshall v. State of New York Div. of State Police, 952 F. Supp. 103 (N.D. N.Y. 1997).

[112] Thomas v. Municipal Court of Antelope Valley Judicial District of California, 878 F.2d 285, 288 (9th Cir. 1988).

[113] *See* Manoir-Electroalloys Corp. v. Amalloy Corp, 711 F. Supp. 188 (D.C. N.J. 1989); Marketti v. Fitzsimmons, 373 F. Supp. 637 (W.D. Wis. 1974). Sometimes implied consent will be found, as where the former client knew of the new representation, failed to object to it after having ample opportunity to object, and there would be great hardship to the new client if disqualification were ordered. *See, e.g.,*

Your consultation in connection with obtaining his or her consent should involve not only an explanation of the conflicts that may arise, but also their implications.[114]

Finally, it is important to emphasize that although conflict-of-interest questions might be raised by the trial judge or opposing counsel, the primary responsibility for resolving such questions rests with you, and you are obligated to adopt reasonable office procedures to determine in both litigation and non-litigation matters the parties and issues involved and to determine whether there are actual or potential conflicts of interest.[115] If a disqualifying conflict arises after you have undertaken the representation, you should take appropriate steps to withdraw (*see* § 6.11). If more than one client is involved and a conflict arises after representation, you may even have to withdraw from the representation of *both* clients if required by Rule 1.16.[116]

## § 6.10  SETTING ATTORNEY'S FEES

Entering into a fee agreement with your client is an integral part of establishing the attorney-client relationship in terms of clarifying the services you will render and how your client will pay for them. This Section discusses setting fees on an hourly rate or in a fixed amount. Ethical considerations in connection with contingent fees are discussed in Section 9.04.

Model Rule 1.5 provides in part:

(a) A lawyer shall not make an agreement for, charge, or collect an unreasonable fee or an unreasonable amount for expenses. The factors to be considered in determining the reasonableness of a fee include the following:

(1) the time and labor required, the novelty and difficulty of the questions involved, and the skill requisite to perform the legal service properly;

(2) the likelihood, if apparent to the client, that the acceptance of the particular employment will preclude other employment by the lawyer;

(3) the fee customarily charged in the locality for similar legal services;

(4) the amount involved and the results obtained;

(5) the time limitations imposed by the client or by the circumstances;

(6) the nature and length of the professional relationship with the client;

(7) the experience, reputation, and ability of the lawyer or lawyers performing the services; and

---

River West Inc. v. Nickel, 234 Cal. Rptr. 33 (Ct. App. 1987); Cox v. American Cast Iron Pipe Co., 847 F.2d 725 (11th Cir. 1988); Donohoe v. Consolidated Operating & Production Corp., 691 F. Supp. 109 (N.D. Ill. 1988).

[114] *See* First Wisconsin Mortgage Trust v. First Wisconsin Corp., 422 F. Supp. 493 (E.D. Wis. 1976); Florida Insurance Guaranty Association Inc. v. Carey Canada Inc., 749 F. Supp. 255 (S.D. Fla. 1990).

[115] Comment to Rule 1.7 at paragraph [3].

[116] Comment to Rule 1.7 at paragraph [5].

(8) whether the fee is fixed or contingent.

(b) The scope of the representation and the basis or the rate of the fee and expenses for which the client will be responsible shall be communicated to the client, preferably in writing, before or within a reasonable time after commencing the representation, except when the lawyer will charge a regularly represented client on the same basis or rate. Any changes in the basis or rate of the fee or expenses shall also be communicated to the client.

The Comment to the Rule instructs in part:

[1] Paragraph (a) requires that lawyers charge fees that are reasonable under the circumstances. The factors specified in (1) through (8) are not exclusive. Nor will each factor be relevant in each instance. Paragraph (a) also requires that expenses for which the client will be charged must be reasonable. A lawyer may seek reimbursement for the cost of services performed in-house, such as copying, or for other expenses incurred in-house, such as telephone charges, either by charging a reasonable amount to which the client has agreed in advance or by charging an amount that reasonably reflects the cost incurred by the lawyer.

[2] When the lawyer has regularly represented a client, they ordinarily will have evolved an understanding concerning the basis or rate of the fee and the expenses for which the client will be responsible. In a new client-lawyer relationship, however, an understanding as to fees and expenses must be promptly established. Generally, it is desirable to furnish the client with at least a simple memorandum or copy of the lawyer's customary fee arrangements that states the general nature of the legal services to be provided, the basis, rate or total amount of the fee and whether and to what extent the client will be responsible for any costs, expenses or disbursements in the course of the representation. A written statement concerning the terms of the engagement reduces the possibility of misunderstanding . . . .

[4] A lawyer may require advance payment of a fee, but is obligated to return any unearned portion. *See* Rule 1.16(d) . . . .

[5] An agreement may not be made whose terms might induce the lawyer improperly to curtail services for the client or perform them in a way contrary to the client's interest. For example, a lawyer should not enter into an agreement whereby services are to be provided only up to a stated amount when it is foreseeable that more extensive services probably will be required, unless the situation is adequately explained to the client. Otherwise, the client might have to bargain for further assistance in the midst of a proceeding or transaction. However, it is proper to define the extent of services in light of the client's ability to pay. A lawyer should not exploit a fee arrangement based primarily on hourly charges by using wasteful procedures.

The touchstone of a valid fee is reasonableness. In this regard, the eight factors enumerated in Rule 1.5(a) are general guidelines to be considered in setting the amount of a fee. Although the factors do not add up to some mandatory formula that must be followed in establishing either the type or amount of your fee, courts routinely consider these factors when reviewing the reasonableness of a fee agreement.[117]

A court always has the inherent power to review the reasonableness of fees and to refuse to enforce any contract involving excessive or unreasonable fees.[118] For example, a contract calling for a fee in excess of that permitted by statute will not be enforced.[119] In addition, courts have consistently prohibited lawyers from charging general overhead expenses to clients in addition to a fee, or from separately charging clients for rote "housekeeping" activities such as organizing and labeling files or delivering documents.[120]

Comment [4] above allows you to require your client to advance money for legal fees or to pay a retainer fee. There are three types of retainers:

1. With a special retainer, a client agrees to pay a specified fee for a specified service, which can be calculated on an hourly or percentage basis, and may be paid in advance or as billed.

2. A nonrefundable retainer permits a lawyer to keep advance payments regardless of the specified services provided.

3. Under a general retainer, the client agrees to pay a lawyer a fixed sum in exchange for the lawyer's promise to be available to perform legal services at an agreed price during a specific period. Because a general retainer is given in exchange for the lawyer's availability, it is a charge separate from the fee incurred for services actually provided.[121]

A special retainer is essentially an advance fee payment where the outstanding balance of the advance is reduced as you perform legal services for your client and earn the fee. If you withdraw from the representation or are discharged, you must return any unearned portion of the advance fee payment.[122] A nonrefundable retainer, by definition, need not be returned to your client if you withdraw or are discharged and have not yet earned the advance payment.[123] However, many jurisdictions prohibit nonrefundable retainers on public-policy grounds and require the unearned portion of the fee to be returned to the client in the event of your withdrawal or discharge.[124] A general retainer, sometimes called a "classic" or "true" retainer,[125] is a payment that is considered separate from a fee for services

---

[117] *See* Fourchon Docks, Inc. v. Milchem, Inc., 849 F.2d 1561 (5th Cir. 1988).

[118] Pfeifer v. Sentry Ins., 745 F. Supp. 1434 (E.D. Wis. 1990); Beatty v. NP Corp., 581 N.E.2d 1311 (Mass. App. 1991); In re Kidney Ass'n of Oregon, Inc. v. Ferguson, 843 P.2d 442 (Or. 1992).

[119] *See, e.g.,* In re Harney, 3 Cal. St. Bar Ct. Rptr. 266 (Review Dep't 1995) (fee in excess of state-law cap on fees in medical malpractice case); Committee on Legal Ethics of W. Va. State Bar v. Burdette, 445 S.E.2d 733 (W. Va. 1994) (fee in excess of that permitted in workers' compensation case); In re Estate of Konopka, 498 N.W.2d 853 (Wis. App. 1993) (fee in excess of that permitted by statute in estate matter).

[120] *See, e.g.,* Spicer v. Chicago Bd. Options Exch., 844 F. Supp. 1226 (N.D. Ill. 1993); Keith v. Volpe, 644 F. Supp. 1317 (C.D. Cal. 1986).

[121] Wong v. Michael Kennedy, P.C., 853 F. Supp. 73 (E.D. N.Y. 1994).

[122] Comment to Rule 1.5 at paragraph [4]; Rule 1.16(d) (*see* § 6.11).

[123] *See* Pa. Bar Ass'n Comm. on Legal Ethics and Professional Responsibility, Formal Op. 85-120 (1985); Alaska Bar Ass'n Ethics Comm. Op. 87-1 (1987).

[124] *See, e.g.,* In re Cooperman, 591 N.Y.S.2d 855 (App. Div. 1993); Jennings v. Backmeyer, 569 N.E.2d 689 (Ind. App. 1991); Texas Ethics Op. 431 (1986); Ala. State Bar Gen. Counsel Op. RO-93-21 (1993).

[125] *See* In re National Magazine Publishing Co., 170 B.R. 329 (Bankr. N.D. Ohio 1994).

rendered and is provided solely to ensure your availability to handle the client's case. The nonrefundable nature of such a retainer is recognized in a number of jurisdictions.[126]

Although Rule 1.5 does not require that the fee agreement with your client be in writing, the safest practice is to provide your client with a simple letter or memorandum concerning the fee to reduce the possibility of any misunderstanding.[127] Whether your agreement is made orally or reduced to writing, it should clearly specify (1) the specific client or clients you are representing;[128] (2) the services you have agreed to provide on your client's behalf;[129] (3) any limits on the scope of your services,[130] such as whether your representation includes any appeal;[131] (4) how the fee will be computed and how your client will be billed;[132] (5) any anticipated change in the fee rate in the future, and what different rates will be charged for paralegals or other lawyers who work on the case;[133] and (6) what costs and expenses (e.g., charges for court filings, expert witnesses, investigators, stenographers, transcriptions, photocopying, travel, computer assisted research, etc.) your client will be responsible for paying.[134]

## § 6.11  DECLINING OR WITHDRAWING FROM REPRESENTATION

Except when you are appointed by the court to represent a client, ordinarily you have no obligation to accept the representation of a client and may even limit the scope of your representation as a condition of agreeing to accept the client's case.[135] However, once you undertake to represent a client, the discretion to decline the case is replaced with a duty to diligently pursue your client's objectives until you have completed the matter you were hired to undertake.[136] Notwithstanding this duty, there are certain circumstances in which you are *required* to decline representation or withdraw from representing your client, and there are other circumstances in which you *may*, but are not required to, withdraw from the

---

[126] *See, e.g.*, Mass Bar Ass'n Ethics Comm. Op. 95-2 (1995); In re Disciplinary Action Against Lochow, 469 N.W.2d 91 (Minn. 1991); Richmond v. Nodland, 501 N.W.2d 759 (N.D. 1993).

[127] Comment to Rule 1.5 at paragraph [2].

[128] *See* Stern v. Wonzer, 846 S.W.2d 939 (Tex. App. 1993).

[129] *See* Connecticut Informal Ethics Op. 92-31 (1992); Iowa Ethics Op. 86-13 (1987).

[130] *See, e.g.*, New York State Ethics Op. 604 (1989) (representation may be limited to discreet matter or particular stage of proceedings).

[131] *Compare* Joseph E. Di Loreto Inc. v. O'Neill, 1 Cal. Rptr. 2d 636 (Ct. App. 1991) (fee contract specified lawyer was not obligated to pursue appeal), *with* Maryland Attorney Grievance Comm. v. Korotki, 569 A.2d 1224 (Md. App. 1990) (appeal should be pursued if fee contract silent about the matter).

[132] *See* Comment to Rule 1.5 at paragraph [2]; ABA Formal Ethics Op. 93-379 (1993); Kansas Ethics Op. 81-28 (1981).

[133] *See* Severson, Werson, Berke & Melchior v. Bolinger, 1 Cal. Rptr. 2d 531 (Ct. App. 1991); ABA Business Law Section, Task Force on Lawyer's Business Ethics, *Statement of Principles in Billing for Legal Services* (1995); New Mexico Ethics Op. 1990-4; Los Angeles County Ethics Op. 391 (1981).

[134] *See* ABA Business Law Section Task Force on Lawyer Business Ethics, *Statement of Principles in Billing for Disbursements and Other Charges* (1995); Alaska Ethics Op. 93-5 (1993).

[135] Model Rule 1.2(c) (*see* § 6.03).

[136] *See* Model Rule 1.3 and Comment to that Rule at paragraph [4] (*see also* § 6.04[b]); Tormo v. Yormark, 398 F. Supp. 1159 (D.C. N.J. 1975); Anderson, Calder & Lembke v. District Court, 629 P.2d 603 (Colo. 1981).

representation. Regardless of whether the grounds for withdrawal are mandatory or permissive, if you are the client's attorney of record in litigation, your withdrawal is subject to the approval of the court.[137]

Model Rule 1.16 provides:

(a) Except as stated in paragraph (c), a lawyer shall not represent a client or, where representation has commenced, shall withdraw from the representation of a client if:

(1) the representation will result in violation of the Rules of Professional Conduct or other law;

(2) the lawyer's physical or mental condition materially impairs the lawyer's ability to represent the client; or

(3) the lawyer is discharged.

(b) Except as stated in paragraph (c), a lawyer may withdraw from representing a client if:

(1) withdrawal can be accomplished without material adverse affect on the interests of the client;

(2) the client persists in a course of action involving the lawyer's services that the lawyer reasonably believes is criminal or fraudulent;

(3) the client has used the lawyer's services to perpetrate a crime or fraud;

(4) the client insists upon taking action that the lawyer considers repugnant or with which the lawyer has a fundamental disagreement;

(5) the client fails substantially to fulfill an obligation to the lawyer regarding the lawyer's services and has been given reasonable warning that the lawyer will withdraw unless the obligation is fulfilled;

(6) the representation will result in an unreasonable financial burden on the lawyer or has been rendered unreasonably difficult by the client; or

(7) other good cause for withdrawal exists.

(c) A lawyer must comply with applicable law requiring notice to or permission of a tribunal when terminating a representation. When ordered to do so by a tribunal, a lawyer shall continue notwithstanding good cause for terminating the representation.

(d) Upon termination of representation, a lawyer shall take steps to the extent reasonably practicable to protect a client's interests, such as giving reasonable notice to the client, allowing time for employment of other counsel, surrendering papers and property to which the client is entitled and refunding any advance payment of fee or expense that has not been earned or incurred. The lawyer may retain papers relating to the client to the extent permitted by other law.

---

[137] *See* Vander Voort v. Texas State Bar, 802 S.W.2d 332 (Tex. App. 1990); Lutes v. Alexander, 421 S.E.2d 857 (Va. App. 1992).

The Comment to the Rule provides in part:

[1] A lawyer should not accept representation in a matter unless it can be performed competently, promptly, without improper conflict of interest and to completion . . . .

[2] A lawyer ordinarily must decline or withdraw from representation if the client demands that the lawyer engage in conduct that is illegal or violates the Rules of Professional Conduct or other law. The lawyer is not obligated to decline or withdraw simply because the client suggests such a course of conduct; a client may make such a suggestion in the hope that a lawyer will not be constrained by a professional obligation.

[3] When a lawyer has been appointed to represent a client, withdrawal ordinarily requires approval of the appointing authority . . . Difficulty may be encountered if withdrawal is based on the client's demand that the lawyer engage in unprofessional conduct. The court may wish an explanation for the withdrawal, while the lawyer may be bound to keep confidential the facts that would constitute such an explanation. The lawyer's statement that professional considerations require termination of the representation ordinarily should be accepted as sufficient . . . .

[4] A client has a right to discharge a lawyer at any time, with or without cause, subject to liability for payment for the lawyer's services . . . .

[5] Whether a client can discharge appointed counsel may depend on applicable law. A client seeking to do so should be given a full explanation of the consequences. These consequences may include a decision by the appointing authority that appointment of successor counsel is unjustified, thus requiring self-representation by the client.

[6] If the client has severely diminished capacity, the client may lack the legal capacity to discharge the lawyer, and in any event the discharge may be seriously adverse to the client's interests. The lawyer should make special effort to help the client consider the consequences and may take reasonably necessary protective action as provided in Rule 1.14. [*See* Sec. 6.06].

[7] A lawyer may withdraw from representation in some circumstances. The lawyer has the option to withdraw if it can be accomplished without material adverse effect on the client's interests. Withdrawal is also justified if the client persists in a course of action the lawyer reasonably believes is criminal or fraudulent, for a lawyer is not required to be associated with such conduct even if the lawyer does not further it. Withdrawal is also permitted if the lawyer's services were misused in the past even if that would materially prejudice the client. The lawyer also may withdraw where the client insists on taking action that the lawyer considers repugnant or with which the lawyer has a fundamental disagreement.

[8] A lawyer may withdraw if the client refuses to abide by the terms of an agreement relating to the representation, such as an agreement concerning fees or court costs or an agreement limiting the objectives of the representation.

For the most part, the provisions of Rule 1.16 are fairly self-explanatory. The most ambiguous provisions concern the permissive withdrawal situations where the "client insists upon pursuing an objective that the lawyer considers repugnant or with which the lawyer has a fundamental disagreement" under subsection (b)(4), where "the representation . . . has been rendered unreasonably difficult by the client" under subsection (b)(6), and where "other good cause for withdrawal exists" under subsection (b)(7).

It has been suggested that the "repugnant" language provides you with a certain degree of professional independence to withdraw when the client's conduct, though not unlawful, violates community interests or your sense of public policy or personal morals.[138] For example, it has been held that a lawyer could properly withdraw on grounds of repugnancy where he or she could not, in good conscience, continue to represent a defendant who wanted to forgo appeals and accept the death penalty.[139] Similarly, repugnancy may permit you to withdraw if your client insists on a course of action or objective that is contrary to your advice and your client would not be prejudiced by your withdrawal.[140]

Withdrawal on the ground that your client has rendered the representation "unreasonably difficult" may be justified when your client refuses to communicate or cooperate in the case,[141] or tensions between you and your client have led to a complete breakdown of the trust and loyalty necessary for an effective attorney-client relationship.[142] An antagonistic breakdown in the attorney-client relationship may also constitute "other good cause" for withdrawal.[143] In addition, it has been held that "other good cause" for withdrawal may exist when it has become clear that the client's case is without merit,[144] the client has filed a grievance against the lawyer,[145] or the client has deliberately disregarded a fee obligation.[146]

---

[138] *See* Gillers, What We Talked About When We Talked About Ethics: A Critical View of the Model Rules, 46 Ohio St. L. J. 243, 260 (1985).

[139] Red Dog v. State, 625 A.2d 245 (Del. 1993). *See also* Tenn. Sup. Ct. Bd. of Professional Ethics Comm. Op. 96-F-140 (1996) (withdrawal may be permitted if lawyer's representation impaired by his moral or religious beliefs).

[140] *See* Spero v. Abbott Laboratories, 396 F. Supp. 321 (D. Ill. 1975); Kannewurf v. Johns, 632 N.E.2d 711 (Ill. App. 1994) (refusal to follow advice regarding settlement). *But see* May v. Seibert, 264 S.E.2d 643 (W. Va. 1980) (acceptance of settlement terms is solely within client's province, and thus client's refusal to settle is not adequate ground for lawyer's withdrawal).

[141] *See, e.g.*, Statute of Liberty-Ellis Island Foundation Inc. v. International United Industries, 110 F.R.D. 395 (S.D. N.Y. 1986) (refusal to cooperate); Sobol v. District Court of Aprahoe County, 619 P.2d 765 (Colo. 1980) (client withheld material information, repeatedly contacted opponent's lawyers, and was critical of counsel); Hancock v. Mutual of Omaha Insurance, 472 A.2d 867 (D.C. App. 1984) (client unresponsive to phone calls and letters).

[142] *See, e.g.*, McGuire v. Wilson, 735 F. Supp. 83 (S.D. N.Y. 1990) (client alleged lawyer mishandled case, coupled with vituperative letters between client and counsel evidencing "sad state" of relationship); In re Admonition Issued in Panel File No. 94-24, 533 N.W.2d 852 (Minn. 1995) (client's anger and refusal to cooperate with lawyer showed client had no confidence in lawyer); Kolomick v. Kolomick, 518 N.Y.S2d 413 (App. Div. 1987) (breakdown of relationship made representation impossible).

[143] *See, e.g.*, McGuire v. Wilson, 735 F. Supp. 83 (S.D. N.Y. 1990); Chaleff v. Superior Court, 138 Cal. Rptr. 735 (Ct. App. 1977); Lasser v. Nassau Community College, 457 N.Y.S.2d 343 (App. Div. 1983).

[144] *See* Kirsch v. Duryea, 146 Cal. Rptr. 218 (Ct. App. 1978).

[145] *See* In re Anonymous, 379 S.E.2d 723 (S.C. 1989).

[146] Commonwealth v. Sheps, 523 A.2d 363 (Pa. 1987).

If you are discharged by your client or withdraw from the representation, you have a duty under subsection (d) of the Rule to take reasonable steps to mitigate any damage to your client's interests. As that subsection states, this means giving your client reasonable notice of your intent to withdraw, allowing time for your client to employ other counsel, surrendering papers and property to which your client is entitled, and refunding any advance payment of a fee not yet earned. In addition, you should advise your client about the importance of hiring substitute counsel,[147] and diligently cooperate with substitute counsel in responding to inquiries and handing over the client's file.[148]

## § 6.12   DEALING WITH PERSONS OTHER THAN YOUR OWN CLIENT

In representing a client, Model Rule 4.2 addresses the extent to which you may communicate with another person who is represented by counsel in the same legal matter, and Rule 4.3 addresses your dealings with unrepresented persons. Rule 4.4 otherwise deals with your conduct towards third persons.

Model Rule 4.2 provides that "[i]in representing a client, a lawyer shall not communicate about the subject of the representation with a person the lawyer knows to be represented by another lawyer in the matter, unless the lawyer has the consent of the other lawyer or is authorized to do so by law or a court order." The Comment to the Rule explains in part:

[2] This Rule applies to communications with any person who is represented by counsel concerning the matter to which the communication relates.

[3] The Rule applies even though the represented person initiates or consents to the communication. A lawyer must immediately terminate communication with a person if, after commencing communication, the lawyer learns that the person is one with whom communication is not permitted by this Rule.

[4] This Rule does not prohibit communication with a represented person, or an employee or agent of such a person, concerning matters outside the representation. For example, the existence of a controversy between a government agency and a private party, or between two organizations, does not prohibit a lawyer for either from communicating with nonlawyer representatives of the other regarding a separate matter. Nor does this Rule preclude communication with a represented person who is seeking advice from a lawyer who is not otherwise representing a client in the matter. A lawyer may not make a communication prohibited by this Rule through the acts of another. *See* Rule 8.4(a). Parties to a matter may communicate directly with each other, and a lawyer is not prohibited from advising a client concerning a communication that the client is legally entitled to make. Also, a lawyer having independent justification or legal

---

[147] *See* In re Palmer, 380 S.E.2d 813 (S.C. 1989); In re Kaufman, 567 P.2d 957 (Nev. 1977).

[148] In re Tos, 576 A.2d 607 (Del. 1980); In re Sumner, 665 A.2d 986 (D.C. App. 1995); In re Dils, 646 N.E.2d 667 (Ind. 1995); In re Swerine, 513 N.W.2d 463 (Minn. 1994).

authorization for communicating with a represented person is permitted to do so . . . .

[7] In the case of a represented organization, this Rule prohibits communications with a constituent of the organization who supervises, directs or regularly consults with the organization's lawyer concerning the matter or has authority to obligate the organization with respect to the matter or whose act or omission in connection with that matter may be imputed to the organization for purposes of civil or criminal liability. Consent of the organization's lawyer is not required for communication with a former constituent. If a constituent of the organization is represented in the matter by his or her own counsel, the consent by that counsel to a communication will be sufficient for purposes of this Rule . . . .

[8] The prohibition on communications with a represented person only applies in circumstances where the lawyer knows that the person is in fact represented in the matter to be discussed. This means that the lawyer has actual knowledge of the fact of the representation; but such actual knowledge may be inferred from the circumstances. *See* Rule 1.0(f). Thus, the lawyer cannot evade the requirement of obtaining the consent of counsel by closing eyes to the obvious.

This Rule, sometimes called the "anti-contact" rule, is designed to prevent lawyers from taking advantage of laypersons and to preserve the integrity of the attorney-client relationship.[149] Although the Rule applies only when you have "actual knowledge" that the other person is represented, Comment [8] above makes clear that you cannot avoid the Rule by simply "closing [your] eyes to the obvious" in circumstances where there is substantial reason to believe that the other person is represented.[150] Accordingly, some cases have held that in doubtful situations you have a duty to ask the layperson whether he or she is represented.[151]

The Rule does not prohibit represented parties from speaking with one another without lawyer consent, but you cannot "mastermind" the inter-party communications by, for example, using your client as a conduit to initiate a conversation with the other party and then take over the conversation with the other party without his or her lawyer's consent.[152] In addition, it has been held that a lawyer who merely "listens" to an adverse party who initiates a conversation with the lawyer violates the Rule if the interaction occurs without the consent of the adverse party's lawyer.[153]

---

[149] *See* United States v. Lopez, 4 F.3d 1455 (9th Cir. 1993); Polycast Tech. Corp. v. Uniroyal Inc, 129 F.R.D. 621 (S.D. N.Y. 1990); Michaels v. Woodland, 988 F. Supp. 468 (D. N.J. 1997); ABA Comm. on Ethics and Professional Responsibility, Formal Op. 95-396.

[150] ABA Standing Committee on Ethics and Professional Responsibility, Formal Op. 95-396 (1995).

[151] *See, e.g.*, Monsanto Co. v. Aetna Cas. & Sur. Co., 539 A.2d 1013 (Del. 1990); Upjohn v. Aetna Cas. & Sur. Co., 768 F. Supp. 1186 (W.D. Mich. 1990). *Contra* Colo. Bar Ass'n Comm. on Professional Ethics, Rev. Op. 69 (1987) (no duty to inquire).

[152] *See* Trumball County Bar Ass'n v. Makridis, 671 N.E.2d 31 (Ohio 1996) (lawyer for plaintiff reprimanded when he suggested his client call defendant, and during call, plaintiff handed phone to lawyer who continued conversation with defendant). *Cf.* State Bar of Cal. Standing Comm. on Professional Responsibility and Conduct, Formal Op. 1993-131 (lawyer may confer with client about strategy to be pursued in client's communications with other party, but content of communication must originate with client, not lawyer).

[153] *See, e.g.*, In re Howes, 940 P.2d 159 (N.M. 1997).

The Rule, however, does not preclude you from interviewing witnesses of another party.[154] Also, when a governmental agency is the represented party, the Fifth Amendment right of petition permits you to discuss the controversy with government officials without consent of counsel for the Government.[155]

In criminal cases, the courts have repeatedly held that the Rule is inapplicable to communications entered into by a prosecutor, his or her agents, or informants with a represented criminal suspect, so long as those communications occur in a non-custodial setting and *before* the initiation of formal charges.[156] With respect to federal prosecutors, the United States Justice Department has established specific guidelines governing prosecutor contacts with represented persons.[157]

In dealing with an unrepresented person, Rule 4.3 provides:

> In dealing on behalf of a client with a person who is not represented by counsel, a lawyer shall not state or imply that the lawyer is disinterested. When the lawyer knows or reasonably should know that the unrepresented person misunderstands the lawyer's role in the matter, the lawyer shall make reasonable efforts to correct the misunderstanding. The lawyer shall not give legal advice to an unrepresented person, other than the advice to secure counsel, if the lawyer knows or reasonably should know that the interests of such a person are or have a reasonable possibility of being in conflict with the interest of the client.

It is important to note that this Rule covers any communications directed to *any* unrepresented person by a lawyer acting on a client's behalf, including other parties to a proposed transaction, potential witnesses, and opposing parties in planned or pending litigation.

Rule 4.3 prohibits you from giving advice to an unrepresented person other than the advice to obtain counsel if the person's interests might conflict with those of your client.[158] In addition, although the Rule does not prohibit you from interviewing an unrepresented person (whether a witness or prospective adverse party),[159] when seeking or conducting an interview, you should clearly identify your role as lawyer for your client.[160] A number of jurisdictions have held that if the unrepresented person is a potential adverse party, you should notify him or her that a lawsuit is possible or contemplated;[161] and if a lawsuit has already been filed and the

---

[154] *See* McCallum v. CSX Transp.Inc, 149 F.R.D. 104 (M.D. N.C. 1993); Cole v. Appalachian Power Co., 903 F. Supp. 975 (S.D. W. Va. 1995).

[155] *See* Camden v. State of Maryland, 910 F. Supp. 1115 (D. Md. 1996); N.C. State Bar Ass'n Ethics Comm. Op. 219 (1995).

[156] *See* United States v. Marcus, 849 F. Supp. 417 (D. Md. 1994); United States v. Balter, 91 F.3d 427 (3d Cir. 1996).

[157] *See* 28 C.F.R. § 77 (1994) (permitting, before charge, arrest, or indictment, *ex parte* contacts with persons known to be represented in the matter being investigated).

[158] Comment to Rule 4.3 at paragraph [2].

[159] *See, e.g.*, Pennsylvania Ethics Op. 96-145 (1996); Mississippi Ethics Op. 141 (1988); New York State Ethics Op. 607 (1990).

[160] *See, e.g.*, Arizona Ethics Op. 87-25 (1987); Pennsylvania Ethics Op. 93-156 (1993).

[161] *See, e.g.*, Arizona Ethics Op. 87-25 (1987); Pennsylvania Ethics Op. 93-156 (1993). When interviewing an unrepresented present or former employee, some jurisdictions have established special protocols to be followed by lawyers. *See, e.g.*, McCallum v. CSX Transp. Inc., 149 F.R.D. 104 (M.D. N.C. 1993) (requiring interviewing lawyer to disclose his representative capacity, nature of interview, and to

unrepresented party does not know about it, you should reveal that information.[162]

Finally, Rule 4.4(a) provides that "[i]n representing a client, a lawyer shall not use means that have no substantial purpose other than to embarrass, delay, or burden a third person, or use methods of obtaining evidence that violate the legal rights of such a person." This Rule essentially commands that, when representing a client, you must act with civility towards all third persons such as opposing counsel,[163] the opposing party,[164] witnesses,[165] and the court.[166] In dealing with third persons, you are also obligated to be truthful when making any statements "of material fact or law." (*See* § 9.06 and its discussion of Rule 4.1).

---

inform employee of right to refuse interview and have counsel present). *See also* Kan. Bar Ass'n Ethics/Advisory Services Comm. Op. 97-07 (1992).

[162] *See* Brew v. Stern, 603 A.2d 126 (N.J. 1991).

[163] *See, e.g.*, St. Paul Fire & Marine Ins. Co., 828 F. Supp. 594 (C.D. Ill. 1992); In re Belue, 76 P.2d 206 (Mont. 1988); Principe v. Assay Partners, 586 N.Y.S.2d 182 (1992).

[164] *See, e.g.*, In re Golden, 496 S.E.2d 619 (S.C. 1998); In re Bechhold, 771 P.2d 563 (Mont. 1988).

[165] *See, e.g.*, In re Golden, 496 S.E.2d 619 (S.C. 1998).

[166] *See, e.g.*, Kentucky Bar Ass'n v. Waller, 929 S.W.2d 184 (Ky. 1996); In re Vincenti, 704 A.2d 927 (N.J. 1998).

# PART II
## NEGOTIATING

# Chapter 7

# INTRODUCTION AND ACADEMIC APPROACHES TO NEGOTIATION

## § 7.01  THE RELATIONSHIP BETWEEN COUNSELING AND NEGOTIATING

Negotiation is a process by which parties try to resolve their differences or common problems in order to reach some mutually satisfactory agreement. Of course, parties routinely negotiate in a non-dispute context when they seek to engage in a business relationship for the sale of goods or services or to consummate a transaction. When a dispute is involved, parties almost always initially seek to resolve their differences through negotiation, and it is estimated that over 90% of all lawsuits are settled.[1]

Counseling and interviewing are integral to representing a client in negotiations, whether those negotiations occur in the context of a dispute or not. That is, the skills of establishing a counseling relationship with your client, obtaining information relevant to the decision to be made by your client, analyzing the decision to be made, advising your client about the decision, and implementing the decision are all employed when representing a client in an effort to reach an agreement with another. In addition, counseling and negotiating are inexorably interrelated in that you cannot ethically and effectively represent your client in negotiations without providing appropriate counseling. Thus, in learning negotiating skills you must apply all that you have learned about counseling. Although negotiation is a separate subject from counseling in that the former is a means towards achieving your

---

[1] *See* Herbert M. Kritzer, *Let's Make a Deal* 3 (1991).

client's ends that have been developed through the latter, counseling your client does not stop when negotiations start. All aspects of negotiating involve your client's interests, and therefore it is necessary to continue to counsel your client throughout the entire negotiating process.

## § 7.02  ACADEMIC APPROACHES TO UNDERSTANDING NEGOTIATION

For many years, academicians have sought to understand negotiating through game theory and from the perspectives of disciplines such as economics, anthropology, sociology, and psychology. Attempts at categorizing, quantifying, and systematizing the negotiating process have proven difficult and sometimes have led to more confusion than clarity. Part of the problem is that much of the literature has become permeated by a specialized nomenclature that must be sorted out before one can understand what is being said. Another part of the problem may be that attempts to employ quasi-empirical analyses and models to the negotiating process are inherently difficult given that negotiating is an extremely complex form of human behavior that is often characterized by irrational as well as rational considerations. Empirical or quasi-scientific methodologies and theories (as contrasted with more "anecdotal" approaches) tend to give us a greater sense of comfort and certainty that we understand a subject, and therefore it is difficult to concede that these ways of understanding why people do what they do may often be limited. Nevertheless, disciplined research about the negotiating process should not be discounted even by those who go so far as to characterize a good bit of the theoretical literature as being unnecessarily abstract, esoteric, or ethereal. Ongoing and imaginative research may well add more to our understanding of negotiating in the long run.

Provided below is a selected (not exhaustive) summary of some of the most often-cited multi-disciplinary commentary about negotiating. As indicated above, these approaches may serve as a catalyst for on-going research. In any event, providing at the outset this summary of existing theory serves as a useful introduction to the overall subject of negotiating and may also be of help in thinking more creatively about the subject.

## § 7.03  GAME THEORY AND THE PRISONER'S DILEMMA

Game theory[2] is an experimental tool used by a number of theorists to study negotiation.[3] Probably the most widely known game is the "Prisoner's Dilemma." While there are many variations of this game, it essentially involves two persons (*e.g.*, Smith and Jones) who are taken into custody by the police and charged with a serious felony.[4] Smith and Jones are separated from one another for purposes of interrogation, and each must decide whether to confess to the felony and turn State's evidence against the other or not to confess. Both prisoners know that if neither confesses, the State will not have enough evidence to convict them of the

---

[2] The seminal work on game theory is J. Von Neumann & O. Morgenstern, *Theory of Games and Economic Behavior* (1944).

[3] *See* D. Pruitt, *Negotiation Behavior*, 102–110 (1981); H. Raiffa, *The Art and Science of Negotiation*, 123–126 (1982); *see generally*, A. Rapoport, *Two-Person Game Theory: The Essential Ideas* (1966).

[4] *See* E. McGinnis, *Social Behavior: A Functional Analysis*, 417–418, 423–424 (1970).

felony and each will receive only a 1-year sentence for a misdemeanor. If both confess (*i.e.*, plead guilty so that there is no need for one to turn State's evidence against the other), both will go to jail for the felony but will receive a reduced sentence of 7 years in return for pleading guilty. However, if one confesses and the other does not (*i.e.*, one turns State's evidence and the other does not confess and pleads not guilty), the former will be released and the latter will go to jail for 10 years. Thus, each prisoner's choice of confessing or not confessing will result in different outcomes depending not only upon his own decision, but also upon the decision made by his fellow prisoner. Because the prisoners are not permitted to communicate with one another, neither knows what the other will do.

The different outcomes or "payoffs" may be illustrated by the following matrix:

### Jones

|               | Does not Confess | Confesses |
|---------------|---------------------------------|----------------------------------|
| **Does not Confess** | Smith gets 1 year<br>Jones gets 1 year | Smith gets 10 years<br>Jones is released |
| **Confesses** | Smith is released<br>Jones gets 10 years | Smith gets 7 years<br>Jones gets 7 years |

**Smith**

The "dilemma" faced by Smith and Jones is that while both will be better off if neither confesses (*i.e.*, each gets 1 year) than if both confess (*i.e.*, each gets 7 years), neither wants to be the "sucker" who pleads not guilty when the other has confessed and turned State's evidence (*i.e.*, the "sucker" will get 10 years). Thus, without being able to communicate with one another, the incentives tend to pressure both into confessing such that "the pursuit of self-interest leads to a poor outcome for all"[5] (*i.e.*, each prisoner ends up with a 7-year jail term).

This result is apparent when one considers the various alternatives available to Smith if Jones confesses on the one hand, or does not confess on the other:

(1) <u>Assume Jones confesses</u>: Here, if Smith does not confess, Smith gets a 10-year sentence. If Smith also confesses, then Smith gets a 7-year sentence. Thus, assuming Jones confesses, Smith is better off by confessing.

(2) <u>Assume Jones does not confess</u>: Here, if Smith confesses, Smith is set free. If Smith also does not confess, then Smith gets a 1-year sentence. Thus, assuming Jones does not confess, Smith is better off by confessing.

If Jones applied the same analysis *vis a vis* the choices available to Smith, Jones would also conclude that his best option would be to confess.

In the context of studying negotiating, the Prisoner's Dilemma game illustrates the fact that cooperation and competition are inherent in two-party bargaining.

---

[5] R. Axelrod, *The Evolution of Cooperation* 7 (1984).

Cooperation is necessary to achieve a voluntary agreement, but competition usually occurs over the terms of a final agreement. Analogizing Smith and Jones as opposing negotiators, if Smith *cooperates* with Jones by *not confessing*, Smith is gambling that Jones is to be trusted to reciprocate by also not confessing. However, Jones might *compete* by *confessing* (*i.e.*, "defecting" as it is called in the game-theoretic nomenclature) and thereby exploit Smith's cooperation such that Jones is released at Smith's expense. Thus, the game suggests that the best outcome for any one negotiator (prisoner) is to engage in competitive behavior (*i.e.*, to confess and serve no jail time) when the other engages in cooperative behavior (*i.e.*, does not confess and receives a 10-year sentence). The game also suggests that if both negotiators engage in cooperative behavior (*i.e.*, both do not confess), a reasonable, albeit less than ideal result occurs (*i.e.*, both get a 1-year sentence). If both engage in competitive behavior (*i.e.*, both confess), the result is largely undesirable for both (*i.e.*, both get a 7-year sentence).

There is extensive theoretical literature analyzing what happens when two players repeatedly play the game.[6] One prominent theorist held two computer tournaments in which professional and amateur game theorists submitted computer programs to compete against one another in repeated plays of the Prisoner's Dilemma where the number of rounds was not predetermined. The winner was the simplest of all strategies submitted, "Tit for Tat." Under this strategy, the player started out by cooperating and then did whatever the opposing player did on the previous move. In this way, Tit for Tat used cooperation at first instance, but switched to competitive behavior (defection) in response to competitive moves by the other side.[7]

Along with different variations on the Prisoner's Dilemma, numerous other games and game-theoretic models have been developed which, generally speaking, illustrate and analyze the tension between cooperative and competitive behavior.[8] These heuristic devices to understanding negotiating are often divorced from reality because of the strict "rules of the game." For example, most of the games involve only two parties who are the principals to the negotiation, and thus there is no accounting for the involvement of agents such as lawyers[9] or the involvement of third-party neutrals such as mediators. The games also heavily restrict other circumstances attendant to the negotiation, such as the type and number of potential outcomes or payoffs, the extent to which the players are able to communicate with one another, and the choice of strategies that may be employed (*e.g.*, cooperating or competing by "defecting"). There are usually no time constraints, and the bargainers are only concerned about the instant negotiation to the exclusion of factors such as past or future dealings between the parties, linkage to

---

[6] *See, e.g.*, Roger B. Myerson, *Game Theory: Analysis of Conflict*, 308–310, 337–42 (1991); Jean-Francois Mertens, "Repeated Games," in *The New Palgrave: Game Theory* 205 (1989); R. Duncan Luce & H. Raiffa, *Games and Decisions: Introduction and Critical Survey*, 97-102 (1957).

[7] *See* R. Axelrod, *The Evolution of Cooperation* 27–54 (1984); D. Lax & J. Sebenius, *The Manager as Negotiator: Bargaining for Cooperation and Competitive Gain* 157–160 (1986).

[8] *See, e.g.*, O. Young, Bargaining (1975) (summarizing various game-theoretic and economic models); James P. Kahan, "Experimental Studies of Bargaining as Analogues of Civil Disputes," (Rand Paper Series, Rand Corp. 1983) (bilateral monopoly game and others); H.M. Kritzer, *Let's Make a Deal* 88–98 (1991) (summarizing various models); J. Rubin & B. Brown, *The Social Psychology of Bargaining and Negotiation* 19–32 (1975) (summarizing various games).

[9] *See* R.J. Gilson & R.H. Mnookin, Disputing Through Agents: Cooperation and Conflict Between Lawyers in Litigation, 94 Colum. L. Rev. 509 (1994).

other transactions or problems faced by the parties, or the effects of establishing precedents through settlements, etc. Finally, the overall control placed over the form of game-theoretic bargaining makes any individual and interpersonal variables such as emotion, irrationality, and the personal situations of the parties essentially irrelevant to the negotiation.[10]

In short, the paradigms of game-theoretic analysis markedly limit the utility of these approaches to understanding negotiating in the real world.[11] However, this is not to say that these approaches are completely useless or unworthy of continued research. As one scholar tactfully put it:

> One criticism of [game-theoretic analysis], to put it bluntly, is that it often represents a "painful elaboration of the obvious." In fact, what appears to be obvious in retrospect is frequently less clear before the elaboration. More important, the game theoretic models serve to systematize what are often disparate bits and pieces of common wisdom (and perhaps wisdom that is not so common) and to provide a useful, albeit perhaps only heuristic, framework for thinking about bargaining. Such models also point to the basic fact that negotiations do involve a substantial component of gamesmanship.[12]

## § 7.04 ECONOMIC APPROACHES

Often related to game-theoretic analyses are economic theories of negotiating.[13] Economic theory essentially focuses on a "cost-benefit" approach to analyzing the outcome of negotiations inasmuch as the predominant commodity at stake in most negotiations is money. On the one hand, in negotiations involving business transactions where there is no legal dispute to be resolved, this analysis involves straightforward economic considerations that dictate the course and outcome of bargaining based upon the extent to which the parties believe that a deal would be profitable. In the context of negotiations to resolve a legal dispute, economic theory essentially posits that the likelihood of a settlement depends on the extent to which the parties calculate or otherwise perceive that the benefit to be achieved by settling the case outweighs the cost of resolving the dispute through litigation.

The thrust of the latter analysis is that a settlement will occur if the bottom-line amounts of money that the respective parties are willing to settle for create a "zone of overlap" where the minimum amount the plaintiff will accept is less than the maximum amount the defendant will pay.[14] In the most straightforward formulation, these bottom-line amounts (often referred to as "resistance points") are arrived at by calculating an *expected outcome* for the case by multiplying the

---

[10] *See* H. Scott Bierman & Luis Fernandez, *Game Theory with Economic Applications*, 68–70 (1993); H. Raiffa, *The Art and Science of Negotiation* 3–4, 54 (1982).

[11] *See* O. Young, *Bargaining* 36–37 (1975) ("[T]he models of game theory have not produced good predictions in empirical terms. That is, the outcomes predicted by these logical models do not correspond well with the actual outcomes that occur in related real-world situations even though a number of models are logically and mathematically elegant.").

[12] H. M. Kritzer, *Let's Make a Deal*, 92–93 (1991).

[13] *See* O. Young, *Bargaining* (1975) (summarizing a number of classical economic models).

[14] *See generally*, Richard A. Posner, An Economic Approach to Legal Procedure and Judicial Administration, 2 J. Legal Studies 399 (1973); Alan E. Friedman, An Analysis of Settlement, 22 Stanford L. Rev. 67 (1969); John P. Gould, An Economic Analysis of Legal Conflicts, 2 J. Legal Studies 279 (1973).

gross outcome that could be obtained at trial by the probability that the gross outcome will occur, and then subtracting (for plaintiffs) or adding (for defendants) the non-shiftable costs a court would not tax against the losing party which would be incurred in obtaining that outcome ("transaction costs").

For example, if the Plaintiff estimates that the gross outcome he could obtain at trial is $100,000, that he has approximately a 75% chance of obtaining such a verdict in light of the particular circumstances of the case, and that it will cost him approximately $5,000 in non-shiftable litigation expenses to obtain that verdict, his bottom-line settlement amount (resistance point) would be $70,000 (*i.e.*, $100,000 ×.75 = $75,000; $75,000 − $5,000 = $70,000). On the other hand, the Defendant might estimate that Plaintiff has only a 60% chance of obtaining $100,000 at trial, and that it will cost her (the Defendant) $20,000 in non-shiftable expenses to try the case. Thus, her bottom line (resistance point) would be to pay Plaintiff no more than $80,000 to settle the case (*i.e.*, $100,000 ×.60 = $60,000; $60,000 ∓ $20,000 = $80,000). Here, because the minimum amount the Plaintiff will accept ($70,000) is less than the maximum amount the Defendant will pay ($80,000), a settlement is theoretically most likely to occur somewhere within the $10,000 zone of overlap between $70,000 and $80,000.

A fundamental difficulty with this type of analysis is estimating "what the case is worth" when one chooses a gross amount that a jury might award and a probability that such a verdict would be realized. In addition, the amount of non-shiftable litigation costs in a given case may be quite difficult to estimate. To some extent, these uncertainties may be mathematically taken into account if each party considers a variety of possible jury verdicts (*e.g.*, from $0 to $10,000 to $20,000, etc. up to $100,000), assigns a probability to each (where the total of the percentages equals 100%), multiplies each possible jury verdict by the particular probability assigned to it to arrive at a set of "expected values," and then adds the expected values together to arrive at an overall expected outcome. The same procedure could be followed to arrive at an overall estimate of expected costs. The expected costs would then be subtracted (for the plaintiff) or added (for the defendant) to the overall expected outcome. However, the prophetic accuracy of this method of calculation is still dependent upon the relative accuracy of the various probabilities that the parties assign to different jury verdicts and cost estimates. Moreover, and perhaps most importantly, the utility of this method is limited to the extent that the parties or their lawyers are able and willing to think in these arithmetic calculations of the various probabilities.

Apart from the difficulty of arriving at an expected value for a case, numerous other uncertainties exist that affect the reliability of economic analyses of potential settlements. For example, the extent to which the parties are psychologically willing to gamble on going to trial versus settling the case (commonly referred to as "risk aversion") usually has a profound impact on the negotiating process and its outcome. Similarly a party might have different reasons why she would prefer a trial or settlement of the case, and the particular concession behavior of a party may significantly affect the negotiating behavior of the other party. In various ways, economic theorists have struggled to incorporate these and other variables into intricate mathematical models in an on-going effort to understand different types of negotiations and their potential outcomes.[15]

---

[15] For an excellent summary of many of these models, *see* Robert D. Cooter & Daniel T. Rubinfield,

The foregoing discussion of economic theory has assumed a type of bargaining that is frequently called "distributive" bargaining, having a "zero-sum" nature. That is, where there is a single issue such as money, the consequence of negotiating is that the more money or gain one side gets, the less the other side gets.[16] Another line of economic theory, however, conceptualizes "integrative" bargaining, having "positive-sum" results. Here,

> . . . [in] such bargaining, in which there are two parties and several issues to be negotiated, . . . [t]he parties are not strict competitors. It is no longer true that if one party gets more, the other necessarily has to get less; they both can get more. They can cooperate in order to enlarge the pie that they eventually will have to divide.[17]

One way of conceptualizing integrative bargaining is through the model of the so-called "efficient frontier" or "Pareto Optimal Frontier," developed by the Italian economist Vilfredo Pareto.[18] This model may be graphically represented as follows:[19]

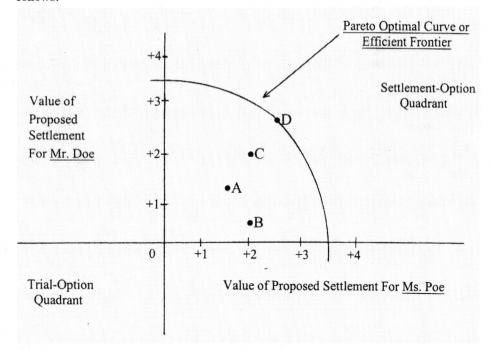

In this graph, the point symbols designated by ● with their accompanying letters represent different settlement proposals. The horizontal axis represents increases in the value of a settlement proposal for Ms. Poe in an easterly direction, and the vertical axis represents increases in the value of a settlement proposal for Mr. Doe in a northerly direction. A settlement proposal perceived by one or both of

Economic Analysis of Legal Disputes and Their Resolution, 27 J. Econ. Literature 1067 (1989).

[16] H. Raiffa, *The Art and Science of Negotiation* 33 (1982).

[17] H. Raiffa, *The Art and Science of Negotiation* 131 (1982).

[18] *See* H. Raiffa, *The Art and Science of Negotiation*, 138–142, 148–165 (1982).

[19] This graph is adapted from the one found in Jonathan M. Hyman, Trial Advocacy and Methods of Negotiation: Can Good Trial Advocates be Wise Negotiators?, 34 UCLA L. Rev. 879 n.34 (1987).

the parties to be of less value than what could be obtained at trial would not give rise to a settlement and would fall within the southwest "Trial Option Quadrant." The parties will only settle the case if a particular proposal falls within the northeast quadrant.

Within this "Settlement-Option Quadrant," there are theoretically three types of settlement proposals that could be made: (1) proposals that are of greater value to one party but simultaneously reduce value to the other party, (2) proposals that are of greater value to one party but do not reduce value to the other, or (3) proposals that are of *maximum* value to each party without reducing value to any party. The latter settlement proposals are said to be "Pareto-optimal" or most "efficient." That is, at some level, it will not be possible to fashion a settlement that will increase value for at least one party without reducing value to the other, and this level is represented by the "Pareto Optimal Curve or Efficient Frontier." Thus, no settlements exist to the north or east of the curve, but from any position within the area bounded by the curve it is theoretically possible to find a settlement along the curve line that is better for at least one party without reducing value to the other.

For example, if, after Mr. Doe has proposed a settlement of comparable value to both parties at point A, Ms. Poe proposes a settlement at point B which is of greater value to her, the latter proposal will be rejected by Mr. Doe because it reduces the value of the settlement he would have received through proposal A. If either party thereafter proposes a settlement at point C, such a settlement would be more efficient than B because proposal C would increase value for Mr. Doe without decreasing value for Ms. Poe. In this way, proposal C is said to be "pareto superior" to proposals A or B. However, a settlement at point C is not "pareto optimal" in the face of proposal D that would be of yet further value to both parties without reducing value to any one party.

The theory of the efficient frontier is that, particularly in situations where the parties are bargaining over a number of issues rather than merely the question of how much money one party will pay and the other will get, an optimal settlement is one that is most efficient in the sense of providing the most gain to each party without diminishing the value received by any one of them through some other or earlier settlement proposal. The theory presupposes and prescribes that the parties explore and share their various interests, needs, goals, and values underlying the subject matter of the negotiation. In this way, they are more likely to arrive at an optimal settlement that is of greater net benefit to both of them than would otherwise be the case if they engaged in myopic "positional" bargaining that did not take into account their underlying interests, needs, goals, and values.

As a simple example, if Ms. Poe and Mr. Doe are in a dispute about custody, child support, and alimony, Ms. Poe's initial position might be that she will have sole "legal and physical custody" of their child, that Mr. Doe must pay her $X in child support, and that he should pay $Y in fault-based alimony each month because he committed adultery. Mr. Poe's initial position might be that he should have sole custody of the parties' child or will pay only $Z in child support if Ms. Poe has custody, and in no event will he pay any alimony notwithstanding his adultery. If the parties essentially maintain these initial positions and limit their bargaining solely to the payment amounts regarding child support and alimony, they might never reach agreement. On the other hand, if they share their underlying interests, needs, goals, and values with one another (*e.g.*, through their lawyers or a mediator), they may be successful in reaching an agreement that each perceives to have more positive-sum than zero-sum aspects. For instance, the parties might agree to have "joint legal custody" of their child with Ms. Poe having primary "physical" custody, and Mr. Doe might agree to pay more in child support than he otherwise was willing to pay (or would statutorily be obligated to pay) in exchange for Ms. Poe's agreement to forego receiving any alimony. In short, these various tradeoffs between the parties will more closely reflect the differing needs and values that the parties place upon parental status, the most appropriate care for their child, the relative importance of admitting fault in the break up of the marriage, and considerations of immediate or longer-term financial security for the child and/or the spouses.

This multi-dimensional approach of integrative bargaining as conceptualized through the search for pareto-optimal settlements has become commonly referred to as "problem-solving" negotiation in contrast to purely distributive, "adversarial" negotiation.[20] The attributes and limitations of each approach have been vigorously debated among scholars.[21] Essentially, this debate reflects the tension between (1) the reality that most negotiations are exclusively concerned with how much money one party will receive and the other will pay, and (2) the "principled" view that parties might achieve greater mutual satisfaction if they cooperate or collaborate to either enlarge the pie they can divide or fashion an agreement that places a premium on satisfying both parties' true interests, needs, goals, and values.

## § 7.05  ANTHROPOLOGICAL & SOCIOLOGICAL APPROACHES

Game theory and economic theory focus primarily, though not exclusively, on the outcome of negotiations rather than on their process. Much of the anthropological and sociological literature, on the other hand, focuses on identifying and exploring typologies of negotiating that are descriptive (and to some extent prescriptive) about the process of negotiating. These typologies tend to combine analyses of the structure of negotiations with analyses of different styles used in them to explore the interrelationship between the ends and means involved in negotiating.

For example, one prominent anthropologist has developed what is essentially a seven-phase model of the negotiating process based upon research in different cultural settings.[22] These phases may be summarized as follows:

(1) <u>The search for an arena</u>. The negotiators begin by choosing a forum to engage in negotiations, whether that forum is a particular place where discussions are held in person or under circumstances where negotiations take place over the telephone, Internet, or in writing.

(2) <u>Composition of agenda and definition of issues</u>. The negotiators decide what issues need to be addressed and the agenda for the negotiation.

---

[20] *See generally*, R. Fisher & W. Ury, *Getting to Yes* (1981); C. Menkel-Meadow, Toward Another View of Legal Negotiation: The Structure of Problem Solving, 31 UCLA L. Rev. 784 (1984).

[21] *Cf., e.g.,* James J. White, Review Essay: The Pros and Cons of "Getting to Yes" by Roger Fisher & William Ury, 31 J. Legal Education 115 (1981) *with* Roger Fisher, Comment on James White's Review of "Getting to Yes," 31 J. Legal Education 128 (1981).

[22] P.H. Gulliver, *Disputes and Negotiations: A Cross-Cultural Perspective* (1979).

(3) Establishing maximal limits to issues in dispute. The negotiators limit the key issues and stake out their positions on those issues.

(4) Narrowing the Differences. The negotiators begin to narrow their differences, and the negotiation shifts from differences and antagonism to coordination and even cooperation. When multiple issues are involved, differences are narrowed through strategies such as following a simple agenda, focusing on the most important issues, reducing issues to the attributes of a single objective, solving the less difficult issues, and/or considering matters to trade or package deals.

(5) Preliminaries to final bargaining. To the extent that the negotiators, in the process of narrowing their differences, identify sub-issues or other matters that need to be resolved to reach an agreement, information is exchanged and these issues are also addressed to bring the negotiators closer to final agreement.

(6) Final bargaining. The negotiators close the deal, disposing of the few issues or problems that remain to be resolved.

(7) Ritual Affirmation. Upon reaching a final agreement, the negotiators engage in any customary ritual that acknowledges or memorializes it, whether a simple hand shake, elaborate ceremony, or celebration.

This anthropological model was developed from a cross-cultural perspective. In the context of negotiating legal disputes, one scholar has reduced the negotiating process to a series of four stages that roughly complement many of the phases given above. Those stages are (1) "orientation and positioning" (during which the negotiating attorneys establish a relationship and their opening positions); (2) "argumentation" (during which the attorneys present their positions in the light most favorable to their respective side, define the issues, seek to discover the "real" position of the other side, and make concessions); (3) "emergence and crisis" (during which the attorneys recognize that one or both of them must make further concessions to prevent deadlock, further concessions are made, "crisis" is reached when neither side wants to make yet further concessions, and one of the parties either accepts the other's final offer or an impasse occurs); and (4) "agreement or final breakdown" (during which a settlement is formalized if an agreement is reached, or a decision is made to go to trial if no agreement is reached).[23] Taken together, the cross-cultural and legal typologies provide an overall portrait of the major features of the process of negotiating in terms of moving from initial discussions to final agreement.

In addition, much of the sociological literature (and legal literature) has been devoted to identifying key variables or factors that permeate or differentiate negotiations. Among the more important factors that have been routinely discussed include:[24]

- The effects of the location where the negotiation takes place and the

---

[23] Gerald R. Williams, *Legal Negotiation and Settlement* 70–72 (1983).

[24] *See generally,* J. Rubin & B. Brown, *The Social Psychology of Bargaining and Negotiation* (1975); D. Druckman, *Negotiations: Social Psychological Perspectives* (1977); S. Bacharach & E. Lawley, *Bargaining: Power, Tactics, and Outcomes* (1981); A. Strauss, *Negotiations: Varieties, Contexts, Processes and Social Order* 237–238 (1978); H. Raiffa, *The Art and Science of Negotiation* 11–19 (1982); G. Lowenthal, A General Theory of Negotiation Process, Strategy, and Behavior, 31 U. Kan. L. Rev. 69

particular physical arrangements at the site of negotiations;

- The number of parties involved in the negotiation and whether any coalitions exist;
- The number and complexity of the issues involved in the negotiation;
- The nature of the stakes in the negotiation;
- The effect of time constraints or time-related costs on the parties;
- The relative bargaining power possessed by the parties;
- Whether the negotiations are public or private;
- Whether there are any persons other than the parties ("audiences") to whom the negotiators are beholden or accountable, or whether there are any constituencies that may be affected by the negotiation;
- Whether a third-party neutral assists or intervenes in the negotiation;
- Whether the negotiations are one-shot or multiple events, or are linked;
- The effects on the negotiation of any continuing relationships between the parties or their negotiators after the negotiation is concluded;
- The alternatives available to the parties in the absence of reaching an agreement;
- The personalities of the parties and their negotiators;
- The interests, needs, goals, and values of the parties and their negotiators;
- The extent of information sharing between the parties and their negotiators, and their ability to communicate with one another.

Another major line of research and analysis concerns the impact of the negotiator's style or strategy in negotiating upon negotiator effectiveness and the outcome of negotiations. Much of this research has attempted to compare the effectiveness of negotiators who adopt a "cooperative" approach to bargaining (*e.g.*, by "seeking common ground" and "communicating a sense of shared interests, values, and attitudes using rational logical persuasion as a means . . . to reach a fair resolution of the conflict based on an objective analysis of the facts and law.."[25] with those who employ a "competitive" approach (*e.g.*, by making high initial demands, maintaining a high level of demands during negotiations, making few and small concessions, and having a general high level of aspiration).[26] To the extent negotiator "effectiveness" involves considerations such as the cost of the negotiations, the comprehensiveness of a settlement, the satisfaction of both parties, the quality of the outcome, and observing the "rules of the game," one study concluded that cooperative negotiators are generally more effective than competitive negotiators. However, the author of this same study ultimately concluded " . . . neither pattern has an exclusive claim on effectiveness. Use of the cooperative pattern does not guarantee effectiveness, any more than does the use of the competitive pattern. An attorney can be very effective or very ineffective within the constraints of

---

(1982); C. Menkel-Meadow, Review Essay: Legal Negotiation: A Study of Strategies in Search of a Theory, 4 Am. Bar. Found. J. 927–928 (1983).

[25] Gerald R. Williams, *Legal Negotiation and Settlement* 53 (1983).

[26] Id. *See also* D. G. Gifford, A Context-based Theory of Strategy Selection in Legal Negotiation, 46 Ohio St. L. J. 41 (1985) (distinguishing "cooperative," "competitive," and "integrative"); G.T. Lowenthal, A General Theory of Negotiation Process, Strategy and Beahvior, 31 U. Kan. L. Rev. 69 (1982) (distinguishing between "competition" and "collaboration"); D. Lax & J. Sebenius, *The Manager as Negotiator: Bargaining for Cooperation and Competitive Gain* (1987) (distinguishing between negotiating to "claim value" and to "create value"); H. Raiffa, *The Art and Science of Negotiation* (distinguishing between "distributive" and "integrative" bargaining).

either."[27]

In terms of the effect of a cooperative or competitive style or strategy upon the "outcome" of negotiations (*i.e.*, the result achieved in relation to what was initially sought), a number of scholars have suggested that a competitive negotiator will fare better when pitted against a cooperative negotiator, particularly if the latter does not recognize his counterpart's competitive tactics.[28] This is because, given that competitive negotiators tend to take tougher positions and make fewer concessions, it has been statistically shown that "[h]igh initial demands (relative to stakes) by plaintiffs and low initial offers (again, relative to stakes) by defendants are related to [more positive] success for the relevant side."[29] However, when the negotiators for both sides take the same approach, whether competitive or cooperative, there would not seem to be any theoretical reason why one style should lead to consistently better outcomes when the only issue is money. On the other hand, as mentioned previously in connection with the discussion of Pareto Optimal solutions, there is extensive debate about whether the ends of a negotiation are better served by employing a "problem-solving" model of negotiating through cooperative means, as contrasted with engaging in "adversarial" bargaining through competitive means.

## § 7.06  PSYCHOLOGICAL APPROACHES AND FACTORS

The psychological theories that are most often drawn upon in the academic literature about negotiating relate to how people "communicate" with one another and how negotiators can overcome common barriers to effective communication. Another line of psychological theory (or social-psychological theory) that is useful to understanding negotiation, and which is less intuitively understood than communicative considerations, involves how people make decisions under conditions of uncertainty. Because negotiations usually require parties to make choices under circumstances of risk, provided below are some of the more important psychological factors affecting such decision-making.

### [1]    Risk Aversion

A critical factor in a party's decision whether to settle a case depends upon that party's willingness to gamble that the alternative to settlement (*e.g.*, taking the case to trial) will yield a better result. This is typically referred to as "risk aversion" — the degree to which a party is psychologically disinclined to take risk.

In the litigation context, a risk-averse plaintiff is one who theoretically will settle the case for something less than his calculation of the "expected outcome" for the case (*i.e.*, his estimate of the gross outcome that could be obtained at trial multiplied by the probability that the gross outcome will occur). That is, when faced with a final settlement offer, if Plaintiff estimates that there is a 75% chance

---

[27] *See* Gerald R. Williams, *Legal Negotiation and Settlement* 18–19 (1983).

[28] *See* Gerald R. Williams, *Legal Negotiation and Settlement* 54 (1983); Gary T. Lowenthal, A General Theory of Negotiation Process, Strategy, and Behavior, 31 U. Kan. L. Rev. 82–83, 109–110 (1982); Donald G. Gifford, A Context-Based Theory of Strategy Selection in Legal Negotiation, 46 Ohio St. L. J. 60–62 (1985); Hazel Genn, *Hard Bargaining: Out of Court Settlement in Personal Injury Actions* 48 (1988).

[29] H. M. Kritzer, *Let's Make a Deal* 54, 79 (1991).

of obtaining a $100,000 verdict at trial (*i.e.,* an expected outcome of $75,000), he will reduce that expected outcome further by an amount that reflects the extent to which he is intuitively averse to gambling upon getting a better result at trial. This discount would be in addition to the non-shiftable litigation costs that he would subtract from the expected outcome to arrive at his potential bottom-line settlement amount (resistance point). Similarly, a risk-averse Defendant will theoretically settle the case for something more than her calculation of the expected outcome for the case. That is, along with adding her estimated litigation costs to her calculation of the expected outcome for the case, Defendant will make a further adjustment to the bottom-line settlement amount she is willing to pay by the extent to which she is intuitively averse to gambling upon getting a better result at trial. In short, the parties' bottom-line settlement amounts (resistance points) are often adjusted downwards (for plaintiffs) and upwards (for defendants) depending upon their respective levels of risk aversion.

Of course, a party might be "risk neutral" or be a "risk preferer." If a party is risk neutral, that party will make no adjustment of the sort described above. If the Plaintiff is a risk preferer, he might adjust his bottom-line settlement demand *upwards*, not downwards; and if the Defendant is a risk preferer, she might adjust her bottom-line settlement offer *downwards*, not upwards. Most significantly, if one party is risk averse and the other is a risk preferer (or is risk neutral), the latter will have an advantage over the former in that the latter will theoretically be able to extract greater concessions from the former than would otherwise be the case.

This advantage frequently exists where one party is a "repeat player" in the type of litigation involved, and the other party is a "one-shot" player.[30] For example, in personal injury cases, an insurance company — which is, for all practical purposes, the paying defendant in such cases — is a repeat player in that it is involved in settling and litigating personal injury claims all the time. On the other hand, the injured plaintiff is a one-shot player. The important difference between the parties is that the insurance company has experience and significant financial resources available to it that may not be available to the plaintiff, particularly if she is represented by an inexperienced lawyer or one who is not willing or able to advance the costs of the litigation. As a repeat player, the insurance company is likely to be risk neutral (or even a risk preferer) because any loss resulting from a particular case will, at some level, be offset by wins in other cases. However, the injured plaintiff is more likely to be risk averse because she has only "one shot" at receiving compensation; there is no averaging out of wins and losses over a series of cases. Thus, if the insurance company has a lower aversion to risk than the plaintiff, the company is likely to hold out for a settlement on terms that are more favorable to it than to the plaintiff.

Whether a party will have a tendency to be risk averse and therefore be more inclined to settle the case than go to trial, or have a tendency to be risk preferring and thus be more inclined to gamble on a trial outcome, sometimes depends upon whether the risk is perceived as one of gaining or losing a sum of money. There is growing research to indicate that a party who perceives her situation in terms of

    [30] *See* D. Wittman, Dispute Resolution, Bargaining, and the Selection of Cases for Trial: A Study of the Generation of Biased and Unbiased Data, 17 J. Legal Studies 322 (1988); M. Galanter, Why the 'Haves' Come Out Ahead: Speculations on the Limits of Legal Change, 9 Law & Society Review 95 (1974).

losing money will often prefer to gamble to avoid what otherwise would be a sure loss, even if the expected loss from the gamble is larger. On the other hand, a party who perceives her situation in terms of gaining money will usually be less inclined to gamble on obtaining a greater amount, even if the expected gain from the gamble is larger. That is, parties who stand to lose money may have a tendency to be "loss averse" and risk preferring — more willing to prevent or minimize loss by taking their chances at trial; but parties who stand to gain money are generally more risk averse — less willing to gamble on getting more money at trial.[31]

As an example of this phenomenon, suppose that a person is faced with the choice of (a) a sure gain of $15,000, or (b) an 80% chance of winning $20,000 and 20% chance of getting $0. Here, even though the expected value of choice (b) is $16,000 (i.e., .80 × $20,000 ∓ .20 × $0), most people would choose the sure gain of $15,000. On the other hand, if a person is given the choice of (a) a sure loss of $15,000, or (b) an 80% chance of losing $20,000 and a 20% chance of losing nothing, studies suggest that most people will choose option (b).[32] To the extent this phenomenon is at work in a particular case, it suggests that, absent other factors that might affect the parties' risk preferences, plaintiffs will generally opt to accept a smaller gain through settlement rather than gamble on winning a larger sum at trial, whereas defendants will be more prone to risk a larger possible loss at trial in lieu of incurring a sure, albeit smaller, loss by settling a disputed case.[33]

## [2]  Reference Points and Framing Effects

Whether one views a matter as a gain or loss largely depends upon one's "reference point" (i.e., the situation from which the gain or loss is measured) and how the matter is "framed" (i.e., whether the issue, problem, or choice is presented as a "gain" or "loss").[34] This is also true in negotiating. A party will view a particular proposal as a gain or loss (which, in turn, may affect that party's level of risk aversion) based on that party's reference point — usually his resistance point — and the manner in which the proposal is framed. Thus, negotiators routinely try to induce one another to change their resistance points and risk preferences by "framing" the situation in terms of gain or loss as best suits the negotiators' respective objectives.

For example, in buyer-seller negotiations, the seller may prevail upon the buyer to purchase an item for an amount that the buyer thinks he cannot afford (a loss) by characterizing the purchase as an "investment" (a gain). Similarly, a worker may be convinced to switch jobs in the face of taking a pay cut (a loss) if she is made to see the new job as a stepping stone to greater, long-term career

---

[31] *See* P. J. van Koppen, Risk Taking in Civil Law Negotiations, 14 Law and Human Behavior 151–167 (1990); Amos Tversky & Richard Thaler, Anomalies Preference Reversals, 4 J. Econ. Perspectives 201 (1990); Amos Tversky, et. al., The Causes of Preference Reversals, 80 Am. Econ. Rev. 204 (1990); Robert H. Mnookin, Why Negotiations Fail: An Exploration of Barriers to the Resolution of Conflict, 8 Ohio St. J. Disp. Res. 243–245 (1993); M. Neal & M. Bazerman, The Effects of Framing and Negotiator Overconfidence on Bargaining Behaviors and Outcomes, 28 Acad. Mgmt. J. 34, 37–38 (1985).

[32] *See* G. Goodpaster, Rational Decision-Making in Problem-Solving Negotiation: Compromise, Interest-Valuation, and Cognitive Error, 8 Ohio St. J. Disp. Res. 346–347 (1993).

[33] *See* H. M. Kritzer, *Let's Make a Deal* 76 n. 19 (1991).

[34] *See generally*, D. Kahneman, et. al., *Judgment Under Uncertainy: Heuristics and Biases* (1982); D. Kahneman & A. Tversky, Prospect Theory: An Analysis of Decision Under Risk, 47 Econometrica 263 (1979).

advancement (a gain). On the other hand, a bargainer might seek to emphasize what she stands to lose from a particular proposal in order to induce the other party to forgo a greater gain, or, more frequently, emphasize what the other party stands to lose if she is unwilling to make further concessions. In either case, the overriding effort is to manipulate the other party's perspective on the situation in terms of acquiring gain or incurring loss.

Another implication of framing a proposal as an opportunity to maximize gain (which may cause a party to be risk averse) or minimize loss (which may cause a party to be loss averse) is that a party seeking to maximize gain may take a more cooperative approach to the negotiation to achieve a settlement in preference to going to trial, whereas a party seeking to minimize loss may take a more competitive approach due to a greater willingness to take the case to trial. In adversarial bargaining, where a gain to one side is viewed as a corresponding loss to the other, a party who is loss averse and thus risk-preferring and more competitive is likely to have an advantage in the negotiation if the other party is risk averse and thus more cooperative. On the other hand, the parties might take a problem-solving approach to the negotiation, in which case each would cooperate with one another by viewing the negotiation as an opportunity for both parties to maximize gain and minimize loss. In theory, the potential effects of these different factors on a settlement may be illustrated by the following matrix:

|  | **Jones** | |
| --- | --- | --- |
|  | Maximize<br>Gain | Minimize<br>Loss |
| **Smith** Maximize Gain | Problem Solving<br>Smith is risk neutral & cooperative<br>Jones is risk neutral & cooperative<br>(Better settlement for both) | Adversarial Bargaining<br>Smith is risk averse & cooperative<br>Jones is loss averse (risk preferring)<br>& competitive<br>(Better settlement for Jones) |
| Minimize Loss | Adversarial Bargaining<br>Smith is loss averse (risk preferring)<br>& competitive<br>Jones is risk averse & cooperative<br>(Better settlement for Smith) | Problem Solving<br>Smith is risk neutral & cooperative<br>Jones is risk neutral & cooperative<br>(Better settlement for both) |

## [3] Sunk Costs

A common psychological barrier to rational decision-making under conditions of uncertainty is the tendency to allow past events which one cannot change to govern one's choices about the future. In negotiations, this barrier frequently occurs when one or both of the parties becomes entrapped by "sunk costs" — *i.e.* lost no matter what the party does but which the party vainly seeks to justify or recoup in making a choice about settlement or trial.[35]

For example, before attempting to settle a case, the parties may have incurred substantial expenditures in pretrial litigation. If they have become psychologically entrapped by these investments, they may forgo any possibility of settling the case

---

[35] *See* Robyn M. Dawes, *Rational Choice in an Uncertain World* 22 (1988).

out of a belief that going to trial is the only way to justify or recoup that investment. In this way, the parties may only escalate the conflict, persist in spiraling litigation, and end up sustaining losses that far surpass the benefits of any favorable trial outcome. Conversely, a party may become psychologically entrapped by the time, effort, and resources expended in seeking to settle the case. Unwilling to abandon this investment, the party might irrationally agree upon a settlement that ends up costing far more than the alternative of going to trial.[36]

In short, rational decision-making generally involves an assessment of the benefits that may be realized or losses that may be minimized when looking toward the future, rather than the past. Past events or investments, to the extent they are truly "sunk" in the sense that they cannot be realistically recouped through a settlement or some reasonable alternative to a negotiated agreement, should be abandoned unless there is some other, overriding reason to honor those past events or investments.[37]

## [4]    Reactive Devaluation

The phenomenon of "reactive devaluation" relates to the sometimes-irrational inferences that parties draw from one another's offers or concessions made during negotiations. This phenomenon, which is commonly observed and has been empirically verified, refers to the tendency of a party to devalue a settlement proposal or compromise simply because it originated with the other side.[38] That is, a compromise or concession made unilaterally by a party is often valued less highly than one that is initially withheld and subsequently extracted through reciprocal proposals or concessions. Thus, a party might reject a seemingly gratuitous offer that is beneficial to her by misinterpreting it as a sign of weakness by the other side that warrants yet greater concessions from the other side. This misinterpretation may, in turn, result in a gross miscalculation that causes an otherwise desirable settlement to end in deadlock.

Reactive devaluation is not to be confused with a reasoned assessment about what a party's particular proposal means about his overall approach to the negotiation and concession behavior. For example, depending upon the overall context in which it is made, a unilateral concession may be a good indicator of the conceding party's resistance point. However, to *automatically* devalue a proposal or concession solely because the other side makes it is irrational. Thus, a party who is the recipient of such a proposal should act upon it to the extent it advances her objectives, rather than allow her objectives to be undermined by a gut reaction that is based on purely speculative assumptions about the other side's motives in making the proposal.

If a party is concerned that his proposal may be erroneously devalued by the other side, he might frame it as emanating from some objective criterion such as an independent standard, custom, rule, or measure of damage under applicable law, rather than as stemming from his purely individual intentions. Alternatively, any

---

[36] *See* Charles B. Craver, *Effective Legal Negotiation and Settlement* 277–278 (3d ed. 1997).

[37] *See* G. Goodpaster, Rational Decision-Making in Problem-Solving Negotiation: Compromise, Interest-Valuation, and Cognitive Error, 8 Ohio St. J. Disp. Res. 356 (1993).

[38] *See* R. H. Mnookin, Why Negotiations Fail: An Exploration of Barriers to the Resolution of Conflict, 8 Ohio St. J. Disp. Res. 246–247 (1993).

effect of reactive devaluation is likely to be greatly diminished if the proposal is communicated through a third-party neutral such as a mediator.

## § 7.07  TRANSLATING ACADEMIC APPROACHES INTO PRACTICE

The foregoing summary of the major academic approaches to understanding negotiation underscores the fact that the study of negotiation is essentially an interdisciplinary field. There is no single discipline or intellectual perspective that has a monopoly on useful insights into the subject, and likewise there is no single theory, model, or typology that is most descriptive and instructive about it. However, taken together, the various academic approaches provide a useful introduction to learning about negotiating because they help us to understand *why* certain negotiations are successful when others are not.

By the same token, the academic approaches are useful from a prescriptive standpoint. That is, understanding the fundamental dynamics of negotiating also tells us a lot about *how* to negotiate effectively. For example, the game-theoretic interplay between cooperation and competition in bargaining implicates the relative merits of employing cooperative or competitive means in achieving problem-solving or adversarial ends to negotiating. The cost-benefit analyses underlying economic theory are highly useful in valuing a case when choosing between the options of settlement or trial. The social-psychological literature is instructive about effective negotiating styles, tactics, and techniques that may be employed to foster rational decision-making under circumstances of risk and uncertainty. In short, in varying forms and degrees, all of these theoretical approaches may be translated into practical application.

Finally, as indicated at the outset of this Chapter, the academic research may encourage us to push the intellectual envelope to consider more expansive and imaginative approaches to negotiating. This is important because, as in the application of other practical skills, lawyers too often form the habit of adopting a largely singular negotiating approach in client representation. Although a routine approach may be comfortable and workable in many circumstances, the genius of the most effective lawyers is their ability to adopt and adapt to different approaches to negotiation as may be warranted by the particular circumstances of a case. Encouraging this ingenuity is perhaps the most practical contribution of the academic literature.

# Chapter 8

## NEGOTIATING MODELS, STRATEGIES AND STYLES

## § 8.01   INTRODUCTION

As introduced in the preceding chapter, the existing academic literature about the negotiating process has given rise to two distinct models of negotiating that are particularly helpful in understanding what negotiators do and what they ought to do. These descriptive and prescriptive models are useful frameworks for bridging the gap between theory and practice in that they provide a conceptual overview of the negotiating process that is eminently practical in deciding what overall negotiating approach to use in particular circumstances.

## § 8.02   THE ADVERSARIAL MODEL

The adversarial model of negotiation (sometimes called "competitive," "zero-sum," "individualistic," or "distributive bargaining") is the most commonly used approach to legal negotiations. It focuses on "winning" in the sense of maximizing the likelihood the client will prevail and what the client receives upon prevailing. Each side strives to get as much of the thing bargained for (usually money), and the more one side gets, the less the other side gets. Adversarial negotiators engage in a largely competitive and manipulative process in which a series of concessions is made from initial, polarized positions to arrive at a compromise point which is perceived to be either roughly equivalent to what a court would award or more desirable than taking the risk of what might happen in court.

Adversarial negotiation usually involves five stages. First, each party prepares for the negotiation by establishing her "target" and "resistance" points, and estimating the target and resistance points of the other side. A "target point" is the best result a party realistically expects she can obtain, and her "resistance point" is the point below which she will not make any further concessions and will resort to her best alternative to negotiation such as going to trial. From these target and resistance points, the parties plan their first offers (which are set somewhere beyond their target points), and establish their concession patterns in light of the ultimate "settlement zone" created by the overlap between the parties' resistance points.

For example, if P sues D for personal injuries sustained due to the alleged negligence of D, the parties' target and resistance points, first offers, concession patterns, and settlement zone may look like the following:

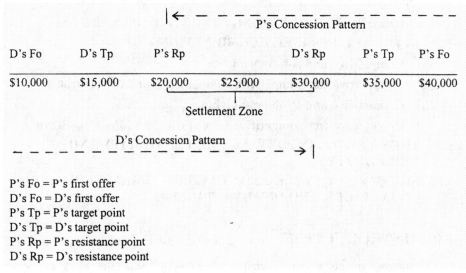

P's Fo = P's first offer
D's Fo = D's first offer
P's Tp = P's target point
D's Tp = D's target point
P's Rp = P's resistance point
D's Rp = D's resistance point

In the second stage, the parties define the issues and often make their first offers or proposals. Third, the parties exchange information in the course of presenting their varying positions and arguments in support of those positions. Fourth, they bargain toward compromise by analyzing and making concessions. And fifth, the parties conclude the negotiation by executing settlement documents or releases if an agreement has been reached, or, if no agreement can be reached, by resorting to their best alternative to negotiation such as going to trial.

The adversarial model is based on four assumptions. First, the model assumes that the parties desire the same goals, items, or values (*e.g.,* money). Second, the model assumes that the parties are in conflict because they are bargaining over the same "scarce" goals, items, or values. Third, it is assumed that the matters to be bargained for are limited to those that a court would award, whether money or something that the law may compel a party to do or not to do. Finally, the model assumes that the best solution is predicated upon a division of and compromise over the goals, items, or values at issue. As summarized by one scholar:

> The adversarial paradigm is based almost exclusively on the simple negotiation over what appears to be one issue, such as price in a buy-sell transaction, or money damages in a personal injury or breach of contract suit. The common assumption in these cases is that the buyer wants the lowest price, the seller the highest; the plaintiff wants the money demanded in the complaint and the defendant wants to resist paying as much as possible. Each dollar to the plaintiff is a commensurate loss to the defendant; the same is true with the buyer and seller. Given this description of the paradigmatic negotiation, the negotiator's goal is simply to maximize gain by winning as much of the material of the negotiation as possible. Underlying this general assumption are really two assumptions: first, that there is only one issue, price; and second, that both parties desire equally and exclusively the thing by which that issue is measured, in most cases, money.[1]

Critics of the adversarial model contend that its underlying assumptions and method of negotiating often limit the quality of the solution to the parties' problem or dispute. By assuming that the parties desire the same goals, items, or values (such as money) and therefore are limited to bargaining over the same scarce resource, the parties may overlook the fact that they really value these goals or items unequally or have completely different goals in mind. When these differences are not taken into account, the parties may fail to consider alternative solutions, such as trading a smaller sum of money for the performance of an act or service by the other side. Moreover, by assuming that the matters to be bargained for are limited to those that a court would award, the parties often limit their solutions to purely "legal" ones without considering extra-judicial alternatives that may better satisfy both parties' goals, values, or needs.

For example, if a former husband and wife are in dispute about an appropriate increase in the amount of alimony the wife should receive, and the wife contends she needs $300 more per month than the husband says he is able to afford without straining his cash-flow situation, a strict application of the adversarial model may result in the parties splitting the difference at $150 more a month or some other amount they think a court might award. However, if the wife's underlying need for the additional $300 is to allow her to make payments on a new car over a two-year period, and the former husband is the owner of a car dealership, he may be able to give her a car from his inventory in exchange for the wife's agreement to forego a $300 increase in monthly support payments. In this way, the wife receives the item that is of greater value to her (the immediate use of a dependable car), and the

---

[1] C. Menkel-Meadow, Toward Another View of Legal Negotiation: The Structure of Problem Solving, 31 U.C.L.A. L. Rev. 784 (1984).

husband obtains the goal that is most important to him (preserving his future cash-flow situation).

Critics of the adversarial model also contend that the process by which adversarial negotiations are conducted tends to undermine the quality of potential solutions in two ways. First, the process of exchanging offers, counteroffers, and concessions may not be helpful when the parties are faced with multiple issues. Second, the competitive nature of adversarial negotiation tends to result in argumentation, manipulation, and deception that may inhibit creativity in finding solutions, leave the parties resentful even if an agreement is reached, and impair their future relationship.

## § 8.03   THE PROBLEM-SOLVING MODEL

The problem-solving model of negotiation (sometimes called "cooperative," "accommodative," "collaborative," or "integrative bargaining") focuses on identifying the parties' underlying interests or needs to develop a broad range of potential solutions from which an agreement can be fashioned that satisfies as many of the parties' mutual needs as possible. Unlike the adversarial model, which emphasizes maximizing individual gain at the expense of the other side, problem solving emphasizes maximizing the parties' joint gain. Problem-solving negotiators engage in a largely cooperative and collaborative process that strives to create a mutually satisfactory solution that is not necessarily limited to traditional judicial remedies.

The problem-solving model is based on four assumptions. First, the model assumes that the usual objective of obtaining money damages is actually a proxy for more basic interests or needs apart from merely those things that money can buy. Second, the model assumes that the parties' interests or needs are often not mutually exclusive. Third, it assumes that by identifying the parties' underlying interests or needs, the parties can come up with a greater number of possible solutions. And fourth, the model assumes that by exploring a greater number of possible solutions, the parties are more likely to find a solution that mutually satisfies their interests or needs.

The problem-solving model is usually applied in five stages of so-called "principled negotiation."[2] First, the parties plan for the negotiation by identifying each side's underlying interests or needs. These interests, which essentially constitute the underlying *reasons* for the parties' objectives or goals, are identified in light of the financial situation of the parties, their social and psychological needs, their moral perspectives, and the legal issues in the case.

Second, the parties make a conscientious effort to "separate the people from the problem" — a mindset that attacks the problem, not each other. Instead of focusing on stated "positions," they discuss and share information about each other's interests or needs to see where they are shared or in conflict.

Third, the parties engage in a "brainstorming" session to generate as many solutions as possible that may satisfy the interests or needs of both parties. Fourth, the parties choose the most reasoned solution that maximizes their mutual gain. Concessions might be made by trading off different interests or needs, and, where interests conflict, the parties strive to resolve their differences based on some

---

[2] *See* R. Fisher & W. Ury, *Getting to Yes* 4, 17–98 (1981).

objective standard (such as market values, expert opinions, customs, industry standards, or the law) which is independent of the naked will of either side. Finally, the parties conclude the negotiation by executing settlement documents or releases if an agreement is reached, or, if no agreement can be reached, by resorting to their "best alternative to a negotiated agreement" (BATNA) such as going to trial.

Even the strongest proponents of the problem-solving approach acknowledge its limitations. As summarized by one scholar:

> Several difficulties may confront the skeptical problem solver. First there is the problem of perceiving resources as finite. In some legal disputes, for example, a case involving a simple transfer of limited dollars or other valued items from one side to the other, it may appear impossible to expand what is available to both parties. A second barrier may be the perceived inequality of power between the negotiating parties. If one side has power in the legal, economic or psychological sense during the negotiation, the weaker party may have insufficient leverage to use problem-solving techniques where the stronger party knows it can gain a great deal by exercising power in a conventional negotiation. Third, an attempt to satisfy needs may itself thwart the problem-solving approach in a situation where, for example, one of the parties has a need for revenge or punishment. Fourth, there may be limited psychological resources. Where one of the parties is used to a competitive style of negotiation, the execution of a problem-solving method may be viewed as impossible unless the other party becomes a problem solver. Finally, a problem-solving model based on a theory of needs has its own limitations. It will not solve all negotiation dilemmas, but it still offers a potentially more systematic and effective way of thinking about negotiation.[3]

## § 8.04  FACTORS AFFECTING THE UTILITY OF THE ADVERSARIAL AND PROBLEM-SOLVING MODELS[4]

Many negotiations involve neither a purely adversarial nor a purely problem-solving approach. Thus, negotiators frequently use more than one of these approaches in a single negotiation. For example, the parties might start with an adversarial approach and then move to a problem-solving one, or they may apply different approaches to distinct issues in the case. While it sometimes may be psychologically difficult to shift between approaches, particularly when a highly competitive adversarial approach is taken at the outset and the parties then try to engage in problem solving after egos have been frayed or hurt, the willingness to be flexible in shifting one's approach often makes the difference between reaching and not reaching a satisfactory agreement.

In deciding which negotiating model may be most effective in a particular case, the following factors should be considered:

---

[3] C. Menkel-Meadow, Toward Another View Of Legal Negotiation: The Structure of Problem Solving, 31 U.C.L.A. L. Rev. 829–30 (1984).

[4] See D. G. Gifford, a context-based theory of strategy selection in legal negotiation, 46 Ohio State L. J. 58–93 (1985). See generally, D. Pruitt, Negotiation Behavior (1981).

## [1] The Nature of the Dispute or Problem

The nature of the parties' dispute or problem often has a significant impact on the relative effectiveness of the adversarial or problem-solving approach. For example, the adversarial model may be better suited when the parties are bargaining solely over a fixed and finite matter such as money. If the only issue is how much one party will pay the other, and the gain to one party will necessarily be at the expense of the other, this "zero-sum" controversy rarely provides an opportunity or incentive for the parties to collaborate in expanding the resources they might divide or trade to their mutual gain. Thus, if the only issue between a buyer and seller is the price of a single item, or the only issue between the plaintiff and the defendant is the amount of property damage, the adversarial model is likely to be more appropriate.

On the other hand, the problem-solving model may be more useful to the extent the nature of the dispute or problem does not have zero-sum aspects. This is particularly true if the parties are negotiating over multiple issues that they value differently. For example, if the parties are in dispute over the issues of child custody, visitation, and support, it is more likely that a problem-solving approach will produce a more mutually satisfactory solution if the parties consider options such as joint or split custody, and how various visitation arrangements may affect appropriate amounts of child support. Similarly, if the issue between a buyer and seller is not merely price, but involves considerations such as quantity, time of delivery, and manner of payment, the problem-solving approach may be more productive in reaching an agreement addressing these multiple elements. In practice, problem solving is used more frequently in domestic relations, business regulation, and government action cases.[5]

## [2] The Other Side's Negotiating Approach

A party's negotiating approach will often be affected by the particular approach taken by the other side. For example, if the other side is unwilling to engage in a problem-solving approach, attempts to employ that model will be largely ineffective because the model presupposes information sharing and collaboration between the parties. This does not mean that a problem-solving negotiator should not try to encourage the other side to use a problem-solving approach. However, if the effort is unsuccessful, it is unlikely the problem solver will be able to make any headway in the negotiation unless he is willing to accommodate the other side's adversarial bargaining.

Sometimes the other side's negotiating approach conforms to some generally accepted convention or norm that is endemic to a particular geographical area or type of case. In simple personal injury cases, for example, most lawyers and insurance adjusters routinely engage in adversarial bargaining; and plaintiffs' lawyers who enter into contingency fee arrangements, whereby their fee is a percentage of the monetary amount received in settlement or at trial, may be less motivated to engage in problem solving if that approach would produce a settlement that is not exclusively resolved by the payment of money.

In addition, the parties may be reluctant to share their true needs or interests upon which expanded options for a resolution might be explored. For example, a

---

[5] *See* Herbert M. Kitzner, *Let's Make a Deal*, 42–43 (1991).

party might be psychologically or financially distressed as a result of the dispute and not want to reveal these matters out of embarrassment or fear of demonstrating weakness. Similarly, particularly when litigation is contemplated or has already commenced, a party might not want to reveal certain information to give "free discovery" to the other side. In either of these circumstances, the parties may be more likely to resort to adversarial bargaining than problem solving.

## [3]    Differences in Bargaining Leverage

Negotiating leverage stems from the perception of the negative consequences that a party can inflict on his opponent if an agreement is not reached, or from the benefits that a party can bestow on the other if an agreement is reached. The extent of this leverage is largely dependent upon the alternatives available to each party in the absence of an agreement. Generally, the side that possesses the most viable alternative in the event that an agreement is not reached will have greater power over the other side.

A negotiator who possesses greater bargaining leverage over his opponent may adopt an adversarial approach on the theory that his threats will be perceived as more credible and he will thus be able to extract greater concessions from his opponent. Conversely, the negotiator with less bargaining power will often choose the problem-solving model to offset or neutralize the adversarial bargainer's emphasis on a purely concession-based settlement. In essence, the lower-power negotiator will attempt to appeal to the more powerful negotiator's sense of fairness and justice to counteract the latter's tendency to believe that his bargaining position is superior and that any concessions on his part are unwarranted.

When both negotiators have high aspiration levels and possess relatively equal bargaining leverage, rigid adherence to the adversarial model may often result in deadlock. Deadlock may motivate the parties to abandon an adversarial approach and adopt a problem-solving approach.

## [4]    Future Dealings Between the Parties or Negotiators

The extent to which the parties or their negotiators are likely to have an on-going relationship after the negotiation often affects the incentive for adopting an adversarial or problem-solving approach. The adversarial model sometimes gives rise to distrust and ill will, and thus the problem-solving approach is more frequently used when the parties or their representatives expect to have future dealings with one another. On the other hand, if the parties or their negotiators are merely engaged in a one-shot transaction or encounter, there will be less incentive to avoid the adversarial model with its concomitant risk of impairing future relations.

## [5]    Pressures to Reach an Agreement

The pressures placed on the parties to reach an agreement may affect their choice of negotiating approach. For example, a party might want to settle quickly because she needs the settlement proceeds immediately, desires to limit legal fees or other expenses, or wants to avoid the psychological stress of protracted controversy. Similarly, court deadlines or heavy caseloads may pressure the negotiators to expedite an agreement.

Generally, the problem-solving model's emphasis on sharing information to identify the interests or needs of the parties and brainstorming to develop possible solutions is more time consuming than the offer-counteroffer and response-counter-response method of adversarial negotiation. Thus, the greater the time pressure placed on the parties, the more likely they are to resort to adversarial bargaining through the swifter device of reciprocal concessions.

## § 8.05   NEGOTIATING STRATEGIES AND STYLES

In practice, negotiating strategy is simply the conceptual model or approach chosen in conducting the negotiation — whether adversarial, problem solving, or some combination of the two. Negotiating style, on the other hand, refers to the negotiator's *interpersonal behavior* in the negotiating setting, and often will be affected by the particular strategy chosen. Generally, there are three types of negotiating styles: (1) competitive (hardball), (2) cooperative (softball), or (3) a combination of competitive and cooperative (hardball and softball).[6] Each has its advantages and disadvantages that should be assessed in choosing an appropriate style.

## § 8.06   COMPETITIVE (HARDBALL) STYLE

The competitive style is typically characterized by aggressiveness and a confrontational approach. Winning is everything, and personal feelings and interpersonal relationships are viewed as essentially irrelevant. Threats, intimidation, and Machiavellian tactics are sometimes employed.

The advantage of this style is that it tends to pressure the adversary into making concessions, particularly when he is easily intimidated or inexperienced; and extreme demands and hard-nosed positions may sometimes give rise to larger settlements. In addition, the competitive negotiator develops a reputation of strength and toughness that is attractive to many clients. On the other hand, a competitive style frequently alienates the other side and produces mistrust, misunderstanding, and more frequent deadlocks. It often polarizes positions and causes overreaction. Personal relationships may be impaired or destroyed, thus making future negotiations with the same party or negotiator more difficult.

The competitive style may be effective when dealing with an inexperienced negotiator or where the parties and their representatives are involved in a one-time adversarial relationship. On the other hand, if the parties intend to have an ongoing relationship, the competitive style is undesirable because of its propensity to cause mistrust and alienation. For example, this style is generally not well suited for business negotiations.

The negotiator who adopts a highly competitive style can minimize its negative effects by focusing on the subject matter of the negotiation rather than on personalities, and after an agreement is reached, by initiating an effort to repair

---

[6] *See generally,* Gerald R. Williams, *Legal Negotiation and Settlement* 18–39 (1983); Gary T. Lowenthal, A General Theory of Negotiation Processs, Strategy, and Behavior, 31 Univ. of Kansas L. Rev. 69-114 (1982); D. Gifford, *Legal Negotiations: Theory and Applications,* 8–11 (1989).

any damage that has been caused to personal relationships.

## § 8.07   COOPERATIVE (SOFTBALL) STYLE

The cooperative style is the antithesis of the competitive style. The cooperative negotiator places a premium on interpersonal relations, and strives for common ground, shared interests, and understanding between the parties. The style is typically sincere, accommodating, and low key. While it should not be confused with weakness, it often conveys that image.

The advantage of this style is that it tends to reduce the risk of deadlock and produces faster and more long-lasting agreements. In addition, the parties usually come away from the negotiation with their egos intact and a disposition to continue their relationship in the future. The disadvantage is that the cooperative negotiator may have a tendency to avoid confrontation and make too many concessions. Sometimes a more favorable agreement is forsaken for the mere goal of reaching an agreement.

The effectiveness of a cooperative style depends upon the willingness of both sides to forthrightly exchange information. If the cooperative negotiator is pitted against a competitive opponent, the latter may gain an unfair advantage by obtaining information from the former without reciprocating. In addition, the competitive bargainer may misinterpret the cooperative style as a sign of weakness and escalate her aggressiveness. Thus, the cooperative negotiator should also understand competitive tactics so that she can offset them in appropriate circumstances.

## § 8.08   COMPETITIVE-COOPERATIVE (HARDBALL AND SOFTBALL) STYLE

The competitive-cooperative style represents a middle ground between hardball and softball. Here, many of the advantages of the competitive and cooperative approaches are combined in a style that is professionally amicable, open-minded, but firm. Under this approach, realistic concessions are made to satisfy the objectives of both parties that are consistent or not mutually exclusive. Conflicting objectives are resolved by compromise or by some creative solution that maximizes as many of the parties' remaining objectives as possible.

The advantage of this style is that it preserves personal relationships and facilitates long-term agreements. The disadvantage is that the approach is largely unworkable unless both sides are genuinely willing to "work together" to resolve their differences — an attitude that may be inherently difficult to adopt in the face of a heated dispute. In addition, the approach requires more time and patience.

The competitive-cooperative approach is usually a waste of time if the other side is unrelentingly competitive. However, this approach may be successful if the competitive negotiator has a weak position.

## § 8.09   CHOOSING A NEGOTIATING STYLE AND STRATEGY

The particular negotiating style and strategy you adopt will depend upon your own personality, the nature of the dispute, the style and strategy employed by the other side, and the client's interests and objectives which you have identified in preparing for the negotiation. In choosing an effective style and strategy, it is important to bear in mind that (1) no particular combination of style and strategy is always more effective; (2) you should consider being flexible in your choice of style and strategy throughout the negotiation process; and (3) your choice of style and strategy should always have everything to do with your client's interests in mind and nothing to do with your own ego.

Understanding the differences among negotiating styles and between negotiating strategies is highly useful in choosing a particular style and strategy. In addition, understanding how different styles and strategies tend to operate together is useful in choosing an effective combination for a particular case.

## § 8.10   STYLE AND STRATEGY COMBINATIONS[7]

### [1]   Competitive and Adversarial

When a competitive (hardball) style is combined with an adversarial strategy, the negotiation is usually characterized by hard, intense bargaining. The positions of the parties are likely to be extreme at the outset and remain fairly rigid throughout the negotiation. Concessions are hard to come by, and bluffs, threats, and even *ad hominem* attacks may permeate the process. Deadlocks are frequent, and, even if the parties reach agreement, they sometimes leave the negotiation dissatisfied and with their personal relationship impaired or destroyed.

### [2]   Cooperative (or Competitive-Cooperative) and Adversarial

When a cooperative (softball) or competitive-cooperative (hardball & softball) style is combined with an adversarial strategy, the prospects of reaching an agreement are enhanced. The negotiation is typically cordial and characterized by a reasoned debate about the various offers and counteroffers presented. Concessions made gradually are "in the spirit of compromise." Bluffs and threats may occur from time to time, but not in the sometimes-acerbic manner employed by purely hardball negotiators. If a settlement is reached, it might include the performance of obligations other than the mere payment of money, and the parties usually will conclude the negotiation with their relationship and egos intact.

### [3]   Competitive and Problem-Solving

A competitive (hardball) style is largely antithetical to a problem-solving strategy. While the competitive problem solver will participate in identifying the needs of the opposing party, he is likely to be less than completely candid about those needs and seek to de-emphasize them in favor of feigning or inflating the

---

[7] *See* Charles B. Craver, *Effective Legal Negotiation and Settlement* 21–25 (3d Ed. 1997).

needs of his own client. In addition, the competitive bargainer is likely to advance solutions that solely benefit his side, rather than entertain broader solutions that accommodate the interests of the other side. In short, the competitive negotiator is primarily motivated to explore mutually beneficial solutions only to the extent they maximize his own client's interests.

### [4]    Cooperative (or Competitive-Cooperative) and Problem-Solving

A cooperative (softball) or competitive-cooperative (hardball & softball) style best complements a problem-solving strategy. The cooperative negotiator genuinely seeks to identify the legitimate interests of both parties, and is willing to explore mutually beneficial solutions in an open-minded manner. A premium is usually placed on the candid exchange of information. The hallmark of the cooperative problem-solver's style is to emphasize common ground and minimize the parties' differences. Generally, when a cooperative style is combined with a problem-solving strategy, the prospects for reaching a mutually satisfactory agreement are at their greatest.

## § 8.11   THE OVERALL IMPORTANCE OF FLEXIBILITY AND CREDIBILITY

Regardless of the negotiating style and strategy you choose for a particular case, you should always be flexible in switching or modifying that style or strategy in appropriate circumstances. It is not unusual for a negotiator to use more than one style or strategy in a single negotiation session or during different stages of protracted settlement discussions. In short, if it becomes clear that a particular strategy or style is counterproductive, it may be beneficial to make an adjustment.

Along with flexibility, your choice of style and strategy must be credible. Persuasion depends largely upon believability. If your style or strategy is strained or disingenuous, it is unlikely you will be effective in successfully negotiating the case. A common mistake made by inexperienced negotiators is adopting a style or strategy that is at odds with their own personality. If credibility depends upon using a particular style or strategy that you are uncomfortable with, ask a colleague who is more skilled in using that style or strategy to join you in the negotiation.

## § 8.12   SUMMARY OF STYLE AND STRATEGY CHARACTERISTICS, ADVANTAGES, AND DISADVANTAGES[8]

#### Competitive (Hardball) Style

*Characteristics*:      (1) aggressive and unfriendly
                 (2) confrontational
                 (3) intimidating
                 (4) Machiavellian
                 (5) negotiates by ultimatum

---

[8] *See* X. M. Frascogna, Jr. & H. L. Hetherington, *Negotiation Strategy for Lawyers* 41–42 (1984).

|                   | (6) makes few concessions |
|-------------------|---------------------------|

*Advantages*:      (1) pressures inexperienced adversaries into making concessions

(2) hard-nosed approach may result in better settlements for one's client

(3) establishes reputation for toughness that is attractive to clients

(4) may produce one-sided agreements that are advantageous if performed

*Disadvantages*:   (1) causes anger, alienation, and mistrust

(2) polarizes positions and causes overreaction or irrationality

(3) impairs or destroys personal relationships

(4) damages future relations between the parties or negotiators

(5) may induce the losing party to breach the agreement

(6) frequently causes deadlocks

## Cooperative (Softball) Style

*Characteristics*:  (1) friendly and mild mannered

(2) strives for common ground

(3) slow to anger

(4) communicates freely

(5) prone to make reasonable concessions

(6) readily considers alternative solutions

*Advantages*:      (1) reduces the risk of deadlock

(2) produces faster, more long-lasting, and creative agreements

(3) maintains personal relationships

(4) preserves future relations between the parties

(5) decisions are made without anger or overreaction

*Disadvantages*:   (1) tends to make concessions too easily

(2) may unnecessarily result in a less favorable agreement for one's side

(3) conveys a weak negotiating image

## Competitive-Cooperative (Hardball and Softball) Style

*Characteristics*:  (1) friendly but firm

(2) open-minded and creative

(3) confrontational when necessary

(4) strives for common ground and mutually beneficial solutions

(5) makes necessary concessions

(6) communicates forthrightly

|                    | (7) analyzes alternative solutions |
| *Advantages*: | (1) usually results in mutually beneficial solutions |
|               | (2) produces more long-lasting and creative agreements |
|               | (3) maintains personal relationships |
|               | (4) preserves future relations between the parties |
|               | (5) controls the competitive negotiator |
|               | (6) encourages concessions from both sides |
| *Disadvantages*: | (1) unworkable if the adversary is unrelentingly competitive |
|                  | (2) difficult to use when the parties dislike or mistrust each other |
|                  | (3) largely unworkable if the parties refuse to cooperate |
|                  | (4) sometimes sacrifices unilateral gains for joint solutions |
|                  | (5) requires time and patience |

## Adversarial Strategy

| *Characteristics*: | (1) most commonly used negotiation strategy |
|                    | (2) emphasizes maximizing the party's gain (usually in terms of money) |
|                    | (3) constitutes a zero-sum game |
|                    | (4) fact and law rationales are manipulated to advance and defend positions |
|                    | (5) based on a strict cost-benefit analysis |
| *Advantages*: | (1) effective when the only matter obtainable is a single objective like money |
|               | (2) works well when the parties dislike or mistrust each other and are not interested in a cooperative solution |
|               | (3) negotiation process is less complex and time consuming |
| *Disadvantages*: | (1) creativity is curtailed in arriving at mutually beneficial solutions |
|                  | (2) the final agreement may not satisfy the parties' true needs or interests |
|                  | (3) parties and negotiators sometimes remain dissatisfied and resentful after agreement |

## Problem-Solving Strategy

| *Characteristics*: | (1) the people are separated from the problem |
|                    | (2) both parties' needs or interests are identified and acknowledged |
|                    | (3) information is freely exchanged |

                  (4) both parties strive for mutually beneficial solutions

                  (5) interests and objectives of both parties are accommodated to the greatest extent possible

*Advantages*:      (1) usually results in greater satisfaction to both parties

                  (2) negotiations are markedly less intense and testy

                  (3) both parties' true needs or interests are often fulfilled

                  (4) preserves personal relationships and future relations between the parties and negotiators

*Disadvantages*:      (1) usually unworkable when only one objective is sought (e.g., money)

                  (2) unworkable if both parties are not committed to finding mutually beneficial solutions

                  (3) negotiations are more complex and time consuming

                  (4) sometimes unnecessarily sacrifices unilateral gains for joint solutions

# Chapter 9

# ETHICAL CONSIDERATIONS IN NEGOTIATION AND SETTLEMENT

SYNOPSIS

## § 9.01  INTRODUCTION

The American Bar Association's Model Rules of Professional Conduct (Model Rules) contain a number of Rules that are particularly applicable to a lawyer's responsibilities in representing a client in negotiations and settlement. These Rules relate to (1) the requisite authority that an attorney must have from the client to make an agreement or settlement on behalf of the client, and the lawyer's responsibilities in advising the client throughout the negotiating process; (2) the lawyer's responsibilities when entering into an aggregate settlement on behalf of multiple clients; (3) the circumstances under which contingent fees are permissible; (4) the extent to which a lawyer is obligated to make truthful statements to others in connection with negotiations or settlement; (5) a lawyer's duty to behave with civility in negotiations; and (6) whether a lawyer may threaten criminal prosecution in negotiating a civil matter. Although the Model Rules have been modified by many states in various respects, these Rules are instructive about the most important ethical considerations attendant to negotiating and settling a case.

## § 9.02  ATTORNEY'S AUTHORITY TO SETTLE AND ADVISING THE CLIENT

Rule 1.2(a) of the Model Rules provides, in part, that "[a] lawyer shall abide by a client's decisions concerning the objectives of representation . . . [and] shall consult with the client as to the means by which they are to be pursued." Although this provision has been interpreted as making a distinction between the client's objectives and the means for achieving them, whereby the lawyer is in charge of "procedural" decisions such as tactics and strategy and the client has the final decision over matters directly affecting the ultimate resolution of the case,[1] as a lawyer, you generally have no authority to enter into a final agreement or settle a case on behalf of a client merely by virtue of the attorney-client relationship or because you have been given general authority to enter into negotiations.[2] Rather, except in rare emergency situations where prompt action by you is necessary to protect your client's interests and consultation with the client is impossible,[3] most courts require that you have *express* authority from your client to enter into a binding agreement or compromise of an action; and Rule 1.2(a) adopts this position by mandating that "[a] lawyer shall abide by a client's decision whether to settle a matter." In many states, this express authority is otherwise prescribed by statute or local court rule.[4]

Generally, the special authority you need to compromise your client's claim can be obtained only when a specific settlement is proposed, or when you have been given prior authority to settle within certain limits.[5] This, of course, presupposes appropriate communication between you and your client. As Model Rule 1.4 provides, in part:

(a) A lawyer shall:

(1) promptly inform the client of any decision or circumstance with respect to which the client's informed consent . . . is required by these Rules; . . . .

(3) keep the client reasonably informed about the status of the matter;

(4) promptly comply with reasonable requests for information; . . . .

(b) A lawyer shall explain a matter to the extent reasonably necessary to permit the client to make informed decisions regarding the representation.

The official Comment to that Rule explains, in pertinent part:

[2] If these Rules require that a particular decision about the representation be made by the client, paragraph (a)(1) requires that the lawyer promptly consult with and secure the client's consent prior to taking action unless prior discussions with the client have resolved what action the client wants the lawyer to take. For example, a lawyer who receives from opposing counsel an offer of settlement in a civil controversy or a proffered plea bargain in a criminal case must promptly inform the client of its substance unless the client has previously indicated that the proposal will be acceptable or unacceptable or has authorized the lawyer to accept or to reject the offer. See Rule 1.2(a) . . . .

---

[1] *See* State v. Debler, 856 S.W.2d 641 (Mo. 1993); State v. Ali, 407 S.E.2d 183 (N.C. 1991); Blanton v. Womancare, Inc., 696 P.2d 645 (Cal. 1985).

[2] *See* Faris v. J.C. Penney Co., 2 F. Supp. 2d 695 (E.D. Pa. 1998); Kaiser Foundation v. Doe, 903 P.2d 375 (Or. App. 1995).

[3] *See* Sockolof v. Eden Point North Condominium Assoc., 421 So. 2d 716 (Fla. App. 1982); Schumann v. Northtown Ins. Agency, Inc., 452 N.W.2d 482 (Minn. App. 1990); Midwest Federal Savings Bank v. Dickinson Econo-Storage, 450 N.W.2d 418 (N.D. 1990).

[4] *See generally*, Annotation, *Authority of Attorney to Compromise Action — Modern Cases*, 90 ALR4th 326 (1991).

[5] *See* Lord v. Money Masters, Inc., 435 S.E.2d 247 (Ga. 1993).

[5] The client should have sufficient information to participate intelligently in decisions concerning the objectives of the representation and the means by which they are to be pursued, to the extent the client is willing and able to do so. Adequacy of communication depends in part on the kind of advice or assistance that is involved. For example, when there is time to explain a proposal made in a negotiation, the lawyer should review all important provisions with the client before proceeding to an agreement. In litigation a lawyer should explain the general strategy and prospects of success and ordinarily should consult the client on tactics that are likely to result in significant expense or to injure or coerce others. On the other hand, a lawyer ordinarily will not be expected to describe trial or negotiation strategy in detail. The guiding principle is that the lawyer should fulfill reasonable client expectations for information consistent with the duty to act in the client's best interests, and the client's overall requirements as to the character of representation.

Thus, you have a duty to disclose to your client all good faith settlement offers,[6] and to adequately explain all ramifications of a proposed agreement or settlement so that your client can make an informed decision.[7] If you settle your client's case without authority, fail to communicate a settlement offer to your client, or fail to adequately advise your client about a potential settlement, you may be subject to discipline by the bar[8] or be liable to the client for malpractice.[9]

## § 9.03 AGGREGATE SETTLEMENTS

An aggregate settlement is one that is made on behalf of two or more clients who are represented by the same lawyer. Rule 1.8(g) of the Model Rules provides, in part:

A lawyer who represents two or more clients shall not participate in making an aggregate settlement of the claims of or against the clients . . . unless each client gives informed consent, in a writing signed by the client. The lawyer's disclosure shall include the existence and nature of all the claims . . . involved and of the participation of each person in the settlement.

This Rule typically applies where "counsel representing several separate plaintiffs with different claims against a single defendant . . . settle[s] all of the

---

[6] *See* In re Cardenas, 791 P.2d 1032 (Ariz. 1990); In re Baehr, 744 P.2d 799 (Kan. 1987).

[7] *See* Hartford Accident & Indemnity Co. v. Foster, 528 So. 2d 255 (Miss. 1988); Ramp v. St. Paul Fire & Marine Ins. Co. 269 So. 2d 239 (La. 1972). *See generally*, Perschbacher, Regulating Lawyers Negotiations, 27 Ariz. L. Rev. 76, 115–119 (1985).

[8] *See, e.g.*, In re Nugent, 624 A.2d 291 (R.I. 1993) (settling personal injury action without client's consent was grounds for discipline); Comm. On Professional Ethics v. Behnke, 486 N.W.2d 275 (Iowa 1992) (lawyer who handled client's personal injury claim by telephone and settled case without discussion with client violated MRPC Rule 1.4); Culpepper v. Mississippi State Bar, 588 So. 2d 413 (Miss. 1991) (lawyer disciplined for misleading client about true bases of settlement reached with opposing counsel in divorce action, and for failing to advise her that agreement filed was different from her previous agreement). *See generally*, Annotation, *Conduct of Attorney in Connection with Settlement of Client's Case as Ground for Disciplinary Action*, 92 ALR3d 288 (1979).

[9] *See, e.g.*, Moores v. Greenberg, 834 F.2d 1105 (1st Cir. 1987) (attorney may be liable for malpractice for failing to inform client of a settlement offer, permitting client to recover damages in the amount of that offer).

claims together."[10] While most of the cases discussing the Rule have involved aggregate settlements of only a small number of clients, the Rule is also acutely applicable in mass tort litigation cases where large numbers of plaintiffs are represented by a single lawyer or law firm. The Rule's prohibition against making an aggregate settlement without each client's informed consent (1) aims to prevent lawyers from favoring one client over another in settlement negotiations,[11] (2) empowers clients to prevent lawyers from putting their own economic self-interest ahead of their clients' interest (given the temptation of some lawyers to accept a relatively cheap, comprehensive settlement at an early stage of the representation rather than invest the time and resources that would be necessary to maximize their clients' recoveries),[12] and (3) reflects the mandates of Rule 1.4 that clients have a right to be fully informed about settlement offers and to control the ultimate settlement decision.[13]

When you represent multiple clients[14] against a single adversary and receive an "all or nothing" lump sum, settlement offer which conditions settlement upon acceptance of the agreement by all or a particular number of your clients, the initial question will be how the lump sum would be allocated among your clients. If you represent a relatively small number of clients, the simplest approach is to help your clients to agree among themselves as to an appropriate division. However, if you represent a large number of clients, it is likely to be much more difficult to achieve unanimous agreement on the division of a lump sum settlement. In that situation, some lawyers utilize the services of special masters or ask a judge to mediate the division.[15]

After determining the amount that would be received by each client, and before acceptance of the settlement, you should confer directly with each client (rather than communicating with one client and expecting that client to confer with the others),[16] to inform each about (1) the total, lump sum settlement amount, (2) the particular amount the client will receive, (3) every other client's share in the settlement,[17] and (4) all other information necessary to enable the client to make an informed decision whether to accept or reject the settlement. The aggregate settlement cannot be accepted unless *all* clients give informed consent, and this requirement cannot be circumvented by some other agreement, such as a retainer agreement, authorizing settlement by majority vote or by some other method.[18] A violation of Rule 1.8(g) may render the settlement unenforceable against the

---

[10] Kelly v. Johns-Manville Corp., 590 F. Supp. 1089, 1092 n.1 (E.D. Pa. 1984).

[11] *See* In re Anonymous Member of South Carolina Bar, 377 S.E.2d 567, 568 (S.C. 1989).

[12] *See* Arce v. Burrow, 958 S.W.2d 239 (Tex. App. 1997); Silver & Baker, Mass Lawsuits and the Aggregate Settlement Rule, 32 Wake Forest L. Rev. 733, 751–752 (1997).

[13] *See* Hayes v. Eagle-Picher Industries, Inc., 513 F.2d 892 (10th Cir. 1975); Quientero v. Jim Walter Homes, Inc., 709 S.W.2d 225 (Tex. App. 1985).

[14] As a threshold matter, the multiple representations must be proper under Model Rule 1.7(b).

[15] *See* Weinstein, Ethical Dilemmas in Mass Tort Litigation, 88 Nw. U. L. Rev. 469, 521 (1994).

[16] *See* Gelb, Common Ethical Problems, 79 Mass. L. Rev. 167, 174 (1994).

[17] *See* In re Anonymous Member of the South Carolina Bar, 377 S.E.2d 567, 568 (S.C. 1989) (lawyer should provide list showing the names and amounts to be received by other settling clients); *accord* Quintero v. Jim Walker Homes Inc., 709 S.W.2d 225, 229 (Tex. Ct. App. 1985).

[18] Hayes v. Eagle-Picher Industries Inc., 513 F.2d 892 (10th Cir. 1975).

non-consenting clients[19] and subject the offending attorney to disciplinary action by the bar.[20]

## § 9.04   CONTINGENT FEES

Many settlements occur in personal injury cases, whether arising out of common law negligence, an intentional tort, or a breach of a duty of care defined by statute. Lawyers often take these cases on a contingent fee basis, whereby the attorney's fee is a percentage of the total monetary amount or interest in property[21] recovered for the client (usually one-third), or a combination of a percentage and an hourly fee.[22] The rationale for contingent fees is that they provide a means by which clients who cannot afford to pay an hourly or fixed fee may compensate their lawyers by giving the lawyer a portion of the winning result. The fact that a lawyer might earn a larger sum of money in charging a contingent fee than would otherwise be earned from a fixed fee or at an hourly rate is balanced against the risk that the lawyer will receive no fee at all if no recovery is obtained for the client.

Model Rule 1.5 provides, in pertinent part:

(c) A fee may be contingent on the outcome of the matter for which the service is rendered, except in a matter in which a contingent fee is prohibited by paragraph (d) or other law. A contingent fee agreement shall be in writing signed by the client and shall state the method by which the fee is to be determined, including the percentage or percentages that shall accrue to the lawyer in the event of settlement, trial or appeal, litigation and other expenses to be deducted from the recovery, and whether such expenses are to be deducted before or after the contingent fee is calculated. The agreement must clearly notify the client of any expenses for which the client will be liable whether or not the client is the prevailing party. Upon conclusion of a contingent fee matter, the lawyer shall provide the client with a written statement stating the outcome of the matter and, if there is a recovery, showing the remittance to the client and the method of its determination.

(d) A lawyer shall not enter into an arrangement for, charge or collect:

(1) any fee in a domestic relations matter, the payment or amount of which is contingent upon the securing of a divorce or upon the amount of alimony or support, or property settlement in lieu thereof; . . .

Like other types of fees, a contingent fee must be reasonable in terms of the percentage the lawyer will receive of the monetary amount recovered for his or her client; and the courts retain overall supervisory power to monitor the reasonable-

---

[19] *See, e.g.*, Knisley v. Jacksonville, 497 N.E.2d 883 (Ill. App. 1986); Quintero v. Jim Walker Homes, Inc., 709 S.W.2d 225 (Tex. Ct. App. 1985).

[20] *See, e.g.*, State ex rel. Oklahoma Bar Assoc. v. Watson, 897 P.2d 246 (Okla. 1994); Butler County Bar Assoc. v. Barr, 591 N.E.2d 1200 (Ohio 1992).

[21] *See, e.g.*, Beatie v. Delong, 561 N.Y.S.2d 448 (Sup. Ct. App. Div. 1990) (upholding 30% of revenues generated by patents whose rights the lawyer recaptured for the client).

[22] *See, e.g.*, Boston and Maine Corp v. Sheehan, Phinney, Bass & Green P.A., 778 F.2d 890 (1st Cir. 1985) (upholding hourly fee plus reduced contingent fee).

ness of such fees.[23] Even when this percentage falls within the usual range of percentages charged in similar types of cases, a court may find the percentage unreasonable if the risk of no recovery by the client is virtually nonexistent or the lawyer can easily resolve the matter without much effort.[24] For example, the courts have repeatedly warned that contingent fees are usually inappropriate in cases involving the collection of insurance proceeds when the client's right to that money is clear and it will take little effort to collect it.[25] On the other hand, even a 50% contingent fee may be permissible, particularly if the case is very complicated, liability is highly questionable, and a favorable outcome of the case will depend upon considerable skill by the lawyer.[26] In addition, by statute or local court rule, some jurisdictions limit the percentages that may be charged in matters such as workers' compensation cases, social security cases, medical malpractice[27] or civil rights actions,[28] or in cases involving the representation of children.[29] These statutory limitations may never be exceeded in a contingent fee contract.

Rule 1.5(c) requires that the contingent fee contract be in writing and signed by the client. The agreement must state the percentage or percentages of the recovery to which you will be entitled if your client's case (1) is settled (making clear whether a different percentage applies if the case is settled during trial, as opposed to prior to trial); (2) goes to trial (or is retried); and (3) is appealed. If a structured settlement is possible, you should state whether the fee will be based on a percentage of the lump sum immediately received by your client plus the present value of the future payments to which your client is entitled, or on a percentage of each future payment received by your client when it is received. In addition, the agreement must state generally the "litigation and other expenses to be deducted from the recovery," and whether your percentage of the recovery will be taken from the gross amount before deduction of expenses or the net amount after deduction of expenses.[30] The agreement might also contain a clause that, in the event you are

---

[23] Thomton, Sperry & Jensen Ltd. v. Anderson, 352 N.W.2d 467 (Minn. App. 1984); West Virginia State Bar Committee on Legal Ethics v. Taterson, 352 S.E.2d 107 (W. Va. Sup. Ct. App. 1986).

[24] *See, e.g.*, In re Gerard, 548 N.E.2d 1051 (Ill. 1989) (lawyer disciplined for collecting contingent fee of 35.2% to locate and collect client's assets to which no adverse claims were made, where it took the lawyer no more than 160 hours to perform the task and contingent fee amounted to approximately $1000 per hour of work).

[25] *See* In re Hanna, 362 S.E.2d 632 (S.C. 1987); West Virginia State Bar Committee on Legal Ethics v. Tatterson, 352 S.E.2d 107 (W. Va. Sup. Ct. App. 1986); Maryland Attorney Grievance Commission v. Kemp, 496 A.2d 672 (Md. App. 1985).

[26] *E.g.*, Sweeney v. Athens Regional Medical Center, 917 F.2d 1560 (11th Cir. 1990); Fraidin v. Weitzman, 611 A.2d 1046 (Md. Ct. Spec. App. 1992). *Cf.* West Virginia State Bar Committee on Legal Ethics v. Gallaher, 376 S.E.2d 346 (W. Va. Sup. Ct. App. 1988) (50% contingent fee excessive where lawyer achieved modest settlement of client's case in less than 17 hours; one-third fee would have been more appropriate); Maryland Attorney Grievance Commission v. Korotki, 569 A.2d 1224 (Md. App. 1990) (even though case was complex and involved a trial and two appeals, successive contracts adding up to 75% contingent fee constituted excessive fee).

[27] *See generally*, Annotation, *Validity of Statute Establishing Contingent Fee Scale for Attorneys Representing Parties in Medical Malpractice Actions*, 12 ALR4th 23 (1982).

[28] *See* Federal Tort Claims Act, 28 USC 2678, limiting contingent fees to 25% (or 20% if the case is settled at the administrative level).

[29] *See generally* Annotation, *Court Rules Limiting Amount of Contingent Fees or Otherwise Imposing Conditions on Contingent Fee Contracts*, 77 ALR2d 411 (1961).

[30] *See* Louisiana State Bar Assoc. v. St. Romain, 560 So. 2d 820 (La. 1990) (attorney privately reprimanded for using retainer agreement that did not specify how expenses would be deducted).

discharged from the case without good cause, you will be entitled to a fee amounting to the reasonable value of your services under *quantum meruit*, expressed as either a reduced percentage of the amount recovered by your client or a fee based on an hourly rate.[31]

Rule 1.5(d)(1) states explicitly that you cannot charge a contingent fee if the contingency is your client's obtaining a divorce, or if the amount of the fee is dependent on what your client is awarded as alimony or child support or in a "property settlement" in lieu of alimony or child support. However, in most states you are permitted to charge a contingent fee where your client's right to alimony or child support has *already* been established judicially and the aim of the representation is the collection of past-due payments of alimony or child support. Jurisdictions are divided about whether the Rule's prohibition against contingent fees in "property settlement" matters embraces equitable distribution cases, some courts holding that a contingent fee in an equitable distribution case is permissible so long as the contract does not simultaneously provide for compensation contingent on securing a divorce, or obtaining alimony or child support.[32]

Finally, Rule 1.5(c) provides that, at the conclusion of the contingent fee representation, you are obligated to provide your client with a written financial accounting of the monies to be disbursed in connection with the case. The disbursement statement must state "the outcome of the matter and, if there is a recovery, show[] the remittance to the client and method of its determination." A failure to abide by this requirement may result in disciplinary action.[33]

## § 9.05  EXAMPLE OF CONTINGENT FEE CONTRACT

### Contingent Fee Contract

The law firm of _____ (Attorneys) is retained and employed by _____ (Client) to represent Client in a claim for damages against _____ or any others who may be liable for injuries that Client sustained on _____ [Date] _____.

1. This is a contingent fee contract and it is agreed that if Attorneys recover no compensation for Client, Client owes Attorneys no fee until a favorable recovery is obtained. If a recovery is obtained on behalf of Client, Attorneys shall receive as attorneys' fees _____% of any recovery obtained, whether by settlement or trial. If an appeal is taken or proceedings are necessary to collect any judgment, the attorneys' fees shall increase to _____%. These percentages shall be calculated and paid based on the gross amount recovered for Client, and before deduction of any costs, litigation expenses, or medical charges and expenses as provided for in paragraphs 3 and 4.

2. If settlement of this case is made by a structured settlement, attorneys' fees shall be based on the present cash value of the settlement as determined by actuarial

---

[31] *See generally*, Annotation, *Limitation to Quantum Meruit Recovery, Where Attorney Employed Under Contingent Fee Contract is Discharged Without Cause*, 92 ALR3d 690 (1979); Annotation, *Circumstances Under Which Attorney Retains Right to Compensation Notwithstanding Voluntary Withdrawal from Case*, 88 ALR3d 246 (1978).

[32] *See* Williams v. Garrison, 411 S.E.2d 633 (N.C. App. 1992).

[33] *See* Florida Bar v. Rood, 633 So. 2d 7 (Fla. 1994).

experts, and such fees shall be paid out of the initial cash lump sum payment.

3. In addition to attorneys' fees, all court costs, expert witness fees, subpoena costs, photographs, depositions, court reporter fees, reports, witness statements, photocopying, telephone, travel, and all other out-of-pocket expenses directly incurred in investigating, preparing, or litigating this claim shall be paid by Client irrespective of the outcome of this case, and Attorneys may deduct those amounts from the Client's share of the proceeds of any recovery.

4. All medical expenses and charges of any nature made by doctors, hospitals, clinics, or Client will pay other health-care providers in connection with the diagnosis or treatment of Client's injuries. In the event that Attorneys recover damages on Client's behalf, Client authorizes Attorneys to pay all such expenses and charges that are unpaid as of that date from Client's share of the recovery.

5. Client agrees not to make any settlement of this case without Attorneys being present and receiving all payments due them under this Contract.

6. Client agrees that Attorneys have made no promises or guarantees about the outcome of this case.

7. Client and Attorneys each have a copy of this Contract, and its terms are acceptable.

This the _____ day of _____, [year].

_____      by: _____
[Client]                      [Attorneys]

## § 9.06   TRUTHFULNESS IN NEGOTIATING

The Preamble to the Model Rules states that "[a]s negotiator, a lawyer seeks a result advantageous to the client but consistent with the requirements of honest dealing with others." Rule 4.1(a) of the Model Rules provides that "[i]n the course of representing a client a lawyer shall not knowingly: make a false statement of material fact or law to a third person." The Comment to that Rule states, in pertinent part:

> [1] A lawyer is required to be truthful when dealing with others on a client's behalf, but generally has no affirmative duty to inform an opposing party of relevant facts. A misrepresentation can occur if the lawyer incorporates or affirms a statement of another person that the lawyer knows is false. Misrepresentations can also occur by partially true but misleading statements or omissions that are the equivalent of affirmative false statements.

> [2] This Rule refers to statements of fact. Whether a particular statement should be regarded as one of fact can depend on the circumstances. Under generally accepted conventions in negotiation, certain types of statements ordinarily are not taken as statements of material fact. Estimates of price or value placed on the subject of a transaction and a party's intentions as to an acceptable settlement of a claim are in this category.

These provisions reflect a tension between the aspiration that lawyers should be honest when negotiating with others and the reality that the parlance of negotiating often includes a certain amount of deception. The failure of Rule 4.1(a) and its Comment to set a bright-line standard of complete truthfulness in negotiating has led one commentator to ruefully remark that these provisions "unambiguously embrace[] 'New York hardball' as the official standard of practice."[34] Thus, some scholars have urged that these provisions should be revised to establish a tighter standard of truthfulness in negotiations,[35] while others recognize that, of necessity, negotiations involve at least some deceptive behavior.[36]

In practice, most experienced lawyers are essentially honest in negotiating. However, they will not mindlessly volunteer or concede weaknesses in their clients' positions and will usually make every effort to portray the facts of the situation in a light most favorable to their clients. Thus, experienced lawyers expect their adversaries will often *characterize* the facts of the case and why their clients are deserving of a more favorable outcome in ways that are less than objectively accurate. Acceptance of this reality, however, should not be interpreted as an endorsement of dishonesty. Rather, it is merely recognition of the fact that part of zealous advocacy involves the ability to tactfully put a favorable "spin" on matters. As the Comment to Model Rule 1.3 provides: "[a] lawyer must also act with commitment and dedication to the interests of the client and with zeal in advocacy upon the client's behalf." Painting one's client's position in the most favorable light is an attribute of lawyer competency that is still consistent with ethical responsibility.

At the same time, most experienced lawyers also expect that their adversaries, if they are also first-rate lawyers, will not conduct themselves in negotiations by engaging in outright prevarication on material matters. This is so because, apart from the prohibition against untruthfulness in Rule 4.1(a), experienced lawyers know that effective client representation depends in large part upon lawyer credibility. Lawyers who lie are usually found out. They are as ineffective in persuading other lawyers as they are ineffective in persuading judges or juries, and persuasion is the lawyer's principal stock in trade, whether in negotiation, litigation, or other aspects of client representation. Moreover, to the extent that actual or perceived "toughness" plays a role in effective representation, experienced lawyers know that the lawyers who have the ability to be truly tough, when necessary, are usually those who also have a strong reputation for credibility through trustworthiness and integrity.

Rule 4.1(a) and its Commentary, in large part reflect these realities. Although you generally have no duty to inform an opposing party of relevant facts such as

---

[34] G. Lowenthal, The Bar's Failure to Require Truthful Bargaining by Lawyers, 2 Geo. J. Legal Ethics 411, 445 (1988).

[35] *See* Rubin, A Causerie on Lawyers' Ethics in Negotiation, 35 La. L. Rev. 577 (1975); Jarvis & Tellam, A Negotiation Ethics Primer for Lawyers, 31 Gonzaga L. Rev. 549 (1995/96); *see also* Steele, Deceptive Negotiating and High-Toned Morality, 39 V and. L. Rev. 1387 (1986).

[36] *See* C. Craver, Negotiation Ethics: How to Be Deceptive Without Being Dishonest/How to Be Assertive Without Being Offensive, 38 S. Tex. L. Rev. 713 (1997); *see also* Hazard, The Lawyer's Obligation to Be Trustworthy When Dealing with Opposing Parties, 33 S.C. L. Rev. 181 (1981); James T. White, Machiavelli and the Bar: Limitations on Lying in Negotiation, 1980 Am. Bar Found. Res. J. 927–928 (1980) ("To conceal one's true position, to mislead one's opponent about one's true settling point, is the essence of negotiation.").

those which would indicate weaknesses in your client's position,[37] and you are not prohibited from zealous advocacy such as by "puffing," giving mere "personal opinions" about the merits of the case, or even embellishing your client's intentions as to what would be an acceptable settlement, you may not go so far as to make any "false statements of material fact or law" to third persons in connection with negotiations on behalf of your client. False statements include those that are written as well as oral, statements by you that repeat or affirm false statements made by your client when you know of their falsity,[38] and may include statements of your intent to do something when you actually have no such current intention.[39] A false statement will also violate the Rule if made in response to a third party's question, and such a statement cannot be excused by the duty to protect client confidences because, if the matter is privileged, you have a duty to decline to answer the question altogether.[40] Moreover, if you make a statement that is literally true but is misleading because you purposefully omit material information, the intentionally deceptive nature of the omission may make it equivalent to an affirmative false statement.[41]

Rule 4.1(a) only prohibits making false statements of "material" fact or law. Although the Model Rules do not define the term "material," a "[r]epresentation relating to a matter which is so substantial and important as to influence [a] party to whom made is 'material.' "[42] For example, it has been held that information about a personal injury client's alcohol use at the time of the accident, which a lawyer deleted from the client's medical records before submitting them to an insurer, was material.[43] A lawyer was disciplined for stating there was only $200,000 in insurance coverage, when documents in the lawyer's possession showed $1 million in coverage.[44] Similarly, a lawyer was disciplined when, during negotiations to settle a hospital's claim for a personal injury client's medical expenses, the lawyer failed to disclose to the hospital the existence of a third insurance policy when the hospital mistakenly believed there were only two insurance policies that provided coverage for the accident.[45] And, it has been held that the death of one's client during

---

[37] *See* Brown v. County of Genesee, 872 F.2d 169 (6th Cir. 1989) (defense counsel had no general ethical duty to tell counsel for plaintiff during settlement negotiations about the latter's factual error; error was not induced or contributed to by defense counsel).

[38] *See, e.g.,* Florida Bar v. Burkich-Burrell, 659 So. 2d 1082 (Fla. 1995) (lawyer notarized false answers to interrogatories on behalf of husband-client, knowing that answers were untrue).

[39] *See* In re Graveley, 805 P.2d 1263 (Mont. 1990); ABA Formal Ethics Op. 94-383 (it is unethical to make a false threat to file disciplinary charges against another lawyer).

[40] *See* People v. Petsas, 262 Cal. Rptr. 467 (Ct. App. 1989) ("distinct difference [exists] between restricting an attorney from divulging information learned in confidence from a client, and proscribing him from knowingly making affirmative false representations regarding a claim or claims of that client."); ABA Formal Ethics Op. 93-370 (1993) (lawyer may decline to answer improper question by judge regarding settlement authority, but is barred by Rule 4.1 from responding with a deliberate misrepresentation or lie).

[41] *See* Florida Bar v. Joy, 679 So. 2d 1165 (Fla. 1996) (lawyer violated Rule 4.1 by making statement that was literally true but intended to mislead opposing counsel); In re Goodsell, 667 So. 2d 7 (La. 1996); Mississippi Bar v. Robb, 684 So. 2d 615 (Miss. 1996); ABA Formal Ethics Op. 93-375 (1993) (attorney representing client in bank examination may not omit information when omission is tantamount to affirmative false statement).

[42] *Black's Law Dictionary* 976 (6th ed. 1990).

[43] In re Zeiger, 692 A.2d 1351 (D.C. 1997).

[44] In re McGrath, 468 N.Y.S.2d 349 (App. Div. 1983).

[45] State ex rel. Nebraska State Bar Assoc. v. Addison, 412 N.W.2d 855 (Neb. 1987).

settlement negotiations is a material fact that must be disclosed to opposing counsel.[46]

Making false statements of law has typically given rise to disciplinary action where the statements were made to non-lawyers. For example, a lawyer was disciplined for falsely telling a debtor that his driver's license would be suspended if he failed to pay a judgment.[47] A lawyer was also held to have violated Rule 4.1(a) for providing false opinion letters to a purchaser regarding title to real property so as to enable his clients to profit from undisclosed double sales of property.[48] On the other hand, rendering a mere "personal opinion" as to the proper interpretation of a statute or case decision would fall outside the scope of the Rule,[49] and it has been said that a lawyer has no ethical duty to inform an opposing party that the statute of limitations has run, so long as the lawyer does not misrepresent the facts or his intent to file suit.[50]

Apart from the disciplinary consequences of violating Rule 4.1(a), the danger of making false statements of material fact or law is that such misrepresentations may also give rise to an action in tort for fraud. For example, it has been held that a lawyer could be sued in tort by the opposing party who alleged that the case was settled for a lower amount in reliance on the lawyer's false representation about applicable insurance policy coverage.[51] A claim for fraudulent misrepresentation was held actionable against a seller's lawyer who allegedly stated to purchasers that they were getting "a lot of property for the money" when the lawyer knew that his client could not convey title.[52] And another court refused to dismiss a complaint for fraud against lawyers who allegedly induced an asbestos manufacturer to settle claims by falsely representing that the claims were valid.[53] Thus, even if misrepresentations of fact or law might not constitute an ethical violation, you should be aware of the risk that such misrepresentations, or even nondisclosure of information in circumstances where the law may impose a duty of disclosure,[54] may give rise to liability in tort.

## § 9.07   CIVILITY IN NEGOTIATING

Rule 4.4(a) of the Model Rules provides, in part, that "[i]n representing a client, a lawyer shall not use means that have no substantial purpose other than to embarrass, delay, or burden a third person." Most of the reported decisions finding a violation of this Rule have involved abusive interpersonal behavior or abusive

---

[46] Kentucky Bar Assoc. v. Geisler, 938 S.W.2d 578 (Ky. 1997); Virzi v. Grand Trunk Warehouse & Cold Storage Co., 571 F. Supp. 507 (E.D. Mich. 1983); ABA Formal Ethics Op. 95-397 (1995).

[47] In re Eliasen, 913 P.2d 1163 (Idaho 1996).

[48] In re Duckworth, 914 P.2d 900 (Ariz. 1996).

[49] *See* J. Moliterno & J. Levy, *Ethics of the Lawyer's Work* 234 (1993).

[50] ABA Formal Ethics Op. 94-387 (1994).

[51] Fire Insurance Exchange v. Bell, 643 N.E.2d 310 (Ind. 1994).

[52] Jeska v. Mulhall, 693 P.2d 1335 (Or. App. 1985).

[53] Raymark Industries Inc. v. Stemple, 714 F. Supp. 460 (D. Kan. 1988). *See also* Sainsbury v. Pennsylvania Greyhound Lines, 183 F.2d 548 (4th Cir. 1950) (setting aside release of personal injury claim that was induced by lawyer's false representation that employees in government service could recover only for pain and suffering).

[54] *See generally,* Restatement (Second) of Torts, § 551 (enumerating circumstances where party has a duty of disclosure in business transactions).

tactics in the litigation context, whether directed against opposing counsel, opposing parties, witnesses, jurors, or court personnel. For example, numerous cases have found violations of the Rule where lawyers were verbally abusive to third persons, or engaged in physical threats or similar types of despicable behavior.[55] In some instances, the courts have found that a violation of Rule 4.4 also comes within the prohibitions on "engag[ing] in conduct that is prejudicial to the administration of justice" under Rule 8.4(d).[56]

Rule 4.4 recognizes that a lawyer's means in representing a client may have more than one purpose. The Rule is violated only when the means used have no other "substantial purpose" than to cause embarrassment, delay, or a burden to another person. By requiring that the other permissible purposes be "substantial," the language of the Rule suggests that the lawyer's purportedly legitimate purposes will be closely scrutinized. A good example of this occurred in *State ex rel. Scales v. West Virginia State Bar Committee on Legal Ethics*, 446 S.E.2d 729 (W. Va. Sup. Ct. App. 1994) where Scales, in representing a woman in a bitter divorce with her husband who was a member of the armed forces, contacted the husband's commanding officer to report that the husband was abusing his wife. The Court rejected the State Bar Committee's contention that Scales' sole purpose in contacting the commanding officer was to harass and embarrass the husband, noting that when the wife had contacted the commanding officer to report the abuse, he had told her he could not do anything unless her lawyer contacted army officials. Thus, the Court held that because Scales' intervention had a substantial purpose other than embarrassment and harassment, there was no violation of Rule 4.4.

As in the litigation context, a violation of Rule 4.4 may occur in the context of negotiations. However, because of the overall importance of lawyer credibility as discussed in Section 9.06, in practice, the vast majority of lawyers negotiate with civility. Resort to abusive interpersonal behavior or obnoxious negotiating tactics is relatively rare and, when they do occur, they are usually a product of the lawyer's personal insecurity, professional immaturity, or both.

---

[55] *See, e.g.*, Castillo v. St. Paul Fire & Marine Insurance Co. (In re Walker), 828 F. Supp. 594 (C.D. Ill. 1992) (lawyer repeatedly obstructed deposition and engaged in "most egregious example of lawyer incivility that this Court has ever seen," including threatening opposing counsel); In re Ramunno, 625 A.2d 248 (Del. 1993) (lawyer referred to opposing counsel in vulgar terms in office conference before judge and engaged in insolent colloquy with judge); In re Bechhold, 771 P.2d 563 (Mont. 1988) (lawyer who represented client on a claim submitted to insurance company, contacted claims department employee seven or eight times a day for several days, was rude, and then attempted to serve papers on insurance company by bringing them to the claims office where lawyer engaged in continual profanity).

[56] *See, e.g.*, In re Schiff, 599 NYS2d 242 (N.Y. Sup. Ct. App. Div. 1st Dept. 1993) (lawyer's conduct of being unduly intimidating and abusive toward opposing counsel, and directing vulgar, obscene, and sexist epithets toward her in deposition reflected adversely on fitness to practice); In re Holmes, 921 P.2d 44 (Colo. 1996) ("undignified, offensive, threatening, and unprofessional" letters to opponents and court employees); In re Stanley, 507 A.2d 1168 (N.J. 1986) (rude stares at judge, laughing, remarking in undertones, shaking finger at judge).

## § 9.08    THREATENING CRIMINAL PROSECUTION IN NEGOTIATING

One negotiating tactic that could arguably run afoul of Rule 4.4 and has received special attention by the American Bar Association is threatening criminal prosecution in connection with negotiating a civil matter. Before the Model Rules were adopted, Disciplinary Rule (DR) 7-105(A) of the ABA Model Code provided that "[a] lawyer shall not present, participate in presenting, or threaten to present criminal charges solely to obtain an advantage in a civil matter."[57] The Code explained the rationale for this provision in Ethical Consideration 7-21 as follows:

> The civil adjudicative process is primarily designed for the settlement of disputes between parties, while the criminal process is designed for the protection of society as a whole. Threatening to use, or using, the criminal process to coerce adjustment of private civil claims or controversies is a subversion of that process; further, the person against whom the criminal process is misused may be deterred from asserting his legal rights and thus the usefulness of the civil process in settling private disputes is impaired. As in all cases of abuse of judicial process, the improper use of criminal process tends to diminish public confidence in our legal system.

The Model Rules, however, deliberately do not contain a corresponding provision to DR 7-105(A). The ABA Ethics Committee addressed the issue for the first time under the Model Rules in *ABA Ethics Opinion 92-363* (1992). That opinion states that you may use the possibility of presenting criminal charges against an opposing party in a private civil matter to gain relief for your client, provided that the criminal matter is related to the civil claim, both the civil claim and possible criminal charge are warranted by the law and the facts of the situation, and you do not attempt to exert improper influence over the criminal process. In addition, the Committee said you may agree, as part of a settlement, to refrain from presenting criminal charges against an opposing party so long as the agreement does not violate applicable law. The opinion explained that requiring the criminal charges to be related to the civil matter "discourages exploitation of extraneous matters that have nothing to do with evaluating the claim."

Thus, as a general rule, it is not unethical to threaten the initiation of criminal prosecution (*e.g.*, to seek the swearing out of a warrant), or agree to refrain from initiating such process, in connection with negotiations. However, you should not seek, as part of a settlement, any compensation that is expressly in exchange for not testifying at a criminal trial.[58] In addition, if you make a *direct* threat to initiate criminal prosecution (as opposed to merely a veiled threat) without any present intention to initiate that process if a settlement is not achieved, you may violate Model Rule 4.1(a)'s prohibition against "making a false statement of material fact"

---

[57] *Cf.* West Virginia State Bar Commission on Legal Ethics v. Printz, 416 S.E.2d 720 (W. Va. Sup. Ct. App. 1992) (decided when DR 7-105(A) was still in effect, and holding that the tactic of threatening criminal charges was not prohibited in legitimate negotiations so long as the lawyer did not seek payment beyond restitution in exchange for foregoing criminal prosecution or seek any payment in exchange for not testifying at a criminal trial).

[58] *See* West Virginia State Bar Commission on Legal Ethics v. Printz, 416 S.E.2d 720 (W. Va. Sup. Ct. App. 1992).

(*see* § 9.06).[59]

---

[59] *See* ABA Formal Ethics Op. 94-383 (unethical to make false threat to file disciplinary charge against another lawyer).

# Chapter 10

## NEGOTIATING TACTICS AND TECHNIQUES

## § 10.01   INTRODUCTION

Negotiators routinely employ a variety of tactics and techniques during the negotiating process to advance their clients' interests. These range from subtle games, to overtly obnoxious behavioral ploys, to well-meaning techniques for reaching a reasoned agreement. Some are geared toward adversarial or competitive bargaining, while others are designed to encourage problem solving or cooperative bargaining. Depending upon how they are used, certain tactics or techniques may run afoul of the ethical prescriptions of truthfulness and civility in negotiating discussed in §§ 9.06 and 9.07.

A glossary of common tactics and techniques variously used in negotiations is provided below in alphabetical order.[1] Further references to them are made throughout this book. This glossary is not provided as an express endorsement of any particular tactic or technique, or, for that matter, to encourage the routine use of special tactics in negotiations generally. Rather, it is provided because understanding these tactics and techniques and how to deal with them are essential to effectively representing your client. Section 10.50 at the end of this Chapter provides a general discussion of how to deal with tactics or techniques used by the other side that are particularly disingenuous or otherwise inappropriate under the circumstances.

You may find some of the tactics or techniques useful to employ in a particular situation. However, before using a special tactic or technique, it is sometimes desirable to advise your client about any advantages or disadvantages of using it so

---

[1] Similar glossaries are contained in numerous works. *See, e.g.*, T.A. Donner & B. L. Crowe, *Attorney's Practice Guide to Negotiations*, Chapters 11–12 (1995); M. Schoenfield & R. Schoenfield, *Legal Negotiations: Getting Maximum Results*, Chapter 5 (1988); C. B. Craver, *Effective Legal Negotiation and Settlement*, Chapter 10 (3rd ed. 1997); Lisnek, *A Lawyer's Guide to Effective Negotiation and Mediation*, Chapter 6 (1993); G. Goodpaster, *A Guide to Negotiation and Mediation*, Chapter 4 (1997).

that your client will be able to advise you about any unanticipated reason why the tactic or technique might be inappropriate under the circumstances. Of course, you should never use a tactic or technique that you believe to be unethical, and it is highly unwise to adopt a tactic or technique that is at odds with your own personality, style, or philosophy. Properly used, tactics and techniques are aids to negotiating a successful agreement in particular circumstances, and should not be used for their own sake.

## § 10.02   ABDICATION

Abdication is sometimes effective in deadlock situations. It occurs when both sides are close to an agreement and each side has put forward its best arguments as to why the other ought to compromise somewhat more. Then, one negotiator abdicates by telling the other that he is at a loss as to what to do further but will agree to a final proposal if the other side can just come up with a more equitable solution. In effect, the abdicator is putting the entire problem into the hands of the other party but is hinting at the same time that he (the abdicator) will accept a fair solution.

This tactic thus puts pressure on the other side to make one more final concession. Particularly if the abdicator styles his abdication with praise for the other side's creativity and good faith in resolving the impasse, the technique will sometimes produce an additional concession by the other side that is agreeable to both parties.

## § 10.03   ADJOURNMENT OR CAUCUS

Sometimes a negotiator may find it beneficial or necessary to take a temporary recess during the negotiation, or stop it altogether to resume discussions at a later date. Adjournment may be beneficial to regroup when momentum has been lost, to evaluate a *Surprise* that has developed, to reflect and relax when you are feeling overly pressured to make an immediate decision, or to change the tone of the negotiation if it has become particularly frustrating, exhausting, or acrimonious. In addition, negotiations might have to be temporarily suspended to consult with your client about a matter. In any event, the primary objective is to temporarily bide time to allow for a clearer assessment of the situation.

## § 10.04   ANGER/AGGRESSIVENESS

A display of anger, whether real or feigned, is often effective in conveying to the other side the seriousness of one's position and may reduce the other party's expectations. On the other hand, particularly if the anger is real, the anger may be dangerous for the angry party in that he may unwittingly reveal his bottom line. For example, if you make an offer to settle for $200,000 and the opposing negotiator angrily responds by exclaiming, "this case can't possibly be worth more than $100,000!," the outburst might well reveal that the negotiator's bottom line is close to $100,000.

Some negotiators use anger as part of an overall pattern of aggressive and abrasive behavior that is designed to brow beat their adversaries into making concessions out of intimidation or simply to conclude the unpleasant interaction.

When faced with such a negotiator, it is often best to let him "blow off steam" rather than try to match the aggressiveness with quid pro quo counter attacks. In short, the best counter measure to unabated aggressiveness is to "keep your cool."

## § 10.05   ASYMMETRICAL TIME PRESSURE

This tactic involves asking the out-of-town opponent about her arrival and departure times, ostensibly to confirm flight schedules and other arrangements. In light of the opponent's time constraints, various social and hospitality events are held to delay the start of negotiations and thus limit the time for discussion before the opponent has to leave. The tactic is designed to induce the opponent to make greater concessions to conclude the negotiation before her departure so as not to return home empty-handed. The most obvious antidote to this tactic is to make alternative flight or other travel arrangements for departure.

## § 10.06   BLAMING OR FAULT FINDING

Another form of *Anger/Aggressiveness* may occur when a negotiator abruptly blames or alleges some fault on the part of the other side for the parties' inability to reach an agreement. Depending upon the relationship between the parties or negotiators, this tactic may result in a further concession induced solely by a sense of guilt or an overriding desire to preserve the relationship. If the accusation of fault has merit, a concession based on that fact would not be irrational. On the other hand, if the accusation is unfounded, you should guard against capitulating on an important point for the mere sake of placating the accuser.

## § 10.07   BLUFFING

Bluffing involves making an assertion or taking a position that is seemingly fixed when that is not true. A negotiator might bluff about an offer or counteroffer, or in making a threat. The obvious drawback to bluffing is that the bluffer will lose credibility in the negotiation if the bluff is exposed.

A negotiator might extricate herself from a bluff by claiming that her seemingly unalterable assertion or position warrants modification or retraction based on new or unanticipated information learned during the negotiation, or in light of a misunderstanding about the facts or law. Similarly, the party who exposes a bluff might allow the bluffer to *Save Face* by acknowledging that the seemingly fixed assertion or position was based on incomplete or erroneous information.

## § 10.08   BR'ER RABBIT

This tactic is drawn from the story of Br'er Rabbit who, after being caught by a fox, repeatedly begs not to be thrown into the brier patch until, in the end, the fox did just that. The tactic might be employed against an opponent who, like the fox, tends to be overly suspicious and distrustful of the other side and has a desire to always gain the upper hand. The negotiator subtly suggests to the fox-like opponent that a particular clause or provision in an agreement might be detrimental to the negotiator's client but advantageous to the opponent's client (even though the matter would actually be of benefit to the former). The overzealous opponent then jumps to agree to this provision without recognizing its value to the other side.

## § 10.09   COALITION

Coalition is the unification of power of two or more parties to increase their leverage in negotiating with a third party. For example, coalition building is often used by consumer groups or in boycott situations. The theory of the tactic is that forming a coalition has the effect of placing more negotiating cards in the hands of its members than would be the case if each member acted independently.

Sometimes the coalition tactic may be effective when the party draws upon or forms an allegiance with a person who may be a key player in the event the negotiation fails. For example, in a domestic custody dispute, having the allegiance of a child psychologist who would testify in court that your client would be the best person to be the primary custodial parent may bring added leverage to a negotiation where custody is the main issue.

## § 10.10   COMPANY POLICY EXCUSE

Some negotiators attempt to justify their position by the glib assertion that "it's company policy." Usually, such a purported "policy" has nothing to do with the applicable law of remedies or other objective criteria upon which the dispute should be reasonably resolved. Thus, when confronted with a company policy excuse, you should probe the reasons underlying the policy and who has the power to change the policy, while steering the other side toward adopting a more objective standard as the basis for negotiating the dispute.

## § 10.11   DEADLINES

Real or perceived deadlines often exert pressure on the negotiating process. Deadlines may be unavoidable and inflexible (such as the statute of limitations), or they may be unilaterally imposed by one of the parties. Creating a deadline within which to conclude negotiations may be particularly effective if the consequence of not agreeing by the deadline is sufficiently serious or risky. In litigation, for example, one party may create a deadline by filing a motion, giving notice of a hearing, or by refusing to consent to a request by the other party to extend the time within which to meet a deadline imposed by the court. (*See* § 15.07).

In setting the length of a deadline, it is important to consider your purpose in exerting pressure on the negotiation process. For example, if your purpose is to induce immediate action, you should set a short deadline, whether an hour, day, or week. Generally, if a deadline exceeds ten days, it will lose its effectiveness for lack of demonstrating urgency. On the other hand, if you are not yet prepared to take immediate action or it is in your best interests to bide time to obtain additional information, you should consider a more flexible deadline of a few weeks or months.

Imposing a deadline is most effective when coupled with concrete sanctions for not meeting the deadline. As with the tactic of using a *Threat*, if you are not willing and prepared to follow through with concrete consequences for noncompliance with the deadline, the deadline tactic will be vacuous.

## § 10.12   DELAY

Delaying negotiations until the most advantageous time is a common tactic. Negotiators frequently delay in order to allow a change in position to occur for a more favorable result, or to time the negotiations with an event that puts maximum pressure on the other side to negotiate. Delay is also used to gain time for obtaining more information pertinent to the negotiation, or to preserve the status quo under circumstances where it is temporarily advantageous to preserve the existing situation of the parties.

## § 10.13   DODGING THE QUESTION THROUGH BLOCKING TECHNIQUES

Sharing information between the parties is integral to the negotiating process, particularly when a problem-solving strategy is adopted. On the other hand, negotiators invariably need to protect certain sensitive or damaging information from the other side and thus seek to evade questions that are directed to such information.

This evasion may occur through any one of five methods, sometimes called "blocking" techniques. The first method is to simply ignore the question and change the topic. The second method is to rule the question out of bounds and provide the other side with a reasonable reason for refusing to answer the question. A third technique is to answer the question by asking another question. Fourth, you might attempt to answer the question by answering another question. This might be done by (a) re-framing the initial question so that the answer will not be damaging, (b) simply answering another question as if it had been asked, or (c) by answering another question that has recently been asked. The fifth and final method is to over-answer or under-answer the question by responding broadly to a particular question or narrowly to a general question. (*See* § 14.11).

Most of these blocking techniques are, in essence, methods of distraction. The key to avoid succumbing to this distraction is to carefully *listen* to the answer and, when necessary, re-ask the question.

## § 10.14   DRAFT DOCUMENT OR SINGLE NEGOTIATING TEXT

Sometimes a negotiator will bring a draft of a potential agreement to the negotiation to set the agenda and serve as a starting point for discussions. This technique may also be effective in multiparty negotiations, particularly where one of the negotiators or a neutral third party submits the draft in advance of formal discussions to the other parties who are asked to submit suggested changes to the draft. The negotiating text is then revised and resubmitted to the other parties for further suggestions.

The process may involve the preparation of numerous drafts before the parties actually sit down together to hammer out a final accord. By the time they do, the single negotiating text is likely to reflect the most important interests of at least most of the parties and greatly reduce the number of issues that remain to be resolved. The process often creates a powerful momentum to reach a final agreement because the parties will usually be reluctant to unravel what the text has already accomplished, and thus they will be more inclined to make reasonable concessions to close a deal.

## § 10.15  ESCALATING DEMANDS

Under this tactic, the negotiator engages in a pattern of raising one of his demands for every concession made on another, or of reopening issues you thought had already been resolved. The effect is to decrease your overall concessions and to induce your side to quickly reach an agreement lest the negotiator escalate one or more of his demands again.

When faced with this tactic, it is usually best not to counter it by engaging in the same conduct. Rather, you should firmly bring the matter to the negotiator's attention and insist that the negotiation proceed in a more principled manner. If the tactic persists, you may be forced to temporarily suspend negotiations or end them altogether.

## § 10.16  EXCESSIVE INITIAL DEMANDS/OFFERS

As mentioned in §12.03[10], it is generally desirable for a negotiator to make a greater initial demand or offer than a more modest one, so long as some reasonable basis can be provided for the more hardened, initial demand. This approach often has the effect of reducing the other party's initial expectations. However, if the initial demand or offer is extreme in the sense of having absolutely no rational basis, the negotiator is likely to quickly lose credibility with the opposing side.

When confronted with a truly excessive initial demand, the best counter tactic is to expose it by probing the purported justification for the demand. Another approach is to directly point out the disingenuousness of the tactic and indicate that you do not intend to employ the same unproductive technique. Yet another alternative is to refuse to disclose your initial offer until the other side has presented a proposal that is justified with some reasonable rationale.

## § 10.17  FACE SAVING

Negotiations frequently reach an impasse not because the particular proposal is unacceptable, but because one party is psychologically unable to accept the proposal for fear of being perceived as having capitulated. Face saving is a technique for inducing a party to change a previously held position in a way that fulfills his needs for self-esteem. In essence, the tactic is designed to make the other party "feel" that he is really not backing down.

For example, if the other party's change of position involves a concession on a legal or factual point, you might acknowledge that absent the complete facts you also would have taken an initial position similar to that taken by the other side. Another approach is to ask questions about the information relied upon by the other side in support of its proposal, and then point out how that information is incomplete. Oftentimes good-natured humor is also an effective face saving technique.

## § 10.18   FAIT ACCOMPLI

"Fait accompli" is a French phrase meaning "an accomplished fact." As a negotiating tactic, it constitutes some action or inaction by a party to change the status quo and put the other side in a weaker position.

For example, insurance adjusters sometimes create a fait accompli by simply sending a check in an amount deemed appropriate for the injury to the injured party's attorney, thus putting the attorney and her client in the position of having to accept the check or continue with litigation. Filing a lawsuit or obtaining a restraining order during the pendency of negotiations creates the choice of either quickly settling the case or expending money in defense of the legal action. Or, in a breach of contract situation, if the breaching party simply discontinues the acts constituting the alleged breach and sells her business to another company, the injured party may be left with having to deal with a new party or with a remedy limited to damages for a past breach. In both instances, the breaching party has weakened the other side's bargaining leverage and economic justification for bringing suit.

## § 10.19   FALSE DEMANDS

During the exchange of information between the parties, a negotiator may discover a matter that is particularly important to the other side but of little or no value to his client. In an effort to take advantage of this knowledge, the negotiator may pretend that this matter is also highly important to his client and includes it as an integral part of his client's initial demand or offer. The negotiator then seeks to enhance his client's position by giving up that matter to the other side in exchange for extracting a more crucial concession. The best way to guard against such false demands is to carefully scrutinize the terms of your opponent's offers to determine whether they contain matters that are of only incidental benefit to your opponent.

## § 10.20   FALSE EMPHASIS

Under this tactic, the negotiator temporarily emphasizes matters of lesser importance to her client and de-emphasizes matters of greater importance to her client. The goal is to mislead the other side about the client's true preferences such that the other side is induced to give up the de-emphasized matter (which is actually the more important matter to the client). For example, by creating the appearance that the most desired object is less desirable, a buyer may be successful in minimizing the cost she would have to pay for the object. Conversely, a seller may be able to increase the price that she can obtain for an item by creating the appearance that the item is much more valuable to her than it is in reality.

## § 10.21   FALSE MULTIPLE CONCESSIONS

During a negotiation session, one party may make multiple, relatively small concessions in rapid sequence to induce the other party to reciprocate with multiple, larger concessions to the latter's detriment. For example, in contemplating a move from an initial demand of $800,000 to a new demand of $700,000, instead of making a single, principled concession of $100,000, the party might first move to $780,000, then move to $740,000 after some discussion, and then move to $700,000. Claiming three separate, unanswered concessions, the party then seeks to have the opposing party make a larger counteroffer than would have been produced in response to a single move from $800,000 to $700,000.

When faced with such consecutive concessions, you should focus on the aggregate movement involved rather than the mere number of concessions made. If you then choose to make a single counteroffer to the other party's consecutive concessions, you should make the same counteroffer you would have made had the aggregate movement been made in one concession.

## § 10.22   FALSE SECURITY

Negotiators sometimes attempt to play on the psychological tendency of people to value a commodity or matter more highly if it is perceived to be scarce or the opportunity of obtaining it is perceived to be limited.[2] Thus, a negotiator might seek to extract a better price for an item by simply claiming that its availability elsewhere at the price stated is nonexistent or rare.

One form of this ploy is to convert what otherwise would be a two-party negotiation over an item into a multiparty negotiation by inviting all prospective buyers to a single negotiation rather than dealing with each potential buyer separately. This auction-like atmosphere might even be set up in the face of each buyer's expectation that he would be the sole person meeting with the seller. The competitiveness induced by the bidding atmosphere may well allow the seller to obtain a higher price than that which could have been obtained by dealing with each potential buyer on an individual basis.

## § 10.23   FLOATING TRIAL BALLOONS AND BRACKETING

This tactic is frequently employed in politics. A politician leaks a particular proposal or contemplated action and waits to see the reaction of his opponent and the public before formally adopting the proposal or implementing the action. The same technique may be used in the negotiating process. The client or a member of his negotiating team privately leaks or "floats" controversial aspects of a potential agreement to test the reaction of the opposing party.

A variant on this tactic, sometimes called "bracketing," might be employed during an actual negotiation session. For example, the negotiator might say, "I know it would be too much for you to pay $50,000, but I also know that no one could get away with paying only $30,000." By presenting these high and low figures, the negotiator tests the opposing party's reaction to each figure to gauge a midpoint range for settlement. In this example, the negotiator may want to negotiate a price between $35,000 and $45,000 even though he knows that the other side desires to pay much less.

---

[2] This is sometimes referred to as "Brehm's theory of psychological reactance": "[l]abeling a resource as scarce may cause reactance . . . and produce more vigorous action to obtain the resource and more dissatisfaction with its unavailability." J. Pfeffer, *Power in Organizations* 83 (1981).

## § 10.24    GOOD GUY-BAD GUY ROUTINE/MUTT AND JEFF

The "good guy-bad guy" (or "Mutt and Jeff") routine is played by a team of two or more negotiators for the same side, one of whom adopts a seemingly reasonable and accommodating approach while the other takes a hard-nosed and intransigent approach. After the good guy heaps praise on the other party for his concessions and it appears that an agreement is close to being reached, the bad guy rejects the proposal as patently unacceptable, and the good guy, in turn, tries to persuade the other party that if only a few additional concessions would be made, the irrational partner may be persuaded to accept the agreement. As a variant on this routine, a single negotiator might play the good guy but insist that greater movement is necessary to satisfy his irrational client.

Law enforcement personnel frequently use the "good guy-bad guy" routine when they are interrogating a suspect. Although not usually described as a "negotiation," the "good guy" interrogator is in effect negotiating with the suspect for additional information (including the names of the other participants in the criminal behavior) in exchange for charging the suspect with a lesser criminal offense. The "bad guy" cop is holding out for more information before agreeing to a negotiated plea to a lesser criminal charge. The suspect often succumbs to the wishes of the "good guy" in order to mollify the "bad guy."

One useful test for determining whether the negotiators for the other side are playing good guy-bad guy, or whether they are genuinely in disagreement with one another, is to watch whether the reasonable negotiator ever assents to an aspect of an agreement without expressing the necessity of obtaining the approval of the unreasonable negotiator. If the reasonable negotiator always seeks the unreasonable negotiator's acquiescence, it is highly probable the game is underway.

When the tactic is employed, it is usually best to simply recognize it rather than openly expose it. If your accusation is wrong, the negotiation may be unnecessarily impaired. If you are right, the opposing negotiators may simply resort to other devious tactics. Thus, place your primary focus on obtaining the assent of the reasonable negotiator. Then, perhaps with the aid of the reasonable negotiator, direct your attention to persuading the unreasonable one.

## § 10.25    LACK OF AUTHORITY OR LIMITED AUTHORITY

A negotiator may claim that she lacks authority or has limited authority from her client for a number of reasons. First, the tactic may serve as the negotiator's "back door" by giving her an excuse to avoid making a decision in the face of a pushy adversary or to guard against making spontaneous or reactionary decisions. Second, the tactic provides an excuse for the negotiator to stall or temporarily suspend negotiations until there is time to consult with another negotiator or higher authority. Third, the tactic allows the negotiator to insulate the client from the heat of battle of the negotiating process so that a final decision may be made on cool-headed analysis rather than on pure emotion.

The intended effect of claiming lack of authority or limited authority, whether real or feigned, is to obtain psychological commitments from the other side when it is negotiating with complete authority, since most people tend to feel bound by tentative agreements they have reached. The negotiator without complete authority is then able to modify the tentative agreement based on new or unexpected demands from the client. When faced with this tactic, it is often useful to suggest that you also lack final authority over the matter. In this way, it is understood from the outset that any agreement is entirely tentative. If it becomes clear that claims of lack of authority or limited authority are making the negotiation unproductive, recess or suspend the negotiation until the other side obtains the requisite authority to substantively negotiate.

## § 10.26   LITTLE OL' COUNTRY LAWYER

Some negotiators deliberately adopt a style of seeming inexperience, disorganization, absent-mindedness, meekness, ineptness, or flattery to lure their unsuspecting adversaries into a false sense of security. They then extract valuable information and concessions from their opponents who have become unwittingly stupefied by their own sense of superiority and self-gratifying desire to accommodate the pathetic "little ol' country lawyer." The best antidote to this tactic is simply to recognize it and maintain a disciplined approach that sticks to your negotiation plan and insists upon the other side's principled participation in the negotiation process.

## § 10.27   LOCK-IN POSITIONS

A tactic particularly common to labor-management negotiations is to have a principal, such as a union president or company executive, give a publicized speech or press conference that "locks in" the party's position in such a way that negotiations cannot effectively proceed until the other side at least acknowledges the party's announced position as a starting point for discussions. For example, a union president might give a speech or call a press conference to proclaim that his membership "will never accept less than a 10% pay increase" to induce management to accept that position as a bottom-line for beginning negotiations. Of course, the representative or chief negotiator for management might also call a press conference and respond with the company's own assertion of a bottom-line.

To counter this tactic, a party's purported lock-in position might simply be ignored, or characterized by the other side as a mere "expectation," "goal," or "discussion point like any other." Alternatively, the party who employed the lock-in tactic might be told that, notwithstanding his public pronouncements, you intend to negotiate the dispute at the bargaining table, not in the press.

## § 10.28   LOW-BALLING

Low-balling is a tactic that takes advantage of the psychological tendency of many people to acquiesce to additional terms of an agreement once they have committed themselves to accepting the underlying transaction.[3] It is a form of *Nibbling*, designed to bait a party into deciding to purchase an item and then increasing the purchase price when it comes time to sign final papers.

As one example of this tactic, a car salesman will induce a person to decide to buy a car on what are represented to be particularly favorable terms. The prospective purchaser might even be permitted to try out the car for a few days so as to "hook" her on it. When the time comes to sign a final purchase contract, the salesman

---

[3] *See* Robert B. Cialdini, *Influence* 102–105 (1984).

claims that there was some mistake or that the manager won't approve the original deal and asks for more money. Since the buyer has become psychologically committed to the idea of owning the car, she may agree to pay the additional money. Of course, the antidote to this tactic is simply to protest the change in terms and threaten to walk away from the deal if the salesman insists on increasing the purchase price.

## § 10.29  MISSTATEMENT

When certain information is difficult to obtain from the other side, a negotiator might make a misstatement of fact to induce the other party to correct the fact and thereby reveal the information sought. For example, if a buyer is negotiating the purchase price of an item, he might say, "We understand that you sold the same machine to X for $35,000." The seller might then correct the misstatement, revealing that the actual sale to X was for $28,000. This may give the buyer leverage to negotiate a price for the same type of machine that is closer to $28,000 than $35,000. The obvious lesson from this tactic is that you must always maintain control over yourself in what you reveal to your adversary.

## § 10.30  NIBBLING

A variation on the *Lack of Authority or Limited Authority* tactic occurs when the negotiator holds herself out as having full authority from her client, but, after concluding the agreement, approaches the other side to sheepishly confess that she really didn't have "complete" authority and her dissatisfied client will only accept the agreement if just one more concession is made.

To counter this "nibbling" tactic, when confronted with a request for a post-agreement concession, you might indicate to your adversary that you are relieved because your own client may be dissatisfied and want to modify a term in the agreement that you had, perhaps too prematurely, agreed upon. If your opponent's post-agreement request is in good faith, she will usually agree to discuss your proposed modification in deference to reciprocity. On the other hand, if your opponent's response is to reject further discussions and to insist upon the terms of the initial agreement, you will know that you have successfully thwarted your adversary's disingenuous attempt at nibbling.

## § 10.31  OFF-THE-RECORD DISCUSSIONS

Negotiators sometimes find it useful to meet informally with one another, without their clients present, to engage in off-the-record discussions about the dispute. In this way, the negotiators are able "to lay their cards on the table" and freely explore options toward an agreement without making any firm commitments to one another. The tactic is particularly beneficial for exploratory discussions before negotiations begin, or to "separate the people from the problem" in circumstances where negotiations have broken down. This tactic is particularly useful in hotly contested and emotionally laden domestic negotiations.

## § 10.32 PERSONAL ATTACKS

Some hardball negotiators deliberately engage in a variety of verbal and nonverbal behavior to insult, belittle, disparage, or otherwise make the opposing party as uncomfortable as possible. The theory is to intimidate the opponent into submission. The best counter measure to this tactic is to tactfully "name the game" and insist that the negotiations proceed on the merits of the parties' respective proposals rather than on personalities.

## § 10.33 PLAYING DUMB

A variation on the *Abdication* and *Little Ol' Country Lawyer* tactics occurs when the negotiator "plays dumb" by persistently picking apart the other party's proposals but never makes a proposal of his own out of a feigned inability to come up with any solution. The tactic is designed to induce the opposition to prove that it can formulate a satisfactory settlement. When the negotiator plays dumb, repeatedly ask him what he wants. If he continues to refuse to make a proposal, indicate that you may have to terminate the negotiation unless he can be more forthcoming in making proposals.

## § 10.34 PRECONDITIONS OR CONDITIONAL PROPOSALS

Some negotiators condition their willingness to negotiate upon the satisfaction of a condition precedent (*e.g.*, "We won't negotiate until you do X."). The unilaterally imposed precondition is essentially presented as a non-negotiable issue or as a threshold concession that must be made by the other side. The precondition might be "procedural" in the sense of how the negotiation will be conducted, "substantive" in the sense of demanding that the other party agree to a particular term in the agreement, or a combination of both (*e.g.*, "We are willing to discuss issue X if agreement is first reached on issue Y.").

A precondition is effective if the demanding party has superior bargaining leverage over the other side on the condition being imposed. On the other hand, the danger of imposing a precondition is that the other side may view the tactic as coercive or tantamount to exacting an unfair concession. This may cause the other party to simply ignore the precondition, flatly reject it, or assert a counter precondition.

Closely akin to preconditions are conditional proposals. The latter are offers which are contingent upon receiving a concession on a specific point, resolving a specified issue first, or resolving all of the remaining issues in the negotiation. For example, X is offered for Y so long as the other party gives up Y, does Z, or W is resolved.

## § 10.35 PROBLEM SOLVING

Negotiators who adopt a problem-solving approach seek to focus on each party's needs or interests rather than on stated "positions." The people are separated from the problem, and solutions are explored for mutual gain based on objective criteria rather than the naked will of any one party.

In furtherance of this approach, problem-solving negotiators employ the following tactics: (1) they shun any temptation to engage in personal attacks or react irrationally to the other side; (2) they seek to diffuse anger, fear, and suspicion by listening, acknowledging the other party's points, and agreeing whenever possible; (3) they deflect hard-line positions by re-framing them in the form of problem-solving questions that explore the needs and reasons underlying the other party's positions and suggest alternative solutions; (4) they adopt the role of a mediator, trying to identify and satisfy the other side's unmet interests; and (5) instead of employing threats or force, they seek to educate the other party to the costs of not reaching an agreement, and reassure him that the goal of the negotiation is mutual satisfaction, not victory.[4] (*See also* Sec. 14.14).

## § 10.36  PUBLICITY

Efforts at using the media to exert pressure on the other side to negotiate or compromise are sometimes used in labor disputes, class actions, or other high-profile cases. Typical examples of these efforts include using press releases, granting newspaper or magazine interviews, and making public pronouncements over the TV or radio. ( *See also, Lock-in Positions*).

The extent to which a lawyer may make statements to the media is limited by ethical constraints. Rule 3.6 of the ABA Model Rules of Professional Conduct provides, in pertinent part:

(a) A lawyer who is participating or has participated in the investigation or litigation of a matter shall not make an extrajudicial statement that a reasonable person would expect to be disseminated by means of public communication if the lawyer knows or reasonably should know that it will have a substantial likelihood of materially prejudicing an adjudicative proceeding in the matter.

(b) Notwithstanding paragraph (a), a lawyer may state:

(1) the claim, offense or defense involved and, except when prohibited by law, the identity of the persons involved;

(2) information contained in a public record;

(3) that an investigation of a matter is in progress;

(4) the scheduling or result of any step in litigation;

(5) a request for assistance in obtaining evidence and information necessary thereto;

(6) a warning of danger concerning the behavior of a person involved, when there is reason to believe that there exists the likelihood of substantial harm to an individual or to the public interest . . .

. . . .

(c) Notwithstanding paragraph (a), a lawyer may make a statement that a reasonable lawyer would believe is required to protect a client from the substantial undue prejudicial effect of recent publicity not initiated by the

---

[4] *See* W. Ury, *Getting Past No* (1991); R. Fisher & W. Ury, *Getting to Yes* (1981).

lawyer or the lawyer's client. A statement made pursuant to this paragraph shall be limited to such information as is necessary to mitigate the recent adverse publicity.

(d) No lawyer associated in a firm or government agency with a lawyer subject to paragraph (a) shall make a statement prohibited by paragraph (a).

Lawyers wishing to achieve publicity for their clients without offending Rule 3.6 frequently include extensive details about their clients and the injuries they have suffered in the clients' complaints and answers. Because these pleadings are public records, the details are available to the press. Those lawyers who wish to avoid publicity for their clients should engage in early negotiations to stave off litigation and the creation of a "public record" available to the press.

## § 10.37  QUESTIONS TO FACILITATE AGREEMENTS

Skillful negotiators often use different forms of questions to facilitate an agreement. Examples of these different types of questions include the following:[5]

*(1) Questions to get the negotiation started*:

- What are the facts of the situation from your perspective?
- What do you consider to be the major issues?
- What are your primary interests and concerns?
- What proposals or solutions are you thinking about?

*(2) Questions to obtain specific information*:

- Who, what, which, when, where, why, how?
- What do you mean by . . . ?
- Would you explain that further?

*(3) Questions to invite clarification*:

- How will your proposal work?
- Who will do what, when, where, and how?
- How will this solve the problem?

*(4) Questions to reflect understanding*:

- Do you mean that . . . ?
- Do I understand you to be saying that . . . ?
- Am I correct in assuming that . . . ?

*(5) Questions to explore or suggest alternative solutions*:

- What would you think if we tried to . . . ?
- Is it possible to consider . . . ?
- Are there other ways to address that concern?
- What option do you think is better?

*(6) Questions to focus on the key issues*:

- What does all this lead to?
- Where do we go from here?

---

[5] *See also,* John M. Hayes, *The Fundamentals of Family Mediation* 185–186 (1994).

- How might we resolve the issue of . . . ?
- Why do you think we are blocked on this issue?

*(7) Questions to bring closure to and confirm the agreement*:

- So, as I understand it, have we agreed to . . . ?
- Can you think of anything we have left out in our agreement?

## § 10.38   QUESTIONING BY SOCRATIC METHOD

Some skillful negotiators adopt the "Socratic method" of asking a series of logical questions that are designed to expose the weaknesses in the opposing party's proposals and lead to a particular result. This approach often allows the negotiator to obtain a series of agreements about certain concepts or principles that should underlie a resolution of the dispute. The goal is to induce the other side to participate in the negotiator's reasoning process that leads to a particular result.

This tactic should not be viewed as unfair or illegitimate. If the parties exchange thoughtful questions and answers, they are more apt to understand each other's interests and objectives and develop a solution based on reason rather than naked desire. On the other hand, excessive use of this tactic may come across as patronizing.

## § 10.39   REVERSING POSITION

The tactic of reversing position may be as effective in breaking a deadlock as in solidifying one. Here, when faced with a stalemate, the negotiator abruptly declares that she has made too many concessions and can no longer live with what she has already offered. She then withdraws some of her concessions. This is intended to serve as a huge blow to the other party who has worked so hard to establish headway but now finds himself "back to square one." The tactic often results in either successfully reducing the other party's aspiration level so that progress resumes, or in solidifying the stalemate unless the negotiator who reversed position reaffirms her previous concessions and offers a new proposal.

## § 10.40   SALAMI

The "salami" tactic stems from the metaphor that if you want to eat the salami on the other person's plate, you should proceed one slice at a time. That is, it is usually more palatable for the other side to end up paying a larger sum or conceding on a greater number of matters if the issues are defined and addressed in smaller, bite-size portions. For example, it may be easier to justify a total settlement of $600,000 if it is comprised of separately negotiated amounts for past medical expenses, future medical expenses, past lost wages, reduction in earning capacity, past pain and suffering, future pain and suffering, and the like.

## § 10.41   SNOW JOB/ALLEGED EXPERTISE

In an attempt to gain psychological leverage, some negotiators seek to display their high level of expertise about the subject matter of the negotiation, or shower their adversaries with a highly detailed presentation of facts and figures to dominate and overwhelm the other side. If the other side is relatively unprepared, this factual "snow job" or display of expertise is effective in conveying the message that the negotiator is prepared to go to trial or take other alternative action if no agreement is reached.

When faced with this tactic, you should be careful to evaluate whether your opponent's professed expertise is real or illusory, and whether the detailed presentation is really substantive or irrelevant. Often times, slick and detailed presentations are cluttered with meaningless factual and legal minutiae in order to disguise a proposal's true weaknesses. Avoid being hurried into accepting your adversary's data and consider asking him to summarize his position without unnecessary resort to details. In this way, you will be able to keep your focus on the key components of the proposal to evaluate its overall acceptability.

## § 10.42   SPLITTING THE DIFFERENCE

Splitting the difference is probably the most common form of concluding an agreement in adversarial bargaining. For example, one party makes concessions down to $20,000, the other party concedes up to $10,000, and the parties settle on $15,000.

The appropriateness of splitting the difference depends largely on the reasonableness of the parties' respective opening offers and concession behavior. For example, if a reasonable settlement range is between $10,000 and $20,000, and X makes an opening offer of $90,000 and Y opens with $4,000, if X thereafter makes multiple concessions down to $30,000 and Y makes a single concession up to $10,000, it would be inappropriate for X to claim that the parties should split the difference at $20,000 because she has conceded $60,000 and Y has only conceded $6,000. The point is that splitting the difference only becomes reasonable after the negotiation process has effectively negated X's extreme initial demand. In addition, once X is at $30,000 and Y is at $10,000, if Y nevertheless proposes to split the difference at $20,000, Y should not allow X to disingenuously treat the $20,000 as a separate offer to split with $30,000 and arrive at an excessive final settlement of $25,000.

## § 10.43   SURPRISE

Regardless of how thorough you are in preparing for the negotiation, from time to time the unexpected occurs and you are suddenly confronted with either a welcome or unwelcome surprise. For example, during the course of negotiations, you may unexpectedly discover some damaging information against the other side or find out about an event or fact that undercuts your position.

If the surprise is welcome news, it is often better to gently use it as an additional tool to reinforce and advance your overall objectives rather than to dramatically spring it upon the other side in an effort to extract an immediate, extraordinary concession. This is because a dramatic and hasty use of the surprise may backfire and eliminate its utility if the other side is unable to save face and recoils by suspending or terminating negotiations. On the other hand, if the surprise is damaging to your side, delaying the negotiations is effective in fending off any short-term advantage that may be gained by the opposition. By buying time, you can usually regroup and analyze the situation to minimize the surprise or neutralize its immediate impact.

## § 10.44   TAKE-IT-OR-LEAVE-IT

A "take-it-or-leave-it" approach,[6] particularly if literally styled that way, often comes across as obnoxious and arrogant, and frequently results in indignant rejection. However, some negotiators who use this tactic genuinely don't intend to create that reaction, but insist upon making a single offer that they deem fair which the other side is simply free to accept or reject. This approach may be particularly effective if the offeror possesses considerable bargaining leverage over his opponent.

When faced with a take-it-or-leave-it offer, you might choose to ignore it, divert it by changing the subject, or try to counter it by pointing out what the offeror stands to lose if no agreement is reached. If the offeror refuses to budge, evaluate the offer dispassionately. After all, you should not automatically assume that a better result could be obtained through ritualistic, give-and-take bargaining.

Because the take-it-or-leave-it approach often results in instinctive rejection, it is usually best not to use it even if you possess far superior bargaining power over your adversary. The more power you have in a negotiation, the more you can afford to engage in its "process." Allowing the other party to participate in protracted bargaining usually has the benefit of leaving him more satisfied after a settlement is reached and more likely to stick by and implement the settlement. Perhaps most importantly, it provides you with a hedge against having misjudged the situation. After all, a settlement reached after protracted negotiations may turn out to be more favorable to you than the offer you had planned to have the other party summarily "take or leave."

## § 10.45   THREATS

A threat is vacuous unless it is credible. To be credible, (1) the threat must be understood; (2) the other side must be convinced that you definitely intend to carry out the threat and possess the capability of doing so without undue cost to your client; and (3) the other side must believe that it would be less costly to comply with your demands than to suffer the consequences that would follow if you carried out the threat. Threats tend to be most effective (a) when styled without hostility but as an unfortunate and unavoidable necessity, (b) when coupled with a deadline and some visible preparatory actions taken by your client to carry out the threat, and (c) when made without anticipation by the other side.

Threats can be countered in a variety of ways. First, you can respond with a threat of your own, but you should recognize that this tactic might cause the negotiation to degenerate into an escalating spiral of additional threats. Second, you can simply ignore the threat. Third, you can act as if the threat were unauthorized or made in the heat of passion. Fourth, you can characterize the threat as something else, such as a purely hypothetical course of action. Fifth, you can attempt to refute the other side's perception of the cost your client will incur if the threat is carried

---

[6] The approach is sometimes called "Boulwarism," named after Lemuel R. Boulware, a vice-president of General Electric, who used the tactic in connection with labor negotiations by bypassing GE's union representatives to make a "first, fair, firm, and final" offer directly to the company's workers. The National Labor Relations Board ultimately declared the tactic an "unfair labor practice" because it undermined the union as a representative of workers in the collective bargaining process. General Electric Co and IUE, 150 N.L.R.B. 192 (1964), aff'd NLRB v. General Electric Co., 418 F.2d 736 (1969).

out, or try to convince the other side that it has underestimated its own costs if the threat is carried out. Finally, you can simply dare the other side to carry out the threat to demonstrate its lack of meaning to your client. Of course, the best choice among these options will depend upon the particular circumstances.

## § 10.46 TIMING

Negotiators routinely attempt to conduct or conclude negotiations at times that are most advantageous to their clients. A particular event or particular time pressures placed upon the parties may trigger the most opportune timing. Negotiating when the other party is in the weakest position or your client is in the strongest position will enhance your prospects for a favorable settlement.

Jockeying for the best time to negotiate involves using tactics such as *Asymmetrical Time Pressure, Deadlines, Delay*, or taking preemptive action to create conditions through a *Fait Accompli*. Generally, if a party is operating under a particular time constraint, he should try to withhold that fact from his opponent. If this is not practical, the party may have to communicate a deadline within which negotiations must be completed in order to deprive his adversary of using this time pressure as leverage.

Finally, in a particular case, a negotiator might even consider the best day of the week or time of day to negotiate. If a negotiator is able to pick a particular day or time of day to negotiate that places a special time pressure upon the other side, he may enhance his prospects for obtaining a more favorable settlement.

## § 10.47 TWO AGAINST ONE

Most negotiations are conducted on a one-on-one basis with a single individual representing each side. Sometimes, however, a party may create a negotiating team of two or more representatives to "take on" a single negotiator for the other side. This might be done to permit the team to employ a *Good Guy-Bad Guy Routine* or otherwise to exert psychological pressure upon the opponent. When this occurs, the single negotiator might simply refuse to negotiate with more than one counterpart, or bring in one or more additional negotiators on behalf of her side to counterbalance the opposing party's team.

## § 10.48 WALKOUT

Walking out in the middle of a negotiation may appear somewhat dramatic and adolescent, but if done in a genuine and non-hostile manner it may be effective in breaking a deadlock. A walkout is often accompanied by some ultimatum about what will be required to resume negotiations. It is usually best to word such an ultimatum with sufficient ambiguity so that you have the option of walking back into the negotiation if necessary. If the other party is truly committed to on-going negotiations, he will realize that he has simply pushed matters too far and the negotiation may resume after a short recess or at a later time.

## § 10.49   WORD-SMITHING

Negotiators are word smiths. That is, they often couch what they say in language that is designed to subtly signal their intentions or concerns. Thus, you must be sensitive to the verbal cues given by your counterpart's expressions. The following are just a sampling of what certain expressions, depending upon the context, might really mean:

- *Our initial demand is $125,000* = We are prepared to make a lower offer.
- *Our counteroffer is $25,000 . . . If you have any further information, we will of course consider it* = We need further factual justification to increase our offer.
- *I have no authority to accept less than $85,000 at this time* = I probably can get authority to accept less that $85,000.
- *My client is not inclined to . . .* = My client doesn't like the idea but might be persuaded otherwise.
- *For the sake of discussion, what would you think about a value of this case in the range of $75,000 to $85,000?* = Is your resistance point $80,000? Mine might be. Let's settle for $80,000.
- *Our final offer is to pay no more than $75,000* = Your resistance point [in the preceding example] is really $75,000, so that's going to be my bottom line.
- *Well, our final counteroffer is that we will accept no less than $77,500* = You might have been correct that our resistance point was $75,000, but you will settle the case for $2,500 more rather than go to the expense of a trial.

## § 10.50   DEALING WITH DISINGENUOUS OR INAPPROPRIATE TACTICS OR TECHNIQUES

A tactic or technique may be inappropriate to a negotiation either because it is disingenuous (and perhaps even unethical), or because you believe it otherwise would be counterproductive in the particular circumstances. Generally, there are four ways you can deal with such tactics or techniques. However, no one method is invariably better than the other, and thus you should simply choose the method (or combination of methods) you think best in the particular situation.

*[a] Rule the tactic or technique out of bounds before negotiations start or when it arises during the negotiation*

Ruling the tactic or technique out of bounds before negotiations start may be appropriate if your counterpart has already employed the tactic or technique before formal negotiations begin or you are certain the tactic or technique will be employed when negotiations begin. On the other hand, this method may come across as condescending or patronizing if used when your counterpart never had any intention in the first place of employing the tactic or technique you want to foreclose. Thus, if you are unsure whether the tactic or technique will be used, it is better to rule it out of bounds at the time it first arises during actual negotiations rather than before they start.

Either way, it is important to be *tactful* in ruling a tactic or technique out of bounds. The goal is to foreclose the tactic or technique without unnecessarily foreclosing negotiations by disparaging or insulting your counterpart. For example, compare (untactful negotiator):

— *Listen, John, we're not interested in any "Getting to Yes by Getting Past No" problem-solving type of stuff here-*

*. . . This case is about bucks, only bucks, and nothing but bucks . . . So, the only thing I'm interested in knowing is where your bucks stop.*

— *George, let me tell you at the outset that if you guys truly want to negotiate this contract, I'm not going to tolerate any "lock-in" tactics in the press . . . If you guys want to do that, you and I might just as well get in front of the cameras now and lock horns . . .*

with (tactful negotiator):

— *John, I may be wrong, but I really don't think we can "problem solve" this case . . . For better or worse, my client's only interest is the amount of money she might receive.*[7]

— *George, let me share with you one concern I have before next week's meeting. In these types of cases, I'm always concerned that the press might undermine a deal before we even have a chance to sit down and talk. I can prevent that on my end. Can you give me any help on that from your end?*

### [b] Deflect the tactic or technique by ignoring it

Deflecting a tactic or technique by ignoring it does not mean that you act as if you are naively unaware of it. For example, you might show your awareness of the tactic through subtle body language expressing your irritation, or by making some casual remark indicating that you know the tactic or technique is being employed (see also *[c]* below). Deflecting a tactic or technique by ignoring it simply means that you proceed with the negotiation as if the tactic or technique were not being used. This approach essentially shows the other side that you are not interested in playing his or her game, and that you intend to proceed with your own principled approach to the negotiation.

### [c] Expressly expose the tactic or technique

Expressly exposing the tactic or technique involves directly mentioning it to your counterpart when it arises during the negotiation, hoping this will be enough to cause him to abandon the tactic. This approach differs from *[a]* above only in that when you expose the tactic you might not say anything about your unwillingness to proceed with the negotiation if the tactic continues to be used. Again, when expressly exposing the tactic or technique, try to be tactful so that your counterpart will not be unnecessarily embarrassed or lose face. For example, if your counterpart persists in *Dodging the Question* through one or more "blocking techniques,"

---

[7] A tactful problem solver might respond, "I understand. I would just like to explore for a minute the possibility that each side could benefit by . . . "

it may be more effective to explain why a candid answer to your question is important to the negotiation rather than to confront your counterpart with, "Why do you always answer my question with a question or with some answer to a question I never asked?"

## [d] Respond to the tactic or technique in kind

If you counter a disingenuous tactic or technique by employing the same or similar tactic or technique, the negotiation may rapidly result in deadlock. On the other hand, retaliating in this way may be enough to cause your counterpart to abandon the unproductive behavior. For example, when faced with a *Good Guy-Bad Guy Routine* or a *Two Against One* tactic, you might indicate to your adversaries that you may need to temporarily suspend the negotiation until another colleague can join you in continuing discussions. Similarly, as mentioned previously, a sudden claim of *Lack of Authority or Limited Authority* by your counterpart might be countered with a suggestion that you too may need to confer further with your client before a final agreement can be reached.

# Chapter 11

# VALUING CASES FOR NEGOTIATION AND SETTLEMENT

## SYNOPSIS

## § 11.01  INTRODUCTION

The vast majority of cases in the litigation context involves a dispute over money and therefore is usually negotiated through adversarial bargaining. In these negotiations, because the ultimate decision to settle rests with your client, you will often be asked to advise whether it would be in your client's best interests to settle the case or take it to trial. This requires valuing the case in terms of its likely outcome at trial as compared with the outcome of accepting the opposing party's final settlement offer. It also involves taking into account how willing your client is to gamble on the outcome of a trial versus accepting a settlement and your client's other motivations affecting the choice between trial and settlement. This Chapter discusses a variety of analyses that you might draw upon in valuing a case for negotiation and settlement. In addition, these analyses may be drawn upon to help formulate the offers and concessions that your client might make during adversarial negotiations, which is discussed more fully in Chapter 12.

## § 11.02  TARGET AND RESISTANCE POINTS

As introduced in § 8.02, in adversarial bargaining, the parties prepare for negotiation by establishing "target" and "resistance" points. From the Plaintiff's perspective, his "target point" will be the highest amount of money he realistically believes he could obtain if everything in the case went his way. From the Defendant's perspective, her "target point" will be the lowest amount of money she realistically believes she would have to pay if everything in the case went her way. The Plaintiff's "resistance point" will be the lowest amount of money he will accept in settlement; and if he does not receive at least that sum, he will take his chances at trial. On the other hand, the Defendant's "resistance point" will be the highest amount of money she is willing to pay to settle the case; and if the Plaintiff insists on a settlement that is greater than that amount, she will take her chances at trial.

Target points should not be confused with opening offers made in negotiations. The Plaintiff will usually make an opening offer to settle the case for an amount that is greater than his target point, and the Defendant will make an opening offer for an amount that is lower than her target point. Each party will thereafter make concessions (downwards for the Plaintiff and upwards for the Defendant) to propose settlement amounts that approach their respective target points. Usually, further concessions will be made such that the Plaintiff will end up offering to settle for an amount below his target point and the Defendant will end up offering to settle for an amount above her target point. However, in no event will the Plaintiff settle for an amount that is less than his resistance point, nor will the Defendant settle for an amount that is greater than her resistance point. The significance of the parties' resistance points is that a settlement will occur only if they overlap, where the minimum amount that the Plaintiff will accept is less than or equal to the maximum amount that the Defendant will pay.

For example, assume that the Plaintiff sets his target point at $70,000, resistance point at $30,000, and plans to make an opening offer of $90,000. The Defendant sets her target point at $20,000, resistance point at $50,000, and plans to make an opening offer of $10,000. As shown in the chart below, Plaintiff's "settlement range" thus falls between $70,000 and $30,000, and Defendant's "settlement range" falls between $20,000 and $50,000. Plaintiff will gradually make concessions downward from his opening offer of $90,000, but never below his resistance point of $30,000; and Defendant will gradually make concessions upward from her opening offer of $10,000, but never above her resistance point of $50,000. The amount overlapping the parties' resistance points ($50,000 to $30,000), constitutes the anticipated "settlement zone" — the range within which the parties are most likely to reach final agreement. If there is no overlap between the parties' resistance points, no settlement can be achieved unless one or both of the parties revise their resistance points to expand the settlement zone.

The foregoing example may be illustrated as follows:

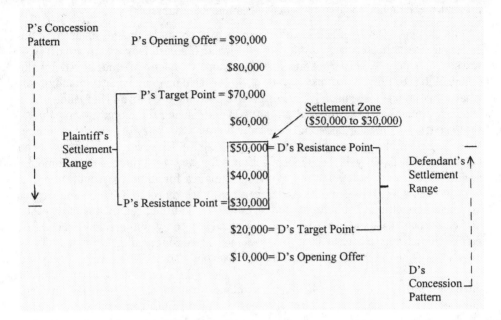

In light of the foregoing, in advising your client about settlement and in preparing for adversarial bargaining, you must be in a position to recommend a "settlement range" represented by a resistance point and target point. Ideally, and from a purely *economic* standpoint, when the only alternative to settling the case is going to trial, an accurate resistance point for the Plaintiff would be an amount that is less than what a jury would award; and an accurate resistance point for the Defendant would be an amount that is greater than what a jury would award. Thus, you must have some analytical method to determine an appropriate resistance point that your client might adopt in connection with negotiations in the litigation context. Once this "bottom line" is established, the goal of bargaining will be to settle the case in an amount that is better than one's resistance point and as close as possible to one's target point.

## § 11.03   INTUITIVE "CASE WORTH" ANALYSIS

To advise a client about an appropriate resistance point, many lawyers engage in an essentially intuitive analysis of "what the case is worth" in terms of the net recovery to the client if the case were tried. This analysis is "intuitive" in the sense that it is largely based on the lawyer's experience and best judgment. It essentially involves predicting what a likely jury verdict would be in light of all the circumstances of the case, and then adjusting that verdict expectancy downward (for plaintiffs) or upwards (for defendants) by the amount that it is likely to cost the client to litigate the case. The resulting figure may serve as the client's resistance point. In making this analysis, lawyers typically consider (1) the cause of action that would be brought and the elements of proof and damages that the substantive law provides for that cause of action; (2) the relative strength of the evidence in support of and in opposition to the client's contentions about liability and damages; (3) the amount of money that could be reasonably argued to a jury in light of the foregoing factors and jury verdicts in similar cases; and (4) the cost of gathering and presenting the evidence in a persuasive manner to a jury.[1]

The particular cause of action and elements of proof and damages involved in the case will affect the accuracy of determining what the case is worth in a variety of ways. For example, in a contract dispute where damages are measured by the financial loss to the plaintiff as a result of the breach, or in a property damage suit where the damages are usually the difference between the fair market value of the property immediately before and after the event causing the damage, the value of the case from a jury-verdict standpoint may be relatively easy to forecast assuming that the essential facts and liability are not in dispute. However, even if there is no question about liability, if the cause of action is for personal injury in an automobile accident case, or for defamation involving damages for injury to reputation and punitive damages, the elements of damage are much more amorphous and cannot be calculated with any real degree of certainty. In addition, regardless of whether the case involves damages that are objectively or only subjectively calculable, determining what the case is worth becomes increasingly difficult if liability is questionable or the facts relating to damages are in dispute. Moreover, forecasting the most likely result at trial may be even more difficult if the burden of proof involves "clear, cogent, and convincing evidence" rather than the usual "preponderance of the evidence" standard, the case involves multiple issues with shifting burdens of persuasion and production, or existing law is unclear about whether liability may be imposed under the particular facts of the case.

Similarly, trying to determine what a case is worth is complicated by the quantum and quality of the evidence available in the case. For example, factors such as the availability of corroborating witnesses and the extent of their credibility, whether one or both parties have "jury appeal," and whether the particular facts of the case would cause a jury to be more sympathetic to one side or the other all have a bearing on the value of the case but are not capable of any precise calculation. Similarly, the cost of finding and preparing expert witnesses in a difficult case is hard to calculate.

Nevertheless, under an intuitive "case worth" analysis, a lawyer will take into account all of these factors, notwithstanding their uncertainties, to arrive at a "best judgment" about what a jury would do if the case were tried. In this connection, particularly if the damages are amorphous, some lawyers consult sources on prior verdicts in similar cases such as the *Personal Injury Valuation Handbooks* (Jury Verdict Research, Inc., Cleveland Ohio), *The National Jury Verdict Review and Analysis* (Jury Verdict Review Publications, Inc. Newark, New Jersey), the *JVR Case Evaluation Software for the Evaluation of Personal Injury Cases* (Jury Verdict Research, Inc., Solon, Ohio), the *ATLA Law Reporter* (Association of Trial Lawyers of America, Washington, D.C.), or local bar publications that report jury verdicts in the particular jurisdiction to estimate the value of the case at hand. In addition, lawyers frequently confer with other experienced trial lawyers to solicit their views about what a jury might award in the particular circumstances, even though, when consulted about the same facts, highly experienced lawyers special-

---

[1] Some lawyers also consider the relative experience and trial skills of opposing counsel as a factor that may affect the value of the case. However, unless opposing counsel is particularly inexperienced, this factor is usually less important than some lawyers might prefer to think. In any event, when negotiations are conducted prior to the filing of a lawsuit, and the negotiator for the other side is not the person who will represent the opposing party in the event suit is brought, the factor is irrelevant because the opposing litigator is unknown.

izing in litigating the same type of case will often have wide differences of opinion about what a jury would do.[2]

After the value of the case is estimated from the standpoint of a most likely jury verdict, the lawyer will estimate the costs to the client of achieving that verdict (*i.e.*, litigation expenses, and lawyer's fees if based on an hourly rate) that the law in the particular jurisdiction will not shift to the opposing party as taxable court costs in the event of a favorable judgment. These expenses will then be subtracted (for plaintiffs) from the estimated jury verdict, or added (for defendants) to the estimated jury verdict. After consultation with the client, the resulting figure may become the client's resistance point, and the target point is then set at a higher figure (for plaintiffs) or a lower figure (for defendants) based on an estimate of the *best possible* verdict that might be obtained if everything in the case went the client's way.

## § 11.04　RULE-OF-THUMB VALUATION

In personal injury cases, some lawyers and insurance adjusters consider certain crude "rules of thumb" as a starting point in valuing a case. The most common of these is to estimate the settlement value of the case by multiplying the "special damages" (*i.e.*, the gross amount[3] of the medical bills and other expenses incurred as a result of the accident) by a factor of three. For example, if the Plaintiff's gross doctors' bills are $4,500 and drug expenses are $500, $5,000 × 3 yields a potential settlement figure of $15,000. Although lost wages are part of special damages, insurance adjusters normally do not triple the lost wages, but instead add them after the multiplier is applied to the medical bills and other expenses. Thus, if the Plaintiff also has lost wages in the gross amount (*i.e.*, before taxes and other deductions and regardless of the use of sick leave or vacation time) of $3,000, the final settlement estimate would be $18,000 ($15,000 ± $3,000).

This crude calculus is most frequently considered when liability is undisputed and the Plaintiff has not suffered any extraordinary pain or significant permanent injury. If the pain and suffering is relatively severe or permanent injury exists, the multiplier applied to the special damages might be increased to five, ten, or more. Generally, however, this multiplier, "rule-of-thumb" approach is only considered in minor personal injury cases.

---

[2] *See, e.g.,* Gerald R. Williams, *Legal Negotiation and Settlement* 5–6 (1983) (widely divergent settlement results were reached by 20 pairs of lawyers, all of whom practiced in the same community and were given information about the same case); D. Rosenthal, *Lawyer and Client: Who's in Charge?* 202–207 (1974) (widely divergent results reached by a panel of two plaintiffs' lawyers, two insurance adjusters, and one attorney who handled both plaintiffs' and defendants' cases, when each was asked to independently evaluate cases presented in the study); R. Haydock, *Negotiation Practice*, § 2.3 (1984) (30 experienced personal injury lawyers who were asked to evaluate a simulated personal injury case came up with widely divergent valuations).

[3] This is the total of the medical and other expenses, regardless of whether the plaintiff has been or will be reimbursed for them from his private health insurance carrier or from some other independent source.

## § 11.05   COMPUTER-GENERATED VALUATION

Today, most liability insurance companies utilize a computer software program to aid in the valuation of bodily injury claims.[4] The most widely used program is called "Colossus," although there are other programs.[5] These programs, which contain closely-held proprietary information by their users, aim primarily to compute the general, non-economic damages of a personal injury claim. Adjusters using such a program typically rely upon its dollar valuation of the case in establishing a resistance-point range for settlement.

In the case of Colossus, in particular, the focus of valuation is on general damages, such as pain and suffering, the effects of permanent impairment, and the impact upon the claimant's lifestyle, to which the adjuster then adds objectively verifiable special damages such as medical bills and lost wages to make a final calculation of proposed compensation. Four steps are utilized to establish a Colossus valuation.

First, the particular insurance company establishes, from its claims' experience, specific monetary values (or ranges of value) for different types and severities of injury. Second, the insurance adjuster enters into the Colossus program the claimant's age, where the injury occurred, and all diagnosed and accident-related injuries. Third, through a series of "interactive questions," the adjuster enters into the program additional data about treatment, prognosis, pre-existing conditions, injury symptoms, duration of injury, subjective complaints, impairment of activities, and the like. Fourth, based on these entries and the monetary values ascribed for different types and severities of injuries as initially established by the insurance carrier, Colossus calculates a recommended range of value for the injured claimant's general-damages claim.

Colossus evaluates approximately 600 injuries and some 10,000 factors. The Colossus valuation depends entirely upon the specific entries made by the adjuster into the program; and typically, the claimant's medical records are the only source of information that adjusters are permitted to enter into Colossus, other than information from their own personal observations of the claimant. Thus, it is essential that the claimant's attorney not merely submit to the adjuster all medical records, but also obtain and submit additional *medical documentation* that specifically addresses the factors considered by Colossus.[6]

As examples only, additional medical-report documentation might be needed for:

- The location and severity of ancillary injuries, such as bruising, headaches, and the like;
- Specific *diagnoses* for *each* subjective or objective medical finding;
- Specific "listings" of the injured person's "subjective" complaints;

---

[4] *See generally* Bonnet, Dawn R., *The Use of Colossus to Measure the General Damages of a Personal Injury Claim Demonstrates Good Faith Claims Handling*, 53 Clev. St. L. Rev. 107 (2005–2006); "Colossus" http://www.csc.com/industries/insurance/mds/mds221/408.shtml (Apr. 12, 2007); *see* Steele, Jeanine, "The Truth about Colossus: Are you just a Magnetic Image?" http://settlementcentral.com/page0405.htm (Apr. 13, 2007); Frey, Joe, "Putting a Price on Auto Injuries: How software called Colossus evaluates your pain," June 26, 2000; http://www.Badfaithinsurance.com/PC/0023a.htm (Apr. 14, 2007).

[5] *E.g.*, "Claims Outcome Advisor;" "Injury Claims Evaluation;" and "InjuryIQ."

[6] As a starting point for understanding the factors, see www.colossusbooks.com.

- Separate diagnoses and prognoses for *each* injured area;
- A permanent impairment rating under the latest edition of the AMA Guidelines to the Evaluation of Permanent Impairment;
- Specific details about the need for, type, and extent of, future treatment;
- Specific documentation of the injured person's activities or performance while in pain or impaired;
- Who referred the injured person to another health-care provider and why;
- The need, nature of, and duration of use for medical aids, such as walkers, crutches, cervical collars, and the like;
- Specific reasons for gaps in treatment;
- Detailed explanations for loss of enjoyment of life;
- Detailed explanations for inability to work;
- Specifics about any pre-existing condition and how the instant injury aggravated that condition;
- Specific details about all pain, depression, and/or anxiety; and
- Specific details about the need for, frequency, and duration of, prescribed medications.[7]

In essence, when the claimant's attorney in a personal injury case is dealing with a claims adjuster who is valuing the case based largely on a software program like Colossus, the contents of a Settlement Brochure (*see* §§ 13.05–13.06) must provide the adjuster with all pertinent information that will allow the adjuster to "enter" all appropriate data into the computer program. This means that the claimant attorney's "Summary" of "Medical Treatment," "Lost Earnings," "Pain and Suffering and Permanent Injury" (*see* § 13.05[3]–[5]) must be fully and specifically documented by official medical records or additional documentation obtained from relevant health-care providers.

For the attorney hired by an insurance carrier that utilizes a computerized program like Colossus, effective representation in valuing a case based on that program will require an evaluation as to whether all of the relevant factors affecting the injured party's damages have been properly accounted for by the entries made into the program. Without such an evaluation, the Colossus valuation will be misleading at best and may result in a jury verdict in an amount far in excess of the Colossus valuation for the simple reason that factors introduced into evidence at trial were not "entered into" the computer program.

In sum, the use of computer software programs by insurance companies in estimating the value of amorphous damages like pain and suffering and permanent impairment is becoming routine. The effort to provide more "objectivity" to the assessment of general damages may, however, be fraught with gross miscalculation because computerized estimates are only as good as the data entered into the program. If the initial ranges of value plugged into the program for particular injuries and factors are flawed, or if the adjuster "enters" incomplete data into the program, the resulting valuation will be useless.

Moreover, no computer program can fully account for the often quintessential "personal" factors and dynamics that govern a jury's decision about the amount of general damages — *e.g.*, the "jury appeal" of the claimant, the circumstances surrounding liability and injury, the credibility of witnesses, and the like. Thus, even though an adjuster may be bound by a general "policy" of the insurance

---

[7] *See* 41 Trial, No. 4 (April 2005).

carrier to adhere to the computerized valuation, a lawyer hired by the carrier to represent the defendant (and the lawyer for the claimant) should always bear in mind the inherent limitations on the utility of any computerized valuation. This means, at bottom, that, from the lawyers' perspective in terms of advising the client about valuation, the results of a computerized valuation should only be considered as an "aid" to valuation, rather than as an unyielding resistance point.

## § 11.06    TRADITIONAL ECONOMIC ANALYSIS

The traditional economic analysis of valuing cases for settlement involves computing an "expected outcome" by multiplying the gross outcome by the probability that it will occur, and then adjusting for "transaction costs" that would be incurred in obtaining that outcome. Assuming you represent the Plaintiff, this analysis consists of four calculations:

(1) First, an average verdict expectancy is estimated assuming that the Plaintiff client will prevail on liability. For example, if a reasonable verdict range for the particular kind of case is $35,000 to $45,000, the average verdict expectancy would be $40,000.

(2) Second, the $40,000 average verdict expectancy is adjusted by the probability (expressed as a percentage) that the Plaintiff will be successful in actually obtaining that amount. This results in an "*expected* outcome" for your client. For example, if you estimate that there is a 50% chance on the law and the facts that your client will win $40,000, the "expected outcome" becomes $20,000. This outcome, under probability theory, is "expected" in the sense that if the case were tried 100 times, approximately 50 trials would result in a verdict for your client and 50 would result in a verdict for the defendant; and the average recovery would be 50 Plaintiff's victories multiplied by $40,000 per victory or $2,000,000, plus 50 losses multiplied by $0 per loss, divided by 100 cases for an average recovery of $20,000. (When the analysis is conducted for the Defendant, in *theory*[8] she might use the same average verdict expectancy of $40,000 but will adjust it by her own estimate of the probability that the Plaintiff will be successful in obtaining that amount).

(3) Third, an estimate is made of all non-shiftable litigation expenses and hourly lawyer's fees that your client will incur if the case goes to trial, and these costs and hourly fees are also deducted from the average verdict expectancy. Thus, if your client is expected to incur a total of $4,000 in litigation expenses and hourly lawyer fees combined, the bottom-line settlement value of the case becomes $16,000. (When the analysis is conducted for the Defendant, the expenses and fees are added.)

(4) Fourth, the time value of money is sometimes considered because an amount received now is worth more than the same amount received much later. If your client is not expected to obtain a verdict for a number of years, and the investment yield on a prudent investment is currently X% per year, the amount of money received in a year is worth about X% less than if received now. Thus, for the Plaintiff, this time value of money would also be applied to adjust the $16,000 depending upon how much time is likely to transpire from the point an offer of settlement is made until a judgment would be obtained at a trial. The resulting

---

[8] Needless to say, the Defendant's estimate of the average verdict expectancy for the case may be quite different than the Plaintiff's estimate, and disputes about this matter exist in the vast majority of cases.

figure may serve as your client's resistance point.

Setting aside a calculation for the time value of money, the basic formula for establishing the Plaintiff's and Defendant's resistance points may be expressed as follows:

| P's Resistance Point | = Average Verdict Expectancy | × P's % Estimate of P's Probability of Winning at Trial | – P's Cost of Going to Trial |
|---|---|---|---|
| or: | (AVE | × PPW) | – PC |
| D's Resistance Point | = Average Verdict Expectancy | × D's % Estimate of P's Probability of Winning at Trial | + D's Cost of Going to Trial |
| or | (AVE | × PPW) | + DC |

Theoretically, a settlement will occur only if Plaintiff's Resistance Point ≤ Defendant's Resistance Point.[9]

Taking the example above, Plaintiff's resistance point of $16,000 was calculated based on $40,000 (the Average Verdict Expectancy) × .50 (P's % Estimate of P's Probability of Winning at Trial) = $20,000 (P's expected outcome) – $4,000 (P's Cost of Going to Trial). Assume that the Defendant calculates her resistance point as follows: $40,000 (the Average Verdict Expectancy) × .40 (D's % Estimate of P's Probability of Winning at Trial) = $16,000 (D's expected outcome) + $5,000 (D's Cost of Going to Trial) = resistance point of $21,000. Since Plaintiff's resistance point of $16,000 is less than Defendant's resistance point of $21,000, a settlement would theoretically occur within the $5,000 zone of overlap.[10]

In the parlance of management science, the resistance-point calculation for the Plaintiff or Defendant may be expressed in the form of a "decision-tree" analysis commonly used in business and public-policy decision-making.[11] To illustrate, assume that in the example above the Defendant ultimately makes a settlement offer of $20,500. In deciding whether to accept this offer, Plaintiff's decision tree might look like the following:

---

[9] Expressed another way, a settlement will occur only if the Average Verdict Expectancy × P's % Estimate of P's Probability of Winning at Trial (P's expected outcome) (the Average Verdict Expectancy × D's % Estimate of P's Probability of Winning at Trial (D's expected outcome) ≥ P's Cost of Going to Trial ± D's Cost of Going to Trial.

[10] Under the formula given in the preceding note, a settlement will theoretically occur because Plaintiff's expected outcome of $20,000 ($40,000 × .50) minus Defendant's expected outcome of $16,000 ($40,000 × .40) amounts to $4,000, which is less than the sum of the costs of going to trial for the two sides of $9,000 ($4,000 for Plaintiff + $5,000 for Defendant).

[11] See David P. Hoffer, *Decision Analysis as a Mediator's Tool*, 1 Harv. Negotiation L. Rev. 113 (1996). *See generally*, H. Raiffa, *Decision Analysis: Introductory Lectures on Choices Under Uncertainty* (1968).

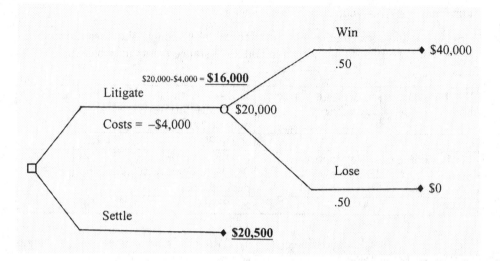

This tree is organized chronologically from left to right. The □ symbol is the "decision node," denoting the point at which the decision-maker must choose between two or more options. The O symbol is the "chance node," denoting the point where the decision maker is faced with an event over which he has no control and to which a probability is assigned that reflects the most likely result of the event. The ◇ symbol is the "terminal node," which denotes the result of an option or particular event.

Here, Plaintiff has two choices — litigate or settle — as shown by the branches stemming from the decision node, □. If Plaintiff accepts Defendant's settlement offer, Plaintiff will receive $20,500 as shown next to the terminal node, ◇, at the end of the branch representing the settlement option. If Plaintiff chooses the litigation option, he is expected to incur $4,000 in non-shiftable trial costs as shown under the branch denominated "Litigate."

The expected outcome of a trial, represented by the "Win" and "Lose" branches stemming from the chance node, O, is calculated with reference to the probabilities of achieving that outcome. That is, Plaintiff estimates he has a 50% (.50) chance of winning an average jury verdict expectancy for the type of case of $40,000, and therefore a 50% (.50) chance of getting $0.[12] The expected outcome of $20,000 shown to the right of the chance node, O, is calculated by: (1) multiplying the 50% probability of winning by the average jury verdict expectancy of $40,000; (2) multiplying the 50% probability of losing by the $0 payoff of defeat; and (3) adding the two together. Thus, .50 × $40,000 ± .50 × $0 = $20,000 as the expected outcome.

Finally Plaintiff's resistance point of $16,000 (as shown above the "Litigate" option) is calculated by subtracting from the expected outcome of $20,000 the $4,000 in trial costs. Since the option of accepting Defendant's settlement offer of $20,500 yields a greater recovery than the option of going to trial which yields only $16,000, Plaintiff would be best off to accept the settlement offer.

---

[12] To make the arithmetic work, the sum of the probabilities assigned to the branches stemming from any chance node *must* equal 100%.

If you were to construct a decision tree for the Defendant using the hypothetical given above, the expected non-shiftable trial costs would be $5,000; the Defendant's estimate of the probability of Plaintiff winning $40,000 at trial would be 40% (.40); and the Defendant's estimate of the probability of Plaintiff getting $0 at trial would be 60% (.60). Thus, .40 × $40,000 ± .60 × $0 = $16,000 as the expected outcome at trial. To this number, the Defendant would then *add* her expected trial costs of $5,000 to arrive at a resistance point of $21,000. If Plaintiff were to make a final settlement offer that is equal to or less than $21,000, Defendant should settle the case.

In short, this decision-tree analysis is substantively the same as Traditional Economic Analysis. However, because the "form" of the analysis is a management tool routinely taught in business schools and continuing education courses in management, it may serve as a more familiar method of presenting the settlement value of a case to a business executive who is making a decision on behalf of a corporate party.

## § 11.07　FAIR SETTLEMENT RANGE FORMULA

The Fair Settlement Range Formula[13] for valuing cases is essentially a refinement on traditional economic analysis. Under this formula, an over-all fair settlement range for the case is established, after which the Plaintiff might set his initial resistance point at the low end of the range and the Defendant might set her initial resistance point at the high end of the range. The components of the formula are as follows:

**AVE** = The Average Verdict Expectancy assuming the plaintiff will prevail on liability.

**PPW** = The Probability the Plaintiff Will Win the Average Verdict Expectancy, considering the law and facts of the particular case.

**UPV** = The Uncollectible Portion of the Verdict (*e.g.*, where some defendant is uninsured, underinsured, or is partially or completely judgment proof).

**PC** = The Plaintiff's Cost of going to trial.

**DC** = The Defendant's Cost of going to trial which the defendant would be willing to contribute to settlement.

**SIF** = Special Intangible Factors (expressed as a $ amount) that may increase or decrease the verdict (*e.g.*, the particular "jury appeal" of the case for one party or the other).

**FSV** = The Fair Settlement Value of the case.

**FSR** = The Fair Settlement Range of the case.

The formula may be expressed as follows:

**(AVE × PPW) – UPV – PC + DC ± SIF = FSV**

**Then, FSV + (10% of FSV) = FSR (upper end of range)**

**FSV – (10% of FSV) = FSR (lower end of range)**

---

[13] *See* John W. Cooley, *Mediation Advocacy*, § 3.12 (NITA 1996).

For example, drawing upon the hypothetical estimates given for the Plaintiff in § 11.06, the figures that would be computed in the formula would be:

- AVE = $40,000.

- PPW = 50% (.50).

- UPV = $0 (*i.e.,* assuming the Defendant is not uninsured or underinsured).

- PC = $4,000.

- DC = $3,000 (assuming the Defendant's total cost of going to trial would be $5,000 and it is estimated she would be willing to contribute $3,000 of the costs towards settlement, thereby saving $2,000 in costs).

- SIF = $5,000 in favor of Plaintiff (*e.g.,* assuming he has much greater jury appeal than does the Defendant).

Applying the foregoing to the formula yields the following:

**(AVE × PPW) − UPV − PC ± DC ± SIF = FSV**

- ($40,000 × .50) − $ 0 − $4,000 ± $3,000 ± $5,000 = $24,000

Then, to establish a Fair Settlement Range, 10% of the Fair Settlement Value is added to and subtracted from that Value to arrive at a range:

**FSV ± (.10 × FSV) = FSR (upper end of range)**

- $24,000 ± (.10 × $24,000) = $26,400 (upper end of range), and

**FSV − (.10 × FSV) = FSR (lower end of range)**

- $24,000 − (.10 × $24,000) = $21,600 (lower end of range).

Based on the foregoing, the Plaintiff might set his initial resistance point at $21,600. He might then set his target point at $27,000 and opening offer at $75,000. In the usual case, the Defendant's calculation of the formula is likely to be quite different from the Plaintiff's calculation. However, assuming the Defendant arrives at the same Fair Settlement Range arrived at by the Plaintiff, the Defendant might set her initial resistance point at $26,400, her target point at $20,000, and opening offer at $7,000.

## § 11.08   ANALYSIS OF THE CLIENT'S AVERSION TO RISK AND MOTIVATIONS

The foregoing methods of valuation largely assume that the client's decision to settle or go to trial will be made solely on the basis of which course of action will yield the best result from a rote economic standpoint. However, choosing between settlement and trial is not purely an economic process. Whether a client will accept a final settlement offer or take his chances at trial largely depends on that client's psychological propensity or aversion to risk — that is, how willing the client is to gamble on losing at trial versus the certainty of receiving the amount offered in final settlement. (*See also* § 7.06[1]).

This risk averseness varies from individual to individual and will often vary for each individual at different points in time. For example, most people are less willing to "roll the dice" with an "all or nothing" outcome at trial where liability is questionable if the amount at stake is a million dollars versus $10,000. Similarly, a wealthy client is more likely to gamble on his chances at trial when the amount at stake is $10,000, whereas an indigent client faced with the same amount at stake may be content to settle for the certainty of receiving $5,000.

In addition, risk aversion largely explains why many settlements occur on the eve of trial and some occur literally on the courthouse steps. When a trial is a year or more away, the consequences of an adverse verdict appear more abstract.[14] On the other hand, those consequences often take on a different reality during the weekend before trial, with the result that many clients will at that time prefer the certainty of an agreed-upon settlement to the risk of an undesirable verdict.

Clients also have various motivations that will affect their decision to settle the case or take it to trial. For example, settlement may be preferred to avoid the emotional strain and time demands of a trial, to preserve the personal or business relationship between the parties, to avoid unwanted publicity, to avoid an adverse legal or factual precedent, or to obtain an immediate source of funds if the client is in financial distress. On the other hand, a client might prefer a trial over settlement out of a desire to inflict punishment on the opposing party, to publicly vindicate a principle by having one side declared the winner and the other the loser, to establish a legal precedent or policy (*e.g.*, to discourage nuisance suits), or to simply delay payment of a claim for lack of sufficient funds to pay it.

Thus, you must always analyze the extent of your client's aversion to risk and other motivations that may affect the desirability of settling the case or trying it. These factors may be analyzed by (1) identifying the various risks and personal motivations bearing upon the choice between settlement and trial, (2) reducing these to a set of consequences of settling the case on the one hand, and trying it on the other, and (3) asking your client to place a monetary value on the overall consequences in light of his preferences and values to determine how much he is willing to accept or forgo for those consequences.[15] This amount might then be applied to increase or decrease the client's resistance point that was otherwise established based on a purely economic type of analysis.

As a simple example, assume that resistance points of $30,000 for the Plaintiff and $50,000 for the Defendant are arrived at by Intuitive "Case Worth" Analysis, the Sindell Formula, Traditional Economic Analysis, or the Fair Settlement Range Formula. If the Plaintiff does not want to go through the emotional trauma of a bitter trial, he might lower his resistance point by an additional $10,000 to $20,000. On the other hand, if the Defendant is more willing to take the case to trial because she has received adverse publicity from the suit and wants to vindicate herself from any wrongdoing, she might adjust her resistance point such that she will pay no more than $30,000. In this scenario, what otherwise would have likely resulted in a settlement of approximately $40,000 (*i.e.*, the midpoint of a $30,000 to $50,000 settlement zone) is now likely to result in a settlement of approximately $25,000 (*i.e.*, the midpoint of a $20,000 to $30,000 settlement zone).

---

[14] *See* D. Waterman & M. Peterson, Evaluating Civil Claims: *An Expert System Approach* 8 (1985) (one study found that the value of a personal injury case just before trial may be as much as 20% greater than the value of the case two years before trial).

[15] *See* P.T. Hoffman, Valuation of Cases for Settlement: Theory and Practice, 1 J. Disp. Res. 38–40 (1991).

## § 11.09 ADOPTING A HOLISTIC ANALYSIS AND ADVISING THE CLIENT

Most lawyers do not employ a standard mathematical formula in valuing cases for negotiation and settlement. Although a strict empirical approach may be tempting and comforting from the standpoint of providing some "objective" analysis, certainty in valuing cases for settlement is almost always illusory. The typical case presents too many factors and unknowns to reconcile through some rote computation. Indeed, if one applies, for example, Traditional Economic Analysis or the Fair Settlement Range Formula to the same case, the resulting computations will likely be very different. Moreover, if there were some fool-proof formula to valuing cases, there would be no need for negotiation at all because cases would then simply be settled by applying that formula to the particular facts and arriving at a result.

Thus, most lawyers adopt a "holistic" analysis to valuing cases for settlement that essentially draws upon the various factors considered in Intuitive "Case Worth" Analysis, Traditional Economic Analysis, the Fair Settlement Range Formula, and an analysis of the Client's Aversion to Risk and Motivations. Depending on the particular type of case and the values and preferences of the client, holistic analysis considers the factors variously emphasized in the other approaches, giving those factors more or less weight as the circumstances warrant. In the process of considering and weighing these factors, however, holistic analysis does not attempt to plug them into some standard mathematical formula, but attempts to arrive at a multi-faceted, reasoned judgment about a reasonable "settlement zone" for the case (*i.e.*, the distance between the parties' resistance points) and a reasonable "settlement range" for each side (*i.e.*, the distance between each party's resistance point and target point).

In this process, it is explicitly recognized that the predictions made are uncertain, may well change over time, and may well be revised during actual negotiations. These limitations on the prophetic accuracy of valuing a case are accepted as a reality and reconciled under the assumption that if the lawyer and client engage in an on-going assessment of the advantages and disadvantages of settling the case versus trying it, the final decision — which should always be made by the client — will turn out to be the best decision in the end.

It follows that in advising the client about a reasonable settlement zone and settlement range, most lawyers express their opinions about these matters as a *tentative* prediction or estimate. The reason for this is not, as some might cynically believe, to somehow exonerate the lawyer from making a bad prediction relied upon by the client. Rather, the tentativeness of the prediction or estimate is, as mentioned above, a candid concession to the inherent complexity and difficulty of valuing cases for settlement. It is consistent with the ethical prescription that a lawyer has a duty to advise his client according to the lawyer's best overall judgment and to place the ultimate decision whether to settle the case with the client. Indeed, a lawyer should explain this to the client in just these terms.

In light of the foregoing, in employing a holistic analysis to case valuation and advising your client about that analysis, you might follow the following 6 steps:

*(1) Estimate the "Average Jury Verdict Expectancy" for the type of case, by evaluating:*

- The cause of action;
- The burdens of proof for the cause of action;
- The legal elements and measure of damages for the cause of action;
- Jury verdicts in the same type of case, drawn from one's own experience, the experience of other lawyers, or from publications reporting jury verdicts.

*(2) Adjust the Average Jury Verdict Expectancy (upwards or downwards) to arrive at an "Estimated Jury Verdict for the Case" that reflects the particular legal and factual circumstances of the case, by evaluating:*

- Any uncertainties in the law about whether the case is actionable or damages are recoverable;
- The relative strength of the evidence in support of and in opposition to establishing liability;
- The relative strength of the evidence in support of and in opposition to establishing damages;
- What damages may be calculated as a sum certain (*e.g.*, special damages);
- What damages are amorphous (*e.g.*, pain and suffering, permanent injury, punitive damages);
- The extent to which the case has any special "jury appeal" for one side or the other.

*(3) Adjust the Estimated Jury Verdict for the Case (downwards for the Plaintiff and upwards for the Defendant) by the amount of the client's non-shiftable costs of obtaining that verdict to arrive at a "Potential Resistance Point," by evaluating:*

- All out-of-pocket expenses the client will likely incur and which the court will not tax against the party who loses at trial (*e.g.*, hourly attorney's fees, and costs associated with case investigation and preparation);
- The time value of money if a trial would not take place for a number of years.

*(4) Adjust the "Potential Resistance Point" (upwards or downwards) based on the Client's aversion to risk and personal motivations, by evaluating:*

- The client's financial, social, psychological, and other personal circumstances;
- The various risks and personal motivations of the client bearing on the choice between settlement and trial;
- The important consequences to the client of settling the case or trying it;
- Any monetary value that the client would place on settling the case in preference to trial or vice versa.

*(5) Adjust the "Potential Resistance Point" further, if appropriate, based on an evaluation of the factors under steps (3) and (4) above from the other party's perspective.*

*(6) Based on the Potential Resistance Point as adjusted, advise the client about a tentative resistance point and tentative target point, leaving the final decision on these matters to the client.*

These steps in holistic analysis are similar to the Fair Settlement Range Formula, but place a greater premium on the effects that intangible factors play in evaluating whether it is in the client's best interest to settle the case or take it to trial. The analysis also embodies a more fluid reasoning process that is more in keeping with how most clients and lawyers think about case valuation — *i.e.*, through a process of weighing multiple factors, probabilities, and preferences together, rather than through some rote, algebraic calculation of seemingly independent variables.

This does not mean that the mathematical calculations employed in the Fair Settlement Range Formula (or Traditional Economic Analysis) are inappropriate to consider when conducting holistic analysis. For example, many lawyers find it useful to arrive at an "Estimated Jury Verdict for the Case" in Step 2 above by multiplying the "Average Jury Verdict Expectancy" by the probability, expressed as a percentage, that it will occur (*i.e.*, AVE × PPW in the Fair Settlement Range Formula). Similarly, after arriving at the "Potential Resistance Point" in Step 5 of holistic analysis, it may be useful to consider a fair settlement range by establishing a bracket whose endpoints are 10% on either side of the Potential Resistance Point — *i.e.*, the Potential Resistance Point ± (10% of the Potential Resistance Point) = Upper end of Range; and the Potential Resistance Point − (10% of the Potential Resistance Point) = Lower end of Range. In sum, in an appropriate case, holistic analysis might draw upon or be combined with certain aspects of the Fair Settlement Range Formula or some other valuation method in arriving at a potential resistance point and target point.

## § 11.10  EXAMPLE OF HOLISTIC ANALYSIS

Assume that a Town has decided to build a water supply reservoir to meet the demands of the Town's growing population. The site chosen for the reservoir is located approximately ten miles outside the Town limits. This is a predominantly rural area consisting mostly of farm land, but some residential subdivision development has occurred in the general area in recent years.

To acquire the land for the reservoir, the Town has given statutory notice to affected landowners that it intends to use its power of eminent domain to condemn eight separate properties, each of which consists of approximately 100 acres of vacant, unsubdivided, and undeveloped land, and is owned by different landowners. However, before filing condemnation actions to officially "take" each of the eight properties, the Town has decided to negotiate with the affected landowners to purchase their properties at current fair market value. This has been somewhat successful to date in that three of the landowners have already sold their properties to the Town for $7,000 per acre, which is the current fair market value estimated by an independent appraisal firm hired by the Town. The other five landowners remain opposed to the reservoir project, but negotiations with them are still under way.

Ms. Jessica Dalton, a relatively poor, elderly widow, is one of the five landowners who has not yet settled with the Town. Her property also consists of 100 acres of vacant, undeveloped land. However, unlike all the other properties being acquired for the reservoir, Dalton had planned to subdivide her property into 10 contiguous lots (10 acres a piece) for eventual sale to third-party purchasers who would build their homes on the lots. In connection with these plans, last year she spent $50,000 (constituting almost all of the proceeds of her late husband's modest life insurance policy) on surveying and various engineering costs to finalize a plat for the subdivision. She ended up not recording the plat with the County Register of Deeds office once she was given formal notice that the Town planned to acquire her property as part of the reservoir project. Had she simply recorded the plat, while this would not have affected the Town's right to condemn her property, her subdivision would have been complete because there were no other local-governmental requirements for approval of this type of subdivision.

The Town is still waiting for a response to the offers it has made to the four other landowners who were extended purchase offers based on $7,000 per acre. Because of Dalton's frustrated subdivision plans and expenditure of $50,000, the Town Council thinks her situation might be unique and has asked its attorney to estimate the value of Dalton's property for settlement purposes before the Town makes her a purchase offer.

Tracking the 6 steps set out in § 11.09, the Town attorney's holistic analysis of the settlement value of Dalton's property might be as follows:

### (1) An estimate of the "Average Jury Verdict Expectancy" for the condemnation case:

Although the Town would be the named plaintiff in a condemnation action, for all other litigation purposes it would actually occupy the position of a defendant. The burden of proof is on the landowner to establish (by a preponderance of the evidence) the fair market value of the condemned property as of the date of the "taking," which is the date the Complaint is filed. When a lawsuit is filed, the Town must simultaneously deposit with the clerk of court the amount of money the Town estimates to be the current fair market value of the property (which amount is not admissible as evidence at a trial), and the landowner may immediately receive that money from the clerk notwithstanding the pendency of the lawsuit.

At trial, the jury decides the issue of "just compensation" (i.e., the fair market value of the property on the date of taking), and the judge decides all other issues. If the verdict exceeds the amount that the Town deposited with the clerk, the Town must pay the landowner the amount awarded in excess of the deposit. If the verdict is for less than the amount deposited, the landowner must pay back to the Town the difference between the amount deposited and the verdict. So long as the verdict is greater than the amount of the deposit, the law requires the Town to pay all litigation expenses of the landowner (e.g., costs of appraisals, appraisers' expert-witness fees, court-reporter costs for depositions, etc.), but not attorney's fees. Landowners are usually represented on a contingent fee basis, whereby the lawyer's fee is a percentage of the amount obtained for the landowner that exceeds the amount the Town deposited with the clerk.

"Fair market value" as the measure of damages is the amount that a willing buyer and willing seller would most likely agree upon for the property, where the buyer is not compelled to buy and the seller is not compelled to sell. Fair market value is also determined based on the "highest and best use" of the property, which means the most economically viable use to which the property may be put, even if that is not how the property was being used at the time of the taking. However, the jury is not permitted to award compensation to the landowner based on a purely speculative use, or for sums such as lost profits from some intended future use. In addition, no compensation may be awarded for specific amounts paid by the landowner to improve her property (such as the $50,000 that Dalton spent), or for general damages such as those stemming from any inconvenience to the landowner, or emotional distress, or the like occasioned by the taking. In sum, the sole measure of compensation is the fair market value of the property on the date of taking, considering its "highest and best use."

Jury verdicts in condemnation cases typically favor the landowner and result in awards that are higher than the fair market value contentions of the condemnor such as a Town. This is usually the case even if the jury essentially rejects the testimony of the landowner's appraisers. Notwithstanding that the burden of proof is on the landowner, juries tend to give the landowner the benefit of the doubt in any valuation, and they are frequently prone to reject the appraisals of both parties altogether, and independently arrive at a determination of fair market value based on the differing "comparable sales" data submitted to them at trial. Apart from this general experience with jury verdicts, there are no reliable statistics that can be drawn upon to predict the average percentage by which verdicts exceed the fair market value contentions of the condemnor.

In the case at hand, because no condemnation suits have yet been filed by the Town, there are no verdicts to draw upon to estimate an "Average Jury Verdict Expectancy" for the per-acre value of the properties being acquired for the reservoir. The best information currently available is that all of the properties being acquired for the reservoir have a fair market value of approximately $7,000 per acre as determined by the appraisal firm hired by the Town. This figure does not appear to be an unreasonable benchmark because three landowners have already accepted this valuation. Thus, an Average Jury Verdict Expectancy for Dalton's 100 acres would be at least $700,000.

### (2) Adjustment of the Average Jury Verdict Expectancy to arrive at an "Estimated Jury Verdict for the Case" that reflects the particular legal and factual circumstances of the case:

Estimating what a jury would most likely find to be the fair market value of Dalton's property is complicated by a legal question about the proper appraisal method that may be used in valuing that property. On the one hand, the Town's appraiser is likely to employ the "comparable sales" method of valuation to appraise the fair market value of the property based on actual sales of other approximately 100-acre tracts of undeveloped, unsubdivided land in the general vicinity of the reservoir area. There is no question that an appraisal based on this method would be admissible into evidence. The result would be a value of approximately $7,000 per acre for a total of $700,000.

However, Dalton's appraiser is likely to appraise her property on the assumption that it consisted of a subdivision of 10 lots, and therefore the fair market value should be determined based on the aggregate of the prices that could have been obtained for the 10 lots, less the costs of developing the subdivision and other costs that would have been incurred until all the lots had been sold. The case law in the jurisdiction is arguably conflicting about whether an appraisal based on this "development approach" to valuation would be admissible under the circumstances of the instant case. On the one hand, the law is clear that a landowner may not value unsubdivided, undeveloped land as if it were subdivided or developed. On the other hand, the law is equally clear that if a final plat has been recorded to subdivide the property, it may be valued as a subdivision. In Dalton's situation, the only reason her plat was not recorded was due to the futility of this act in light of the Town's plans to acquire the property for the reservoir project, and the law would not now permit her to record the plat because she has received formal notice of the Town's condemnation plans.

Notwithstanding Dalton's situation, it is unlikely that the appellate courts of the instant jurisdiction would hold that a "development approach" to valuation would be admissible in valuing her property. However, because the resolution of this issue remains uncertain in the jurisdiction, there is a 50% chance that a trial judge would permit an appraisal based on that approach to be admitted into evidence in the case. If that were to occur, the jury would be presented with evidence that the fair market value of the property is approximately twice as much as that estimated by the Town's appraiser — *i.e.*, as high as $14,0000 per acre for a total of $1.4 million dollars.[16] Even if Dalton's appraisal based on the "development approach" were not admitted into evidence, she would still be able to introduce the fact that there was one sale of a large tract in the general vicinity of the reservoir area that sold for $8,000 per acre.

Even assuming that Dalton's appraisal of $1.4 million were admitted into evidence, it is highly unlikely that a jury would accept this amount as the fair market value because there is nothing to differentiate Dalton's property from the comparable sales in the $7,000–$8,000 per-acre range, except for the fact that Dalton had prepared a plat to subdivide her property into 10 lots. That is, the mere preparation of the plat (or the recording of it, had that occurred) did not result in any specific physical improvements to the property. Nevertheless, the jury is likely to be highly sympathetic to the fact that Dalton has now essentially lost the $50,000 she expended in surveying and engineering costs to prepare the plat. Although it is unlikely a jury would specifically include this amount in its verdict (given a trial judge's explicit instruction that this element of damage is not compensable), most jurors would have this loss in the back of their minds during deliberations.

From a "jury appeal" standpoint, everything about the case favors Dalton. She is an elderly widow of modest means who is being forced to give up her land. There will be no evidence that she will benefit in any way from the reservoir. Thus, consistent with the typical condemnation case, the jury is likely to give her the benefit of the doubt in any reasonable calculation of fair market value.

In light of the foregoing, even though it is unlikely a jury would give Dalton a "bonus" of $50,000 over and above what it otherwise determines to be the fair market value of her property, it is reasonable to predict that a jury would calculate the fair market value at approximately $7,500 per acre. This would be justified given

---

[16] In appraisal "theory," at least, an application of the "development approach" and "comparable sales" method should yield the same result, assuming the "highest and best use" is residential development. In reality, however, this is almost never the case in light of the numerous variables considered in a "development approach" which may be manipulated to produce much higher values.

that $8,000 per acre is the upper end of the available comparable sales data. The "Estimated Jury Verdict for the Case" is thus $750,000.

### (3) Adjustment of the Estimated Jury Verdict for the Case by the amount of the Town's non-shiftable costs of obtaining that verdict to arrive at a "Potential Resistance Point":

It is expected to cost the Town approximately $35,000 in lawyer's fees, expert-witness fees, and other litigation expenses combined. In addition, it is estimated that the Town will have to pay Dalton approximately $10,000 of Dalton's litigation expenses. This totals $45,000 which, when added to the Estimated Jury Verdict for the Case of $750,000, results in a "Potential Resistance Point" of $795,000.

### (4) Adjustment of the "Potential Resistance Point" based on the Town's aversion to risk and motivations:

The Town Council is primarily concerned about the *de facto* precedent that might be established if Dalton were paid much more than $7,000 per acre. This is so not only because three of the landowners have already accepted purchase offers from the Town at $7,000 per acre and might publicly accuse the Council of treating them disparately if Dalton were paid more than $7,000 per acre, but because there remain (apart from Dalton) four other landowners who might not agree to accept less than the per-acre value that is given to Dalton. This problem could not be resolved by including a confidentiality clause as part of a settlement with Dalton because the Town is a governmental entity that has a duty to disclose how public funds are expended.

On the other hand, even though Dalton's property has no special characteristics that, from a fair market value standpoint, distinguish it from the tracts of land owned by the other seven landowners, unlike them, she has now lost the $50,000 she spent in preparing the subdivision plat. Out of fairness, the Council is not philosophically opposed to paying her this amount in addition to the reasonable fair market value of her property, even though she would not be legally entitled to recover the $50,000 at trial. Whether in a contract to purchase her property or in a settlement agreement, the Town could denominate the additional $50,000 as an equitable reimbursement for her special loss, thereby distinguishing it from the amount paid to her strictly for the fair market value of her property.

The Town's overriding interest is to settle all cases as close to the $7,000 per acre benchmark as possible because this is the figure that can be justified to the public based on the Town's appraisal. Moreover, the budget is extremely tight. Thus, the Council is not afraid to spend the $45,000 it would cost to try the case in an effort to establish a possible verdict precedent of approximately $7,000 per acre. If a jury awarded Dalton $7,500 per acre, she would receive $50,000 more than she otherwise would receive at $7,000 per acre, and this additional amount could be publicly explained as an equitable result in light of Dalton's loss of the $50,000 she incurred in preparing the subdivision plat. Paying her as much as $750,000 in settlement would be equivalent to the "Estimated Jury Verdict in the Case" and save the Town $45,000 in litigation expenses.

Thus, taking into account the Town Council's motivations, the "Potential Resistance Point" of $795,000 (*i.e.*, $45,000 in non-shiftable costs ∓ a $750,000

"Estimated Jury Verdict for the Case") might be adjusted downward to $750,000. This amount would (a) be consistent with the Council's goal of settling all cases at $7,000 per acre, (b) equitably reimburse Dalton for her special $50,000 loss which she otherwise would not be entitled to recoup at trial, and (c) save the Town $45,000 in litigation expenses that would be incurred in obtaining the "Estimated Jury Verdict for the Case" of $750,000.

*(5) Adjustment of the "Potential Resistance Point" further, if appropriate, based on an evaluation of the factors under Steps (3) and (4) above from Dalton's perspective:*

Not all of Dalton's litigation expenses are shiftable to the Town in the event of a trial. The trial judge will only award her "reasonable" litigation expenses. For example, if an appraiser charges her a particularly large amount of money to conduct an appraisal or testify at trial, the judge may tax only a portion of that charge against the Town. Moreover, she may incur some litigation-related costs that are not taxable against the Town at all (*e.g.*, the costs of preparing certain illustrative exhibits or preparing a professional video-tape of the property). However, it is unlikely that her non-shiftable costs will be great enough to warrant any adjustment to the Town's "Potential Resistance Point."

Dalton's aversion to risk and personal motivations are not known. However, it is reasonable to assume that given her age she might prefer to settle the case rather than wait out the trial process and an additional number of years if the case is appealed. In addition, it is reasonable to assume that she is aware of the settlements that the Town has reached with three of her neighbors. Regardless of what feelings she might have about their willingness to accept $7,000 per acre, it is also reasonable to assume that she wants to be compensated for her special loss of $50,000 in addition to receiving the fair market value of her property. None of these assumptions, however, warrant any adjustment to the Town's "Potential Resistance Point."

*(6) Based on the Potential Resistance Point as adjusted, advise the Town Council about a tentative resistance point and tentative target point, leaving the final decision on these matters to the Council:*

Based on the evaluations in Steps (1) through (5) above, a tentative resistance point for the Town would be not to pay Dalton more than $750,000. A tentative target point would be to pay her $700,000 based on $7,000 per acre. Because the Town has extended purchase offers to all of the other landowners based on $7,000 per acre, an initial offer to Dalton should not be less than this amount.

Chapter 12

# PREPARING FOR NEGOTIATION

§ 12.06  ILLUSTRATION OF NEGOTIATION PREPARATION OUTLINE
(PROBLEM-SOLVING APPROACH)

§ 12.07  THE ROLE OF THE CLIENT AND ADVISING THE CLIENT

## § 12.01  INTRODUCTION

Thorough preparation is indispensable for effective negotiation. Before commencing negotiations, you must (1) obtain all information relevant to understanding what may reasonably be obtained for your client through negotiation, and (2) transpose that information into a working outline from which an overall negotiating approach can be developed and employed.

## § 12.02  INFORMATION TO OBTAIN

Generally, you should obtain all information that may be pertinent to the entire negotiation process. This information should serve as the raw material from which you can identify: (1) what further information you need to find out; (2) what information to reveal during the course of negotiating; (3) what information to protect from disclosure; (4) the underlying interests of each party; (5) the primary, secondary, and incidental objectives of each party; (6) possible solutions that may satisfy each party's interests and objectives; (7) each party's best alternatives to a negotiated agreement (BATNA); (8) each party's strongest and weakest factual and legal leverage points; (9) the "target" and "resistance" points for each party; (10) each party's negotiating strategy and style; (11) the specific offers or proposals that may be presented by each party; and (12) the particular tactics each party may employ during the negotiation process. In obtaining this information, consider the following categories.

### [1]  Information from the Client

Obviously, your client is a critical source of information. You need to know all the facts and circumstances surrounding your client's problem. Carefully probe your client's objectives: what would she want in a final agreement if she could obtain everything she hoped to achieve in the negotiation? And, if everything went against her in the negotiation, what would be the very least she would accept to conclude an agreement? What are her long-term and short-term goals?

Apart from objectives or goals, encourage your client to share her underlying "interests." That is, what are her real needs, desires, concerns, fears, and feelings? Many clients are hesitant to disclose these more deeply rooted matters for fear that revealing them will display some personal weakness or insecurity. However, a candid exploration of these matters may well give rise to alternative and more creative solutions for satisfying your client's objectives.

### [2]  Information About the Other Party

Just as you need to know all the facts and circumstances surrounding your client's problem from her perspective, it is also essential to understand all the facts and circumstances from the other party's perspective. The latter information will provide a basis for anticipating the other party's objectives and underlying interests. In short, you must be willing to put yourself in the shoes of the opposing party.

In obtaining information about the other party, be sure to obtain information about his personal and financial situation, and emotional or psychological needs and dispositions. In addition, particularly when the opposing party is a corporation or governmental entity, identify the principal decision-makers who will play the most important roles in fashioning and deciding upon an agreement, and identify the particular pressures and interests that may affect their input into the negotiating process.

When obtaining information about an individual, don't overlook sources such as the Internet, criminal records, records of prior judgments, biographies, *Who's Who* books, clubs, professional societies, trade associations, or other attorneys or parties who have had prior dealings, disputes, or litigation with the individual. In the case of a corporation, useful information might be obtained from sources such as the Internet, the Consumer Protection division or Better Business Bureau of a state, annual and quarterly reports, reports of stockholders meetings, *Dun and Bradstreet, Moody's, Standard & Poors*, speeches of executives, company press releases, newspapers, or information supplied to governmental entities or public stock exchanges.

## [3]    Information About the Opposing Negotiator

Obtaining information about the negotiator for the opposing side is particularly important in choosing an appropriate negotiating style and strategy. Find out about the opposing negotiator's personality, style, level of competence, experience as a negotiator, reputation as a trial lawyer, and overall approach to negotiating.

If the opposing negotiator is a lawyer, it is also often useful to consider his likely fee arrangement with his client. For example, if the opposing party is being represented on a contingency fee basis, his lawyer may be primarily interested in a settlement that includes an up-front cash payment rather than a purely structured settlement with payments made over time. On the other hand, if the fee is based on an hourly rate, you will be able to estimate the pressure that mounting legal costs may impose on the opposing party throughout the negotiation process.

In addition, knowing about opposing counsel's general workload and trial schedule may be useful. For example, if opposing counsel is overworked, consumed by a pressing trial schedule, or is facing crucial deadlines in the case at hand or in other cases, these factors may markedly affect his disposition toward settlement at different times during the negotiation process.

## [4]    Information About the Law

Thoroughly researching the law applicable to your client's problem is essential. To be effective in negotiating you must not only know the factual strengths and weaknesses of the case, but the legal strengths and weaknesses as well. In addition, when appropriate, you should research any legal issues that may arise from the particular terms of a potential or final agreement.

## [5]    Other Information

Apart from the foregoing, you should obtain any other information that may be pertinent to the particular negotiation. In this era of information explosion and ever-expanding resources such as the Internet, your ability to obtain information is almost as limitless as your imagination.

## § 12.03   PREPARING A NEGOTIATION PREPARATION OUTLINE

Once you have obtained as much of the foregoing information as possible, you should evaluate and transpose that information into a working outline (a Negotiation Preparation Outline like that shown in § 12.04) from which an overall negotiating approach can be developed and employed. In preparing this outline, use the twelve steps presented below:

## [1]    <u>Step 1</u>: From the Perspective of Each Party, Make a List of Information To Obtain, Information To Reveal, and Information To Protect

*Information To Obtain*

An integral aspect of the negotiating process is finding out information from the other side that you have been unable to obtain independently. Having as complete information as possible about the other party's interests, objectives, possible solutions, best alternatives to a negotiated settlement, factual and legal leverage points, target and resistance points, offers or proposals, and particular tactics is essential in shaping your particular approach to the negotiation. Thus, based on the information you already possess, make a list of information you need to find out from the other party.

Next, make a list of information you expect the other party will want to find out from you that is not readily obtainable from independent sources. This may or may not include information that you will be willing to reveal to the other side.

*Information To Reveal*

Make a list of information you want to reveal to the other party (whether or not the other side knows about it already), and a separate list of types of information you expect the other side will gratuitously reveal to you. Information to reveal may consist of each side's strong factual or legal leverage points that will be itemized in Step 6 below, or other important information that each party wants the other to know in order to understand one another's particular interests, objectives, possible solutions, and offers or proposals.

*Information To Protect*

Finally, make a list of information you want to protect from disclosure to the other side, and a separate list of types of information you expect the other party will not want to reveal to you. Information to protect may include damaging factual or legal points (*see also* Step 6 below), or sensitive information such as trade secrets, work product, or the like.

## [2]     <u>Step 2</u>: Make a List of Each Party's Interests

Conceptually, a party's "interests" are to be distinguished from her "objectives," even though the two often overlap or end up being the same. A party's objectives are the specific *matters* she wants to obtain from the negotiation, whereas interests are the underlying *reasons* for the party's objectives. There may be multiple interests underlying any one objective, or multiple objectives that are related to a single interest.

To identify the interests of your client or the other party, ask "why" she desires a particular objective. Focus on her underlying *needs, desires, concerns, fears, philosophies*, and *feelings*. What are the personal, psychological, ideological, and emotional motivations behind her goals? Does she have any special needs for power, prestige, acceptance, security, economic well-being, belonging, or control over her life? When listing the interests of your client and the other party, rank those interests from most important to least important, and note which interests may be shared between the parties, as well as those which conflict.

For example, consider the plaintiff in a defamation or wrongful death case. While in both cases the single "legal" objective would be money, the primary interest of the plaintiff in the defamation case might be to restore her reputation, and the primary interest of the plaintiff in the wrongful death case might be to ensure that the accident that killed the decedent would never happen again. These interests may give rise to alternative objectives and solutions apart from the mere payment of money. In the defamation case, the plaintiff's interest in restoring her reputation may give rise to the objective of obtaining a public retraction and apology. This might not be at odds with the defendant's interests if the retraction and apology are styled in terms of the defendant having made a mistake in making the defamatory statement, and if a payment of a smaller sum is made to the plaintiff in exchange for making the recantation public. Similarly, in the wrongful death case, the interests of the plaintiff and defendant in preventing a future accident will undoubtedly be shared, and this may lead to a possible solution in which the defendant promises to undertake specific steps to correct the product's defect in exchange for paying a smaller sum to the plaintiff.

## [3]     <u>Step 3</u>: Make a List of Each Party's Primary Objectives, Secondary Objectives, and Incidental Objectives (to Exchange)

As mentioned above, a party's objectives are what she specifically wants out of an agreement, whereas her interests constitute the reasons underlying her objectives. In other words, objectives are the outgrowth of interests. While objectives and interests are conceptually distinct, objectives are quite often nothing more than interests formulated into statements of specific goals.

Based on the interests of both parties identified in Step 2 above, list each party's primary, secondary, and incidental objectives (or objectives to exchange). A "primary" objective is a specific matter that must be obtained if an agreement is to be reached at all. A "secondary" objective is an important but not necessarily vital matter that a party may choose to forgo if the primary objective is resolved in a satisfactory manner. An "incidental" objective is a lower-priority goal that a party would be pleased to obtain, but which will not have a substantial effect on the overall success or failure of the final agreement. In addition, an incidental objective may serve as a matter to trade with the other party for something of greater value. After listing each party's objectives, compare them to note those which are shared, which conflict, and which do not conflict.

## [4]    Step 4: Make a List of Possible Solutions for Each Party (from most preferred to least preferred)

In light of the interests and objectives of each party, make a list of possible solutions for each side. In formulating possible solutions, it may be useful to first consider the primary, secondary, and incidental objectives of each party that are shared or do not conflict, and then consider those which do conflict.

Particularly when thinking about solutions to the parties' conflicting objectives, try to develop solutions based on objective criteria that are fair and independent of each party's mere desires. For example, in a property damage dispute, a reasonable solution is more likely to be found if the parties focus on objective criteria such as appraisals or "book values" to establish fair market value, rather than on a sum that one party merely wants to receive or the other is merely willing to pay. Similarly, in a construction contract dispute, a solution might be based on industry-wide standards, rather than on the mere preferences or practices of the particular parties. Depending upon the case, other sources of objective criteria might include what a court might decide, professional standards, moral standards, expert opinions, precedent, costs, efficiency, tradition, and the like.

At this stage, it is particularly important to "brainstorm" and list all possible solutions. These will later be refined into more concrete offers or proposals in Step 10 below.

## [5]    Step 5: Make a List of Each Party's Best Alternatives to a Negotiated Agreement (BATNA)

The purpose of negotiation is not only to reach an agreement that satisfies your client's objectives and interests, but also to protect your client from an agreement that would be harmful or counterproductive to his interests and objectives. In understanding the dividing line between an acceptable and unacceptable agreement, you must understand your client's Best Alternative to a Negotiated Agreement (BATNA), and whether that "walk-away" option would be better than anything that could be achieved from an agreement.

Knowing your client's BATNA and forecasting the other party's BATNA is essential to understanding the relative negotiating strength of each party. If you know in advance what your client's alternatives are if an agreement is not reached, you will not be negotiating in the dark. Instead, you will have the strength and confidence to walk away from the bargaining table if the best alternative is more attractive than the final agreement. Similarly, the relative negotiating power of the other party will primarily depend on his BATNA.

Understanding the BATNA of both parties also makes it easier to realistically estimate what you can expect from the negotiation. If your BATNA is greater than the other side's BATNA, you will have greater leverage over the terms of any negotiated agreement. Conversely, if the other side's BATNA is greater than yours, you may have to reduce your expectations and modify your objectives accordingly.

### [6]    Step 6: Make a List of Each Party's Factual and Legal Leverage Points (Strong and Weak)

Factual and legal leverage points are the strong and weak aspects of the case that shape the parties' target and resistance points (see Step 7 below), and the rationales for each party's offers or proposals (*see* Step 10 below). As such, these factual and legal leverage points are used by the parties in arguing for or against various terms of an agreement.

Each party's strong and weak factual and legal leverage points often correspond, respectively, to the information "to reveal" and information "to protect" listed in Step 1 above. In listing these factual and legal leverage points, it is important to maintain an objective perspective. Because you are intimately familiar with your client's situation and may know much less about the other side's situation, it is sometimes tempting to unduly focus on the weaknesses of your own case without recognizing that those weaknesses may not be actually apparent to the other party. Thus, remember that your assessment of the strong and weak points for each party is necessarily limited by the extent of the information possessed by you.

### [7]    Step 7: Identify Each Party's Potential Target and Resistance Points

As discussed in § 11.02, a party's "target point" is the best result she realistically hopes to achieve from the negotiation. It is not to be confused with a party's opening offer (see Step 10 below), which is the point at which a party begins negotiations and thereafter moves, through a series of concessions, toward the target point but not below her "resistance" point. A party's "resistance" point is her "bottom line" — the point below which she would cut off negotiations and resort to her Best Alternative to a Negotiated Agreement (BATNA). In other words, it is the point below which the party is unwilling to make any further concessions or compromises.

Estimating target and resistance points depends upon an overall evaluation of the case in light of all the factors considered in Steps 1 through 6 above. Drawing upon those factors and the valuation methods discussed in Chapter 11, you should establish not only the target and resistance points of your client, but consider and list alternative target and resistance points that may be adopted by the other side so that you can estimate different ranges of potential settlement zones.

### [8]    Step 8: Identify Each Party's Negotiating Strategy: Adversarial or Problem-Solving

As discussed in Chapter 8, there are generally two types of negotiating strategies: "adversarial" or "problem-solving." Each has its advantages and disadvantages that should be considered in light of the particular case. Taking into account these considerations and the matters developed in Steps 1 through 7 above, identify the particular strategy you intend to adopt in the negotiation and the one you expect will be employed by the other party.

[9]     Step 9: Identify Each Party's Negotiating Style:
         Competitive (Hardball), Cooperative (Softball), or
         Competitive-Cooperative (Hardball and Softball)

Also as detailed in Chapter 8, there are generally three types of negotiating styles: (1) "competitive" (hardball), (2) "cooperative" (softball), or (3) a combination of "competitive and cooperative" (hardball and softball). Like the different negotiating strategies, the different negotiating styles have their distinct advantages and disadvantages. In addition, there are particular advantages and disadvantages to different style and strategy combinations such as "competitive and adversarial," "cooperative (or competitive-cooperative) and adversarial," "competitive and problem-solving," or "cooperative (or competitive-cooperative) and problem-solving." In light of these considerations and the anticipated negotiating strategy of each side listed in Step 8 above, identify the particular negotiating style you plan to use in the negotiation, and the one you expect will be used by the opposing party.

[10]    Step 10: Make a List of Each Party's Offers or
          Proposals in the Order They May be Presented

The specific offers or proposals of each party should be formulated in light of all the matters developed in Steps 1 through 9 above. In deciding your opening offer and fall-back offers in descending order to your final offer, the target and resistance points and potential concession patterns developed in Step 7 above are particularly important. In addition, for every offer or proposal you make, you should draw upon the factual and legal leverage points listed in Step 6 above to back up each offer or concession with well-reasoned rationales.

In choosing an opening offer, it is important to note that a number of studies have shown that negotiators frequently obtain more satisfactory outcomes when they start with more extreme rather than more moderate demands (*i.e.*, higher initial demands by plaintiffs or lower initial offers by defendants). In this regard, experience has shown that in choosing an initial offer, many successful negotiators first forecast the best result they reasonably expect to achieve in the negotiation, and then deliberately *increase this goal* or target point in setting an opening offer.[1]

On the other hand, if your initial offer or proposal is too extreme and cannot be backed up with sensible reasons, you are likely to quickly lose credibility with the opposing party. In that event, the negotiation may collapse at the outset, or, if it nevertheless proceeds, it will be more difficult for you to justify the meaningfulness of your concessions to the other side. In short, your opening offer and each subsequent offer should be supported by non-frivolous rationales.

In developing your fall-back offers and concession pattern, consider (1) the extent of the information possessed by each side and the extent to which the factual and legal aspects of the case have been developed; (2) how protracted the negotiation is likely to be in light of the relative complexity of the case; and (3) the particular negotiating strategy and style (*see* Steps 8 and 9 above) of the opposing

---

[1] *See* C. Karrass, *The Negotiating Game* 17–18 (1970); J. Rubin & B. Brown, *The Social Psychology of Bargaining and Negotiation* 267 (1975); M. Bazerman & M. Neale, *Negotiating Rationally* 28 (1992); Charles B. Craver, *Effective Legal Negotiation and Settlement* 63–66 (3rd ed. 1997); Herbert M. Kritzer, *The Justice Broker: Lawyers and Ordinary Litigation*, 143–155, 159–161 (1990).

party. Generally, the more thoroughly developed the case is in terms of the overall information possessed by each side, the less room you need to leave to maneuver between your opening offer and final offer. Similarly, if the negotiation is not expected to be long or complex, and the opposing party does not take a highly competitive (hardball) approach to the negotiation, it is less important to preserve substantial maneuvering room between your initial proposal and bottom line. On the other hand, if the negotiations start out when the parties possess limited information about each other's interests and objectives, or if the opposing party adopts a highly adversarial strategy and competitive style, you should prepare a concession pattern that leaves ample room within which to maneuver from your opening offer to your final one.

Finally, it is essential to forecast the potential offers and concession pattern of the opposing party. This perspective will help you to anticipate and formulate balanced counter-offers and alternatives to the other side's proposals.

## [11]    Step 11: Consider Each Party's Particular Tactics

Negotiators invariably employ a variety of particular tactics throughout the negotiating process to advance their clients' objectives. The most common tactics are discussed in Chapter 10. Thus, in preparing for negotiation, you should consider any particular tactics you might employ, and anticipate any tactics that might be used by the other party so that you will be prepared to meet and counter those tactics.

## [12]    Step 12: Revise All of the Foregoing Matters Throughout the Negotiating Process

The foregoing Steps are designed to systematically develop an overall approach to the particular negotiation. You can then prepare a Negotiation Preparation Outline for use in all stages of the negotiating process. While the outline may serve as a blueprint or road map for the negotiation, you should always be prepared to revise any aspect of it, in whole or in part, as circumstances warrant.

## § 12.04    FORMAT FOR NEGOTIATION PREPARATION OUTLINE

There are many ways to format a Negotiation Preparation Outline. One format is as follows:

| | YOUR CLIENT | OTHER PARTY |
|---|---|---|
| 1. INFORMATION | | |
| To Obtain: | 1. | 1. |
| | 2. | 2. |
| | 3. | 3. |
| | 4. | 4. |
| To Reveal: | 1. | 1. |
| | 2. | 2. |
| | 3. | 3. |
| To Protect: | 1. | 1. |
| | 2. | 2. |

                              3.              3.

2. INTERESTS (from most important to least important)

                              1.              1.
                              2.              2.
                              3.              3.
                              4.              4.

3. OBJECTIVES

Primary:                      1.              1.
                              2.              2.

Secondary:                    1.              1.
                              2.              2.

Incidental:                   1.              1.
(to exchange)                 2.              2.

4. POSSIBLE SOLUTIONS (most preferred to to least preferred)

                              1.              1.
                              2.              2.
                              3.              3.

5. BEST ALTERNATIVES TO A NEGOTIATED AGREEMENT
(BATNA)

                              1.              1.
                              2.              2.

6. FACTUAL AND LEGAL LEVERAGE POINTS

Strong points:                1.              1.
                              2.              2.
                              3.              3.
                              4.              4.

Weak points:                  1.              1.
                              2.              2.
                              3.              3.
                              4.              4.

7. POTENTIAL TARGET AND RESISTANCE POINTS

Target Points:                1.              1.
                              2.              2.

Resistance Points:            1.              1.
                              2.              2.

8. OFFERS OR PROPOSALS

                              1st:            1st:
                              2nd:            2nd:
                              3rd:            3rd:
                              4th:            4th:

9. PARTICULAR TACTICS

                              1.              1.
                              2.              2.
                              3.              3.

## § 12.05   ILLUSTRATION OF NEGOTIATION PREPARATION OUTLINE (ADVERSARIAL APPROACH)

Assume you represent Polly Pierce, a very attractive nineteen-year-old woman, who lives in Hopeville, a small town in rural North Carolina. Polly's father is a tobacco farmer who has recently been diagnosed with cancer, and her mother is a homemaker.

Polly has just finished her first semester at a small four-year college, the Gordon College of Dance & The Arts in Bakersfield, North Carolina, which is nationally known for training some of the best performing dancers in the country. Although Polly is considered by her instructors to have a promising career and is one of the best dancers the college has seen in the past decade, she is only on a partial scholarship and her parents are struggling to pay the balance of her tuition and other expenses which total approximately $20,000 per year.

On the evening of December 12, Polly went to a party with some of her classmates to celebrate the end of the first semester. At the party, she had four beers during a two-hour period. As she was about to leave and drive back to the college, one of her classmates, Missa Sulick, asked Polly if she was able to drive. Missa was concerned that Polly had too much to drink. Polly said that she was fine and proceeded to drive back to the college which was approximately 15 miles away. Other classmates at the party would testify that, while they could tell that Polly had been drinking, she was not too intoxicated to drive.

While driving back to the College, Polly was hit head-on by Donald Doan, who lost control of his car while speeding and crossed the centerline into Polly's lane of travel. Polly was not speeding. The accident happened on a lightly traveled road in Bakersville County. There were no independent witnesses to the accident.

Polly was taken by ambulance to Bakersville Memorial Hospital where she was diagnosed with multiple fractures to her right leg and ankle. Her blood alcohol level taken approximately one hour after the accident was 0.07, just below the legal limit. She spent 10 days in the Hospital during which she had surgery and the doctors put a pin in her leg to secure one of the fractures. Her medical and physical therapy bills totaled $30,000. Because Polly had no insurance, the Hospital has asserted a statutory lien in that amount on any personal injury funds she recovers. That is, the $30,000 will have to be paid back to the Hospital out of any personal injury compensation that Polly receives.

Polly was able to attend the spring semester on crutches, and her fractures were healed by the end of April. She has a 25% permanent partial disability rating of her right leg and ankle. She is able to walk without a cane, but has a permanent limp and a slightly visible four-inch scar on her right leg from the surgery. Her doctors expect that she is at high risk for developing potentially debilitating arthritis later in life, but they have no estimate of what this might mean in terms of future medical costs. Her prospects for any dancing career are now over. She had no medical problems before the accident, except that when she was 18 she was diagnosed with early degenerative disc disease in her back which may or may not have hampered her future dancing career. According to standard mortality tables, she has an average life expectancy of an additional 53 years.

The top dancing graduates from Gordon usually earn between $30,000 and $40,000 per year for the first two to three years, and for the next five to ten years they may earn up to $100,000 or more per year depending upon their success. Polly has now decided to switch her major from dance to art history, and either teach art history in high school or at the college level upon graduating from Gordon.

Doan was miraculously not injured in the accident. He admitted to the police that he had "been going a bit over the speed limit." He was charged with speeding and driving while left of center of the roadway, and pled guilty to these traffic violations. Doan is a member of the Bakersville County Board of Commissioners, and it is rumored that he might run for Chairman of the Board in the next election that is six months away. To date, there has been no media coverage of the accident. It is also rumored that Doan recently inherited a sizeable sum of money that is believed to be in excess of $500,000.

You have undertaken to represent Polly on her personal injury claim on a contingency fee basis, which is 1/3 of the gross recovery regardless of any medical liens. You have already given notice of your representation to Doan's insurance carrier. The adjuster handling the claim, Arnold Aaron, is based at the carrier's headquarters in Dallas, Texas. Aaron is a senior claims adjuster who is rumored to be an extremely hard-nosed negotiator. Polly's property damage claim for her car has already been resolved.

No lawsuit has yet been filed in the case. If a lawsuit is filed, it will be filed in Bakersville where jury verdicts are significantly lower than in larger cities such as Dallas, Texas. You have found out that at least one recent jury verdict in Dallas on similar facts totaled $600,000.

Polly is still quite angry about the accident and how it has foreclosed her promising career in dance. She plans to finish her college education at Gordon, but she does not want her tuition and expenses for the remaining three years (approximately $60,000) to be a burden on her family, particularly in light of her father's declining health. She is also very concerned about her long-term physical condition in light of the prognosis of early arthritis and because any health insurance she might now obtain would most likely exclude her leg and ankle injury as a pre-existing condition. She is also concerned about how she will pay the $30,000 hospital lien. While Polly is not afraid of a jury trial, she would very much prefer to settle the case and get it over with before beginning her second year at Gordon, which starts in four months. She does not care whether the terms of any settlement are kept confidential, and she also doesn't care if the settlement is "structured" (whereby she would receive payment over a number of years) so long as she receives an initial lump sum that will cover her remaining college education and the hospital lien after attorney's fees are paid.

North Carolina law requires that all motorists carry liability insurance of at least $50,000, but you do not know the specific limits on Doan's policy that may be considerably more than $50,000. In addition, North Carolina is a pure contributory negligence jurisdiction, which precludes a claimant from recovering *any* amount on a personal injury claim if she is in any way contributorily negligent.

You estimate that the best monetary result you can realistically obtain for Polly is $479,000 calculated as follows: $30,000 for the medical bills ∓ $25,000 for pain and suffering from December through April ∓ $424,000 for permanent disability, future pain and suffering, and loss of the dancing career (53 years x $8,000 per year). Your rough guess is that Aaron will not settle for an amount over $300,000, particularly in light of the potential contributory negligence problem.

It is now early May, five months after the accident. You have told Aaron that in the near future you will provide him with an initial offer along with pertinent documentation about Polly's claim. Aaron already has a copy of the accident report by the police, and a copy of Polly's medical records and bills since December 12 from Bakersville Memorial. You expect that if the case is to be settled in the next three to four months, all of the negotiation is likely to be conducted with Aaron in writing and over the telephone.

Based on the foregoing, your Negotiation Preparation Outline might include the following:

|  | YOUR CLIENT | OTHER PARTY |
|---|---|---|
| **1. INFORMATION** | | |
| To Obtain: | 1. D's insurance policy limit. | 1. P's past medical history. |
| | 2. Whether D will run for re-election. | 2. Facts about P's drinking at the party. |
| | 3. D's financial situation. | 3. P's jury appeal. |
| To Reveal: | 1. P's jury appeal. | 1. P's .07 alcohol level. |
| | 2. P's promising dance career. | 2. P has recovered from her injuries. |
| | 3. P's disability rating. | |
| | 4. P is uninsured. | |
| | 5. $600,000 Dallas verdict. | |
| To Protect: | 1. P prefers to settle. | 1. D's financial situation. |
| | 2. P's prior medical history. | |

| **2. INTERESTS (from most important to least important)** | | |
|---|---|---|
| | 1. Not to burden family with college expenses. | 1. Aaron will want to minimize any pay out. |
| | 2. Concerned about future physical problems. | 2. D doesn't want publicity. |
| | 3. Pay off hospital lien. | 3. D doesn't want a judgment in excess of policy limits. |
| | 4. Settle the case. | 4. D probably wants to settle. |

| **3. OBJECTIVES** | | |
|---|---|---|
| Primary: | 1. $ to pay remaining college expenses and lien. | 1. Aaron wants to pay as little $ as possible. |

|  | | |
|---|---|---|
| | 2. Future medical insurance. | 2. D doesn't want a judgment in excess of policy limits. |
| Secondary: | 1. $ to compensate for future pain and suffering. | 1. Settle the case. |
| | | 2. Include confidentiality clause in settlement. |
| Incidental: (to exchange) | 1. No confidentiality clause in settlement. | 1. -------------------- |

---

4. POSSIBLE SOLUTIONS (most preferred to to least preferred)

| | | |
|---|---|---|
| | 1. Lump-sum settlement. | 1. Structured settlement. |
| | 2. Part lump-sum and part structured settlement. | 2. Part lump-sum and part structured settlement. |
| | 3. Carrier to provide P with future insurance. | |

---

5. BEST ALTERNATIVES TO A NEGOTIATED AGREEMENT (BATNA)

| | | |
|---|---|---|
| | 1. Binding arbitration or mediation. | 1. Jury trial. |
| | 2. Jury trial. | 2. Binding arbitration or mediation. |

---

6. FACTUAL AND LEGAL LEVERAGE POINTS

| | | |
|---|---|---|
| Strong points: | 1. P's jury appeal. | 1. P's potential contributory negligence. |
| | 2. Permanent disability. | 2. P is fully recovered. |
| | 3. $30,000 in special damages. | 3. Speculative future medicals. |
| | 4. Promising career is destroyed. | 4. Lower verdict expectancy In Bakersville. |
| | 5. Dallas jury verdict of $600,000. | |
| Weak points: | 1. P's potential contributory negligence. | 1. P's jury appeal. |
| | 2. Dancing career speculative. | 2. P's permanent disability. |
| | 3. Future medicals speculative. | 3. Promising career destroyed. |

4. Lower verdict ex-
pectancy in Bakers-
ville.

---

## 7. POTENTIAL TARGET AND RESISTANCE POINTS

Target Points:       1. $479,000          1. $100,000
Resistance Points:   1. $150,000          1. $300,000
                     (Settlement Zone = $150,000 to
                     $300,000)

---

## 8. OFFERS OR PROPOSALS

1st: $600,000              1st: $90,000
2nd: $500,000              2nd: ?
3rd: ?                     3rd: ?
4th: $350,000              4th: $300,000
(not lower than $150,000)
— Consider structured settlement for
any amount over $150,000
— Trade confidentiality clause for more
$
— Trade less $ for carrier insuring P
for leg and ankle (P to pay premiums)

---

## 9. PARTICULAR TACTICS

1. Threaten lawsuit     1. Aaron may
in 30 days if case not  delay until he
settled.                gets discovery
                        relevant to con-
                        tributory negli-
                        gence.

2. Send a videotape
of P to Aaron.

3. Send Aaron affida-
vits from students
who say P was able
to drive.

# § 12.06   ILLUSTRATION OF NEGOTIATION PREPARATION OUTLINE (PROBLEM-SOLVING APPROACH)

Assume you represent Coble Inc., a small midwestern fertilizer manufacturer. Coble has one plant in the Midwest and has recently developed an improved fertilizer for commercial farming. Coble wants to expand its market for the new fertilizer by establishing new plants throughout the country. While Coble's first plant has been profitable, the company does not have the capital to build new plants of its own and has decided against seeking traditional financing for fear that incurring additional debt in the foreseeable future would strain the company's resources. Moreover, Coble still does not have a well-developed management team with the capability of managing multiple plants in different areas of the country.

Consequently, over the past year Coble has entered into licensing agreements with two other companies, one in the southeast and one in the northeast. Under these agreements, Coble has granted each company an exclusive right to manufacture and sell the new fertilizer (and any improvement to the product that is made or acquired by Coble) within a 250-mile radius of the licensee's plant. Each company paid Coble an initial fee in the form of a nonrefundable advance against royalties, which provided Coble with immediate cash to expand its own plant and engage in continuing research and development. To prevent the licensees from developing a substitute to Coble's fertilizer and thus avoid payment of additional royalties in the future, the licensees were required to assign all of their improvements in fertilizer substitutes to Coble so that it could remain in control of the business and receive royalties on any improvements to the product that were manufactured and sold by any licensee.

Through these licensing arrangements, Coble's on-going plan is to obtain additional plants throughout the country that are run by management supplied by licensees. The licensees would have the benefit of exclusively manufacturing and selling a top-quality product, and generate earnings based on the success of their sales and plant operations.

Although Coble has done well by its Midwestern plant and licensees in the southeast and northeast, it has not yet been able to expand its market into the farm belts of the central states such as Nebraska and Kansas. However, Coble has recently been contacted by Baxter, Inc., a manufacturer and seller of pesticides. Baxter owns and operates two plants, one in the southeast and the other in Nebraska, and is interested in entering into a licensing agreement with Coble to manufacture and sell the new fertilizer from both of Baxter's plants.

Representatives of Coble and Baxter have already held preliminary discussions about a potential licensing arrangement. Coble has learned that while Baxter has never been in the fertilizer business, the company has an interest in developing its own line of fertilizers sometime in the near future and would not want to assign those products to Coble and pay royalties on them. Coble has also learned that Baxter has a large share of the pesticide market in the southeast and central states (including Nebraska, Kansas, Oklahoma, and the Dakotas), and virtually all of its customers would be potential buyers of the new fertilizer. Finally, Baxter has made clear that in order to enter into a licensing agreement, Baxter must be permitted to manufacture and sell Coble's new fertilizer from both of Baxter's plants.

Coble is concerned that if Baxter develops new fertilizers in the future and pays no royalties on them, Coble will be in the ironic position of having put Baxter into the fertilizer business, only to lose the ability to earn money from a business initially created by Coble's creative efforts. In addition, while granting Baxter a license in the southeast would not violate Coble's specific territorial agreement with its southeastern licensee, Coble is concerned that competition between two licensees in that region might reduce overall profits. Notwithstanding the latter concern, Coble has also had some exploratory discussions with Fulton, Inc. of Atlanta, Georgia, which is interested in a licensing agreement on the same terms as those that Coble negotiated with its current southeastern licensee. However, Coble is more interested in making a deal with Baxter because of its broad customer base not only in the southeast but throughout the central states.

Coble's strong preference is to negotiate a licensing agreement with Baxter along the same terms as Coble has negotiated with its other licensees. While Coble intends to be flexible, in no event will it enter into an agreement that does not provide some protection against Baxter's domination of the commercial fertilizer business through the development of its own line of fertilizers. Because Coble's cash flow situation is now much better than it was a year ago, Coble is prepared to be flexible about requiring Baxter to pay a nonrefundable initial fee.

The lead negotiator for Baxter is its in-house attorney, Malcolm Sears. Sears has a reputation for being smart, forthright, and easy going. A meeting has been scheduled between you and Sears in ten days to see if the basic elements of a licensing agreement can be worked out.

Based on the foregoing, your Negotiation Preparation Outline might include the following:

|  | YOUR CLIENT | OTHER PARTY |
|---|---|---|
| **1. INFORMATION** | | |
| To Obtain: | 1. Number of B's potential customers for fertilizer. | 1. History of gross sales of fertilizer. |
| | 2. B's ability to convert plants for fertilizer mfg. | 2. Other licensees and the terms of their agreements. |
| To Reveal: | 1. C's strong sales. | 1. B's broad customer base. |
| | 2. Discussions with Fulton. | 2. B's ability to manufacture and sell fertilizer. |
| To Protect: | - - - - - | - - - - - |

| **2. INTERESTS** (from most important to least important) | | |
|---|---|---|
| | 1. Expand market into central states. | 1. Expand into fertilizer mfg. and sales at both plants. |
| | 2. Protect control over product and future royalties. | 2. Retain all rights to B's own line of fertilizers. |
| | 3. Maintain cash flow for on-going R and D. | 3. Pay lowest royalties and initial fee as possible. |

| **3. OBJECTIVES** | | |
|---|---|---|
| Primary: | 1. Enter into licensing agreement with B, particularly to expand market into central states. | 1. Enter into licensing agreement with C for both of B's plants. |
| | 2. Protect control over product and future royalties. | 2. Pay no royalties on any fertilizers developed by B. |

| Secondary: | 1. Require B to pay the same royalties as are being paid by other licensees. | 1. Pay lowest royalties and initial fee as possible. |
| Incidental: (to exchange) | 1. Amount of initial fee. | 1. - - - - - |

---

## 4. POSSIBLE SOLUTIONS (most preferred to to least preferred)

| | |
| --- | --- |
| 1. Licensing agreement on the same terms as those negotiated with C's other licensees. | 1. Licensing agreement without assignment to C of any fertilizers developed by B alone. |
| 2. Licensing agreement without assignment to C of fertilizers developed by B alone, but B must share any of its improvements/ substitutes with C and permit C and its other licensees to use them without cost. | 2. Licensing agreement without assignment to C, but B still gets to manufacture and sell any improvements to C's product that are made or acquired by C or its other licensees. |
| 3. Licensing agreement without assignment to C, but B only gets to manufacture and sell improvements to product made by C alone and not acquired by C from its other licensees. | 3. Reduction in initial fee. |
| 4. Reduction in initial fee. | |

---

## 5. BEST ALTERNATIVES TO A NEGOTIATED AGREEMENT (BATNA)

| | |
| --- | --- |
| 1. Grant a license to Fulton. | 1. Develop a fertilizer product on B's own. |
| 2. Find other licensees in the central states. | 2. Find another licensor. |

---

## 6. FACTUAL AND LEGAL LEVERAGE POINTS

| Strong points: | 1. C's strong sales. | 1. B's broad market and customers. |
| | 2. Fulton is a potential licensee. | 2. B has 2 plants. |
| | 3. C already has a licensee in the southeast. | 3. B has ability to manufacture and sell C's product. |
| | 4. B has never been in the fertilizer business. | |
| Weak points: | 1. C has no market in the central states. | 1. C already has a licensee in the southeast. |
| | 2. B has many customers. | 2. B has never been in the fertilizer business. |

|  |  | 3. Fulton is a potential licensee. |
|---|---|---|

**7. POTENTIAL TARGET AND RESISTANCE POINTS**

| Target Points: | 1. Licensing agreement on the same terms as those negotiated with C's other licensees. | 1. Licensing agreement for both plants. |
|---|---|---|
| Resistance Points: | 1. Licensing agreement with some protection against B dominating the fertilizer market. | 1. Licensing agreement without assignment to C of any fertilizers developed by B. |

**8. OFFERS OR PROPOSALS**

| | | |
|---|---|---|
| | 1st: Licensing agreement on the same terms as those negotiated with C's other licensees. | 1st: Licensing agreement without assignment to C of any fertilizers developed by B alone. |
| | 2nd: Licensing agreement without assignment to C of fertilizers developed by B alone, but B must share all of its improvements/ substitutes with C and permit C and its other licensees to use them without cost. | 2nd: Same as C's 2nd offer, but B still gets to manufacture and sell any improvements to C's product that are made or acquired by C or its other licensees. |
| | 3rd: Same as B's second offer, but B only gets to manufacture and sell improvements to product made by C alone and not acquired by C from its other licensees. | 3rd: Same as C's 3rd offer, but C must reduce its initial fee. |
| | 4th: Same as B's 3rd offer, and initial fee to be 75% of that charged to C's other licensees. | 4th: Same as B's 4th offer, but initial fee to be 66% of that charged to C's other licensees. |

**9. PARTICULAR TACTICS**

| | | |
|---|---|---|
| | 1. Induce B to make the first offer. | 1.<br>- - - - - |

## § 12.07 THE ROLE OF THE CLIENT AND ADVISING THE CLIENT

The client's role in the negotiation is integral to preparation and the overall approach taken to the negotiation. Some studies have indicated that the dollar outcomes of certain settlements are consistently higher when the client is not only regularly informed about the progress of the negotiation, but actively participates in the overall process (even if he is not actually present during the negotiations). Similarly, attorney-client misunderstandings have been found to be the single largest factor resulting in unsuccessful settlements.[2]

Of course, the ultimate decision whether to accept or reject a settlement negotiated by a lawyer rests with the client, and a lawyer generally has a duty to inform his client of all settlement offers. Within this restriction, however, the client may give you broad authority not only over the process of the negotiation, but over what offers or counteroffers to make and what proposals to accept or reject. Thus, it is imperative that there be a clear understanding between you and your client about the extent of your authority throughout the negotiation process. (*See* § 9.02).

Generally, in informing and advising the client about the negotiation, you should cover: (1) the procedural and substantive process of the negotiation, including its different phases, the goals of the particular negotiation, and expected time frames; (2) how, when, and to what extent your client may be involved at different stages of the process or during the actual negotiation; (3) when and how your client will receive status reports about the progress of the negotiation; (4) all alternatives to the negotiation process and the relative advantages and disadvantages of those alternatives; and (5) all expenses and attorney fees that are likely to be incurred in negotiating the case or resolving it by other means such as trial. Because negotiation is a dynamic and changing process, it is essential that you regularly advise your client of any reassessments about the foregoing matters as the situation warrants.

In addition, it is imperative that you establish a strong relationship of trust with your client. Never inflate your client's expectations about what may be accomplished through the negotiation, and always inform him that your representation is aimed at achieving the best result consistent with his objectives and interests. A relationship grounded in honesty and trust in your skill and judgment is essential to effective representation.

---

[2] *See* G. Williams, *Legal Negotiation and Settlement* 58–60 (1983).

# Chapter 13

# NEGOTIATING IN WRITING AND OVER THE TELEPHONE

## § 13.01  INTRODUCTION

Many negotiations are conducted exclusively in writing, over the telephone, or through a combination of both. This is particularly true for small business deals or disputes, domestic disputes, and non-catastrophic personal injury cases. Typically, one party initiates the negotiation by mailing, faxing, or e-mailing a proposal or demand letter, and the other party responds in writing or negotiations proceed over the phone. Particularly in personal injury cases, lawyers usually start negotiations by sending the insurance adjuster a "settlement brochure" that details the client's contentions about liability and damages, and provides an initial settlement "demand." There are certain advantages and disadvantages to negotiating in writing and over the telephone. In addition, there are a variety of techniques that can enhance the effectiveness of these methods of negotiation.

## § 13.02  NEGOTIATING IN WRITING — ADVANTAGES AND DISADVANTAGES

The principal advantage of negotiating in writing is that it creates a paper record that leaves less room for misunderstanding, and allows the other party to carefully review what is being said and share it with other persons involved in the negotiation. Also, correspondence is often more articulate. Strong points can be emphasized, and weak points carefully downplayed or refuted. Matters that might be difficult to say face to face can be controlled through delicate wording and phrasing. Moreover, writing is an efficient and unmistakable way of conveying instructions, sanctions, time frames, and deadlines.

The principal disadvantage of negotiating in writing is that it is impersonal and does not lend itself to interpersonal or emotional appeals. Moreover, a sloppily worded or ambiguous letter can create false impressions, confusion, or misunderstandings that may be more difficult to erase later. Writing also takes time, not only from the standpoint of preparing the correspondence or other documentation, but by slowing down the pace of the negotiation.

## § 13.03  TECHNIQUES FOR EFFECTIVE CORRESPONDENCE

Whether writing an initial business proposal, pre-litigation demand letter, or response to either, you should consider the following:

### [1]  Send the Letter By Registered or Certified Mail

Consider sending the letter by registered or certified mail, return receipt requested. This will inevitably grab the attention of the recipient and foreclose any contention that the letter was not received. If you choose this form of mailing, be sure to designate on the first page of the letter that it was sent by certified mail, return receipt requested. If you fax the letter, be sure to keep the printout showing that the fax went through to the recipient.

### [2]  Copy the Letter to Other Persons

Particularly if the letter is being sent to a business or governmental entity, consider copying the letter to any individual who is likely to be directly or indirectly involved in the negotiation. This is likely to exert pressure on the recipient and increase the chances of getting a corporation or governmental entity to act promptly. However, this tactic should not be employed if it will unnecessarily alienate the addressee or other persons to whom a copy of the letter is sent. Do not send a copy to the opposing party if counsel represents him, because of course you cannot correspond with a represented party.

### [3]   Identify Your Authority to Represent

In the first paragraph of your letter, clearly identify the subject matter of your representation and authority to represent. This is an essential formality that will require the other side to respond directly to you.

### [4]   Adopt an Appropriate Style and Tone

Adjust the style and tone of your letter to the particular recipient and anyone else who might read the letter. For example, if you are writing directly to an unrepresented party, you should avoid unnecessary legalese. If the letter is sent to the other side's lawyer, always assume that the letter will be read by his client.

Avoid using language from which any personal attack or insult might be inferred. Although, in an appropriate case, your letter should be firm, your overall style and tone should be identical to that which you would consider professional if you were the recipient of the letter. In this regard, particularly if you are writing to a person you do not know, consider concluding the letter with, "I look forward to hearing from you and working with you on this matter." Similarly, in responding to a letter, you should regulate the tone as well, regardless of the tone used by the other side. For example, you might begin your response with, "This will acknowledge and thank you for your letter of . . . "

### [5]   Highlight the Pertinent Facts and Law

Be sure to educate the other side to the relevant facts. It is best to state them in an objective tone rather than by editorializing or being argumentative. Because your understanding of the facts is often limited to what your client has told you, leave yourself maneuvering room in the event that your client's version is not totally accurate. This can be accomplished by prefacing your factual recitation with, "According to our client, . . . " In addition, if you need an immediate response from the other side to verify your understanding of the facts (as where you are contemplating injunctive relief), you might write: "To prevent any misunderstanding about the facts surrounding this matter, please advise us immediately if our understanding is incorrect" [or] "If I do not hear from you on or before . . . , I will assume that the facts related by my client are accurate."

Educate the other side to your legal position. This might be stated by quoting the particular language of a contract or court order at issue, or by summarizing or citing to specific statutory or case law supporting your legal contention. Also, consider attaching to your letter a copy of any pertinent documentation, legal authority, or even a draft complaint or motion.

Of course, you should highlight the facts and law most favorable to your client. While you should never deliberately misrepresent the facts or law, you have no obligation to disclose weak facts or adverse legal authority in the negotiation context. If your letter cannot summarily deal with weak points, it is often best to deal with them at a later stage of the negotiation. The structure of your letter, word selection, and choice of points to emphasize or omit can help you put the best light on your client's situation.

## [6]    Convey a Specific Proposal or Course of Action

A business proposal or pre-litigation demand letter is essentially meaningless if it does not specifically convey what you propose or what you are asking the other side to do or not to do. In addition, the terms of your proposal or demand should not be vague or ambiguous unless you have a deliberate reason for leaving matters open ended or imprecise. Thus, in stating a particular proposal or demand, make sure that it appropriately answers who, what, which, when, where, why, and how.

## [7]    State a Time Frame for Action and Consequences for Inaction

Consider including in your letter a time frame or deadline within which you expect the other side to act. Imposing a time constraint on the other party will exert pressure on the negotiating process. In choosing a time frame or length of a deadline, you must bear in mind whether your purpose is to induce immediate action or to bide time (*see Deadlines* in Chapter 10).

In addition, setting a time frame for action is most effective when coupled with an indication or specific statement of the consequences that could occur or sanctions that could be imposed if the other side is unresponsive. Thus, it is often desirable to educate the other side to these consequences or what you will be forced to do in the event that no timely agreement is reached (*see Threats* in Chapter 10). For example, a pre-litigation demand letter might say: "If we do not hear from you by . . . p.m. on . . . , we will have no alternative but to immediately institute appropriate legal proceedings. If that should become necessary, in addition to the principal amount of $_____, we will request that the court award reasonable attorneys' fees, interest, and all court costs pursuant to [cite statute]."

## § 13.04    ILLUSTRATION OF A DEMAND LETTER

June 7, [year]

|                          |                  |
|--------------------------|------------------|
| Mr. Franklin Sinclair,   | CERTIFIED        |
| Esq. Suite 300, Bartlett | MAIL RE-         |
| Building 210 N. Jones    | TURN RE-         |
| Street Raleigh, North    | CEIPT            |
| Carolina 27602           | REQUESTED[1]     |

RE: <u>Unauthorized Sale of Marital Home of Ida L. Doe and Austin T. Doe</u>

Dear Mr. Sinclair:

Our law firm represents Ms. Ida. L. Doe in connection with her recent separation from her husband, Austin T. Doe, who I understand you represent. Ms. Doe has authorized me to contact you regarding your client's apparent plans to sell the parties' marital home and potentially defeat Ms. Doe's interest in it as distributable marital property under G.S. 50-20 *et. seq.*[2]

As you may know, the parties separated on May 17, [year], and since then Mr. Doe has been in possession of the marital home at 3629 Briarwood Court in Raleigh,

---

[1] *See* § 13.03 at [1]. A letter such as this might also be faxed.

[2] *See* Id. at [3].

and Ms. Doe has been living with her mother in Charlotte. The marital home was purchased for $106,000 on March 6, [year] during the marriage of the parties, but for some unexplained reason title was placed solely in Mr. Doe's name. (*See* Attachment 1). There is currently no mortgage or other indebtedness on the home, and, according to Ms. Doe, each of the parties paid one-half of the $15,000 down payment from their separate, premarital funds. Accordingly, the home constitutes distributable marital property under G.S. 50-20, notwithstanding that title is in Mr. Doe's name alone. *See Smith v. Smith*, 314 N.C. 80, 331 S.E.2d 682 (1985) (equal division of marital property is generally mandatory even though title to marital assets may be listed in the name of only one spouse during the course of the marriage).[3]

Ms. Doe has informed me that on June 6, [year] at approximately 7:30 p.m., Mr. Doe telephoned my client from Canada where he is currently on a two-week business trip. During the conversation, the parties apparently had an argument, and Mr. Doe said he intends to put the marital home up for sale immediately upon his return to Raleigh on June 22. Ms. Doe reports that Mr. Doe also said he wants to sell the home by no later than August 1, [year] does not care if the home is sold at a depressed price, and that he will "fix it" so that Ms. Doe will not get any of the proceeds from the sale. According to Ms. Doe, your client indicated further that he intends to list the house for only $180,000 even though the latest tax value alone is $200,000. (*See* Attachment 2).[4]

This letter serves as formal notice of Ms. Doe's objection to any listing or sale of the marital home at 3629 Briarwood Court without her consent. Any unauthorized sale of the home by Mr. Doe (or anyone on his behalf) will be considered unlawful conversion and waste of a marital asset in which Ms. Doe has at least a one-half interest. Ms. Doe is requesting that the parties immediately execute a written agreement that prohibits the listing or sale of the marital home without the consent of both parties and which acknowledges Ms. Doe's interest in the home as distributable marital property under G.S. 50-20. (*See* draft of proposed Agreement at Attachment 3).[5]

If I do not hear from you by 4:00 p.m. on or before June 19, [year], I will assume that the facts set forth in this letter are accurate and that Mr. Doe has no intention of entering into an agreement like that proposed above. If a satisfactory agreement cannot be reached on or before that date and time, we will be forced to seek immediate injunctive and other relief under G.S. 50-20 (i); G.S. 1A-1, Rule 65; G.S. 1-485; and G.S. 1-116 *et. seq.*[6]

Notwithstanding the circumstances giving rise to the parties' separation, Ms. Doe wishes to resolve all matters respecting the parties' rights as cooperatively and amicably as possible. I look forward to hearing from you and working with you on this case.[7]

**Sincerely,** _____

---

[3] *See* Id. at [5].

[4] *See* Id.

[5] *See* Id. at [6].

[6] *See* Id. at [5] and [7].

[7] *See* Id. at [4].

## § 13.05  SETTLEMENT BROCHURES

A settlement brochure is a document that sets out the legal and factual basis for a claimant's claim and details her damages. The brochure may be in the form of a letter or a more formal, bound document that contains extensive exhibits. Brochures are often used by plaintiffs' lawyers in personal injury cases to establish the basis for initial settlement demands and to define the issues for ensuing negotiations.

The brochure is often sent to the adjuster for the defendant's liability insurance carrier before any lawsuit is filed. The adjuster then responds to the claimant's initial offer in writing or over the telephone. After an exchange of one or more counteroffers, the case is often settled without the parties or their representatives having engaged in any face-to-face negotiations. If in-person negotiations do occur, the plaintiff's lawyer often uses the brochure in an effort to structure the negotiation agenda.

Effective brochures usually contain extensive documentary and illustrative exhibits to back up the claimant's assertions about the facts, liability, and damages. Broad disclosure is justified on the theory that the materials contained in the brochure would otherwise be revealed through discovery, and meaningful settlement discussions cannot occur without substantiating the claim. If these exhibits are voluminous, the brochure might contain an index of them. Such documentation lends credibility to the brochure and shows the opposing side that the claimant is prepared to litigate the case if necessary. Supporting documentation also serves to "paper" the defense representative's file to justify the amount of a final settlement.

While much of the documentation in a brochure will consist of materials that would be admissible at trial, you should not limit yourself to revealing strictly admissible evidence. So long as the information is pertinent to the claim, it should be included regardless of technical rules of evidence. Although, in the event of litigation, formal discovery will require you to reveal certain information that may be damaging to your client's case, weak aspects of your client's claim may usually be omitted from the brochure unless the opposing side already knows about these weak points and they can be effectively countered in the brochure. On the other hand, you should never make a false statement of material fact in the brochure (*see* § 9.06).

The format and content of a brochure are limited only by your imagination. Most brochures take the form of a written summary or narrative that makes reference to the documents or exhibits collected at the end of the brochure. However, some brochures are organized in a sequence of documents, photographs, and other materials that are arranged under captions and interspersed with commentary to provide a dramatic, pictorial presentation of the client's case. In addition, some attorneys will include a videotape that reenacts the accident or displays the client's injuries and physical limitations. Occasionally, video footage from television news stations or from the highway patrol might be included. Regardless of the particular format chosen for the brochure, you should usually include within it the following elements:

## [1]    Introduction to Brochure/Cover Letter

Your brochure should contain an introduction or be accompanied by a prefatory letter that provides a general introduction to the case and specifies any restrictions or limitations on the use of the brochure. These might include: (1) a statement that the brochure is being provided for settlement purposes only (*see* Fed. R. Evid. 408 and § 17.11); (2) a statement that the brochure is the property of your client, may not be copied without permission, and must be returned upon demand; (3) a date specified for a reply, after which the settlement offer will expire or be withdrawn; (4) an expression of willingness to settle the case reasonably; and (5) an offer to discuss the case further or to meet for future negotiations.

## [2]    Statement of Facts and Liability

The brochure should detail the facts giving rise to your client's claim and the basis for the defendant's liability. This statement of facts and liability should be written as a narrative, and refer, whenever possible, to exhibits such as police or accident reports, private investigative reports, witness statements (whether by affidavit or recorded interview), diagrams or photos of the accident scene or instrumentality causing the injury, or newspaper articles, etc. In addition, it is important to humanize your client and provide appropriate information about his background, such as age, marital status, family, education, military service, avocational interests, awards, commendations, financial status, work history, and the like.

When liability is clear, it is unnecessary to discuss the applicable law. Even when liability is disputed, many attorneys avoid any specific discussion of the law because the representative for the defendant is usually aware of the applicable legal principles and might be offended or feel patronized by counsel's citation to legal authority. On the other hand, if the recipient of the brochure is unlikely to be familiar with the applicable law, or if a discussion of the law otherwise seems appropriate, the legal grounds for liability should be set out and supported by accurate citations to case law and statutory authority. In this regard, some attorneys also include a copy of the plaintiff's proposed complaint.

## [3]    Summary of Medical Treatment

The brochure should contain a chronological summary of your client's pertinent medical treatment. This might be written in narrative form or by quoting verbatim the most important portions of the medical records. A copy of all relevant medical records (including test results and x-rays) should be included as an exhibit and indexed if the records are voluminous. Any letters from physicians that are not part of the formal medical records and that discuss the extent and nature of your client's future medical treatment, future medical costs, prognosis, and extent of disability should also be summarized and included as an exhibit. If the medical records contain references to a medical condition or course of treatment that is wholly unrelated to the accident, the summary should omit those matters.

### [4]     Summary of Lost Earnings

If your client has incurred lost wages due to her injury, or will incur future lost wages or a reduction in earning capacity, these elements of damage should be described with particularity. In the case of past lost wages, the brochure should include a statement from your client's employer showing your client's gross wage rate, time out of work due to the accident, and total lost wages. In the event of future lost earnings or a reduction in earning capacity, the brochure might include a report prepared by an economist that calculates the future lost wages and fringe benefits, reduced to present value.

### [5]     Summary of Pain and Suffering and Permanent Injury

Your client's general damages for past, present, and future pain and suffering and permanent injury, as applicable, should be vividly described in narrative form. The description should cover all pertinent aspects of your client's life, including physical, psychological, social, and economic effects. Whenever possible, this description should be accompanied by photographs of your client before and after the accident and during different stages of recovery. Particularly in catastrophic injury cases, a day-in-the-life video of your client may be highly effective. If permanent injury is involved, your client's life expectancy should be stated based on standard mortuary tables.

### [6]     Damages Summary and Initial Demand

The conclusion of the brochure should provide an itemized summary of your client's damages along with an initial demand or first offer. Each item of damage, whether special or general, should be separately enumerated and supported by available statements, bills, receipts, or other documentation. Special damages might include: (1) medical expenses, (2) future medical expenses, (3) lost wages, (4) future lost earnings and benefits, and (5) miscellaneous expenses (past and future).

Items of general damage should also be separately enumerated when appropriate. These might include: (1) past pain and suffering (including humiliation and emotional distress), (2) future pain and suffering, and (3) loss of life's pleasures or other damage resulting from permanent disfigurement or disability. In an appropriate case, some attorneys also set out the amount that would be sought at trial for punitive damages.

At the conclusion of the brochure, the special and general damages should be combined to produce a single figure representing an initial settlement demand or first offer.

## § 13.06   ILLUSTRATION OF SETTLEMENT BROCHURE (PERSONAL INJURY CASE)

**SETTLEMENT BROCHURE**
**Prepared on behalf of**
**JANE R. POOLE**
**June 14, [year]**
**By:**
**John W. Doe, Jr.**
**DOE & DOE**
**Suite 344, 30 Columbia Avenue**
**Charlotte, North Carolina 28212**
**Telephone: (704) 333-2868**
**Fax: (704) 221-8685**
**E-Mail: jwdoe@lightspeed.com**

June 14, [year]

Mr. Donald Delaney
Senior Claims Adjuster
All-Care Insurance Company
629 Bellview Road
West Newton, Massachusetts 02165

RE:     My Client: Ms. Jane R. Poole Our File
        No.: JWD-2392 #1 Your Insured:
        Winslow S. Hall Date of Collision:
        January 4, [year]

Dear Mr. Delaney:

As I mentioned to you in my letter of January 10, [year], I represent Ms. Jane R. Poole in her personal injury claim arising out of an automobile collision on January 4, [year] in Charlotte, North Carolina caused by your insured, Mr. Winslow S. Hall. This settlement brochure summarizes Ms. Poole's personal injury claim, and all information provided herein is intended for settlement purposes only. You are free to copy the brochure if you wish, but it is the property of Ms. Poole and DOE & DOE law firm and is returnable to us on demand.[8]

### FACTS AND LIABILITY

There is no question about liability in this case. On Monday, January 4, [year], at approximately 8:30 a.m., Ms. Poole was on her way to work, traveling east on Harnette Avenue in Charlotte, North Carolina. She stopped at a stoplight at the intersection of Harnette Avenue and St. Mary's Street. Mr. Hall, who was also traveling east on Harnette Avenue, lost control of his vehicle and crashed into the rear of Ms. Poole's car at an estimated speed of 45 miles per hour in a 35 mile per hour zone. (*See* Charlotte Police Accident Report at Exhibit 1).

Mr. Milton Reeves, who was traveling in a car behind Mr. Hall, witnessed the accident and will testify that Mr. Hall was "speeding," driving "erratically," and "weaving" in the road just before the impact. (*See* statement of Milton Reeves at

---

[8] Here, there is no reason to prohibit copying of the brochure because all of the materials contained in it would be discoverable in the event of litigation and there is no reason to suppose that the adjuster will inappropriately disseminate the contents of the brochure. Thus, the requirement that the brochure be returned to the claimant's lawyer upon demand is, in this case, a purely *pro forma* safeguard.

Exhibit 2). Officer T. L. Fennell, who responded to the accident scene and prepared the police report, charged Mr. Hall with "Failure to Reduce Speed to Avoid an Accident" to which Mr. Hall entered a plea of guilty on March 6, [year]. (*See* Citation at Exhibit 3). Although the accident report also notes that the rear brake lights on Ms. Poole's car were not working at the time of the accident, under the circumstances of this case no jury would find that this fact was a contributing or proximate cause of the accident.[9]

Upon impact, even though Ms. Poole was wearing her seatbelt, she was thrown violently forward and backward in her seat, and her left knee slammed into the dashboard. The force of the impact broke the driver's seat. Her car was nearly totaled. (*See* photographs at Exhibit 4).[10]

## MEDICAL TREATMENT

Ms. Poole was taken by ambulance to the emergency room at Hopeview Memorial Hospital in Charlotte. The following are the most pertinent, verbatim portions of her medical records during her five-month course of treatment (*See* medical records at Exhibit 5):[11]

1/4/yr:     Emergency Room, Hopeview Memorial Hospital.
Chief complaints: low back pain and stiffness; numbness; soreness in neck; left knee pain from impact with dashboard.
Thorough examination.
Small contusion, bruising to medial left knee.
DIAGNOSIS: Musculoskeletal pain.
DISCHARGE INSTRUCTIONS:
1. Expect to be sore.
2. Advil for pain.
3. Heating pad for pain.
4. No strenuous activity for next 2–3 days, then advance as tolerated.
5. Return immediately if problems develop or symptoms worsen.

1/8/yr:     Dr. Bruce Cooper, MD, Charlotte Family Medicine Center, P.A.
New patient.
Chief complaints: development of increased lower back pain and left upper back pain; persistent pain in right lower rib cage; difficulty in sleeping.

---

[9] If there was any real doubt about this proposition, the attorney might cite an appropriate appellate decision.

[10] For purposes of effect, the attorney might put the photographs immediately following this paragraph rather than including them in an attached exhibit.

[11] This approach would not be practical if the medical records were particularly voluminous. In that event, the attorney might summarize the course of treatment in a narrative and make specific reference to key medical records such as surgical procedures or discharge summaries.

EXAM: Neck reveals some mild left trapezial tightness; tenderness; mild to moderate paralumbosacral tenderness over both iliac crests; point moderate to severe tenderness over mid-thorzic right rib cage and around T7–8.

ASSESSMENT: Neck and back strain; probable fractured rib.

PLAN: Will obtain rib x-rays. Sent to Spellman Radiology for x-rays. Recommend local ice packs to rib cage; gentle flexible exercises, avoiding any activities that exacerbate any of her pain; avoid high impact activities. Prescribed: Advil for pain; Ambien 10 mg for sleep. Follow-up recheck in one week.

1/9/yr:     Spellman Radiology, Dereck S. Spellman, MD.

X-rays taken of right ribs: reveal nondisplaced fracture of right 10th rib.

1/14/yr:     Dr. Bruce Cooper, MD, Charlotte Family Medicine Center, P.A.

Follow-up examination. Slight "clicking" left hip; some occasional discomfort on that side with walking. Slight pressure lower back.

Examination of lower back reveals some mild paralumbosacral tenderness over left superior anterior iliac crest. Mild-moderate tenderness over right lateral rib cage.

ASSESSMENT: Mild left hip, low back strain; rib fracture.

PLAN: Encourage patient to get back into normal exercise program at 50% level and slowly increase. Recommend hot packs and stretching. Recheck in 3 weeks. Consider physical therapy. Advise patient to expect several weeks to heal but she should have complete resolution of symptoms.

2/16/yr:     Dr. Bruce Cooper, MD, Charlotte Family Medicine Center, P.A.

Follow-up examination.

No longer has pain in rib cage; now has most of pain in neck: right side greater than left. Neck gets tired upon flexion or leaning forward. Occasional blurring of vision, but no apparent visual field defects. Examination of neck reveals some mild-moderate tenderness on right paracervical ridge.

Noted that patient saw her gynecologist for pregnancy test: positive a week ago, but negative serum test four days ago. Apparently since accident she has also had galactorrhea which is being monitored by her GYN.

ASSESSMENT: Neck strain secondary to motor vehicle accident.

PLAN: Get baseline cervical spine x-rays; send to physical therapy with follow-up in one month.

ASSESSMENT: Galactorrhea; possible spontaneous abortion.

PLAN: Follow-up with GYN. Galactorrhea could be due to emotional trauma of

motor vehicle accident causing patient's hormone imbalance.

2/20/yr:     Spellman Radiology, Dereck S. Spellman, MD

Cervical Spine x-rays: minor straightening of cervical spine which could represent muscle spasm.

3/16/yr:     Dr. Bruce Cooper, MD, Charlotte Family Medicine, P.A.

Follow-up. Gets occasional sharp pain in head and neck; some stiffness in lower back. Will be starting on regular exercise aerobic program soon and will be seeing Ian Tersky, Physical Therapist for strengthening and flexibility exercises. Galactorrhea apparently resolved. No new symptoms.

Low back reveals some slight limitation in forward flexion.

ASSESSMENT: Resolving neck and back strain.

PLAN: Physical therapy to get patient back on road to recovery and help get back to normal full-time activity and exercise. Cervical spine x-rays unremarkable except for slight straightening consistent with spasm. Advised to follow-up when ready to come to closure on this.

3/28/yr:     Ian Tersky, P.T., Charlotte Comprehensive Physical Therapy Center.

Initial evaluation.

Chief complaints: neck/back pain; headaches. Symptoms aching in nature and intermittent. Discomfort caused by symptoms severe in intensity, affecting her most in afternoon and evening.

ASSESSMENT:

Diagnosis: Cervicolumbar strain.

Problem list: Limited cervical range of motion; limited lumbar range of motion; increased density right levator and lumbar myofasia.

GOALS:

Short term: Decrease inflexibility and inflammation; increase cervical range of motion to full.

Long term: Increase lumbar ROM to full; decrease headache frequency and intensity.

PLAN:

Treatment: Ice; facet stretching; massage; and flexibility exercises. Treatment to be followed 2 times per week for approx. 3 weeks.

4/2/yr:     Charlotte Comprehensive Physical Therapy Center. Physical therapy.

4/5/yr:     Charlotte Comprehensive Physical Therapy Center. Physical therapy.

4/10/yr:     Charlotte Comprehensive Physical Therapy Center. Physical therapy.

4/13/yr:    Charlotte Comprehensive Physical Therapy Center.
Physical therapy.

4/17/yr:    Charlotte Comprehensive Physical Therapy Center.
Physical therapy.

5/10/yr:    Dr. Bruce Cooper, MD, Charlotte Family Medicine,
P.A.

Patient here to achieve some closure on her motor vehicle accident. Gets occasional mild tightness in lower
back with rotation. Finds physical therapy helpful.
Examined.

ASSESSMENT: Resolved back and neck strain.

PLAN: Patient to continue as she has been doing. No
need for further physical therapy at this point. Continue with home exercise program.[12]

## MEDICAL EXPENSES

Listed below are Ms. Poole's medical and miscellaneous, pharmaceutical expenses to date (*See* Exhibit 6):

| | |
|---|---|
| MECKLENBURG COUNTY AMBULANCE SERVICE | $250.00 |
| HOPEVIEW MEMORIAL HOSPITAL | $200.00 |
| CHARLOTTE FAMILY MEDICINE CENTER, P.A. | $350.00 |
| SPELLMAN RADIOLOGY | $250.00 |
| CHARLOTTE COMPREHENSIVE PHYSICAL THERAPY CENTER | $500.00 |
| MISCELLANEOUS PHARMACEUTICAL EXPENSES | $80.00 |
| | **$1,630.00** |

## LOST WAGES[13]

Ms. Poole is employed as an Account Technician I at the University of North
Carolina at Charlotte. Due to the accident, she missed 52 hours of work at a gross
wage of $35.00 per hour. (*See* Letter from UNC Personnel and Benefits Office at
Exhibit 7).

TOTAL LOST WAGES        **$1,820.00**

---

[12] If the claimant sustained an injury that required future medical treatment, the next section of the
brochure would summarize that on-going treatment under a heading styled, "FUTURE MEDICAL
TREATMENT."

[13] If the client will sustain future lost wages or a reduction in earning capacity, these matters would
also be detailed here.

## PAIN AND SUFFERING[14]

Prior to the collision, Ms. Poole was a healthy 43-year-old woman. She had no prior history of medical problems like those sustained in this collision. Given the tremendous force of the collision (*see* photos at Exhibit 4), Ms. Poole was fortunate that she was not more seriously injured and that she was able to recover in five months.

As the medical records show, Ms. Poole sustained at least 116 days of continuous pain of varying intensity from January 4, [year] through the end of April [year]. As the physical therapy record of March 28 [year] states, her "discomfort [is] caused by symptoms severe in intensity, affecting her most in [the] afternoon and evening." Accordingly, the jury would be permitted to compensate approximately 80% of Ms. Poole's pain and suffering through a *per diem* calculation.

The medical records objectively show that the elements of her pain and suffering include (1) "a fracture of her right 10th rib," (2) "bruising to medial left knee," (3) "lower back pain,"(4) "upper back pain," (5) "difficulty in sleeping," (6) "avoiding any activities that exacerbate any of her pain," (7) "left hip pain," (8) "neck strain and pain," (9) "blurring of vision," (10) "muscle spasms," (11) "sharp pain in head," (12) "limitation in forward flexion," (13) "headaches," (14) "limited cervical range of motion," and (15) "galactorrhea due to emotional trauma of motor vehicle accident."

Ms. Poole's injuries markedly affected her daily activities. Her sleeplessness, headaches, and blurred vision left her lethargic and at times disoriented. Her rib fracture and cervical and paralumbosacral pain limited her movement. Routine household chores, grocery shopping, and even driving were difficult. Prolonged sitting at work exacerbated her pain in the afternoons and into the evenings. She was forced to markedly limit her social activities. She canceled her aerobics classes, and was forced to restrict other recreational activities. She was under Advil for pain, Ambien for sleeplessness, and variously used heating pads, ice packs, and hot packs to relieve her condition. The prolonged emotional trauma of the collision even manifested itself in a physical hormone imbalance.

## DAMAGES SUMMARY

| | |
|---|---|
| MEDICAL EXPENSES | $1,630.00 |
| LOST WAGES | $1,820.00 |
| PAIN AND SUFFERING | $_____ |
| **TOTAL DEMAND** | $_____ |

**Based on the foregoing, we propose that $_____ would be a reasonable sum to settle this case. After you have had an opportunity to review this brochure, I look forward to hearing from you and working with you on this case.**

**Sincerely,**

_____

**John W. Doe, Jr.**

---

[14] If the claimant has permanent injury or will sustain future pain and suffering, these matters would also be detailed here under a heading such as "PAIN AND SUFFERING AND PERMANENT INJURY."

## § 13.07   NEGOTIATING OVER THE TELEPHONE — ADVANTAGES AND DISADVANTAGES

When negotiations are conducted over the telephone (as contrasted with written communication), communication is enhanced and misunderstandings or misperceptions are reduced. Questions can be asked to clarify ambiguous proposals, and the interests and reasons underlying a party's proposals can be fully explored. The negotiators are able to share each other's views firsthand and focus on the particular matters they consider important. Moreover, even though the negotiators are not meeting face to face, they can usually get a sense of each other's true intentions by discerning changes in tone and voice inflection.

Telephone negotiations also give the parties a greater sense of freedom and security than they otherwise might feel when negotiating face to face. The negotiator is free to choose the time when he is willing to talk, and the pressure to make an on-the-spot response can be simply eliminated with a promise to phone the other party back after his proposal has been reviewed. Moreover, it is easier to say no to the other party over the phone, and discussions can be more gracefully terminated than would be the case if they were being conducted face to face.

On the other hand, because telephone negotiations are less personal than face-to-face interactions, they are almost always more abbreviated than personal meetings. Consequently, it is usually more difficult to create a concerted, psychological commitment to resolve the case over the phone. For the same reason that it is easier to say no over the phone, it is also easier for a party to engage in overtly competitive and deceptive tactics. In addition, notwithstanding that it is easier to come up with a graceful excuse for cutting short a phone conversation, some individuals feel psychologically pressured to negotiate once they are on the phone even though they may be distracted or unprepared. This may lead to hasty concessions and uninformed decisions.

## § 13.08   TECHNIQUES FOR EFFECTIVE TELEPHONE NEGOTIATIONS

Many of the bargaining techniques that are effective in face-to-face negotiations (*See* Chapter 14) apply to telephone negotiations as well. In addition, you should keep the following in mind:

### [1]   Do Not Commit Yourself Unless You Are Prepared

The negotiator who makes the telephone call often has an advantage over the recipient because the former will be prepared and the latter may be caught unawares. This may allow the phoning party to be more persuasive and exact greater concessions than would be possible if the negotiation had been formally scheduled. Thus, the recipient of the phone call should never hesitate to postpone making a response or decision until she is fully prepared to do so. In addition, the recipient should use the call as an opportunity to listen, ask questions, and obtain as much information from the other side as possible. After this information has been fully evaluated, the recipient can always call the other side back to give a response.

## [2]     Do Not Be Afraid to Be "Unavailable"

Of course, the recipient of a call may simply use the excuse that she is "unavailable" to take the call at the particular time. This is the best choice to make if you are so hurried or distracted that you cannot even use the call for the limited purpose of obtaining information from the other side. Moreover, if your objective is to delay negotiations, you can always have your secretary or assistant tell the other side that you will return the call at a later time.

## [3]     Use a Preparation Negotiation Outline

To negotiate effectively over the phone, you should prepare for it as you would for a face-to-face meeting. Thus, it may be useful to use a Preparation Negotiation Outline like that shown at § 12.04. It is also useful to prepare a checklist of items to be discussed to ensure that you present your points in a logical order and important matters are not overlooked.

In addition, take careful notes of the conversation so that you have a record of what was said. Concessions, promises, or other important points can often be forgotten during a protracted discussion. Throughout the conversation, confirm in your own words your understanding of the proposals or points being made by the other side. If an agreement is reached, promptly confirm its terms by fax, E-mail, or a follow-up letter to avoid any misunderstanding.

## [4]     Adjust the Pace and Tone of Your Voice

Unless you are negotiating on a televised conference call, telephone conversations do not, of course, allow the negotiators to observe one another. Thus, to enhance comprehension, you should consciously try to talk more slowly during a telephone negotiation. In addition, try to "put a face" in your voice. Even though the listener cannot see your expressions, if you talk as if he were sitting across the table from you, your tone of voice will convey greater feeling behind your words and enhance the persuasiveness of your presentation.

## [5]     Do Not Be Afraid to Call Back

After a telephone conversation is over, never hesitate to promptly call back if you discover an error or suspect a possible misunderstanding. The more abbreviated nature of telephone negotiations may sometimes cause the parties to overlook important matters or fail to clear up ambiguities in a final settlement offer. Thus, if you have any doubt about a proposal or agreement made over the phone, it is best to immediately call back and clarify the issue in lieu of having to reopen negotiations after a written agreement has been prepared for the parties to execute.

# Chapter 14

## NEGOTIATING FACE TO FACE

## § 14.01  INTRODUCTION

Negotiating face to face is a highly complex form of human behavior. Indeed, to negotiate effectively in person is much more of an art than a science. This effectiveness can be enhanced by understanding (1) how to set the stage for a face-to-face negotiation (*i.e.*, with whom, when, and where to negotiate, and who should attend the negotiation); (2) how to set the tone and agenda for the negotiation (*i.e.*, the negotiating atmosphere and the issues to be discussed); (3) the importance of reading body language during the negotiation; (4) how information is exchanged during the negotiation (*i.e.*, techniques for obtaining, protecting, and revealing information); (5) the process and techniques associated with traditional, adversarial bargaining (*i.e.*, the making of offers, counteroffers, and concessions, and using different forms of persuasion); (6) the process and techniques associated with problem-solving bargaining (*i.e.*, identifying the parties' interests or needs, and brainstorming for mutually beneficial solutions); (7) how to combine adversarial and problem-solving bargaining when appropriate; and (8) how to conclude the negotiation.

## § 14.02  WITH WHOM TO NEGOTIATE

In the vast majority of circumstances, you will have no control over choosing the person with whom you will negotiate. Once the opposing negotiator has been identified, you should conduct appropriate research about his likely style and strategy toward the negotiation (*see* §§ 8.04[2] and 12.02[3]). Sometimes it is desirable to arrange a pre-negotiation get-together to become acquainted with your counterpart and establish rapport. This initial meeting may also be useful to find out preliminary information about others who may be involved in the negotiation, and the general attitude of the other side toward the negotiation.

In the early stage of negotiations, it sometimes may become apparent that the negotiator for the other side actually has little authority to bind his principal. This is an undesirable situation because the success of a negotiation depends far more upon negotiating with a person who can make binding decisions than on negotiating with someone with whom you might feel more comfortable. If it is clear that the other side's agent has little authority, consider suggesting that the negotiation might be expedited by involving the principal or other decision-maker directly in the negotiation. This must be done tactfully so as not to offend the agent, and preferably should be arranged with the cooperation of the agent. If the agent is not agreeable to your suggestion, at the very least try to arrange a meeting or conference call with the agent and his principal.

Either at the outset of negotiations or as they progress, it may become apparent that you and your counterpart simply cannot get along with one another. In this situation, you might also suggest that the principals be directly included in the negotiation. Alternatively, you might suggest that additional negotiators participate in the discussions, or even that it would be in the best interests of both sides that each call upon some other representatives to continue the negotiation.

When the negotiation involves more than two parties, it is necessary to decide with which party you should start negotiations. While there may be myriad factors to consider in making this selection, generally it is desirable to start negotiations with the party who (1) is most likely to accept your position, (2) is most likely to establish a precedent during the negotiations, or (3) possesses the weakest bargaining power.

## § 14.03  WHEN TO NEGOTIATE

Although it is rare to have any choice about the person with whom you will negotiate, you will often have greater control over the timing of negotiations. Generally, you should initiate negotiations when the other party is in the weakest position or your client is in the strongest position. The optimal time for negotiating may be influenced by tactics such as *Asymmetrical Time Pressure*, setting *Deadlines, Delaying,* taking some action to create a *Fait Accompli*, or the development of a *Surprise* (*see* Chapter 10). In addition, you should consider the most optimal day of the week or time of day to negotiate, which should usually be a time when the parties are most apt to be alert or when the opposing side is under a pressing time constraint.

## § 14.04  WHERE TO NEGOTIATE

Whenever possible, you should seize the opportunity to choose the site of the negotiation — usually your own office. The negotiator who negotiates on her "home court" is apt to be more relaxed, confident, and assertive. In contrast, the visiting negotiator occupies the subordinate status of a guest, and is more likely to feel constrained and distracted in unfamiliar surroundings. Because familiar surroundings tend to reduce tension and anxiety, arranging the negotiation on your home turf may be particularly important if your client will attend the negotiation. One circumstance in which you might deliberately choose to hold the negotiation at the opposing party's office is if you believe that you may have to use a *Walkout* tactic in the event the negotiation deadlocks.

If you are unable to arrange the negotiation at your office and have a strong reason for not negotiating at your opponent's office, propose that the meeting take place at a neutral location. If you make all of the arrangements for the neutral site and pay the expenses for its use and refreshments, you will effectively make it an extension of your own office. In addition, gratuitously making these arrangements shows respect for the other side and the importance you attach to the negotiation.

When you are able to control where the negotiation will take place, it is also important to give attention to the overall environment and available seating arrangements. Generally, the negotiating room should be conducive to a relaxed, noncompetitive environment. There should be a conference table if documents are to be reviewed, and if there will be groups of participants, it is desirable to have adjacent rooms available for private caucuses. Refreshments should be made available, and the room should be quiet and free from outside distractions and interruptions, particularly the telephone.

Seating arrangements can also affect the initial tone of the negotiation. For example, a more adversarial atmosphere may be created when participants are seated opposite one another at a rectangular or round table, whereas a more cooperative atmosphere may exist when the participants sit together in an L-shaped configuration at a rectangular table, or together in a semicircle at a round table.[1]

## § 14.05  WHO SHOULD ATTEND THE NEGOTIATION

If a negotiator intends to employ a *Good Guy-Bad Guy Routine/Mutt and Jeff* approach or a *Two Against One* strategy (*see* Chapter 10), it is necessary to have a colleague join him in the negotiation. A negotiator might otherwise choose to have a colleague or assistant join him at the negotiation merely to serve as a passive, objective observer, or to assist in note taking or locating and presenting documentation or other materials during the discussion. An assistant may also provide psychological support and give the lead negotiator the benefit of a detached perspective as the negotiation progresses.

Having your client attend the negotiation presents certain drawbacks. When your client is present: (1) it may be more difficult for you to control the negotiation and prevent inappropriate argumentation between your client and the other side; (2) the emotional aspects of the dispute may be more likely to pervade the negotiation; (3) candor may be inhibited; (4) the other side may not be able to engage in emotional venting as a prerequisite to serious discussions; (5) you may create the impression that your client does not have complete confidence in you; (6) you will be deprived of the convenient excuse of having to *Adjourn or Caucus* with your client; (7) a *Good Guy-Bad Guy Routine/Mutt and Jeff* or *Lack of Authority or Limited Authority* tactic cannot be employed; and (8) it may be difficult to engage in any *Off-the-Record Discussions* with the opposing negotiator (*see* Chapter 10).

On the other hand, having your client and the other side's client present during the negotiation may be useful (1) if the parties expect to have a continuing relationship; (2) if substantive or emotional misunderstandings can be smoothed over in a face-to-face meeting; (3) if the client's presence is necessary to provide technical expertise, clarification of the facts, or input about an unforeseen issue; (4) if it would be beneficial to demonstrate the client's sincerity or jury appeal; or (5) if having the client present will muzzle an obstreperous or irrational negotiator. If your client will attend the negotiation, he must be fully advised about what to expect

---

[1] *See* M. Korda, *Power: How to Get It, How to Use It* (1975).

in terms of his role and your role, the agenda of the negotiation, potential tactics, and the importance of carefully monitoring nonverbal behavior.

If you represent an institution, labor union, or large corporate client, it may be necessary to have client officials present during the negotiation for "political" reasons or to authorize a settlement. In these circumstances, it also is sometimes psychologically desirable to have your audience outnumber the other side's audience. In the absence of an actual audience at the negotiation, the effect of an audience might otherwise exist when a party establishes a *Coalition*, publicly pronounces a *Lock-in Position*, or engages in other *Publicity* by utilizing press releases or news leaks (*see* Chapter 10).

If it is decided that your client will attend the negotiation, generally you will "take the lead" in the negotiation. Your client's role should be carefully restricted to the reasons why he is attending. For example, if his attendance is designed to demonstrate his jury appeal or to smooth over a misunderstanding, at some point during the negotiation you might have your client describe the events surrounding the controversy or permit the other side to ask him appropriate questions about those events. Apart from your client's pre-planned role, it is generally unwise for him to speak during the negotiation, and you might decide to continue the negotiation with the opposing side without your client present. Finally, in lieu of having your client present at the negotiation, you might choose to have him on telephone standby in the event you need to confer with him while the negotiation is underway.

## § 14.06  SETTING THE TONE

Once the stage has been set for the negotiation, the initial phase of the actual face-to-face meeting is a crucial opportunity to set the tone for the ensuing negotiation. This tone or atmosphere should be established from the time that the opposing side literally walks in the door. For example, a host negotiator who greets the other side with a smile, a handshake, and on a first name basis exudes warmth and trust. Greeting the visiting negotiator promptly and personally escorting her to the office or conference room show equality and respect. As mentioned in § 14.04, if the negotiators choose seats next to or adjacent to one another, as opposed to separating themselves by a wide distance or across from one another with a table in between, they will create a more cooperative atmosphere. On the other hand, a more adversarial atmosphere may be created when the negotiators are slow in starting the negotiation, shake hands as a glib formality, address one another as "Mr. _____ or Ms. _____," or deliberately seat themselves so as to create spatial separation, distance, or dominance.

After the initial greeting, the tone of the negotiation may be influenced by the extent to which the negotiators make an effort to engage in appropriate, casual conversation to establish rapport before "getting down to business." This preliminary conversation is useful to humanize the setting, to relax the participants, and to allow them to get to know one another if they have never met before. In this regard, it cannot be overemphasized that in an appropriate situation, making at the outset a genuine apology about the circumstances of the case or dispute may have a dramatic effect on the entire tone and ultimate success of the negotiation. This is so because direct displays of humility, contrition, or apology are rarely expressed in the face of the formalistic, ritualistic, and often nonsensical practice of never admitting fault or liability regardless of the facts. In addition, in an appropriate case, a negotiator should not hesitate to convey at the outset her desire to engage in a cooperative or problem-solving approach to the negotiation. This direct expression of a non-adversarial attitude toward the negotiation is uniquely powerful precisely because of the instinctive, competitive style and adversarial strategy that otherwise permeate most legal negotiations.

## § 14.07   SETTING THE AGENDA

The issues to be resolved in the negotiation and the order in which they will be addressed constitute the agenda for the negotiation. The agenda might be tacit, *ad hoc*, expressly agreed upon before the negotiation begins, or established through discussion or debate at the negotiation session. Whether the agenda is prearranged or established during the negotiation, you should have a specific agenda in mind before the face-to-face meeting.

This agenda should be prepared from your "Negotiation Preparation Outline." If you are able to control the issues to be resolved and the order in which they will be addressed in the negotiation, you will sometimes have an advantage over your opponent, particularly in complex adversarial bargaining. This is because the negotiator who controls how the issues are defined and when they will be discussed is in a better position to dictate the focus of the negotiation by framing the issues in the light most favorable to his client, emphasizing those topics or points of most importance to his client, and de-emphasizing the matters of most importance to the other side.

Most negotiations involve two types of issues: (1) those which center around the parties' "primary objectives" (*i.e.*, those matters which must be obtained to reach an agreement), and (2) those which constitute the parties' "incidental objectives" (*i.e.*, those matters which are of lesser importance and might be traded in order to obtain a primary objective) (*see* § 12.03[3]). The particular outcome of a negotiation may largely depend upon the order in which these different types of issues are presented and discussed.

There are distinct advantages and disadvantages to starting the negotiation with the "primary" issues on the one hand, or "incidental" issues on the other. Adversarial negotiators who put their primary objectives at the forefront of the agenda do so on the theory that it may be easier to resolve these difficult matters at the outset when the negotiators may have a more conciliatory attitude. Putting off the tough issues until the end may make them more difficult to resolve in the face of fatigue and if the parties have already used up most, if not all, of their "bargaining chips" constituting their incidental objectives. Moreover, dealing with the hard issues first creates a challenge that tests the parties' initial willingness to be flexible, and places pressure on them to determine more quickly whether a settlement can be reached or deadlock is inevitable. When problem-solving negotiators take this approach, they are sending the message that it is essential to first address the parties' most important needs or interests in order to reach an accord that accommodates as many of those needs or interests as possible.

The obvious disadvantage of starting with the primary issues is that the negotiation may result in premature deadlock. The haste associated with "cutting to the chase" may cause the negotiators to become discouraged and abandon the negotiation before giving it a chance to work its course. In addition, if the primary issues are resolved first, the bargainers may not have a chance to use their "bargaining chips" to optimal advantage by trading them for a more favorable resolution of a primary issue.

Adversarial negotiators who put the incidental issues at the top of the agenda theorize that resolving these easier matters at the outset builds an atmosphere of trust, cooperation, and conciliation between the parties, and establishes a positive momentum for subsequently tackling the tougher, primary issues. Similarly, problem-solving negotiators may start with the less difficult issues to demonstrate to the other side how a mutual effort to accommodate the parties' varying needs or interests may be effectively employed in resolving the remaining harder issues.

The principal disadvantage to this approach is that it may create the false impression that the party initiating the resolution of the easier issues at first instance is being flexible, accommodating, and anxious to reach agreement because of weakness. This misperception may cause the opposing side to take a more hardened, demanding, and unrealistic approach to the primary issues and cause the negotiation to unnecessarily deadlock. Moreover, if both parties have exhausted their "bargaining chips" at the outset, neither side may be left with any matters to trade once the bargaining turns to the toughest issues.

In light of the relative advantages and disadvantages of starting the negotiation with either the primary or incidental issues, many negotiators strive to balance the discussion of these different matters throughout the negotiation. In this way, the risks associated with the "all or nothing" approach of starting with the primary issues, or the "easy does it" approach of beginning with the incidental issues are minimized. The adversarial negotiator's technique of controlling the agenda is thus tempered with a willingness to be flexible in discussing the various issues in whatever order promotes ultimate progress in the negotiation.

From the problem solver's standpoint, so long as the parties are focusing on their real needs or interests, it matters less whether those interests involve primary or incidental issues at any particular stage in the negotiation. Indeed, many problem-solving negotiators use the tactic of allowing the other side to dictate the agenda as a means of finding out what interests are most important to the opposing party and may be compatible with one's own interests. It is only when the opposing party deviates from focusing on the joint needs or interests of the parties and becomes entrenched in positional bargaining that the problem solver becomes more concerned about controlling the agenda. In that event, the problem solver will strive to refocus the parties' attention back to their respective needs or interests, by trying to "separate the people from the problem," and using "brainstorming" to arrive at mutually beneficial solutions based on objective criteria (*see* § 14.14[2]).

Setting the agenda at the negotiation usually takes the form of one party suggesting that the discussion begin with a particular issue. Alternatively, a party might simply begin discussing some issue without expressly stating the issue as a starting point. The advantage of the subtlety of the latter approach is that it disguises the party's attempt at agenda control and obviates a mini-negotiation over what will be negotiated and how. Sometimes, particularly in complex business or labor negotiations involving numerous participants, the agenda will have been pre-negotiated and reduced to writing such as through a *Draft Document or Single Negotiating Text* (*see* Chapter 10).

## § 14.08  READING BODY LANGUAGE

To be a skilled negotiator you must not only be sensitive to understanding what is being said at a negotiation and "reading between the lines" of what is being said and not being said, but you must be sensitive to the other party's nonverbal thoughts and feelings expressed through body language. Some negotiators become so consumed with the ritualistic aspects of making and meeting offers and concessions that they unwittingly ignore what they can learn intuitively from the nonverbal reactions of the other side. It is essential to keep in mind that what the other party "feels" during the negotiation is often integral to the bottom-line outcome.

Reading body language is much more instinctive than scientific. It is essentially grounded in experienced intuition. That experience cautions that many people react differently under different circumstances, and the mannerisms displayed by one person may mean something quite different when displayed by another. Thus, reading body language accurately must be done contextually and holistically.[2]

## § 14.09  EXCHANGING INFORMATION

After the "small talk" has set the tone for the negotiation and the agenda has been explicitly or implicitly established, the substantive portion of the negotiation usually begins with the parties exchanging information that is relevant to their ensuing bargaining. This "information stage" (sometimes called the "assessment stage") is, from a conceptual standpoint, often viewed as a distinct component of the negotiation process that is followed by the so-called "persuasion" and "exchange" stages during which the parties make their offers, counteroffers, and concessions toward a final agreement.[3] While these stages provide a useful analytical framework for understanding the negotiation process, it is important to emphasize that they are invariably intertwined and permeate the entire negotiation process.

In general, the parties exchange information during the negotiation in order to (1) predict what each one will do, (2) understand what each is proposing, (3) determine the accuracy or truthfulness of what is being said, and (4) evaluate what matters are of greater or lesser importance to each party. In addition, information is used to persuade in that it forms the basis for the reasons underlying the parties' offers, counteroffers, concessions, needs or interests, and proposed solutions. Where competitive, adversarial bargaining is involved, the ability to control critical information about the strengths and weaknesses of the parties' respective positions is integral to the successful outcome of the negotiation. For cooperative problem solvers, exchanging information is essential to identifying the parties' varying needs or interests and in fashioning mutually beneficial solutions.

---

[2] *See generally*, D. Morris, *Bodytalk* (1994); D. Druckman, et. al., *Nonverbal Communication: Survey, Theory and Research* (1982); A. Mechrabian, *Nonverbal Communication* (1972).

[3] *See* R. Condlin, Cases on Both Sides: Patterns of Argument in Legal Dispute-Negotiation, 44 U. Md. L. Rev. 65 (1985).

## § 14.10 OBTAINING INFORMATION

As detailed in Chapter 12, prior to commencing the negotiation, you should obtain as much information as possible from your client, the other party, and the opposing negotiator that is pertinent to (1) the underlying needs or interests of each party; (2) the primary, secondary, and incidental objectives of each party; (3) the possible solutions that may satisfy each party's interests and objectives; (4) each party's best alternatives to a negotiated agreement (BATNA); (5) each party's strongest and weakest factual and legal leverage points; (6) the target and resistance points of each party; (7) each party's negotiating strategy and style; (8) the specific offers or proposals that may be presented by each party; and (9) the particular tactics each party may employ during the negotiation. This information may be contained in a Negotiation Preparation Outline for use during the face-to-face negotiation. The Outline will also contain an "Information" category that lists information "to obtain" from the other side, information "to reveal" to the other side, and information "to protect" from the other side (*see* § 12.04).

During the face-to-face negotiation, you will need to confirm and obtain information from the other side about one or more of the nine categories listed above. Thus, these categories serve as a useful checklist of information that is relevant to both adversarial and problem-solving bargaining.

In obtaining information from the other side during the negotiation, in addition to the technique of using *Questions to Facilitate Agreements* in Chapter 10, it is useful to keep the following matters in mind:

### [1]  Ask Broad, Open-ended Questions When Seeking Maximum Information

The best technique for obtaining maximum information is to ask broad, open-ended questions (*e.g.*, "Tell me how the contract came about . . . "), as opposed to directed or leading questions that call for a "yes" or "no" answer (*e.g.*, "Did you propose the purchase price?" or "You proposed $20,000, didn't you?"). Open-ended questions invite the other negotiator to talk, and the more she talks, the more information you are likely to obtain.

### [2]  Use Silence, Encouragement, and Questions that Call for Elaboration

Using silence and not interrupting the speaker are also effective in obtaining maximum information. In addition, you can indirectly encourage the speaker to elaborate by using utterances that indicate attention, such as "I see," "hmmm," "uh huh," or by asking open-ended follow-up questions that call for elaboration, such as "Could you explain that?" or "What happened next?" You may also find that reflecting feelings encourages the speaker to continue talking. Phrases such as, "That must have upset you," or "I understand," convey your focus on the listener and facilitate the continued exchange of information.

### [3]    Listen Intently and Patiently

Part of the art of information gathering (and effective questioning) is listening. While this point is obvious, many negotiators are habitually prone to talk more than to listen. Effective listening requires patience and a willingness not to hurry through the negotiation. So long as the other side is talking, even if what is being said is repetitive or rambling, patience may yield additional relevant information. Moreover, it is difficult to listen effectively if you are distracted by excessive note taking or overly preoccupied with thinking about your response to what is being said.

### [4]    Ask Specific Questions to Clarify, Pin Down, and Confirm Information

Specific or leading questions are most useful to clarify information, pin down ambiguous responses, or to confirm the accuracy of information you already possess. When taking a deposition, for example, many lawyers use a so-called "funnel" technique whereby the examiner begins with open-ended questions that elicit a plethora of information metaphorically represented by the wide mouth of the funnel, and then asks a series of more specific questions to clarify and pin down the details of what is being said which is represented by the bottom tip of the funnel.[4] Information can also be clarified or confirmed by recapitulating what has been said (*e.g.*, by responsively saying, "So, if I understand your point, it is . . . ").

### [5]    Insist upon the Necessity of Receiving Crucial Information

If the other side is being evasive or refuses to reveal information that is essential to the negotiation, do not hesitate to point out why the requested information is important and why the failure to supply it will make further negotiation unproductive or impossible. An appeal to fairness and reciprocity is often successful. Alternatively, if the other negotiator is being unreasonably secretive, you might explain to him that his evasiveness has forced you to assume the facts in the light least favorable to his client. Notwithstanding the risks associated with this confrontational approach, it may be enough to cause the other side to be forthcoming.

## § 14.11  PROTECTING INFORMATION

Although sharing information is integral to the negotiating process, negotiators must protect privileged information; and they invariably avoid revealing other sensitive or damaging information whenever possible. This occurs even in the most cooperative, problem-solving negotiations.

When protecting privileged information or avoiding the disclosure of damaging information, a negotiator should never engage in outright misrepresentation. As discussed previously (*see* § 9.06), it is unethical to make false statements of material fact, and if a misrepresentation is exposed, the negotiator's credibility will be severely if not irreparably impaired. To avoid revealing information without

---

[4] *See* David M. Malone & Peter T. Hoffman, *The Effective Deposition*, 70–78 (1993).

misrepresentation, negotiators sometimes employ one or more of the so-called *Blocking Techniques* introduced in Chapter 10. The most common blocking techniques are as follows:

## [1] Ignore the Question and Change the Topic

Because many listeners become so caught up in what they are being told, they often forget the question they asked. Thus, if you are faced with a question that asks for information you do not want to reveal, it is often effective to simply ignore the question and continue the conversation on a different topic. The effectiveness of this technique is enhanced if your response relates to a matter of importance to the other side, notwithstanding its unresponsiveness to the particular question asked.

## [2] Answer the Question by Asking Another Question

Sometimes asking a question in response can deflect a question. For example, suppose your opponent asks, "What tax returns do you have to support your client's claim for lost wages?" If you want to avoid revealing your client's tax returns (or non-existence of them), you might respond: "Don't you think that my client's W-2 statement accurately shows his earnings before the accident?"

## [3] Answer the Question by Answering Another Question

If you are asked a compound question (*e.g.*, "How has the boycott affected local sales and your last year's contract with Corporation X?") you can choose which part of the question to answer and ignore the other part. Alternatively, you might attempt to answer the question by answering another question. This may be done by re-framing the question in a way that the answer will not be damaging, by answering another question that has recently been asked, or by simply answering another question as if it had been asked (*e.g.*, "If you're asking about the nationwide effect on our business, I can tell you it has been devastating . . . over a dozen suppliers have canceled their contracts with us.").

## [4] Over-Answer or Under-Answer the Question

Giving broad, general responses can often deflect specific questions. Similarly, giving narrow responses can often deflect general questions. This technique of over-answering a specific question or under-answering a general question is a variation of the technique in [3] above.

## [5] Rule the Question Out of Bounds

If a question is asked that calls for revealing privileged information, such as confidential attorney-client communications or work-product material, do not hesitate to explain that you are not at liberty to reveal such information. However, be careful to be consistent about the types of information you claim to be privileged. Revealing certain portions of information claimed to be privileged but declining to reveal other information on the same subject will be construed as disingenuous.

## § 14.12 REVEALING INFORMATION

Exchanging relevant information is, of course, essential to the negotiating process. Generally, there are five categories of information you will want to reveal: (1) your client's interests or needs; (2) your client's objectives; (3) possible solutions to the dispute or problem at hand; (4) your strongest factual and legal leverage points; and (5) your specific offers or proposals. All of this information should be contained in your "Negotiation Preparation Outline." In short, these types of information are necessary to educate and persuade the other side to the result you hope to obtain through the negotiation.

Revealing information is a dynamic process that occurs throughout the negotiation. Information is most effectively revealed through a dialogue rather than a monologue. While some negotiators prefer to start the substantive phase of a face-to-face negotiation with an "opening statement" that essentially "lays all of the cards on the table," this is usually undesirable. Notwithstanding the directness of this approach, opponents are often suspicious of wholesale voluntary disclosures, and sometimes view them as patronizing, disingenuous, self-serving, and even manipulative. (*See also, Reactive Devaluation* at § 7.06[4]).

Thus, it is usually best to err on the side of divulging important information gradually. Allow the other side to extract information through her questions. In this way, the other side is more likely to listen to your information. When appropriate, you can always emphasize or reveal additional information in responding to particular questions.

The effective exchange of information occurs in a fluid, mutual, and cooperative process. It is conversational and sharing in nature, not a structured presentation of alternating opening speeches or a staid question-and-answer session. In sum, it is most effective when conducted in an open, free-flowing discussion.

## § 14.13 ADVERSARIAL BARGAINING

In adversarial bargaining, after the parties have set the tone and agenda and exchanged pertinent information, the negotiation proceeds into the so-called "persuasion" and "exchange" stages whereby the parties make offers, counteroffers, and concessions in an effort to reach a final agreement. The process and techniques associated with these aspects of the negotiation are discussed below.

### [1]  Making Offers

#### [a]  *Who Should Make the First Offer*

While negotiators frequently try to induce their adversaries to make the first offer, there is no empirical evidence that making the first offer results in a less favorable outcome to the negotiation. Quite often, one party will simply decide to "get the ball rolling" by making a first offer, or, out of custom, the party who initiated the claim or the negotiation will make the first offer.

Negotiators who prefer to induce the other side to make the first offer adopt this approach for four reasons. First, making the first offer may give the appearance that one is overly eager to reach an agreement and has a weak position. This reason for not making the first offer is largely overstated. After all, no negotiation can proceed unless someone makes the first offer.

Second, it is asserted that if the party making the first offer has miscalculated the value of the case, he will find himself at a distinct disadvantage if his initial offer falls close to the other party's bottom line or resistance point. For example, if the plaintiff in a personal injury case makes a first offer of $75,000 and the defendant (having a bottom line of $70,000) would have started with $30,000 had he made the first offer, in hindsight the plaintiff will realize he woefully underestimated the value of the case and his first offer should have been far in excess of $75,000.

Third, the negotiator who can induce the other side to make the first offer can adjust his initial counteroffer to make it appear that his goal is the mid-point between the two opening offers. For example, if one's goal is to obtain $50,000 and the other side makes a first offer of $10,000, an initial counteroffer of $90,000 will keep the target point of $50,000 in the middle.

Fourth, inducing the other party to make the first offer will frequently induce that party to make the first concession after the responding party makes his initial counteroffer. There is some statistical evidence to suggest that the party who makes the first concession does less well in the negotiation,[5] perhaps because an initial concession provides the first forecast of the conceding party's concession strategy and potential target and resistance points.

In the final analysis, with the exception of the situation where you are unsure about the value of the case, it makes little difference which party makes the first offer. Indeed, the party making the first offer will have the advantage of observing the other party's initial reaction to the proposal and thus may learn something about his potential settlement range.

Nevertheless, if you have a good reason to induce the other party to make the first offer, you should try to do so. If your opponent steadfastly declines to make the first offer, you can always protect yourself against a miscalculation by (1) making an opening offer that is more extreme than the one you originally planned to make, or (2) expressing your first offer in the form of a dollar range (*e.g.*, "I would estimate that this case is worth anywhere from $100,000 to $200,000."). Moreover, in the unfortunate event that you discover that your first offer was a gross miscalculation, don't be afraid to substitute it with a revised offer and an explanation for your original miscalculation. Despite the embarrassment and loss of credibility that this retraction may cause, it may be the only way to avoid a bad agreement for your client.

### [b] *When to Make the First Offer*

Before making a first offer, you should be sure that during the face-to-face negotiation you have obtained as much information as possible from the other party about (1) his underlying needs or interests; (2) his primary, secondary, and incidental objectives; (3) possible solutions that may satisfy his interests and objectives; (4) his best alternatives to a negotiated agreement (BATNA); (5) his strongest and weakest factual and legal leverage points; (6) his potential target and resistance points; and (7) his potential offers or proposals (*see* § 12.03). While, prior to the face-to-face meeting, you will have forecasted these matters in your

---

[5] R. M. Bastress & J. D. Harbaugh, *Interviewing, Counseling, and Negotiating* 493 (1990).

Negotiation Preparation Outline, you must appropriately revise the information in your Outline based on what you have learned first-hand at the meeting. Once you have taken into account any revisions to your Outline, you will be in a position to make your first offer.

### [c]    The Amount of the First Offer

Setting the amount of your first offer (or responsive counteroffer) depends upon the estimate you have made in your Negotiation Preparation Outline of both parties' target and resistance points. As mentioned previously, studies have shown that a negotiator might obtain a better outcome if her first offer represents a goal that is greater than her estimated target point (*see* § 12.03[10]). Thus, in a damages case, if the plaintiff's target point is $70,000 and her resistance point is $30,000, and the defendant's target is to pay only $20,000 and his resistance point is $50,000, the plaintiff might make a first offer of $90,000, and the defendant might make an initial counteroffer of $10,000 (*see* diagram at § 11.02). Generally, for the purpose of making first offers, it would be disadvantageous for either party to make an opening offer that falls within the parties' "settlement zone" of $50,000 to $30,000 (*i.e.*, the range between the parties' respective resistance points).

However, it is also unwise for a party to make an opening offer that is extreme in the sense of being wholly devoid of any rational basis. An outrageous opening offer may result in premature deadlock and loss of credibility. If you are confronted with an outrageous opening offer, it is usually best to summarily reject it and resume preliminary discussions or the exchange of further information. After your opponent is given some time to save face, you can either induce him to make another first offer or make your own first offer.

### [d]    Communicating Offers

The cardinal rules about making any offer are to make it (1) succinct, (2) specific, and (3) justifiable.[6] Brevity is important in order to avoid unnecessary elaboration or a slip of the tongue that might reveal your resistance point or concession strategy. Too often a negotiator will make the mistake of excessively elaborating upon the reasons for her offer such that she unwittingly reveals more information underlying the offer than she intended. This sometimes has the ironic effect of exposing fallacies in the basis of the offer itself.

Second, the offer should be specific rather than vague. As applicable, all essential terms about timing and performance should be spelled out. Specificity avoids misunderstandings and demonstrates the negotiator's commitment to the offer.

Third, every offer must be justifiable. This means that you must be prepared to provide precise and persuasive reasons for your offer based on your strongest factual and legal leverage points contained in your Negotiation Preparation Outline. When communicating your offer, it is usually desirable to provide the other side with specific reasons for your proposal (*e.g.*, "Our $11,668 offer is based on $5,000 in lost wages, $2,668 in medical expenses, and $4,000 for four months of pain and suffering during which Mr. Smith was undergoing regular treatment."). Avoid giving a lecture about your reasons. You can always amplify upon your

---

[6] *See* R. M. Bastress & Joseph D. Harbaugh, *Interviewing, Counseling, and Negotiating* 507 (1990).

reasons in response to questions from the other side. (*See also* § 14.13[4][a]).

## [2]    Making Counteroffers

Like opening offers, all counteroffers should be made with brevity, specificity, and justifiable reasons. However, before making a counteroffer, you should carefully evaluate the other side's offer in terms of understanding (1) exactly what is being offered, and (2) the other party's reasoning behind his offer. Do not hesitate to ask follow-up questions about any specifics of the offer and why the other party considers his proposal reasonable.

When probing the rationale for an offer, you will often recognize fallacies or weaknesses in the other party's position or analysis. This will provide you with an opportunity to expose and discuss those weaknesses to (1) lower your opponent's aspiration level, and (2) formulate and justify your counteroffer. It is important to re-emphasize that although you will have prepared one or more counteroffers in your Negotiation Preparation Outline, you should appropriately revise any counteroffers in light of the additional information you have learned about your opponent's offers and emerging concession strategy.

## [3]    Making Concessions

### [a]    *When to Make Concessions*

Concessions are an integral part of negotiation. They may be triggered by any number of the tactics or techniques discussed in Chapter 10 such as *Abdication, Asymmetrical Time Pressure, Br'er Rabbit,* the formation of a *Coalition, Deadlines* or other time pressures, *Escalating Demands,* a *Fait Accompli, False Demands, False Emphasis, False Multiple Concessions, Lock-in Positions, Low-Balling, Nibbling, Preconditions* or *Conditional Proposals, Reversing Position, Splitting the Difference, Surprise,* a *Take-it-or-Leave-it* approach, *Threats,* or a *Walkout.* In addition, a party's mere desire to put an end to the dispute, preserve good will, or accede to the advice of a third party such as a judge or mediator often results in concession behavior.

Generally, concessions are appropriate when your use of argument, persuasion, threats, promises, or other tactics have been unsuccessful, and you still have some distance between your latest offer or counteroffer and your resistance point. In any event, in the absence of a concession by one party or the other, there will be no further movement toward an agreement. Thus, you should be willing to make concessions so long as you believe that the outcome of the negotiation will be better than your best alternative to a negotiated agreement.

Whether to make the first concession or wait for the other party to do so is a controversial issue. As mentioned in § 14.13[1][a], there is some statistical evidence suggesting that the party who makes the first concession does less well in the negotiation. However, if you make one or more minor concessions at the outset without losing bargaining leverage, you may have greater success later on in extracting more important concessions from the other party who has been psychologically induced to reciprocate out of a sense of fairness. That is, it often pays to give the appearance of generosity and cooperativeness by initiating one or more small concessions that do not equal a major concession. In this way, the purported generosity doesn't cost much.

## [b]   *Concession Strategy*

Effective negotiators tentatively plan out their concession strategy in advance of the face-to-face negotiation. This strategy should be reflected in the 1st, 2nd, 3rd, and 4th "Offers or Proposals" contained in your Negotiation Preparation Outline. Each successive offer will reflect one or more additional concessions. Your planned concession pattern will also be based on the successive offers or proposals that you anticipate will be made by the other party.

Some research suggests that when one party's concessions are few and small, the opposing party is more likely to reduce her aspirations and make both greater and more frequent concessions. Thus, as a general rule, negotiators tend to be more successful if they make both fewer and smaller concessions than their adversaries.[7] As summarized by one authority:

> The research data suggest you can construct an effective concession pattern as an adversarial negotiator by doing the following: Be sure your rate of concession is not too rapid, nor the size of the concessions too great, nor the number too many. Consistent with the research, taking a strong stand on a moderately high or low opening offer with one or, at most, a few concessions to your resistance level will produce the most effective results. Finally you should attempt to accurately identify the minimum your opponent will accept to settle the matter [*i.e.*, his resistance point] and then position yourself just outside that point, resisting a further concession for as long as possible.[8]

Consider the following example:

---

[7] *See* C. Karrass, *The Negotiating Game* 18–19 (1970).

[8] R. M. Bastress & J. D. Harbaugh, *Interviewing, Counseling, and Negotiating* 520 (1990). *See also,* M. Saks & R. Hastie, *Social Psychology in Court* 124 (1978) (advocating "extreme initial offers, well above (or below) one's resistance point, making concessions few, small, reciprocal, and each one rationalized, explained, justified on some basis other than mere pursuit of agreement.").

**Example 1**

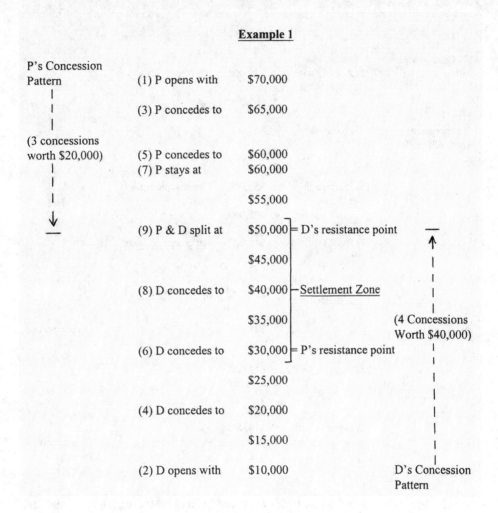

In this example, the settlement zone is $30,000 to $50,000, with P's resistance point at $30,000 and D's resistance point at $50,000. The following exchange steps occur: (1) P makes an opening offer of $70,000; (2) D makes an opening offer of $10,000; (3) P makes a first concession to $65,000; (4) D makes a first concession to $20,000; (5) P makes a second concession to $60,000; (6) D makes a second concession to $30,000; (7) P refuses to move from his latest offer of $60,000; (8) D grudgingly makes a third concession to $40,000; and (9) P proposes to split the difference by conceding to $50,000 and D agrees by conceding to $50,000. The net result is that P has made slower, smaller, and fewer concessions than D. That is, P has made a total of 3 concessions worth $20,000 (while holding out at $60,000 for a time), and D has made 4 concessions worth $40,000 (while never resisting a concession). Although the mid-point of the settlement zone is $40,000, P managed to achieve a settlement of $50,000 that constituted D's resistance point, as compared with P's resistance point of $30,000.

Consider, however, another example:

**Example 2**

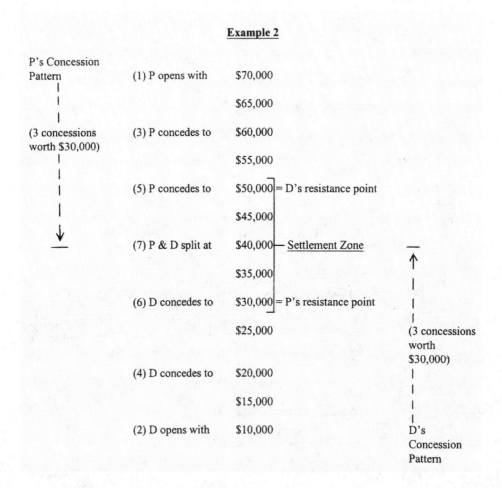

| P's Concession Pattern | | |
| --- | --- | --- |
| | (1) P opens with | $70,000 |
| | | $65,000 |
| (3 concessions worth $30,000) | (3) P concedes to | $60,000 |
| | | $55,000 |
| | (5) P concedes to | $50,000 = D's resistance point |
| | | $45,000 |
| | (7) P & D split at | $40,000 — Settlement Zone |
| | | $35,000 |
| | (6) D concedes to | $30,000 = P's resistance point |
| | | $25,000 |
| | (4) D concedes to | $20,000 |
| | | $15,000 |
| | (2) D opens with | $10,000 |

(3 concessions worth $30,000)

D's Concession Pattern

In this example, the settlement zone is still $30,000 to $50,000, with P's resistance point at $30,000 and D's resistance point at $50,000. The following exchange steps occur: (1) P makes an opening offer of $70,000; (2) D makes an opening offer of $10,000; (3) P makes a first concession to $60,000; (4) D makes a first concession to $20,000; (5) P makes a second concession to $50,000; (6) D makes a second concession to $30,000; and (7) P and D split the difference by each conceding an additional $10,000 to settle at $40,000. The net result is that neither party has made slower, smaller, or fewer concessions than the other. That is, each party has made 3 concessions worth $30,000 and settled at the mid-point of the settlement zone ($40,000), which is the mid-point of their respective resistance points.

The foregoing examples teach that you can generally prevent the other side from having an undue advantage by (1) keeping careful track of the number and value of the other side's concessions, (2) seeking to extract reciprocal concessions in number and value, and (3) modifying your planned concession strategy in light of the particular concessions made by the other side. Monitoring the other side's concession behavior will also gradually reveal how close that side is coming to its resistance level and the relative impact that one's efforts at persuasion and use of various tactics are having upon the other side's concession pattern.

Patience in making concessions is important because it is estimated that as much as 80% of position changes tend to occur during the last 20% of the negotiation.[9] Being too hasty in making concessions may thus cause you to make a greater, aggregate compromise at the end of the negotiation than you would have made had your earlier concessions been fewer in number and value. In addition, impatience with the negotiating process may cause you to become frustrated and angry with your more cautious and grudging adversary, and become psychologically entrapped by the negotiation "game" such that you feel compelled to reach an agreement regardless of the cost.[10] This entrapment can be avoided by always keeping your resistance point and best alternative to a negotiated agreement (BATNA) in mind, regardless of the time, effort, and energy expended in attempting to reach an accord. There is nothing wrong with failing to reach an agreement, but it is poor advocacy to acquiesce to an agreement on behalf of your client simply for the sake of reaching an agreement.

This does not mean that in an appropriate situation you should not adjust your initial resistance point. If the negotiation process reveals that you have misjudged your pre-planned bargaining limits or that the consequences of non-settlement are more onerous than a negotiated result, you should be flexible in reassessing your resistance point. On the other hand, if it remains apparent that a negotiated agreement would be more costly than your best alternative to negotiation, and you are unable to convince the other party that a settlement on your terms would be better than his best alternative to a negotiated agreement, do not hesitate to tell the other side that you cannot make any further concessions. If negotiations deadlock at that point and thereafter do not resume, you can resort to your best alternative option.

### [c]    *Communicating Concessions*

Inasmuch as concessions are almost always embodied in counteroffers, your concessions should be communicated with brevity, specificity, and justifiable reasons (*see* § 14.13[1][d]). Providing one or more reasons for your concessions demonstrates to the other party that you are not simply engaging in a ritualistic offer, counteroffer, response, counter-response march along the bargaining scale toward your ultimate resistance point. Rather, you want to demonstrate that your concessions are based on a rational assessment of the dispute or problem at hand and form a modified proposal to which you are committed.

Your reason for making a concession might stem from a persuasive point made by the other side, an effort to accommodate a particular need or interest of the other side, additional information you were not previously aware of, or a mere willingness to engage "in the spirit of compromise." Be succinct in giving your reasons and avoid being defensive.

Sometimes, particularly when there are multiple issues in the negotiation, it may be useful to forecast your willingness to make a possible concession in exchange for a specific concession from the other side (*e.g.,* "We might agree to make a larger lump sum payment if you are willing to accept our non-compete clause."). Using flexible language in communicating a concession makes it easier to

---

[9] *See* R. Dawson, *Roger Dawson's Secrets of Power Negotiating* 144 (1995).

[10] *See generally,* J. Brockner & J. Rubin, *Entrapment in Escalating Conflicts: A Social Psychological Analysis* (1985).

retract your position and resurrect the concession at a later time. However, the excessive use of ambiguity in suggesting concessions may lead to misunderstandings and undermine your credibility for lack of committing yourself to making firm concessions.

## [4]    Forms of Persuasion

### [a]    Argument[11]

Argument as a form of persuasion permeates the making of offers, counteroffers, and concessions. Effective arguments contain six elements.

First, the argument should be based on some normative standard or objective criterion that is independent of the naked will of either side. Thus, the argument might be based on applicable law, the facts of the dispute or problem at hand, economic considerations, custom, ethical norms, expertise, analogy, or rule. These should be included as part of the "Factual & Legal Leverage Points" in your Negotiation Preparation Outline (see § 12.03[6]). The most effective arguments are based on as many of these normative standards or objective criteria as possible.

Second, the argument must show how the normative standard or objective criterion chosen applies to the parties' situation. That is, the legal, factual, or other reason asserted must be rationally related to the case at hand.

Third, the normative standard or objective criterion chosen must be credible or authoritative in the sense of being supported by appropriate evidence or other proof. Such evidence or proof might be based on indisputable or verifiable facts, logical presumptions, or so-called "customary proofs" such as generally accepted assumptions, beliefs, or values.

Fourth, the argument must be "balanced" in the sense of taking into account the other party's legitimate contentions. If you fail to be evenhanded or distort the merits of the other side's arguments, your own arguments will be unpersuasive. When possible, you must be prepared to distinguish away the strongest points advanced by the other party, or persuasively show how his standards or criteria are inappropriate, inapplicable to the situation at hand, or based on inadequate evidence or proof.

Fifth, when appropriate, your argument should be emphasized by highlighting and amplifying upon key points, without muddling the force of your argument with minutiae or ancillary matters. In addition, arguments should be emphasized by repeating them in different forms, and they should be expressed with tact and controlled emotion that takes into account the legitimate feelings of the parties.

Sixth, although it is usually best to be relatively brief when communicating an offer, your justification for it will have more persuasive force if you give multiple reasons for your proposal. That is, if you can show that no matter which way one looks at the problem the best solution always seems to be the same, your proposal will be much more convincing. This also means that you should be prepared to

---

[11] See R. Condlin, "Cases on Both Sides": Patterns of Argument in Legal Dispute-Resolution, 44 Md. L. Rev. 65 (1985); C. Perelman & L. Obrechts-Tyteca, The New Rhetoric: A Treatise on Argumentation (1971).

provide detailed factual information that supports the multi-dimensional reasoning behind your proposal.[12]

### [b] Exhibits

Exhibits, such as models, diagrams, charts, photos, slides, or videos may be highly effective in presenting arguments or proposals. Of course, proper attention to considerations such as format, placement, layout, size, and style is essential. Similarly, careful attention should be given to the use of color schemes in exhibits to make them easy to read and understand.[13]

### [c] Emotional Appeals

In contrast to rational argumentation, emotional appeals are directed to the other party's psychological needs and motivations. People need and are often motivated by (1) sensory rewards such as feeling good or free from anger, fear, tension, and anxiety; (2) social rewards such as prestige, acceptance, and love; and (3) ego-supporting rewards such as self-esteem and meaning in life. Cooperative negotiators frequently appeal to these psychological rewards through positive behaviors such as altruism, good will, friendship, humor, flattery, and the like. Conversely, some highly competitive negotiators employ a variety of negative behaviors or tactics, such as *Anger/Aggressiveness, Blaming or Fault-Finding, Escalating Demands, Reversing Position,* or *Threats* (*see* Chapter 10), that are designed to create frustration, guilt, embarrassment, discomfort, indebtedness, or other unpleasant pressures upon their adversaries. Whether emotional appeals are made through deliberately positive or negative behavior, the ultimate goal is the same — to induce the other party to enter into an agreement more favorable to one's own terms, either under circumstances where the other party will feel good about himself in reaching an agreement, or under circumstances where he would prefer to conclude an agreement in lieu of having to further endure the unpleasant encounter.

### [d] Threats and Promises

Threats and promises, whether express or implied, are commonly used forms of persuasion. A threat is intended to induce the other party to believe that the cost of disagreement outweighs the cost of reaching a particular agreement. Threats are negative in the sense that they forecast preplanned negative consequences if carried out. As such, threats tend to elicit greater feelings of hostility and competitiveness.

An affirmative promise, on the other hand, is a proposal to act in a beneficial way toward another if she takes certain action (*e.g.,* "We would be willing to do X if you would be willing to accommodate us on Y."). Promises imply reciprocal cooperation. Accordingly, in contrast to threats, positive promises tend to elicit greater feelings of conciliation and cooperativeness. Thus, it is not surprising that the prospects for reaching a mutually satisfactory agreement are greater when

---

[12] *See* Thomas F. Guernsey, *A Practical Guide to Negotiation* 101–102 (1996).

[13] For a discussion about using color in negotiations, *see* Cheskin, *Color Guide for Marketing Media* (1955); Cheskin, *Color for Profit* (1957).

affirmative promises are employed in lieu of negative threats.[14]

The elements of a credible threat and techniques for responding to threats are set out in § 10.45. In addition, whenever possible, negotiators should consider using a "warning" in lieu of an express threat. A warning might take the form of a strong word of caution, argument, or an appeal to the other side about the consequences that might result in the event an agreement is not reached. In contrast to a formal threat, such a warning does not presage specific, adverse action on the part of the declarant, but forecasts undesirable consequences that will independently occur in the absence of an accord.

## § 14.14  PROBLEM-SOLVING BARGAINING[15]

The substantive stages of problem-solving bargaining involve the identification and sharing of the interests or needs of both parties, and brainstorming to develop as many solutions as possible that may satisfy those needs and maximize the parties' mutual gain. The making of offers, counteroffers, and concessions is deliberately tied to this objective. The process and techniques of this problem-solving approach are given below.

### [1]    Identifying and Sharing Interests or Needs

Since the aim of problem solving is to reach an agreement that is mutually satisfactory to both parties, this approach to negotiation is predicated upon a cooperative effort between the parties to identify and share each other's underlying interests or needs. A party's "interests" are akin to his "objectives" in that the former constitute the *reasons* underlying his specific negotiation goals. Identifying interests involves asking "why" one desires a particular objective. The focus is on the *needs, desires, concerns, fears, philosophies,* and *feelings* that shape a party's personal, psychological, ideological, or emotional motivations underlying his negotiation goals. For example, consider the following potential interests:[16]

• Ego or psychological interests: recognition, status, personal satisfaction, career satisfaction, sense of power or authority, self-esteem and self-respect, freedom from anxiety or stress

• Moral or ideological interests: reputation, good will, integrity, fairness, religious or political beliefs

• Economic or efficiency interests: financial security, short-term or long-term profits, reducing costs or inefficiency, developing new business opportunities, establishing or avoiding certain precedents

• Relationship interests: fostering better interpersonal relationships, working with others, ending detrimental relationships, developing new relationships or contacts

The interests (and objectives) of both parties should be listed in your Negotiation Preparation Outline, ranked from most important to least important, and evaluated to determine which are shared between the parties, which are

---

[14] *See* J. Rubin & B. Brown, *The Social Psychology of Bargaining and Negotiation* 286 (1975).

[15] *See generally,* R. Fisher & W. Ury, *Getting to Yes* (1981); W. Ury, *Getting past No* (1991).

[16] *See* G. Goodpaster, *A Guide to Negotiation and Mediation* 95–96 (1977).

independent of each other but do not conflict, and which conflict. When the parties exchange information during problem-solving negotiation, they (1) consciously strive to "separate the people from the problem" through a mindset that attacks the problem, not each other; and (2) focus on each other's interests, as against the mere "wants" reflected in each side's stated "positions."

If one side is resistant to these efforts, the other party will (1) shun any temptation to participate in personal attacks or react irrationally to the other side; (2) seek to diffuse anger, fear, and suspicion by listening and acknowledging the other side's points and concerns; (3) deflect hard-line positions by re-framing them in the form of problem-solving "why" and "what if" questions that explore the interests and reasons underlying the other side's positions; (4) adopt the role of a mediator, trying to identify and satisfy the other side's unmet interests; and (5) instead of employing threats or force, seek to educate the other side to the costs of not reaching an agreement and emphasize that the overriding goal of the negotiation is mutual satisfaction, not victory.

## [2]   Brainstorming for Solutions

After the parties identify and share their interests or needs, they jointly brainstorm for as many solutions as possible that may satisfy their mutual needs. These potential solutions should be drawn and developed from the "Possible Solutions" listed in your Negotiation Preparation Outline.

In brainstorming for possible solutions, it has been suggested that the parties employ the following techniques:[17]

(1) They should initially spend time thinking of all possible solutions by promoting broad discussion and agreeing to outlaw negative criticism of any kind. (These potential solutions might be outlined on a chart for all to see).

(2) They should clarify at the outset that each party's mere listing of solutions is not an expression of an official position. The point is to generate as expansive a list as possible, which can later be refined for detailed discussion.

(3) They should strive to broaden the potential options that might be considered, rather than look for a single answer.

(4) Multiple options might be generated by identifying (i) the overall problem at hand, (ii) potential causes of or barriers to solving the problem, (iii) theoretical solutions, (iv) solutions that might be proposed by experts or persons from the perspective of different professions or disciplines, and (v) specific steps that might be taken to deal with the problem.

(5) The parties should consider which options might be more desirable or workable than others, distinguishing among those that are substantive versus procedural, comprehensive versus partial, and unconditional versus contingent.

(6) Options for mutual gain should be explored based on shared interests and the possibility that the parties' divergent interests can be mutually

---

[17] *See* R. Fisher & W. Ury, *Getting to Yes* (1981); W. Ury, *Getting Past No* (1991).

satisfied without undue cost to any particular party.

(7) Each party should consciously consider potential options from the other side's point of view.

(8) The parties should be particularly advertent to possible solutions that are based on normative standards or objective criteria, such as the facts at hand, applicable law, economic considerations, custom, industry standards, ethical norms, expertise, analogy, or rule, rather than the naked will of any one party.

## [3]     Making Problem-Solving Offers, Counteroffers, and Concessions

After developing a broad list of potential solutions, the parties will, of course, have to decide which solution or combination of solutions to formally propose or adopt. In contrast to negotiators engaged in strictly adversarial bargaining, problem solvers are much less hesitant to initiate first offers, and they are less inclined to view subsequent offers as incremental steps in a pre-established concession strategy toward a defined resistance point. This is because the problem solver often uses the making of offers to encourage joint problem solving by analyzing what the other party's responses to those offers mean about the other party's underlying interests or needs. Therefore, it is not unusual for problem solvers to make multiple offers at the same time. By gauging the other party's reaction to these offers and engaging in a discussion about them, more specific proposals can be fashioned that maximize mutual gain.

Consistent with this approach, unlike adversarial bargainers, problem solvers tend to make offers, counteroffers, and concessions that are more general and expansive. Specificity is replaced with generality (at least at the outset), and brevity is replaced with a willingness to expansively share explanations and rationales for what is being proposed. Once again, in this way the problem solver is able to reveal and reinforce the needs of her own client and simultaneously demonstrate a willingness to recognize the legitimate interests or needs of the other side. Purely singular solutions are shunned, and fervent commitment to any particular proposal is avoided in order to invite open, honest, and legitimate criticism. The goal is that, through joint sharing, exploring, and discussion, a concrete proposal will emerge that best satisfies as many of the interests or needs of both parties as possible.

In freely making offers, counteroffers, and appropriate concessions, however, the problem solver, like the adversarial bargainer, buttresses them with justifiable reasons. Thus, arguments are based on normative standards or objective criteria that are rationally related to the case at hand, are credible or authoritative in the sense of being supported by appropriate evidence or other proof, are "balanced" in light of the legitimate points made by each side, and are appropriately emphasized and highlighted whenever possible (see § 14.13[4][a]). In addition, notwithstanding the problem solver's disposition to seek solutions that maximize the mutual gain of the parties, she still guards against becoming entrapped by the negotiation process and keeps in mind her best alternatives to a negotiated agreement (BATNA).

# § 14.15   COMBINING ADVERSARIAL AND PROBLEM-SOLVING BARGAINING

Few negotiations are either purely adversarial or purely problem solving. Many negotiators combine the two approaches to different aspects of a single negotiation, where the salient features of each strategy best complement the dispute or problem at hand or otherwise enhance the prospects for a favorable agreement. In addition, some negotiators might start with a wholly adversarial approach and, when it becomes plain that the negotiation is stalling or near deadlock, pursue a largely problem-solving approach. The mere fact that the adversarial and problem-solving models are analytically and conceptually distinct is not a reason to employ only one to the exclusion of the other. Negotiation is a complex and dynamic form of human interaction which often requires flexibility to achieve a successful outcome.

As a practical matter, in most negotiations there is an on-going tension between "win-win" cooperative efforts to create solutions for an agreement, and "win-lose" competitive efforts to claim the best solutions for one's own side.[18] In this sense, problem solving "giveth" and adversarial bargaining "taketh." The tension can be counterproductive and subject to abuse in that win-lose tactics often impede the creation of desirable solutions, and win-win tactics — while tending to promote creative solutions — may be exploited by a disingenuous problem solver who changes his approach in midstream and adopts an adversarial posture to reap the fruits of cooperatively created solutions for his unilateral benefit. From the perspective of purely "zealous advocacy," this type of giving with the right hand and taking with the left is clever (and arguably creative) negotiating — *i.e.,* problem solve to create and then compete to take.

To effectively deal with this tension and create cooperative solutions without being vulnerable to exploitation, a so-called TIT-FOR-TAT or "conditionally open" approach has been suggested.[19] Under this approach, problem-solving and adversarial bargaining are combined in that the negotiator (1) warily seeks mutual cooperation at first instance; (2) engages in competitive tactics when the other party does so; (3) resorts back to cooperative behavior when the other side appears so inclined; and (4) attempts to induce an overall problem-solving approach by developing a reputation for being a consistently "principled" negotiator who nevertheless is not a push-over but is willing and able to meet highly competitive tactics in kind when necessary. This "conditionally open" approach is a form of "tough love," whereby the negotiator genuinely exemplifies cooperativeness and fairness along with appropriate firmness and subsequent forgiveness if the other party transgresses into overly disingenuous and exploitive conduct.

Alternatively, the parties might find it mutually productive to adopt a problem-solving approach towards certain issues in the case or during certain phases of the negotiation, and an adversarial approach towards other issues or during other phases. For example, problem solving might be used for those issues where the parties are capable of exchanging or trading a variety of items or matters, whereas adversarial bargaining might be employed where the issue is merely how much money one party receives and the other pays. Alternatively, the parties might choose to deliberately engage in problem-solving to understand each other's

---

[18] *See* D. Lax & J. Sebenius, *The Manager as Negotiator* 29–41, 158–166, 91–105 (1981).

[19] *See* Id., R. Axelford, *The Evolution of Cooperation* 109–124 (1984).

underlying interests or needs and the issues at hand, and thereafter engage in adversarial bargaining when it comes time to constructing a specific agreement. There is nothing wrong with or undesirable about bifurcating and then combining adversarial and problem-solving bargaining in these ways, so long as each party is expressly or implicitly aware which playing field is being used for any particular issue or at any particular time during the negotiation.

## § 14.16   CONCLUDING THE NEGOTIATION

In every negotiation there comes a time when it becomes apparent to the parties either that an agreement is likely to be reached or that the negotiation will conclude in an impasse or final deadlock. If an impasse occurs, or even if a deadlock seems inevitable, it is usually best to indicate that you are willing to "keep the door open" for future negotiations. In addition, you should close the stalled or deadlocked negotiation with civility.

If it appears that the parties are close to reaching an agreement, it is essential to avoid being caught up in the anticipation of the moment. As mentioned previously, the most significant concessions tend to be made toward the end of the negotiation (*see* § 14.13[3][b]), and thus it is not uncommon for a negotiator to become overly anxious to conclude an agreement by forfeiting at the last moment much of what she had gained by patience throughout the balance of the negotiation session. Accordingly, effective negotiators tend to be particularly patient, cautious, and persistent when making final offers, counteroffers, or concessions toward the end of the bargaining session. This means always keeping in mind one's resistance point and best alternative to a negotiated agreement.

In light of the psychological tendency of many negotiators to accelerate and increase their concessions toward the end of the negotiation, you might be able to capitalize on this tendency by (1) applauding the other party for the movement or position changes he has made thus far, (2) encouraging him to continue his conciliatory behavior for the sake of reaching a final agreement, or (3) providing him with appropriate face-saving reasons for making one or more additional concessions. Even in problem-solving bargaining, the most successful negotiators tend to be more competitive than cooperative during the closing phase of the negotiation.

Sometimes, negotiators seek to accelerate the closing phase of a negotiation through tactics discussed in Chapter 10 such as *Abdication, Asymmetrical Time Pressure,* creating *Deadlines,* using other *Timing* pressures, *Escalating Demands,* creating a *Fait Accompli, Reversing Position,* offering to *Split the Difference,* announcing a *Take-it-or-Leave-it* position, or engaging in a *Walkout.* In general, to protect yourself against such tactics you should (1) not allow the other side to press for a closing until you are ready to close, (2) not press for a closing yourself until you are ready to close, and (3) not press for a closing when the other side is likely to view your pressure with mistrust or suspicion.

After you have reached an agreement, and before you leave the face-to-face meeting, it is desirable to repeat the major terms of the transaction or reduce them to a memorandum of understanding to obviate any misunderstandings. If any exist, they should be dealt with on the spot so as not to lose the momentum toward closure. In addition, you should be careful to clarify any details attendant to the execution of the agreement. These matters might include (1) time frames for performing the agreement; (2) any follow-up action to be taken by the parties; (3) what information or documents are needed to effectuate the agreement; (4) whether any third parties need to be notified of the agreement; (5) details regarding the preparation and submission of appropriate releases, pleadings, or other documents; (6) contingency plans in the event either client rejects the agreement (assuming final client approval is necessary); and (7) who will bear any applicable expenses such as court costs, legal fees, and expenses.

If the agreement is to be formalized in writing, and particularly if its terms are complex, you should volunteer to draft the final documentation. This reduces the risk that the other party will insert new terms or provisions into the agreement that were not discussed or agreed upon during the negotiation. In addition, if you are the draftsman, the other party is more likely to be at a psychological disadvantage if she requests any significant changes, additions, or deletions to your draft. That is, if such changes are demanded, you might be in a better position to exact some additional concessions from the other party in exchange for modifying the draft.

On the other hand, if you do not prepare the final documentation, you must carefully review it to ensure that it accurately and completely reflects the agreement reached at the face-to-face meeting. If it does not, firmly insist upon appropriate changes to the draft, and, if the other side repeatedly resists your modifications, volunteer to take over the final drafting process yourself.

Finally, conclude the face-to-face meeting with appropriate parting salutations and professionalism. If you have achieved a particularly advantageous agreement for your client, do not gloat; and if the final agreement was less desirable than you hoped for, do not pout. In either case, by graciously commending your counterpart for her efforts in handling the negotiation, you will bolster your reputation for integrity and professionalism in any future dealings.

# Chapter 15

# NEGOTIATING DURING CIVIL LITIGATION

## SYNOPSIS

## § 15.01   INTRODUCTION

Approximately 90% of all lawsuits are settled,[1] and it is likely that this percentage will increase with the growth of court-annexed mediation and other forms of alternative dispute resolution. Litigation is expensive, risky, and time consuming, and the economic and emotional drain on the parties is usually considerable. Because settlement is so prevalent during litigation, lawyers should not hesitate to initiate settlement discussions as a rule rather than as an exception.

Much of the discussion in the preceding chapters is relevant to negotiating during litigation. However, given below are some additional considerations that you should bear in mind in connection with settling before trial and settling during or after trial.

## § 15.02   GENERAL CONSIDERATIONS ABOUT PREPARATION

As in any negotiation context, to effectively prepare for a lawsuit settlement you should develop a Negotiation Preparation Outline like that discussed in Chapter 12. In addition, in developing an overall approach to settlement, it is particularly important to obtain information about the opposing lawyer, not only as a negotiator, but also as a trial advocate. After all, in the litigation context, the parties' best

---

[1] *See also* H.M. Kritzer, *Let's Make a Deal* 1 (1991) ("If one were to include the cases that never get through the door of the court *house*–cases that are settled between the parties before a formal court action is even started — the settlement figure approaches 99 percent!").

alternative to a negotiated agreement usually will usually be trial, and the outcome of a trial may have much to do with the relative trial skills of the parties' lawyers.

Particularly when settlement discussions are initiated before the filing of a lawsuit, it is also important to obtain information about the settlement attitudes and practices of any insurance carrier or other entity that will be involved in the negotiation. For example, if you represent the plaintiff and the particular carrier or entity has a reputation for routinely taking a hard-line position to initial settlement overtures, it may be preferable to file a lawsuit before initiating any discussion of settlement. On the other hand, if you represent the defendant under circumstances where liability seems clear, and the plaintiff's lawyer has a reputation of being reluctant to try cases and a disposition to settle quickly, you might choose to be more active in initiating or responding to settlement proposals. In either case, the simplest way to find out about the general settlement attitudes of the other side is to ask lawyers or other persons who have had prior dealings with your counterpart.

## § 15.03  GENERAL CONSIDERATIONS ABOUT PRETRIAL STRATEGY AND STYLE

As mentioned previously, lawsuit negotiations are usually adversarial and competitive. This is because, in many instances, once lawyers have become involved and litigation is contemplated or underway, the parties' relationship has become badly strained or even destroyed. In addition, both sides are aware that, regardless of who prevails in the lawsuit, each is still a potential loser. A victory for the plaintiff may be offset by the costs of time and money in pursuing his claim, and a victory for the defendant in preserving the status quo may be offset by substantial legal fees and other costs. Perhaps most importantly, both sides have already begun to sustain the emotional costs of stress, pressure, anxiety, and animosity. Thus, once the parties have come to recognize that their dispute might only be resolved through litigation, they are often, as a purely "human" rather than rational matter, less inclined to adopt a problem-solving and cooperative approach to settlement.

The litigation process itself aggravates this adversarial and competitive atmosphere. After initial settlement discussions have broken down, the plaintiff and defendant often engage in the following series of actions and counteractions: (1) the plaintiff files his complaint; (2) the defendant takes as long as permissible to answer, and interposes a counterclaim if possible; (3) the plaintiff initiates discovery (*i.e.*, by taking depositions, submitting interrogatories and requests to produce documents, etc.); (4) the defendant responds in kind and often initiates even more discovery; (5) the plaintiff files dispositive motions; (6) the defendant responds or counters with her own dispositive motions; (7) one side or the other calendars the case for trial; (8) the other side sometimes seeks to delay the trial; and (9) after trial, the losing party appeals and, if she loses on the initial appeal, an appeal is taken to the jurisdiction's highest court. In sum, each party seeks to wear down the other through pressure, counter-pressure, action, counter-action, delay, and spiraling expense.

Against this background, settlement discussions tend to occur when one or both parties begin to realize (1) that it may be more advantageous to substitute the certainty of a settlement for the uncertainty of a trial outcome, or (2) that the time and expense associated with the litigation process is becoming unbearable. Of course, there is no standard point in the litigation process when either of these realizations will be triggered. However, in general, the strategy often employed by the plaintiff is to exert maximum pressure on the defendant through the litigation process until the latter realizes that the plaintiff is prepared to go the distance. Conversely, an often used strategy for the defendant is to erect as many barriers as possible to the plaintiff's pursuit of his claims with the hope that he will significantly reduce his expectations and settle the case cheaply, or even abandon his case altogether due to the financial costs of continuing to pursue the case. In the end, the party who possesses the greatest persistence, patience, and economic and emotional wherewithal is most likely to effectuate the most advantageous settlement.

This description of the effects of the litigation process on settlement should not be interpreted as an endorsement of engaging in such a highly competitive and adversarial approach as a matter of course. A more cooperative approach is often instrumental in blunting the adversarial instincts inherent in the litigation setting, and a problem-solving strategy is neither conceptually nor practically inappropriate after a lawsuit has been filed. Particularly when the parties' dispute involves multiple issues, may be resolved through a variety of solutions other than the mere payment of money, or requires ongoing dealings between the parties, a problem-solving approach is often the best means for settling litigation.

## § 15.04   FILING THE COMPLAINT AND ANSWER

As discussed in Chapter 13, many lawyers initially try to resolve disputes through a demand letter, settlement brochure, or negotiations over the telephone. A lawsuit is typically not filed until negotiations break down or unless initiating them would be fruitless at the outset. On the other hand, a number of experienced litigators advocate filing a lawsuit at first instance, or, at the least, sending the other side a draft of the complaint when initiating settlement discussions. The rationale for this approach is that it demonstrates the plaintiff's preparedness and seriousness about his claims.

Once the decision has been made to file a lawsuit, there are a number of considerations to take into account for settlement purposes. First, when possible, the plaintiff's lawyer should bring the suit in the most convenient place for his client and most inconvenient place for the defendant. For example, if the defendant lives in Wyoming but the transaction took place in New York where your client lives, the forum of choice would be New York. The inconvenience and expense to the defendant of having to litigate the case away from home may exert significant settlement pressure.

Second, despite the bare requirements of "notice pleading," for settlement purposes it is sometimes desirable to draft a complaint that sets forth one's factual allegations and calculation of damages in extra detail. This has the benefit of beginning to educate defense counsel to the merits of your case at the outset, rather than gradually revealing them later on through a drawn-out discovery process. Additional specificity in your complaint also shows the other side that you are not bluffing about the bases for your causes of action, which are often otherwise expressed in rather conclusory terms. However, you should always bear in mind that filing a complaint for an improper purpose or with frivolous factual or legal allegations is unethical and otherwise may expose you or your client to potential sanctions by the court.[2]

Third, when possible, causes of action that are ancillary to the main claim should be included in the complaint. For example, if the defendant's negligence was accompanied by extreme and outrageous conduct resulting in severe emotional distress, additional causes of action for negligent and/or intentional infliction of emotional distress should be included. Similarly, if such outrageous behavior involved willful, wanton, reckless, or malicious conduct, a claim for punitive damages should be added even if the applicable insurance would not cover exemplary damages. In short, the greater the number of causes of action and claims for damages, the greater the defendant's potential exposure becomes.

Fourth, in an appropriate case, seeking a temporary restraining order or preliminary injunction might increase bargaining leverage. Even if an *ex parte* TRO is not granted, the climate for settlement might be enhanced pending a hearing on the motion for a preliminary injunction. If injunctive relief is granted, the plaintiff will have scored a *Fait Accompli* (*see* Chapter 10) by changing the status quo to require the defendant to refrain from certain action or take certain action to protect the plaintiff.

Fifth, including a demand for a jury trial in the complaint may increase bargaining leverage because jury verdicts and awards are much less predictable than decisions and awards rendered by judges. From the plaintiff's standpoint, a jury trial is particularly important when the defendant is a so-called "target defendant," such as a large corporation or governmental entity for whom the jury may have little sympathy.

Sixth, even the choice of how to effect service of the complaint upon the defendant may exert psychological pressure toward settlement. For example, serving a defendant by sheriff at the defendant's home or office will generate greater stress and anxiety than serving her by registered or certified mail, return receipt requested.

In answering the complaint, the defendant should, when permissible, first consider moving for an extension of time within which to answer. This is important not only to gain time to conduct an adequate investigation into the plaintiff's allegations, but may be desirable as part of an overall strategy to preserve the status quo as long as possible.

Second, when applicable, the defendant's answer should detail all available counterclaims against the plaintiff. Apart from compulsory counterclaims which must be raised to avoid waiver,[3] it is often desirable for settlement purposes to plead all permissive counterclaims[4] in order to reduce the plaintiff's expectation of recovery. In addition, any appropriate cross-claims or third-party impleader or interpleader should be raised.[5]

Third, just as the plaintiff should consider including in his complaint all potential causes of action, the defendant should consider raising all affirmative defenses and allege factual bases for those defenses in extra detail. In this regard, instead of

---

[2] *See* Fed. R. Civ. P. 11(b) and (c).

[3] *See* Fed. R. Civ. P. 13(a).

[4] *See* Fed. R. Civ. P. 13(b).

[5] *See* Fed. R. Civ. P. 13(g), 14, and 22.

making mere general denials of the plaintiff's allegations, the defendant should consider, when permissible, expanding upon her denials by stating the relevant facts that contradict the plaintiff's averments.

Fourth, the defendant should raise in the answer (or by motion, when appropriate) any pertinent defenses such as lack of jurisdiction, improper venue, insufficiency of process or service of process, failure to state a claim on which relief can be granted, or failure to join a party.[6] In addition, if the plaintiff's complaint contains any redundant, immaterial, impertinent, or scandalous matter, a motion to strike should be made;[7] and if the allegations are vague or ambiguous, a motion for a more definite statement should be filed.[8]

Filing the complaint and answer usually puts a temporary hold on settlement discussions. Thereafter, the attorneys usually allow the discovery process to proceed at least for a while before negotiations resume. Once the parties have a clearer understanding of the factual and legal issues in the case and begin to feel the effects of time pressures and expense, there is a heightened incentive to discuss settlement possibilities.

## § 15.05   USING DISCOVERY

Discovery may be effectively used formally or informally to induce settlement. Informal discovery essentially occurs when the plaintiff details his claims, along with supporting documentation, in a demand letter or settlement brochure. Sometimes, as in negotiations with an insurance adjuster, the plaintiff's lawyer might allow his client to be interviewed by the other side to demonstrate the plaintiff's jury appeal. Alternatively, both sides might agree to freely exchange information and documentation that would otherwise be discoverable in order to evaluate the prospects for settlement. Given the breadth of information that is otherwise discoverable under the formal discovery rules, exchanging information informally is usually a desirable method for educating the parties about settlement possibilities.

Promptly taking depositions is another effective method for moving a case toward settlement. The deposition is the most useful discovery device for obtaining information, testing legal theories, evaluating a witness's demeanor, gathering impeachment material, setting up the case for possible summary judgment, and asking about facts which are not directly related to the lawsuit but which may lead to the discovery of admissible evidence. A videotape deposition may be particularly effective for revealing the extent of a party's injuries or the jury appeal of a party or crucial witness.

The usual goal of a deposition is to obtain information for use at trial and not to provide the witness with a rehearsal of what it will be like at trial. However, for settlement purposes, it is sometimes useful to depose the opposing party with the specific intention of giving her a taste of what it will be like when she is cross-examined or called as an adverse witness before the jury. A particularly destructive cross-examination of a party opponent during a deposition may cause

---

[6] *See* Fed. R. Civ. P. 12(b).

[7] *See* Fed. R. Civ. P. 12(f).

[8] *See* Fed. R. Civ. P. 12(e).

her to seriously rethink the desirability of settling the case in lieu of the embarrassment and discomfort she will incur when taking the witness stand. A similar approach might be used when deposing a key witness for the other side.

Submitting interrogatories, requests for admissions, or requests for production of documents not only demonstrates a commitment to prepare for trial, but may reveal information that will induce the parties to settle. For example, obtaining information about applicable insurance policy limits or requesting extensive financial records from a party against whom punitive damages are sought may dramatically change the prospects for settlement.

Litigants often engage in extensive "paper" discovery and various obstructionist tactics to thwart discovery requests in an effort to wear down the opposition. Motions to compel and motions for protective orders are still commonplace. However, this is changing in many jurisdictions in light of revisions to discovery rules and the growing intolerance of judges to discovery abuses. For example, the requirements under the federal rules to provide "initial disclosures" and "pretrial disclosures," along with limitations on the number of interrogatories that may be submitted and depositions that may be taken,[9] have tended to curtail abuses and hence the use of the discovery process to overwhelm less wealthy litigants.

## § 15.06 MAKING OFFERS OF JUDGMENT

Rule 68 of the Federal Rules of Civil Procedure provides:

> At any time more than 10 days before the trial begins, a party defending against a claim may serve upon the adverse party an offer to allow judgment to be taken against the defending party for the money or property or to the effect specified in the offer, with costs then accrued. If within 10 days after service of the offer the adverse party serves written notice that the offer is accepted, either party may then file the order and notice of acceptance together with proof of service thereof and thereupon the clerk shall enter judgment. An offer not accepted shall be deemed withdrawn and evidence thereof is not admissible except in a proceeding to determine costs. If the judgment finally obtained by the offeree is not more favorable than the offer, the offeree must pay the costs incurred after the making of the offer. The fact that an offer is made but not accepted does not preclude a subsequent offer. When the liability of one party to another has been determined by verdict or judgment, but the amount or extent of the liability remains to be determined by further proceedings, the party adjudged liable may make an offer of judgment, which shall have the same effect as an offer made before trial if it is served within a reasonable time not less than 10 days prior to the commencement of the hearings to determine the amount or extent of liability.

A number of states have similar rules, and some states even permit plaintiffs to make offers of judgment.[10] However, under Fed. R. Civ. P. 68, only a defendant or

---

[9] *See* Fed. R. Civ. P. 26, 30, and 33.

[10] *See* Solimine & Pacheco, State Court Regulation of Offers of Judgment and Its Lessons for Federal Practice, 13 Ohio St. J. Disp. Res. 51, 63–69 (1997).

a plaintiff defending against a counterclaim[11] may make an offer of judgment. The offer must be in writing and served upon the adverse party (usually the plaintiff), and the rule is not satisfied by a mere oral offer made in settlement negotiations or an offer made before suit is filed.[12]

The defendant's offer of judgment may be for non-monetary relief such as to allow a judgment for entry of an injunction or the granting of other equitable relief.[13] The offer may also disclaim liability[14] or be conditioned upon acceptance by all plaintiffs where multiple plaintiffs are involved.[15] The essential effect of rejecting an offer of judgment is that, if the ultimate judgment for the plaintiff is identical to[16] or less favorable than the offer, the plaintiff is obligated to pay all of the defendant's post-offer statutory "costs" (*e.g.*, filing fees, witness fees, and court reporter costs).[17] In determining whether the plaintiff's judgment exceeds the offer, the total monetary recovery (*i.e.*, compensatory and punitive damages) is included, along with plaintiff's pre-offer costs.[18] However, the rule is inapplicable if the defendant wins altogether because, in that situation, there has been no "judgment finally obtained by the [plaintiff] offeree," at all.[19] The defendant's costs in that situation may be recouped in the discretion of the court under Fed. R. Civ. P. 54(d).

When making an offer of judgment, the offer must specify a definite sum that will be paid on the underlying action (or other relief for which a judgment may be entered) and include a provision for "costs then accrued," although the defendant may leave the amount of the costs for later determination by the court. That is, an offer may take one of three forms — a lump-sum offer including substantive relief and costs, a sum for substantive relief while leaving the amount of costs for the court's determination, or separate specified sums for substantive relief and costs.[20]

Ordinarily, attorney's fees are not part of "costs." However, under certain federal statutes, such as those governing civil rights actions or employment discrimination cases, attorney's fees are expressly included as part of costs.[21] In such cases, if the offer of judgment expressly and unambiguously[22] states that it includes attorney's fees up to the date of the offer as part of costs, a plaintiff who accepts the offer or rejects it and obtains a judgment that is less than the total offer

---

[11]　Simon v. Intercontinental Transport (ICT) B.V., 882 F.2d 1435 (9th Cir. 1989).

[12]　Clark v. Sims, 28 F.3d 420 (4th Cir. 1994); Cox v. Brookshire Grocery Co., 919 F.2d 354 (5th Cir. 1990).

[13]　*See* Liberty Mut. Ins. Co. v. EEOC, 691 F.2d 438 (9th Cir. 1982) (injunction); Mallory v. Eyrich, 922 F.2d 1273 (offer of judgment for finding a violation of Voting Rights Act); Spencer v. General Electric Co., 894 F.2d 651 (4th Cir. 1990) (offer of judgment to reinstate plaintiff in sexual harassment case).

[14]　Staples v. Wickesberg, 122 F.R.D. 541 (D. Wis. 1988).

[15]　Lang v. Gates, 36 F.3d 73 (9th Cir. 1994).

[16]　*See* Id., Hutchison v. Wells, 719 F. Supp. 1435 (D. Ind. 1989).

[17]　*See* 28 U.S.C. § 1920; Fed. R. Civ. P. 54(d).

[18]　*See* Grosvenor v. Brienen, 801 F.2d 944 (7th Cir. 1986).

[19]　Delta Air Lines, Inc. v. August, 450 U.S. 346, 101 S.Ct. 1146, 67 L.Ed2d 287 (1981).

[20]　*See* Simon, The New Meaning of Rule 68: Marek v. Chesney and Beyond, 14 N.Y.U. Rev. of Law and Social Change 475, 508–509 (1987); Marek v. Chesney, 473 U.S. 1, 105 S.Ct. 3012, 87 L.Ed2d 1 (1985).

[21]　*See* 42 U.S.C. §§ 1983, 1988, & 2000 *et. seq. See also* the listing of such federal statutes in Marek v. Chesney, 473 U.S. 1, 105 S.Ct. at 3035–36, 87 L.Ed2d 1 (1985).

[22]　*See* Bevard v. Farmers Ins. Exchange, 127 F.3d 1147 (9th Cir. 1997).

cannot apply to the court for otherwise recoverable fees incurred after the date of the offer.[23] If the offer of judgment does not expressly include attorney's fees where they are statutorily included as part of costs, then the plaintiff who accepts the offer[24] or rejects it and obtains a judgment in excess of the offer may recover post-offer attorney's fees. If the applicable statute provides for attorney's fees separately from costs, an offer of judgment that is rejected by the plaintiff who fails to obtain a judgment in excess of the offer does not automatically cut off the prevailing plaintiff's right to seek post-offer attorney's fees, but such fees are likely to be significantly reduced by the court in light of the fact that the plaintiff's post-offer legal work produced a net loss.[25]

Finally, in federal civil rights and employment discrimination cases, even if the defendant may shift its post-offer "costs" to the plaintiff under Rule 68, the defendant's attorney's fees cannot be shifted to the plaintiff. This is so because, in such suits, the defendant may only receive attorney's fees if the action was "frivolous, unreasonable, or without foundation."[26]

Although there is no current empirical evidence that Rule 68 has, as it was designed to do,[27] increased the rate of settlements,[28] if you represent the defendant, making an offer of judgment may cause the plaintiff "to 'think very hard' about whether continued litigation is worthwhile"[29] in certain types of cases. For example, an offer of judgment may exert significant pressure on a plaintiff to settle if liability is clear, the costs of the litigation will be high, the plaintiff's damages will be difficult to prove or are very uncertain, or the plaintiff is in need of immediate funds or is otherwise not disposed to bear the time and stress of lengthy litigation. The defendant may make an offer of judgment at any time after suit is filed and need not wait until the plaintiff has completed discovery,[30] and there is no limit on the number of offers that the defendant may make. Finally, particularly where the plaintiff's cause of action permits him to recover attorney's fees as part of costs, an early offer of judgment that expressly includes fees up to the date of the offer should cause him to seriously consider the offer in the face of the prospect that no post-offer fees will be recoverable if he fails to obtain a judgment in excess of the offer.

## § 15.07  USING TIMING AND DEADLINES

The most opportune times for engaging in pretrial negotiations are influenced by numerous factors and circumstances. Among them are the following:

---

[23]  Herrington v. County of Sonoma, 12 F.3d 901 (9th Cir. 1993); Guerrero v. Cummings, 70 F.3d 1111 (9th Cir. 1995).

[24]  Fulps v. City of Springfield, 715 F.2d 1088 (6th Cir. 1983); Chambers v. Manning, 169 F.R.D. 5 (D. Conn. 1996).

[25]  See Haworth v. State of Nevada, 56 F.3d 1048, 1052 (9th Cir. 1995); Sheppard v. Riverview Nursing Center, Inc., 88 F.3d 1332 (4th Cir. 1996).

[26]  Grossman v. Marcoccio, 800 F.2d 329 (1st Cir. 1986); EEOC v. Bailey Ford Inc., 26 F.3d 570 (5th Cir. 1994); See Hughes v. Rowe, 449 U.S. 5, 101 S.Ct. 173, 66 L.Ed2d 163 (1980).

[27]  See Delta Air Lines, Inc. v. August, 450 U.S. 346, 101 S.Ct. 1146, 67 L.Ed2d 287 (1981).

[28]  See Rowe & Anderson, One-Way Fee Shifting Statutes and Offer of Judgment Rules: An Empirical Experiment, 36 Jurimetrics J. 225 (1996).

[29]  Marek v. Chesny, 473 U.S. 1, 11, 105 S.Ct. 3012, 3017, 87 L.Ed2d 1 (1985).

[30]  See Grossman v. Marcoccio, 800 F.2d 329 (1st Cir. 1986) (offer made 21 days after suit filed).

(1)   If the parties are attempting to avoid litigation and the statute of limitations on the plaintiff's claim is drawing near, negotiation efforts may be accelerated.

(2)   Sometimes negotiations will be triggered merely by the filing of the complaint, or when the defendant aggressively asserts a counterclaim, cross-claim, or seeks to add additional parties to the lawsuit.

(3)   Settlement discussions are influenced by the extent to which the discovery process reveals particular strengths or weaknesses in a party's case, and whether engaging in discovery is becoming cost prohibitive for one or both of the parties.

(4)   If the trial judge denies the defendant's motion for summary judgment but otherwise indicates that the plaintiff's case is tenuous, the prospect for settlement is likely to increase.

(5)   The extent to which the trial judge encourages the parties to settle or pushes the case to trial will often influence the parties' disposition toward settlement.

(6)   If the plaintiff is in need of money, he is more likely to settle for a smaller sum now than gamble on recovering a larger sum later at trial.

(7)   If a party is receiving adverse publicity about the case or her litigation position, she may be induced to negotiate a settlement.

(8)   The outcome of another lawsuit or appellate decision on issues similar to those being litigated between the parties may induce settlement.

(9)   Corporate parties may be more receptive to settlement toward the end of the calendar or fiscal year either for tax purposes or because the resolution of the case can be announced in the corporation's annual report.

(10)   The arrival of the holiday season toward the end of the year may cause the parties to be more inclined to discuss settlement, and an indigent plaintiff might accept a lesser sum than he might otherwise accept in order to buy Christmas or Chanukah presents.

(11)   The unexpected postponement of a trial after the parties have strenuously prepared for trial may cause them to consider settlement possibilities.

(12)   Settlement prospects may be affected by factors such as the illness of a party or her attorney, the extent to which a party is really prepared to go to trial, whether the party is being represented on an hourly or contingent fee basis, or whether a party's witnesses have become unavailable or difficult to secure for trial.

(13)   Establishing deadlines can also exert pressure on the parties toward settlement. For example, a party might notify the other side that numerous depositions will have to be noticed by a certain date if no settlement is reached by that date, obtain a court order for a deadline within which discovery must be completed, make a calendar request to schedule the case for trial, obtain a court order that peremptorily sets the case for trial, or file a motion for a pretrial conference with the judge.

## § 15.08   USING PRETRIAL SETTLEMENT CONFERENCES

A pretrial settlement conference with the trial judge or magistrate is frequently an appropriate time to advance the settlement of a case. Many jurisdictions require pretrial settlement conferences or make them available upon motion of a party.[31] Sometimes clients are required to attend along with the lawyers. In cases where a conference is not required, requesting one is particularly useful when the other party is being recalcitrant. After all, a judge is not likely to look with favor upon a party who refuses to discuss settlement.

Judges vary in their approaches to pretrial settlement conferences. Many are constrained to merely encourage the parties to seriously consider settlement possibilities. Others take a more active role by asking the parties to explain their most recent offers, probing the factual and legal contentions of each side, and even giving a gratuitous assessment of the case or suggesting a possible compromise.

The local rules of some jurisdictions require the parties to submit written settlement conference statements to the court in aid of the conference. These rules vary in terms of what should be included in the statements, whether they are to be filed with the court or only "lodged" with it (*i.e.*, submitted solely to the judge without becoming part of the official record of the case), and whether they are to be served on opposing counsel. Experienced judges advise that, in general, these written statements should (1) be brief and to the point (*i.e.*, not exceed ten pages and not include voluminous exhibits), (2) reflect candor by appropriately acknowledging the weaknesses in your case, (3) clearly state the *reasons* for your settlement contentions, (4) avoid emotionalism, and (5) avoid taking a "nickel and dime" approach in making offers or counteroffers.[32] Except as the applicable local rule might otherwise prescribe, your written statement should include:

(1)   A brief summary of the facts giving rise to the lawsuit (including an itemization of damages) and the anticipated trial evidence in support of those facts;

(2)   A summary of your legal contentions about liability and damages in light of the facts and anticipated evidence;

(3)   A summary of the procedural status of the litigation (i.e., the extent of discovery conducted in the case and the pendency of any pretrial motions);

(4)   A summary of any settlement offers or counteroffers that have already been made in the case; and

(5)   A summary of your client's current settlement position in terms of a specific settlement amount or settlement range, and your specific reasons justifying that amount or range.

How to best conduct yourself at the pretrial settlement conference will, of course, largely depend upon the style of the presiding judge. In general, however, with or without a written settlement conference statement, you should be prepared to (1) summarize the past and current offers of the parties; (2) explain your strongest factual and legal points, while appropriately acknowledging your weaker ones; (3) show the judge any admissible documentation or key exhibits that substantiate your claims or defenses; (4) provide rational reasons for your offer or propose a modification of your latest offer; (5) downplay any emotionalism or acrimonious

---

[31]   *See* Fed. R. Civ. P. 16.

[32]   *See* E.F. Lynch, et. al., *Negotiation and Settlement* 391–398 (1992).

history of the litigation; and (6) avoid using any deceptive tactics.

If you demonstrate some willingness to compromise, it is likely that the judge will look to the other side to reciprocate. However, as in the closing phase of a face-to-face negotiation, it is best to be patient and cautious in making final concessions. If you appear overly eager to compromise, the judge may end up exerting more pressure on your side to effectuate a final settlement.

Finally, unless you know in advance that the judge would flatly decline to do so, you should not hesitate to ask her for her general assessment of the case for settlement purposes. While most judges are reluctant to give a direct opinion on this subject, some will at least indicate their instincts about the general settlement value of the controversy, or use your question as a springboard to actively encourage settlement. Of course, this does not mean that you should feel bound by any assessment the judge might make, but the opinion of a trial judge who has seen hundreds of verdicts and awards is worth careful consideration.[33]

## § 15.09   SETTLING AT THE LAST MINUTE

Last minute settlements — whether at the courthouse steps, during trial, or while an appeal is being contemplated or pending — are not unusual. No matter how thoroughly prepared you are for trial, unexpected events invariably occur. A party might be induced to settle (1) the night before or minutes before the trial starts, (2) after the judge has ruled on a critical pretrial motion such as a motion *in limine*, (3) after an unfavorable jury has been empanelled, (4) after one or more key witnesses fails to show up for trial, (5) after a particularly destructive cross-examination, (6) after a witness gives unexpected or surprise testimony, (7) after the plaintiff has rested his case and before the defendant makes a motion for a directed verdict, (8) during or after the defendant's evidence, (9) after the judge has made his rulings at the jury instruction conference, or (10) after the closing arguments and before the jury returns from the jury room to announce its verdict and award. In short, nearly every trial has its own pressure points that may cause the parties to settle.

If the trial has not gone well either party and both sides have been unable to reach agreement on a settlement amount, you still might be able to force a last-minute agreement. For example, as the jury is returning from the jury room to render a verdict, you might inform the judge of your final settlement offer. The judge is likely to give the other side a few minutes to accept the settlement or hear the verdict. The pressure of this "last ditch" effort, coupled with the certainty of a reasonable settlement, may induce the other party to accept.

Alternatively, after the closing arguments and while the jury is deliberating, the parties might consult with the judge about a last-minute settlement. Obtaining the judge's perception about the presentation of the evidence and the risks to each party in gambling on the jury's verdict may facilitate a final agreement.

Even after the jury verdict, a settlement might be reached while the losing party contemplates filing an appeal or while an appeal is pending. The appellate process

---

[33] For an interesting survey about the attitudes of judges and lawyers toward various techniques that might be used in a pretrial settlement conference, *see* Rude & Wall, Judicial Involvement in Settlement: How Judges and Lawyers View It, 72 Judicature 175 (1988).

is likely to take years, and the parties may choose to forgo the time, expense, and uncertainty of the outcome on appeal. This is so even for the party who prevailed at trial. If an objective assessment of the outcome on appeal indicates that a reversal and remand for a new trial is likely, serious consideration should be given to renewing settlement discussions.

## § 15.10   HIGH-LOW AGREEMENTS

In connection with last-minute settlements, the parties will sometimes enter into a so-called "high-low" agreement that provides for a floor and a ceiling on a settlement amount that is tied to the jury's verdict or award. For example, if the plaintiff believes that his case is worth $250,000, and the defendant thinks that she might prevail at trial but is concerned about being faced with a large verdict by a run-away jury, the parties might agree that if the jury finds liability, the plaintiff will receive $150,000; and if no liability is found, the plaintiff will receive $50,000. Alternatively, it might be agreed that if the jury returns an award of $100,000 or more, the plaintiff will get $150,000, but if the jury renders any verdict below $100,000, the plaintiff will receive $50,000. This type of agreement guarantees the plaintiff a reasonable award but protects the defendant from an excessive verdict.

## § 15.11   "COLLABORATIVE LAW" AGREEMENTS

"Collaborative Law" is a new model of dispute resolution that is gaining attention in the family law arena.[34] In this model, a husband and wife who are contemplating separation or divorce and their respective attorneys enter into a pledge or agreement at the outset of the case promising to participate in the settlement process in good faith with full disclosure. The agreement also includes a provision that each of the four parties to the agreement (husband, wife, husband's attorney, and wife's attorney) understand and agree that if the settlement process breaks down prior to resolution, the attorneys cannot represent either party in any future legal proceedings.

During the "Collaborative Law" process, both clients and their respective attorneys meet in several "four-way conferences" to exchange documents and discuss resolution of the parties' issues. As a rule, prior to each four-way conference, the attorneys meet to discuss areas of conflict that may act as "triggers" for their clients. They then develop an agenda for each meeting as well as an overall plan that will give the clients a sense of accomplishment early in the process so that movement towards a settlement will not stop when the difficult issues must be tackled.

The attorneys also meet with their respective clients to train them in various communication techniques that will allow them to better understand one another's needs. According to one commentator: "Collaborative communication is critical throughout the process. How language is used is very important in this negotiation

---

[34] Angela L. Haas, "The Difference Between Practicing Law Collaboratively and Practicing Collaborative Law", CLE Manuscript for "Getting to Equal Protection," LGBT Legal Issues in N.C., Apr. 22, 2005, RTP, N.C. p. V-2. Stuart Webb, an attorney in Minnesota first started practicing collaborative law in the early 1990s in Minnesota. Since then workshops have been held in several states. *See* Pauline H. Tessler, "Collaborative Law: What It Is and Why Family Attorneys Need to Know about It." (2001, www.collaborativefamilylawofUtah.com) for a history of the collaborative law movement.

model. Using words such as 'we', 'let's', 'and', 'our', and 'together' create a sense of cooperation and teamwork and decrease the feelings of competition."[35] The attorneys work with their respective clients to get them to express their concerns about the future and to focus on long-lasting practical solutions. If the parties need expert advice during their negotiations, the parties jointly choose and retain the experts.

The attorneys who practice "Collaborative Law" do not see themselves as "negotiators" for their clients, but instead as "facilitators" of the needs-based discussions that will allow "their clients to negotiate in a respectful, non-competitive environment."[36]

A few state legislatures have enacted statutes and rules of practice delineating the parameters of "Collaborative Law" for attorneys practicing in the domestic area.[37] The American Bar Association has also described the "Collaborative Law" process in its Handbook for Clients:

> Collaborative Law: Each person retains his or her own trained collaborative lawyer to advise and assist in negotiating an agreement on all issues. All negotiations take place in "four-way" settlement meetings that both clients and both lawyers attend. The lawyers cannot go to court or threaten to go to court. Settlement is the only agenda. If either client goes to court, both collaborative lawyers are disqualified from further participation. Each client has built-in legal advice and advocacy during negotiations, and each lawyer's job includes guiding the client toward reasonable resolutions. The legal advice is an integral part of the process, but all the decisions are made by the clients. The lawyers generally prepare and process all papers required for the divorce.[38]

Although the concept of "Collaborative Law" originated in the family law arena, Pauline Tesler in her article, *Collaborative Law: What It Is and Why Family Law Attorneys Need to Know about It*, recommends its use "in any situation where preservation of an ongoing relationship between the parties is an important objective."[39]

---

[35] Angela L. Haas, "The Difference Between Practicing Law Collaboratively and Practicing Collaborative Law", CLE Manuscript for "Getting to Equal Protection," LGBT Legal Issues in N.C., Apr. 22, 2005, RTP, N.C. p. V-4.

[36] Angela L. Haas, "The Difference Between Practicing Law Collaboratively and Practicing Collaborative Law", CLE Manuscript for "Getting to Equal Protection," LGBT Legal Issues in N.C., April 22, 2005, RTP, N.C. p. V-4.

[37] *See* N.C.G.S. § 50–70 *et seq.*; Tex. Fam. Code § 6.603; and Minn. Gen. R. Prac. § 111.05 (2008).

[38] American Bar Association, Appendix C: Handbook for Clients (2001).

[39] Tesler, footnote 34.

# Chapter 16

# NEGOTIATING DURING MEDIATION

    **[7]   Make Reasonable Settlement Offers Supported by Sound Reasons**

    **[8]   Hold Back Some Strong Leverage Points Until the Final Caucuses**

    **[9]   Suggest Mediator Tactics and Techniques that May Help Forge an Agreement**

    **[10]  Confer Alone with the Mediator and Opposing Counsel, If Necessary**

    **[11]  Do Not Make the Mediator's Fee an Element of the Settlement**

    **[12]  Be Patient With the Mediation Process and Take Time to Confer Privately With Your Client**

**§ 16.13   CONCLUDING THE MEDIATION**

## § 16.01  INTRODUCTION

Mediation is an informal, non-adversarial alternative dispute resolution process, whereby a neutral third party, who is either selected by the parties or is appointed from an approved list of mediators eligible to mediate the type of case at hand, encourages and facilitates the parties to voluntarily resolve their dispute. The mediator does not decide what the outcome should be. The process is different from arbitration, in which a neutral third party hears evidence and arguments from the parties and makes a binding or non-binding decision about how the parties' dispute should be resolved. In mediation, the parties themselves make the decision; and if they do not voluntarily resolve their dispute, they may resolve it through some other alternative dispute resolution process or, if the case is actionable, litigate it.

Virtually all jurisdictions — by statute, agency rule, or court rule — mandate mediation or otherwise formally make it available in certain types of cases. Illustrative are family-law disputes, collective bargaining and other labor-law disputes, personal injury cases, medical malpractice actions, products liability cases, civil rights actions, contract cases, wrongful discharge cases and other employment-related disputes, landlord-tenant cases, small claims actions, toxic tort cases, consumer complaints, environmental disputes, professional conduct and licensing cases, neighborhood or community disputes, farm mortgage disputes, housing disputes, agricultural producer-distributor bargaining, geothermal energy development disputes, criminal misdemeanor cases (*see* § 19.12), and rule-making disputes.[1] Many jurisdictions mandate mediation in a broad range of civil cases as a prerequisite to taking the case to trial. These "court-annexed" mediation programs have burgeoned as a means of easing the backlog of cases and reducing the time and expense of litigation. In short, the "mediation explosion" has permeated our society in the both the public and private sector.

Studies have shown that mediation has a number of advantages over traditional inter-party or lawyer-to-lawyer negotiations.[2] First, mediation provides a structured opportunity to bring the parties together, not just to exchange demands and positions, but to discuss and explain their interests, needs, and emotions in a setting where the parties can feel that another person (the mediator) has heard their side

---

    [1] *See* Nancy H. Rogers & Craig A. McEwen, *Mediation: Law, Policy & Practice* (2d ed. 1994) (setting forth in Appendices state-by-state legislation governing mediation in different types of cases).

    [2] *See* Robert A. Baruch Bush, "What Do We Need a Mediator For?": Mediator's "Value-Added" For Negotiators, 12:1 Ohio St. J. on Dispute Res. 13–26 (1996); Nancy H. Rogers & Craig A. McEwen, *Mediation: Law, Policy & Practice* § 4:04 (2d. ed. 1994).

of the story and given them a "fair shake." Second, mediation structures the negotiating process in ways that increase more reliable information sharing and better understanding between the parties so that they can better decide how to resolve their dispute. Third, skilled mediators can help facilitate an agreement by breaking down cognitive and emotional barriers between the parties through a variety of tactics and techniques that help to diffuse suspicion and irrationality, and help to promote reality testing and face saving. Fourth, mediation gives the parties a greater sense of participation and control over their case through a process in which they can address the issues they themselves feel are most important. In sum, the advantages of mediation are consistent with the well-established fact that clients are often at least as much concerned with how they are treated in dispute resolution as they are with its results. That is, the very *process* of how the parties go about resolving their dispute is often of integral importance to them.

Often mediation will occur after traditional negotiations have failed to produce an agreement. Sometimes, however, the parties will choose mediation as a means of first resort in trying to resolve their dispute. This chapter focuses on how you can negotiate effectively during mediation, whether you are engaging in the process as part of a mandatory program or as a matter of choice.[3]

## § 16.02  THE MEDIATION PROCESS, IN GENERAL[4]

Mediation typically occurs in a conference room at a neutral location or at a lawyer's office agreed upon by the parties and the mediator. Present are the mediator (or perhaps co-mediators in a multi-party or highly complex case), the individual parties (or a designated representative of a party if it is a corporation or governmental entity), and their lawyers. If there is insurance coverage in the case, an insurance adjuster will usually also attend. In many court-annexed mediations, all of the foregoing persons are required to attend. Sometimes, by agreement between the parties, other support persons (*e.g.*, a spouse of a party, or a person who has some special expertise or is otherwise integrally involved in the case) might attend all or part of the mediation or be on telephone standby for consultation. Because the process is private, no stenographers, court personnel, news reporters, or other observers attend the mediation.

The mediator begins the mediation in a joint session in the presence of all participants. After the mediator introduces herself, and all participants have introduced themselves to one another, she will make some brief introductory remarks that explain her role and the over-all mediation process. Typically, these remarks will explain that:

(1)  Mediation is an informal process where the rules of evidence and other formal rules of procedure do not apply;

(2)  The mediator is neutral and impartial in the case and has no conflict of interest;

(3)  The mediator has reviewed any pre-mediation submissions that the parties

---

[3] The focus is not on how to be an effective mediator, a subject typically relegated to a "mediation" or "alternative dispute resolution" course. Among the numerous instructive works for mediators, *see* Christopher W. Moore, *The Mediation Process — Practical Strategies for Resolving Conflict* (2d ed. 1996); John W. Cooley, *The Mediator's Handbook* (NITA 2000).

[4] *See also* "General Suggestions to Mediators for How to Mediate a Case" in Appendix B of this book.

may have sent to her in advance of the mediation;

(4)  The mediator's role is to assist the parties in reaching a possible agreement, and not to serve as a judge or jury in the case;

(5)  Generally, most things said or done during the mediation are confidential in the sense that they cannot later be used by one side against the other in litigation (*see* § 17.11);

(6)  If a party privately shares anything with the mediator that the party expressly states he wants kept confidential, the mediator is prohibited from disclosing that information to the other side or to anyone else unless required by law;

(7)  The mediator is prohibited from giving any legal advice during the mediation;

(8)  Each side will be given an opportunity at the outset to make an opening statement about the case;

(9)  Each side might then wish to ask some clarifying questions of the other to bring as much non-confidential information to the table as early as possible in the mediation process;

(10)  After the case is discussed in joint session, the mediator typically will hold multiple private caucuses, separately with each party, to clarify information, and to discuss underlying interests, feelings, objectives, possible solutions to the dispute, and particular proposals offered by the parties that might resolve the case;

(11)  If a settlement is reached, the mediator will have all participants reconvene in a joint session at which she will summarize the terms of the agreement and make sure the parties understand what steps will be taken to prepare and execute any settlement documents;

(12)  If no agreement is reached, it is the mediator's duty to declare an impasse; and

(13)  The fees for the mediation will be borne equally between the parties unless they have otherwise agreed about how those fees will be paid.

After the mediator has made her introductory remarks and answered any questions about her role or the overall mediation process, each side will make an opening statement, usually beginning with the claimant. The lawyers typically give these opening statements, which generally set forth the parties' factual and legal contentions. Sometimes, however, the clients will participate in the opening statements by explaining certain parts of "the story" (*see* §§ 16.08[4] and 16.11). After the opening statements, the mediator might ask some clarifying questions, might allow the parties to share further information between one another, or might let the parties engage in a free-flowing discussion of the dispute. If there are multiple issues in the case, the mediator might devote part of the joint session to establishing an appropriate agenda.

When it becomes apparent that discussions in a joint session are no longer productive, the mediator will begin private caucusing through separate, *ex parte* meetings with each side. Usually, she will hold the first private meeting with the claimant and his attorney or the side that is in the position to respond to the latest offer or proposal, and then caucus with the opposing side. In most cases, private caucusing will begin shortly after the parties have given their opening statements, and the mediator will hold numerous private meetings with each side. Indeed, in the mediation of legal disputes, it is common for the balance of the time spent during mediation to consist of these alternating private caucuses through which the mediator acts as a sort of "shuttle diplomat" between the opposing sides. On the other hand, after holding a number of private caucuses with each side, the mediator might decide to bring the parties back together in a joint session if, for example, they express a desire to do so, or if exchanging certain information or discussing a particular proposal would be more efficient in a joint meeting.

During the private caucuses, the mediator will engage in five overlapping functions or stages:

(1)    Obtaining information about the facts, the law, the issues, the parties' underlying feelings, interests or needs (*e.g.*, emotional, psychological, economic, physical, or social), the parties' primary, secondary, and incidental objectives, potential solutions or proposals, and the reasons supporting particular proposals, offers, and counteroffers;

(2)    Generating and discussing potential solutions or proposals in light of the parties' interests and objectives;

(3)    Assessing, selecting, and communicating specific proposals, offers, and counteroffers of the parties;

(4)    Creating movement in the negotiations by encouraging the parties to compromise and consider the risks, costs, and alternatives to not reaching an agreement; and

(5)    Forging and finalizing the terms of an agreement.

Throughout these stages, the mediator will engage in a variety of tactics and techniques to encourage the parties to be cooperative and realistic in the bargaining process.

Most mediation sessions last between one and five hours, but it is not uncommon for a mediation to last for a day or more in multi-party or particularly complex cases. In addition, the mediator and the parties might agree to hold more than one mediation session to allow the parties to use the time in between to formulate or consider new settlement proposals or obtain additional information.

## § 16.03   FACILITATIVE V. EVALUATIVE MEDIATION

As a matter of mediation philosophy, mediators often distinguish between so-called "facilitative" and "evaluative" mediation, and some jurisdictions permit only "facilitative" mediation in court-annexed mediation programs. Strictly speaking, in "facilitative mediation," the mediator assists the parties to arrive at their own decision about a reasonable settlement or solution under circumstances where the mediator neither offers an opinion about the settlement value of the case nor recommends how the case should be resolved. In contrast, in "evaluative mediation," the mediator is permitted to give a non-binding opinion or recommendation about the settlement value of the case or how the case should be resolved. In a combined facilitative-evaluative mediation, the mediator will usually first try to achieve a resolution through pure facilitation, and if that is unsuccessful, will then offer an opinion or recommendation about how the case should settle. In selecting a mediator, the parties are usually free to choose which type of mediation they prefer for their case.

It is important to emphasize that even in strictly "facilitative" mediations, the mediator still engages in important evaluative functions throughout the mediation. For example, mediators constantly evaluate the body language of the parties, the relative importance of their feelings, needs, interests and objectives, the reasons behind their offers and counteroffers, the costs and risks associated with not reaching an agreement, and the extent to which the parties' negotiating positions are realistic. This is because an on-going evaluation of these matters is critical to the mediator in deciding what styles, strategies, and tactics and techniques to employ in helping the parties reach an agreement. Thus, although the strictly "facilitative" mediator will never *directly* render an opinion about the settlement value of the case or how the case should be resolved, she will inevitably indicate her views or sense about these matters by *indirection* — through the questions she asks the parties, the information she shares between one side and the other, and the various matters she emphasizes with each side in an effort to encourage the parties to compromise and forge a satisfactory agreement.

## § 16.04   MEDIATOR STYLES AND STRATEGIES

Mediators may engage in styles of interpersonal behavior that range from being fairly passive to being quite aggressive. In mediation training programs, mediators are typically taught to act in a mild-mannered and low-key way, to keep their emotions under control, and to place a premium on being sensitive to the feelings and concerns of the parties through focused questioning, "active listening," and empathetic understanding.

In connection with the overall goal of trying to bring the parties together to reach an agreement, mediators employ different strategies or methodologies that, in turn, may affect their interpersonal style. In general, these different strategies or conceptual approaches to mediating have been usefully described as "trashing," "bashing," or "hashing it out."[5]

Under the "trashing" approach, the mediator uses the private caucuses to "tear apart" each side's case by asking pointed questions about its strengths and weaknesses. In this way, the parties are forced to take a hard look at the merits of the case from a more objective factual and legal standpoint. Despite the bombastic-sounding term "trashing," this strategy of facilitating honest case assessment may be employed by mild-mannered as well as more aggressive mediators. After each side's case has been "torn down," the mediator proceeds to press both sides to put more "realistic" proposals or settlement figures on the table. The mediator then continues to shuttle back and forth between the parties in private caucuses to help forge an agreement out of their more reasonable proposals or positions.

Many lawyers appreciate this sometimes blunt, "no-nonsense" approach to mediating, particularly in adversarial cases where money is the sole or primary issue and the lawyers' or parties' egos have prevented them from making realistic assessments of the value of the case or coming up with viable settlement options. The effectiveness of the strategy, however, largely depends upon the litigation experience of the mediator and her ability to accurately point out the strengths and weaknesses of the case from a trial standpoint. Although the approach may also be used in problem-solving situations, it is likely to be less effective when the parties are not particularly concerned with analyzing settlement prospects from a cost-

---

[5] James J. Alfini, Trashing, Bashing, and Hashing it Out: Is this the End of "Good Mediation"? 19 Fla. St. Univ. L. Rev. 47 (1991).

benefit perspective, but rather are driven by matters such as establishing precedent or obtaining vindication.

Under the "bashing" strategy, the mediator (who might, for example, be a retired judge) spends much less time discussing the relative strengths and weaknesses of the parties' cases, and instead "bashes away" at the initial settlement offers of the parties to try to get the parties to settle somewhere in between. The basher draws upon her trial experience to emphasize the risks and costs of litigation, and then aggressively exhorts the parties to compromise. The ensuing mediation becomes a sort of "mad dash for the middle." As explained by one basher:

> The plaintiff wanted $75,000. The defendant told me he would pay $40,000. I went to the plaintiff and said to him, "They're not going to pay $75,000. What will you take?" He said, "I'll take $60,000." I told him I wasn't sure I could get $60,000 and asked if he would take $50,000 if I could get it. He agreed. I then went back to the defendant and told him I [sic] couldn't settle for $40,000, but "you might get the plaintiff to take $50,000" and asked if he would pay it. The answer was yes. Neither of them were bidding against themselves. I was the guy who was doing it, and that's the role of the mediator.[6]

Some lawyers welcome this highly aggressive approach, which tends to expeditiously "hammer sense" into the parties. The drawbacks of the strategy are that it is not conducive to problem solving, is largely inappropriate for complex or multiparty cases, and sometimes fails to encourage the parties to carefully evaluate their cases beforehand to make reasonable initial settlement offers from which concessions are made based on reasoning rather than out of raw submission.

Under the "hashing it out" approach, the mediator places greater reliance on direct communication between the parties and takes a less directive role in pressing them toward an agreement. The preference is for the parties to communicate freely and hash out an agreement by themselves. If the parties have difficulty communicating with one another, they communicate through the mediator. The mediator variously plays the roles of "facilitator, orchestrator, referee, sounding board, [and] scapegoat."[7] Unlike the trashers and bashers, hashers tend to be more flexible in their approach to the mediation process by varying their styles and use of caucusing as best fits the particular circumstances of the case and the parties. If the parties are not making headway toward an agreement and wish to terminate the mediation, the hasher will usually accede to the voluntariness of the process and not press the parties to reach an agreement.

Hashers thus tend to take a somewhat more passive role in the mediation process. The strategy is well suited for problem-solving and works particularly well when the parties are willing to engage in non-adversarial and cooperative bargaining. On the other hand, because of the hasher's penchant not to vigorously "push" the parties toward an agreement, the parties may end up abandoning the mediation process prematurely.

These different mediator strategies are not necessarily mutually exclusive. That is, in a particular mediation, a mediator might first hash, then trash, and finally bash. Similarly, a mediator might adopt a more passive style at the outset of the

---

[6] Id. at 70.

[7] Id. at 71.

mediation and then employ a more aggressive style later if the parties appear able to reach an agreement but are having difficulty achieving closure. In short, different strategies and styles have their own advantages and disadvantages depending on the particular case, the parties involved, and where the parties are in the mediation.

## § 16.05  WHAT CASES TO MEDIATE AND WHEN TO MEDIATE

If your client has filed a lawsuit and the jurisdiction requires that the case be mediated as a predicate to maintaining the suit, your client will have no choice but to engage in mediation unless the applicable statute, agency rule, or court rule otherwise allows the parties to waive mediation by mutual agreement or for good cause. Even if mediation is not required, it is important to decide whether to nevertheless voluntarily engage in mediation either after negotiations have failed or in lieu of traditional negotiations. If you decide to pursue mediation, it is also necessary to consider at what stage of the case mediation would be most productive.

The option of mediating a case is typically not considered until after traditional negotiations have broken down. However, in circumstances where (1) the parties or their lawyers have a particularly strained relationship, (2) multiple parties are involved, or (3) there are numerous or complex issues in dispute, it may be beneficial to mediate the case at the outset in lieu of engaging in traditional negotiations. Assuming you are considering mediation, either in lieu of traditional negotiations or after they have failed, provided below are "Favorable Situations for Mediation" and "Unfavorable Situations for Mediation" to aid in deciding whether to mediate and at what stage of the case mediation might be most productive.

### [1]   Favorable Situations for Mediation

- The parties or their lawyers are finding it difficult to engage in negotiations, or negotiations are deadlocked.
- The parties want to settle the case confidentially.
- The parties want to avoid establishing judicial precedent.
- Communication between the parties is poor, or their emotional involvement in the case is preventing settlement.
- The parties want to minimize litigation costs.
- The interests or needs of the parties are interdependent, and they would benefit from each other's cooperation in satisfying those interests or needs.
- The parties want or will have to maintain a relationship after the dispute is resolved.
- The parties have different perceptions about the facts of the case, or disagree about what data or other information is needed to resolve it.
- The parties are divided over different values or interests.
- There are multiple parties in the case, or there are a number of other persons whose input is necessary or would be desirable in resolving the dispute.
- There are multiple issues in the case and the parties disagree about the order in which the issues should be addressed.
- The parties are considering a non-monetary remedy or some other remedy that a court cannot provide.

- The parties are unable to agree on an acceptable forum or structure for negotiations.
- Stereotyping, prejudices, misunderstandings, or other misperceptions are preventing the parties from resolving their dispute.
- The parties are having difficulty evaluating the factual or legal merits of the case or its value, or have unrealistic views about those matters.
- The parties desire to resolve at least some, if not all, issues in the case.
- The parties wish to engage in informal discovery, or want to evaluate each other's credibility or jury appeal.

## [2]    Unfavorable Situations for Mediation

- The parties have a need for formal discovery that has not yet been completed, and they are unable to provide necessary information to one another through the mediation process.
- The parties want a judicial resolution of the dispute because they want to establish a precedent, want a court to resolve ambiguous or conflicting law, or want vindication.
- The sole issues dividing the parties are ones of "principle."
- Punitive damages are an indispensable issue in the case.
- The events giving rise to the parties' dispute were so traumatic that the parties are not yet psychologically able to discuss a possible resolution of their dispute (*e.g.*, in the family law area, where domestic violence has been involved in the dispute).
- Negotiations have been so acrimonious or unproductive that the parties have essentially decided to take the case to trial.
- The parties stand to gain from a strategy of delay.
- There are numerous parties involved in the dispute and one or more of them is unwilling to mediate.
- The parties' dispute affects the public interest and the government is not represented.

## § 16.06   CHOOSING A MEDIATOR

In jurisdictions that mandate mediation in certain types of cases, the parties are usually free to select their mediator by mutual agreement. If they cannot agree, a mediator will usually be appointed from a list of mediators eligible to mediate the particular type of case. Typically, these eligible mediators have been "certified" to mediate cases after completing a mandatory mediation-training course.

One scholar has summarized the qualities and abilities of a good mediator as a person who is "capable of appreciating the dynamics of the environment in which the dispute is occurring, intelligent, effective listener, articulate, patient, non-judgmental, flexible, forceful and persuasive, imaginative, resourceful, a person of professional standing or reputation, reliable, capable of gaining access to necessary resources, non-defensive, person of integrity, humble, objective, and neutral with regard to the outcome."[8] When choosing a mediator, in addition to these qualities and abilities, you should consider whether the prospects for settling the case would

---

[8]   Joseph B. Stulberg, The Theory and Practice of Mediation: A Reply to Professor Susskind, 6 Vt. L. Rev. 94 (1981).

be enhanced by a "facilitative" or "evaluative" mediator, and whether the particular mediator has a style and strategy that would complement the case.

Along with the foregoing considerations, it may be useful to know that, for many lawyers, the most sought-after mediators are those who are "willing and able to 'push' the parties, not in an antagonistic or hostile sense, but in the positive sense of inviting, supporting, encouraging, motivating, and urging the parties to work [toward an agreement]."[9] This overall attribute of "pushing" the parties involves pushing them (1) to obtain, disclose, and consider all information relevant to resolving the dispute; (2) to carefully assess the importance of any missing pieces of information in deciding whether and how to proceed in the absence of complete information; (3) to identify and consider all possible options for resolving the issues before focusing on specific options and making actual decisions; (4) to consider and fully understand the consequences of reaching an agreement or not reaching an agreement; (5) to articulate clearly their positions and the reasons behind them; and (6) to hear and understand each other's positions and the reasons underlying them.[10] In sum, many lawyers appreciate mediators who are willing to be persistent in the mediation process by engaging in a diligent effort to push *for* the parties to reach an agreement and push *with* them toward that end. This role of the effective mediator may be accomplished through any number of different mediator styles or strategies.

Finally, in unusually complex cases or where there are numerous parties and issues, it may be desirable to have co-mediators conduct the mediation. In selecting co-mediators, you might consider whether gender, racial, or ethnic balance would enhance the mediation. In addition, you might select one mediator for her rote skills as an effective mediator, and the other for his special expertise in the subject matter of the case to be mediated.

## § 16.07   MEDIATOR TACTICS AND TECHNIQUES

### [1]   Tactics and Techniques Drawn from Traditional Negotiating

It is often said that good mediators are good negotiators. Accordingly, mediators routinely employ a variety of tactics and techniques that are similar to those employed in inter-party negotiations. Thus, mediators may use a number of the "Negotiating Tactics and Techniques" discussed in Chapter 10. However, good mediators will not use those tactics and techniques which are designed to mislead or exert undue pressure upon a party, or which are otherwise disingenuous or unethical.

Based on the list of Negotiating Tactics and Techniques given in Chapter 10, the following chart separates the particular tactics and techniques that mediators will not use in mediation from those they might use in mediation:

---

[9] Robert A. Baruch Bush, Efficiency and Protection, or Empowerment and Recognition? The Mediator's Role and Ethical Standards in Mediation, 41 Fla. L. Rev. 277 (1989).

[10] Id. at 278–281.

Negotiating Tactics and Techniques Mediators Will Not Use:

- Anger/Aggressiveness
- Blaming or Fault Finding
- Bluffing
- Br'er Rabbit

- Coalition

- Company Policy Excuse
- Dodging the Question

- Escalating Demands
- Excessive Initial Demands/Offers

- Fait Accompli
- False Demands
- False Multiple Concessions

- False Scarcity
- Good Guy-Bad Guy Routine/Mutt and Jeff
- Lack of Authority or Limited Authority
- Little Ol' Country Lawyer
- Lock-in Positions
- Low-Balling
- Misstatement
- Nibbling
- Personal Attacks
- Playing Dumb
- Publicity
- Reversing Position
- Snow Job/Alleged Expertise
- Take-it-or-Leave-it
- Threats
- Two Against One
- Walkout

Negotiating Tactics and Techniques Mediators Might Use:

- Abdication
- Adjournment or Caucus
- Deadlines
- Delay (in a constructive application)
- Draft Document or Single Negotiating Text
- Face Saving
- Floating Trial Balloons and Bracketing
- Off-the-Record Discussions
- Preconditions or Conditional Proposals
- Problem-Solving
- Questioning by Socratic Method
- Questions to Facilitate Agreements
- Salami
- Splitting the Difference

- Surprise

- Timing
- Word-Smithing

In addition to the foregoing negotiating tactics and techniques that mediators sometimes employ, there are a number of other tactics and techniques that mediators commonly use which are important to understand when you prepare for mediation and negotiate during mediation. These mediator tactics and techniques are summarized below under the five overlapping functions or stages that mediators engage in during mediation: (1) Obtaining Information; (2) Generating and Discussing Potential Solutions; (3) Assessing, Selecting, and Communicating Specific Proposals; (4) Creating Movement in the Negotiations; and (5) Forging and Finalizing the Terms of an Agreement.

## [2]     Tactics and Techniques for Obtaining Information

Mediators consider it essential to obtain complete information from both parties about the facts; the law; the issues; the parties' underlying feelings, interests or needs (*e.g.*, emotional, psychological, economic, physical, and social); the parties' primary, secondary, and incidental objectives; potential solutions or proposals; and the reasons supporting particular proposals, offers and counteroffers. This information serves as the raw material from which the mediator can understand the issues in the case, and then proceed to explore potential solutions, discuss specific proposals, create movement in the negotiations, and hopefully forge and finalize an agreement.

Sometimes these types of information are discussed openly in a joint session, but more often than not, the mediator will seek to obtain this information during private caucusing. In doing so, the mediator might:

- Ask direct questions about the facts, law, issues, and the parties' interests, objectives, and possible solutions (*see also* §10.37);
- Ask "why" the parties have the particular interests and objectives that they do;
- Ask the parties to rank, from most important to least important, their interests, objectives, the issues in the case, and general elements of a potential agreement;
- Explore the extent to which the interests and objectives of the parties are mutually exclusive, competing, compatible, or identical;
- Allow the parties to vent their emotions;
- Ask for counsels' analysis of the merits of the case and what might resolve it.

In this information-gathering stage, the mediator is primarily concerned with building rapport with the parties, understanding all factors underlying the dispute, and identifying the key issues in the case. If the parties are unable to agree on an appropriate agenda for dealing with the issues, the mediator might call upon the parties to (a) alternate in choosing the issues to be discussed, (b) pick one or two issues that both parties consider of greatest importance and place them at the top of the agenda, (c) identify the "easier" issues and place them at the top of the agenda, (d) negotiate first those issues that are a necessary or logical predicate to resolving other issues, or (e) negotiate a number of issues simultaneously through packaged proposals containing multiple-issue solutions.

## [3]     Tactics and Techniques for Generating and Discussing Potential Solutions

Mediators often encourage the parties to problem-solve by generating as many potential solutions to the dispute as possible before making a specific proposal or offer. (*See also* § 14.14[2]). The overall objective is to encourage the parties to consider solutions that may satisfy their mutual interests or needs, and to discourage the parties from engaging solely in positional bargaining. Consistent with this objective, mediators frequently request that the parties not reveal their bottom lines (*i.e.*, resistance points) to the mediator until late in the mediation process. This is to prevent the parties from becoming psychologically committed to bottom-line outcomes that may result in deadlock when their settlement ranges do not overlap, and to prevent them from being reluctant to modify their bottom lines in light of the information they learn during the mediation process that may change their assessment of the case.

In helping the parties generate and discuss a broad range of potential solutions, the mediator might:

- Encourage the parties to explore non-monetary as well as monetary solutions to the case;
- Engage in "brainstorming for solutions" (*see* §14.14[2]) either in a joint session or during the private caucuses;
- Ask each party to consider the opposing party's interests and views about the dispute;
- Pose hypothetical solutions to the parties to test their reaction to alternative ways of resolving the dispute;
- Ask the parties what elements of an agreement they might be willing to trade in exchange for obtaining certain other commitments in an agreement;
- Ask the parties (if they have an ongoing or past relationship) to identify those aspects of their relationship that have worked well, and whether any of those aspects might be incorporated into an agreement;
- Encourage the parties to consider objective standards such as custom, industry standards, ethical norms, or expertise in generating possible solutions;
- Suggest that the parties consider incorporating into an agreement the elements of any "model agreements" that other persons have used to resolve similar disputes.

## [4]   Tactics and Techniques for Assessing, Selecting, and Communicating Specific Proposals

After the parties have generated and discussed potential solutions, they will begin the bargaining phase of the mediation by making specific proposals, offers, and counteroffers, which the mediator will communicate to the parties usually by shuttling back and forth between them in private caucuses. Sometimes this will occur in a joint session when, for example, a party's proposal contains multi-faceted elements that require detailed explanation or discussion.

In assisting the parties to assess and select specific proposals, the mediator might:

- Help the parties value the case through any of the valuation methods discussed in Chapter 11;
- Ask the parties to articulate specific reasons for their particular proposals or offers;
- Encourage the parties to make reasonable first offers and counteroffers;
- Suggest that the parties work from a *Draft Document or Single Negotiating Text* (*see* § 10.14);
- Suggest that the parties consider incorporating into a proposal, as might be appropriate:
    - a payment in kind (*e.g.*, a transfer of goods or property, or a performance of services) instead of in money;

—  a structured settlement (*see* § 17.09) or payment in installments;

—  payment of a portion of the settlement to a mutually acceptable charity or other public-interest organization;

—  a future business arrangement or relationship (*e.g.*, in a contract dispute);

—  a change in an employee's title or work status in lieu of, or in exchange for, a smaller pay increase (*e.g.*, in an employment dispute);

—  an undertaking to provide a warning label on a product in a products liability case, or a promise to take certain corrective action to prevent the recurrence of the type of accident that occurred in the instant case;

—  a substitution of goods (*e.g.*, in a dispute involving a purchase or lease of goods);

—  an apology for what happened;

—  a confidentiality clause in the agreement;

—  a provision to abide by the recommendation of a suitable third party who has special expertise in the matter in dispute (*e.g.*, the recommendation of a child psychologist in a child custody or visitation dispute).

In communicating specific proposals being made by one party to the other, the mediator might:

- Present the proposal as if it were the mediator's own idea so as to keep the party to whom the proposal is made from rejecting it out of hand due to "reactive devaluation" (*see* § 7.06[4]);

- Make a proposal conditional without communicating a commitment on the part of the offering party (*e.g.*, "If I can get the other side to do X, will you do Y?");

- Time the communication of a particular proposal to coincide with that point in the process when presentation of the proposal will have the greatest impact;

- Explain the parties' reasons for their particular offers, or their reasons for rejecting or modifying particular proposals.

## [5]  Tactics and Techniques for Creating Movement in the Negotiations

Creating movement in the negotiations in the sense of encouraging the parties to make reasonable concessions toward an agreement is, of course, the mediator's most difficult task. To this end, as discussed in § 16.04, a mediator might employ a "trashing," "bashing," or "hashing it out" strategy, or a combination of these strategies. As specific tactics and techniques for bringing the parties closer together and reducing their commitment to unreasonable or unrealistic positions, the mediator might:

- Directly or indirectly indicate the mediator's views about the merit or lack of merit of a particular proposal or position;

- Engage in *Questioning by Socratic Method* (*see* § 10.38) by asking a series of logical questions that are designed to expose the weaknesses in a party's proposals or positions;

- Suggest that counsel for the parties phone another lawyer or a law professor they respect to render an opinion about the relative merits of a novel or controversial legal theory advanced in the case;
- Ask what evidence would be introduced at trial in support of a particular factual or legal theory in the case;
- Inquire about the extent of the parties' "aversion to risk" and willingness to actually take the case to trial (*see* § 7.06[1]);
- Point out the economic and emotional costs of taking the case to trial or of pursuing the parties' other BATNAs;
- Point out the irrationality of failing to reach an agreement due to a preoccupation with "sunk costs" — *i.e.*, past expenditures of money or emotional capital which are lost no matter what the parties do but which they vainly seek to justify or recoup in making a choice about settlement or trial (*see* § 7.06[3]);
- Point out that a party's interests or positions may not be as important as originally believed, or that the other party's interests or positions may be more important than originally believed;
- Engage in an off-the-record, private discussion solely with the parties' lawyers to discuss the barriers that are preventing settlement (*see also* § 16.12[10]);
- Suggest that the mediation be temporarily adjourned so that the parties might reconsider their positions or try to come up with new proposals;
- Ask a variety of questions designed to moderate the parties' positions, such as:

  — If you were in the other party's situation, would you accept the proposals that you are making now, or would you expect that more should be offered in exchange for an agreement?
  — Is your offer fair? Will those whom you respect, the community or the public, perceive it as such?
  — Is your offer in line with community, legal, or other norms?
  — Is the demand that you are making in line with other negotiated settlements or court decisions on similar issues under similar conditions?
  — Do you have the power to force the issue?
  — What are the benefits to you of pursuing your present course? Are there any risks?
  — How certain are you that you can win in court? Ninety percent? Seventy-five percent? Fifty percent?
  — What if you lose in court? What will your life be like then?
  — What impact do you think your victory in court will have on your on-going relationship with the other party? Will you ever be able to work together again? Who else might be affected?[11]

---

[11] Christopher W. Moore, *The Mediation Process — Practical Strategies for Resolving Conflict*, 276, 331 (2d ed. 1996).

## [6]    Tactics and Techniques for Forging and Finalizing the Terms of an Agreement

When the parties are on the verge of reaching an agreement, mediators often become somewhat more aggressive in helping to forge the terms of a final settlement. For example, the mediator might press harder in applying the tactics and techniques set forth in subsection [5] above. In addition, the mediator might:

- *Abdicate* by pressing one or more of the parties to come up with a final concession (*see also* § 10.02);
- Provide one or more of the parties with a rationale for changing position that allows the party to save face in making a final concession;
- Ask one or more of the parties to make a specific concession proposed by the mediator who serves as the scapegoat for the concession, such that the party making it can say that he did so solely at the request of the mediator and not because the party initiated the concession or was forced into it by the other side;
- Suggest that the parties split the difference.

As mentioned previously, if the parties reach an agreement, the mediator will usually reconvene in a joint session to summarize the terms of the agreement and seek clarification about any "loose ends" and appropriate arrangements for preparing and executing final settlement documents. In many court-annexed mediation programs, the mediator is required to have the parties sign a memorandum of understanding about the terms of the settlement before leaving the mediation session.

## § 16.08   PREPARING FOR MEDIATION

Preparing for mediation is much like preparing for negotiation. You need to (1) prepare a Mediation Preparation Outline from which an overall negotiating approach can be developed and employed during the mediation; (2) decide whether to hold a pre-mediation conference with the mediator or opposing counsel; (3) decide who should attend the mediation for your side and what roles those participants will play; and (4) prepare the client for the mediation session.

### [1]    Preparing a Mediation Preparation Outline

In preparing a Mediation Preparation Outline, you should follow the same twelve steps and format used for preparing a Negotiation Preparation Outline as set forth in §§ 12.03 and 12.04. These steps, with a few additional considerations pertinent to the mediation process, are as follows:

**Step 1:** *From the Perspective of Each Party, Make a List of Information to Obtain, Information to Reveal, and Information to Protect.* Any special information you decide "to reveal" to the other side would presumably be information you would want to reveal to the mediator as well. Under "information to protect," list any information that you do not want to disclose to the mediator, even in confidence, and any information that can be disclosed to the mediator but not to the other side.

**Step 2:** *Make a List of Each Party's interests.*

**Step 3:** *Make a List of Each Party's Primary Objectives, Secondary Objectives, and Incidental Objectives (to Exchange).*

**Step 4:** *Make a List of Possible Solutions for Each Party (from most preferred to least preferred).*

**Step 5:** *Make a List of Each Party's Best Alternatives to a Negotiated Agreement (BATNA).*

**Step 6:** *Make a List of Each Party's Factual and Legal Leverage Points (Strong and Weak).*

**Step 7:** *Identify Each Party's Potential Target and Resistance Points.*

**Step 8:** *Identify Each Party's Negotiating Strategy: Adversarial or Problem Solving.*

**Step 9:** *Identify Each Party's Negotiating Style: Competitive (Hardball), Cooperative (Softball), or Competitive-Cooperative (Hardball and Softball).* Also identify the mediator's most likely style and strategy during the mediation — *e.g.*, passive or aggressive, and "trasher," "basher," or "hasher" (*see* § 16.04).

**Step 10:** *Make a List of Each Party's Offers or Proposals in the Order They May Be Presented.*

**Step 11:** *Consider Each Party's Particular Tactics.* Also consider any special tactics and techniques that might be effectively used by the mediator during the mediation (*see* § 16.07).

**Step 12** *Revise All of the Foregoing Matters Throughout the Mediation Process.*

Because mediation often occurs after the parties have already engaged in negotiations and filed a lawsuit, it is particularly important to review the case file when preparing your Mediation Preparation Outline. This means reviewing all pleadings, formal admissions, responses to interrogatories and requests for production of documents, transcripts of depositions, correspondence setting forth the history of prior settlement discussions and any instructions from your client about your settlement authority, and any other important documents in the case (*e.g.*, medical reports, medical bills, statements showing lost earnings, reports of expert witnesses or investigators, documents that might be introduced at trial, etc.). If your review of the case file shows that certain documentation is incomplete or that you need additional information to support your client's case, this information should be obtained in advance of the mediation.

## [2]    Holding a Pre-mediation Conference With the Mediator or Between Counsel

It is sometimes desirable to hold a pre-mediation conference, by telephone or in a meeting, with the mediator or opposing counsel. Such a conference may be useful:

- To work out the agenda, format, or logistics of the mediation;
- To brief the mediator about the issues in the case, prior settlement discussions, the status of the litigation, and the basic positions of the parties;

- To determine whether there is any essential information that the parties need to obtain or submit to the mediator in advance of the mediation;
- To forewarn the mediator about any delicate aspects of the controversy that may impede a resolution of the case;
- To provide the mediator with insights about any special ways in which the mediation session might be structured or conducted to best facilitate a resolution of the dispute;
- To discuss the need for having any third persons attend the mediation or be on telephone standby for consultation on questions of settlement authority or to provide certain expertise during the mediation;
- To apprise the mediator of any technical, legal, or sensitive information so as to save time or awkwardness in discussing these matters at the mediation session;
- To suggest that the mediator meet in advance with one or more persons who have information relevant to the dispute but who will not be able to attend the mediation;
- To suggest that, where numerous parties are involved or the parties are particularly emotional about the dispute, the mediator meet privately with each party in advance of the mediation to understand the issues and, as appropriate, calm the parties; or
- To discuss any other matters that may enhance the overall efficiency of the mediation session and the prospects for resolving the case.

The foregoing types of matters are typically discussed between counsel before deciding whether it would be useful or necessary to raise any of them with the mediator in advance of the mediation. Moreover, counsel's pre-mediation discussions about these matters help them to prepare for the mediation and to ensure that both sides have all necessary information to meaningfully evaluate the case. In most situations, you will find that an informal pre-mediation discussion with opposing counsel will be sufficient to pave the way for an effective mediation session, and that it is unnecessary to hold a formal pre-mediation conference with the mediator. As a matter of practice, a lawyer for a party generally should not have any *ex parte* pre-mediation meetings or conversations with the mediator about substantive issues or positions in the case without opposing counsel's knowledge.

## [3]  Who Should Attend the Mediation

As mentioned previously, many court-annexed mediation programs require the following persons to attend the mediation: the individual parties (or a designated representative of a party if it is a corporate or governmental entity), an insurance company representative if there is insurance coverage in the case, the parties' lawyers, and the mediator (or co-mediators). The goal is to ensure that all persons who are necessary to reaching a workable and binding settlement be present.

However, even in jurisdictions that prescribe the persons who must attend the mediation, the parties are usually permitted, by mutual agreement and the consent of the mediator, to excuse the attendance of a person who otherwise is required to attend. For example, in automobile personal injury cases where liability is not in issue, the parties will often agree that the defendant who caused the accident need not be present, given that the defendant's insurance carrier paying the claim will be represented at the mediation by a claims adjuster and by defense counsel hired by the carrier.

When your client's attendance at the mediation is not mandatory, it is unwise for him not to attend unless there are compelling reasons for his nonattendance. In most cases, active client participation in the mediation (particularly during the private caucuses) is instrumental to reaching a settlement. Given that for many clients the very *process* of resolving a dispute is important, there can be no exposure to that "process" if your client does not attend the mediation. Moreover, your client's attendance at the mediation helps give effect to the ethical prescription that he alone must make the final decision about whether to settle the case. Finally, his attendance makes it easier for you to fulfill your ethical responsibility of ensuring that he is reasonably informed about all essential matters relevant to making that decision (*see* § 9.02).

In addition to these reasons for having your client attend the mediation, his attendance may be particularly useful as an opportunity to display his credibility and likeability to the opposing side. This is important because many mediations occur before the lawyers have deposed any of the parties. Even if your client does not have a personality that readily radiates these qualities, his mere presence at the mediation will tend to humanize the case. In short, a client's demonstration of "jury appeal" can go a long way towards achieving a favorable settlement when the only alternative to settlement is taking the case to trial.

On the other hand, if your client does not want to attend the mediation and seems incapable of controlling negative behaviors that would impede the mediation process, you should seriously consider obtaining his consent not to attend the mediation. That is, if he is simply unable to control his distinct lack of jury appeal (even in a relatively short joint session before private caucusing), you might discuss with him the option of not attending the mediation and making himself available for private consultation with you by telephone during the mediation. Of course, discussing this option with your client is a difficult matter if he nevertheless wants to be present at the mediation. In that event, the best approach is to be straightforward but tactful about the matter, pointing out that some clients — through no fault of their own — are so emotionally affected by a dispute that their overall interests might be better served if they are not physically present at the mediation. This same explanation would be given to the other side and the mediator to obtain their consent to your client's nonattendance. However, if your client still insists on attending the mediation, you must honor that choice.

Sometimes a client will want a family member or close friend to be physically present during the mediation session as a support person. This may be permitted with the consent of the opposing party and the mediator, but rarely occurs in practice. More often, the support person will be permitted to come to the office where the mediation is being held to confer privately with the client when breaks are taken or when the mediator is holding private caucuses with the other side.

Parties sometimes also find it useful to have certain experts attend the mediation or, more commonly, be on telephone standby for consultation during the mediation. Examples of such experts include structured settlement experts, accountants or tax lawyers, medical experts, psychologists (*e.g.*, in a child custody or visitation dispute), or economists (*e.g.*, to explain lost future earnings). If one side has an expert attending the mediation, mediators usually prefer that the other side also have an expert present or available for consultation by telephone. That is, mediators are particularly sensitive to maintaining a "level playing field" for both parties.

Finally, some jurisdictions provide that third parties who have a lien or other claim on the proceeds of a settlement (*see* § 17.10) have the right to attend the mediation or be on telephone standby for consultation. As a practical matter, lienholders or similar claimants rarely send a representative to attend the mediation; and mediators otherwise usually prefer that such third parties not attend, given that the assertion of their economic interests during the mediation may greatly complicate the process and undermine the prospects for a settlement. On the other hand, the participation of a lienholder at the mediation may be important where, for example, the defendant is unwilling to pay the plaintiff more than the amount of the lien and the lienholder, hearing this, thus decides to reduce its lien to ensure at least some recovery for itself and for the plaintiff.

## [4]    Preparing the Client for Mediation

In preparing your client for mediation (or any other person who will attend the mediation for your side), you should explain the overall mediation process (*see* §16.02); whether the mediation will be "facilitative" or "evaluative" (*see* § 16.03); and the general style and strategy of the particular mediator (*see* § 16.04), including her background and qualifications. In particular, emphasize that:

- The process is not a trial and will be conducted in an informal atmosphere that is designed to make all parties feel comfortable;
- The offers and counteroffers or proposals discussed at the mediation are not admissible as evidence at a trial;
- The mediator (even in "evaluative" mediation) does not serve as a judge or jury to decide the case, but is trained to assist both sides to consider each other's perspectives about the controversy to make an informed and voluntary decision about whether to settle the case, and if so, how to settle it;
- The ultimate decision whether to settle the case is your client's, but that you will be providing advice to your client throughout the mediation to help him make that decision;
- In the private caucuses with each side, the mediator is likely to "play the devil's advocate" — not to criticize your client's interests or positions, but to encourage a realistic assessment of the case and discussion of all possible solutions;
- Particularly in the private caucuses, the mediation process is designed to encourage free-flowing discussion and open information sharing;
- Many mediations last for the better part of the day (or even longer), and experience has shown that patience and open-mindedness in the process often leads to a satisfactory settlement of the case; and
- During the mediation session there will be ample opportunity for you and your client to confer privately.

Irrational or inflated client expectations about the value or outcome of the case are common problems that lawyers face when representing a client in mediation. If you have these problems with your client, stress the knowledge and experience of the mediator, and that the mediation process provides a unique opportunity to listen to the mediator and draw upon her special skills and experience as you and your client assess the case and the prospects for a reasonable settlement. In short, point out that consistent with the ultimate task of deciding whether it is in your client's best interests to settle the case or take it to trial, the input of an impartial and neutral mediator is worth careful consideration when one is trying to make a decision that will not later be regretted.

After explaining the overall mediation process and the role of the mediator, you should review and discuss your Mediation Preparation Outline with your client. As appropriate, make any changes or additions to it. Be sure to emphasize to your client that the Outline is only a general "game plan" for the mediation, and not an inflexible blueprint of unalterable interests, objectives, positions, and bottom lines. Explain that it is typical to discover new information or perspectives about the case during the mediation process that may cause both parties to significantly depart from their pre-planned approach to the mediation and reconsider their earlier assessment about what would be a reasonable settlement of the dispute. In sum, emphasize that the *sine qua non* of effective advocacy in the mediation setting is to resist becoming entrapped by entrenched positions, and to keep an open mind and willingness to be flexible in considering different solutions to the case and engaging in appropriate compromise.

Next, discuss with your client the specific roles he will play during the mediation. In the joint session, this role may range from saying nothing to making pre-planned remarks as part of the opening statement or answering questions of the other side. For example, if your client is articulate, credible, likeable, and persuasive, you might have him participate in the opening statement by explaining certain facts or events in connection with the case, explaining how he has been affected by those events, or sharing his general perspectives or feelings about the dispute. Conversely, if your client's personality or emotional involvement in the case would make it inappropriate or uncomfortable for him to participate in the presentation of the opening statement or respond to questions of the other side, he should be advised to let you do all of the talking in the joint session.

Similar considerations apply in determining the extent to which your client should speak during the private caucuses. In this setting, however, your client's active participation is much "safer" in that what he says, and how he says it, is known only to the mediator and can be shielded from the other side. Therefore, it is generally a good idea to encourage your client to speak freely during the private caucuses, particularly in responding to questions asked directly to him by the mediator. This will enhance the mediator's understanding of your client's feelings and views about the case, and any "venting" or other emotional displays by your client are more likely to be viewed by the mediator as being the product of a candid attempt to respond to her questions, rather than as manifestations of an irrational or unstable personality. In any event, you can always take a recess from a private caucus if you think that your client is engaging in counterproductive or other inappropriate behavior.

Notwithstanding the usual desirability of encouraging your client to speak freely during the private caucuses, you should specifically advise your client:

- Not to reveal any information that both of you have agreed to keep confidential from the mediator;
- Not to reveal any attorney-client privileged information, such as your negotiating strategy;

- Not to get into an argument with the mediator or anyone else at the mediation session;
- Not to engage in exaggeration, hyperbole, speculation, or misrepresentation;
- Not to interrupt when another person is speaking; and
- Not to display any verbal or non-verbal reactions to any settlement proposals or offers in a way that may reveal or otherwise undermine your negotiating strategy.

These cautionary instructions also apply, of course, to any joint session during the mediation.

As for your role during the mediation, explain that your overall responsibility is to "take the lead" for your client's side. Make clear that your role as an advocate during mediation is quite different from your advocacy role at a trial or in an arbitration. That is, during mediation, you will not be engaging in the formal presentation of evidence, cross-examining any witnesses, or delivering a closing argument. Rather you will be engaging in a respectful dialogue with the other side and the mediator, where you will be doing at least as much listening as talking. Moreover, explain that consistent with your goal to advance the best interests of your client and negotiate a favorable settlement on his behalf, you will be utilizing the mediation process as part of an on-going assessment of your client's case to give him your best judgment and advice from which he can make an informed decision about settlement.

## § 16.09   EFFECTIVE ADVOCACY DURING MEDIATION, IN GENERAL[12]

To be an effective advocate during the mediation process, it is important to understand (1) how to prepare a pre-mediation submission to the mediator; (2) how to present your opening statement; and (3) what to do during the private caucuses. In addition to these matters, it is essential to bear in mind that to be an effective advocate during mediation you must use the mediation process to *actively negotiate* with the other side, and not rely upon the mediator to do this work for you. As mentioned previously, while a good mediator is one who is also a good negotiator, her role is not to resolve the parties' dispute. Rather, her negotiating skills are used to facilitate *your* negotiations with the other side and vice versa. Therefore, it is essential that you draw upon and apply all of the concepts, skills, and techniques of effective negotiating discussed in the preceding chapters of this book when representing your client during mediation.

## § 16.10   PREPARING A PRE-MEDIATION SUBMISSION

The primary purposes of a pre-mediation submission are to educate the mediator about the general nature of the dispute, to identify the issues to be addressed, and to set out the basic contentions of the parties. It is essentially an introductory purview of the case that gives the mediator a general idea of what the dispute is about before the mediation takes place. The submission is often useful in helping

---

[12] *See also,* John W. Cooley, *Mediation Advocacy* (1996).

the mediator to move more quickly in assisting the parties to reach a resolution during the mediation.

Some mediators invite or even require that the parties submit a pre-mediation submission. Other mediators expressly prohibit or prefer not to receive any pre-mediation materials out of a fear that such submissions might taint their impartiality in the case. Still others have no standard practice about the matter and will review any pre-mediation materials sent to them. Therefore, as a threshold matter, it is important to find out your mediator's preferences about pre-mediation submissions and whether the applicable jurisdiction has any special rules governing them.

If you are not prohibited from making a pre-mediation submission, it is often a good idea to send one to the mediator (with a copy to opposing counsel), bearing in mind the limited purposes of a submission mentioned above. Consistent with those purposes, in the vast majority of cases, the submission should be very brief — *i.e.*, no more than a two or three page synopsis of the case. In a letter, succinctly set out in a non-argumentative style:

(1)   The basic facts of the case or events giving rise to the dispute, including the amount of any special damages;

(2)   If a lawsuit has been filed, the basic legal claims and defenses involved;

(3)   If no lawsuit has been filed, the basic contentions of your client;

(4)   The nature of the issues to be addressed if they are not otherwise apparent from the foregoing;

(5)   The status of any prior negotiations and the latest settlement offers of the parties if mentioning those offers would be instructive to the mediator in understanding the dispute;

(6)   A reference to any documents attached to the letter (*e.g.*, a copy of the contract involved, accident report, governing statute if the law is not generally known, or copy of the pleadings if reading them is essential to understanding the case, etc.); and

(7)   A concluding sentence that confirms the time and place of the upcoming mediation, along with an expression of your hope that the mediation might be successful in resolving the case.

It cannot be overemphasized that, in the routine case, brevity is the hallmark of an appropriate submission. Mediators do not want to read (and rarely will read) prolix or voluminous pre-mediation materials. Accordingly, do not send the mediator packages or boxes of medical records, medical bills, or documentary trial exhibits, etc. If, before the mediation, it is absolutely necessary for the mediator to understand certain matters contained in voluminous records, summarize that information in a short attachment to your letter submission. Remember that at the mediation you will have your complete file in the case, from which you can show the mediator any pertinent document or set of documents that may become the focal point of discussion.

In extremely complex cases or multi-party cases, however, your pre-mediation submission may have to be more detailed. In these situations, your pre-mediation submission might include, for example, an indexed notebook containing important documentary evidence, portions of discovery, court orders, legal memoranda, or even copies of appellate decisions. If the case being mediated is on appeal, it may be necessary for the mediator to read such matters as the final judgment and any

Memorandum Opinion, the jury instructions, any special verdicts, rulings on any post-trial motion, portions of the trial transcript, and the appellate briefs and record on appeal if they have been filed.

Unless otherwise agreed between the parties, you should send a copy of your pre-mediation submission to opposing counsel. Because this means that the opposing counsel's client will read your submission, it is important to be as objective as possible in your summary of the facts and contentions, and to draft your submission in a way that does not unnecessarily escalate the dispute or otherwise impair the prospects for constructive negotiations during the mediation. Even if it is agreed that your submission will be sent to the mediator *ex parte*, your submission should not be written in an excessively argumentative or acerbic tone that will undermine your credibility with the mediator.

Finally, when reviewing the case file and preparing your pre-mediation submission, if you discover any new documents or additional information that are pertinent to the dispute and have not yet been furnished to the other side (*e.g.*, updated medical records, year's-end financial statements, etc.), send a copy of this information to opposing counsel as appropriate. In addition, before sending a copy of your pre-mediation submission to opposing counsel, it is often desirable to phone him to find out whether there is any further information he needs from you to evaluate settlement prospects in the case. In the same conversation, you can ask for any additional information you still need from him that is necessary for your complete evaluation of the case. Like a pre-mediation conference (*see* § 16.08[2]), this pre-mediation contact between counsel can help ensure that the parties have exchanged as much pertinent information as possible before the mediation takes place.

## § 16.11  MAKING THE OPENING STATEMENT

Mediation is, of course, not a trial. In mediation, there is no judge or jury, no burden of proof, no restrictions on the admissibility of evidence, and no verdict. At trial, the opening statement is a forecast of what will be proven, and the closing argument is a summary of what has been proven. Both speeches are designed to convince the fact finder that one side must win and the other must lose. In mediation, however, there is no fact finder to decide the case. Thus, in mediation there is no such thing as a case that may be won or lost.

Although these distinctions are obvious, they are critical to bear in mind because many lawyers who are inexperienced in mediation unwittingly equate mediation with a trial. For instance, many lawyers will deliver an opening statement at mediation that sounds much like a trial opening statement and closing argument wrapped into one: the facts are meticulously set out; the key points of law are explained; the facts are applied to the law; the other side's proof is attacked; and the presentation is concluded with a pronouncement to the effect that there can be no other logical conclusion but that the lawyer's client is the winner, and the other party is the loser. The advocate then turns and looks at the mediator, as if looking at a jury to say, "Please render a verdict in our favor."

The inappropriateness of this approach is that it is designed to ask the mediator to do the very thing she cannot do — decide the case and declare a winner and a loser. Such an opening statement is entirely at odds with the mediator's role as an impartial facilitator of an agreement, as against a fact finder who renders a verdict.

Unlike a trial, where the objective is an all-or-nothing decision on the merits, in mediation the only all-or-nothing matter is whether there will be an agreement or no agreement. If no agreement is reached, neither side leaves the mediation with a verdict that pronounces victory or defeat.

Therefore, lawyers who are experienced in mediation know that the primary objectives of an effective opening statement are not to convince the mediator about which side should win or lose, but rather are: (1) to convince the opposing party to enter into a satisfactory agreement, and (2) to motivate the opposing party to do so. These are the only tangible things that can be obtained through mediation.

This means that an opening statement in mediation should not be delivered as if to "prove a case," where the facts, the law, and imaginative themes are woven together in a presentation that supports a forecast of what will be proven and attacks the other side's forecast of proof. Rather, the opening statement should present the facts, law, and themes of the controversy in a way that points to a possible resolution of the dispute and encourages the other party to seek the same. This means that the content and tone of an effective opening statement must (a) treat the other party with respect; (b) avoid personal attacks; (c) convey a willingness to fairly consider the other side's points of view so that it will fairly consider yours; (d) avoid threats or ultimatums; and (e) allow the other party to consider the case from the perspective of your client's real needs and interests — *i.e.*, "why" he has taken a particular position, and "why" a particular resolution is important to him.

These elements of an effective opening statement should be incorporated throughout a presentation that otherwise appropriately addresses the facts of the case, pertinent legal considerations, the facts and legal aspects of the case that are strongest for your side, potential ways for settling the case, potential outcomes if the case went to trial, and the risks and costs of not reaching an agreement. However, in addressing these matters, the target audience is the *opposing side* because only it, not the mediator, can agree to settle the case. In short, if the opening statement is presented in a way that is aimed at disparaging the opposing side (as is implicitly intended in an opening statement at trial), you may end up "losing" in the mediation process by making it impossible to obtain the only thing mediation can give you — a final settlement offer from the other party that is better than anything you could obtain at trial or through some other means.

Assuming that counsel for the parties have adequately prepared for the mediation and have a fairly good understanding of the case, each opening statement will usually last between fifteen and thirty minutes. However, for cases that are unusually complex, an opening statement may take an hour or more. In a routine case, such as a non-catastrophic personal injury case, the opening statement for plaintiff's counsel will usually consist of the following:

(1) A brief summary of how the accident occurred;
(2) An explanation of the plaintiff's theory of liability (if liability is in issue);
(3) A brief summary of the plaintiff's course of medical treatment;
(4) A summary of the diagnosis and prognosis for the plaintiff's injuries, including the extent of any permanent injury;
(5) A summary of how the plaintiff's injuries have affected his life;
(6) An itemization of the plaintiff's special damages (*e.g.*, medical expenses, lost wages, etc.); and

(7)     An expression of willingness to fairly consider all aspects of the case from the perspectives of both sides to the end that the case might be settled through the mediation process.

If counsel and the plaintiff have decided that the plaintiff will participate in the opening statement, counsel might call upon his client (either in the middle of counsel's opening statement or after it is over) to explain, for example, how the accident occurred or how the plaintiff's injuries have affected his life.

Defense counsel's opening statement will then usually consist of the following:

(1)     An explanation of any additional facts about how the accident occurred;

(2)     An explanation of the defendant's theory of liability (if liability is in issue);

(3)     A summary of any time gaps in the course of the plaintiff's medical treatment, or any medical treatment that appears to have been unnecessary under the circumstances of the case;

(4)     Any references in the medical reports to a pre-existing medical condition, or any ambiguities in the reports about diagnoses, the plaintiff's prognosis, or extent of permanent injury;

(5)     An itemization of any special damages that seem unwarranted in the case;

(6)     An expression of apology to the plaintiff or similar expression of regret about how the accident has affected the plaintiff; and

(7)     An expression, like that of plaintiff's counsel, of a willingness to fairly consider all circumstances of the case with the hope that it might be resolved by agreement.

When delivering the opening statement, most advocates use a low-key, non-argumentative style. In addition, most advocates will primarily make eye contact with the mediator, even though they are consciously addressing their remarks to the opposing side. There are two reasons for this. First, part of the function of an opening statement is to educate the mediator about the case. Second, and most importantly, advocates often correctly intuit that if the opening statement is delivered by making too much direct eye contact with opposing counsel's client, the opening statement may come across as a lecture to the opposing party who may then "reactively devalue" (see § 7.06[4]) what is being said. In short, many clients do not like lawyers, particularly the opposing party's lawyer. Thus, from a body-language standpoint, the opening statement is directed at the mediator precisely so that the opposing party might be more receptive to what is being said.

The particular type of case involved, the gravity or delicacy of the dispute, and the dynamics of the parties must all, of course, be taken into account in deciding what would be most appropriate to say in the opening statement and how to present it. For example, in an appropriate case, consider the following:

•     Using audiovisual aids such as models, charts, diagrams, photos, a video, a chalkboard, a power point slide presentation, a tape recording, a computerized simulation, etc.;

•     Showing potential trial exhibits, such as a day-in-the-life video of the injured plaintiff or the metal rod that the surgeons removed from his leg;

•     Providing all participants with a notebook containing pertinent documents to refer to during the opening statement;

•     Suggesting an appropriate agenda, or outlining the parameters of a potential settlement or other proposal that may resolve the dispute;

- Acknowledging at the outset certain strengths in the case for the opposing party, but pointing out that there are two sides to the story and that the risks and costs of litigation for both sides warrant a reasoned effort to try to resolve the case by agreement;
- Making an initial offer or concrete proposal and explaining the reasons behind the offer or proposal;
- Declining to make an initial offer or proposal at the outset until after there has been an opportunity for private caucusing;
- Suggesting that at the conclusion of the opening statements, both sides engage in a free-flowing, uninhibited discussion about the dispute and possible ways to resolve it;
- Extending a sincere (not canned) apology for the events giving rise to the dispute;
- Establishing a deadline for completing the mediation session by mentioning that counsel will have to leave the mediation by a certain time to meet a another commitment.

## § 16.12   USING THE PRIVATE CAUCUSES

In the vast majority of cases (except in family-law disputes), the private caucuses are the most important part of the mediation process. As discussed previously (*see* § 16.07), it is here that the mediator works her craft in obtaining information; generating and discussing potential solutions; assessing, selecting, and communicating specific proposals; trying to create movement in the negotiations; and helping to forge and finalize the terms of an agreement. Effective advocacy during the private caucuses requires (1) that you actively participate in all of these functions of private caucusing as you negotiate with the opposing party, and (2) that you try to *assist* the mediator, rather than try to manipulate her, when negotiating through the private caucuses.

Trying to manipulate the mediator through misrepresentation or the use of disingenuous tactics such as *bluffing, escalating demands, false demands, false emphasis, false scarcity, reversing position*, or the like (*see* Chapter 10) is a bad idea for three reasons. First, attempts at such manipulation are likely to be unavailing because most mediators are trained to recognize them, and experienced mediators can otherwise spot them immediately.

Second, although the mediator cannot decide the case in your favor or compel the other party to settle the case on your terms, you do want the mediator "on your side" in the sense of having respect for you as a credible advocate who has a realistic assessment of the case and is making reasonable offers or proposals toward a potential settlement. As mentioned in § 16.03, even mediators who hold a most stringent "facilitative" philosophy about mediation, engage in a constant process of evaluating the extent to which a party's interests, objectives, analysis of the case, and proposals are realistic. Thus, your credibility for realism and reasonableness will invariably have an effect on how fervently the mediator will "push" the other side to seriously consider your offers or proposals. Although even a "basher" cannot and will not "force" the other side to see matters your way, even a "hasher" may be induced to engage in some "bashing" with your opponent if she is convinced of the genuineness and rationality of your negotiating efforts.

Third, attempts at manipulating the mediator will only undermine her ability to create movement in the negotiations by impairing her ability to assist the other party to understand and be more willing to accommodate the interests and objectives of your client. The standard tactics and techniques used by mediators to facilitate productive negotiations can only be effectively employed with the other side if you assist the mediator in providing her with the benefit of all your information, reasoning, and analysis which serve as the raw material for utilizing those tactics and techniques. Needless to say, trying to manipulate the mediator is antithetical to assisting her in this effort.

For the foregoing reasons, it is also futile to call upon the mediator to threaten or otherwise play hardball with the other side. Mediators will simply not do that, and they are heavily schooled in cooperative and principled problem-solving negotiation. On the other hand, this does not mean that you should be weak or irresolute in your analysis of the case and representation of your client. Mediators appreciate firmness in well-considered and well-grounded positions and proposals. As in negotiation, in mediation you should always remember that a settlement should never be entered into simply for its own sake. Although an agreement is often the most desirable way of resolving a dispute, it is not the only legitimate way. If the offers you make during the mediation process do not give rise to an agreement that is acceptable to your client, you should not hesitate to take the case to trial or resort to your client's other best alternative to dealing with the dispute.

In using the private caucuses to negotiate with the other side and assist the mediator in those negotiations, consider the approaches and techniques provided below.

## [1]   Assist the Mediator in Obtaining Information

As mentioned in § 16.08[4], particularly if your client is articulate, credible, likeable, and persuasive, it is generally a good idea to allow him to freely respond to the mediator's questions and otherwise actively participate in the private caucuses. Even if your client is angry about the events giving rise to the dispute, the mediator will better understand your client's feelings and views about the case if you permit him to appropriately "vent" his feelings. Your client's "humanity" and likeability will often have a favorable psychological effect on the mediator; and if your client is otherwise credible and persuasive, these qualities are likely to be mentioned by the mediator when she privately caucuses with the other side.

If your client is reticent or uncomfortable in actively participating in the private caucuses, you should intercede in responding to the mediator's requests for information. Moreover, because private caucusing is essentially a discussion rather than a question-and-answer session, you should not hesitate to volunteer all pertinent information that may help the mediator understand the dispute. In this regard, remember that the mediator will often want to know "why" your client has taken a particular position or thinks that a particular objective is important. These "why" questions are usually designed to assess the possibility of non-monetary solutions to the dispute, and they may even be relevant in a case that appears to be solely about money given that a monetary settlement might still include some non-monetary commitments.

In addition, you should not hesitate to point out to the mediator important information that you need from the other side. Explain to the mediator why this information is essential, and encourage her to ask the other side about it. In most situations, the mediator will follow up on your suggestion and will ask for the information without specifically mentioning to the other side that the request came from you. In sum, use the private caucuses not only to give information but to obtain information as well.

## [2]    Discuss the Strengths and Weaknesses of the Case

Private caucusing is a safe opportunity to recognize reality. Each case has its strengths and weaknesses, and understanding both is critical to making a sound decision about settling the case or taking it to trial. Therefore, it is only sensible to acknowledge the weaknesses in your case as well as its strengths. It is useful to discuss weaknesses for three reasons.

First, the mediator is likely to play the devil's advocate at some point during the private caucuses, and acknowledging weaknesses enhances your credibility with the mediator. Second, the relevance of a weakness depends not only upon the extent to which it *in fact* hurts your case, but upon the extent to which the other side *perceives* that the matter hurts your case. A candid, private discussion about weaknesses may reveal that you either underestimated or overestimated the particular weakness and may require that you adjust your negotiating strategy accordingly. Third, even when there are significant weaknesses in your case, they might well be offset by equally significant strengths. Therefore, in the course of acknowledging certain weaknesses, you also have the opportunity to put a positive spin on them by pointing out to the mediator how they pale in contrast to the strengths of your case, and why the other side's perception of those weaknesses is overblown. These points, if well taken, are likely to be emphasized by the mediator to the other side.

When weaknesses in your case are not readily apparent to the other side, it is usually best not to volunteer weaknesses in your case at first instance. Wait until the subject is prompted by the mediator's questions to you or her comments about the other side's views of the case. In this way, you can hedge against unnecessarily revealing weaknesses that are unknown to the other side, and you can keep them in the back of your mind when you consider whether it is worthwhile to make a particular concession at a crucial point during the negotiations.

## [3]    Specify Confidential Information

When the mediator caucuses with the other side, you should assume that it is fair game for her to share with them anything you or your client have said to her during the private caucuses that you have not specified as strictly confidential. This does not mean that she will invariably share everything you have told her with the other side. Rather, mediators tend to be quite selective about what information they share between one side and the other, depending on the extent to which the mediator believes that sharing the particular information will advance the prospects of reaching an agreement.

However, because of the mediator's general license to share with one side what she has learned from the other, it is essential that you make very clear to her what information you want her to keep confidential from the other side. Accordingly, before the mediator leaves a caucusing session with you to caucus with the other side, remind her of what information you wish to keep in strict confidence.

## [4]      Listen to the Mediator's Cues and Clues

Mediators are wordsmiths. They try to *tell* you things, usually indirectly through their questions and sometimes even through their body language. That is, mediators often give you cues and clues about their views about the case and, most importantly, what might be acceptable to the other side in resolving it. These usually subtle (and sometimes not so subtle) hints are routinely given by mediators, and even by those who profess to engage in strictly "facilitative" mediation.

For example, consider a mediator who asks: (1) "Are you aware of any six-figure jury verdicts for this type of case?" (2) "Do you think the other side would perceive your offer as being fair?" Or (3) "What would you say if the other side offered to do X?" On the one hand, these questions might be asked strictly for the purpose of obtaining information, without intending to suggest anything about the mediator's views or what she knows from the other side. On the other hand, depending upon the context of the discussion in which the questions are asked, they may actually mean: (1) "The value you have placed on the case is way out of line"; (2) "Your offer is unreasonable and unrealistic"; and (3) "The other side has told me that they are willing to do X, but you must give them something in return."

Thus, it is essential to carefully consider the context in which the mediator asks her questions and otherwise makes comments during the private caucuses. Asking rhetorical questions is the primary device that mediators use to indicate their assessment of the case, the viability of your settlement proposals, and what is going on in the mind of the other side. Needless to say, an ability to accurately read between the lines of what the mediator is asking or saying may be of significant strategic assistance in negotiating with the other side.

## [5]      Invite the Mediator's Perspectives About the Case

Except in "evaluative" mediation, mediators will not *directly* express their views about the value of the case or how it should be resolved. This is true in "facilitative" mediation even if you specifically ask the mediator how she would value the case or settle it. However, as mentioned in subsection [4] above, most mediators will at least *indicate* their views about these matters through the context in which their questions are asked or otherwise through subtle comments or body language. This disciplined refusal to give a direct response to a party's question about the value of the case or how to settle it is consistent with the role of the mediator as a neutral and impartial facilitator of an agreement that should be fashioned and owned by the parties, not the mediator.

This does not mean, however, that a mediator will be unresponsive to your requests for assistance in resolving the case. It is entirely legitimate for you to invite the mediator's *general* perspectives about the case in terms of your analysis and the other party's analysis of its strengths and weaknesses, value, and possible solutions. After all, the whole mediation process involves the interplay between these differing analyses of the dispute. In connection with these analyses, the mediator's perspective — precisely because she is neutral and impartial — is often integral to helping the parties reach an agreement.

The mediator's willingness to reveal her general perspectives about these matters will largely depend on whether she perceives that you are asking for her assistance in understanding the viewpoints of the other side to assess the overall case, or are asking for her *personal opinion* about the merits of your positions or how to resolve the case. For example, if you ask her, "What do you think a jury would do in this case?" or "How do you think we can settle this case?," she is most likely to respond, "What do you think?" On the other hand, if you ask her to help you "think through" an evaluation of the case by engaging in a Fair Settlement Range Formula calculation (*see* § 11.07) or constructing a Decision Tree (*see* § 11.06), or by asking questions such as, "How can we best think through this aspect of the dispute?" "What might we do to accommodate the other side about X?" or "I wonder if there is anything more we should be thinking about to resolve this matter?" she is likely to be more directive in her responses. Even if she persists with a glib, "Well, what do you think?" response, generating a *discussion* about these matters is likely to encourage her to be more forthcoming in sharing her perspectives about the case.

If the mediator is a "trasher" or "basher," or otherwise is not hesitant to help "push" the parties toward an agreement, you might be able to be more direct in soliciting her perspectives. For example, you might ask, "What is your sense of how a jury might react to X fact, Y theory, or Z theme?" "What can we do to encourage the other side to make more movement in the case?" or "How can we encourage the other side to consider X?" Alternatively, you might invite her responsiveness by musing: "I'm having difficulty seeing how a jury would react to the fact that . . . " or "I'm having trouble coming up with something else to offer . . . I wonder what more we can do?"

When inviting the mediator's perspectives about the case, bear in mind that your requests for assistance must be carefully couched so that the mediator does not feel that her responses would be tantamount to being perceived as "taking sides" in the case. The aim is to encourage her to see that you are earnestly willing to be educated about the relative strengths and weaknesses of the overall case and possible ways to resolve it.

## [6]    Do Not Disclose Your Bottom Line Up Front

If you represent the plaintiff, it is unwise in the initial caucuses to tell the mediator the minimum amount you would accept to settle the case; and if you represent the defendant, it is unwise to reveal up front the maximum amount you would be willing to pay. There are four reasons for this.

First, the opposing party might have evaluated the case much differently from what you had thought, and therefore might be willing to settle the case on terms that are much more favorable to your client than you had anticipated. Second, during the caucusing process, you might learn critical information that will cause you to change your bottom line. Third, by providing the mediator with your bottom line, you will lose significant control over the negotiating process by effectively causing the mediator to "play" within your bottom-line constraint. And fourth, you may place the mediator in the awkward position (if not troubling ethical dilemma) of how to candidly respond to a question about whether the other party has "any further flexibility" if the party asking the question is about to make a final offer that is less (for plaintiffs) or more (for defendants) than what would be acceptable to the other side. That is, if the plaintiff is contemplating making a final offer of $30,000 when the mediator knows that the defendant will pay as much as $60,000, or the defendant is contemplating making a final offer of $60,000 when the mediator know that the plaintiff is willing to settle for $30,000, the mediator's dilemma is whether to disclose to the plaintiff that more money is available from the defendant, or whether to disclose to the defendant that the plaintiff is willing to accept less than the defendant's bottom line.

Along with not disclosing your bottom line up front, it is unwise to reveal to the mediator that your client will not, in any event, take the case to trial. For example, in many relatively minor automobile personal injury cases, the plaintiff will decide at the outset that he does not want to go through the delay, expense, and inconvenience of litigation, but simply wants to use the mediation process to obtain as much money from the defendant's insurance carrier as it might be willing to pay on the claim. If the mediator knows that this is the plaintiff's sole goal, the mediator is much less likely to "push" the defendant to consider making higher settlement offers.

## [7]    Make Reasonable Settlement Offers Supported by Sound Reasons

A major function of the mediator is that she serves as a conduit for your negotiations with the other side. As in traditional inter-party negotiations, making an initial offer that is extreme and beyond reason is likely to insult the other side, impair your credibility, and may cause the mediation to unnecessarily end in deadlock.

Whenever you make a settlement offer or a concession through a counteroffer, provide the mediator with specific reasons for your proposal so that these may be conveyed to the other side. (*see also* § 14.13). If you can, try to incorporate into your proposals something that the other side wants, or provide reasons for why your proposal would have some benefit to the other side. In these ways, you will assist the mediator in explaining to the other side that your proposals are principled and rationally based, and that your counteroffers are similarly principled and not simply made in the course of an auction-like bargaining process.

## [8]    Hold Back Some Strong Leverage Points Until the Final Caucuses

One of the mediator's most difficult tasks is helping to forge the final terms of a settlement when the parties are close to an agreement but are unwilling to make any further concessions. In helping the mediator bring closure to an agreement, it is sometimes useful to have held back one or two important items of information (*e.g.*, an important document, the fact that one of the opposing party's key witnesses has a criminal record, etc.) until late in the caucusing process. These leverage points might then be raised with the mediator toward the end of the negotiations to provide her with exactly what she needs to encourage the opposing side to make an additional deal-clinching concession.

As a practical matter, this technique is unlikely to be available in most cases. That is, if counsel for both sides have carefully prepared for the mediation, they are likely to know in advance about critical favorable or unfavorable matters affecting the case. Moreover, even if you have certain critical leverage points that are unknown to the other side in advance of the mediation, it will often be best to raise those matters earlier rather than later in the mediation process, so as to create a psychological commitment of movement and momentum toward an agreement. That is, holding back a particularly strong leverage point until near the end of the mediation presupposes that meaningful compromise will not occur during the process unless you "drop a bombshell" at the last minute.

## [9]    Suggest Mediator Tactics and Techniques that May Help Forge an Agreement

As discussed in § 16.07, the mediator will invariably employ a variety of tactics and techniques in an effort to help the parties reach a satisfactory agreement. Quite often, the mediator will use these tactics and techniques *sua sponte*, without any express prompting from the parties. However, if you perceive that one or more of these tactics or techniques may be particularly helpful in forging a satisfactory agreement, suggest them to the mediator. For example, in an appropriate case, you might suggest:

- A payment in kind instead of in money;
- A structured settlement or payment in installments;
- Payment of a portion of the settlement to a mutually acceptable charity or other public-interest organization;
- A future business arrangement or relationship;
- A change in an employee's title or work status in lieu of, or in exchange for, a smaller pay increase;
- An undertaking to provide a warning label on a product, or to take certain corrective action to prevent the recurrence of the type of accident that occurred in the instant case;
- A substitution of goods;
- An apology for what happened;
- A confidentiality clause in the agreement;
- A provision to abide by the recommendation of a suitable third party who has special expertise in the matter in dispute;
- That the mediator present a proposal to the other side as if it were her own idea;
- That the mediator make a proposal conditional without communicating a commitment on your part (*e.g.,* "If I can get the other side to do X, will you do Y?");
- That the mediator present a particular proposal at a certain time during the mediation process when the proposal will have the greatest impact;
- That counsel for the parties phone another lawyer or a law professor they respect to render an opinion about the relative merits of a novel or controversial legal theory;
- That the mediator hold a private discussion solely with the parties lawyers to discuss the barriers that are preventing settlement (*see also* subsection [10] below);
- That the mediation be temporarily adjourned so that the parties might reconsider their positions or try to come up with new proposals;
- That the mediator provide the other side with a particular rationale for changing position that allows that party to save face;
- That the parties split the difference;
- That the parties reconvene in joint session to discuss the case.

## [10]    Confer Alone With the Mediator and Opposing Counsel, If Necessary

It is not unusual for you and opposing counsel to be faced with equally irrational or emotionally distraught clients who are making it tremendously difficult for the mediator to engage in constructive private caucuses with each side. In these circumstances, it is sometimes useful for you and opposing counsel to meet with the mediator, without the clients present, to discuss the sources of their irrationality or psychological inability to meaningfully participate in the medation process.

It is best to make this suggestion to the mediator outside the presence of your client, for example, during a break in the session. If it is decided that you and opposing counsel will meet privately with the mediator, explain to your client (or preferably have the mediator explain) that the mediator has asked for the private meeting as an additional way to discuss how to get the settlement discussions back on track. Assure your client that nothing will be decided about settling the case without his full knowledge and consent, and that he will be briefed about the meeting after it is over. When the meeting is over, either you or the mediator can summarize for your client what was discussed and any suggestions that arose about how to resume more constructive negotiations.

## [11]    Do Not Make the Mediator's Fee an Element of the Settlement

Typically, the mediator's fee is split evenly between the parties. Sometimes, in an effort to exact yet one additional concession from the other side, a party will propose that the other side pay the mediator's entire fee. This is usually not a good idea. Such a proposal is embarrassing to the mediator and puts her in the uncomfortable position of appearing to have a monetary stake in the final agreement. Moreover, such a proposal may inhibit the mediator from devoting the amount of time she believes is appropriate to the mediation out of a fear that the other side might construe her on going caucusing as a way of unnecessarily prolonging the session to obtain a greater fee. Nevertheless, on occasion, a party might agree to bear the entire cost of the mediator's fee in an effort to seal a final settlement.

## [12]    Be Patient With the Mediation Process and Take Time to Confer Privately With Your Client

As mentioned in § 16.01, the principal advantage of mediation over traditional inter-lawyer negotiations is that it provides a "process" through which the clients have an opportunity to be directly involved in resolving their dispute; and for many clients, the very *process* of how they go about resolving their differences is often very important to them. Working through this process takes time, and therefore you must be patient with it even though hours may pass before the mediation begins to "get to the point" of substantive negotiations over specific terms of a potential agreement. In short, if you hurry the process, you may defeat its fundamental purpose.

In addition, after each private caucus with the mediator, take the time to confer privately with your client. As appropriate, discuss the matters raised during the caucus and consider your "next move." If during a caucusing session you or your client wants to talk privately (*e.g.,* to decide what counteroffer you want the mediator to present to the other side), do not hesitate to temporarily recess the session to confer. Above all, remember that even though you and your client have established a game plan for the mediation through your Mediation Preparation Outline, you should use all that you learn during the mediation to modify that plan as the circumstances warrant. Indeed, this modification may be as significant as entirely changing what you earlier thought was an appropriate bottom line.

## § 16.13 CONCLUDING THE MEDIATION

As mentioned previously, if an agreement is reached during the mediation, the mediator will typically bring the parties back together in a joint session to summarize the terms of the settlement and discuss arrangements for the preparation of final settlement documents. At the joint session, be sure that the mediator's summary of the terms of the agreement is accurate, and clarify any ambiguities or loose ends with opposing counsel. For considerations about preparing final settlement documents, *see* §§ 17.12 through 17.14.

If no agreement is reached, leave the mediation with civility toward the other side. In an appropriate case, indicate to opposing counsel your willingness to resume the mediation or further lawyer-to-lawyer negotiations at some later time. Always bear in mind that in many cases where mediation has failed to produce an agreement, the parties still end up settling the case in lieu of taking it to trial or resorting to what they thought was their other best alternative to a negotiated agreement.

# Chapter 17

# Legal Considerations in Settlement

## § 17.01   INTRODUCTION

This chapter discusses some of the more important legal considerations that must be taken into account when negotiating a settlement on behalf of a client. These legal considerations include: (1) the professional duty of care you owe to your client in negotiating a settlement, (2) your responsibilities in settlement negotiations if you are hired by an insurer to represent an insured tortfeasor, (3) the implications of particular types of settlement agreements where joint tortfeasors are involved, (4) what kinds of settlements require judicial approval, (5) what portion of settlement funds are taxable, (6) differences between lump-sum and structured settlements, (7) your responsibilities to health-care providers or other entities which have asserted statutory liens on settlement funds for medical services or benefits provided to an injured party, (8) the extent to which settlement agreements and settlement discussions may be kept confidential, and (9) how to finalize and enforce a settlement agreement.

## § 17.02  DUTIES OF ATTORNEYS IN SETTLEMENT

As discussed in § 9.02, it is unethical for an attorney to (1) settle a case on behalf of a client without requisite authority from the client, (2) fail to disclose to the client all good-faith settlement offers, or (3) fail to adequately explain all ramifications of a proposed settlement so that the client can make an informed decision about whether to settle. In addition, it is unethical for an attorney who represents multiple clients to enter into an aggregate settlement on their behalf unless each client consents after full consultation (*see* § 9.03). Along with these ethical duties, you have a legal duty to exercise a reasonable degree of care and skill when settling a case on behalf of your client, and a breach of this duty (as well as any one of the foregoing ethical duties) may give rise to liability for malpractice.

It is often broadly stated that because the relationship between an attorney and client is fiduciary in nature, an attorney owes his client a high degree of fidelity and good faith.[1] More precisely, the attorney's duty to his client is to exercise the knowledge, skill, and ability ordinarily possessed and exercised by members of the legal profession similarly situated.[2] This duty does not require an attorney to act with extraordinary diligence,[3] and he will not be liable for a mere error in judgment so long as he acts with due care and in good faith, and honestly believes that his acts and advice are well founded and in the best interests of his client.[4] That is, an attorney is not an insurer or guarantor of a successful result for his client, and he will not be liable for acting upon or giving mistaken advice about a legal matter that has not been clearly decided by a court of last resort or about which other informed lawyers may have different opinions.[5]

However, an attorney who breaches this standard of exercising "reasonable care"[6] in representing his client may be liable for any actual losses incurred by the client as a result of the breach.[7] The elements of a legal malpractice action, whether grounded in tort or breach of contract, are typically defined as follows:

> In an action against an attorney for negligence or breach of contract, the client has the burden of proving the existence of the relationship of attorney and client; the acts constituting the alleged negligence or breach of contract; that it was the proximate cause of the damage; and that but for such negligence or breach of contract the client would have been successful in the prosecution or defense of the action.[8]

The proximate cause element will be satisfied so long as the attorney's negligence was a "substantial factor" in the client's loss, and it need not be the sole

---

[1] *See, e.g.,* Coleman v. Moody, 372 S.W.2d 06 (Tenn. App. 1963).

[2] Zalta v. Billips, 81 Cal. App.3d 183, 144 Cal. Rptr. 888 (1978); Frank H. Taylor & Son Inc. v. Shepard, 344 A.2d 344 (N.J. Super. 1975); Hughes v. Klein, 427 A.2d 353 (Vt. 1981).

[3] *See* Glenn v. Haynes, 66 S.E.2d 509 (Va. 1951).

[4] *See* Woodruft v. Tomlin, 616 F.2d 924 (6th Cir. 1980); Cook v. Irion, 409 S.W.2d 467 (Tex. Civ. App. 1966).

[5] *See* Hodges v. Carter, 80 S.E.2d 144 (1954); Babbitt v. Bumpus, 41 N.W. 417 (Mich. 1889).

[6] Lysick v. Walcom, 258 Cal. App.2d 136, 65 Cal. Rptr. 406 (1968); Nause v. Goldman, 321 So.2d 304 (Miss. 1975).

[7] *See* Pete v. Henderson, 269 P.2d 78 (Cal. App. 1954); Freeman v. Rubin, 318 So.2d 540 (Fla. App. 1975).

[8] Glenna v. Sullivan, 245 N.W.2d 869, 871 (Minn. 1976).

cause of the loss.[9] However, in proving loss, the client must show that she sustained an actual, ascertainable loss[10] that would have been obtainable and collectible in the case but for her attorney's negligence.[11] Thus, for example, if the client alleges that as a result of her attorney's negligence she agreed to an undesirable settlement of the case, she must make a non-speculative showing that any reasonable jury would have given her a better result at trial and that this amount (in the case of a plaintiff) would have been collectible from the defendant.[12]

In representing a client in settlement negotiations, the legal duty of care you owe to your client (coupled with ethical prescriptions) dictates the following:

(1) You should never settle a case without having requisite authority from your client.[13]

(2) You should always communicate to your client all settlement offers extended by the other side.[14]

(3) You should fully advise your client of her right to trial and all ramifications of a proposed settlement.[15]

(4) You should conduct an adequate investigation of the case and initiate, as well as respond to, settlement offers on behalf of your client when appropriate.[16]

(5) You should adequately advise your client about whether to accept or reject a settlement offer, but emphasize to your client that the ultimate decision whether to settle and in what amount rests with her.[17]

(6) When effectuating a comprehensive settlement on behalf of your client, you should exercise reasonable care that all issues in the case are resolved by the settlement.[18]

---

[9] *See* Lysick v. Walcom, 258 Cal. App.2d 136, 65 Cal. Rptr. 406 (1968).

[10] *See* Glenna v. Sullivan, 245 N.W.2d 969 (Minn. 1976); Murphy v. Edwards & Warren, 245 S.E.2d 212 (N.C. App. 1977); Freeman v. Rubin, 318 So.2d 540 (Fla. App. 1975).

[11] *See, e.g.,* Hoppe v. Ranzini, 385 A.2d 913 (N.J. Super. 1978).

[12] *See* Glenna v. Sullivan, 245 N.W.2d 869 (Minn. 1976); Nause v. Goldman, 321 So.2d 304 (Miss. 1975); Becker v. Julien, Blitz & Schlesinger P.C., 406 N.Y.S.2d 41 (Sup. Ct. 1977), *aff'd* 411 N.Y.S.2d 17 (1978).

[13] *See generally,* Annotation, *Authority of Attorney to Compromise Action-Modern Cases,* 90 ALR4th 326 (1991).

[14] *See* Moores v. Greenberg, 834 F.2d 1105 (1st Cir. 1987); Rogers v. Robson, Masters, Ryan, Brumund and Belom, 407 N.E.2d 47 (Ill. 1980).

[15] *See* Ramp v. St. Paul Fire and Marine Ins. Co., 269 So.2d 239 (La. 1972); Ishmael v. Millington, 241 Cal. App. 2d 520, 50 Cal. Rptr. 592 (1966).

[16] *See* Lysick v. Walcom, 258 Cal. App. 2d 136, 65 Cal. Rptr. 406 (1968); Smiley v. Manchester Ins. & Indem. Co. of St. Louis, 375 N.E.2d 118 (Ill. 1978).

[17] *See* Nioso v. Aiello, 69 A.2d 57 (D.C. 1949).

[18] *See* Zalta v. Billips, 81 Cal. App. 3d 183, 144 Cal. Rptr. 888 (1978).

## § 17.03   DUTIES OF INSURERS TO DEFEND AND SETTLE

Under a standard liability insurance policy, an insurer is required to defend any action against the insured or another person who is covered by the policy on the claim asserted.[19] Even in the absence of a policy provision that expressly requires the insurer to defend, a duty to defend may be implied if the policy gives the insurer the right to control the defense.[20] Generally, this duty to defend exists as long as the plaintiff's claims arguably or potentially fall within the coverage of the policy[21] and even if the action is fraudulent or groundless.[22] Thus, the duty to defend exists unless it is absolutely clear from the plaintiff's complaint that her claims fall outside the coverage of the policy or, during the course of the litigation, it becomes clear that despite the allegations in the complaint, none of the plaintiff's claims are within the policy's coverage.[23]

If an insurance carrier wrongfully refuses to defend, the insured is relieved of any obligation to comply with the provisions of the insurance contract and may independently hire an attorney to defend the case and attempt to settle it.[24] If the case is tried, the insurer will be liable to the insured for legal fees incurred in defending the action and the amount of any judgment rendered against the insured that is within the policy limits.[25] Similarly, if the insured settles the case in a reasonable manner, the insurer will be required to pay the insured's legal fees as well as the amount of the settlement itself.[26] In some jurisdictions, the insurer may even be liable to the insured for other consequential or punitive damages for wrongfully failing or refusing to defend.[27]

Related to the duty to defend, an insurer also has a duty to engage in "good faith" in settling a case on behalf of an insured or any other person entitled to the benefits of the liability policy.[28] That is, an insurer who wrongfully fails or refuses to settle a lawsuit brought against a person covered by the policy may be liable to the

---

[19] *See, e.g.,* Maryland Casualty Co. v. Armco, 822 F.2d 1348 (4th Cir. 1987); Missionaries of Co. of Mary, Inc. v. Aetna Cas. & Sur. Co., 230 A.2d 21 (Conn. 1967).

[20] *See* Id. *But see* American Casualty Co of Reading v. Federal Deposit Ins. Corp., 677 F. Supp. 600 (N.D. Iowa 1987).

[21] *See, e.g.,* Ellis v. Transcontinental Ins. Co., 619 So.2d 1130 (La. App. 1993); Aetna Casualty & Sur. Co. v. Centennial Ins. Co., 838 F.2d 346 (9th Cir. 1988); Brown v. State Auto. & Cas. Underwriters, 293 N.W.2d 822 (Minn. 1980); Brooklyn & Queens Allied Oil Burner Ser. Co. v. Security Mut. Ins. Co., 27 Misc.2d 401, 208 N.Y.S.2d 259 (1960).

[22] *See, e.g.,* Cole's Restaurant, Inc. v. North River Ins. Co., 105 Misc2d 754, 432 N.Y.S.2d 844 (1980); Novak v. Insurance Administration Unlimited Inc., 414 N.E.2d 258 (Ill. App. 1980).

[23] *See e.g.,* Lee v. Aetna Cas. & Sur. Co., 178 F.2d 750 (2d Cir. 1949); Touchette Corp. v. Merchants Mut. Ins. Co., 76 A.D.2d 7, 429 N.Y.S.2d 952 (4th Dept. 1980); First American v. Nat. Union Fire Ins., 695 So. 2d 475 (Fla. App. 1997).

[24] *See, e.g.,* Krutsinger v. Illinois Cas. Co., 141 N.E.2d 16 (Ill. 1957); Milbank Mut. Ins. Co. v. Wentz, 352 F.2d 592 (8th Cir. 1965).

[25] *See, e.g.,* United States Fid. & Guar. Co. v. Capfer, 406 N.Y.S.2d 201 (1978) *aff'd* 424 N.Y.S.2d 356, 400 N.E.2d 298 (1979); Landie v. Century Indem. Co., 390 S.W.2d 558 (Mo. App. 1965); Nat'l Steel Constr. Co. v. Nat'l. Union Fire Ins. Co., 543 P.2d 642 (Wash. App. 1975); Executive Aviation Inc. v. National Ins. Underwriters, 94 Cal. Rptr. 347 (Cal. App. 1971).

[26] *See, e.g.,* Servidone Const. Corp v. Security Ins. Co., 64 N.Y.2d 419, 477 N.E.2d 441 (1985); Zander v. Casualty Ins. Co. 259 Cal. App. 2d 793, 66 Cal. Rptr. 561 (1968).

[27] Annotation, *Insurer's Tort Liability for Consequential or Punitive Damages for Wrongful Failure or Refusal to Defend Insured,* 20 A.L.R.4th 23 (1983).

[28] *See generally,* Annotation, *Liability Insurer's Negligence or Bad Faith In Conducting Defense as*

insured or his assignee for the full amount of an ultimate judgment, including any portion of the judgment in excess of the policy limits.[29] The courts have variously based this liability on breach of a fiduciary duty between the insurer and its insured,[30] breach of an implied covenant of good faith and fair dealing,[31] or, more commonly, on a finding that the insurer's failure or refusal to settle was in "bad faith," was negligent, or both.[32] Moreover, many states have passed specific statutes that variously set forth the standard for liability and types of damages that may be recovered if the insurer breaches its duty to settle.

Under the "bad faith" doctrine, an insurer may be liable for its refusal to accept a reasonable settlement offer if the insurer fails to consider, in good faith, the insured's interests as well as its own when making a decision about settlement.[33] Bad faith, as the absence of good faith, essentially means any frivolous or unfounded refusal to pay a reasonable settlement demand and, in the view of most bad-faith courts, does not require a showing that the insurer engaged in fraud, misrepresentation, or deceit.[34] Of course, bad faith will be found if the insurer's refusal to accept a reasonable settlement offer resulted from a dishonest purpose, moral obliquity, or conscious wrongdoing such as fraud or malice,[35] but most courts will uphold a jury finding of bad faith under circumstances where there was (1) no lawful basis for the refusal to settle coupled with actual knowledge of that fact, or (2) an intentional failure by the insurer to determine whether there was any lawful basis for the refusal.[36]

However, courts that adopt the bad-faith test will not impose liability against an insurer for a failure to settle that results from *mere* negligence or bad judgment.[37] Nevertheless, evidence of the insurer's negligence in handling the claim is frequently permitted as circumstantial evidence of bad faith.[38] The overall thrust of

---

*Ground of Liability to Insured*, 34 ALR3d 533 (1970); Kent D. Syverd, The Duty to Settle, 76 Va. L. Rev. 1113 (1990)

[29] *See, e.g.*, Torrey v. State Farm Mut. Auto. Ins. Co., 705 F.2d 1192 (10th Cir. 1982); Hall v. Brown, 526 A.2d 413 (Pa. Super. 1987); Bollinger v. Nuss, 449 P.2d 502 (Kan. 1969).

[30] *See, e.g.*, Hazelrigg v. American Fid. & Cas. Co., 241 F.2d 871 (10th Cir. 1957); Evans v. Florida Farm Bur. Cas. Ins. Co., 384 So. 2d 959 (Fla. App. 1980).

[31] *See, e.g.*, Automobile Ins. Co. of Hartford Conn. v. Davilla, 805 S.W.2d 897 (Tex. Ct. App. 1991); Critz v. Farmers Ins. Group, 230 Cal. App.2d 788, 41 Cal. Rptr. 401 (1964), 12 ALR2d 1142 (1967); Smith v. American Family Mut. Ins. Co., 294 N.W.2d 751 (N.D. 1980).

[32] *See, e.g.*, Tacket v. State Farm Fire & Casualty, 558 A.2d 1098 (Del. 1988) (bad faith); Gelinas v. Metropolitan Prop. & Liab. Ins. Co., 551 A.2d 962 (N.H. 1988) (negligence); Spencer v. Aetna Life & Cas. Ins. Co., 611 P.2d 149 (1980) (duty of good faith and duty to exercise reasonable care).

[33] Cappano v. Phoenix Assur. Co., 28 A.D2d 639, 280 N.Y.S.2d 695 (4th Dep't. 1967).

[34] State Farm Mut. Auto. Ins. Co. v. White, 236 A.2d 269 (Md. 1967); United Services Auto. Ass'n. v. Carroll, 486 S.E.2d 613 (Ga. App. 1997); United States Fid. & Guar. Co. v. Lembke, 328 F.2d 569 (10th Cir. 1964).

[35] *See, e.g.*, World Ins. Co. v. Wright, 308 So.2d 612 (Fla. App. 1975); Slater v. Motorists Mut. Ins. Co., 187 N.E.2d 45 (Ohio 1962).

[36] *See* Motorists Mut. Ins. Co. v. Said, 590 N.E.2d 1228 (Ohio 1992); James v. Aetna Life & Casualty Co., 326 N.W.2d 114 (Wis. 1982); Miglico v. HCM Claim Corp., 672 A.2d 266 (N.J. Super 1995).

[37] *See, e.g.*, Steedly v. London & Lancashire Ins. Co. Ltd, 416 F.2d 259 (6th Cir. 1969); Aetna Cas. & Sur. Co. v. Price, 146 S.E.2d 220 (1966); Delaune v. Liberty Mut. Ins. Co., 314 So. 2d 601 (Fla. App. 1975).

[38] *See, e.g.*, Liberty Mut. Ins. Co. v. Davis, 412 F.2d 475 (5th Cir. 1969); Kohlstedt v. Farm Bur. Mut. Ins. Co., 139 N.W.2d 184 (Iowa 1965); Kunkel v. United Sec. Ins. Co., 168 N.W.2d 723 (S.D. 1963); Holt v. Continental Ins. Co., 440 F.2d 652 (6th Cir. 1971).

the duty of good faith is that an insurer has an obligation to fairly evaluate and act upon a reasonable settlement offer in the case. As summarized by two decisions:

> [Good faith] requires that the defense of [the action] be evaluated in terms of the reasonable expectations that that defense will prevail and the amount of the verdict if it does not. The settlement offers must then be viewed in light of those expectations, with equal consideration being given to the financial exposure of both the insured and the insurer.[39]

> \*    \*    \*

> If the insurance company, then, was guilty of an intentional disregard of [the insured's] interests, in hoping to escape full liability under the policy, it was guilty of bad faith; if it did not exercise an honest judgment as to the merits of the case, and whether it should be settled, it was guilty of bad faith; if the circumstances suggested to the jury that the insurance company was indifferent to the trust imposed by the policy to guard [the insured's] rights equally with its own, the jury might find bad faith; if the insurance company abandoned [the insured's] interests merely because it faced the prospect of a full loss under the policy, it was guilty of bad faith; if the insurance company was guilty of arbitrary and capricious denial of settlement within the policy limits, its action might have been found to amount to bad faith.[40]

Most jurisdictions, as an alternative to the bad-faith test, employ a negligence test (or incorporate a negligence standard into the bad-faith test)[41] to require insurers to exercise reasonable care in evaluating and acting upon settlement offers extended in the case, and liability may be imposed upon an insurer for a breach of this duty of care.[42] Examples of the numerous factors that a jury might consider in this regard include whether the insurer adequately investigated the case, whether the insurer reasonably evaluated the merits of the case in terms of liability and damages, whether the insurer engaged in serious settlement negotiations, whether the insurer kept its insured reasonably informed about settlement offers in the case, and whether the insurer followed the recommendations of its attorney in rejecting a settlement offer.[43]

Regardless of how the duty to settle is defined — whether in terms of exercising good faith, reasonable care, or both — the courts essentially require that an insurer put itself in the shoes of the insured and act as if the insurer faces potential,

---

[39] Heges v. Western Cas. & Sur. Co, 408 F.2d 1157 (8th Cir. 1969).

[40] Tennessee Farmers Mut. Ins. Co. v. Wood, 277 F.2d 21 (6th Cir. 1960).

[41] *See, e.g.,* State Farm Mut. Auto. Ins. Co. v. Jackson, 346 F.2d 484 (8th Cir. 1965); United States Fid. & Guar. Co. v. Evans, 156 S.E.2d 809 (Ga. App. 1967); Gernocky v. Indemnity Ins. Co. of North America, 216 N.E.2d 198 (Ill. App. 1968); Anderson v. St. Paul Mercury Indem. Co., 340 F.2d 406 (7th Cir. 1965); Kabatoff v. Safeco Ins. Co., 627 F.2d 209 (9th Cir. 1980); Kinkel v. United Sec. Ins. Co., 168 N.W.2d 723 (S.D. 1969).

[42] *See generally,* Allan D. Windt, *Insurance Claims and Disputes,* § 5.13 at 259 (2d ed. 1988).

[43] *See, e.g.,* Hodges v. State Farm Mut. Auto. Ins. Co., 488 F. Supp. 1057 (D. S.C. 1980); Board of Educ. of Bor. of Chatham v. Lumbermen's Mut. Cas. Co., 293 F. Supp. 541 (D. N.J. 1968); Daniels v. Horace Mann Mut. Ins. Co., 422 F.2d 87 (4th Cir. 1970). *See generally,*Annotation, *Liability Insurer's Negligence or Bad Faith in Conducting Defense as Ground of Liability to Insured,* 34 ALR3d 533 (1970).

unlimited liability from an adverse claim.[44] If the insurer refuses a settlement demand within the policy limits and a judgment results in excess of that demand, the insurer will not be liable for the excess judgment merely because it miscalculated the situation, but liability will exist if the insured (or, more commonly, the third-party claimant who has accepted an assignment of the insured's rights in satisfaction of the judgment)[45] proves by a preponderance of the evidence that the insurer's refusal to settle was outside the realm of any reasoned judgment. In addition, apart from liability for the amount by which the judgment exceeds the policy limits, a number of jurisdictions treat the wrongful failure or refusal to settle as a tort rather than a mere breach of contract, and thus permit the insured to recover other economic losses, emotional distress, and even punitive damages in an appropriate case.[46]

The foregoing is only a general summary of a highly complex area of the law that varies significantly among the jurisdictions. Nevertheless, if you represent an insurer or are hired by an insurer to defend an insured on a claim covered by a liability policy, the existing decisional law about an insurer's obligations regarding settlement is instructive in the following respects:

(1) An insurer has an obligation to adequately investigate the case in terms of liability and damages and to determine whether a judgment in excess of the policy limits is likely.[47]

(2) An insurer should promptly inform the insured of all settlement offers by the plaintiff, particularly when damages in excess of the policy limits are being sought.[48]

(3) If the insurer is aware that damages may exceed the policy limits, it should notify the insured to allow her to retain counsel to protect her interests by contributing towards any settlement.[49]

(4) An insurer should attempt to negotiate a settlement in an appropriate case even if the plaintiff has not made any offer to settle.[50]

---

[44] *See, e.g.,* Voccio v. Reliance Ins. Co., 703 F.2d 1 (1st Cir. 1983); Herges v. Western Cas. & Sur. Co., 408 F.2d 1157 (8th Cir. 1969); Davis v. Cincinnati Ins. Co., 288 S.E.2d 233 (Ga. App. 1982).

[45] *See generally,* Annotation, *Right of Injured Person Recovering Excess Judgment Against Insured to Maintain Action Against Liability Insurer for Wrongful Failure to Settle Claim,* 63 ALR3d 677 (1975).

[46] *See, e.g.,* Crisci v. Security Ins Co. of New Haven, 426 P.2d 173 (Cal. 1967); Kunkel v. United Security Ins. Co., 168 N.W.2d 723 (S.D. 1969); Farmers Group, Inc. v. Trimble, 658 P.2d 1370 (1982), *aff'd* 691 P.2d 1138 (Colo. 1984); Gibson v. Western Fire Ins. Co. 682 P.2d 725 (Mont. 1984). *See generally,* Annotation, *Recoverability of Punitive Damages in Action By Insured Against Liability Insurer for Failure to Settle Claim Against Insured,* 85 ALR3d 1211 (1978).

[47] *See* State Farm Mut. Auto Ins. Co v. Zubiate, 808 S.W.2d 590 (Tex. App. 1991); Tennessee Farmers Mut. Ins. Co. v. Wood, 277 F.2d 21 (6th Cir. 1960); Boston Old Colony Ins. Co. v. Gutierrez, 386 So.2d 783 (Fla. 1980); Baker v. Northwestern Nat'l. Cas. Co., 132 N.W.2d 493 (Wis. 1965).

[48] *See* Keith v. Conco Ins. Co, 574 So.2d 1270 (La. Ct. App. 1991); National Farmers Union Property & Cas. Co. v. O'Daniel, 329 F.2d 60 (9th Cir. 1964); Baker v. Northwestern Nat'l. Cas. Co., 132 N.W.2d 493 (Wis. 1965); State Farm Mut. Auto Ins. Co. v. White, 236 A.2d 269 (Md. 1967).

[49] *See* Martin v. Hartford Accident & Indem. Co, 228 Cal. App. 2d 178, 39 Cal. Rptr. 342 (1964); Kaudern v. Allstate Ins. Co., 277 F. Supp. 83 (D. N.J. 1967); Young v. American Cas. Co., 416 F.2d 906 (2d Cir. 1979).

[50] *See* Steward v. State Farm Mut. Ins. Co., 392 F.2d 723 (5th Cir. 1968); Kohlstedt v. Farm Bur. Mut. Ins. Co, 139 N.W.2d 184 (Iowa 1965); Abernathy v. Utica Mut. Ins. Co., 373 F.2d 565 (4th Cir. 1967).

(5) Even after an excess judgment has been entered against the insured, the insurer has a continuing duty to attempt to reasonably settle the case within the policy limits if possible.[51]

(6) If liability is clear and damages exceed the policy limits, an insurer generally should accept a settlement offer within the policy limits unless the insurer reasonably believes that the jury would not award damages in excess of those limits.[52]

(7) When multiple claimants have brought claims against the insured arising out of a single event, the insurer should consider whether it is in the best interests of the insured to negotiate a comprehensive settlement with all claimants rather than a settlement with only some of the claimants that exhausts the policy limits.[53]

(8) An insurer should not disregard the settlement recommendations of its attorney or claims adjuster without compelling reasons to do so.[54]

(9) An insurer's failure to disclose its policy limits may be evidence of bad faith.[55]

## § 17.04   SETTLEMENTS WITH AND CONTRIBUTION AMONG JOINT TORTFEASORS

Multiple defendants may be jointly and severally liable to a plaintiff if her injuries were caused by concerted action of the defendants or their failure to perform a common duty, or if separate but concurring acts of the defendants caused a single and indivisible harm to the plaintiff.[56] Generally, under the doctrine of joint and several liability, each tortfeasor who contributed to the plaintiff's injuries is liable to her for her entire damages, irrespective of proportionate responsibility; and the plaintiff may thus obtain full satisfaction from one or more of the joint tortfeasors.[57] As a practical matter, this doctrine allows the plaintiff to proceed

---

[51] *See* State Farm Mut. Auto Ins. v. Smoot, 381 F.2d 331 (5th Cir. 1967); Foundation Reserve Ins. Co. v. Kelly 388 F.2d 528 (10th Cir. 1968); State Farm Mut. Auto Ins. Co. v. Brewer, 406 F.2d 610 (9th Cir. 1968).

[52] *See* Comunale v. Traders & Gen. Ins. Co., 328 P.2d 198 (Cal. 1958), 68 ALR2d 833 (1959); Boerger v. American Gen. Ins. Co., 100 N.W.2d 133 (Minn. 1959).

[53] *See* Liberty Mut. Ins. Co. v. Davis, 412 F.2d 475 (5th Cir. 1969).

[54] *See generally*, Annotation, *Reliance on, or Rejection of, Advice of Counsel as Factor Affecting Liability in Action Against Liability Insurer for Wrongful Refusal to Settle Claim*, 63 ALR3d 725 (1975). *See also* General Star Nat'l. Ins. v. Liberty Mut. Ins., 960 F.2d 377 (3d Cir. 1992); Commerical Union Ins. Co. v. Liberty Mut. Ins. Co., 393 N.W.2d 161 (Mich. 1986).

[55] Cernocky v. Indemnity Ins. Co. of North America, 216 N.E.2d 198 (Ill. App. 1966); Coppage v. Firemen's Fund Ins. Co., 379 F.2d 621 (6th Cir. 1967).

[56] *See* In re One Meridian Plaza Fire Litig., 820 F. Supp 1492 (E.D. Pa. 1993); Employers Mut. Cas. Co. v. Petroleum Equip. Inc., 475 N.W.2d 418 (Mich. App. 1991); General Accident Ins. Co. of America v. Schoendorf & Sorgi, 549 N.W.2d 429 (Wis. 1996).

[57] A few courts have distinguished "joint tortfeasors" (*i.e.*, those who jointly commit a wrong resulting in a single injury) from "concurrent tortfeasors" (*i.e.*, those who commit separate and distinct acts which concur to cause a single injury) to hold that the single-satisfaction rule is inapplicable where liability is concurrent. *See, e.g.*, Phillips v. Cincinnati Traction Co. v. Griffith, 120 N.E. 207 (Ohio 1918). However, most jurisdictions apply the doctrine of joint and several liability to both classifications where the wrongs result in a single injury. *See, e.g.*, Pillo v. Reading Co., 232 F. Supp. 761 (E.D. Pa. 1964);

against the "deep pocket" defendant for full satisfaction of a claim even though that particular defendant's culpability may have been less than that of other defendants who are less able to pay the claim.

A plaintiff's settlement prior to trial with some but not all joint tortfeasors raises three major issues. First, if the plaintiff enters into a partial settlement with one joint tortfeasor, under what circumstances and to what extent may she thereafter also proceed against one or more other non-settling joint tortfeasors? Second, if one joint tortfeasor has settled with the plaintiff, under what circumstances and to what extent may that tortfeasor seek contribution from a non-settling joint tortfeasor? And third, if one joint tortfeasor has settled with the plaintiff, under what circumstances and to what extent may the non-settling joint tortfeasors seek contribution from the settling joint tortfeasor?

Under the common law, the answer to the first issue — under what circumstances and to what extent a plaintiff may proceed against a non-settling joint tortfeasor after settling with one joint tortfeasor — depends upon whether the plaintiff's settlement agreement with the settling tortfeasor is a "covenant not to sue" or a "release." A "covenant not to sue" is an agreement by which the injured plaintiff promises not to bring or enforce an existing cause of action against the covenanting tortfeasor; and although the agreement operates as a promise not to sue between the parties to it, it preserves the injured plaintiff's claim against other joint tortfeasors who are not joined in the agreement.[58] However, if the injured plaintiff thereafter sues a joint tortfeasor who was not joined in the agreement, the liability of that tortfeasor will usually be reduced by the amount that had been paid to the plaintiff by the covenanting tortfeasor.[59]

On the other hand, a "release" at common law is an agreement by which the injured plaintiff relinquishes a cause of action against a tortfeasor but the release, unlike a covenant not to sue, has the effect of entirely extinguishing the cause of action by discharging *all* tortfeasors from liability.[60] Thus, a true release may be pleaded by any joint tortfeasor as a defense to any claim brought on the cause of action[61] under the rule that an unqualified release of one tortfeasor generally operates to discharge all parties liable for the same harm.[62]

However, most jurisdictions have abolished this distinction between a release and a covenant not to sue and abrogated or modified the common-law rule that a general release given to one tortfeasor discharges all others. For example, under the latest version of the Uniform Contribution Among Tortfeasors Act (UCATA)[63]

---

McLeod v. American Motors Corp., 723 F.2d 830, *reh'g denied*, 729 F.2d 1468 (11th Cir. 1984).

[58] Raye Korte Chevrolet v. Simmons, 571 P.2d 699 (Ariz. Ct. App. 1977); Menzel v. Morse, 362 N.W.2d 465 (Iowa 1985); Hood v. Williamson, 499 P.2d 68 (Wash. App. 1972).

[59] Wirth v. Miller, 580 A.2d 1154 (Pa. Super. 1990); Asbridge v. General Motors Corp., 797 S.W.2d 775 (Mo. Ct. App. 1990).

[60] Taggart v. United States, 880 F.2d 867 (6th Cir. 1989); Sanderson v. Hughes, 526 S.W.2d 308 (Ky. Ct. App. 1975); Aljian v. Ben Schlossberg, Inc., 73 A.2d 290 (N.J. Super. 1950).

[61] Gronquist v. Olson, 64 N.W.2d 159 (Minn. 1954); Collins v. Fairways Condominiums Ass'n, 592 A.2d 147 (R.I. 1991).

[62] Hayman v. Patio Products, Inc., 311 S.E.2d 752 (Va. 1984); Beck v. Cianchetti, 439 N.E.2d 417 (Ohio 1982).

[63] The Uniform Contribution Among Tortfeasors Act of 1955 (UCATA) is a product of the National Conference of Commissioners on Uniform State Laws. *See* Richard M. Dunn, David R. Hazouri &

adopted by a number of states, a release or covenant not to sue one joint tortfeasor does not operate to discharge the other tortfeasors from liability unless it so provides, "but it reduces the claim against the others to the extent of the greater of either (a) any amount stipulated by the release or the covenant, or (b) the amount of consideration paid for it."[64] Similarly, some other states have adopted the Uniform Joint Obligations Act under which a release of one joint tortfeasor will not discharge other joint tortfeasors if the release expressly reserves the injured party's rights against the other tortfeasors.[65] Only a small minority of states still speak of the traditional common-law rule that a general release executed in favor of one charged with a wrong extinguishes the right of action against all those jointly liable for the same wrong.[66]

Most jurisdictions also take the view that the release of one tortfeasor does not release others unless (1) this is the actual intention of the parties as evidenced in their written agreement, or (2) the plaintiff has, in fact, received full compensation for her entire claim in exchange for the release.[67] For example, the release of one tortfeasor will not release all if the court finds that the agreement is, in essence, a covenant not to sue,[68] or if the release is construed to reserve a cause of action under a finding that the plaintiff did not intend to accept full satisfaction for her entire injury when receiving payment under the release.[69] Usually, whether the consideration for a release was received or intended as full compensation for the plaintiff's claim is a question of fact for the jury.[70]

Thus, where a plaintiff chooses to settle with one joint tortfeasor in partial settlement of a larger claim, the safest practice is to include language in the agreement that expressly reserves her rights against the non-settling tortfeasors if she intends to proceed against them to recover additional compensation towards full satisfaction of her claim. If the agreement reserves these rights, the amount the plaintiff will be permitted to recover from a non-settling tortfeasor at trial will nevertheless be reduced in one of several ways. In jurisdictions that have adopted the UCATA, the plaintiff's claim against the non-settling tortfeasor will be reduced by deducting the greater of the amount stipulated by the release given to the

---

Raquel M. Gonzalez, *Defending Against Contribution Actions: Using the UCATA Bar to Advantage*, 68 Def. Counsel J. 403 (2001).

[64] UCATA § 4(a), 12 U.L.A. 57 (1975). *See also* Annotation: *Uniform Contribution Among Tortfeasors Act*, 34 A.L.R.2d 1107 (1954).

[65] *See, e.g.*, Melo National Fuse and Powder Co., 267 F. Supp. 611 (D.C. Colo. 1967) (applying Utah law); State Farm Mut. Auto. Ins. Co. v. Continental Casualty Co., 59 N.W.2d 425 (Wis. 1953); Moore v. Missouri Pacific Railroad, 299 Ark. 232, 773 S.W.2d 78 (1989).

[66] *See, e.g.*, Young v. Hoke, 493 N.E.2d 1279 (Ind. Ct. App. 1986); Grundy County Nat'l. Bank v. Olsen, 534 N.E.2d 196 (Ill. App. 1989); Moore v. Missouri Pacific Railroad, 299 Ark. 232, 773 S.W.2d 78 (1989). Supreme Court of Arkansas held that a release discharging "any and all other persons, associations and corporations, whether herein named or referred to or not" was not an effective release unless the tortfeasors were specifically identified.

[67] *See, e.g.*, Richardson v. Eastland Inc., 660 S.W.2d 7 (Ky. 1983); Mickle v. Blackman, 166 S.E.2d 173 (S.C. 1969); Weldon v. Lehmann, 84 So. 2d 796 (Miss. 1956).

[68] *See, e.g.*, Western Spring Co v. Andrew, 229 F.2d 413 (10th Cir. 1956); Florkiewicz v. Gonzales, 347 N.E.2d 401 (Ill. App. 1976); Gronquist v. Olson, 64 N.W.2d 159 (Minn. 1954).

[69] *See, e.g.*, Johnson v. Harnisch, 147 N.W.2d 11 (Iowa 1966); Mallet v. Credo Oil & Gas, 534 So. 2d 126 (La. Ct. App. 1988); Freeman v. Myers, 774 S.W.2d 892 (Mo. Ct. App. 1989).

[70] *See* Murphy v. Indiana Harbor Belt R.R., 289 N.E.2d 167 (Ind. App. 1972); Hargreaves v. American Flyers Airline Corp, 494 P.2d 229 (Wash. App. 1972).

settling tortfeasor or the amount actually paid under the release (*pro tanto* method).[71] Other jurisdictions deduct an amount equal to the settlor's proportionate share of liability or culpability for the injury (comparative fault method),[72] or deduct an amount equal to the settler's share of the verdict (*pro rata* method).[73]

For example, if plaintiff sues joint tortfeasors A, B, and C and settles with A for $200,000, and if the jury finds plaintiff's total damages to be $300,000 in a trial against B and C, under a strict *pro tanto* method, plaintiff would recover $100,000 ($300,000–$200,000) from B and C collectively, whereas under a strict *pro rata* method, she would recover $200,000 ($300,000–$100,000) with B and C each paying their $100,000 share. Thus, the particular method used in the applicable jurisdiction must be carefully considered by the plaintiff in deciding whether to enter into a partial settlement and, if so, with which tortfeasor to settle and which tortfeasor to take to trial.

If the plaintiff settles with one joint tortfeasor, the second major issue is under what circumstances and to what extent that tortfeasor may seek contribution from a non-settling joint tortfeasor. Generally, the doctrine of contribution gives a joint tortfeasor the right to recover from another joint tortfeasor that amount for the liability that the other ought to pay.[74] Although at common law there was a very limited right to contribution between joint tortfeasors (under the theory that no person should be allowed to profit from his own wrong),[75] most states now permit contribution actions by joint tortfeasors in broader circumstances and so long as the tortfeasor seeking contribution did not engage in intentional or willful or wanton conduct in contributing to the plaintiff's injury.[76] Where the right of contribution exists, generally the jurisdictions establish the amount of contribution based on (1) a *pro rata* or equal sharing among the tortfeasors having common liability,[77] or (2) the comparative fault of the joint tortfeasors where damages are apportioned in proportion to the tortfeasors' respective degrees of fault in causing the plaintiff's injuries.[78]

---

[71] *See, e.g.*, Martinez v. Lopez, 476 A.2d 197 (Md. 1984); Lafayette v. County of Los Angeles, 162 Cal. App. 3d 547, 208 Cal. Rptr. 668 (1984); Salim v. LaGuire, 361 N.W.2d 9 (Mich. App. 1984).

[72] *See, e.g.*, Cooper Mountain, Inc. v. Poma of America Ins., 890 P.2d 100 (Colo. 1995); Cartel Capital Corp v. Fireco of N.J., 410 A.2d 674 (1980); Bartels v. City of Williston, 276 N.W.2d 113 (N.D. 1979). *See also* Uniform Comparative Fault Act, § 6, 12 U.L.A. at 54.

[73] *See, e.g.*, Wall v. Am. Employers Inc. Co, 386 So. 2d 79 (La. 1980); Palestine Contractors, Inc. v. Perkins, 386 S.W.2d 764 (Tex. 1964).

[74] *See* Partin v. First Nat'l Bank & Trust Co., 283 N.W. 408 (Minn. 1939); Barth v. Keffer, 464 S.E.2d 570 (W. Va. 1995).

[75] *See* Merryweather v. Nixan, 8 Term Rep. 186, 101 Eng. Rep. 1337 (K.B. 1799).

[76] *See, e.g.*, UCATA § 1(c) (1955 Revised Act), 12 U.L.A. (1975); Ziarko v. Soo Line R.R., 641 N.E.2d 402 (Ill. 1994); Savage v. Booth, 468 S.E.2d 318 (W.Va. 1996); Blackburn, Inc. v. Harnischfeger Corp., 773 F. Supp. 296 (D. Kan. 1991) (punitive damages are not recoverable in an action for contribution). *See also* Sorrano v. N.Y. Life Ins. Co., 2005 U.S. Dist. LEXIS 30962 (D. Ill. 2005) (concluding that even if common law contribution survived enactment of the Illinois Joint Tortfeasors Contribution Act, it does not apply to intentional torts); Murray v. Chicago Youth Center, 224 Ill.2d 213, 239, 864 N.E.2d 176, 191 (2007) (Interpreting the *Ziarko* plurality holding: "Accordingly, the court found that contribution principles could be applied in cases when one defendant is found guilty of negligence and another of willful and wonton acts not rising to the level of intentional misconduct. *Ziarko*, 161 I.2d at 280, 204 Ill. Dec. 178, 641 N.E.2d 402.").

[77] *See, e.g.*, Economy Eng'g Co. v. Commonwealth, 604 N.E.2d 694 (Mass. 1992); Sanchez v. City of Espanola, 615 P.2d 993 (N.M. App. 1980).

[78] *See, e.g.*, Dunn v. Praiss, 656 A.2d 413 (N.J. 1995); Bervoets v. Harde Ralls Pontiac-Old, Inc., 891

In the specific context of a settling tortfeasor's attempt to seek contribution from a non-settling joint tortfeasor, some states — for example, New York[79] and Texas[80] — do not recognize a right of contribution where a tortfeasor has obtained a release from liability. On the other hand, states that have adopted the most recent version of the UCATA will allow a settling tortfeasor to recover contribution from another joint tortfeasor (1) if the settling tortfeasor settled with the plaintiff in "good faith" (*i.e.*, entered into a reasonable settlement without collusion or fraud)[81] and paid more than his *pro rata* share of the common liability; (2) if the settlement agreement clearly extinguished not only the liability of the settling tortfeasor but that of the other tortfeasors from whom contribution was sought (*e.g.*, as some courts have said, where the release specifically named the joint tortfeasors whose liability was extinguished);[82] (3) if the settling tortfeasor did not intentionally cause or contribute to the plaintiff's injury; and (4) only for that amount which the settling tortfeasor paid in excess of his *pro rata* share.[83] The settling tortfeasor has the burden of proving all of the foregoing.[84]

If there is no judgment against the settling tortfeasor seeking contribution, the UCATA provides that the tortfeasor's right of contribution is barred unless he or she has either "discharged by payment the common liability within the statute of limitations period applicable to claimant's right of action against him and has commenced his action for contribution within one year after the payment" or, prior to judgment in an action against him, he or she has agreed to discharge the common liability and has actually paid the liability and commenced a contribution action within one year of so agreeing.[85]

With respect to a liability insurer who settles with the plaintiff on behalf of an insured-tortfeasor, the UCATA provides that if the insurer has discharged in full or in part the liability of the insured and thereby has discharged in full its obligation as insurer, it is subrogated to the insured's right of contribution to the extent the insurer has paid in excess of the insured's *pro rata* share of the common liability.[86]

In addition, the UCATA provides that the Act does not apply to or impair any right of indemnity under existing law, and the indemnity obligor is not entitled to

---

S.W.2d 905 (Tenn. 1994). *See also* Petrolane Inc. v Robles, 154 P.3d 1014, 1021 (Alaska 2007) ("Indeed allowing full offsets under several liability would discourage settlement because a rational defendant would delay resolving the case in the hopes that another defendant's settlement would reduce or eliminate his liability. Our strong policy favoring settlement as a positive method of case resolution is a further reason to favor proportionate (*pro rata*) offset." (Footnotes omitted.)).

[79] N.Y. Gen. Oblig. Law § 15-108(c). *See* Gonzles v. Armac Indus. Ltd, 611 N.E.2d 261 (N.Y. 1993); Rosado v. Proctor & Schwartz, Inc., 484 N.E.2d 1354 (N.Y. 1985).

[80] *See* Sherwin-Williams Co. v. Trinity Contractors, Inc., 852 S.W.2d 37 (Tex. Ct. App. 1993); Beech Aircraft Corp. v. Jinkins, 739 S.W.2d 19 (Tex. 1987).

[81] *See* Reynolds v. Southern R.R., 320 F. Supp. 1141 (N.D. Ga. 1969); Cooper Mountain Ins. v. Poma of America Inc., 890 P.2d 100 (Colo. 1995).

[82] *See, e.g.*, Albright Bros. Contractors, Inc. v. Hull-Dobbs Co., 209 F.2d 103 (6th Cir. 1953); United States v. Reilly, 385 F.2d 225 (10th Cir. 1967) (applying New Mexico law).

[83] *See, e.g.*, O'Keefe v. Baltimore Transit Co., 94 A.2d 26 (Md. 1953).

[84] *See* Reynolds v. So. R.R., 320 F. Supp. 1141 (N.D. Ga. 1969); Young v. Steinberg, 250 A.2d 13 (N.J. 1969).

[85] UCATA § 3(d), 12 U.L.A. 63 (1975).

[86] UCATA § 1(e), 12 U.L.A. 63 (1975).

contribution from the obligee for any portion of the indemnity obligation.[87] This is because indemnity, unlike contribution, does not seek an equitable sharing of joint and several liability, but arises by an express agreement or by operation of law (*e.g.*, as through vicarious or derivative liability under the doctrine of *respondeat superior*)[88] such that the entire loss borne by one party who has been forced to pay is shifted to one who should bear it instead, either by virtue of a contract or some special relationship between the parties.[89]

In those jurisdictions that have not adopted the UCATA, the settling tortfeasor may have to meet other requirements to obtain contribution from a non-settling joint tortfeasor. For example, under Michigan law, a settling tortfeasor is not entitled to recover contribution unless he makes a reasonable effort to notify the person from whom he seeks contribution about the pendency of settlement negotiations with the plaintiff, and gives the potential contributor a reasonable opportunity to participate in the settlement negotiations.[90]

Finally, the third major issue presented by a joint tortfeasor's pretrial settlement with the plaintiff is whether the settling tortfeasor may have to contribute to the amounts the other tortfeasors have to pay. This issue is addressed by the UCATA, which provides that when a release or covenant not to sue is given in "good faith" to a joint tortfeasor, "[i]t discharges the tortfeasor to whom it is given from all liability for contribution to any other tort-feasor."[91] This rule that a settling tortfeasor is protected from liability for contribution fosters the public policy of encouraging settlements,[92] and thus has even been applied by states that have not adopted the UCATA.[93]

Much of the litigation in this area has concerned whether, under the UCATA, the joint tortfeasor entered into the particular release in "good faith" so as to preclude contribution.[94] In most jurisdictions, good faith essentially means the absence of fraud, collusion, or dishonesty by the plaintiff and the settling tortfeasor. A tortfeasor seeking contribution from a settling tortfeasor bears the burden of proving lack of good faith in the earlier settlement. The courts typically examine the

---

[87] *See, e.g.*, Owens v. Truckstops of America, 915 S.W.2d 420 (Tenn. 1996).

[88] *See* In re Consolidated Vista Hills Retaining Wall Litig., 893 P.2d 438 (N.M. 1995).

[89] *See* Hermeling v. Minnesota Fire & Cas. Co., 548 N.W.2d 270 (Minn. 1996); Keil v. United States, 705 F. Supp. 346 (E.D. Mich. 1988); Fucher v. First Vt. Bank & Trust Co., 821 F. Supp. 916 (D. Vt. 1993).

[90] *See, e.g.*, Klawiter v. Reurink, 492 N.W.2d 801 (Mich. App. 1992).

[91] UCATA § 4, 12 U.L.A. 98. *See also* Uniform Comparative Fault Act, § 6, 12 U.L.A. at 57. *See, e.g.*, Schreier v. Parker, 415 So. 2d 794 (Fla. Dist. Ct. App. 1982); Bartles v. City of Williston, 276 N.W.2d 113 (N.D. 1979); Baker v. Clouse, 591 N.E.2d 722 (Ohio App. 1990); Robert C. Weill, A Primer on Contribution & Indemnity, 26 NO.2 Trial Advoc. W. 18 (Spring 2007). For additional reading, see Richard M. Dunn, David R. Hazouri & Raquel M. Gonzalez, *Defending Against Contribution Actions: Using the UCATA Bar to Advantage*, 68 Def. Counsel J. 403 (2001).

[92] *See* Cooper Mountain Inc. v. Poma of America, Inc., 890 P.2d 100 (Colo. 1995); Gouty v. Schnepel, 795 So. 2d 959 (Fla. 2001); Petrolane Inc. v Robles, 154 P.3d 1014 (Alaska 2007).

[93] *See, e.g.*, Hardy v. Gulf Oil Corp., 949 F.2d 826 (5th Cir. 1992) (applying Texas law and general maritime law); Cook v. Iowa, 476 N.W.2d 617 (Iowa 1991); Cook v. Stansell, 411 S.E.2d 844 (W. Va. 1991).

[94] *See* Cohen v. Univ. of Dayton, 164 Ohio App.3d 29 34, 840 N.E.2d 1144, 1148 (2005) ("a trial court must be accorded substantial discretion to limit the scope of discovery in cases involving good faith settlement defenses to contribution, lest they become mini-trials on the individual liability of alleged tortfeasors").

"totality of the circumstances" in determining the question.[95] Some courts also predicate a finding of good faith on at least some showing that the amount paid in settlement fell within a "ballpark" or reasonable range estimate of the settling tortfeasor's liability in the case.[96]

Some states that have not adopted the UCATA have enacted statutes providing that a release by the plaintiff of one joint tortfeasor will not preclude contribution to another joint tortfeasor unless the release (1) is given before the right of the other tortfeasor to secure a money judgment for contribution has accrued, and (2) provides for a reduction, to the extent of the *pro rata* share of the released tortfeasor, of the plaintiff's damages recoverable against all other tortfeasors.[97]

The legal effects of a settlement involving fewer than all joint tortfeasors is quite complex, particularly because of the wide variations in the law among different jurisdictions. The foregoing highlights only the major issues and principles. This means, of course, that whenever you represent a party in connection with a partial settlement involving joint tortfeasors, it is imperative to have a complete understanding of the applicable law in the relevant jurisdiction.

If you represent a plaintiff who has been injured by multiple defendants in a jurisdiction that follows the latest version of the UCATA, the following are some of the major considerations to keep in mind when negotiating a settlement of the case:

(1) When possible, it is of course desirable for a plaintiff to enter into a comprehensive settlement that resolves her entire claim against multiple tortfeasors. In that event, all parties "buy their peace" without the uncertainty of a trial and potential issues of contribution.

(2) Assuming a comprehensive settlement cannot be obtained, a partial settlement that resolves the liability of one tortfeasor benefits the plaintiff in that she is thereby assured of at least some compensation for her injuries, and the compensation she receives might otherwise provide her with a fund to finance her litigation against the non-settling torfeasors.

(3) However, if the plaintiff settles with one joint tortfeasor, she will thereafter have no further recourse against that defendant and will be relegated to pursuing other, perhaps less solvent defendants at trial to obtain complete compensation for her damages. This underscores the importance to the plaintiff of negotiating a particularly satisfactory settlement if the only tortfeasor willing to settle is the "deep pocket" in the case.

(4) If the plaintiff enters into a settlement agreement releasing one tortfeasor and intends to take the others to trial, it is imperative that she include language in the agreement that expressly reserves her rights against the non-settling tortfeasors. In this regard, the safest practice is to include in the settlement agreement the specific names of those tortfeasors

---

[95] *See, e.g.,* Smith v. Monongahela Power Co., 429 S.E.2d 643 (W. Va. 1993); Sterling v. Gil Soucy Trucking, Ltd., 146 N.C. App. 173, 552 S.E.2d 674 (2001).

[96] *See, e.g.,* Tech-Bilt, Inc. v. Woodward-Clyde & Assoc., 698 P.2d 159 (Cal. 1985); City of Tucson v. Superior Court, 778 P.2d 1337 (Ariz. 1989). See *Troyer v. Adams*, 102 Haw. 399, 77 P.3d 83 (2003) for an extensive discussion of the three basic standards used in different jurisdictions to determine whether a settlement was given in "good faith."

[97] *See, e.g.,* McBride v. Chevron U.S.A., 673 So. 2d 372 (Miss. 1996), *superseded by statute as stated in J & J Timber Co. v. Broome*, 932 So. 2d 1 (Miss. 2006).

against whom the plaintiff reserves her rights (see example at Section 17.05).

On the other hand, if you represent a defendant joint tortfeasor who is negotiating a potential settlement with the plaintiff, the following are some major considerations to bear in mind:

(1) A settlement with the plaintiff is desirable because, assuming the UCATA applies, a full release from the plaintiff will insulate the defendant from having to make contribution to any other joint tortfeasor.

(2) However, when settling with the plaintiff, the defendant must avoid any terms in an agreement that may be construed as evidencing collusion with the plaintiff to pay her a cheap sum in exchange for cooperating with her to maximize her recovery against the other joint tortfeasors. This means, among other things, that the amount of the settlement should be reasonably related to a good-faith assessment of the defendant's share of potential liability, taking into account jury verdicts in similar cases.

(3) If the defendant undertakes to settle with the plaintiff by paying her more than the defendant's *pro rata* share of the common liability and intends thereafter to seek contribution from the non-settling tortfeasors, it is imperative that the settlement agreement include language that makes it absolutely clear that the plaintiff is releasing all other joint tortfeasors from liability. In this regard, it is desirable for the agreement to specifically name all known potential joint tortfeasors who are being released from liability by the plaintiff (see example at Section 17.05).

(4) If the settling defendant intends to seek contribution from the other joint tortfeasors, the requirement that the settlement agreement release all joint tortfeasors from liability to the plaintiff will be in direct conflict with the plaintiff's interests if she wishes to preserve her rights in the agreement to proceed against the non-settling tortfeasors herself. The resolution of this conflict will undoubtedly be reflected in the amount of the settlement and influenced by the relative bargaining power of the parties. If the plaintiff refuses to release all joint tortfeasors in the settlement agreement, one option for the defendant is to insist on an indemnification provision in the agreement by which the plaintiff undertakes to hold the defendant harmless from any contribution claim brought against him by a non-settling joint tortfeasor. However, as a practical matter, the value of such an indemnity provision to the defendant will only be as good as the solvency of the plaintiff to be bound to it.

## § 17.05  EXAMPLE OF SETTLEMENT AGREEMENT AND RELEASE [WITH RESERVATION OF RIGHTS]

Settlement Agreement And Release [With reservation of Rights][98]

In consideration of the payment to the undersigned, . . . . . . . . . . , of $_____, the receipt of which is acknowledged, the undersigned, being legally

---

[98] *See also* Beaver v. Harris' Estate, 409 P.2d 143 (Wash. 1965); Morris v. Millers Mut. Fire Ins. Co. of Texas, 343 S.W.2d 269 (Tex. Civ. App. 1961); Miles v. Inter Island Tel. Co., 416 P.2d 115 (Wash. 1966).

competent and of lawful age, releases and forever discharges, for myself, heirs, executors, administrators, and assigns, the following persons: . . . . . . . . . . . . . . . . . . . , and, except as otherwise provided herein, all other persons, firms, or corporations from any causes of action, claims, demands, damages, costs, loss of services, expenses and compensation on account of, or in any way growing out of, any known and unknown personal injuries and property damage resulting or to result from the accident that occurred on the . . . . . . . . . day of . . . . . . . . . at or near . . . . . . . . . in . . . . . . . . . .

[This Settlement Agreement and Release reserves to the undersigned all rights of action, claims and damages against the following: . . . . . . . . . . . . . . . . . . ]

[This Settlement Agreement and Release does not include the subrogation interest of the . . . . . . . . . I nsurance Company.]

The undersigned understands that the injuries sustained may be permanent and progressive, that any recovery from them is uncertain and indefinite, and that any recovery at law for those injuries or other damages is uncertain and indefinite. The undersigned understands and agrees that, in making this Settlement Agreement and Release, I rely wholly on my judgment, belief, and knowledge, and that I have not been improperly influenced in any way by anyone in making this Settlement Agreement and Release.

The undersigned understands that this settlement is the compromise of a doubtful and disputed claim, and that the payment is not to be construed as an admission of liability on the part of the persons, firms, and corporations hereby released, by whom liability is expressly denied.

[The undersigned further agrees to forthwith file a dismissal with prejudice in favor of the defendant, . . . . . . . . . . . , in the lawsuit filed as . . . . . . . . . . v. . . . . . . . . . . in the court of . . . . . . . . . ]

[The undersigned further agrees that any liens outstanding in favor of any medical or health-care provider or governmental agency which would prevent the direct payment to the undersigned of the settlement proceeds received under this Settlement Agreement and Release will be satisfied out of the proceeds of this settlement, and the undersigned agrees to indemnify and hold harmless . . . . . . . . . . for any claim by any lienholder against these settlement funds.][99]

This Settlement Agreement and Release contains the entire agreement between the parties, and the terms of this Settlement Agreement and Release are contractual and not a mere recital.

The undersigned states that I have signed this Settlement Agreement and Release as my own free act, and before doing so I have fully informed myself of its contents by reading it or having it read to me.

This Settlement Agreement and Release shall be construed under the laws of the State of . . . . . . . . . .

Signed this the . . . . . . . . . day of . . . . . . . . . . . . . . . . . .

---

[99] *See* § 17.10.

Caution: Read Before Signing. _____

## § 17.06   MARY CARTER AND LOAN-RECEIPT AGREEMENTS

Assume that P, after being injured in an automobile accident, sues A, B, and C, all of whom were driving separate trucks. Assume also that, at the time of the accident, B and C were working for the same company employer. Prior to trial, P enters into a written agreement with A which specifies that the agreement is not to be revealed to anyone unless ordered by the court. The agreement provides that A's maximum liability to P will be $12,500, and that A will remain a party-defendant in the suit. It is understood (though not expressly "agreed") that A will testify that the fault for the accident lies with B and C. The agreement further provides that if the jury awards P more than $37,500 from the joint tortfeasors (*i.e.*, $12,500 multiplied by the three defendants), P will seek satisfaction of the judgment only from B and C's employer (who is also a named defendant in the suit and would be liable under the doctrine of *respondeat superior*), and A will owe nothing to P. If the jury awards P less than $37,500 from B and/or C only, A will owe P an amount, not exceeding $12,500, to make up the difference between the verdict and $37,500. If P loses the case entirely, A will pay $12,500 to P. These facts are roughly what occurred in Booth v. Mary Carter Paint Co., 202 So.2d 8 (Dist. Ct. App. Fla. 1967). After the jury awarded $15,000 to P, the Florida District Court of Appeal upheld the agreement by which A was obligated to pay $12,500 to P.

This type of agreement is commonly called a "Mary Carter" agreement.[100] While it may have many variations, it typically has three features. First, the contracting defendant remains a party throughout the litigation and provides testimony at trial that is favorable to the plaintiff in her effort (and the contracting defendant's effort) to pin all liability and large damages upon the non-agreeing defendants. Second, the contracting defendant promises to pay the plaintiff a predetermined, maximum amount of money (*e.g.*, the $12,500 in the *Mary Carter* case) if the plaintiff's recovery at trial is less than that predetermined amount or if the plaintiff fails to win a judgment altogether; and if the judgment equals or exceeds the predetermined maximum amount of money guaranteed by the contracting defendant and all co-tortfeasors are found liable, the plaintiff promises to enforce the judgment only against the non-agreeing defendants. In addition, or alternatively, the plaintiff and the contracting defendant may agree that the contracting defendant's ultimate payment to the plaintiff will be calculated on a "sliding scale" in proportion to the size of the recovery that the plaintiff obtains against the non-agreeing defendants (*e.g.*, in the *Mary Carter* case, the difference between $37,500 and the amount of the verdict, not exceeding $12,500). Either way, the amount the contracting defendant ultimately pays the plaintiff is determined by the success of the plaintiff's action against the non-agreeing tortfeasors. And third, the agreement between the contracting defendant and the plaintiff is kept secret in that it is not voluntarily revealed to any non-agreeing defendant.

---

[100] *See generally*, Annotation: *Validity and Effect of "Mary Carter" or Similar Agreement Settling Maximum Liability of One Cotortfeasor and Providing for Reduction or Extinguishment Thereof Relative to Recovery Against Nonagreeing Cotortfeasor*, 22 A.L.R.5th 483 (1994). Some courts variously describe such agreements as guarantee agreements, sliding-scale agreements, "Gallagher Covenants," (*see, e.g.*, City of Tucson v. Gallagher, 383 P.2d 798 (Ariz. App. 1971), *vacated*, 493 P.2d 1197 (Ariz. 1972)) or "Pierringer releases" (*see, e.g.*, Lochthowe v. C.F. Peterson Estate, 2005 ND 40, 692 N.W.2d 120).

Stated in a more shorthand way, the prototypical Mary Carter agreement is a confidential agreement that places a limit on the maximum liability of the contracting defendant, which will be reduced or extinguished depending upon the amount the plaintiff recovers at trial from the non-agreeing defendants. In addition, the plaintiff agrees not to execute on any judgment found by a jury against the contracting defendant but to seek recourse against only the non-agreeing defendants; and the contracting defendant agrees to continue as a party-defendant in the trial of the action.

Thus formulated, a Mary Carter agreement is neither a "release" nor a "covenant not to sue," nor even a true "settlement." (*See generally*, § 17.04). That is, the agreement does not release any party from liability with the common-law effect of extinguishing the plaintiff's entire cause of action against all joint tortfeasors. The agreement is also not a covenant not to sue because the contracting defendant in a Mary Carter agreement remains an active party-participant in the suit with a strong financial interest in its outcome, whereas a covenant not to sue discharges the settling tortfeasor as a party-defendant who then has no tangible stake in the outcome of the case. At most, a Mary Carter agreement is only a "partial" settlement in the sense that the contracting defendant guarantees the plaintiff a minimum sum of money, yet the litigation continues as if no settlement had been reached at all.

A Mary Carter agreement presents distinct advantages for the plaintiff. She is guaranteed at least a minimum recovery from the contracting defendant even if she entirely loses the case at trial. Particularly if she receives her guaranteed funds up front, she will have greater resources to fund the litigation and can marshal them with those of the contracting defendant in engaging in discovery and other pretrial preparation. Most importantly, the contracting defendant will be her ally at trial and will be cooperative in presenting testimony and other evidence that points the finger for liability and damages upon the non-agreeing defendants. The overall scheme is that the plaintiff and contracting defendant will team up against the non-agreeing defendants with a united litigation front.

For the contracting defendant, the greatest advantage of a Mary Carter agreement is the assurance that his liability will be limited to a predetermined amount, and thus he will not run the risk of becoming victim to an adverse, run-away verdict. In addition, if the agreement not only places a predetermined cap on the contracting defendant's liability but provides that his *ultimate* liability will be reduced as the size of the judgment increases, such a "sliding-scale" provision may have the effect of significantly reducing, or entirely erasing, what he ultimately has to pay the plaintiff depending on the extent to which the judgment against the non-agreeing defendants exceeds the predetermined cap. Finally, if the contracting defendant's maximum liability is limited to an amount that falls within his insurance coverage, he will not be faced with an uninsured loss, and his insurer will favor the arrangement because it will tend to negate the possibility of eventual liability for an amount in excess of the policy limits on the basis of a bad-faith failure to settle.[101] (*See generally* § 17.03).

For any non-agreeing defendant, the effects of a Mary Carter agreement present a litigation nightmare. He faces not only the plaintiff as an adversary, but the deceptive contracting defendant who he ordinarily would assume to be his ally

---

[101] *See* Tucsan v. Gallagher, 493 P.2d 1197 (Ariz. 1972).

but who now has pooled his resources with the plaintiff to pin all liability in the case upon the non-agreeing defendant alone. The effects are particularly invidious if he is unaware of the secret agreement. At every stage of the litigation, whether pretrial or during trial, the plaintiff and contracting defendant are — "behind the non-agreeing defendant's back," so to speak — cooperating in discovery and pretrial motions, and cooperating during jury selection and in the presentation of evidence and overall courtroom strategy.[102] This not only significantly increases the chances that the jury will render a verdict against the non-agreeing defendant (and perhaps a larger verdict than otherwise would be awarded against him), but the plaintiff will look to him alone to pay the entire judgment if the damage award is above the minimum amount that the contracting defendant has agreed to pay to the plaintiff.

Because Mary Carter agreements give the contracting defendant a financial interest in the outcome of the trial and a motive to advance the plaintiff's cause, they can promote unethical collusion, skew the trial process, mislead the jury, and create the likelihood that a less culpable non-agreeing defendant will be burdened with the full payment. Thus, by statute or judicial fiat, some jurisdictions (including now Florida) have banned these types of agreements altogether as being in violation of public policy,[103] or have invalidated them as being champertous (*i.e.*, containing a promise for a payment of compensation for the subject matter of the suit),[104] or as failing to satisfy the "good faith" requirement necessary under the Uniform Contribution Among Tortfeasors Act to discharge the contracting defendant from any obligation of contribution.[105] Other jurisdictions, however, have not found these types of agreements invalid *per se*.[106]

Most jurisdictions that have permitted Mary Carter agreements, have established prophylactic procedural rules to protect the non-agreeing defendants and the integrity of the trial process. For example, a number of jurisdictions either make such agreements and their terms subject to discovery[107] or require their disclosure

---

[102]  *See* Note, "It's a Mistake to Tolerate the Mary Carter Agreement," 87 Colum. L. Rev. 368 (1987).

[103]  *See, e.g.,* Dosdourian v. Garsten, 624 So.2d 241 (Fla. 1993); Elbaor v. Smith, 845 S.W.2d 240 (Tex. 1992); Cox v. Kelsey-Hayes Co., 594 P.2d 354 (Okla. 1978); American Nat'l. Bank & Trust Co. v. Bic Corp., 880 P.2d 420 (Okla. App. 1994) (dictum). *See also* J.M. Krupar Const. Co., Inc. v. Rosenberg, 95 S.W.3d 322, 332 (Tex. App. Houston 1st Dist. 2002), where the court held that "[u]nlike the typical Mary Carter agreement, if [the agreement in question] gives the *plaintiff* a stake in the recovery of the *settling defendant-cross plaintiff* against the non-settling defendant, thereby making it in the interest of the plaintiff and the settling defendant to maximize the settling defendant's recovery, such an agreement is as violative of public policy as a typical Mary Carter agreement."

[104]  *See, e.g.,* Lum v. Stinnett, 488 P.2d 347 (Nev. 1971). *See also Simpson v. Matthews,* 274 Ill. Dec. 25, 790 N.E.2d 401 (App. Ct. 5th Dist. 2003) for a discussion of the history of Mary Carter cases in Illinois.

[105]  *See, e.g.,* Brandner by Brandner v. Allstate Ins. Co., 512 N.W.2d 753 (Wis. 1994); *Re Waverly Acci. of February 22–24, 1978,* 502 F. Supp. 1 (M.D. Tenn. 1979) (applying Tennessee law); Reager v. Anderson, 371 S.E.2d 619 (W. Va. 1988).

[106]  *See, e.g.,* Howard v. ICRR, 709 So.2d 1044 (La. App. 1998); Abbott Ford Inc. v. Superior Court, 741 P.2d 124 (Cal. 1987) (sliding-scale agreements specifically addressed by statute); General Motors Corp. v. Lahocki, 410 A.2d 1039 (Md. 1980); Pacific Indem. Co. v. Thompson-Yaeger, Inc., 260 N.W.2d 548 (Minn. 1977); Carter v. Tom's Truck Repair, Inc., 857 S.W.2d 172 (Mo. 1993); Vermont Union School Dist. v. H.P. Cummings Constr. Co., 469 A.2d 742 (Vt. 1983); Shell Oil Co. v. Christie, 607 P.2d 21 (Ariz. App. 1979).

[107]  *See* Firestone Tire & Rubber Co. v. Little, 639 S.W.2d 726, *appeal after remand,* 662 S.W.2d 473 (Ark. 1982). Corn Exchange Bank v. TriState Livestock Auction Co., 368 N.W.2d 596 (S.D. 1985).

to the court and the non-agreeing defendants.[108] A significant number of jurisdictions allow the fact of the existence of the agreement (albeit usually not its specific monetary terms) to be disclosed to the jury so that the jurors can evaluate the credibility or bias of the parties to the agreement.[109] Finally, some courts have suggested that to preserve the non-agreeing defendant's right to a fair trial, he should be allowed to have the trial of the case against him severed from the trial against the contracting defendant.[110]

Another type of agreement similar to a Mary Carter Agreement is a "loan-receipt" agreement.[111] Here, the contracting defendant gives a non-interest bearing loan to the plaintiff who is obligated to repay all or a portion of the loan if the plaintiff either recovers from a non-agreeing defendant or the recovery from the non-agreeing defendant exceeds the amount of the loan. For example, P might settle with and release defendant A from liability in exchange for a loan from A to P of $25,000, none of which is to be repaid to A if P loses her case against B at trial, but which is repayable to A to the extent of the amount P recovers from B. Thus, if P gets a $15,000 verdict against B, P repays that amount to A but keeps the original $25,000. Alternatively, P might settle with A for a loan of $25,000, repayable to A only to the extent P gets a verdict against B that exceeds the amount of the loan. Thus, if P gets a verdict against B for $15,000, P owes A nothing and nets $40,000; if the verdict is $35,000, P nets $50,000 with A being repaid $10,000; if the verdict is $100,000, P nets $75,000 after repaying to A all of the $25,000 loan.

To the extent such an agreement otherwise contains the common features of a Mary Carter agreement (e.g., the obligatory participation of the contracting defendant as a continuing party in the suit), a loan-receipt agreement might be prohibited on public policy grounds.[112] However, under the usual loan-receipt agreement, the contracting defendant enters into a true settlement with the plaintiff in the sense of being discharged from the case as a party-defendant,

---

[108] See, e.g., Gum v. Dudley, 505 S.E.2d 391 (W. Va. 1997); Ratterree v. Bartlett, 707 P.2d 1063 (Kan. 1985); Johnson v. Moberg, 334 N.W.2d 411 (Minn. 1983); Cox v. Kelsey-Hayes Co., 594 P.2d 354 (Okla. 1978).

[109] See, e.g., Thibodeaux v. Ferrellgas Inc., 717 So.2d 668 (La. Ct. App. 3d Cir. 1998); Franklin v. Morrison, 711 A.2d 177 (Md. 1998); Stam v. Mack, 984 S.W.2d 747 (Tex. App. 1999); Ratterree v. Bartlett, 707 P.2d 1063 (Kan. 1985); L.J. Vontz Constr. Co. v. Alliance Industries Inc., 338 N.W.2d 60 (Neb. 1983); Cox v. Kelsey-Hayes Co., 594 P.2d 354 (Okla. 1978); Hatfield v. Continental Imports, Inc., 610 A.2d 446 (Pa. 1992); Riggle v. Allied Chemical Corp., 378 S.E.2d 282 (W. Va. 1989); Corn Exchange Bank v. TriState Livestock Auction Co., 368 N.W.2d 596 (S.D. 1985); Poston v. Barnes, 363 S.E.2d 888 (S.C. 1987); Carter v. Tom's Trucking Repair, Inc. 857 S.W.2d 172 (Mo. 1993); Fullenkamp v. Newcomer 508 N.E.2d 37 (Ind. App. 1987); Gatto v. Walgreen Drug Co., 337 N.E.2d 23 (Ill. 1975); Firestone Tire & Rubber Co v. Little 639 S.W.2d 726 (Ark. 1982); Sequoia Mfg. Co. v. Halee Const. Co., 570 P.2d 782 (Ariz. 1977); Bohna v. Hughes, Thorsness, Gantz, Powell & Brundin, 828 P.2d 745 (Alaska 1992). Where the agreement contains self-serving language that would be prejudicial to the non-agreeing defendant, that language would be excised from disclosure to the jury. See, e.g., General Motors Corp. v. Lahocki, 410 A.2d 1039 (Md. 1980); Carter Tom's Truck Repair, Inc., 857 S.W.2d 172 (Mo. 1993). 84 U. Det. Mercy L. Rev. 61 (Fall 2006), "Tort Law — Settlement Agreements — With "Mary Carter-Style" Agreements, Fairness Served by Disclosure to the Jury must be Weighed Against the Countervailing Interest of Encouraging Settlements. Hashem v. Les Stanford Oldsmobile, Inc. 697, N.W.2d 558 (Mich. Ct. App. 2005)."

[110] See Burkett v. Crulo Trucking Co., 355 N.E.2d 253 (Ind. App. 1976).

[111] See generally, Annotation: Validity and Effect of "Loan Receipt" Agreement Between Injured Party and One Tortfeasor, for Loan Refundable to Extent of Injured Party's Recovery from a Cotortfeasor, 62 A.L.R.3d 1111 (1975).

[112] See 22 A.L.R.5th 483 at 498 n. 8 (1994).

although he might be called to testify as a witness in the plaintiff's action against one or more non-agreeing defendant-tortfeasors. Largely because of this difference between a loan-receipt agreement and Mary Carter agreement, the courts have refused to invalidate the former on public policy grounds, particularly if the loan must be disclosed to the court and opposing counsel and if the fact of the existence of the loan agreement may be admitted into evidence in the plaintiff's trial against the non-agreeing defendant.[113] The courts have also rejected contentions that loan-receipt agreements should be declared invalid on grounds of unlawful maintenance or champerty (*i.e.*, the common-law rule that one having no interest in a suit may not fund the plaintiff's action or do so in return for receiving a portion of the plaintiff's recovery),[114] or as an illegal sale of a tort claim.[115]

Many jurisdictions hold that a loan-receipt agreement is nothing more than an enforceable loan, and therefore it has neither the effect of discharging all non-agreeing joint tortfeasors from liability nor the effect of allowing them to receive a *pro tanto* reduction in liability corresponding to the amount of the loan if they are sued by the plaintiff.[116] On the other hand, some jurisdictions have construed loan-receipt agreements as covenants not to sue, thereby requiring that any verdict the plaintiff recovers against a non-agreeing defendant must be reduced by the amount advanced under the loan-receipt agreement between the plaintiff and the contracting defendant.[117]

It should be apparent from the foregoing that Mary Carter agreements are much more controversial than loan-receipt agreements. Even if you are permitted to enter into a Mary Carter agreement on behalf of your client, you will usually be required to disclose the terms of the agreement to counsel for the non-agreeing defendant and to the court, and the plaintiff and the contracting defendant can be rigorously cross-examined at trial about the existence of the agreement to undermine their credibility. This may significantly, though not entirely, undercut the benefits of such an agreement to the contracting parties.

On the other hand, loan-receipt agreements are far less controversial. For the plaintiff and contracting defendant, such an agreement has many of the same advantages as a Mary Carter agreement, so long as the particular jurisdiction does not treat the loan-receipt agreement as a covenant not to sue so as to reduce the non-agreeing defendant's liability to the plaintiff by the amount advanced under the loan. Even though some jurisdictions also permit the non-agreeing defendant to cross-examine the plaintiff and contracting defendant about the existence of their agreement, this impeachment is likely to be somewhat less destructive than in the Mary Carter situation because the contracting defendant in a loan-receipt agreement will not be a "party" at trial and might not even be called as a witness at trial.

---

[113] *See, e.g.*, Reese v. Chicao, B & Q. R. Co., 303 N.E.2d 382 (Ill. 1973); State v. Ingram, 399 N.E.2d 808 (Ind. App. 1980).

[114] *See, e.g.*, Cullen v. Atchison, T. & S.F.R. Co., 507 P.2d 353 (Kan. 1973).

[115] *See, e.g.*, Biven v. Charlie's Hobby Shop, 500 S.W.2d 597 (Ky. 1973).

[116] *See, e.g.*, Reese v. Chicago B. & Q. R. Co., 303 N.E.2d 382 (Ill. 1973); American Transport Co. v. Central I.R. Co, 264 N.E.2d 64 (Ind. 1970); Crocker v. New England Power Co., 202 N.E.2d 793 (Mass. 1964); Biven v. Charlie's Hobby Shop, 500 S.W.2d 597 (Ky. 1973).

[117] *See, e.g.*, Bolton v. Ziegler, 111 F. Supp. 516 (Iowa 1953); Cullen v. Atchison T. & S.F.R. Co., 507 P.2d 353 (Kan. 1973); Jensen v. Beaird, 696 P.2d 612 (Wash. App. 1985). *See also* Bohna v. Hughes, et. al., 828 P.2d 745 (Alaska 1992).

If you represent the non-agreeing defendant in a case where a Mary Carter or loan-receipt agreement might be afoot between the plaintiff and another tortfeasor, you should engage in appropriate discovery to determine whether either of these agreements is at play. If so, in jurisdictions which require that the terms of the agreement be disclosed to you, you may be able to learn much about the plaintiff's target and resistance points which may give you added leverage in negotiating a potential settlement with the plaintiff. In addition, the fact that you will usually be permitted to cross-examine the plaintiff and contracting defendant about the existence of the agreement at trial may induce the plaintiff to ultimately accept a reasonable settlement with your client.

## § 17.07   SETTLEMENTS REQUIRING JUDICIAL APPROVAL

A settlement made on behalf of a minor or incompetent, whether made before or after a lawsuit is filed, is subject to court approval. Although the procedures for judicial approval vary among jurisdictions, most require a hearing before the judge who decides (1) whether the proposed settlement is reasonable in light of the minor's or incompetent's damages; (2) the amount of attorney's fees that should be paid out of the settlement funds for the minor's or incompetent's lawyer; (3) the amount of any settlement funds that should be applied to satisfy unpaid medical expenses and the interests of any lienholder (*see* § 17.10), or be paid to a parent, guardian, or conservator for reimbursement for medical or other expenses incurred on behalf of the minor or incompetent; and (4) how the net settlement proceeds will be held for the benefit of, or distributed to, the minor or incompetent.

If the proposed settlement is agreed upon before a lawsuit has been instituted, usually a *pro forma* complaint and answer is filed, along with a motion or petition requesting judicial approval of the settlement. If the proposed settlement is reached after litigation has commenced, the motion or petition is simply filed in the cause. In either case, a guardian *ad litem* (if there is no guardian of the estate) must be appointed to represent the minor's interests, and that guardian will usually be a parent of the child. The guardian ad litem and the lawyers typically attend the hearing on the motion to approve the settlement for the minor and defendant, and some jurisdictions require that the minor or incompetent also attend.

If the court fails to approve the settlement and no satisfactory alternative settlement is approved, the case must be tried. If the court approves the settlement on behalf of a minor, the net settlement proceeds are usually placed in a "blocked account" (*e.g.*, an account in a federally insured bank, savings and loan, credit union, or trust company) in the name of the guardian *ad litem* as trustee for the minor. The funds may not be removed from the account without court approval prior to the minor's reaching the age of majority. In some jurisdictions, if the settlement proceeds to the minor do not exceed a certain amount (*e.g.* $5,000), the court may allow the funds to be paid directly to the guardian *ad litem*, without bond, to be held in trust for the minor until the minor reaches majority age. In the case of an incompetent who is not a minor, the funds may be delivered in trust to the guardian *ad litem* or some other trustee to be held and used for the benefit of the incompetent.

Finally, settlements in class actions also require judicial approval. The principal plaintiff in a class-action suit has a fiduciary obligation to the other class members and may not compromise the group's interests for personal gain. Thus, the federal courts[118] and most state jurisdictions require that notice of the proposed settlement be provided to all members of the class who are then afforded a hearing on any objections they may have to the settlement before the court decides whether to approve or reject it.[119] In determining whether the proposed settlement is fair, adequate, and reasonable, the court will consider such factors as (1) the views of the class members, (2) the views of class counsel, (3) the extent of and any reasons for opposition to the settlement, (4) the existence of any improper collusion behind the settlement, (5) the current stage of the litigation, (6) the likelihood of success at trial, (7) the complexity, expense, and likely duration of the lawsuit, and (8) the range of potential recovery.[120]

## § 17.08    TAXATION OF SETTLEMENT FUNDS

Under federal law, § 104(a)(2) of the Internal Revenue Code excludes from gross income damages received on account of "personal physical injuries or physical sickness."[121] The exclusion applies regardless of whether the funds are received from a judgment or by settlement, or are received in a lump sum or as periodic payments (*e.g.*, through a structured settlement).[122] The exclusion applies except in the case of amounts attributable to and not in excess of deductions for medical expenses permitted under § 213 of the Code. Thus, generally, compensatory damages received from the settlement of a physical personal injury case are not taxable.

However, under § 104(a)(2) of the I.R.C., punitive damages are generally not excludable from gross income and are thus taxable. Also, "emotional distress" (including physical symptoms thereof such as insomnia, headaches, stomach disorders, etc.) does not fall within the definition of "personal physical injuries or physical sickness." Thus, for example, if damages for emotional distress are not attributable to a physical injury or sickness but are merely awarded in connection with a claim for employment discrimination or injury to reputation, the emotional distress damages are generally taxable. However, if the damages for emotional distress paid by the tortfeasor constitute reimbursement to the plaintiff for medical expenses incurred for treatment of the emotional distress, such damages are excludable from income provided they have not otherwise been deducted from income by the plaintiff.[123] On the other hand, if damages for emotional distress are attributable to a physical injury or sickness proximately caused by a tortfeasor, the emotional distress damages are generally excludable from gross income.

In addition, any income derived from the investment of the payment received from a lump-sum settlement or from the investment of periodic payments received under a structured settlement is generally taxable. For example, if the plaintiff receives a $100,000 lump-sum settlement for physical personal injuries and places that sum in an investment account that yields 10% annually, the $100,000 is not taxable but the $10,000 earned in the first year and all interest earned in subsequent

---

[118]  *See* Fed. R. Civ. P. 23(e).

[119]  *See generally,* Boyd v. Bechtel Corp., 485 F. Supp. 610 (N.D. Cal. 1979).

[120]  Austin v. Hopper, 15 F. Supp. 2d 1210 (M.D. Ala. 1998).

[121]  26 U.S.C. § 104(a)(2) (1996).

[122]  Id.

[123]  *See* Id., § 104(a) last sentence.

years is taxable. By contrast, if the plaintiff has negotiated a structured settlement providing for total compensation of $1 million to be paid in periodic payments over a number of years, so long as the plaintiff is only entitled to receive each periodic payment as it becomes due and has no control over the funding source or ability to change the amount or timing of the payments,[124] neither the $1 million nor the amount of any periodic payment is taxable, although any income the plaintiff derives from investing any periodic payment is taxable. (*see also* § 17.09).

Where a settlement is in part a satisfaction of a claim for personal physical injury and in part for a non-physical injury claim, the written settlement agreement should specifically distinguish between the non-taxable amount of the settlement being paid for the physical injury and the taxable amount being paid for the non-physical injury. Generally, a tax court will accept such an allocation so long as it results from arm's length negotiations.[125] In the absence of an express allocation in the settlement documentation, the I.R.S. will generally allocate the taxable versus non-taxable portions of the settlement in proportion to the amounts prayed for in the complaint.[126] For example, if a complaint contains a first cause of action in tort for $100,000 in (non-taxable) compensatory damages on account of physical injury or physical sickness and a second cause of action for breach of contract for $900,000 in (taxable) lost profits, any settlement — in the absence of explicit settlement documentation to the contrary — will generally be allocated one-tenth to non-taxable damages and nine-tenths to taxable damages. Such a result would seriously undermine the value of the settlement to the plaintiff if the parties did not intend this allocation.

Tax law is, of course, a highly complex, changing, and specialized field. Thus, unless you possess independent expertise in the subject, you should always consult a tax lawyer if tax implications may be important in negotiating a settlement. Similarly, after a settlement has been finalized, if you are uncertain about whether or to what extent your client's settlement funds may be taxable, you should advise him to consult a tax specialist. Providing erroneous tax advice in connection with settlement may constitute malpractice.

## § 17.09   LUMP-SUM AND STRUCTURED SETTLEMENTS

The most common type of monetary settlement in the litigation context is the payment of a single lump-sum in exchange for the dismissal of the legal claim. The advantages of this type of settlement are simplicity and finality. After both parties execute the agreement, there is no need for them to monitor any future performance under it.

On the other hand, particularly in personal injury cases where extensive damages are involved, the parties will sometimes enter into a "structured settlement" by which, after an initial lump-sum (or "front money") is paid, the plaintiff will receive future periodic payments on a monthly, quarterly, semi-annual, or annual basis that are paid for a specified number of years or over the plaintiff's lifetime. The amounts of these future payments are predetermined, but they may be set to increase or decrease over time. A structured settlement thus requires

---

[124]   *See* H.G. Miller, *Art of Advocacy-Settlement*, § 10:32[4] (1999).

[125]   *See* Seay v. Commissioner, 58 T.C. 32 (1972).

[126]   Rev. Rul. 85-98, 1985-2 C.B. 55.

on-going performance by the payor and mechanisms by which the plaintiff will be reasonably assured that the payor will not default on its future obligations.

The most common type of structured settlement is the "single-premium immediate annuity." An annuity is a contract between the defendant or the defendant's insurance carrier and an annuity issuer (usually a life insurance company), whereby, in exchange for the defense's payment of a single premium to the annuity issuer, the issuer promises to make specified payments to the plaintiff on specified dates. The defendant or its insurance carrier owns the annuity, and the plaintiff is the sole beneficiary unless the settlement documents designate some other beneficiary upon the plaintiff's death. The annuity is "immediate" in the sense that all of its terms regarding the amount and timing of payments are immediately known at inception.

Ordinarily, if the annuity issuer defaults on making the payments to the plaintiff, the defendant or its insurer will remain ultimately liable for the payments. Quite often, however, and subject to the express approval of the plaintiff, the defendant or its insurer will absolve itself from any liability for a default by assigning that liability to a "Qualified Assignee" as permitted by § 130 of the Internal Revenue Code. To do this, the defendant or its insurer pays the qualified assignee (usually a bank or some corporate affiliate of the life insurance company issuing the annuity) the premium to purchase the annuity and an assignment fee. The assignment corporation then pays the premium to an annuity issuer who, in turn, issues an annuity contract and makes the periodic annuity payments directly to the plaintiff on behalf of the assignment corporation. Under this arrangement, the assignment corporation becomes the ultimate obligor for the future payments in the event of a default by the annuity issuer, and all liability of the defendant or its insurer is extinguished.

Apart from the single-premium immediate annuity, there are a number of other, albeit less common, methods for managing and funding a structured settlement. For example, the defendant or its liability carrier might establish a trust administered by an independent trustee who assumes liability for and makes the future payments to the plaintiff with monies funded by United States Treasury bonds, and the plaintiff is given a security interest in the bonds held by the trust. In lieu of this arrangement, the defendant or its carrier might establish and fund a "reversionary trust" which obligates the defense to pay additional amounts into the trust to meet unforeseen care costs for the plaintiff, but all funds in the trust revert back to the defense in the event of the plaintiff's death. Yet another alternative is a "settlement fund management trust" by which the defendant-carrier's policy limits are paid over to an independent trustee who invests the funds and makes periodic payments to or for the benefit of the plaintiff in a way that roughly emulates the payment stream that would be paid by an annuity issuer.

For the defendant or its liability carrier, the principal advantage of a structured settlement through a single-premium immediate annuity is that a large annuity to be paid over a number of years can be purchased for less than what it would cost the defense to pay a single lump-sum settlement to the plaintiff. The advantages to the plaintiff are that the periodic payments are tax free (which is not the case with respect to any income the plaintiff earns from investing a single lump-sum); the periodic payments may be flexibly designed to meet the plaintiff's anticipated needs (albeit this flexibility ceases once the structure is established); and there is little risk that the plaintiff will mismanage or squander the entire settlement — an outcome that would be particularly disastrous if lifelong medical or custodial care is necessary. On the other hand, a structured settlement might not be desirable for a plaintiff who is elderly, who otherwise wants or has a special need to receive a large sum immediately, or who is capable of wisely investing a lump-sum. In addition, because a structured settlement involves fixed payments that are not changeable once agreed upon at the outset, the purchasing power of those payments will be undercut in the event of future inflation, and the value of the overall settlement to the plaintiff will be reduced if interest rates rise substantially in the future.

In formulating or evaluating a proposal for a structured settlement, many plaintiffs' lawyers employ the services of a structured-settlement consultant, and defendants' lawyers often rely on the expertise of an annuity broker who sells annuity products. Even the most experienced personal-injury lawyers often utilize such an expert in evaluating the case, designing an appropriate structure, and advising or assisting in negotiations. Apart from the desirability of drawing upon a specialist in the field, some of the conventional wisdom about considerations that should be taken into account in connection with structured settlements includes the following:[127]

(1) For the plaintiff, a structured settlement is often desirable when the injuries call for long-term or life-long care; the plaintiff is a minor or incompetent; or the plaintiff is either inexperienced in managing a large sum of money or has spendthrift propensities.

(2) A structured settlement may be inappropriate for a plaintiff who is experienced in managing a large sum of money or who is willing to have a third person such as a trustee manage the investment of a lump-sum. If most of the payments from a structured settlement will be spent on tax-deductible medical care, the tax advantage of structured payments may be illusory because the investment interest earned from a lump-sum settlement can be offset by the large tax deduction of the medical expenses.

(3) For the defense, a structured settlement is often desirable as a means of settling the case in a way that meets the plaintiff's special needs, and the defense should be expected to save at least 5% to 10% of the fair settlement value of the case on the structured portion of the settlement.

(4) It is imperative that plaintiff's counsel research the financial stability of the *ultimate obligor* of the periodic payments — *i.e.*, the defendant or its carrier in the event it will be the owner of the annuity, or the qualified assignee in the event the defendant or its carrier will assign (with the plaintiff's permission) the ultimate liability for the payments to an assignment corporation. That is, the plaintiff should not agree to any qualified assignment to an entity that does not have a high financial rating; and if the defendant carrier remains as the ultimate obligor and has a low financial rating, the plaintiff should insist that the carrier assign its liability to a highly-rated assignment corporation.

(5) If the defendant or its insurer remains the ultimate obligor for the structured payments, it should purchase the annuity only from a highly rated annuity issuer. In most situations, the defendant or its carrier will

---

[127] *See* H. Miller, *Art of Advocacy-Settlement*, Chapter 10 (1999); Schoenfield & Schoenfield, *Legal Negotiations*, § 7.03 (1988).

want to extinguish its ultimate liability and close the file by entering into a qualified assignment with an assignment corporation.

(6) When plaintiff's counsel negotiates the amount of initial "front money" paid apart from and in advance of the periodic payments, counsel should be sure that this amount is sufficient to cover any liens of health-care providers or other entities (*see* § 17.10), unpaid medical and litigation expenses, attorney's fees on the structured portion of the settlement calculated on the cost or present value of the annuity whichever is lower,[128] and the immediate needs of the plaintiff.

(7) To ensure that the periodic payments received by the plaintiff are not taxable, the structured settlement should not give the plaintiff any right to (a) control the funding source or the investment of the funding medium, (b) own the annuity or change the beneficiary of the annuity, or (c) accelerate, increase, or decrease the periodic payments.[129] However, where a qualified assignment is involved, the plaintiff may perfect a "security interest" in the annuity contract under applicable state law so long as the plaintiff has no ownership rights in the contract and cannot assign or otherwise use it as any form of collateral.[130]

(8) To guard against the adverse effects of inflation, the structured settlement might include an escalator provision that increases the amount of the periodic payments each year (*e.g.*, an escalator of 3%–5% per annum), or include a so-called "step rate" or "plateau plan" by which the amount of the periodic payments are increased every certain number of years (*e.g.*, $4,000 per month for the first five years; $4,100 per month for the next five years; $4,200 per month for the next five years, etc.).

(9) Plaintiff's counsel should insist upon disclosure of the actual cost of the premium that will be paid to purchase the annuity contract,[131] and be sure that the annuity being purchased represents fair market value.

(10) The structured settlement agreement should be in writing and carefully drafted to preserve the tax-exempt status of periodic payments.

---

[128] *See* Wyatt v. United States, 783 F.2d 45 (6th Cir. 1986); Danninger & Palfin, How to Evaluate Proposals; Avoid Fee Disputes, 24 Trial 38 (Dec. 1988) (citing the position of the Board of Governors of the Association of Trial Lawyers of America).

[129] The importance of these limitations is to prevent the plaintiff from being deemed in "constructive receipt" of the principal of the structured settlement payments in which event they would be taxable under § 451(a) of the Internal Revenue Code. *See* Treas. Reg. § 1.451-2(a); Rev. Rul. 77-230, 1977-2 C.B. 214; Rev. Rul. 79-220, 1979-2 C.B. 74; Rev. Rul. 79-313, 1979-2 C.B. 75.

[130] *See* I.R.C. § 130; I.R.S. Priv. Ltr. Rul. 92-53745 (October 6, 1992).

[131] Obtaining this information in no way impairs the tax-exempt status of the periodic payments received by the plaintiff. *See* I.R.S. Priv. Ltr. Rul. 83-33035 (May 16, 1983).

## § 17.10   LIENS OF HEALTH-CARE PROVIDERS AND OTHER ENTITIES ON SETTLEMENT FUNDS

The vast majority of jurisdictions, usually by statute or sometimes through the common law, recognize the right of a hospital,[132] physician or other health-care provider[133] to assert a lien upon the settlement funds received by an injured person from a tortfeasor to the extent of the reasonable value of medical services that the health-care provider rendered to the injured person on account of the tortfeasor's negligence and for which the health-care provider has not been paid. Statutes vary significantly in terms of when and how such a lien may be asserted, the permissible extent or amount of the lien, for what type of injuries the lien may be asserted, and the means by which and the persons against whom the lien may be enforced. In addition, if the injured person has received benefits from a public health-care provider or program, it also may have subrogation or associated lien rights on settlement funds, and it even may have a right to participate in settlement negotiations or approve settlements between the injured plaintiff and the tortfeasor.[134]

Significantly, many statutes provide that any person who has proper notice of the lien and thereafter disburses settlement funds to the injured person without first satisfying the lien may be liable to the health-care provider for its unpaid charges. For example, such liability may be imposed upon the tortfeasor or his insurer,[135] or upon the attorney representing the injured party.[136] In any event, a health-care provider may also sue the injured party for payment of the unpaid charges.

Workers' Compensation statutes also provide for liens upon settlement funds paid by third-party tortfeasors in certain circumstances. Typically, workers' compensation statutes provide medical benefits and partial wages to employees who are out of work as a result of being injured on the job, irrespective of the fault of the employer or employee in causing the injury. If an employee while working in the course and scope of her employment is injured as a result of the negligence of a third-party tortfeasor, she may independently seek damages against the tortfeasor and also avail herself of any workers' compensation benefits that she is otherwise entitled to receive from employer. In this situation, workers' compensation statutes variously provide that the employer (or its workers' compensation insurance carrier) has a right to be reimbursed for the benefits it has paid which are attributable to the fault of the third-party tortfeasor, and a right to a credit against

---

[132] *See, e.g.,* Parnell v. Adventist Health System/West et al., 35 Cal. 4th 595, 109 P.3d 69 26, Cal. Rptr. 3d 569, (2005); Nodak Mutual Insurance Co. et al. v. Stegman, 2002 ND 113, 647 N.W.2d 133; and Tankersley v. Parkview Hospital, Inc., 791 N.E.2d 201 (Ind. 2003). *See generally,* Annotation: *Construction, Operation, and Effect of Statute Giving Hospital Lien Against Recovery from Tortfeasor Causing Patient's Injuries,* 16 A.L.R.5th 262 (1993).

[133] *See, e.g.,* Midwest Neurosurgery, P.C. v. State Farm Insurance Companies, 268 Neb. 642, 686 N.W.2d 572 (2004); Blankenbaker, D.C., dba Vax-D Medical Centers v. Jonovich, 205 Ariz. 383, 71 P.3d 910 (2003). *See generally,* Annotation: *Physicians' and Surgeons' Liens,* 39 A.L.R.5th 787 (1996).

[134] *See, e.g.,* The Federal Medical Recovery Act, 42 U.S.C. 2651 *et. seq.,* 7 A.L.R. Fed. 289.

[135] *See, e.g.,* Charlotte-Mecklenburg Hosp. Auth. v. First of Ga. Ins. Co., 455 S.E.2d 655 (N.C. 1995); National Ins. Ass'n. v. Parkview Memorial Hosp., 590 N.E.2d 1141 (Ind. App. 1992); St. Luke's Hosp. v. Consolidated Mut. Ins. Co., 32 Misc.2d 657, 217 N.Y.S.2d 843 (1961); Republic Ins. Co. v. Shotwell, 407 S.W.2d 864 (Tex. Civ. App. 1966).

[136] *See, e.g.,* Charity Hosp. Of Louisiana v. Band, 593 So.2d 1392 (La. App. 1992); Elizabeth General Hosp. & Dispensary v. Longobardi, 116 A. 471 (N.J. 1933).

paying future benefits to the extent of the net settlement recovered by the employee in the third-party action. A similar right of reimbursement exists in favor of the United States under the Federal Employees' Compensation Act.[137] In some state jurisdictions, the amount of the lien or credit is adjusted in proportion to any fault attributed to the employee or employer in causing the injury.[138]

Thus, if you represent the injured party, it is imperative that you have a complete understanding of any statutory obligations you may have to first reimburse a lienholder for medical charges or benefits before distributing the proceeds of any settlement to your client. Similarly, you must thoroughly understand these obligations if you represent the tortfeasor or his insurer. As a matter of practice in many jurisdictions, insurers will insist that in exchange for making a settlement payment to the injured party, the injured party must sign a Settlement Agreement and Release that includes an indemnity clause by which she agrees to hold the insurer and insured-tortfeasor harmless from the claims that any private or public lienholder may have upon the settlement funds. (*See* example of such a clause in § 17.05).

## § 17.11  CONFIDENTIALITY OF SETTLEMENTS AND SETTLEMENT DISCUSSIONS

Approximately three-fourths of the states have adopted rules of evidence that are substantially similar to the Federal Rules of Evidence. Rule 408 of the Federal Rules provides:

> Evidence of (1) furnishing or offering or promising to furnish, or (2) accepting or offering or promising to accept, a valuable consideration in compromising or attempting to compromise a claim which was disputed as to either validity or amount, is not admissible to prove liability for or invalidity of the claim or its amount. Evidence of conduct or statements made in compromise negotiations is likewise not admissible. This rule does not require the exclusion of any evidence otherwise discoverable merely because it is presented in the course of compromise negotiations. This rule does not require exclusion when the evidence is offered for another purpose, such as proving bias or prejudice of a witness, negativing a contention of undue delay, or proving an effort to obstruct a criminal investigation or prosecution.

Consistent with the public policy of encouraging settlement of disputed claims,[139] under this rule, evidence of an offer to settle,[140] acceptance of that offer, or the

---

[137] *See generally*, Annotation, *Construction and Application of Provisions of Federal Employees' Compensation Act (5 U.S.C. § 8132) Requiring Compensation Beneficiary Who Recovers from Third Person or Receives Money in Settlement of Claim, to Refund to United States Amount of Compensation Paid, After Deducting Cost of Suit and Reasonable Attorney's Fee*, 17 A.L.R. Fed. 494 (1973).

[138] *See generally*, A Larson, *Workmen's Compensation Law* § 71 (1990).

[139] *See* Cheyenne River Sioux Tribe v. United States, 806 F.2d 1046, 1050 (Fed. Cir. 1986); Morley-Murphy Co. v. Zenith Electronics Corp., 910 F. Supp. 450, 456 (W.D. Wis. 1996). *See also* 4 Wigmore, *Evidence*, § 1061 at 36 (Chadbourn rev. 1972) (true reason for excluding offers of compromise is that they are essentially irrelevant as manifesting "merely a desire for peace, not a concession of wrong done.").

[140] Pierce v. F.R. Tripler & Co. 955 F.2d 820, 827 (2d Cir. 1992); Winchester Packaging, Inc. v. Mobile Chemical Co., 14 F.3d 316, 319 (7th Cir. 1994) (a demand for payment is not an offer to settle).

settlement itself[141] of a disputed claim[142] is not admissible at trial to prove liability, or invalidity of the claim or its amount.[143] Evidence of conduct or statements made in settlement negotiations is also inadmissible.[144] The rule applies to settlements and settlement negotiations regardless of whether they were between the parties in the instant suit or involved a third party,[145] and extends to conduct or statements of parties, their agents, and their lawyers.[146]

The rule's exclusion is limited, however, only to "disputed" claims (*i.e.*, in situations where there is "an apparent difference of opinion between the parties as to the validity of a claim").[147] For example, the rule does not apply to an offer to settle a claim that has not been asserted,[148] to a mere "demand" for payment, to mere payment in the face of a demand,[149] or to mere "business discussions" about a matter that has not ripened into a dispute.[150] In addition, the rule does not exclude evidence of facts or documents merely because they were presented or revealed in the course of settlement negotiations if such evidence is otherwise discoverable through the discovery process[151] or obtainable from independent sources. Thus, a party cannot render evidence inadmissible under the rule simply by presenting it during settlement.[152] However, statements made during negotiations or documents prepared as a result of them are barred.[153]

Evidence in connection with a settlement may be admissible for a relevant purpose *other* than to prove liability or invalidity of the claim or its amount, such as to prove bias or prejudice,[154] to impeach one who has entered into a Mary Carter or loan-receipt agreement (*see* § 17.06), to negate a contention of undue delay (*e.g.*, evidence that good faith settlement discussions were underway to rebut a contention that a party purposefully delayed certain action to the detriment of another),[155] or to prove an effort to obstruct a criminal investigation or prosecution (*e.g.*,

---

[141] Dolese v. United States, 605 F.2d 1146 (10th Cir. 1979); Burns v. City of Des Peres, 534 F.2d 103, 112 n. 9 (8th Cir. 1976); Hudspeth v. C.I.R., 914 F.2d 1207, 1213 (9th Cir. 1990).

[142] McCormick, *Evidence*, § 266 at 194 (4th ed. 1992); Affiliated Manufacturers, Inc. v. Aluminum Co. of America, 56 F.3d 521, 527–28 (3d Cir. 1995).

[143] Deere & Co. v. International Harvester Co., 710 F.2d 1551, 1557 (Fed. Cir. 1983).

[144] *See* Russell v. PPG Indus. Inc, 953 F.2d 326, 333–34 (7th Cir. 1992) (information from mock trial used to motivate parties to settle was inadmissible); Ramada Dev. Co. v. Rauch, 644 F.2d 1097, 1106 (5th Cir. 1981) (exclusion of architect's report used for settlement negotiations)

[145] Kennon v. Slipstreamer, Inc., 794 F.2d 1067, 1069 (5th Cir. 1986); McInnis v. A.M.F. Inc., 765 F.2d 240, 247–251 (1st Cir. 1985); Missouri Pacific Ry. Co. v. Arkansas Sheriff Boy's Ranch, 655 S.W.2d 389, 394–395 (Ark. 1983).

[146] *See* Pierce v. F.R. Tripler & Co., 955 F.2d 820, 827 (2d Cir. 1992).

[147] Alpex Computer Corp. v. Nintendo Co., 770 F. Supp. 161, 163 (S.D. N.Y. 1991).

[148] *See* Cassino v. Reichhold Chemicals, Inc. 817 F.2d 1338 (9th Cir. 1987).

[149] *See* United States v. Hooper, 569 F.2d 219 (7th Cir. 1979); In re B.D. International Discount Corp., 701 F.2d 1071, 1074 (2d Cir. 1983); Winchester Packaging Inc. v. Mobile Chemical Co., 14 F.3d 316, 319 (7th Cir. 1994).

[150] Big O Tire Dealers Inc. v. Goodyear Tire & Rubber Co., 561 F.2d 1365, 1372–73 (10th Cir. 1977).

[151] *See, e.g.*, Ramada Dev. Co. v. Rauch, 644 F.2d 1097, 1107 (5th Cir. 1981).

[152] *See* Center for Auto Safety v. Dept. of Justice, 576 F. Supp. 739, 749 & n. 23 (D.D.C.1983).

[153] Ramada Dev. Co. v. Rauch, 644 F.2d 1097, 1107 (5th Cir. 1981).

[154] Hudspeth v. Commissioner of IRS, 914 F.2d 1207, 1213–14 (9th Cir. 1990).

[155] California & Hawaiian Sugar Co. v. Kansas City Terminal Warehouse Co., 602 F. Supp. 183, 188 (W.D. Mo. 1985).

evidence of trying to "buy off" the prosecution or a prosecution witness).[156] The rule's list of admissible purposes is not exclusive.[157] Thus, for example, proof of a settlement and its terms are admissible in a contract action to enforce a settlement agreement as long as the suit does not embrace an issue about the validity of the underlying claim.[158]

Because Rule 408 applies only to evidence at trial between the actual litigants before the court and is limited to proof regarding "liability for or invalidity of the claim or its amount," the rule provides only narrow protection against the disclosure of settlements and matters occurring during settlement discussions. The rule does not prohibit disclosure of such matters outside of the courtroom, provides no blanket protection against formal discovery of such matters in the litigation process,[159] and generally does not provide a litigant with protection against the disclosure of other information he might want to protect such as trade secrets or other proprietary data.[160] In addition, as mentioned above, the rule is entirely inapplicable to parties who are negotiating over a matter that does not involve a disputed claim.

In light of these limitations under Rule 408, parties negotiating either a disputed claim or non-litigation matter will sometimes enter into a confidentiality agreement regarding their negotiations or settlement. For example, they might agree not to disclose the fact that negotiations are occurring, the participants in the negotiations, certain information furnished by either side during negotiations, or the terms of a settlement if one is reached. To deter a breach of such an agreement, the parties might include a clause that permits enforcement by injunctive relief and provides for liquidated damages in the event of a breach. As between the signatories to such an agreement, the courts will generally enforce it[161] as well as any liquidated damages provision so long as those damages approximate actual damages.[162]

However, a confidentiality agreement may have limited force if a nonparty discloses the information that the contracting parties wished to protect, or a nonparty seeks disclosure of the confidential information for her own use in unrelated litigation or for some other purpose like "the public's right to know." A nonparty will generally not be bound by the agreement, and some courts have held

---

[156] *See* United States v. Gonzales, 748 F.2d 74, 78 (2d Cir. 1984); Advisory Committee Note to Rule 408.

[157] *See, e.g.,* United States v. Havert, 40 F.3d 197, 200 (7th Cir. 1994) (prior audit settlement admissible to show knowledge of duty); Johnson v. Hufo's Skateway, 949 F.2d 1338 (4th Cir. 1991) (consent decree admissible to show intent or motive to racially discriminate); Belton v. Fibreboard Corp., 724 F.2d 500 (5th Cir. 1984) (evidence of prior settlements admissible to show plaintiffs had been exposed to products of other defendants); Urico v. Parnell Oil Co., 708 F.2d 852 (1st Cir. 1983) (testimony about prior settlement negotiations admissible to show defendant prevented plaintiffs from mitigating their damages).

[158] Cates v. Morgan Portable Bldg. Corp., 780 F.2d 683, 691 (7th Cir. 1985); Catullo v. Metzner, 834 F.2d 1075, 1079 (1st Cir. 1987).

[159] *See, e.g.,* Uinta Oil Refining Co. v. Continental Oil Co., 226 F. Supp. 495 (D. Utah 1964).

[160] *See, e.g.,* Cipollone v. Liggett Group, Inc. 785 F.2d 1108, 1121 (3rd Cir. 1986). *See* Wigmore, *Evidence* § 2212 (McNaughten rev. 1991). On the other hand, a protective order might be sought under Rule 26(c) of the Federal Rules of Civil Procedure to prevent disclosure of such information.

[161] *See, e.g.,* Doe v. Roe, 93 Misc2d 201, 400 N.Y.S.2d 668 (1977).

[162] *See* Uniform Commercial Code, § 2-718; Farnesworth, *Contracts* § 12.18 (1982).

that the contracting parties to a confidentiality agreement may not "foreclose others obtaining, in the course of litigation, materials that are relevant to their efforts to vindicate a legal position."[163] Moreover, a third party may be able to compel disclosure of information otherwise protected by a confidentiality agreement if nondisclosure would violate public policy as where, for example, a public-records disclosure statute is applicable.[164]

With the burgeoning increase in court-annexed mediation and other dispute resolution programs, many jurisdictions have now enacted statutes or court rules that protect the confidentiality of settlement discussions through mediation privilege laws. The protection of confidentiality through a "privilege" may be much broader than the protection afforded by an evidentiary rule like Rule 408 because privileges usually bar persons subject to them from disclosing information not only in the course of adjudicative hearings but also in other contexts. Thus, a privilege may prevent not only the admissibility of certain evidence at trial, but may block the disclosure of information in discovery and in other proceedings or settings not governed by the rules of evidence. The growth of mediation privilege laws and rules stems from the public-policy view that extended confidentiality will encourage the use of mediation or other dispute resolution processes as a means for resolving disputes where traditional, two-party negotiations have failed.

State mediation privilege statutes and rules vary significantly in terms of what processes and persons are covered, the scope and sources of information protected, whether the privilege is qualified or absolute, who may invoke the privilege, in what settings the privilege may be asserted, and in what circumstances the privilege is inapplicable.[165] In most jurisdictions, for example, the mediation privilege applies only in certain publicly administered programs, such as child custody and visitation mediation or state labor department mediation. Other jurisdictions have a more generic privilege that extends to court-annexed mediation of civil or even criminal disputes, or to mediation programs having certain certification requirements for mediators.

Usually, the information that is privileged consists of all matters — whether oral, written, or expressed through conduct — that arise during the mediation. Other statutes more broadly protect the names of the participants to the mediation, communications with nonparties during the mediation, all information in control of the mediator or mediation agency, and sometimes the mediated agreement itself.[166] When the privilege applies, it usually prevents disclosure or use of the protected information in any proceeding in the jurisdiction — whether in discovery, in pretrial proceedings, at trial, or in administrative proceedings — and may be asserted by the mediator or any of the parties or other participants.[167]

---

[163] Grumman Aerospace Corp. v. Titanium Metals Corp., 91 FRD 84, 87–88, 32 FR Serv2d 1520 (E.D. N.Y. 1981). *Cf.*, Hinshaw, et al. v. Superior Court, 51 Cal. App. 4th 233, 58 Cal. Rptr. 2d 791 (6th Dist. 1966) (prohibiting nonsignatories from obtaining income information about physicians contained in confidentiality agreement).

[164] *See, e.g.,* Anchorage School Dist. v. Anchorage Daily News, 779 P.2d 1191 (Alaska 1989), later proceeding 803 P.2d 402 (1989).

[165] For a comprehensive compilation of state mediation privilege statutes and rules, *see* Nancy H. Rogers & Craig A. McEwen, *Mediation: Law, Policy and Practice*, Appendices (2d ed. 1994).

[166] *See* Nancy H. Rogers & Craig A. McEwen, *Mediation: Law, Policy & Practice*, § 9:12 (2d ed. 1994).

[167] *But see* Fenton v. Howard, 575 P.2d 318 (Ariz. 1978) (only mediator holds the privilege); In re

A number of statutes expressly provide for exceptions to the privilege, as where a governmental subdivision or agency is a party to the mediation and is subject to a "sunshine" or "open-meetings" law requiring that the affairs of the governmental entity be open to public scrutiny, where information obtained during the mediation gives rise to evidence of a felony or perjury, or where disclosure is necessary in a suit between a party and a mediator for damages arising from the mediation.[168] Other limitations on the extent of the privilege may exist where the courts interpret it as being "qualified" rather than absolute, as where disclosure is necessary to protect a criminal defendant's constitutional confrontation rights,[169] to otherwise prevent "manifest injustice" in a case or public harm,[170] or to preserve the public's First Amendment right of access to information about adjudicative proceedings.[171] Moreover, many jurisdictions have statutes that require certain professionals to report information about possible child abuse, child neglect, or certain felonies, and these statutes may override or operate independently from any mediation privilege.[172]

In sum, the current state of the law regarding the confidentiality of settlement agreements and settlement discussions outside of the trial setting remains to be more fully developed as states, the federal government, and the judiciary continue to promote various alternative dispute resolution programs and processes. On the one hand, there is wide recognition that confidentiality is a critical component to successful extra-judicial dispute resolution, but the public policy of promoting settlement must be balanced against competing public policies about the costs of confidentiality to the due process rights of litigants, the public's interest in preventing and punishing crime, and the public's interest in access to information to preserve the integrity of adjudicative proceedings. Thus, you must be alert to the fact that this is a rapidly developing and changing area of the law as legislatures and the courts continue to struggle to resolve the tension among competing public policies implicated by confidentiality in settlements and settlement discussions.

## § 17.12    FINALIZING SETTLEMENTS AND DISBURSING SETTLEMENT FUNDS

In the vast majority of cases, the terms of a settlement are, at first instance, orally agreed to between counsel for the plaintiff and counsel for the defendant or, as in most personal injury cases, between plaintiff's counsel and the insurance adjuster for the defendant's insurer. Ordinarily, oral agreements are binding unless

---

Marriage of Rosson, 178 Cal. App.3d 1094, 224 Cal. Rptr. 250 (1986) (same).

[168] *See* Nancy H. Rogers & Craig A. McEwen, *Mediation: Law, Policy & Practice*, § 9:12 (2d ed. 1994).

[169] *See, e.g.,* Davis v. Alaska, 415 U.S. 308, 94 S.Ct. 1105, 39 L.Ed2d 347 (1975) (holding that the confidentiality of juvenile records must yield to the criminal defendant's right to confront and cross-examine prosecution witnesses); Pennsylvania v. Ritchie, 480 U.S. 39, 107 S.Ct. 989, 94 L.Ed2d 40 (1987) (disclosure of privileged information may be necessary to protect a criminal defendant's due process right to exculpatory information).

[170] *See, e.g.,* Federal Administrative Alternative Dispute Resolution Act, 5 U.S.C. 584 (1990). *See also,* Project: Government Information and the Rights of Citizens, 73 Mich. L. Rev. 971 (1975)

[171] *See, e.g.,* FTC v. Standard Financial Management Corp., 830 F.2d 404 (1st Cir. 1987); SEC v. Van Waeyenberghe, 990 F.2d 845 (5th Cir. 1993); Janus Films Inc. v. Miller, 801 F.2d 578 (2d Cir. 1986).

[172] *See generally,* Gibson, Confidentiality in Mediation: A Moral Reassessment, 1992 J. Disp. Res. 25 (1992).

they fall within the statute of frauds,[173] the parties contemplate that the oral agreement will be reduced to writing,[174] or there is a court rule requiring that the oral settlement be in writing to be effective.[175] Notwithstanding the enforceability of many oral settlements, the parties will typically memorialize their agreement through one or more settlement documents.

Usually there is no need for you to confirm in writing the terms of an oral settlement agreed to between you and opposing counsel in advance of having closing settlement documents prepared and executed. However, if you have any doubt that the terms agreed to in an oral settlement discussion might be misunderstood or abrogated prior to the execution of final settlement documents, you should promptly confirm your understanding of the terms of the settlement in a letter or by E-mail to the other side. If an oral agreement is reached during trial, the best practice is to state the complete terms of the agreement on the record before the trial judge.

Following an oral agreement as to the terms of the settlement, defense counsel will usually send plaintiff's counsel (1) a Settlement Agreement and Release like that shown in § 17.05 or some other pertinent settlement agreement or documents (*e.g.* a structured-settlement agreement, contract, or deed, etc.), (2) a settlement check made payable to the plaintiff and plaintiff's counsel if the consideration for the settlement involves the payment of money, and (3) a dismissal to be signed and filed with the court if a lawsuit was previously filed. After these documents are received, the responsibilities of plaintiff's counsel are typically as follows:

(1) Counsel should carefully review the settlement documents to ensure that they comport with all terms of the settlement. If any changes to the documents are necessary, whether in form or substance, the incorporation of those changes should be coordinated with defense counsel.

(2) Counsel should carefully review the final settlement documents with the plaintiff so that the plaintiff has a complete understanding of them.

(3) Counsel should have the plaintiff endorse the settlement check,[176] which must then be deposited in counsel's trust account maintained for the safekeeping of client funds.

(4) Once the check "clears" the trust account, and before any funds are paid out of that account, counsel should prepare a Settlement Statement that provides to the plaintiff an accounting for the disbursement of all settlement funds to be paid from the account. This statement will usually set forth (a) the gross settlement amount, (b) the amount disbursed as attorney's fees, (c) the amounts disbursed for costs and other litigation expenses, (d) the amounts paid to lienholders or other third parties, and (e) the net settlement proceeds disbursed to the plaintiff. For example, if there is a Contingent Fee Contract like that shown in § 9.05, the foregoing maters might be set forth as follows:

---

[173] *See* B-Mall Co. v. Williamson, 977 S.W.2d 74 (Mo. Ct. App. W.D. 1998); Sims v. Purcell, 257 P.2d 242 (Idaho 1953).

[174] *See* Kreling v. Walsh, 176 P.2d 965 (Cal. App. 1947).

[175] *See* Moore v. Gunning, 328 So.2d 462 (Fla. App. 1976).

[176] *See* In re Deragon, 495 N.E.2d 831 (Mass. 1986) (lawyer publicly censured for endorsing check made out to his client).

<u>Settlement Statement</u>

Client: _____

File No.: _____

| | |
|---|---|
| (a) Gross settlement amount . . . . . . . . . . . . . . | $90,000 |
| (b) Less Attorneys' fee (33 1/3% of gross recovery). . . . . . . . . . . . . . . . . . | ($30,000) |
| (c) Less costs and litigation expenses advanced by Attorneys | |
| (see attached itemization) . . . . . . | ($1,000) |
| (d) Less payments to lienholders or other third parties | |
| (see attached itemization) . . . . . . | ($2,000) |
| (e) Net recovery & balance paid to client . . . . . . . . . . . . . . . . . . . . . . . . . | $57,000 |

Approved and signed, this the _____ day of _____ .

Client: _____.

Attorney: _____.

(5) Counsel should review the Settlement Statement and all other settlement documents with the plaintiff. If the plaintiff approves them, the plaintiff should then sign the Settlement Statement, the Separation Agreement and Release (or other settlement papers), and any dismissal of the lawsuit if the plaintiff's signature on the dismissal is necessary.

(6) Counsel must then write and deliver the appropriate checks out of the trust account in accordance with the disbursements set out in the Settlement Statement. In the Settlement Statement example above, this would mean paying the $57,000 to the plaintiff, the $2,000 to the various lienholders, and the attorney's fees and reimbursement for costs and litigation expenses advanced totaling $31,000 to counsel's separate, attorney account.

(7) Counsel must send an original of all executed settlement documents (except the plaintiff's Settlement Statement and the checks) to defense counsel. As a matter of common practice, defense counsel will usually arrange for the actual filing of any dismissal of the action.

Of course, defense counsel should also review all pertinent settlement documents with the defendant. In addition, depending upon the terms of the settlement, defense counsel may have to prepare a Settlement Statement for the defendant and follow the foregoing trust-account procedures for safeguarding and disbursing the defendant's funds.

The proper safekeeping and disbursement of settlement funds is ethically mandated. For example, under the ABA Model Rules of Professional Conduct, Rule 1.15, entitled "Safekeeping of Property," provides:

(a) A lawyer shall hold property of clients or third persons that is in a lawyer's possession in connection with a representation separate from the lawyer's own property. Funds shall be kept in a separate account maintained in the state where the lawyer's office is situated, or elsewhere with the consent of the client or third person. Other property shall be identified as such and appropriately safeguarded. Complete records of such account funds and other property shall be kept by the lawyer and shall be preserved for a period of [five years] after termination of the representation.

(b) Upon receiving funds or other property in which a client or third person has an interest, a lawyer shall promptly notify the client or third person. Except as stated in this rule or otherwise permitted by law or by agreement with the client, a lawyer shall promptly deliver to the client or third person any funds or other property that the client or third person is entitled to receive and, upon request by the client or third person, shall promptly render a full accounting regarding such property.

(c) When in the course of representation a lawyer is in possession of property in which both the lawyer and another person claim interests, the property shall be kept separate by the lawyer until there is an accounting and severance of their interests. If a dispute arises concerning their respective interests, the portion in dispute shall be kept separate by the lawyer until the dispute is resolved.

The official Comment to that Rule provides, in pertinent part:

[2] Lawyers often receive funds from third parties from which the lawyer's fee will be paid. If there is a risk that the client may divert the funds without paying the fee, the lawyer is not required to remit the portion from which the fee is to be paid. However, a lawyer may not hold funds to coerce a client into accepting the lawyer's contention. The disputed portion of the funds should be kept in trust and the lawyer should suggest means for prompt resolution of the dispute, such as arbitration. The undisputed portion of the funds shall be promptly distributed.

[3] Third parties, such as client's creditors, may have just claims against funds or other property in a lawyer's custody. A lawyer may have a duty under applicable law to protect such third-party claims against wrongful interference by the client, and accordingly may refuse to surrender the property to the client. However, a lawyer should not unilaterally assume to arbitrate a dispute between the client and the third party.

In sum, the foregoing prescribes that when you receive settlement funds that belong to your client or with respect to which a third party such as a health-care provider has a lien, you essentially have six fiduciary duties regarding the funds: (1) segregation, (2) safeguarding, (3) notification, (4) record-keeping, (5) delivery to your client or a third person when he is entitled to delivery, and (6) rendering an accounting when asked to by the client or third person. A violation of any one of these duties may result in malpractice or disciplinary action by the bar.[177]

---

[177] *See, e.g.,* In re James, 452 A.2d 163 (D.C. Ct. App. 1982) (lawyer's failure to pay funds on behalf of client in settlement of litigation); In re Feder, 442 N.E.2d 912 (Ill. 1982) (lawyer's failure to pay medical expenses as agreed from funds received on client's behalf); In re Hedrick, 725 P.2d 343 (Or. 1986) (lawyer disciplined for keeping money when client disputed that lawyer was entitled to that money as a fee); In re Strnad, 505 N.W.2d 134 (Wis. 1993) (lawyer may not withdraw funds from trust account as partial payment of disputed fee); In re Waldron, 790 S.W.2d 456 (Mo. 1990) (lawyer disciplined for collecting medical payment and holding it "hostage" for alleged fee); State ex rel. Oklahoma Bar Assoc. v. Watson, 897 P.2d 246 (Okla. 1994) (lawyer failed to provide proper accounting to clients in connection

Rule 1.15 and its Comment are somewhat ambiguous about your duties when you are in possession of settlement funds owed to your client and a dispute develops between your client and a third person (*e.g.*, a lienholder or creditor) as to who is entitled to those funds. Subparagraph (b) of the Rule provides that you must deliver to your client the funds which belong to him, but that you must also deliver to a third person those funds that the third person "is entitled to receive." Paragraph [3] of the Comment notes that third persons may have "just claims" against client funds, in which event you may have a duty "under applicable law" (*e.g.* a statute providing for a health-care provider lien or some other subrogation right) to protect those claims against "wrongful interference" by your client by refusing to surrender the funds to your client.

Assuming there is a dispute between your client and a third party as to who is entitled to particular funds, the question is under what circumstances you should deliver the funds to one or the other. Many courts and state ethics opinions hold that if you have actual knowledge that a third party has a properly perfected statutory lien or has some other clearly valid legal interest in a portion of the settlement funds (*e.g.*, by virtue of a court order or a valid contract), you must deliver that portion to the third party even if your client objects,[178] and the failure to do so may constitute fraudulent conduct.[179] Similarly, if you have properly entered into an express agreement with a third party about the disposition of funds in which the third party has an interest, you must honor that agreement.[180] If you ignore your duty to the third party in either of these circumstances, you may be liable to the third party for the funds owed to it.[181]

On the other hand, if the third-party's interest was not properly perfected pursuant to statute[182] or some other legal requirement,[183] or constitutes the mere

---

with distribution of settlement funds); In re Arrieh, 496 N.W.2d 601 (Wis. 1993) (failure of lawyer to deposit client funds in trust account and maintain adequate records).

[178] *See, e.g.,* Aetna Casualty & Surety Co. v. Gilreath, 625 S.W.2d 269 (Tenn. 1981) (lawyer has duty to honor statutory workers' compensation lien); California Formal Ethics Opinion 1988-101 (where client agreed to pay recovery proceeds to health-care provider, attorney may not disburse all monies to client); Ohio Ethics Opinion 95-12 (1995) (similar); Maryland Ethics Opinion 94-19 (1994) (similar); South Carolina Ethics Opinion 94-20 (1994) (lawyer must deliver funds owed to third party who has valid doctor's lien); Rhode Island Ethics Opinion 95-29 (1995) (lawyer must honor valid Medicare lien).

[179] *See, e.g.,* Cleveland Ethics Opinion 87-3 (1988); Rhode Island Ethics Opinion 90-31 (1990); South Carolina Ethics Opinion 81-14 (1981).

[180] *See, e.g.,* Florida Bar v. Neely, 587 So.2d 465 (Fla. 1991); In re Edwards, 448 S.E.2d 547 (S.C. 1994) (lawyer disciplined for failing to deliver funds to medical providers as agreed); South Carolina Ethics Opinion 93-14 (1993); Iowa Ethics Opinion 89-32 (1989); Washington Ethics Opinion 185.

[181] *See, e.g.,* Kaiser Foundation Health Plan Inc. v. Aguiluz, 54 Cal. Rptr. 2d 665 (Cal. App. 1996); Herzog v. Irace, 594 A.2d 1106 (Me. 1991); Berkowitz v. Haigood, 606 A.2d 1157 (N.J. 1992); Leon v. Martinez, 638 N.E.2d 511 (N.Y. 1994). *But see* American State Bank v. Enabit, 471 N.W.2d 829 (Iowa 1991); Twin Valley Motors Inc. v. Morale, 385 A.2d 678 (Vt. 1978).

[182] *See, e.g.,* Arizona Ethics Opinion 88-6 (1988) (unperfected third-party lien or assignment); Colorado Ethics Opinion 94 (1993) (lawyer should distribute funds to client in absence of statutory lien, contract, or court order); Maryland Ethics Opinion 97-20 (1997) (lawyer may deliver funds to client where medical lien not properly perfected).

[183] *See, e.g.,* South Carolina Ethics Opinion 89-13 (1989) (lawyer not required to deliver funds to client's ex-wife under divorce decree where lawyer not served with process as required by decree); Janson v. Cozen & O'Connor, 676 A.2d 242 (Pa. Super. Ct. 1996) (lawyer owes no fiduciary duty to third person who has no agreement with client).

assertion of a claim in the absence of clear evidence as to its validity,[184] you generally have no duty to investigate that interest and should deliver the funds to your client.[185] In this situation, however, you should always advise your client about the liability he may face in the event that the third-party's claim turns out to be legally enforceable.[186]

However, if there is a non-frivolous dispute between your client and a third person regarding entitlement to the funds, and particularly if your client makes a non-frivolous objection to any payment of the funds to a third party,[187] you "should not unilaterally assume to arbitrate [the] dispute between [your] client and [the] third party"[188] but should advise your client (preferably in writing) that you will keep the disputed funds in your trust account until the dispute is resolved by agreement or by the court.[189] The essential practical point is that, if you have any doubt about who is entitled to the disputed funds, the safest practice is to retain them in trust. Furthermore, in uncertain situations, you may be best able to protect yourself and your client from liability by conferring with ethics counsel for the State Bar in your jurisdiction before making a decision about whether to disburse the funds to your client or the third party or retain the funds in your trust account.

## § 17.13   ENFORCING SETTLEMENTS AND DRAFTING SETTLEMENT AGREEMENTS

A settlement agreement is a contract that is (1) entered into between parties with the requisite authority and capacity, (2) neither illegal nor entered into by fraud, duress, or undue influence, (3) a product of a "meeting of the minds" through a definitive offer and acceptance, and (4) supported by adequate consideration — *i.e.,* the compromise of a bona fide dispute, whether or not in litigation.[190] Thus, a settlement agreement may be rescinded or avoided in the same manner and on the same grounds as other contracts, and the construction and operation of the agreement will be governed by the legal principles applicable to contracts generally.[191] As mentioned in § 17.12, although the vast majority of settlement agreements are memorialized through settlement documents, oral settlement agreements may be enforced unless they are subject to the statute of frauds, the parties

---

[184] *See, e.g.,* Connecticut Informal Ethics Opinion 95-20 (1995) (lawyer has no duty to act on mere assertions of third-party interests); Maryland Ethics Opinion 97-9 (1997) (lawyer may deliver funds to client even though two other lawyers asserted claims to proceeds for services in unrelated matter).

[185] *See, e.g.,* South Carolina Ethics Opinion 93-31 (1993).

[186] *See, e.g.,* Cleveland Ethics Opinion 87-3 (1988); South Carolina Ethics Opinion 93-31 (1993).

[187] *See* Connecticut Informal Ethics Opinion 95-20 (1995) (lawyer cannot pay money to third person over client's objection); Pennsylvania Ethics Opinion 92-89 (1992) (lawyer whose client was ordered to pay arrearage in child support cannot release escrow proceeds without client's consent).

[188] Comment to ABA Model Rule 1.15 at paragraph [3].

[189] *See, e.g.,* Alaska Ethics Opinion 92-3 (1992); Arizona Ethics Opinion 88-6 (1988); California Formal Ethics Opinion 1988-101; Maryland Ethics Opinion 96-16 (1996); Michigan Informal Ethics Opinion 61 (1990); Ohio Ethics Opinion 95-12 (1995); Oregon Ethics Opinion 1991-52 (1991); Philadelphia Ethics Opinion 90-16 (1990); Tennessee Formal Ethics Opinion 87-F-110 (1987).

[190] *See* Marks-Foreman v. Reporter Pub. Co, 12 F. Supp. 2d 1089 (S.D. Cal. 1998); Harding v. Will, 500 P.2d 91 (Wash. 1972); Walker-Neer Machine Co v. Acmeline Mfg. Co., 279 S.W.2d 156 (Tex. Civ. App. 1955); Berger v. Lane, 213 P. 45 (Cal. 1923).

[191] *See* Penn Dixie Lines, Inc. v. Grannick, 78 S.E.2d 410 (N.C. 1953); Smith, Hinchman & Grylls Associates, Inc. v. Board of County Road Comrs., 229 N.W.2d 338 (Mich. App. 1975).

contemplated a writing, or there is a court rule requiring documentation.[192]

Generally, when a settlement agreement is breached under circumstances where no lawsuit was filed on the underlying dispute, the agreement may be enforced through an action for breach of contract, usually by specific performance. If a party breaches a settlement agreement that terminates pending litigation, generally the agreement may be enforced not only through a separate breach of contract action but also through a motion in the original lawsuit to have the court enter a judgment in accordance with the terms of the settlement.[193] The appropriate enforcement procedure will be dictated by the law in the applicable jurisdiction and will depend upon precisely when and how the settlement agreement was reached and breached.

The hallmarks of an enforceable settlement agreement are that it (1) be comprehensive in the sense of covering all pertinent aspects of the parties' obligations under it, and (2) be unambiguous in setting forth those obligations. These basic elements of completeness and clarity should be your primary goals when drafting an agreement. Of course, the agreement must otherwise contain all pertinent technical provisions to effectuate its particular purposes under applicable law, such as to effectuate certain tax consequences or to preserve certain other rights of the parties. Thus, there is no boilerplate "form" that may be used in all circumstances, and each agreement must be carefully tailored to the particular facts and law governing the situation at hand.

With this caveat in mind, when drafting a settlement agreement, it is nevertheless useful to consider the following matters that are frequently contained in many settlement agreements:[194]

(1) The date of the agreement and the identity of the parties. Along with the date of the agreement and names of the parties, a signatory who is acting in a representative or fiduciary capacity should be designated as such.

(2) The identity of counsel. If counsel represents the parties, the names of counsel should be included.

(3) A description of the nature of the dispute. If a lawsuit has been filed, specific reference should be made to the case caption and court file number, along with a brief description of the nature of the case. If no lawsuit has been filed, there should be a brief description of the events of the dispute sufficient to identify the matters that are being settled.

(4) Definitions of technical words or phrases. If the agreement uses terms of art or other words or phrases that are intended to have a special or broader meaning, it is useful to define them at the outset in a single section.

(5) Language reciting consideration for the agreement. Because the consideration for the agreement is usually nothing more than the mutual agreement of the parties to compromise and settle a bona fide dispute, "The obligations of each party" in (6) below are often prefaced by a comprehensive phrase such as: "In consideration of the mutual promises and undertakings of the parties and other consideration made

---

[192] See B-Mall Co. v. Williamson, 977 S.W.2d 74 (Mo. App. 1998); Sims v. Purcell, 257 P.2d 242 (Idaho 1953); Kreling v. Walsh, 176 P.2d 965 (Cal. App. 1947); Moore v. Gunning, 328 So.2d 462 (Fla. App. 1976).

[193] See, e.g., TNT Marketing Inc. v. Agresti, 796 F.2d 276 (9th Cir. 1986); Harrop v. Western Airlines, Inc., 550 F.2d 1143 (9th Cir. 1997); Ozyagcilar v. Davis, 701 F.2d 306 (4th Cir. 1983).

[194] See E.F. Lynch, et. al., *Negotiation and Settlement* § 11:28 (1992).

by each party to the other, the receipt and sufficiency of which is acknowledged, the parties agree as follows: . . . " However, if the applicable law requires some special or additional consideration, it should be specifically stated.

(6) The obligations of each party. The time, manner, and place of payment or other performance of each party should be explicit. If the payment under the agreement is made in part for a claim for "personal injury or sickness" (which is not taxable to the recipient) and in part for a non-personal injury claim (which is taxable to the recipient), the agreement should specifically designate the amount being allocated for each claim (*see* § 17.08). If the agreement is subject to the terms of another document (*e.g.*, an annuity contract or qualified assignment where a structured-settlement agreement is involved), the agreement should specifically incorporate that document by reference. This also should be done if the agreement utilizes exhibits defining the obligations of the parties.

(7) How the litigation will be concluded. If a lawsuit has been filed, the agreement typically will prescribe that the plaintiff (and the defendant, if he interposed a counterclaim) will file a dismissal of all claims. Sometimes the parties might prescribe that only certain causes of action will be dismissed, or that a partial judgment will be entered against one party. In addition, because a statutory right to recover costs and attorney's fees in an action may be waived by a settlement agreement,[195] the parties will often include in their agreement a provision that each party will bear its own costs, expenses, and attorney's fees, or that one party will be responsible for certain costs, expenses, or fees of the other.

(8) A confidentiality provision. The parties might include a provision that the agreement and its terms will remain confidential except to the extent disclosure is required by law or limited disclosure is necessary for conducting the personal or business affairs of the parties such as filing tax returns. (*See also* § 17.11).

(9) The identification and extent of claims being released. The claims being released under the agreement and any claims being reserved under it should be clearly specified. (*See, e.g.*, the "Settlement Agreement and Release [With Reservation of Rights]" in § 17.05).

(10) Remedies for breach of the agreement. The parties will often specify that in the event of a breach of the agreement, the non-breaching party will be entitled to certain remedies or to reactivate the lawsuit settled by the agreement. Such a provision typically provides that the prevailing party in an enforcement action will be entitled to recover reasonable costs, expenses, and attorney's fees from the non-prevailing party.

(11) A disclaimer of liability. A clause disclaiming any liability of one party to the other is typical because a settlement agreement is usually a resolution of a doubtful or disputed claim, and non-admission of liability is sometimes important to defendants to avoid potential *res judicata* issues or adverse decisions by insurance carriers regarding renewal of insurance for defendant-insureds.

(12) An integration clause. An integration clause makes it clear that the parties intend that the written agreement constitutes their entire agreement, thus pre-

---

[195] *See, e.g.,* Wray v. Clarke, 151 F.3d 807 (8th Cir. 1998) (waiver of attorney's fees under 42 U.S.C. § 1988 in civil rights action).

cluding a party from later contending that the written agreement was modified or supplemented by some oral agreement.

(13) A choice-of-law provision. Such a provision specifies the jurisdiction whose laws will govern in the event of a breach of the agreement or if a court is called upon to interpret the agreement.

(14) A severability clause. A severability clause provides that, in the event a particular provision of the agreement is found to be invalid, all other valid provisions will remain enforceable.

(15) An anti-waiver clause. When the agreement calls for multiple or periodic performance, as where one party is obligated to make payments over time, a party may sometimes waive strict compliance by, for example, accepting a late payment from the payor. An anti-waiver clause makes clear that a party's decision to waive strict compliance on one or more occasions in lieu of declaring a breach of the agreement does not constitute a waiver of any subsequent breach of the agreement.

(16) A stipulation that the agreement was entered into freely and voluntarily. Such a stipulation is designed to preclude a party from later claiming that the agreement was procured by fraud, duress, or undue influence.

(17) A recital of joint preparation. A recital that the agreement was jointly drafted by the parties is designed to prevent a court from applying the rule of construction that an ambiguity in the agreement should be construed against the party who drafted it.

(18) A stipulation about the facts on which the agreement is based. A stipulation that the parties accept the facts of the situation as they appeared at the time of the execution of the agreement is designed to foreclose a party from later contending that it entered into the agreement based on some mistake of fact or incomplete understanding of the facts.

(19) A warranty of legal capacity and non-assignment of claims. This provision warrants that each party has the legal capacity to execute the agreement and that neither party has assigned to any third party any claims or right surrendered under the agreement.

(20) A provision to cooperate in executing the terms of the agreement. Such a provision calls upon the parties to cooperate in executing all documents and taking other steps necessary to give effect to the agreement.

(21) The effective date of the agreement and a provision for counterpart execution. The agreement should always specify when it becomes effective, and it might provide that the agreement will be effective even if both parties do not sign the same copy of the agreement.

## § 17.14    EXAMPLE OF COMMON SETTLEMENT AGREEMENT PROVISIONS

The types of provisions enumerated in paragraphs (1) through (21) in §17.13 above are illustrated in paragraphs (1) through (21) of the following Settlement Agreement:

## Settlement Agreement

(1) This Settlement Agreement ("Agreement") is entered into as of _____[date], between John J. Jones of Raleigh, North Carolina and Sandra S. Smith of Roanoke, Virginia.

(2) In connection with this Agreement, Jones is represented by Don D. Doe, Esq. of Raleigh, North Carolina, and Smith is represented by Rhonda R. Rowe, Esq. of Roanoke, Virginia.

(3) There is pending in the Civil Superior Court division in Wake County, North Carolina an action entitled "John J. Jones v. Sandra S. Smith," Court File No: 2000 CVS 1210 ("Action"). In this Action, Jones alleged a First Claim for Relief against Smith for breach of contract, praying for compensatory damages for lost profits, and a Second Claim for Relief against Smith for personal physical injury. Smith timely filed an Answer to Jones' Complaint, denying all of its material allegations.

(4) As used in this Agreement:

(a) "Jones" means John J. Jones, and his employees, representatives, and agents of any kind, and his heirs, assigns, and successors in interest of any kind.

(b) "Smith" means Sandra S. Smith, and her employees, representatives, and agents of any kind, and her heirs, assigns, and successors in interest of any kind.

(c) "Claim(s)" mean all claims, demands, obligations, damages, actions, and causes of action of any kind, for any relief, on any basis, whether known or not, asserted or not, fixed or contingent.

(d) "Party(ies)" means Jones and Smith.

(5) In consideration of the mutual promises and undertaking of the parties to this Agreement and other consideration made by each party to the other, the sufficiency of which is acknowledged, the parties agree as follows:

(6) Within ten business days of the execution of this Agreement, Smith shall (1) pay to Jones $45,000 by delivering a cashier's check in that amount made payable to "John J. Jones and Don D. Doe, attorney" to the office of Don D. Doe at 6256 Springfield Ave., Raleigh, N.C. 27602; and (2) transfer title to the RX-Z Sailboat owned by Smith and having a fair market value of $55,000 by executing the title documents attached as Exhibit A to this Agreement in favor of "John J. Jones" and delivering the executed title documents to the office of Don D. Doe. The parties agree that, of the total $100,000 in cash and property, the $45,000 in cash is allocated as a settlement of the lost profits alleged in the First Claim for Relief in the Action (45% of total), and the $55,000 representing the fair market value of the Sailboat is allocated as a settlement of the personal physical injuries alleged in the Second Claim for Relief in the Action (55% of total).

(7) Within 20 days of the execution of this Agreement, and if Smith has fully performed her obligations under Paragraph 6, Jones shall file with the Wake County Civil Superior Court a Voluntary Dismissal With Prejudice of all claims in John J. Jones v. Sandra S. Smith, 2000 CVS 1210. Each party shall bear its own costs, expenses, and attorney's fees in the Action.

(8) The parties agree that all provisions of this Agreement shall remain confidential between the parties, and its provisions shall not be disclosed to anyone except to the extent that either party is legally obligated to disclose them, disclosure is reasonably necessary for the conduct of the personal or business affairs of the parties (such as disclosure to attorneys, accountants, or tax authorities), or disclosure is necessary in any proceeding to enforce this Agreement.

(9) In consideration of the obligations and undertakings of the parties in paragraphs (6) through (8), each party releases the other from all Claims arising from or connected in any way with the events alleged in the Action and all claims that could have been raised by either party in the Action.

(10) Any breach of this Agreement will entitle the non-breaching party to all legal and equitable remedies for the breach; and if either party brings an action on account of an alleged breach of this Agreement, the prevailing party shall be entitled to recover all of its reasonable costs and expenses of any kind, and reasonable attorney's fees.

(11) This Agreement is the result of a good-faith compromise of disputed claims and shall never or for any purpose be considered an admission of the correctness of the allegations or claims asserted in the Action by either party, each of whom denies all allegations and claims made by the other party.

(12) This Agreement supersedes all previous agreements between the parties, contains the entire Agreement between the parties, and may not be modified except in writing.

(13) This Agreement was negotiated in Raleigh, North Carolina, is to be performed in North Carolina, and the laws of North Carolina shall govern its interpretation and enforcement.

(14) If any part of this Agreement is held to be invalid, unenforceable, or non-binding, all remaining portions shall remain in effect.

(15) The waiver by any party of a breach of a particular provision in this Agreement shall not constitute a waiver of any subsequent breach of the same provision or any other provision.

(16) Both parties stipulate that they have had the advice of counsel throughout the proceedings and negotiations leading to the preparation and execution of this Agreement, that they have read this Agreement and understand its terms, and that they enter into this Agreement freely and voluntarily without any fraud, duress, or undue influence.

(17) The text of this Agreement is the product of negotiations between the parties and their counsel and is not to be construed as having been prepared by one party or the other.

(18) Both parties stipulate that if the facts with respect to which this Agreement is executed should be later found to be different than now believed, this Agreement will nevertheless remain effective; and it is stipulated that neither party has relied on any representations not explicitly set forth in this Agreement.

(19) Each party warrants that as of the date of execution of this Agreement, each has the legal capacity and sole right and authority to execute it, and has not sold, assigned, or otherwise transferred any Claim relating to any right surrendered by this Agreement.

(20) The parties agree to execute all documents and take any further actions reasonably necessary to accomplish the provisions of this Agreement.

(21) This Agreement becomes effective when executed by both parties, and the Agreement may be executed in counterparts and be as valid and binding as if both parties signed the same copy.

_____

[Signatures and dates]

[Witness or notary, if required]

# Chapter 18

# CROSS-CULTURAL NEGOTIATIONS AND NEGOTIATING BETWEEN GENDERS

## SYNOPSIS

## § 18.01  INTRODUCTION

A natural byproduct of our global economy has been the growth of multinational business enterprises and a dramatic increase in cross-cultural business negotiations. This increase in transnational bargaining has required American business executives to learn how to recognize and accommodate wide-ranging cultural differences when negotiating with their counterparts in other countries.

The subject of how cultural differences affect bargaining interactions is complex.[1] Much of the difficulty is that an instructive treatment of the subject depends upon the particular culture or society one is talking about, whether in a country from Eastern or Western Europe, Asia, Latin America, or Africa. The first part of this Chapter, rather than trying to summarize the specific negotiating styles endemic to particular countries or cultures,[2] provides an overall analytical framework for considering how differences in cultures may affect cross-cultural negotiations. The factors set out in this framework are useful to consider before undertaking negotiations in any international setting.

---

[1] *See generally*, G. Faure & J. Rubin, *Culture and Negotiation* (1993); R. Cohen, *Negotiating Across Cultures* (1991); J. Salacuse, *Making Global Deals* (1991); I.W. Zartman, *International Multilateral Negotiation* (1994).

[2] For summaries of such styles, *see, e.g.*, H. Binnendijk, *National Negotiating Styles* (Foreign Service Institute, U.S. Dept. of State 1987); V. Kremenyuk, (ed.), *International Negotiation* (1991).

The second part of this Chapter discusses considerations about negotiations between men and women. This too is a complex subject that is fraught with difficulties of over-generalization and potential misunderstanding. Nevertheless, a discussion of some of the more important factors that affect negotiations between genders may be useful in guarding against erroneous stereotyping that sometimes impedes negotiations between persons of the opposite sex.

## § 18.02   CROSS-CULTURAL NEGOTIATIONS

It is axiomatic that meaningful negotiations require communication and understanding. For negotiators to truly "understand" one another, however, they must be able to recognize critical differences in the cultural norms, customs, rules, and verbal and nonverbal behavior that underlie each other's ways of communicating. In the absence of appreciating these differences, communication is impaired, and misunderstandings may make negotiations extremely difficult if not impossible.

This problem can be particularly acute in cross-cultural negotiations. As a simple example, consider the situation where a person raised in white Anglo-Saxon American culture is negotiating with a person brought up in the Native American culture. The Anglo-Saxon American may have learned as a child, "[n]ever trust someone who can't look you in the eye and give you a firm handshake," whereas the Native American may have been taught that direct eye contact was rude and insulting. Here, in the absence of understanding each other's cultural differences, the two negotiators are likely to mistrust one another before the first offer is even made.

Writing about cross-cultural differences is difficult because of the dangers of stereotyping and oversimplification. However, persons who engage in cross-cultural negotiations need an analytical framework to identify potential barriers or impediments to negotiating in the international setting.[3]

Professor David A. Victor, a noted scholar on the subject of cross-cultural communications, has developed one such framework. He uses the acronym "LESCANT" to describe the most common factors that account for cultural differences in communicating and negotiating. The acronym stands for differences in "Language," "Environment and Technology," "Social Organization," "Contexting," "Authority Conception," "Nonverbal Behavior," and "Temporal Conception."[4] These factors are summarized below.

---

[3] Jeswald W. Salacuse, *Making Global Deals* (Houghton Mifflin 1991) describes 10 specific cultural characteristics that affect negotiations: the negotiating goal (contract or relationship); the negotiating attitude (win/lose or win/win); personal style (formal or informal); communication (direct or indirect); sensitivity to time (high or low); emotionalism (high or low); form of agreement (general or specific); building an agreement (inductive or deductive); team organization (one leader or consensus), and risk taking (high or low). *See also* Robert C. Circillo & Adam Fremantle, and Jeanne Hamburg, "International Negotiations: A Cultural Perspective," *The ABA Guide to International Business Negotiations: A Comparison of Cross-Cultural Issues and Successful Approaches*, 43 (2d ed. 2000).

[4] David A. Victor, "Cross-Cultural Awareness," *The ABA Guide to International Business Negotiations: A Comparison of Cross-Cultural Issues and Successful Approaches*, 98 (2d ed. 2000).

## [1] Language Barriers

Most United States citizens speak only one language, while citizens of other countries are often versed in several languages. Because language creates an "in group" of those who understand and an "outcast group" of those who do not, language barriers often create an "us" versus "them" division. When a U.S. negotiator speaks only English but his or her opponent is conversant in several languages, the U.S. negotiator may find himself or herself isolated and dependent upon a translator, while his or her counterpart freely shares information and bonhomie. Anyone who has sat through the tedious translation of a joke in another language will readily understand this social ostracization.

Language divisions may also be a political statement. Even though the U.S. negotiator may feel that he or she is a member of the "outcast group" who speaks only English, he or she may find himself or herself, as an English speaker, to be viewed as a member of the culture of oppression in some countries. The British Empire stretched across the world during the 19th and 20th centuries. In countries such as South Africa, which were once a part of the British Empire, English was generally spoken by the ruling class. Even though English is now one of the 11 officially recognized languages of South Africa,[5] negotiators need to be cognizant of the political implications that may be involved with a choice of language.

Not being conversant in multiple languages may lead U.S. negotiators, however, to overestimate the importance of language as a cultural barrier.[6] Although the language barrier may be an obstacle, it usually may be overcome through the use of a translator. In addition, even when the negotiator from another culture is able to communicate in English, it may be helpful to the U.S negotiator to hire a translator to assist in negotiations.

Although U.S. negotiators may initially overcome the language barrier through the use of competent translators, even the best translators cannot translate the complete context and nuance of what is being said in the foreign language. For example, one scholar has described this problem by contrasting the different interpretations of the word "corruption" in English and Korean. Although the word has negative connotations in both languages, subtle variations in its meaning evoke different associations in the two countries. For those in the United States, corruption implies immoral and even criminal behavior. For Koreans, however, while corruption may have unfortunate social consequences, it is not considered morally wrong. The distinction appears to turn on differing views about the duties of a civil servant. In the United States, a civil servant is expected to be impartial and loyal to the entire community and thus, for instance, is not permitted to take bribes. In Korea, on the other hand, it is an accepted practice to give gifts to officials because they have obligations to family and friends that take precedence over any abstract duty to society.[7] In this example, one can imagine the difficulties

---

[5] According to Chapter 1 of the Constitution of the Republic of South Africa, adopted in 1996, "The official languages of the Republic are Sepedi, Sesotho, Setswana, siSwati, Tshivenda Xitsonga, Afrikaans, English isiNdebele, isiXhosa and isiZulu."

[6] *Id.* at 99.

[7] *See* Lorand B. Szalay, "Intercultural Communication: A Process Model," 5 *International Journal of Intercultural Relations*, 133–146 (1981); Raymond Cohen, *Negotiating Across Cultures: International Communication in an Interdependent World* 28 (1991).

in translating the different meanings of the word "corruption" when it is being used in a negotiation between a U.S. and a Korean negotiator.

Any cross-cultural negotiation between people who do not speak the same language may also include inaccuracies and even unintended insults as the translator interprets one language into the other. The problem arises most often when the translator, though proficient with word-for-word translation, is unfamiliar with colloquial idioms in one of the languages.

For example, consider the story of a young man from a Kentucky farm who returned from a semester abroad in France to recount his cultural faux-paux at a formal French dinner in his host's home. After being offered a second helping of a delicious roast lamb, he respectfully declined, announcing in his halting French that he could not eat another bite because, "Je suis plein" — a term which he had carefully translated from his phrase book as meaning, "I am full." At first the guests were dumbfounded and then began to titter. Finally, someone explained to him that the phrase he had used was an idiom meaning, "I am pregnant." Although the young man's self-effacing laughter eased the situation, one can easily imagine how different the situation would have been had this student been an unmarried young woman traveling abroad.

An additional problem with translation arises when a phrase conveys a meaning in one language that has no comparable translation in another language. For instance, a U.S. negotiator might say to an opponent, "I think we just hit a home run when we raised that point." The baseball analogy is, of course, meaningless to someone from a country where baseball is not played. An even more difficult problem arises when the use of language results in an unintended but painful insult to one of the parties. For instance, the colloquial U.S. expression, "I think we just dropped a bomb when we gave them that fact," could be perceived as an insult to a Japanese negotiator who has sensitivities to the memories of the atomic bombing of Nagasaki and Hiroshima. Translation of one language into another provides at best "a rough equivalence of meaning," and "in the law where words constitute the most accurate rendering of meaning, a rough equivalence of translated meaning can add a whole new dimension to legal interpretation."[8]

In addition to issues related to the particular meaning of a word or phrase being translated, cultural differences arise when language is used not just as a means to communicate but also as a social lubricant. For example, those who are accustomed to using language solely as a means of conveying information can be frustrated with lengthy exchanges of pleasantries, which, in some cultures, may be customarily appropriate or necessary before any concrete information can be discussed. Impatience with the time spent on "useless visiting" can prevent the listener from investing the time necessary to build trust with the speaker.

In a culture such as the U.S. that values directness, explicitness is sought and indirectness is avoided. However, in a culture in which language is a social lubricant, indirectness is valued, nonverbal messages are read and showcased, and language is used as a means to preserve and promote social interests. For example, a negotiator from the United States may totally misunderstand his or her Japanese counterpart's message if he or she does not know that a common characteristic of

---

[8] David A. Victor, "Cross-Cultural Awareness," *The ABA Guide to International Business Negotiations: A Comparison of Cross-Cultural Issues and Successful Approaches*, 100 (2d ed. 2000).

the negotiation process in Japan is an emphasis on consensus building and an avoidance of confrontation. A Japanese negotiator might never use the word "no" in his or her communication, but those experienced with the Japanese know that the presentation of a counterproposal or a failure to act or respond to a proposal may in fact be a polite, but definite "no" from the Japanese negotiator.[9]

## [2]    Environmental and Technological Differences

Negotiators must determine "where" true negotiation takes place in a culture. In some instances, negotiations are customarily conducted behind closed doors around a boardroom table. In other cases, only the formal positions are stated in the boardroom and the actual negotiations may occur on the golf course or at meals. For example, U.S. State Department officials have described negotiations with Mexican officials as occurring over long lunches rather than at formal negotiating sessions.[10] Thus, when negotiating in cross-cultural settings, one must be prepared for variations in the negotiation environment and be attuned to accepting the luncheon invitation as well as the request to play golf.

Similar sensitivities must be shown when negotiations are occurring in cultures where access to modern office equipment is unavailable. If fax machines and e-mail capabilities are not yet routinely used in a particular country, it is important that the more technologically sophisticated negotiator not impose such equipment on the negotiation process. In some cultures, even telephones may be expensive luxuries. Therefore, a negotiator must not rush to assume that a deal has not been reached when a timely response has not been communicated. It may well be that all communication had been interrupted while a telephone wire was being repaired or electricity was being re-established in a remote area of a third-world country. In these situations, negotiators must be alert to the impracticality of requiring "a faxed acceptance" to a contract proposal by a certain date, or automatically canceling an offer when a timely acceptance is not made.

Although negotiators may be able to conduct their discussions through e-mail or video-conferencing in countries where the technology is available, they should be alert to the reluctance of some people to use these new technologies. In countries where the initial contact between the negotiators is viewed as a courtship to establish trust, the use of impersonal e-mail instead of face-to-face contact may inhibit rather than facilitate a successful negotiation. In countries with a history of an active intelligence community and intrusive government surveillance, people are often hesitant to allow any oral or video commemoration of discussions.[11] In addition, international negotiators need to be attuned to any history of economic espionage that may cause concern to the negotiators. "In certain countries, such as Russia, Romania, Ukraine, and even France, economic espionage is thought to be common, with not only phone lines being intercepted but international hotel rooms and conference rooms being bugged."[12] In order to gain the trust of the other side,

---

[9] Robert C. Circicillo, Adam Femantle, & Jeanne M. Hamburg, "International Negotiations: A Cultural Perspective," *ABA Guide to International Business Negotiations*, 48 (2d ed. 2000).

[10] Raymond Cohen, *Negotiating Across Cultures*, 140 (1997).

[11] Jeanne Hamburg, "Negotiating Across Cultures in the New Millenium," *The ABA Guide to International Business Negotiations: A Comparison of Cross-Cultural Issues and Successful Approaches*, 60 (2d ed. 2000).

[12] Jeanne Hamburg, "Negotiating Across Cultures in the New Millenium," *The ABA Guide to*

U.S. negotiators need to follow the lead of the other side as to the use of "safe technology" for the negotiations. What may appear "safe" in this country may in fact not be safe in another. If one side of the negotiation perceives a lack of safety in the communications, their representatives may refuse to propose compromise positions.

Finally, even if the negotiator decides that e-mail is appropriate for the conduct of the negotiation, the American negotiator needs to pay attention to the tone of his or her e-mail. E-mail correspondence in this country is notoriously informal and abbreviated. The U.S. negotiator may unintentionally offend the more formal international recipient with the casual tone of his or her e-mail correspondence.

## [3]    Differences in Social Organization

"Social organization" refers to the common institutions and collective activities shared by members of a culture.[13] Before one can be an effective negotiator in a foreign culture, one must first understand one's own culture and then study the relevant social organization for the particular foreign culture. Professor Victor has identified six organizational variables most likely to affect legal transactions and negotiations across cultures: (1) kinship and family ties; (2) friendship ties; (3) education; (4) class and social stratification; (5) perception of work and the law; and (6) gender differences.[14]

In some societies, kinship and family ties determine who may be trusted. In such situations, the negotiator may be at a disadvantage unless he or she can find kinship relationships to utilize in the negotiating process. In other societies, friendship determines who may be trusted. Although negotiators obviously cannot make themselves into "kin" or "longstanding friends," they may be able to find appropriate persons who have the requisite kinship or friendship to act as intermediaries in such situations.

In other societies, educational or class ties may determine potential business connections. For instance, in Great Britain, attendance at the same "public" school (which would be called a private university in the United States) will often serve as a resource for networking.

Similarly, those of the same social class who attend the same social functions frequently form business relationships based on those contacts. In some countries, there are formal divisions based on class, caste, or tribe. International negotiators need to recognize that these formal and/or informal divisions may affect who is represented at the negotiation table and who is not. Even in the United States where we take pride in the absence of a formal class or caste system,[15] many a business deal has been negotiated at an exclusive country club that will not admit others based on class, race, or religion.

*International Business Negotiations: A Comparison of Cross-Cultural Issues and Successful Approaches*, 61 (2d ed. 2000).

[13] David A. Victor, "Cross-Cultural Awareness," *The ABA Guide to International Business Negotiations: A Comparison of Cross-Cultural Issues and Successful Approaches*, 102 (2000).

[14] David A. Victor, "Cross-Cultural Awareness," *The ABA Guide to International Business Negotiations: A Comparison of Cross-Cultural Issues and Successful Approaches*, 102 (2000).

[15] David A. Victor, "Cross-Cultural Awareness," *The ABA Guide to International Business Negotiations: A Comparison of Cross-Cultural Issues and Successful Approaches*, 103 (2000).

Perceptions about work and work settings also vary among cultures. For instance, in the United States, most people identify themselves by their profession, not the particular organization in which they practice their profession. When a person in the U.S. is asked about her employment, the response is more likely to be, "I'm a lawyer," or "I'm a teacher," but not, "I work for the attorney general's office" or "I work at Smithwick elementary school." In the U.S., members of a profession often feel their closest ties to others who are practicing in the same profession as opposed to a special closeness to other employees within the same organization. This type of identification contrasts sharply with the Japanese who are more likely to identify themselves by the company where they work, or Mexicans who are more likely to identify themselves primarily by the family to whom they belong.[16]

Gender issues also may affect negotiations (*see also* § 18.03). Each society has developed its own views of the proper roles for each gender, and there is no society in which women and men are acculturated to behave identically.[17] Several studies indicate that children may learn their opinions regarding gender-linked roles before they learn to speak.[18] Although various cultures make distinctions between gender roles, there is considerable similarity among the stereotypes ascribed to men and women regardless of the particular culture. In a study of 29 different countries, for example, it was found that people in each country attached the same sex stereotypes to the same gender. Men were seen to be adventurous, dominant, forceful, independent, and strong-willed. On the other hand, women were classified as emotional, sentimental, submissive, and superstitious.[19] Although these stereotypes may have no connection with the attitudes or temperament of an individual negotiator, those who are planning negotiations should be aware of the particular culture's view of gender differences and the consequent conclusions that might be drawn regarding the importance of the negotiation depending on the gender of the person who has been assigned to conduct it.

## [4]   Differences in Contexting and Face-Saving

"Contexting" is a term coined by Edward T. Hall to describe the extent to which people look beyond what is being literally said and consider what is being said in the context of surrounding circumstances.[20] Put more plainly, it refers to "reading between the lines" of what someone is saying. In some cultures, such as in the United States, negotiators are more likely to focus on the actual words communicated rather than on the context in which the words are spoken. Accordingly, the United States has been referred to as a "low-context" culture.

On the other hand, some other cultures rely heavily on *how* something is said or written and the circumstances surrounding the communication in order to derive the meaning of the exchange. These cultures are referred to as "high-context"

---

[16] David A. Victor, "Cross-Cultural Awareness," *The ABA Guide to International Business Negotiations: A Comparison of Cross-Cultural Issues and Successful Approaches*, 104 (2000).

[17] David A. Victor, "Cross-Cultural Awareness," *The ABA Guide to International Business Negotiations: A Comparison of Cross-Cultural Issues and Successful Approaches*, 104 (2000).

[18] David A. Victor, "Cross-Cultural Awareness," *The ABA Guide to International Business Negotiations: A Comparison of Cross-Cultural Issues and Successful Approaches*, 104 (2000).

[19] J.E. Williams and D. Best, *Measuring Sex Stereotypes: A Thirty Nation Study* (1982).

[20] Edward T. Hall, *The Silent Language* (1959).

cultures. In a high-context culture, negotiations may be based more on what is tacitly understood than what is expressly said. China, Japan, and Egypt are typical examples of high-context cultures.

In low-context cultures, like the United States and France, negotiators, regardless of legal training, are apt to perceive themselves as conscientiously and objectively representing the interests of their client. They aspire to make logical arguments that they hope will persuade the opponent to their point of view. The model that many U.S. negotiators emulate is that of a courtroom in which an unbiased jury will ultimately make a reasoned decision based on the evidence and persuasive arguments of counsel. Although impassioned arguments may be made, it is assumed that most of the emotion expressed is done for histrionic purposes to enhance the logical arguments.[21] The entire focus of this type of negotiation may be the drawing up of a detailed contract that sets out the precise terms that the negotiators have hammered out in a methodical manner. The exact wording of the contract is of the utmost importance.

On the other hand, those coming to the negotiating table from a high-context culture focus less on details such as the drafting of a precisely worded contract, than on the relationship between the negotiators. That is, they are concerned with communal harmony. For instance, the Japanese view debate as an unwelcome threat to communal harmony[22] and are not comfortable with the adversarial, auction-like approach to bargaining used by many Americans. Instead, the Japanese often expect the parties to a dispute to "do the right thing" as defined by obligations implicit in the parties' relationship as opposed to the promises made in a contract.[23]

A key difference in the views that a person from a high-context culture brings to the negotiation table is the differing view of the use of the courts as a remedy. In a high-context culture, courts are viewed as a resolution of last resort, whereas in a low-context culture, such as the United States, legal action may be viewed as the first recourse to resolve a dispute.[24]

Integral to many high-context cultures is the concept of "saving face." When one is negotiating against an opponent in a "high-context face-saving" culture, one must be alert to the appearance as well as the actual result of any deal. That is, in a face-saving culture, the outcome must often appear favorable to those not directly involved in the negotiation, and the high-context negotiator must be able to leave the table with dignity and respect even though the actual result of the negotiation may not be totally favorable for him or her. For the high-context negotiator, this may require that changes in position be skillfully explained away or ignored so that there is no appearance of a concession. It may also require that the high-context negotiator be given permission to leave the table before the details of an agreement are decided in order to have the opportunity to consult with those of more senior status.

---

[21] Raymond Cohen, *Negotiating Across Cultures*, 135–136 (1991).

[22] Raymond Cohen, *Negotiating Across Cultures*, 137 (1991).

[23] Roger W. Benjamin, Images of Conflict Resolution and Social Control: American and Japanese Attitudes toward the Adversary System, Journal of Conflict Resolution 19 (1975).

[24] David A. Victor, "Cross-Cultural Awareness," *The ABA Guide to International Business Negotiations: A Comparison of Cross-Cultural Issues and Successful Approaches*, 107 (2000).

## [5]    Differences in Authority Conception

The management style of an organization varies from culture to culture and sometimes from organization to organization within a given culture. For instance, in the United States, the management style of law firms varies immensely. In some firms, an authoritarian managing partner makes all promotion and salary decisions, while other firms favor a more participatory management committee or even the inclusion of all personnel in management decisions. The same can be said of corporations. In short, different organizations in different cultures prefer and employ varying styles of authority.

Negotiators, therefore, need to be particularly aware of the status of the person with whom they are negotiating. In strictly authoritarian societies, the negotiation should usually occur between those of similar rank. In authoritarian societies, the person who is negotiating may have little, if any, power and must cloak any particular agreement with the understanding that someone of a higher rank must approve every position. The constant need to stop the negotiation for approval from those having more senior status can grow tedious, but it may be a necessary part of the process to reach an agreement.

A person negotiating with someone from an authoritarian culture needs to be particularly attuned to the unspoken meaning of a person of higher rank than the negotiator coming into the room where the negotiation is taking place. The higher ranking person's entrance may not be to participate in the negotiation but instead to communicate his or her unspoken support for the negotiator. In this situation, one should consider whether a similar show of support from someone outside the room may be necessary to level the playing field.

## [6]    Differences in Nonverbal Behavior

Each society has its own way of communicating in a nonverbal manner.[25] All of us are familiar with the stereotypes of the "expansive gestures" of the Italians, the "stoic calm" of the Japanese, and the "stiff upper lip" of the British. Yet, despite these stereotypical descriptions, most of us are unaccustomed to observing, understanding, and explaining the nonverbal behavior of another culture. Professor Victor has classified cultural variations in nonverbal communication in six distinct areas: kinesics (body movement and facial gestures); proxemics (distance); oculesics (eye movements and eye contact); haptics (touching behavior); paralanguage (tone of voice and non-language sounds); and appearance (dressing and grooming).[26]

The negotiator who wishes to be effective in international negotiations must observe how the target culture varies from his or her particular culture in these six areas. For instance, most Americans who have grown up in an individualistic society, where personal space is valued and direct speech is encouraged, will have a difficult time negotiating with someone from a culture where people routinely stand near each other and speak in lowered voices. Those who have grown up in a

---

[25] David A. Victor, "Cross-Cultural Awareness," *The ABA Guide to International Business Negotiations: A Comparison of Cross-Cultural Issues and Successful Approaches*, 109 (2000).

[26] David A. Victor, "Cross-Cultural Awareness," *The ABA Guide to International Business Negotiations: A Comparison of Cross-Cultural Issues and Successful Approaches*, 109–110 (2000).

society where people routinely touch each other during a conversation are in danger of offending someone from a culture where touching is avoided except in the most intimate relationships.

The difficulty in deciphering the meaning of nonverbal behavior is further magnified by the reluctance of most people to ask for an explanation of the specific behavior. Perhaps, because of the mistaken assumption that the meaning of nonverbal behavior is obvious and therefore an inquiry would be rude, or because nonverbal behavior by its very nature is rarely accompanied by a verbal explanation, nonverbal behavior is rarely explicated. The result for the cross-cultural negotiator is often mystification about another's actions. An effective cross-cultural negotiator must therefore strive to understand and thereby demystify his or her counterpart's nonverbal behavior.

## [7]     Differences in Conception of Time

Of all the roadblocks that can occur in cross-cultural negotiations, time may be the least understood but the most important in its ramifications for the participants. There are two major ways that cultures conceive of time.[27] "Monochronic" cultures view time as an inflexible amount that can be subdivided into hours, minutes, and seconds. Members of monochronic cultures typically carry calendars and live their lives according to appointments and schedules. "Polychronic" cultures, however, view time in the cycle of seasons and the patterns of rural life.[28] In a polychronic society, time is measured in days and months, not hours and minutes, and a dividing point in the past is not the number of a year, but whether the event was before or after a natural disaster.

In a monochronic culture like the United States, the focus is often on "getting things done" and life is a "treadmill of achievement."[29] Time is valued by what is accomplished during an hour or a day, not by relationships formed or history recounted. On the other hand, countries with a polychronic concept of time value history and a sense of the past. Members of these cultures are more often focused on the long-term relationship than on the immediate solution.[30]

It is easy to see how conflicts can arise when members of these two cultures attempt to negotiate. Those from a monochronic culture are constantly pressing for scheduled meetings and timely accomplishments aimed towards a final deadline. Those from a polychronic culture, on the other hand, come to the table with a sense of history and a focus on developing a long-lasting and fruitful relationship. Immediate deadlines are of no concern to those from the polychronic culture, whereas the immediate deadline is of all-consuming importance to the person from the monchronic culture.

---

[27] David A. Victor, "Cross-Cultural Awareness," *The ABA Guide to International Business Negotiations: A Comparison of Cross-Cultural Issues and Successful Approaches*, 110 (2000).

[28] Raymond Cohen, *Negotiating Across Cultures*, 34 (1991).

[29] Raymond Cohen, *Negotiating Across Cultures*, 34–35 (1991).

[30] Raymond Cohen, *Negotiating Across Cultures*, 35 (1991).

## [8]　The Utility of the LESCANT Factors

The utility of the LESCANT factors is that they provide a comprehensive set of considerations to be researched by any negotiator who intends to engage in a cross-cultural negotiation. The relative importance of any single factor or combination of factors will, of course, depend upon the particular country and culture where the opposing negotiator resides. As a practical matter, although much can be learned about the particular cultural background and practices of foreign negotiators through reading and study, any U.S. negotiator who is about to engage in a cross-cultural negotiation for the first time would be well advised to consult persons who have had prior personal experience negotiating with others in the particular culture involved.

## § 18.03　NEGOTIATING BETWEEN GENDERS

Professor Charles Craver has said that some male law students in his Legal Negotiating classes have indicated "they are particularly uncomfortable when female opponents obtain extremely beneficial results from them" in a simulated negotiation. Some of these students have even said they would prefer the consequences associated with nonsettlements to the possible embarrassment of "losing" to female opponents.[31] A study of students participating in simulated negotiations in the Lawyering Program at New York University School of Law concluded that "[s]tudents more easily trusted someone of the same gender."[32] Discussions about gender-based comparisons or distinctions in negotiating effectiveness are delicate because they can unintentionally invite the often misleading stereotyping that such discussions are otherwise intended to disabuse. Nevertheless, some discussion of this subject may be useful because, as the foregoing observations indicate, a number of lawyers have great difficulty when interacting with attorneys of the opposite sex.

## [1]　Studies About Negotiating Between Genders

There have been a number of empirical studies about different behavioral characteristics between men and women that may be relevant to negotiating. Most of the existing empirical research indicates that men and women tend to demonstrate the following different characteristics:

| Men | Women |
| --- | --- |
| • More competitive | • Less competitive[33] |
| • More dominant | • More passive and submissive[34] |
| • More rational, objective, and task oriented | • Less rational, objective, and task oriented[35] |

---

[31] Charles B. Craver & David W. Barnes, Gender, Risk Taking, and Negotiation Performance, 5 Mich. J. Gender & L. 299, 315.

[32] Sandra R. Farber & Moica Rickenberg, Under-Confident Women and Over-Confident Men: Gender and Competence in a Simulated Negotiation, 11 Yale J. L. & Feminism 271, 303.

[33] See C. Gilligan, In a Different Voice, 14–15 (1982).

[34] See E. Maccoby & C. Jacklin, The Psychology of Sex Differences, 228, 234 (1974).

[35] See C. Gilligan, In a Different Voice (1982); R. Lewicki, et al., Negotiation, 340–342 (1994).

| Men | Women |
|---|---|
| • Less sensitive to nonverbal signals | • More sensitive to nonverbal signals[36] |
| • Less trusting and trustworthy | • More trusting and trustworthy[37] |
| • More willing to forgive violations of trust | • Less willing to forgive violations of trust[38] |
| • Less concerned with relationships | • More concerned with relationships[39] |
| • Viewed as more competent if physically attractive | • Viewed as more competent if less physically attractive[40] |
| • Employ more "highly intensive" language | • Employ less "intensive language"[41] |
| • Believe in "equitable" bargaining outcomes | • Believe in "equal" bargaining outcomes[42] |

In connection with existing empirical research, one scholar has succinctly observed:

> [D]espite the persistence of stereotypes, the studies of social behavior suggest that there are relatively few characteristics in which men and women consistently differ. Men and women both seem to be capable of being aggressive, helpful, and alternatively cooperative and competitive. In other words, there is little evidence that the nature of women and men is so inherently different that we are justified in making stereotyped generalizations.[43]

This view is consistent with one study that specifically analyzed the impact of gender on clinical negotiating achievement.[44] The view is also consistent with the experiences of the authors of this book in teaching negotiation.

Regardless of the accuracy of different gender-based characteristics in a given situation, there is certainly a difference in the *perception* of abilities that men and women bring to the negotiating table. Carol Gilligan, a noted psychologist, posits a male model of reasoning that she describes as "the logic of the ladder" because of its vertical hierarchy of values. This male model of reasoning is based on abstract universal principles that, in application, create an "ethic of justice." She contrasts

---

[36] *See* J. Hall, *Nonverbal Sex Differences*, 15–17 (1984); N. Henley, *Body Politics: Power, Sex, and Nonverbal Communication*, 13–15 (1977).

[37] *See* J. Rubin & B. Brown, *The Social Psychology of Bargaining and Negotiation*, 171–173 (1975).

[38] *See* J. Rubin & B. Brown, *The Social Psychology of Bargaining and Negotiation*, 171–173 (1975).

[39] *See* R. Lewicki, et al., *Negotiation*, 340–342 (1994).

[40] *See* Cash & Janda, The Eye of the Beholder, Psychology Today 46–52 (December 1984).

[41] *See* Burgoon, Dillard & Doran, "Friendly or Unfriendly Persuasion: The Effects of Violations of Expectations by Males and Females," 10 *Human Communication Research* 284, 292 (1983); Smeltzer & Watson, "Gender Differences in Verbal Communication During Negotiations," 3 *Communication Research Reports* 78 (1986).

[42] See R. Lewicki, et al., *Negotiation*, 330 (1994).

[43] K. Deaux, *The Behavior of Women and Men*, 144 (1976).

[44] C. Craver, The Impact of Gender on Clinical Negotiating Achievement, 6 Ohio St. J. Disp. Res. 1, 12–16 (1990).

this "ethic of justice" with the female "ethic of care" which she describes as similar in structure to a "web." She uses the "web" as a symbol of the interconnected, relational, and contextual form of reasoning that focuses on people as well as the substance of a problem.[45]

Although some commentators have criticized Gilligan's models, in part because of a fear of emphasizing differences in gender to the detriment of women who are often portrayed as weaker,[46] Professor Carrie Menkel-Meadow suggests that women bring to the negotiating table dispositions that are more amenable to problem solving. For her, the problem-solving model of negotiation utilizes the perceived "feminine" attributes of being "less competitive" and more "concerned with relationships" to creatively resolve disputes between the parties as contrasted with the "zero-sum" or adversarial model which focuses on arriving at a solution beneficial to only one party. The adversarial or zero-sum approach is often viewed as more "masculine" because the negotiators are more "competitive" and "less concerned with relationships" than with a result that is beneficial to both parties and places a premium on preserving their future relationship.[47]

Despite the perceived differences based on gender that negotiators bring to the table, empirical studies involving negotiations do not consistently substantiate differences in negotiation outcomes.[48] Psychologists who have utilized the "Prisoner's Dilemma" exercise (see § 7.03) to analyze male-female differences in negotiation have discerned few or no gender differences in outcome.[49] Similarly, a study of male-female performances of students participating in simulated negotiations in the Lawyering Program at New York University School of Law concluded: "We have shown that women and men achieved comparable actual outcomes in this negotiation exercise, and that there were no gender differences in students' perceptions of their outcomes and of their overall performance. Results indicate that women performed as well as men in this exercise, and did not perceive themselves to be less successful in the negotiation than did men."[50]

Although the authors of the study at New York University School of Law concluded there was no difference in the outcomes of simulated negotiations based on gender, they did find that there was a difference in the participants' perceptions about *how* they had negotiated. "When we explored further, however, a more complex picture emerged. Women and men obtained equivalent results, but women

---

[45] Carol Gilligan, *In a Different Voice: Psychology Theory and Women's Development*, 62–63 (1982). *See also* Carrie Menkel-Meadow, Portia Redux: Another Look at Gender, Feminism, and Legal Ethics, 2 Va. J. Soc. Pol'y & L. 75, 76.

[46] *See, e.g.*, Anne M. Coughlin, Excusing Women, 82 Ca. L. Rev. 1, 90–91 (1994); Joan Williams, Deconstructing Gender, 87 Mich. L. Rev. 797, 799–802 (1989).

[47] *See* Carrie Menkel-Meadow, Toward Another View of Legal Negotiation, The Structure of Problem-Solving, 31 U.C.L.A. L. Rev. 754 (1984).

[48] Charles B. Craver and David W. Barnes, Gender, Risk Taking and Negotiation Performance, 5 Mich. J. Gender & L. 299, 317–318.

[49] Charles B. Craver and David W. Barnes, Gender, Risk Taking and Negotiation Performance, 5 Mich. J. Gender & L. 299, 317–318 (citing Eleanor Emmons Maccoby & Carol Ngy Jacklin, *The Psychology of Sex Differences*, 228, 234 (1974) and Jeffrey Z. Rubin & Bert R. Brown, *The Social Psychology of Bargaining and Negotiation*, 172–173 (1975)).

[50] Sandra R. Farber and Monica Rickenberg, Under-Confident Women and Over-Confident Men: Gender and Sense of Competence in a Simulated Negotiation, 11 Yale J. L. & Feminism 271, 302.

left the exercise feeling less confident than did their male peers."[51] This conclusion also correlates with Charles Craver's observations about the performances of students in his Legal Negotiating course at George Washington University: "While male students almost never apologize for their successes, a number of female class members indicate discomfort with their achievements and apologize to opponents whom they have out-performed."[52]

## [2]    The Importance of Awareness About Perceived Gender Differences

When a woman approaches the bargaining table as a negotiator, she faces her own perceptions, the perceptions of her client, the perceptions of the opposing lawyer, and the perceptions of the opposing client. Because of societal stereotypes that women will be less comfortable and less effective in highly competitive circumstances, each of these individuals (including even the woman herself) may suspect that she will be a less successful negotiator. Each of these individuals may make faulty assumptions based on these outdated stereotypes.

For instance, a male attorney who is about to negotiate with a female attorney from a well-respected litigation firm, needs to be alert to a tendency on his part (based on societal stereotypes) to assume that the opposing client and law firm do not place a high value on the case or they would not have assigned the case to a woman. He should prepare for the negotiation aware of this potential misperception because he may discover a highly skilled opponent. Indeed, he may even discover that the opposing firm, client, and attorney intended him to be thrown off guard and initially deceived by the gender of his formidable female opponent.

Negotiators also need to be cognizant of the perceived advantages and disadvantages opponents and clients may attribute to gender. For instance, a female negotiator may find it to her advantage that her male opponent assumes she will not be competitive in her demands. A male negotiator who is operating on the basis of unexamined perceptions instead of the abilities of his opponent may find himself outflanked and outmaneuvered if he enters a negotiation assuming his female opponent will not be competitive in her strategy toward the negotiation. Similarly, a female negotiator who enters into negotiations with the mistaken assumption that her male opponent is adversarial may find herself thrown off balance by the problem-solving techniques he employs.

One scholar has concluded that it is much less important whether women are more cooperative in their negotiation styles than whether "people *think* women are likely to be cooperative types."[53] Successful negotiators must therefore take into account perceived traits and stereotypical assumptions regarding gender when they approach the negotiation table and analyze whether any of these traits or assumptions are at all relevant in a particular case. The fundamental importance of being aware of perceived gender differences in negotiating is that, as repeated

---

[51] Sandra R. Farber and Monica Rickenberg, Under-Confident Women and Over-Confident Men: Gender and Sense of Competence in a Simulated Negotiation, 11 Yale J. L. & Feminism 271, 302.

[52] Charles B. Craver & David W. Barnes, Gender, Risk Taking and Negotiation Performance, 5 Mich. J. Gender & L. at 301.

[53] Carol M. Rose, Bargaining and Gender, 18 Harv. J. L. & Pub. Pol. 547 (1995)

experience has shown, the perception that gender has anything to do with successful negotiation outcomes is belied by the fact that men and women are coequals in negotiating effectiveness.

# Chapter 19

# Plea Bargaining

# § 19.01   INTRODUCTION

Plea bargaining is a form of negotiation by which the prosecutor and defense counsel enter into an agreement resolving one or more criminal charges against the defendant without a trial. The United States Supreme Court has upheld the constitutionality of plea bargaining, encouraged the practice,[1] and summarized its benefits as follows:

> The defendant avoids extended pretrial incarceration and anxieties and uncertainties of a trial; he gains a speedy disposition of his case, the chance to acknowledge his guilt and a prompt start in realizing whatever potential there may be for rehabilitation. Judges and prosecutors conserve vital and scarce resources. The public is protected from the risks imposed by those charged with criminal offenses who are at large on bail while awaiting completion of criminal proceedings.[2]

Approximately 90% of all criminal cases are resolved through plea bargaining.[3]

Plea bargaining may occur before the defendant is formally charged or after formal charges have been brought. Generally, plea negotiations result in one or more of the following: (1) the prosecutor agrees not to charge the defendant; (2) the defendant pleads guilty or *nolo contendere*[4] to a reduced charge or lesser included

---

[1] Santobello v. United States, 404 U.S. 257, 92 S. Ct. 495, 30 L. Ed. 2d 427 (1971).

[2] Blackledge v. Allison, 431 U.S. 63, 97 S. Ct. 1621, 52 L. Ed. 2d 136 (1977).

[3] *See* Brady v. United States, 397 U.S. 742, 752 n.10, 90 S. Ct. 1463, 1471, n.10, 25 L. Ed. 2d 747 (1970); ABA Standards for Criminal Justice 14-5 (2d ed. 1980).

[4] This phrase means literally, "I will not contest it." Piassick v. United States, 253 F.2d 658, 661 (5th Cir. 1958). It is a mere statement of unwillingness to contest and no more, and has the same effect as a

charge; (3) the defendant pleads guilty or *nolo contendere* to a particular charge in exchange for the dismissal of other charges; (4) the defendant pleads guilty or *nolo contendere* as charged or to a lesser charge in return for a sentencing concession by the prosecutor; or (5) the defendant enters a conditional plea of guilty or *nolo contendere,* reserving the right to appeal the judgment and withdraw his plea in the event that the appellate court affords him relief on the adverse determination of a specified pretrial motion. Any one of these bargains might be conditioned upon the defendant's agreement to certain conditions such as cooperating with the government in an investigation, giving testimony for the prosecution against another defendant, completing a rehabilitation program, making restitution to the victim, promising to stay away from the victim, refraining from any further violation of the law, engaging in dispute resolution, or even promising to move out of the jurisdiction.

Generally, the goals of plea bargaining are twofold. First, the defense attorney and the prosecutor seek the most favorable disposition for their respective clients. Second, each side seeks to obtain as much discovery as possible about the other side's case in the event plea negotiations break down and the case goes to trial.

It is important to emphasize that plea bargaining, in contrast to negotiating in the civil context, often involves no negotiations at all. That is, in the majority of criminal cases, although the prosecutor will usually make a plea offer to the defendant that disposes of the case with a penalty that is less harsh than that which the defendant would receive if he were found guilty at trial, that offer is often non-negotiable, and the defendant is simply left with the option of accepting or rejecting the offer. This is so because prosecutors almost always establish uniform policies on pleas that will be extended to defendants in certain types of cases, and those policies are often rigidly applied regardless of the particular circumstances of the case. Thus, the "bargaining" process and techniques discussed throughout this Chapter assume that the prosecutor either has not established an uncompromising plea policy in the particular case or is otherwise open to negotiations with defense counsel in light of special circumstances in the case.

## § 19.02    PLEA BARGAINING STYLES AND STRATEGIES

In the vast majority of plea negotiations, the defense attorney and prosecutor employ an adversarial strategy (*see generally* § 8.02). The adversarial approach is typical because plea bargains are made largely on a cost-benefit analysis that reflects tradeoffs by each side to avoid the financial and emotional costs and uncertainty of a trial. While the process of plea bargaining is not, strictly speaking, a zero-sum game where each gain to one side is a corresponding loss to the other, each side nevertheless seeks to maximize its own gain, and fact and law rationales are manipulated to advance and defend positions. The end result carries benefits to both sides. The prosecution usually secures the certainty of a conviction or some other action by the defendant that acknowledges responsibility for his conduct, and the defendant's exposure to the consequences of the criminal process is usually minimized from what it would be if he were convicted at trial as charged.

---

plea of guilty for purposes of the criminal case. United States v. Wolfson, 52 F.R.D. 170 (D.C. Del. 1971), aff'd, 474 F.2d 1340 (3rd Cir. 1973). The defendant might also decide to plead guilty but maintain his innocence. This is known as an "Alford" plea. North Carolina v. Alford, 400 U.S. 25, 91 S. Ct. 160, 27 L. Ed. 2d 162 (1970).

The pure problem-solving approach of "brainstorming for mutually beneficial solutions" is largely foreign to the plea bargaining process, albeit this does not mean that relatively creative bargains might not be fashioned in certain cases. From the defendant's standpoint in particular, constitutional rights such as the privilege against self-incrimination, due process, and effective assistance of counsel necessarily foreclose the complete and open exchange of information upon which problem solving is based. Moreover, the prosecutor's discretion in plea bargaining often is dictated by internal prosecutorial policies, or limited by statute and what will be acceptable to the court. In short, once the criminal process has been brought to bear against a defendant, the nature of the situation is inherently adversarial and "creative solutions" are limited.

The vast majority of plea bargains are negotiated in a cooperative or competitive-cooperative style (*see generally* § 8.08). Because prosecutors are in exclusive control of the charging process and possess far greater resources than are available to defendants, it is impossible to "brow beat" the prosecutor into a plea bargain through a hardball style. The negotiating power of the prosecutor is almost always greater than that of the defense attorney. Moreover, prosecutors and defense attorneys typically have long-standing professional relationships that would be impaired by Machiavellian interactions. Finally, because plea bargaining is part of the judicial process where both sides have an ethical duty of fair dealing and candor, civility between the prosecutor and defense counsel is expected and required.

## § 19.03   THE PROSECUTOR'S AND DEFENDANT'S INTERESTS AND OBJECTIVES

The prosecutor and the defendant have various interests and objectives that shape the parties' incentives to plea bargain and the terms of a particular bargain. As in other negotiating contexts, identifying these interests and objectives is critical to preparing for plea bargaining and developing an overall approach to plea discussions.

### [1]   Factors Affecting the Prosecutor's Interests and Objectives

As a practical matter, the prosecutor's usual objective is to obtain a plea that is as close to the result that would be obtained if the defendant were convicted as charged. However, this general objective will be affected by a variety of interests and the following factors:[5]

#### [a]   *The Strength of the Prosecution's Case*

The prosecution must prove its case beyond a reasonable doubt. Although probable cause that the defendant committed the particular offense may be strong, no conviction can be sustained on mere suspicion or conjecture, or under the preponderance of the evidence standard which would be sufficient to sustain a civil verdict. Thus, the relative strength of the prosecution's case, the likelihood of an appealable issue, and the relative trial skills of defense counsel and the prosecutor

---

[5] *See generally*, Alschuler, The Prosecutor's Role in Plea Bargaining, 36 U. Chi. L. Rev. 50 (1968).

will all be integral to the decision whether to plea bargain and, if so, what plea to propose.[6]

## [b] The Nature of the Crime and Public Sentiment

The nature of the crime in terms of the harm or injury that occurred, the need for deterrence, and the public's attitude toward the crime will affect the prospects for a plea bargain. Generally, the more heinous or aggravated the crime, the less likely the prosecutor will enter into a plea bargain that is favorable to the defendant. On the other hand, if the offense was committed under circumstances where little or no harm occurred and public sentiment against the crime is not great, the prospects for a plea bargain with a more lenient disposition are enhanced.

## [c] The Feelings of the Victim and the Police

Related to the nature of the crime and public sentiment are the feelings of the victim and the police. While neither the victim nor the police have any legal authority to dictate the prosecutor's discretion in plea bargaining,[7] their views are often given great weight by a prosecutor in plea negotiations.

## [d] The Background and Status of the Defendant

The background of the defendant, including her age, employment, family circumstances, health, "respectability," prior criminal record, and whether she is on bail or in jail pending trial, are often integral factors in plea bargaining. For example, a youthful or first offender is much more likely to obtain leniency than an adult recidivist. A defendant who has been in jail pending trial may be deserving of a sentence for time served. In short, the existence or absence of mitigating factors about the defendant and her role in the crime often has an important bearing upon plea bargaining.

## [e] The Prosecutor's Internal Plea Policies and Limitations of the Law

Virtually all prosecutors establish plea policies in particular types of cases. These policies are often tied to public sentiment about certain classes of crimes or to "sentencing guidelines" established by statute. Thus, the extent to which plea bargaining may be available in a particular case often depends upon where the crime fits into the hierarchy of the types of cases the prosecutor is committed to take to trial or bargain away in light of pre-established prosecutorial policies or statutory guidelines. In addition, many jurisdictions have adopted statutes that limit or preclude the prosecutor from plea bargaining in particular cases.

---

[6] *See* R. Moley, Politics and Criminal Prosecution, 185 (1929) ("It is better not to take a chance of losing a case before a jury but to make certain of at least a small amount of punishment for the offender. Half a loaf is better.")

[7] *See* State v. McDonnell, 794 P.2d 780 (Or. 1990).

### [f]   Budgetary and Resource Constraints

All prosecutors must operate under budgetary, time, and personnel constraints within their own offices and in the face of limited resources available to the police and other investigative agencies. In addition, prosecutors are affected by limited judicial resources in terms of the number of available judges, courtrooms, and support personnel. These constraints, along with statutorily mandated speedy trial rights (where applicable), require prosecutors to prioritize the types of cases that will be prosecuted and to use plea bargaining as a device to control overall case management. Thus, the extent to which a particular case or class of cases will strain prosecutorial or judicial resources will have a significant effect on plea bargaining.

### [g]   The Defendant's Ability to Assist the Prosecutor

Prosecutors often enter into plea bargains in exchange for the defendant's cooperation. This cooperation may take the form of the defendant either assisting in an on-going investigation or testifying for the prosecution against another defendant. The extent of the defendant's willingness and ability to cooperate is often a critical factor in plea bargaining.

### [h]   Personal Motivations of the Prosecutor

In deciding whether to enter into a plea bargain, prosecutors, like other public officials, are frequently motivated by political considerations. Many prosecutors are elected officials or are appointed by the executive branch. Thus, the media and public opinion invariably influence them. Indeed, many prosecutors use their position as a stepping-stone toward attaining other political ambitions. In addition, a prosecutor's attitude toward plea bargaining in a particular case may be affected by purely personal experiences. For example, a prosecutor may be much less inclined to enter into a plea bargain in a case where he knows the victim or in a type of case where he has himself been a victim.

## [2]   Factors Affecting the Defendant's Interests and Objectives

The defendant's ultimate objective in plea bargaining is to have the charge(s) against her dismissed. Failing that, her overall objective is to minimize the consequences of any conviction by (1) having the number of charges against her reduced; (2) pleading to a reduced charge (e.g., to a lesser included offense or to a misdemeanor rather than a felony); (3) avoiding any active incarceration or minimizing the time to be served in prison; and/or (4) obtaining treatment or rehabilitation. These objectives and the reasons or interests underlying them may be influenced by the following factors:

### [a]   The Strength of the Prosecution's Case

The stronger the prosecution's case is against the defendant the more likely she will enter a plea in exchange for an outcome that would be less harsh than that which she would receive if convicted at trial. Conversely, if the prosecution's case is weak or the defendant's defense is strong, the defendant's incentive to enter into a plea agreement is markedly reduced.

### [b]    *The Actual Culpability of the Defendant*

If the defendant is in fact innocent of the charge, it is unlikely she will agree to any plea. In extraordinary circumstances, however, an innocent defendant may nevertheless choose to enter a guilty plea without admitting guilt — a so-called *Alford* plea — and such a plea may be accepted by the court if made intelligently and the prosecution has strong evidence of guilt.[8]

### [c]    *The Financial and Emotional Cost of Trial*

The cost of hiring defense counsel may be considerable. In addition, the criminal process may be lengthy and carry significant emotional costs for the defendant and her family in terms of uncertainty, anxiety, embarrassment, or unwanted publicity. All of these factors will affect the defendant's decision to enter into a plea bargain.

### [d]    *The Desire to Avoid or Minimize Incarceration*

The desire to avoid time spent in prison is, of course, a major inducement for defendants to plea bargain. If the defendant is incarcerated on the charge prior to trial, a plea bargain that would include a sentence for time served is highly attractive. Similarly, pleading to a lesser charge, or even as charged, will be attractive if the plea is exchanged for a sentence that is lighter than would otherwise be the case if the defendant were convicted at trial.

### [e]    *The Nature and Consequences of the Guilty Plea*

The nature of the guilty plea (*e.g.,* whether to a felony or misdemeanor) may affect the defendant's probation or parole, employment or license, eligibility for certain governmental benefits, immigration status, or civil liability. In addition, the nature of the plea may affect whether the record of the conviction will be sealed or expunged, or whether a social stigma is attached to the conviction (*e.g.,* child abuse versus simple assault). All of these matters may affect the defendant's decision to plead.

### [f]    *The Concessions of the Defendant Required by the Prosecutor or Judge*

The nature of the concessions required by the prosecutor in return for a particular plea may be of critical importance. For example, the defendant may have to decide whether she would be willing to cooperate with the government in an on-going investigation or otherwise cooperate by testifying against one or more codefendants. Similarly, when the plea is entered, the presiding judge may require the defendant to make an allocution that might involve an admission of guilt, inculpate a codefendant, or expose the defendant to civil liability.

---

[8] An "Alford plea" is named after North Carolina v. Alford, 400 U.S. 25, 91 S. Ct. 160, 27 L. Ed. 2d 162 (1970). *See also* Fed. R. Crim. P. 11(b) (permitting pleas of nolo contendere with the consent of the court).

### [g]    *The Threat of Additional Charges*

While a prosecutor may not threaten additional prosecution or habitual-offender status for "vindictive" purposes,[9] he may threaten to bring additional charges against the defendant if the defendant does not accept a particular plea offer, so long as there is probable cause for those charges.[10] Thus, the possibility of facing additional charges or being sentenced as a persistent or habitual offender may induce the defendant to enter into a plea bargain.

### [h]    *Personal Motivations of the Defendant*

There may be any number of purely personal or philosophical motivations for a defendant to plead guilty. Quite often, a defendant will decide to plead guilty simply out of remorse or a sense of taking responsibility for her actions, and hope that her forthright attitude will curry leniency with the judge.

## § 19.04   GENERAL CONSTITUTIONAL CONSIDERATIONS

A defendant has no constitutional right to plea bargain.[11] However, a defendant has a Fifth Amendment privilege against compelled self-incrimination, and a Sixth Amendment right to a jury trial.[12] A waiver of either of these rights "not only must be voluntary but must be knowing, intelligent acts done with sufficient awareness of the relevant circumstances and likely consequences."[13] When a defendant enters a plea, the overall test, applicable in state as well as federal courts,[14] is whether the plea represents a voluntary and intelligent choice among the alternative courses of action available to the defendant.[15]

Because of this, when the defendant enters a plea under a plea bargain, generally the court is required to personally advise the defendant of his right to a trial by jury,[16] right to assistance of counsel at trial,[17] right to confront and cross-examine witnesses,[18] right against self-incrimination,[19] and warn him that he will waive his

---

[9] Brady v. United States, 397 U.S. 742, 90 S. Ct. 1463, 25 L. Ed. 2d 747 (1970); Machibroda v. United States, 368 U.S. 487, 82 S. Ct. 510, 7 L. Ed. 2d 473 (1962).

[10] Bordenkircher v. Hayes, 434 U.S. 357, 98 S. Ct. 663, 54 L. Ed. 2d 604 (1978).

[11] Weatherford v. Bursey, 429 U.S. 545, 97 S. Ct. 837, 51 L. Ed. 2d 30 (1977); United States v. Davis, 900 F.2d 1524 (10th Cir. 1990).

[12] Boykin v. Alabama, 395 U.S. 238, 89 S. Ct. 1709, 23 L. Ed. 2d 274 (1969); United States v. Jackson, 390 U.S. 570, 88 S. Ct. 1209, 20 L. Ed. 2d 138 (1968).

[13] The leading United States Supreme Court cases are commonly referred to as the "Brady trilogy." Brady v. United States, 397 U.S. 742, 748, 90 S. Ct. 1463, 1469, 25 L. Ed. 2d 747 (1970); McMann v. Richardson, 397 U.S. 759, 90 S. Ct. 1441, 25 L. Ed. 2d 763 (1970); Parker v. North Carolina, 397 U.S. 790, 90 S. Ct. 1458, 25 L. Ed. 2d 785 (1970). When a minor pleads guilty, no parental consent is required. Ford v. Lockhart, 904 F.2d 458 (8th Cir. 1990).

[14] Boykin v. Alabama, 395 U.S. 238, 89 S. Ct. 1709, 23 L. Ed. 2d 274 (1969).

[15] Parke v. Raley, 506 U.S. 20, 113 S. Ct. 517, 121 L. Ed. 2d 391 (1992).

[16] Streator v. United States, 431 F.2d 567 (5th Cir. 1970). *But see* United States v. Gomez-Cuevas, 917 F.2d 1521, 1525 (10th Cir. 1990).

[17] United States v. Adams, 566 F.2d 962 (5th Cir. 1978).

[18] United States v. Jackson, 627 F.2d 883 (8th Cir. 1980).

[19] United States v. Boone, 543 F.2d 1090 (4th Cir. 1976).

right to trial if the court accepts his plea.[20] In addition, the court must make an on-the-record determination that there is a factual basis for the plea[21] as a condition precedent to exercising the court's discretion to accept or reject the plea.[22] The defendant has no absolute right to have a guilty plea accepted.[23] In examining the factual basis for the plea, the court must determine that the conduct admitted by the defendant constitutes the offense charged, that all elements of the offense are met, and that any requirements of criminal intent are shown by the proffered evidence.[24]

In determining the voluntariness of a plea of guilty or plea of *nolo contendere*, the court has a duty to inquire whether the willingness to plead results from discussions between the defendant or his counsel and the prosecutor.[25] A plea will not be deemed voluntary if it was induced by threats or coercion,[26] was based on unfulfilled[27] or improper promises,[28] or if the defendant was mentally incompetent[29] or under the influence of drugs to the extent that his judgment was impaired.[30] The overall competency standard for entering a plea is whether the defendant has "sufficient present ability to consult with his lawyer with a reasonable degree of rational understanding," and has a "rational as well as factual understanding of the proceedings against him."[31]

A guilty plea or plea of *nolo contendere* is also unconstitutional if the defendant does not have "a full understanding of what the plea connotes and of its consequence."[32] Thus, the court must address the defendant personally in open

---

[20] United States v. Saft, 558 F.2d 1073 (2d Cir. 1977).

[21] Libretti v. United States, 516 U.S. 29, 116 S. Ct. 356, 133 L. Ed. 2d 271 (1995).

[22] Lynch v. Overholser, 369 U.S. 705, 82 S. Ct. 1063, 8 L. Ed. 2d 211 (1962).

[23] United States v. Gomez-Gomez, 822 F.2d 1008 (11th Cir. 1987). However, the court may not arbitrarily reject a guilty plea made pursuant to a plea agreement. United States v. Maddox, 48 F.3d 555 (D.C. Cir. 1995).

[24] McCarthy v. United States, 394 U.S. 459, 89 S. Ct. 1166, 22 L. Ed. 2d 418 (1969); United States v. Boucher, 909 F.2d 1170 (8th Cir. 1990); United States v. Carter, 815 F.2d 827 (1st Cir. 1987); United States v. Lopez, 907 F.2d 1096 (11th Cir. 1990).

[25] McCarthy v. United States, 394 U.S. 459, 89 S. Ct. 1166, 22 L. Ed. 2d 418 (1969); United States v. Riegelsperger, 646 F.2d 1235 (8th Cir. 1981).

[26] United States v. Carr, 80 F.3d 413 (10th Cir. 1996); Walker v. Johnston, 312 U.S. 275, 61 S. Ct. 574, 85 L. Ed. 2d 830 (1941); McMann v. Richardson, 397 U.S. 759, 90 S. Ct. 1441, 25 L. Ed. 2d 763 (1970) (guilty plea involuntary when tainted by a coerced confession).

[27] Machibroda v. United States, 368 U.S. 487, 82 S. Ct. 510, 7 L. Ed. 2d 473 (1962). A guilty plea may be vitiated by unfulfilled promises by the court, law enforcement officials, or attorneys for the prosecution or the defense as to the severity of the sentence that will be imposed. Williams v. United States, 177 F.2d 97 (8th Cir. 1949); Reed v. Turner, 444 F.2d 206 (10th Cir. 1971); United States v. Gonzalez-Hernandez, 481 F.2d 648 (5th Cir. 1973); Stout v. United States, 508 F.2d 951 (6th Cir. 1975).

[28] Brady v. United States, 397 U.S. 742, 90 S. Ct. 1463, 25 L. Ed. 2d 747 (1970) (*e.g.*, bribes).

[29] Chavez v. United States, 656 F.2d 512 (9th Cir. 1981).

[30] United States v. Malcolm, 432 F.2d 809 (2d Cir. 1970).

[31] Bousley v. United States, 523 U.S. 614, 118 S. Ct. 1604, 140 L.Ed.2d 828 (1998) (if defendant is not accurately advised by the court or counsel about the essential elements of the offense charged, the plea is constitutionally invalid); Dusky v. United States, 362 U.S. 402, 402, 80 S. Ct. 788, 789, 4 L. Ed. 2d 824 (1960); Godinez v. Moran, 509 U.S. 389, 113 S. Ct. 2680, 125 L. Ed. 2d 321 (1993).

[32] Boykin v. Alabama, 395 U.S. 238, 89 S. Ct. 1709, 23 L. Ed. 2d 274 (1969); Kercheval v. United States, 274 U.S. 220, 47 S. Ct. 584, 71 L. Ed. 1009 (1929).

court[33] and inform him of the nature of the offense with which he is charged,[34] the range of possible statutory sentences and other penalties for the offense,[35] including the maximum possible sentence,[36] any mandatory minimum sentence,[37] any enhanced punishment under a dangerous special offender statute,[38] the effect of any special parole term that may be imposed,[39] and the terms of any supervised release.[40] However, there is no constitutional requirement that the defendant be advised of so-called "collateral" consequences,[41] such as general information about parole eligibility,[42] the possible revocation of existing parole,[43] the loss of certain civil rights,[44] deportation,[45] the possibility of increased punishment should the defendant repeat the offense,[46] the collateral estoppel effect of a guilty plea in a subsequent civil action,[47] the possibility of a dishonorable discharge from the armed forces,[48] the denial of "good time,"[49] or the fact that the court lacks the power to order that a federal sentence run concurrently with a state sentence.[50]

A defendant has the right to effective assistance of counsel in deciding whether to plead, how to plead, and in entering the plea.[51] However, with the approval of the

---

[33]  United States v. Carter, 662 F.2d 274 (4th Cir. 1981).

[34]  Smith v. O'Grady, 312 U.S. 329, 61 S. Ct. 572, 85 L. Ed. 859 (1941); Henderson v. Morgan, 426 U.S. 637, 96 S. Ct. 2253, 49 L. Ed. 2d 108 (1976); United States v. Allard, 926 F.2d 1237 (1st Cir. 1991); United States v. DeFusco, 949 F.2d 114 (4th Cir. 1991).

[35]  Von Moltke v. Gillies, 332 U.S. 708, 68 S. Ct. 316, 92 L. Ed. 309 (1948).

[36]  Hart v. Marion Correctional Institute, 927 F.2d 256 (6th Cir. 1991).

[37]  United States v. Goins, 51 F.3d 400 (4th Cir. 1995); United States v. Padilla, 23 F.3d 1220 (7th Cir. 1994).

[38]  United States v. Fatico, 458 F. Supp. 388 (D. N.Y. 1978).

[39]  Lucas v. United States, 963 F.2d 8 (2nd Cir. 1992).

[40]  United States v. Good, 25 F.3d 218 (4th Cir. 1994).

[41]  On the other hand, if advice is given about collateral consequences, a guilty plea may be invalid if such advice is materially inaccurate. See United States v. Russell, 686 F.2d 35 (D.C. Cir. 1982); Downs-Morgan v. United States, 765 F.2d 1534 (11th Cir. 1985); People v. Correa, 485 N.E.2d 307 (Ill. 1985); People v. Garcia, 815 P.2d 937 (Colo. 1991).

[42]  See Hill v. Lockhart, 474 U.S. 52, 106 S. Ct. 366, 369, 88 L. Ed. 2d 203 (1986). But see Allen v. Hadden, 536 F. Supp. 586 (D. Colo. 1982); Strader v. Garrison, 611 F.2d 61 (4th Cir. 1979); State v. Davis, 564 P.2d 104 (Ariz. 1977).

[43]  Sanchez v. United States, 572 F.2d 210 (9th Cir. 1977).

[44]  Meaton v. United States, 328 F.2d 379 (5th Cir. 1964).

[45]  United States v. Campbell, 778 F.2d 764 (11th Cir. 1985). But see United States v. Russell, 686 F.2d 35 (D.C. Cir. 1982).

[46]  United States v. Garrett, 680 F.2d 64 (9th Cir. 1982).

[47]  Gray v. C.I.R., 708 F.2d 243, 245 n. 4 (6th Cir. 1983).

[48]  Redwine v. Zuckert, 317 F.2d 336 (D.C. Cir. 1963).

[49]  Johnson v. Dees, 581 F.2d 1166 (5th Cir. 1978).

[50]  United States v. Degand, 614 F.2d 176 (8th Cir. 1980); United States v. Parkins, 25 F.3d 114 (2d Cir.), cert. denied, 115 S. Ct. 530 (1994). But see United States v. Neely, 38 F.3d 458 (9th Cir. 1994) (defendant should be warned that federal judge lacks the power to impose a federal sentence concurrent with a state sentence). See also Commonwealth v. Persinger, 615 A.2d 1305 (Pa. 1992) (defendant should be informed about the possibility of consecutive sentences when he pleads guilty to multiple charges).

[51]  Santobello v. New York, 404 U.S. 257, 92 S. Ct. 495, 30 L. Ed. 2d 427 (1971); McMann v. Richardson, 397 U.S. 759, 90 S. Ct. 1441, 25 L. Ed. 2d 763 (1970); United States v. Taylor, 139 F.3d 924 (D.C. Cir. 1998); United States v. Gwiazdzinski, 141 F.3d 784 (7th Cir. 1998). See generally, Annot., Adequacy of Counsel's Representation of Criminal Client Regarding Plea Bargaining, 8 A.L.R. 4th 660.

court, a defendant may plead guilty without counsel as a matter of free and intelligent choice.[52] Whether the defendant proceeds with or without counsel, the court should always make appropriate inquiries to ensure that the defendant's plea is voluntary, knowing, and intelligent.[53]

## § 19.05    THE ROLE OF THE PROSECUTOR

A prosecutor has a duty to seek justice, not merely to convict.[54] She is given extraordinarily broad discretion in deciding whether to prosecute and what charges to bring,[55] and this discretion is not subject to judicial intervention so long as the charges brought are based on probable cause[56] and the prosecution is not facially discriminatory.[57] This broad power to prosecute includes the power to dismiss or *nolle prosequi* (or "*nol pros*")[58] and to plea bargain.[59]

In deciding whether to press charges, the prosecutor should consider the desirability of a noncriminal disposition,[60] sometimes referred to as "pretrial diversion." In considering such an alternative disposition, the National District Attorneys' Association has said:

> The prosecutor should exercise discretion to divert individuals from the criminal justice system when he considers it to be in the interest of justice

---

[52] Von Moltke v. Gillies, 332 U.S. 708, 68 S. Ct. 316, 92 L. Ed. 2d 309 (1948). *See* Faretta v. California, 422 U.S. 806, 95 S. Ct. 2525, 45 L. Ed. 2d 562 (1975).

[53] Boyd v. Dutton, 405 U.S. 1, 92 S. Ct. 759, 30 L. Ed. 2d 755 (1972).

[54] ABA Standards, The Prosecution Function Std. 3-1.2(c). The American Bar Association's Criminal Justice Section promulgated standards for the "Prosecution Function" (Chapter 3) and "Defense Function" (Chapter 4) in 1992. While the standards are only advisory, *see* Standard 3-1.1, they were apparently influenced by the ABA Model Rules of Professional Conduct, and should be considered as an instructive ethical guide. *See also* National District Attorneys Association (NDAA), National Prosecution Standards, Std. 1.1 (2d. ed. 1991). These NDAA standards are also advisory and many of them were derived from the ABA Standards. It should be noted that the NDAA Standards state that "[t]o the extent that prosecutors are bound by the Rules of Professional Conduct inconsistent with these National Prosecution Standards, prosecutors should endeavor to modify the Rules of Professional Conduct to make them consistent with these Standards." NDAA, National Prosecution Standards, Std. 1.6 (2d ed. 1991).

[55] *See* Pugach v. Klein, 193 F. Supp. 630 (S.D.N.Y. 1961); Newman v. United States, 382 F.2d 479 (D.C. Cir. 1967).

[56] ABA Model Rules of Professional Conduct (RPC) Rule 3.8(a). *See* ABA Standards, the Prosecution Function, Stds. 3-3.4(a) and (c), and 3-3.9(a).

[57] *See* Wayte v. United States, 470 U.S. 598, 105 S. Ct. 1524, 84 L. Ed. 2d 547 (1985); United States v. Relondo-Lemos, 27 F.3d 439 (9th Cir. 1994) (discussing merits of contention that prosecution's plea bargaining decisions were discriminatory and violated equal protection); Annot., What Constitutes Such Discriminatory Prosecution or Enforcement of Laws as to Provide Valid Defense in Federal Criminal Proceedings, 45 A.L.R. Fed. 732; Annot., What Constitutes Such Discriminatory Prosecution or Enforcement of Laws as to Provide Valid Defense in State Criminal Proceedings, 95 A.L.R.3d 280.

[58] United States v. Hastings, 447 F. Supp. 534 (E.D. Ark 1977). *See* Fed. R. Crim. P. 48(a).

[59] *See* ABA Standards, The Prosecution Function Std. 3-3.8 ("The prosecutor should consider in appropriate cases the availability of noncriminal disposition, formal or informal . . . "); NDAA, National Prosecution Standards, Std. 66.1 (2d ed. 1991).

[60] NDAA, National Prosecution Standards, Stds. 66.1 (2d ed. 1991); *See also* ABA Standards, The Prosecution Function, Std. 3-4.1(a) (prosecutor should have general policy of willingness to consult defense counsel about disposing of charges by plea); NDAA, National Prosecution Standards, Stds. 44.1, 44.2, 44.4, 44.5, and 67.1 (2d ed. 1991).

and beneficial to both the community and the individual. Factors which may be considered in this decision include:

   a.   The nature and severity of the offense;
   b.   Any special characteristics or difficulties of the offender;
   c.   Whether the defendant is a first-time offender;
   d.   Whether there is a probability that the defendant will cooperate with and benefit from the diversion program;
   e.   Whether an available program is appropriate to the needs of the offender;
   f.   The impact of diversion upon the community;
   g.   Recommendations of the involved law enforcement agency;
   h.   Whether the defendant is likely to recidivate;
   i.   Consideration for the opinion of the victim;
   j.   Provisions for restitution; and
   k.   Any mitigating circumstances.[61]

If the prosecutor is inclined to charge the defendant, the National District Attorneys' Association advises:

The prosecutor should exercise his discretion to file only those charges which he considers to be consistent with the interests of justice. Factors which may be considered in this decision include:

   a.   The probability of conviction;
   b.   The nature of the offense;
   c.   The characteristics of the offender;
   d.   Possible deterrent value of prosecution to the offender and society in general;
   e.   Likelihood of prosecution by another criminal justice authority;
   f.   The willingness of the offender to cooperate with law enforcement;
   g.   Aid to other criminal justice goals through non-prosecution;
   h.   The interests of the victim;
   i.   Possible improper motives of a victim or witness;
   j.   The availability of adequate civil remedies;
   k.   The age of the offense;
   l.   Undue hardship caused to the accused;
   m.   A history of non-enforcement of a statute;
   n.   Excessive cost of prosecution in relation to the seriousness of the offense;
   o.   Recommendations of the involved law enforcement agency;
   p.   The expressed desire of an offender to release potential civil claims against victims, witnesses, law enforcement agencies and their personnel, and the prosecutor and his personnel, where such desire is expressed after the opportunity to obtain advice from counsel and is knowing and voluntary; and

---

[61] National District Attorneys Association's (NDAA), National Prosecution Standards 44.4. (2d ed. 1991). A practical factor as to whether charges will be brought at all is the extent to which the prosecutor is personally convinced about the defendant's guilt. *Cf.* Freedman, Lawyer's Ethics in an Adversary System, 85 (1975) (prosecutor should be personally convinced of guilt) with Uviller, The Virtuous Prosecutor in Quest of an Ethical Standard, 71 Mich. L. Rev. 1145, 1157–59 (1973) (prosecutor need not be personally convinced).

    q.   Any mitigating circumstances.[62]

Prosecutors are urged to adopt written policies on the exercise of prosecutorial discretion that are available to the public, and this includes standards for plea bargaining.[63] It has been said that in exercising her discretion to plea bargain, a prosecutor should consider the following factors:

(a)   The defendant's willingness to cooperate in the investigation or prosecution of others;

(b)   The defendant's history with respect to criminal activity;[64]

(c)   The nature and seriousness of the offense or offenses charged;

(d)   The defendant's remorse or contrition and his willingness to assume responsibility for his conduct;

(e)   The desirability of [a] prompt and certain disposition of the case;

(f)   The likelihood of obtaining a conviction at trial;

(g)   The probable effect on witnesses;

(h)   The probable sentence or other consequences if the defendant is convicted;

(i)   The public interest in having the case tried rather than disposed of by guilty plea;

(j)   The expense of trial and appeal; and

(k)   The need to avoid delay in the disposition of other pending cases.[65]

A prosecutor may not engage in plea negotiations with a represented defendant without the consent of defense counsel.[66] If the defendant is not represented, the prosecutor should make reasonable efforts to ensure that the accused has been advised of his right to counsel,[67] and the prosecutor should be careful not to give even the appearance of overreaching or coercion.[68] If the prosecutor engages in plea bargaining directly with the defendant, it has been suggested that such plea discussions be recorded or reduced to writing.[69]

If the defendant is convicted, it is a violation of due process for the prosecutor to attempt to punish the defendant by bringing additional or more severe charges in retaliation for appealing the conviction or seeking other post-conviction relief.[70]

---

[62]  NDAA, National Prosecution Standards Stds. 43.6, 10.1 through 10.3, 42.3, 42.4, and 68.1 (2d ed. 1991). *See also* ABA Standards, The Prosecution Function Std. 3-3.9.

[63]  ABA Standards, The Prosecution Function Std. 3-2.5(a); *see* NDAA, National Prosecution Standards Std. 10.1 (2d ed. 1991); White, A Proposal for Reform of the Plea Bargaining Process, 119 U. Pa. L. Rev. 439, 457 (1971).

[64]  Whether the defendant is a "respectable" person in terms of his demeanor, lifestyle, or employment might also be a factor. *See* Newman, Conviction: The Determination of Guilt or Innocence Without Trial, 117–118 (1966).

[65]  J. W. Hall, Jr., Professional Responsibility of the Criminal Lawyer 577 (2d ed. 1996) (citing Department of Justice (DOJ), Principles of Federal Prosecution B(5) (1980), and NDAA, National Prosecution Standards Std. 68.1 (2d ed. 1991)).

[66]  RPC Rules 4.2, 4.3; NDAA, National Prosecution Standards, Std. 24.1 (2d ed. 1991); Department of Justice, Rule on Communications With Represented Persons, 59 C.F.R. 39910, 39930, § 77.8 (1995).

[67]  RPC Rule 3.8(b).

[68]  *See* RPC 3.8(c) (A prosecutor "shall not seek to obtain from an unrepresented accused a waiver of important pretrial rights . . . "); Hood v. State, 546 N.E.2d 847 (Ind. Ct. App. 1989) (defendant's plea not voluntary when prosecutor negotiated with defendant in jail prior to appointment of counsel).

[69]  ABA Standards, The Prosecution Function Std. 3-4.1(b) and Commentary; NDAA, National Prosecution Standards, Stds. 24.3 and 24.4 (2d ed. 1991).

[70]  Thigpen v. Roberts, 468 U.S. 27, 30–31, 104 S. Ct. 2916, 82 L. Ed. 2d 23 (1984).

However, no impermissible "prosecutorial vindictiveness" occurs if the prosecutor threatens to charge the defendant with additional offenses if he fails to enter into a proposed plea,[71] and no presumption of vindictiveness exists if the defendant refuses to plead guilty and additional charges are subsequently brought.[72]

When a prosecutor is negotiating a reduced charge to which the defendant might plead, the charge must bear a reasonable factual relationship to the nature of the defendant's conduct and not adversely affect the investigation and prosecution of others. Similarly, the sentence for the alternative charge should be rationally related to the defendant's conduct,[73] and the prosecutor has a duty to disclose to the court and defense counsel all available information that may be favorable to the accused for sentencing purposes.[74] Whether the plea negotiations involve a prosecutorial concession about one or more charges or length of sentence, the prosecutor should strive to treat similarly situated defendants equally.[75]

Throughout the plea bargaining process, the prosecutor should conduct herself with fairness, impartiality, and an attitude of cooperation with defense counsel, regardless of any prior animosity.[76] This includes a duty to reveal exculpatory information that is material,[77] and a prosecutor "should not knowingly make false statements concerning the evidence in the course of plea discussions."[78] However, a prosecutor is not required to disclose the weaknesses of her case in plea negotiations.[79]

A plea bargain that includes a condition that the defendant will not assert a civil claim in connection with the circumstances giving rise to the charges against him is not *per se* invalid.[80] However, it is unethical for a prosecutor to *insist* upon such a condition as part of a plea bargain or the dismissal of charges.[81] In addition, a plea bargain may not be conditioned upon the defendant's agreement to waive an ethical violation, or forgo a malpractice or ineffective assistance of counsel claim.[82] (*See also* § 19.08[18]).

Prosecutors, defense lawyers, and the police are prohibited from making public statements about the possibility of a guilty plea because such statements have the "substantial likelihood of prejudicing [the] adjudicative proceeding" and are

---

[71] Bordenkircher v. Hayes, 434 U.S. 357, 98 S. Ct. 663, 54 L. Ed. 2d 604 (1978); United States v. Williams, 47 F.3d 658 (4th Cir. 1995).

[72] United States v. Goodwin, 457 U.S. 368, 102 S. Ct. 2485, 73 L. Ed. 2d 74 (1982).

[73] *See* ABA Standards, The Prosecution Function, Std. 3-6.1(a).

[74] *See* NDAA, National Prosecution Standards Stds. 88.4, 88.5 (2d ed. 1991); ABA Standards, The Prosecution Function Std. 3-6.2 and Commentary, and 3-3.11(a).

[75] NDAA, National Prosecution Standards Stds. 66.3, 68.2, and 88.4 (2d ed. 1991).

[76] NDAA, National Prosecution Standards Stds. 25.1, and 25.2 (2d ed. 1991).

[77] Miller v. Angliker, 848 F.2d 1312 (2d Cir.), cert. denied, 488 U.S. 890 (1988).

[78] ABA Standards, The Prosecution Function Std. 3-4.1(c). *See also* RPC Rules 3.3(a) and 4.1.

[79] *See* California District Attorneys Association, Ethics and Responsibility of the California Prosecutor, 95 (1985).

[80] Newton v. Rumery, 480 U.S. 386, 107 S. Ct. 1187, 94 L. Ed. 2d 405 (1987) (upholding a condition barring the defendant from bringing a 42 U.S.C. § 1983 civil rights claim, but not prosecutorial misconduct). *But see* Foley v. Lowell Division of the District Court Dept., 501 N.E.2d 1151 (Mass. 1986) (disapproving of the practice); Cowles v. Brownell, 538 N.E.2d 325 (N.Y. 1989).

[81] NDAA, National Prosecution Standards, Std. 43.5 (2d ed. 1991).

[82] John W. Hall, Jr., Professional Responsibility of the Criminal Lawyer 435–36 (2d ed. 1996).

tantamount to an impermissible publication of an opinion of guilt.[83] Similarly, public statements about a possible plea by a codefendant are prejudicial to the accused and are prohibited.[84]

A prosecutor's plea agreement binds not only her office but other prosecutors in the state as well.[85] If wrongfully breached, the agreement may be subject to specific performance, or, if the prosecutor breaches an executed agreement, the defendant may withdraw his plea for lack of consideration.[86] (*See also* § 19.11). Thus, a prosecutor should not breach a plea agreement unless the defendant does so or there are extenuating circumstances.[87] If a prosecutor cannot fulfill a condition of the plea agreement, she should promptly communicate that fact to defense counsel.[88]

## § 19.06   THE ROLE OF DEFENSE COUNSEL

Like a prosecutor, a defense attorney should explore a non-criminal disposition of his client's case in appropriate circumstances.[89] When a plea bargain would clearly be of benefit to the defendant, the failure to try to negotiate the case may constitute ineffective assistance of counsel upon a showing of prejudice by the defendant.[90] However, for purposes of effective assistance of counsel, a defense attorney has no duty to enter into plea negotiations when the prosecutor has no desire to negotiate.[91]

Also, like the prosecutor, defense counsel has a duty to conduct himself in plea negotiations with candor and to not knowingly make false statements about the evidence to the prosecutor.[92] Statements made during plea discussions with the prosecutor are not admissible at trial,[93] but the defendant may waive this privilege if he takes the stand and testifies about the discussion or otherwise "opens the door" to what occurred during plea negotiations.[94] Defense counsel should not make public statements about the case that he knows or reasonably should know will have a substantial likelihood of prejudicing the criminal proceeding.[95]

---

[83] *See* RPC Rule 3.6; 28 C.F.R. § 50.2(b)(6)(vi) (prohibiting a statement as to "[the possibility of a plea of guilty to the offense charged or to a lesser offense."); ABA Standards, The Prosecution Function, Std. 3-1.4; NDAA, National Prosecution Standards, Stds. 34.1, 34.2, and 35.1.

[84] *See* United States v. Thompson, 615 F.2d 329 (5th Cir. 1980).

[85] State v. Burson, 698 S.W.2d 557 (Mo. Ct. App. 1985).

[86] John W. Hall, Jr., Professional Responsibility of the Criminal Lawyer 430 (2d ed. 1996); Santobello v. New York, 404 U.S. 257, 92 S. Ct. 495, 30 L. Ed. 2d 247 (1971).

[87] ABA Standards, The Prosecution Function Std. 3-4.2(c) and Commentary (extenuating circumstances may exist where the prosecutor discovers facts concerning the defendant's past which were not previously known by the prosecutor).

[88] NDAA, National Prosecution Standards Std. 69.3 (2d. Ed. 1991).

[89] ABA Standards, The Defense Function Std. 4-6.1(a).

[90] *See* Mason v. Balcom, 531 F.2d 717 (5th Cir. 1976); Cole v. Slayton, 378 F. Supp. 364 (W.D. Va. 1974); Walker v. Caldwell, 476 F.2d 213 (5th Cir. 1973).

[91] Burger v. Kemp, 483 U.S. 776, 785–86, 107 S. Ct. 3114, 97 L. Ed. 2d 638 (1987).

[92] ABA Standards, The Defense Function Std. 4-6.2(6).

[93] Fed. R. Evid. 410; Fed. R. Crim. P. 11(f).

[94] *See generally*, Annot., Admissibility of Defense Communications Made in Connection with Plea Bargaining, 59 A.L.R.3d 441; Annot., 60 A.L.R. Fed. 854.

[95] ABA Standards, The Defense Function, Std. 4-1.4 and Commentary; RPC Rule 3.6.

For constitutional purposes, a guilty plea is valid if it was entered knowingly, intelligently and voluntarily.[96] This depends upon the competence of counsel's advice[97] insofar as it affects the defendant's knowledge and understanding.[98] A defendant cannot be bound by her decision to plead guilty if she did not receive reasonably effective assistance of counsel.[99] The test of ineffectiveness is whether counsel's representation fell below an objective standard of reasonableness and whether there is a reasonable probability that, but for counsel's ineffectiveness, the defendant would not have pleaded guilty and would have insisted on going to trial.[100] For example, a plea may be involuntary when counsel materially misinforms the defendant about the applicable law, the consequences of the plea, or the court's probable disposition.[101] However, a mere erroneous estimate of a sentence or sentencing range does not render the plea involuntary, and an erroneous legal opinion regarding the binding effect of the government's promise to make a recommendation as to the defendant's sentence does not render the plea involuntary.[102]

Throughout the plea bargaining process, defense counsel should advise the defendant of the following:[103]

(1) The defendant's sole right and decision to accept the plea bargain or take the case to trial;[104]

(2) All aspects of the merits of the prosecution's case, the defendant's possible defenses, potential defense motions, the applicable law, and a candid assessment of the probable outcome of a trial;[105]

---

[96] Santobello v. New York, 404 U.S. 257, 92 S. Ct. 495, 30 L. Ed. 2d 427 (1971).

[97] United States v. Ramos, 810 F.2d 308 (1st Cir. 1987).

[98] *See* Libretti v. United States, 516 U.S. 29, 116 S. Ct. 356, 133 L. Ed. 2d 271 (1995); Santos v. Kolb, 880 F.2d 941, 944 (7th Cir. 1989); United States v. Frye, 733 F.2d 196 (7th Cir. 1984). *See generally*, Annot., Adequacy of Defense Counsel's Representation of Criminal Client Regarding Guilty Pleas, 10 A.L.R. 4th 8.

[99] United States v. George, 869 F.2d 333 (7th Cir. 1989).

[100] United States v. Calderon, 163 F.3d 644 (D.C. Cir. 1999); Hill v. Lockhart, 474 U.S. 52, 106 S. Ct. 366, 88 L. Ed. 2d 203 (1985); Mangum v. Hargett, 67 F.3d 80, 84 (8th Cir. 1995). (A defendant needs to show that, "but for" counsel's ineffectiveness, the defendant would have had a reasonable chance of success at trial and that the outcome of the case was unreliable or fundamentally unfair).

[101] *See* ABA Standards, The Defense Function, Std 4-6.1(b); United States v. Rhodes, 913 F.2d 839 (10th Cir. 1990); United States v. Sweeney, 878 F.2d 68 (2d Cir. 1989); United States v. Loughery, 908 F.2d 1014 (D.C. Cir. 1990) (failure to advise defendant of recent Supreme Court case that provided basis for dismissal of numerous counts was ineffective and rendered plea involuntary); United States v. Hansel, 70 F.3d 6 (1995) (failure to object to charges barred by the statute of limitations); Finch v. Vaughan, 67 F.3d 909 (11th Cir. 1995); Risher v. United States, 992 F.2d 892 (9th Cir. 1993) (erroneous advice about sentencing); United States v. Michlin, 34 F.3d 896 (9th Cir. 1994) (erroneous prediction by defense counsel concerning sentence does not entitle defendant to challenge guilty plea, but exception may exist if counsel grossly mischaracterizes the likely sentence).

[102] United States v. Khoury, 755 F.2d 1071 (1st Cir. 1985).

[103] *See generally*, Annot., Adequacy of Defense Counsel's Representation of Criminal Client Regarding Plea Bargaining, 8 A.L.R. 4th 660; ABA Standards, The Defense Function, Stds. 4-3.8, 4-6.2(a) and (b); RPC Rule 1.4.

[104] *See* Jones v. Barnes, 463 U.S. 745, 103 S. Ct. 3308, 77 L. Ed. 2d 987 (1983); RPC Rule 1.2(a); ABA Standards, Pleas of Guilty, Std. 14-3.2(a).

[105] ABA Standards, The Defense Function Stds. 4-5.1(a) and (b). *See* State v. Kraus, 397 N.W.2d 671 (Iowa 1986) (inaccurate advice about elements of offense); United States v. Lougherty, 908 F.2d 1014 (D.C. Cir. 1990).

(3)   The general process of plea bargaining and defense counsel's particular plea bargaining strategy in the case;

(4)   All plea offers made by the prosecutor, what they mean, and their relative merits;[106]

(5)   All of the consequences and ramifications of a particular plea, including possible sentences and effects on probation, parole eligibility, immigration status, and the like;[107]

(6)   The actual plea-taking process;[108]

(7)   Any allocution required prior to the court's acceptance of the guilty plea;[109] and

(8)   The process of taking the case to trial if the defendant were to choose that option.

The extent to which defense counsel should try to persuade his client of the wisdom of pleading guilty in a particular case is a controversial subject. As one commentator has observed:

> Most defendants do not understand our system of justice and cannot be made to understand. They are, in the main, too optimistic: they believe that if their attorneys were willing to fight vigorously on their behalf, they might be acquitted. They suspect, however, that the "legal establishment" (including perhaps their own attorney) is conspiring to deprive them of the right to trial, and even when defense attorneys have the time for patient explanations (as they often do not), defendants may not fully realize the extent of the penalty that our system exacts for an erroneous tactical decision. For these reasons, a Chicago public defender observed, "A lawyer shirks his duty when he does not coerce his client," and this statement suggests a fundamental dilemma for any defense attorney working under the constraints of the guilty plea system. When a lawyer refuses to "coerce his client," he insures his own failure; the foreseeable result is usually a serious and unnecessary penalty that, somehow, it should have been the lawyer's duty to prevent. When a lawyer does "coerce his client," however, he also insures his failure: he damages the attorney-client relationship, confirms the cynical suspicions of the client, undercuts a constitutional right, and incurs the resentment of the person whom he seeks to serve. The defense attorney's lot is therefore not a happy one — until he gets used to it.[110]

While there is no constitutional or ethical requirement that defense counsel expressly recommend that his client take a particular course of action,[111] most criminal defense lawyers believe that such advice is desirable beyond merely

---

[106]   ABA Standards, The Defense Function Std. 4-6.2(b); RPC Rule 1.4; McAleney v. United States, 539 F.2d 262 (1st Cir. 1976); Harris v. State, 875 S.W.2d 662, 665–667 (Tenn. 1994).

[107]   *See* ABA Standards, The Defense Function, Stds. 4-8.1(a) and (c); Garmon v. Lockhart, 938 F.2d 120 (8th Cir. 1991); Isble v. United States, 611 F.2d 173 (6th Cir. 1979); Cooks v. United States, 461 F.2d 530 (5th Cir. 1972); Hill v. Lockhart, 474 U.S. 52, 106 S. Ct. 366, 88 L. Ed. 2d 203 (1985); Libretti v. United States, 516 U.S. 29, 116 S. Ct. 356, 133 L. Ed. 2d 271 (1995).

[108]   *See* Isble v. United States, 611 F.2d 173 (6th Cir. 1979); Jennings v. Zahradnick, 455 F. Supp. 495 (W.D. Va. 1978).

[109]   ABA Standards, The Defense Function, Std. 4-8.1(d).

[110]   Alschuler, The Defense Attorney's Role in Plea Bargaining, 84 Yale L.J. 1179, 1310 (1975).

[111]   *See* Jones v. Murray, 947 F.2d 1106 (4th Cir. 1991).

informing the defendant of her bare options.[112] Of course, however, counsel's advice must be reasonably informed,[113] and any efforts at persuasion must not involve improper threats or coercion.[114]

Finally, "[d]efense counsel should not seek concessions favorable to one client by any agreement which is detrimental to the legitimate interests of a client in another case."[115] If defense counsel represents multiple defendants, an impermissible conflict of interest exists if one defendant stands to gain or lose from a plea by a codefendant,[116] and the conflict remains even if the plea bargain is not accepted and the codefendants are tried.[117] However, no conflict of interest exists if all of the defendants represented by the same attorney are aware of the dangers of joint representation, are informed about the direction of the joint defense, and counsel's efforts serve the best interests of each defendant.[118]

## § 19.07 PREPARING FOR PLEA BARGAINING

Of course, thorough preparation is essential to effective plea bargaining. Before beginning to plea bargain, you[119] must (1) obtain all information relevant to understanding what plea may reasonably be obtained for your client,[120] and (2) transpose that information into a working outline — a "Plea Bargaining Preparation Outline" — from which an overall negotiating approach can be developed and employed.

### [1]  Information to Obtain

Generally, you should obtain all information that may be pertinent to the entire plea bargaining process. This information should serve as the raw material from which you can identify (1) what further information to find out; (2) what information to reveal during the course of plea bargaining; (3) what information to

---

[112] *See* Amsterdam, Segal, & Miller, Trial Manual for the Defense of Criminal Cases, 201 (1974).

[113] Strickland v. Washington, 466 U.S. 668, 104 S. Ct. 2052, 80 L. Ed. 2d 674 (1984); *see* Commonwealth v. Thomas, 350 A.2d 847, 850 ("It would be in only the most unusual cases where such advice could be deemed a basis for an ineffective assistance of counsel claim."). *Cf.* Turner v. Tennessee, 726 F. Supp. 1113 (M.D. Tenn.), aff'd, 940 F.2d 1000 (6th Cir. 1991) (counsel's advice to reject plea offer constituted ineffectiveness due to counsel's inflated sense of self optimism and skill as a trial lawyer); Iaea v. Sunn, 800 F.2d 861 (9th Cir. 1986) (counsel's gross mischaracterization of likely sentence constituted ineffective assistance of counsel).

[114] *See, e.g.,* Uresti v. Lynaugh, 821 F.2d 1099 (5th Cir. 1987) (improper for counsel to threaten to abandon client if he did not accept plea); Peete v. Rose, 381 F. Supp. 1167 (W.D. Tenn. 1974) (improper for counsel to excessively exaggerate risks of trial).

[115] ABA Standards, The Defense Function Std. 4-6.2(d).

[116] RPC Rule 1.7 and 1.8(g); ABA Standards, The Defense Function, Stds. 4-3.5(b) and (c) and Commentary, and 4-6.2(e). *See also* Thomas v. Foltz, 818 F.2d 476 (6th Cir. 1987); United States v. Allen, 831 F.2d 1487 (9th Cir. 1987).

[117] Ruffin v. Kemp, 767 F.2d 748 (11th Cir. 1985).

[118] *See* United States v. Carr, 740 F.2d 339 (5th Cir. 1984).

[119] This discussion is primarily written from the defense lawyer's perspective, but should be equally applicable to prosecutors as well.

[120] *See* ABA Standards, The Defense Function, Std. 4-6.1(b) ("Under no circumstances should defense counsel recommend to a defendant acceptance of a plea unless appropriate investigation and study of the case has been completed, including an analysis of controlling law and the evidence likely to be introduced at trial.").

protect from disclosure; (4) the underlying interests of your client and the prosecutor; (5) the primary, secondary, and incidental objectives of your client and the prosecutor; (6) all possible bargains that might be entered into; (7) the strongest and weakest factual and legal leverage points for each side; (8) the specific offers or proposals that may be made by each side; and (9) the tactics each side might employ during the plea bargaining process. In seeking to obtain this information, consider the following categories and factors:

### [a] The Strengths and Weakness of the Prosecutor's Case

- The nature of the charge (*i.e.*, type of offense and whether a misdemeanor or felony).
- The evidence in the case for the prosecution and the defendant.
- The actual guilt or innocence of the defendant.
- The age of the offense.
- Possible defenses and defense motions.
- The defendant's and victim's jury appeal.
- The feelings of the victim and the police.
- Public sentiment.
- Any mitigating circumstances about the defendant or his culpability.
- The probable outcome of a trial.
- Possible appealable issues.
- The likelihood additional charges will be brought.

### [b] The Law Relevant to the Charge and Sentencing, and Consequences of Pleading Guilty

- The legal sufficiency of the charge.
- The existence of lesser included offenses.
- The maximum, minimum, presumptive, or mandatory sentence for the charge.
- The availability of pretrial diversion, expungement, probation, or parole.
- The availability of some other noncriminal disposition (*e.g.*, dispute resolution/community service).
- Any collateral consequences of pleading guilty (*e.g.*, loss of license, employment, etc.).
- The defendant's exposure to civil liability.

### [c] The Background of the Defendant

- The defendant's age, family, education, employment history, and financial circumstances.
- The defendant's health (*e.g.*, any drug/alcohol, psychiatric/physical problems).
- The defendant's prior criminal record (including prior parole or probation).

### [d] The Defendant's Interests and Attitudes Toward a Plea Bargain

- The defendant's needs and fears.
- The defendant's feelings about remorse, acceptance of responsibility, and rehabilitation.

- The defendant's ability to hire defense counsel.
- The defendant's ability to make restitution.
- Any special hardships for the defendant or his family if he is incarcerated.
- The defendant's willingness and ability to cooperate with the government.
- The defendant's attitude toward a polygraph.
- Particular personal, family, economic, and social effects of a guilty plea upon the defendant.
- (*See also* § 19.03[2]).

### [e]  The Prosecutor's Interests and Attitudes Toward a Plea Bargain

- The prosecutor's general attitude and style toward plea bargaining.
- The prosecutor's plea bargaining policies or guidelines.
- The prosecutor's trial skills.
- Whether the prosecutor will negotiate before or after formal charges are instituted.
- Public sentiment and publicity.
- The prosecutor's personal ambitions.
- The prosecutor's resources to try the case and overall case load.
- The attitude of the victim, police, probation officer, and others having input into the bargain.
- (*See also* § 19.03[1]).

### [f]  The Attitude of the Judge

- The judge's attitude toward sentencing and likelihood of accepting a particular plea.
- The judge's requirements about allocution.
- The extent to which the plea might be entered before a different judge.
- The relationship of defense counsel and the prosecutor with the judge.
- (*See also* § 19.09[8]).

## [2]  Sources of Information

For the defense lawyer, the first and most obvious source of information is the client. The client should be interviewed shortly after you are retained or appointed.[121] This is important not only for pretrial bargaining, but for the immediate purposes of determining the client's right to pretrial release or the possibility of obtaining an immediate dismissal of the charges on the basis of insufficient evidence or violations of constitutional rights. Examples of the types of information that should be obtained from the client include the following:

- The client's version of the facts and whether she is in fact innocent.
- The existence of any witnesses to the alleged crime.
- Whether the client's arrest was based on a warrant issued by the police or the prosecutor.
- The factual circumstances of the arrest and whether there were any witnesses to the arrest.

---

[121] ABA Standards, The Defense Function, Std. 4-3.2(a) and Commentary.

- Whether the client was advised of her constitutional rights in connection with her arrest.
- Whether the client has been formally booked and charged.
- Whether the client was interrogated, and all circumstances of the interrogation.
- Whether the client made any statements to the police by way of admissions or confessions.
- Whether the client was promised leniency by anyone.
- Whether the police are relying upon information from any witnesses.
- The client's age, family, education, employment, and financial circumstances.
- The client's physical and mental health (including any drug, alcohol, or psychiatric problems).
- The client's willingness and ability, if any, to provide cooperation.
- The client's prior criminal history.
- The client's needs and/or fears.

After obtaining the foregoing types of information, you should attempt to interview the arresting or other investigating officers. The usefulness of interviewing these persons will, of course, depend upon their willingness to divulge information. That willingness will be affected by the stage of the case (*e.g.*, whether it is still under investigation or has been turned over to the prosecutor), the particular policies of the law enforcement agency and prosecutor's office, and the temperament of the particular police officers involved. Your overall goal should be to obtain as much information as possible about the evidence in the case and the attitude of the arresting or investigating officers to the case.

After your client has been formally charged, you should seek informal and formal discovery from the prosecutor. In addition, you need to know the prosecutor's particular plea policies, general attitude and style toward plea bargaining, and his particular attitude toward the instant case. If you are not personally familiar with the prosecutor, you should consult with other defense lawyers practicing in the particular locality. Similarly, you must familiarize yourself with the attitudes and dispositions of the potential judge who may be involved at different stages of the case.

Finally, you should thoroughly conduct an independent investigation of the case. This means interviewing all potential witnesses, obtaining documentary and other tangible evidence, and talking with those persons who may be involved in sentencing or some alternative disposition to the case *e.g.*, probation officers, those persons involved in potential pretrial diversion programs, the client's family members and close associates, and the like). Particularly in serious cases, an independent investigator may need to be hired.

## [3]  Preparing a Plea Bargaining Preparation Outline

Once you have obtained as much of the foregoing information as possible, you should evaluate and transpose that information into a working outline — a "Plea Bargaining Preparation Outline" — from which an overall negotiating approach can be developed and employed. The components of this Outline are similar to those found in a "Negotiation Preparation Outline" that would be used in a civil case (*see generally* Chapter 12).

Specifically, a Plea Bargaining Preparation Outline contains the following components, which should be listed for both the defendant and the prosecutor:

1. INFORMATION: List information "To Obtain" from the other side, information "To Reveal" to the other side, and information "To Protect" from the other side.

2. INTERESTS (from most important to least important): List each party's underlying societal, personal, psychological, or emotional motivations or reasons that shape the desired terms of the plea bargain. For example, in a case in which the defendant is a first-time offender charged with possession of a controlled substance, the primary objective of the defendant may be to avoid or minimize time spent in prison, and the prosecutor's objective may be to have the defendant serve some active time in custody. However, the primary "interest" of the defendant might be to obtain treatment for his drug habit, and the prosecutor's primary "interest" might be to demonstrate "zero-tolerance" for the crime. The interests of both sides might be satisfied by a plea bargain where the defendant is required to complete a 120-day in-house treatment program in lieu of serving the usual 60 days in jail for such an offense. In this way, the defendant achieves his objective of avoiding prison, and the prosecutor is assured that the defendant is in a controlled setting for twice as long as he otherwise would be if he were incarcerated. Thus, identifying the underlying interests of the defendant and the prosecutor will often be useful in selecting appropriate objectives and possible bargains that will satisfy those objectives.

3. OBJECTIVES: List the "Primary" objectives for each party (i.e., the specific matters that each party must obtain from the bargain if one is to be reached at all); the "Secondary" objectives of each party (i.e., important but not necessarily vital matters that each party might choose to forgo if the primary objectives are resolved in a satisfactory manner); and the "Incidental (To Exchange)" objectives of each party (i.e., those lower-priority goals that each party would like to obtain but which will not have a substantial effect on the decision to accept or reject the plea bargain and which may serve as matters to trade with the other side for something of greater value).

4. POSSIBLE PLEA BARGAINS (Most preferred to least preferred): List each party's "possible" plea bargains — i.e., all potential bargains, however creative, that are not patently out of the question. These will later be refined into specific "Offers or Proposals."

5. FACTUAL AND LEGAL LEVERAGE POINTS: List the "strong points" and "weak points" of each side's case that will shape the rationales for each side's formal "Offers or Proposals."

6. OFFERS OR PROPOSALS: List each party's specific offers or proposals regarding the terms of a plea bargain in the order in which they might be presented.

7. TACTICS: List each party's particular tactics that may be employed in the bargaining process (see § 19.08).

This Outline may then be used as blueprint or road map for plea bargaining with the other side. However, you should always be prepared to revise any aspect of the outline, in whole or in part, as circumstances warrant.

## [4]   Illustration of Plea Bargaining Preparation Outline

Your client, Max. R. Smith, has been indicted in state court for (1) conspiring to traffic in cocaine, (2) trafficking in cocaine by delivery, and (3) trafficking in cocaine by transportation. All offenses involved 28 grams or more but less than 200 grams of cocaine and are felonies. Each offense carries a mandatory, three-year minimum sentence up to a maximum of ten years, and sentences for multiple offenses must be imposed consecutively. However, the judge may suspend any sentence, place the defendant on probation, or impose a sentence that is less than the three-year minimum if the defendant provides "substantial assistance" to law enforcement toward apprehending and convicting other offenders.

Smith is twenty-three years old, has been married for two years, and has a one-year-old daughter. He is a high-school graduate and works for a construction company, framing houses. His employer conducts random drug tests, and Smith tested positive for cocaine eight months ago. As a result, he is on probationary status with the company and will be fired if he tests positive again. His wife works part-time in the evenings as a sales clerk. The couple has little money but they are not on welfare or other public assistance.

Two years ago, Smith was convicted of misdemeanor possession of marijuana. Three years ago, he was convicted of misdemeanor possession of hashish. He served no jail time for those offenses and is currently not on probation. If convicted on any one of the instant charges, and the prosecutor insists, Smith could be sentenced as a habitual drug offender which would raise the mandatory minimum three-year sentence to a minimum of five years for each offense.

Smith is currently out on a $25,000 secured bond. His parents arranged for the bond and live in the same town as Smith. They have the resources to hire defense counsel, but the fee for a trial would essentially use up all of their retirement savings. As indicated previously, Smith has no assets or sufficient income to independently hire defense counsel.

According to the police, the evidence for the State would be as follows. Officer Tom Boles approached Wally Davis at a restaurant and asked if Davis would sell Boles two ounces of cocaine. Davis told Boles to meet Davis at the same restaurant at 10:00 p.m. the next day. At 9:45 p.m. the next day, Officer Leon Fuller took up a surveillance position in his squad car across the street from the restaurant. Fuller saw Smith, who was standing outside the restaurant, walk inside and take a seat. At approximately 9:50 p.m., Fuller saw Davis drive into the parking lot of the restaurant and walk inside. Using binoculars, Fuller saw Davis sit down next to Smith. It appeared to Fuller that Davis and Smith talked for about fifteen seconds. Then, Smith handed Davis a Crown Royal bag and immediately left the restaurant. At 10:03 p.m., Boles arrived and entered the restaurant. He took a seat next to Davis, and Davis handed Boles the Crown Royal bag. Fuller then entered the restaurant and, with the assistance of Boles, arrested Davis. The bag was found to contain 75 grams of cocaine. Smith was arrested the next day.

Davis somehow managed to escape from the county jail a few days after his arrest and has not been found. The police know that Davis is the leader of a local gang, and they believe that he has turned the gang into a major cocaine distribution ring. Because Smith is also a member of the gang, the police believe that he can implicate many of its members and provide information leading to additional charges against Davis.

Your research of the case law in the jurisdiction indicates that, under the so-called "single act" doctrine, Smith's single act of delivering the cocaine to Davis might be insufficient as a matter of law to establish that Smith conspired with Davis to deliver the cocaine to Boles. In addition, some case law in the jurisdiction suggests that convicting Smith of both the delivery and transportation charges would constitute double jeopardy under the so-called "same evidence" test, because there is no meaningful "line of demarcation" between Smith's carrying of the cocaine into the restaurant (*i.e.*, the transportation) and handing the cocaine to Davis (*i.e.*, the delivery). Thus, the State's evidence may run afoul of the rule that double jeopardy exists if the same evidence at trial, regardless of the charges, would sustain a conviction on each charge. In sum, you estimate that there is close to a 50% chance that the conspiracy and transportation charges will be dismissed. If these charges are dismissed, Smith's sentencing exposure (assuming he is not sentenced as a habitual drug offender) would be reduced from 9–30 years to 3–10 years.

Smith does not deny the State's evidence as related by the police. In addition, he has told you that he knew in advance that Davis was going to deliver the cocaine to Boles and agreed to take the cocaine to the restaurant at Davis' request for this purpose. Smith has been involved in a number of other drug transactions with Davis and other members of the gang, and thus Smith could provide the police with concrete information that would incriminate at least five of the gang members (including Davis) on numerous drug-related charges.

Smith is deeply concerned about how his wife and daughter will be able to support themselves if he goes to prison. His parents might be willing to help, but they could not provide much assistance beyond a year. In addition, he has become addicted to cocaine and is concerned that, even though his employer has no standard policy against employing convicted felons, sooner or later he will test positive again on a company drug test and lose his job permanently. He is strongly against the idea of cooperating with the police, but he is willing to do so as a last resort if cooperation would result in a substantially reduced sentence and he could remain employed and support his family.

The prosecutor has a policy against offering misdemeanor pleas where multiple drug felonies are charged. In addition, in recent years, the prosecutor has insisted that all drug felons serve at least some active prison time.

When Davis escaped and Smith was indicted, the county newspaper ran a front-page story that included rumors about the gang's reputed involvement in widespread drug trafficking in the community. The prosecutor is up for re-election in eight months, and, if he is unsuccessful in bringing the gang to justice, he is likely to try to teach the gang a lesson by seeking a particularly lengthy sentence for Smith. The local judge has a penchant for deferring to the prosecutor's recommendations about sentencing.

The jurisdiction has recently implemented an alternative sentencing program for first-time drug felons called "ALT-S." Under ALT-S, a convicted drug felon may attend evening treatment and rehabilitation classes five times a week from one to three months, either in lieu of incarceration altogether (where the defendant provides "substantial assistance" by cooperating with the police), or as part of a reduced active sentence where the offender is employed. In the latter circumstance, the defendant enters the program after he has served his active prison time.

Based on the foregoing, your Plea Bargaining Preparation Outline might include the following:

|  | YOUR CLIENT (D) | THE PROSECUTOR (P) |
|---|---|---|

## 1. INFORMATION

| To Obtain: | 1. P's willingness to plea bargain. | 1. D's willingness and ability to provide substantial assistance. |
|---|---|---|

2. Whether the State has additional evidence on the current charges against D.

3. Whether any additional charges will be brought against D.

| To Reveal: | 1. The weakness of the conspiracy and transportation charges. | 1. D's exposure to habitual offender sentencing. |
|---|---|---|
|  | 2. D's family and employment circumstances. | 2. P's policy that D must serve some active time. |
|  |  | 3. D's ability to provide substantial assistance. |

| To Protect: | 1. D's confidential disclosure of his actual culpability as a conspirator with Davis. | 1. Details of any on-going investigation of the gang. |
|---|---|---|

## 2. INTERESTS
(from most important to least important)

| | 1. To look after the welfare of his family. | 1. To bring Davis and the gang to justice. |
|---|---|---|
|  | 2. To get drug treatment and preserve his job. | 2. To "look good" for re-election. |
|  | 3. To avoid the expense of a trial. | 3. If necessary, to make an example out of D through a harsh sentence. |

## 3. OBJECTIVES

|                          | YOUR CLIENT (D)                                                                 | THE PROSECUTOR (P)                                          |
|--------------------------|--------------------------------------------------------------------------------|------------------------------------------------------------|
| Primary:                 | 1. Serve no more than a one or two-year sentence.                              | 1. D must serve some active time.                          |
|                          | 2. D must provide substantial assistance.                                      |                                                            |
| Secondary:               | 1. Get treatment through ALT-S.                                                | —                                                          |
| Incidental: (to exchange)| 1. Provide substantial assistance.                                             | 1. Seek to have D sentenced as an habitual offender.       |
|                          |                                                                                | 2. Agree to the ALT-S program.                             |

4. POSSIBLE PLEA BARGAINS
(most preferred to least preferred)

|                          | YOUR CLIENT (D)                                                                                                          | THE PROSECUTOR (P)                                                                                                        |
|--------------------------|-------------------------------------------------------------------------------------------------------------------------|--------------------------------------------------------------------------------------------------------------------------|
|                          | 1. D serves 1 yr. or less active time for delivery only, and participates in ALT-S.                                     | 1. D serves 3–5 yrs. active time on each of the 3 counts; provides substantial assistance, and participates in ALT-S.    |
|                          | 2. Same as 1, but D also provides substantial assistance.                                                               | 2. Same as 1, but D serves 3–5 yrs. on one count or each of two counts.                                                  |
|                          | 3. D provides substantial assistance; serves as little active time in excess of 1 yr. as possible; and participates in ALT-S. | 3. Same as 1, but D serves as much active time in excess of 1–2 years as possible.                                       |

5. FACTUAL AND LEGAL LEVERAGE POINTS

|                | YOUR CLIENT (D)                                                        | THE PROSECUTOR (P)                                              |
|----------------|-----------------------------------------------------------------------|----------------------------------------------------------------|
| Strong points: | 1. The weaknesses of the conspiracy and transportation charges.       | 1. Assured conviction on delivery.                             |
|                | 2. D's ability to provide substantial assistance.                     | 2. D's prior criminal record and potential habitual offender status. |
|                | 3. D's family and employment circumstances.                           | 3. Judge will follow P's recommendations                       |

|     | YOUR CLIENT (D) | THE PROSECUTOR (P) |
| --- | --- | --- |
|     | 4. The availability of ALT-S. | |
| Weak points: | 1. No defense to the delivery charge. | 1. The weaknesses of the conspiracy and transportation charges. |
|     | 2. D's prior criminal record and potential habitual offender status. | 2. The need for D's substantial assistance. |
|     | 3. Judge will follow P's recommendations. | |

## 6. OFFERS OR PROPOSALS

|     | | |
| --- | --- | --- |
|     | <u>1st</u>: D serves 6 months active time for delivery only, and participates in ALT-S. | <u>1st</u>: D serves 3–5 yrs. active time on each of 3 counts, provides substantial assistance, and participates in ALT-S. |
|     | <u>2nd</u>: D serves no more than 1 yr. total active time; participates in ALT-S; and provides substantial assistance. | <u>2nd</u>: Same as 1. but D serves no more than 3 to 5 years total active time. |
|     | <u>3rd</u>: Same as 2., but D serves no more than 2 years total active time. | <u>3rd</u>: Same as 1. but D serves no more than 1 or 2 yrs. total active time. |

## 7. PARTICULAR TACTICS

|     | | |
| --- | --- | --- |
|     | 1. Consider pressing for a favorable plea in exchange for substantial assistance before the election when arresting the gang would most benefit P. | 1. Threaten D with habitual offender sentencing. |

## 8. REVISIONS

## [5]  The Role of the Client and Advising the Client

For the defense lawyer, the role of the client is integral to proper preparation and the overall approach taken to the plea bargaining. As mentioned in § 19.06, ethical and constitutional prescriptions generally dictate that counsel advise the defendant of (1) his sole right to accept or reject a proposed plea bargain;[122] (2) all aspects of the merits and demerits of the case and the applicable law;[123] (3) the overall process of plea bargaining and defense counsel's particular strategy in the client's case; (4) all plea offers made by the prosecutor;[124] (5) all consequences of accepting a particular plea bargain;[125] (6) the process of entering a plea before the court; (7) any allocution that the court might require in connection with accepting the guilty plea; and (8) the process of taking the case to trial were the defendant to choose that option. In addition, while engaging in purely preliminary plea discussions does not require client approval, defense counsel should obtain his client's consent before engaging in active plea bargaining.[126]

Of course, properly advising the client assumes that defense counsel is adequately informed about all aspects of the case relevant to entering into a plea bargain. A criminal lawyer has a duty to promptly and thoroughly investigate all aspects of the case, factually and legally, including locating and interviewing witnesses and garnering other evidence, regardless of the accused's admissions to counsel or desire to plead guilty.[127] The duty to investigate extends to determining whether any conflicts of interest exist or will develop, and the client must be informed of any potential or actual conflicts.[128]

When the defendant is incarcerated, counsel should be particularly careful in interviewing and advising the client. The custodial setting often creates feelings of fear and desperation on the part of the accused which may impair his judgment and willingness to be candid. Confidentiality throughout the attorney-client relationship should be fully discussed, and counsel should explain the absolute necessity of candor in order to effectively prepare the case for plea bargaining or trial.[129]

Some defendants erroneously believe that they understand the criminal process. A defense lawyer should never assume that the client adequately possesses this knowledge on his own. All legal and technical jargon should be explained, and the entire pretrial and trial process should be detailed, including practical realties such as delays, inconsequential trial settings, and other nonsubstantive proceedings such as attending administrative calls of the calendar.

Consistent with ethical and constitutional prescriptions, defense counsel should also carefully explain those times in the process when the client will be called upon to make decisions concerning "fundamental rights" (*e.g.*, whether to enter a guilty plea, take the case to trial, or testify),[130] and those times when counsel is called

---

[122] RPC Rule 1.2(a).

[123] *See* ABA Standards, The Defense Function, Std. 4-6.1(b).

[124] RPC Rule 1.4(a).

[125] Libretti v. United States, 516 U.S. 29, 116 S. Ct. 356, 133 L. Ed. 2d 271 (1995).

[126] ABA Standards, The Defense Function, Stds. 4-6.1(b) and Commentary, 4-3.8, 4-6.2(a) and (b).

[127] ABA Standards, The Defense Function, Std. 4-4.1(a) and Commentary. *See* RPC Rule 1.1; Thomas v. Lockhart, 738 F.2d 304 (8th Cir. 1984); Commonwealth v. Baxter, 640 A.2d 1271, 1274–1275 (Pa. 1994).

[128] Holloway v. Arkansas, 435 U.S. 475, 485, 98 S. Ct. 1173, 55 L. Ed. 2d 426 (1978); Glasser v. United States, 315 U.S. 60, 69–70, 62 S. Ct. 457, 86 L. Ed 680 (1942); Cuyler v. Sullivan, 446 U.S. 335, 100 S. Ct. 1708, 64 L. Ed. 2d 333 (1980); RPC Rule 1.7; ABA Standards, The Defense Function, Std. 4-3.5(b).

[129] ABA Standards, The Defense Function, Stds. 4-3.1(a) and 4-3.2(b).

[130] *See* ABA Standards, The Defense Function, Stds. 4-3.1 Commentary, and 4-5.2; Jones v. Barnes,

upon to make purely "strategic decisions" (*e.g.*, what motions to file, witnesses to subpoena, or what to include in a presentence memorandum).[131] The defendant should never be led to believe that defense counsel can work miracles, and all unrealistic expectations that the defendant may have of counsel should be forthrightly disabused. Similarly, a defense lawyer should never overstate his ability to influence the outcome of the case or the likelihood of any given outcome. Worst and best case scenarios should be discussed objectively.[132] All predictions made about the case should be coupled with the caution that the prediction is subject to change in light of changing facts and circumstances, and the client should always be counseled against excessive optimism or pessimism.[133]

This does not mean that defense counsel should hesitate to try to persuade the client toward a particular decision. If entering into a plea bargain appears to be the best choice under the circumstances, that approach should be advocated and explained. On the other hand, the defendant should be assured of counsel's willingness to take the case to trial if the defendant elects that option. Coercing the client is, of course, unethical and unconstitutional. A lawyer is an advocate and an advisor, not a dictator.

When advising the defendant, it is generally desirable for defense counsel to summarize important matters discussed orally with the client through a follow-up letter. This should always be done when the defendant insists upon a course of action that counsel considers unadvisable. In addition, it is recommended that once a plea bargain is agreed upon, if it is not reduced to writing and signed by the client, defense counsel should explain all of the terms of the bargain in a letter to the client. This will protect the client's interests by assuring his informed, intelligent, and voluntary decision to enter into the bargain, and obviate any later contentions by the client that his acceptance of the bargain was done out of ignorance or coercion.

Prosecutors must also be sensitive to the role of certain persons involved in the plea bargaining process and advise them accordingly. Generally, prosecutors have an on-going duty to investigate the merits of a charge and to disclose evidence, favorable or unfavorable, to defense counsel.[134] In addition, although the prosecutor's client is technically the government, she is otherwise accountable to the victim,[135] the police or other investigative agencies, persons involved in probationary[136] or other alternative sentencing programs, and superiors in the prosecutor's office. All of these persons should be appropriately informed and consulted in connection with a particular plea bargain.

---

463 U.S. 745, 103 S. Ct. 3308, 77 L. Ed. 2d 987 (1983); RPC Rule 1.2(a).

[131] *See Id.;* Wainwright v. Sykes, 433 U.S. 72, 97 S. Ct. 2497, 53 L. Ed. 2d 594 (1977).

[132] *See* RPC Rule 2.1.

[133] *See* ABA Standards, The Defense Function, Std. 4-5.1(a) and (b).

[134] RPC Rule 3.8(a) and (d); ABA Standards, The Prosecution Function, Std. 3-3.11(a).

[135] *See* ABA Standards, The Prosecution Function, Std. 3-3.2(g) and (h) (keeping the victim informed); NDAA, National Prosecution Standards, Std. 26.1 (2d ed. 1991).

[136] *See* NDAA, National Prosecution Standards, Std. 28.1.

## § 19.08   PLEA BARGAINING TACTICS

Prosecutors and defense attorneys routinely employ a variety of tactics during the plea bargaining process to advance their clients' goals. Understanding these tactics and how to deal with them is essential to preparing for plea bargaining and implementing an overall approach to plea negotiation. The most common tactics are discussed in alphabetical order below.

### [1]   Coalition

Under this tactic, one party seeks to increase its bargaining leverage by forming an alliance with one or more other persons in negotiating with a third person. For example, in advance of entering into plea discussions, defense counsel might solicit the support or acquiescence of the probation officer, director of an alternative sentencing program, or the investigating police officer toward a particular plea proposal. Armed with this support, defense counsel is more likely to convince the prosecutor to agree to the proposal.

### [2]   Cooperation from the Defendant

As mentioned earlier, one of the most important factors influencing a prosecutor to offer a favorable plea bargain is the ability of the defendant to cooperate by providing information leading to the arrest and conviction of other offenders. Sometimes the defendant is willing to cooperate but possesses little or no useful information. In this situation, defense counsel should argue that her client is no less deserving of a more lenient disposition simply because he possesses little information to cooperate, and that this fact only underscores the defendant's diminished culpability which, by itself, makes him deserving of a reasonable disposition. At other times, the defendant may possess important information but be reluctant to cooperate because of the low esteem associated with being a "snitch," or out of fear of incurring bodily harm from third persons against himself or members of his family as a result of cooperating. In this situation, defense counsel should consider negotiating her client's participation in a witness protection program, or obtain the prosecutor's promise to protect the anonymity of the defendant as an informant to guard against reprisals by codefendants.

### [3]   Deadlines

A prosecutor will often impose a deadline on the defendant to accept a particular plea offer.[137] This is used not only to induce the defendant to accept the particular plea, but to avoid expending further prosecutorial time and resources in the case. If the time-limited offer is rejected, the prosecutor may refuse to make any subsequent offers or only make less attractive offers.

To counter this tactic, defense counsel might argue that she needs additional time to independently investigate the case in order to comply with her constitutional duty to appropriately advise her client and assure that the defendant's acceptance of the plea is knowing and voluntary. If the prosecutor is not inclined to extend the deadline, defense counsel might ask the prosecutor for additional voluntary discovery to expedite defense counsel's investigation. In this

---

[137] *See* NDAA, National Prosecution Standards, Std. 72.1 (2d ed. 1991).

way, defense counsel might be able to obtain additional information about the prosecution's case in the event that the prosecutor rejects the plea offer. (*See also Obtaining Discovery* and *Quick Pleas*).

## [4]    Delay

Delay is a common defense tactic. With the passage of time, prosecution witnesses may become unavailable to testify; the victim may lose interest in the case; publicity may die down; the prosecutor's backlog of cases may increase; or the prosecutor may simply lose his earlier passion for the case. Thus, defense lawyers often seek to delay the case by filing various pretrial motions, such as motions to dismiss, to suppress, for discovery, or for trial continuances.[138] Of course, defense counsel must balance any tactics of delay against the risk of excessively irritating the prosecutor such that he ends up refusing to plea bargain at all. In addition, delay is usually unacceptable to the defendant when he is under pretrial detention.

Sometimes defense counsel and the prosecutor might expressly agree to delay the case to allow the defendant to take certain action that will make a plea agreement or noncriminal disposition more palatable.[139] For example, if the prosecutor takes the view that the defendant's criminal behavior is an aberration and that the defendant is deserving of a "second chance" or an opportunity to avoid a criminal record, but the prosecutor is not yet comfortable with an immediate outright dismissal, the case might be put "on hold" for a period of time during which the defendant might make restitution, obtain counseling, stay out of further trouble, or fulfill other specified conditions. After these conditions have been fulfilled, the case might be dismissed or the prosecutor might agree to a plea that results in a lenient disposition.

## [5]    Illusory Promises

Sometimes a prosecutor will seek to induce a plea bargain through illusory promises that provide no actual benefit to the defendant. For example, a prosecutor might offer to dismiss a charge for which the defendant could not have been convicted, or promise to recommend a concurrent sentence where the defendant could not have received a consecutive one. Some courts have expressly disapproved of such illusory promises.[140] Moreover, it is improper for a prosecutor to offer to recommend a lenient sentence in the event the judge asks for a recommendation when the prosecutor knows that the regular practice of the judge is to never make a request for a recommendation.[141] To guard against illusory promises, defense counsel must know the law and the general practices of the sentencing judge.

---

[138] *See* ABA Standards, The Defense Function, Std. 4-1.3(d) ("Defense counsel should not intentionally use procedural devices for delay for which there is no legitimate basis."); RPC Rule 3.2.

[139] *See* Id.; ABA Standards, The Prosecution Function, Std. 3-2.9(a) and (b) (permitting delay when there is a legitimate basis).

[140] *See, e.g.,* People v. Falkenberg, 333 N.W.2d 616 (Mich. App. 1983); Goodall v. United States, 584 A.2d 560 (D.C. App. 1990); State v. Copeland, 765 P.2d 1266 (Utah 1988); Nash v. State, 429 N.E.2d 666 (Ind. Ct. App. 1981).

[141] *See* McKeag v. People, 131 N.E.2d 517 (Ill. 1956); Dillon v. United States, 307 F.2d 445 (9th Cir. 1962).

### [6]　Image Building

After the defendant is charged, and before entering into plea discussions, a defense lawyer will often take steps to build up the image of her client in order to create factors that may justify a more lenient disposition. For example, defense counsel might urge her client to get a job, make voluntary restitution, obtain psychiatric counseling, or enter a substance abuse treatment program. The overall goal is to demonstrate the defendant's prompt acceptance of responsibility through efforts to rehabilitate himself. When necessary, counsel might deliberately delay plea bargaining in order to allow time to build up the defendant's image.

### [7]　Lack of Authority or Limited Authority

Some assistant prosecutors, genuinely or disingenuously, profess that they lack complete authority to enter into a particular plea bargain. This authority may be limited by the junior prosecutor's need to obtain final approval from a superior, or because the negotiating prosecutor has given the victim or some other third person "veto power" over the plea agreement.[142] To counter these situations, defense counsel might seek to play to the self-esteem of the junior prosecutor and motivate him to "sell" the proposed plea agreement to his superiors or other persons having input into the decision. Alternatively, defense counsel might request the input of the senior prosecutor who possesses complete authority over the case or arrange a joint meeting with the junior prosecutor and his supervisor.

### [8]　Last Minute Pleas

Some defense lawyers believe that plea negotiations should not be initiated until close to the time of trial because the aging of the prosecution's case tends to increase the chances for acquittal (*see Delay*). On the other hand, the closer the case approaches trial, the more likely the prosecutor will have prepared by interviewing witnesses and investing time and resources into the case. Consequently, the prosecutor may be much less inclined to plea bargain at the last minute.

Nevertheless, a plea may be entered during trial, while the jury deliberates, or sometimes even after trial. Any number of events might occur just before the trial begins or during trial that may induce the prosecutor to plea bargain, such as a favorable ruling for the defense on a pretrial motion, the failure of a prosecution witness to answer a subpoena, or the development of an appealable issue. Thus, while prosecutors are generally not inclined to engage in last-minute bargaining, defense counsel might seize the opportunity to make a last-minute offer given a favorable, unexpected pretrial or trial development.

### [9]　Obtaining Discovery

Defense lawyers routinely use the plea bargaining process as an informal discovery device. It is important to know as much as possible about the prosecution's evidence not only to decide upon a plea offer, but to counter the prosecution's case and fashion defenses in the event the case goes to trial. Thus,

---

[142] *But see* State v. McDonnell, 794 P.2d 780 (Or. 1990) (prosecutor may not abdicate his responsibility and give the victim veto power over the plea agreement).

throughout plea discussions, defense counsel should probe for information about the prosecution's case, explaining that this information is necessary in order to assess the outcome of the trial and to intelligently discuss with the defendant the reasoning underlying the prosecutor's plea offer.

## [10] Overcharging

Some prosecutors might overcharge a defendant in an effort to secure an expeditious and advantageous plea. Overcharging is not *per se* unlawful or unethical so long as there is probable cause for each offense charged.[143] For example, if the defendant delivered a controlled substance to another, the defendant might be charged with (1) delivery, (2) transportation, and (3) conspiracy with intent to sell or deliver. When faced with this situation, assuming that defense counsel has no double jeopardy claim, she should stress to the prosecutor that the multiple offenses all arose out of essentially the same event and therefore the defendant should only be punished for his singular conduct.[144]

## [11] Package Deals

When multiple defendants are involved, a "package deal" plea agreement might be proposed. Under this type of plea bargain, codefendants who plead together obtain a more lenient sentence than they would have received had each pled separately. Although package deal plea agreements are not *per se* impermissible,[145] they are fraught with risks of coercion and conflicts of interest, and the court will carefully scrutinize the voluntariness of such agreements.[146] If defense counsel represents multiple defendants, an impermissible conflict of interest exists if one codefendant stands to obtain a more favorable plea at the expense of another codefendant, and package deals should not be entered into unless each defendant consents after full disclosure and consultation.[147]

A package deal plea agreement might also take the form of a so-called "wired," "linked," or "connected" agreement whereby, in exchange for the defendant's guilty plea, the prosecutor promises lenient treatment toward a third person, such as the defendant's spouse or other family member. This type of package deal is also not unconstitutional *per se*, and will not be disturbed absent a showing of bad faith on the part of the prosecutor to generate undue leverage over the defendant who pleads guilty. When such an agreement is before the court, however, "a more searching inquiry" into the voluntariness of the plea is warranted.[148]

---

[143] *See* Bordenkircher v. Hayes, 434 U.S. 357, 98 S. Ct. 663, 54 L. Ed. 2d 604 (1978).

[144] *See* NDAA, National Prosecution Standards, Std. 43.4 (2d ed. 1991) ("The prosecutor should not attempt to use the charging decision only as a leverage device in obtaining guilty pleas to lesser charges."); State v. Compton, 664 P.2d 1370 (Kan. 1993).

[145] *See* United States v. Carr, 80 F.3d 413 (10th Cir. 1996); United States v. Usher, 703 F.2d 956 (6th Cir. 1983); United States v. Ayala, 690 F. Supp. 1014 (S.D. Fla. 1988); State v. Solano, 724 P.2d 17 (Ariz. 1986).

[146] *See* United States v. Castello, 724 F.2d 813 (9th Cir. 1984); United States v. Caro, 997 F.2d 657 (9th Cir. 1993); Thomas v. Foltz, 818 F.2d 476 (6th Cir. 1987); United States v. Wheat, 813 F.2d 1399 (9th Cir. 1987); State v. Horning, 761 P.2d 728 (Ariz. Ct. App. 1988).

[147] RPC Rule 1.8(g); ABA Standards, The Defense Function, Stds. 4-6.2(d) and (e), and Commentary.

[148] United States v. Pollard, 959 F.2d 1011 (D.C. Cir. 1992). *See also* People v. Fiumefreddo, 626 N.E.2d 646 (N.Y. 1993).

## [12]  Plea Policies Excuse

As previously mentioned, prosecutors typically establish standard policies or guidelines for pleas in particular types of cases in order to provide relatively equal treatment for defendants similarly charged. Frequently, a prosecutor will use these policies as an "excuse" for not agreeing to a more favorable plea bargain for a particular defendant. In that situation, defense counsel should stress all relevant factors about the case that would warrant a departure from the policy to justify a more favorable plea bargain for her client. Alternatively, if the prosecutor proposes a plea that is harsher than the particular policy, defense counsel should emphasize the importance of uniform treatment and argue that harsher treatment would effectively set a precedent for violating the prosecutor's policies in future cases.

## [13]  Polygraph Tests

Before entering into plea discussions, a defense lawyer might privately arrange for her client to take a polygraph to show that the defendant did not commit the crime or that his involvement in it was substantially less than what is alleged in the indictment. If the results are favorable to the defendant, they are given to the prosecutor. If the results are inconclusive or indicate that the defendant is prevaricating, they are not revealed. Although the results of polygraphs are generally inadmissible in evidence,[149] many prosecutors will consider the results of these tests in a variety of cases to either dismiss the charges or permit the defendant to enter a plea to a reduced charge. Sometimes a prosecutor will suggest or require a polygraph as a condition to dismissing charges or considering a particular plea.[150]

## [14]  Publicity

Unfavorable publicity toward the defendant and the case makes it exceedingly difficult for defense counsel to negotiate a favorable disposition. Prosecutors frequently invoke the media in announcing a significant indictment, and the resultant public expectation is usually that a hard-line position will be taken. Thus, to the extent possible, a defense lawyer should endeavor to keep the case out of the press, not only to protect her client's ability to obtain a fair trial, but to preserve an unpressured climate within which plea negotiations are possible.

## [15]  Quick Pleas

There are a number of factors that may motivate the defendant or the prosecutor to enter into a "quick plea" shortly after the defendant is charged (*see also* § 19.09[2]). For example, from the defendant's perspective, he may be in custody and unable to make bail, or he may possess information that is useful to the prosecution but the information is getting "stale." In addition, the defendant's plea bargaining leverage may be at its greatest point when he is the first defendant

---

[149] *See* United States v. Gilliard, 133 F.3d 809 (11th Cir. 1998); Miller v. Heaven, 922 F. Supp. 495 (D. Kan. 1996).

[150] *See* Annot., Enforceability of Agreement by State Officials to Drop Prosecution if Accused Successfully Passes Polygraph Test, 36 A.L.R.3d 1280; State v. Best, 703 P.2d 548 (Ariz. 1985) (prosecutor may require defendant to submit to polygraph before offering a plea bargain).

in a multi-defendant indictment to propose turning State's evidence. Similarly, the prosecutor may be inclined to dispose of the case quickly to preserve limited prosecutorial resources, clear a congested case docket, or to accommodate the victim's desire for a quick resolution of the case.

For the defendant, the disadvantage of a quick plea is that it may not allow sufficient time for defense counsel to properly investigate the case and obtain information that may be favorable to the defendant.[151] Thus, as a general rule, quick pleas should be negotiated only in the most simple cases. If the defendant nevertheless insists upon a quick disposition of the case, defense counsel should carefully point out the risks of such an approach and obtain (out of an abundance of caution) the client's written consent to enter the plea in the absence of conducting a complete investigation.

## [16] Take-it-or-Leave-it

Because the prosecutor almost always possesses superior bargaining power over the defendant, defense counsel is often faced with a take-it-or-leave-it plea offer. When this happens, defense counsel might ignore the offer and treat it as a preliminary proposal, or probe the prosecutor's underlying reasons for his offer with the hope that further discussion might cause him to modify it. Alternatively, defense counsel might suspend further plea discussions, delay the case, or attempt to obtain further information or create additional reasons (*see, e.g.*, through *Image Building*) to persuade the prosecutor to reconsider his offer.

## [17] Threats

Prosecutors sometimes threaten to bring additional charges against a defendant or a third person if the defendant refuses to accept a particular plea offer. In addition, prosecutors sometimes threaten to prosecute the defendant as a persistent or habitual offender in order to induce a particular plea. These practices are permissible so long as they are not undertaken for "vindictive" purposes and the prosecutor has a reasonable factual basis for bringing the additional charges or prosecuting the defendant as an habitual offender.[152]

A defense attorney faced with such a threat might choose to ignore it, act as if it was unauthorized or made in the heat of passion, or treat it as a purely hypothetical course of action. Defense counsel will rarely have sufficient bargaining leverage to counter such a threat with a threat of her own. The general strategy should be to refocus the plea discussions on the offenses with which the defendant is currently charged and the various factors and circumstances which warrant entering into a reasonable agreement.

---

[151] *See* ABA Standards, The Defense Function, Std. 4-6.1 (b) (defense counsel should not recommend plea without appropriate investigation).

[152] For an example of overcharging involving improper vindictiveness, *see* State v. Halling, 672 P.2d 1386 (Or. App. 1983).

## [18]    Waiver of Constitutional Rights

As part of a plea agreement, a prosecutor might insist that the defendant specifically waive certain constitutional rights that he otherwise would have in the absence of entering a plea of guilty. For example, a prosecutor might require that the defendant waive his right to file a post-judgment motion or appeal challenging the validity of his guilty plea. Such a provision may not be unlawful *per se* inasmuch as a plea of guilty itself is tantamount to a waiver of constitutional rights such as the privilege against self-incrimination and the right to trial by jury.[153]

However, to the extent a defendant is called upon to waive his fundamental right to "knowingly, intelligently, and voluntarily" enter his plea, such a waiver is likely to be held unconstitutional. Thus, for example, some courts have held that a defendant's guilty plea cannot be deemed intelligent and voluntary if "entered without knowledge of material information withheld by the prosecution"[154] in violation of Brady v. Maryland[155] or if entered with the effect of waiving the right to effective assistance of counsel.[156]

## § 19.09   NEGOTIATING THE PLEA AGREEMENT

Like other forms of negotiation, plea bargaining is a complex form of human interaction that is more of an art than a science. The effectiveness of plea bargaining can be enhanced by understanding (1) with whom to bargain; (2) when to bargain and who should initiate bargaining; (3) where to plea bargain and who should attend; (4) how to set the tone and agenda; (5) how to make offers, counteroffers, and concessions; (6) factors to consider in sentencing; (7) what types of plea provisions to consider and common arguments for the defendant; and (8) how to finalize the bargain, taking into account the ultimate role of the judge.

## [1]    With Whom to Bargain

In virtually all cases, neither defense counsel nor the prosecutor will have any choice about the person with whom she will bargain.[157] The defense lawyer must bargain with the particular prosecutor who is assigned the case, and the prosecutor must bargain with the defendant's lawyer and cannot negotiate directly with the

---

[153] *See, e.g.,* Newton v. Rumery, 480 U.S. 386, 107 S. Ct. 1187, 94 L.Ed.2d 405 (1987) (upholding condition that barred defendant from asserting civil rights claim under 42 U.S.C. 1983, but not prosecutorial misconduct); United States v. Baramdyka, 95 F.3d 840 (9th Cir. 1996); United States v. Schmidt, 47 F.3d 188 (7th Cir. 1995). *But see* United States v. Raynor, 989 F. Supp. 43 (D.D.C. 1997). *See generally,* Annot., Waiver of Right to Appeal as Part of Plea Agreement, 89 A.L.R.3d 864.

[154] Sanchez v. United States, 50 F.3d 1448, 1453 (9th Cir. 1995). *See also* Campbell v. Marshall, 769 F.2d 314 (6th Cir. 1985); White v. United States, 858 F.2d 416 (8th Cir. 1988); United States v. Wright, 43 F.3d 491 (10th Cir. 1997); E. Franklin, Waiving Prosecutorial Disclosure in the Guilty Plea Process: A Debate on the Merits of "Discovery" Waivers, 51 Stan. L. Rev. 567 (1999).

[155] 373 U.S. 83, 83 S. Ct. 1194 (1963).

[156] *See* United States v. Baramdyka, 95 F.3d 840 (9th Cir. 1996).

[157] Some prosecutor's offices assign particular prosecutors to different cases depending on whether the case is submitted to the grand jury or whether pretrial motions are filed. In this situation, defense counsel might have some control over choosing the prosecutor with whom to negotiate by, for example, waiving an indictment or filing certain pretrial motions.

defendant without his lawyer's consent unless the defendant chooses to proceed *pro se*.[158]

Once counsel knows with whom she will be bargaining, she should conduct appropriate research about her adversary's overall style and approach to plea bargaining. If defense counsel does not regularly practice in the particular jurisdiction, she may find it desirable to obtain associate counsel in that jurisdiction to "pave the way" with the local prosecutor. Similarly, if defense counsel has or develops a particularly acrimonious relationship with the prosecutor assigned to the case, defense counsel might choose to associate other counsel to participate in or handle all of the plea bargaining in the case.

Sometimes, particularly when an inexperienced assistant prosecutor is involved, defense counsel might choose to "go over the head" of her adversary. This may be necessary if the junior prosecutor is uncertain about his authority to bargain, or appropriate where the defense lawyer has a particularly close relationship with the chief prosecutor. Of course, in deciding whether to involve the chief prosecutor, defense counsel must weigh this tactic against the risk of antagonizing the junior opponent. (*See also* § 19.08[7]).

## [2]    When to Bargain and Who Should Initiate Bargaining

Generally, counsel should commence plea bargaining when he is in the strongest position and his adversary is in the weakest position. As a practical matter, preliminary bargaining often occurs through casual conversation in courthouse hallways shortly after defense counsel has been retained. However, serious bargaining should never occur until one is adequately prepared.

From the defendant's perspective, any number of factors may tempt him to enter into a plea bargain as soon as possible. For example, he may desire to prevent formal charges before the case is presented to the grand jury; he may be in pretrial custody; he may be concerned about saving substantial legal fees; he may possess information for providing cooperation that might soon become stale and unuseful; or he may simply want "to get the case over with." Similarly, the prosecutor might be interested in an expeditious bargain to clear her docket or save resources. However, particularly for defense counsel, the desirability of entering into a quick bargain must be balanced against the imperative of conducting an adequate investigation, without which the relative strengths and weaknesses of the prosecution's case and hence the propriety of a plea cannot be fully evaluated. Moreover, as mentioned previously, it is often the case that deliberately delaying the plea bargaining and trial process may be particularly advantageous to the defendant (*see* §19.08[4]).

In different jurisdictions, the practice varies as to whether the defense attorney or the prosecutor initiates plea discussions. While it is sometimes contended that initiating plea negotiations is a sign of weakness, this proposition is largely overstated. Many defense attorneys take the view that it is better to wait for the prosecutor to initiate plea discussions because, after all, she was responsible for

---

[158] RPC Rule 4.2, 4.3; ABA Standards, The Prosecution Function, Std. 3-4.1(b). *But see* NDAA, National Prosecution Standards, Stds. 24.2 and 24.4 (2d ed. 1991) (permitting prosecutors to negotiate with represented persons without counsel present "in the best interest of justice" — whatever that means).

bringing the charges in the first place, and it would be useless to engage in bargaining unless the prosecutor indicates her willingness by initiating discussions. On the other hand, a defense lawyer has a duty to explore a plea bargain in an appropriate case, and the party initiating negotiations may be in a better position to set the tone for discussions and define the issues. Moreover, a defense lawyer may be able to obtain valuable information from the prosecutor by initiating plea discussions, even if a bargain is foreclosed at the outset or is not ultimately reached. Thus, there is usually no downside to the party who initiates discussions unless that party does so under circumstances when he is wholly unprepared.

## [3]    Where to Bargain and Who Should Attend

In many misdemeanor cases, plea bargaining often occurs in the courthouse hallways, in the courtroom during a recess, or exclusively over the telephone. In all other cases where the bargaining is not purely perfunctory, when the defense lawyer initiates discussions, he should telephone or write the prosecutor to schedule a meeting. This will give the prosecutor time to review the file in advance and make an initial determination about what plea offer might be extended in the particular case.

If possible, defense counsel should try to arrange the meeting at his own office or at a neutral location such as a coffee shop or restaurant. This avoids the distractions of phone calls or other interruptions that are so common in prosecutor offices, and will create a less formal or authoritarian setting for discussions. However, in the vast majority of cases, plea negotiations are held at the prosecutor's office. If this is the routine practice in the particular jurisdiction, it would be awkward and usually inappropriate to insist upon a different setting. Wherever the meeting takes place, the most important matter is to have the prosecutor's undivided attention.

Virtually all plea bargaining meetings are attended solely by defense counsel and the prosecutor. On the other hand, if the prosecutor does not object, it may sometimes be advantageous for defense counsel to include other persons in the meeting whose views may be integral to the prosecutor's decision about a particular plea offer. For example, in an appropriate case, it may be useful to include in the meeting a sympathetic representative from an alternative sentencing program, or the defendant's probation officer, rehabilitation counselor, or even psychiatrist. The presence of such persons may help defense counsel to establish a *Coalition* (*see* § 19.08[1]). Similarly, sometimes the prosecutor might choose to have an assisting prosecutor, police officer, case investigator, or other person involved in the sentencing process attend the meeting.

## [4]    Setting the Tone and Agenda

Typically the defense lawyer and the prosecutor know each other fairly well, and, because the prosecutor is often under a tight schedule, an initial exchange of pleasantries at the plea bargaining meeting usually yields to "getting down to business" in short order. The prosecutor might begin with, "What will your client take?" or defense counsel might ask, "What do you have in mind about a disposition of this case?" Unlike other types of negotiations where the negotiators might deliberately plan on certain seating arrangements to create a more congenial or cooperative atmosphere (*e.g.*, by choosing seats next to or adjacent to one another), or seek to set a particular agenda for discussion, the defense lawyer usually sits across from the prosecutor's desk, and the issues at hand (*e.g.*, the charges to which the defendant might plead, sentencing options, cooperation, and the like) are usually more predefined.

This does not mean that attempts at agenda control are entirely foreclosed. In an appropriate case, either the defense lawyer or the prosecutor might write a letter to his adversary in advance of a meeting to outline a potential plea bargain. If the defense lawyer adopts this approach, the letter should (1) be non-argumentative, (2) not be "demanding" in tone, (3) propose the terms of a plea in a sufficiently general way to leave flexibility for further discussion and to not unduly "lock in" the defendant's position, and (4) perhaps be copied to the chief prosecutor if defense counsel is dealing with an inexperienced assistant prosecutor. Unless the prosecutor refuses a meeting, it is generally undesirable to engage in plea bargaining exclusively through correspondence.

As mentioned earlier, because defense counsel and the prosecutor usually have an on-going professional relationship and are "officers of the court," plea bargaining is usually conducted in a cooperative or competitive-cooperative style. In light of the fact that the prosecutor, as the charging authority, possesses inherently greater bargaining leverage over the defendant, it is foolish for defense counsel to presume that he can "force" the prosecutor to enter into a particular plea bargain. In sum, the tone of the negotiation should be courteous, professional, and characterized by respectful intellectual equality.

## [5]     Making Offers, Counteroffers, and Concessions

After the "small talk" has opened the meeting, either the prosecutor or defense counsel will usually begin by outlining the terms of a potential plea bargain. The specificity of this outline, however, will largely depend on the extent to which the parties possess the requisite information to make a concrete proposal and respond to one. As discussed in § 19.07, at the meeting you will need to confirm and obtain information from your opponent about his (1) interests, (2) objectives, (3) possible bargains, (4) strongest and weakest factual and legal leverage points, (5) specific offers or proposals, and (6) tactics — all as listed in your "Plea Bargaining Preparation Outline." As each side obtains information from the other during the meeting, the parties will make offers, counteroffers, and concessions toward fashioning a mutually agreeable bargain.

### [a]     *Making Offers*

Many defense lawyers look to the prosecutor to make the first offer because she brought the charges in the first place and any agreement must be consistent with her internal plea policies. In addition, it is advantageous to defense counsel to have the prosecutor make the first offer, particularly if the prosecutor's offer turns out to be more beneficial to the defendant than defense counsel expected. However, in certain types of cases, some prosecutors routinely ask defense counsel to make the first offer. If you are placed in this situation and are unsure what to propose, you might respond with a very general outline of a bargain (*e.g.*, "Perhaps we could discuss a reasonable sentencing cap along with early work release . . . ").

As discussed more fully in §14.13[1][d], the cardinal rules about making any offer is to make it (1) succinct, (2) specific, and (3) justifiable. Brevity is important in order to avoid unnecessary elaboration or a slip of the tongue that might reveal confidential information or your concession strategy. Specificity avoids misunderstandings and demonstrates your commitment to your offer. And making your offer justifiable means that you must be prepared to provide precise and persuasive reasons for it based on your strongest factual and legal leverage points.

### [b]   *Making Counteroffers*

Like opening offers, all counteroffers should be made with brevity, specificity, and justifiable reasons. Before making a counteroffer, however, you should carefully listen to the other side's offer to make sure you understand (1) exactly what is being offered, and (2) the other party's reasoning behind the offer. For example, if you represent the defendant, will the prosecutor specifically "recommend" a particular sentence or merely "not oppose" a particular sentence? How long will the offer remain open? How would the victim feel about an alternative proposal? Never hesitate to ask probing questions about any specifics of the offer and why the other party considers his proposal reasonable. In sum, do not make a counteroffer until you understand as fully as possible the terms of the proposal and its underlying rationale.

### [c]   *Making Concessions*

Concessions in plea bargaining may be triggered by any number of circumstances or tactics. Generally, because prosecutors almost always possess greater bargaining power than defendants, prosecutors tend to make fewer concessions than defense lawyers. However, concessions will be made by both sides so long as they perceive that the desirability of entering into a plea bargain will be more advantageous than going to trial. The most common factors affecting concessions are (1) the strengths and weaknesses of the prosecutor's case; (2) the law relevant to the charge and sentencing, and the consequences of pleading guilty; (3) the background of the defendant; (4) the defendant's interests and attitudes toward a plea bargain; (5) the prosecutor's interests and attitudes toward a plea bargain; and (6) the attitude of the judge.

Sometimes, particularly when there are multiple aspects to a potential plea bargain, it may be useful to forecast your willingness to make a possible concession in exchange for a specific concession from the other side (*e.g.,* "My client might be willing to cooperate if we can agree on a reasonable sentencing cap and parole eligibility."). Using flexible language in communicating a concession makes it easier to retract your position and resurrect the concession at a later time. However, the excessive use of ambiguity in suggesting concessions may lead to misunderstandings and undermine your credibility for lack of committing yourself to making firm concessions.

## [6]   Sentencing Factors

Because the vast majority of plea bargains involve sentencing concessions, it is critical that defense counsel be thoroughly familiar with all sentencing factors pertinent to the particular case and how they may be used to effect a favorable plea agreement for the defendant.[159] As summarized in the *ABA Standards for Criminal Justice*, the Defense Function, Std. 4-8.1(a) (3rd ed. 1993):

> Defense counsel should, at the earliest possible time, be or become familiar with all the sentencing alternatives available to the court and with community and other facilities which may be of assistance in a plan for meeting the accused's needs. Defense counsel's preparation should also include familiarization with the court's practices in exercising sentencing discretion, the practical consequences of different sentences, and the normal pattern of sentences for the offense involved, including any guidelines applicable at either the sentencing or parole stages. The consequences of the various dispositions available should be explained fully by defense counsel to the accused.

Sentencing schemes may involve either "indeterminate" or "determinate" sentences. Under an "indeterminate" sentencing scheme, the legislature specifies the maximum penalty for the offense or class of offenses, and the actual penalty is set in the discretion of the judge, minus statutory or administrative "good time" credits when applicable, and subject to certain actions by the probation office or parole board. Along with the maximum penalty, the legislature might establish a specified "minimum term" of imprisonment (*e.g.*, a maximum of not more that X years and a minimum not exceeding Y years), a "minimum maximum term" (*e.g.*, a maximum of not less than X years nor more than Y years), or a "mandatory minimum term" (*e.g.*, the defendant "shall serve" no less than X months/years).

Under a "determinate" sentencing scheme, the sentence to be served is the one imposed by the court, minus "good time" credits when applicable. A determinate sentence may consist of a "flat-time" sentence, where the defendant serves the exact sentence imposed by the judge or mandated by statute (*e.g.*, two days in jail and a $1,500 fine for a specified misdemeanor). Alternatively, the sentence imposed by the court must fall within a "presumptive" range of permissible months established by statute, and the presumptive sentence may be increased or decreased by the judge from the specified range depending upon a finding of particular aggravating or mitigating factors set forth in so-called "sentencing guidelines." This is essentially the type of sentencing scheme employed in federal law under the *United States Sentencing Guidelines* (USSG).[160]

Under the USSG and those states that have enacted sentencing guidelines, judges are given varying degrees of discretion in determining what sentence to impose and what factors may be considered in imposing a particular sentence. Generally, these guidelines present sentencing options in the form of a two-dimensional grid containing a severity level for the offense and the defendant's criminal history score from which presumptive sentences are given for different felony categories. Typically, sentencing judges are permitted to "depart" from the guidelines, either in terms of disposition (*e.g.*, probation in lieu of imprisonment) or in length of sentence or both, by taking into account various mitigating or aggravating factors prescribed in the guidelines.

---

[159] United States v. Pinkney, 551 F.2d 1241, 1249 (D.C. Cir. 1976).

[160] 18 U.S.C. Sec. 3551 *et. seq. See generally,* T. Hutcheson & D. Yellen, et. al., Federal Sentencing Law and Practice (Current edition). For a detailed discussion of plea bargaining under the U.S. Sentencing Guidelines, *see* G. Nicholas Herman, Plea Bargaining, Chapters 7 and 9 (1997 and current Supp.).

In federal sentencing, the seminal decision in *United States v. Booker*, 543 U.S. 220, 125 S. Ct. 738 (2005), which effectively held that the federal Sentencing Guidelines are only "advisory," paves the way for the consideration of a broad array of additional factors that must be considered. Thus, along with the Guidelines, a federal judge is obligated to also consider (1) the sentencing factors set out in 18 U.S.C. § 3553(a) — the nature and circumstances of the offense, the history, and characteristics of the defendant, the kinds of sentences available, the need to avoid unwarranted sentencing disparities among similarly situated defendants, and the need to provide restitution to any victims of the offense; and (2) the so-called "parsimony" provision of 18 U.S.C. § 3553(a)(2), which requires the sentencing court to "impose a sentence sufficient, but not greater than necessary" to achieve Congress's specific sentencing purposes — a sentence that reflects the seriousness of the offense, promotes respect for the law, provides just punishment, affords adequate deterrence, protects the public from further crimes, and provides the defendant with needed training, medical care, or other correctional treatment. Beyond these requirements, and the procedural requirement that the court give reasons for the sentence it selects, the Sentencing Reform Act as modified by *Booker* places no restriction on the sentence the court may impose within the limits of the statute of conviction. The only restriction *Booker* places on the court is that the sentence be "reasonable."

Although state sentencing statutes or guidelines usually enumerate specific factors that the judge should consider in determining an appropriate sentence, the judge is usually accorded broad discretion to consider "any and all information" that might reasonably bear on the proper sentence for the offense committed,[161] and such information may be drawn from largely unlimited sources.[162] Nevertheless, a sentence may not be founded, even in part, upon material misinformation,[163] and if the information relied upon is contested, it must be established by a "preponderance of the evidence."[164]

In connection with researching the sentencing law in the applicable jurisdiction, counsel should consider the following sentencing categories and factors:

*(1) Terms of Imprisonment*

- Maximum term
- Minimum term
- Minimum-maximum term
- Mandatory minimum term
- Presumptive range/Guideline range
- Grounds for "departure"
- Concurrent/consecutive sentences[165]

---

[161]  Wasman v. United States, 468 U.S. 559, 563, 104 S. Ct. 3217, 82 L. Ed. 2d 424 (1964).

[162]  United States v. Tucker, 404 U.S. 443, 446, 92 S. Ct. 589, 30 L. Ed. 2d 592 (1972).

[163]  Townsend v. Burke, 334 U.S. 736, 741, 68 S. Ct. 1252, 92 L. Ed. 2d 1690 (1948). In some states, prior unprosecuted conduct of the defendant may be considered if there is a factual basis (apart from mere arrest) of the prior offense. *See* State v. Shuler, 780 P.2d 1067 (Ariz. App. 1989); State v. Moore, 345 S.E.2d 217 (N.C. App. 1986).

[164]  McMillan v. Pennsylvania, 477 U.S. 79, 91, 106 S. Ct. 2411, 91 L. Ed. 2d 67 (1986).

[165]  For various factors that a court might consider in deciding whether to impose concurrent or consecutive sentences, *see* State v. Yarbough, 498 A.2d 1239, 1247–1248 (N.J. 1985).

- Split sentence[166]
- Credits for "good time"/"gain time"
- Parole eligibility
- Expungement[167]

### (2) Alternatives to Imprisonment

- Probation[168]
- Parole
- Supervised release
- Work release
- Community service[169]
- Dispute resolution/mediation (See § 19.12)
- Desisting from certain activities[170] /occupational restrictions[171]
- Community confinement
- Home detention/house arrest
- Rehabilitation/treatment programs[172]

### (3) Monetary or Other Sanctions

- Fines/special assessments
- Restitution

---

[166] Under a split sentence, the defendant serves a portion of the sentence imposed and then is placed on probation for the remaining period of the sentence.

[167] See generally, 11 A.L.R. 4th 956.

[168] Various conditions are frequently attached to probation. These may include that the defendant not commit any crime during the term of probation; that the defendant pay a fine, make restitution, or participate in community service; that the defendant not possess illegal controlled substances; that the defendant support his family, refrain from possession of a firearm, remain in the jurisdiction, and regularly report to the probation officer. See 18 U.S.C. 3563.

[169] E.g., United States v. Restor, 679 F.2d 338 (3rd Cir. 1982); United States v. Arthur, 602 F.2d 660 (4th Cir. 1979).

[170] E.g., Malone v. United States, 502 F.2d 554 (9th Cir. 1974) (as a condition of probation, defendant who was convicted of the illegal exportation of firearms to the United Kingdom and who was motivated by a strong commitment to the Irish Republican Army was ordered not to become associated with any Irish organization or movement); State v. Friberg, 435 N.W.2d 509 (Minn. 1989) (defendants convicted of trespass during protest at Planned Parenthood clinic were required to stay 500 feet away from clinic as a condition of probation); State v. Haynes, 423 N.W.2d 101 (Minn. App. 1988) (drug defendant ordered to avoid the area surrounding the drug house where he was arrested). Cf., Burchell v. State, 419 So.2d 358 (Fla. App. 1982) (condition forbidding defendant not to father any children during probationary period violated constitutional right to privacy); Grubbs v. State, 373 So.2d 905 (Fla. 1979) (condition of probation to submit to a warrantless search at any time held violative of the state constitution).

[171] E.g., Wyche v. Madison Parish Police Jury, 769 F.2d 265 (5th Cir. 1985) (defendant convicted of violating civil rights of arrestee and abusing his authority as a deputy sheriff could be forced to give up his profession of law enforcement); United States v. Tonry, 605 F.2d 144 (5th Cir. 1979) (politician convicted of obtaining campaign contributions by promising certain benefits could be ordered not to run for office or participate in political activity for the term of his probation); People v. Burden, 166 Cal. Rptr. 542 (Cal. App. 1980) (defendant convicted of grand theft involving false financial statements to obtain bank loans could be forbidden from obtaining bank loans from financial institutions and from organizing or promoting corporations). Cf., United States v. Sterber, 846 F.2d 842 (2d Cir. 1988) (reversing district court's requirement that pharmacist surrender his license as a condition of probation).

[172] E.g., State v. Watkins, 611 P.2d 923 (Ariz. 1980); Holterhous v. State, 417 So.2d 291 (Fla. App. 1982); United States v. Stine, 675 F.2d 69 (3d Cir. 1982) (defendant required to attend psychological counseling). See also Annot. Jurisdiction of Court to Permit Sterilization of Mentally Defective Person in Absence of Specific Statutory Authority, 74 A.L.R.3d 1210.

- Forfeiture[173]
- License suspension/revocation
- Loss of governmental benefits
- Civil Liability

*(4) Aggravating Factors*

- Role in the offense
- Criminal history
- Habitual/repeat offender status
- Violations of probation/parole/supervised release
- Status or vulnerability of victim
- Extent of harm caused
- Penalty enhancement factors (*e.g.*, use of weapon, use of violence, etc.)

*(5) Mitigating Factors*

- Role in the offense
- Remorse/contrition/acceptance of responsibility
- Cooperation with law enforcement
- Age of defendant
- Education/vocational skills
- Employment record
- Mental/emotional/physical conditions
- Drug/alcohol dependency
- Family and community ties
- Hardships on family
- Record of prior good works of defendant

## [7]    Types of Plea Provisions & Common Defense Arguments

Plea bargains may be composed of a wide variety of provisions. Some of the most common types of provisions to consider include the following:

(1)    A dismissal of all charges.

(2)    A dismissal of one or more, but not all, charges.

(3)    A plea of guilty to one or more charges or a reduced charge.[174]

(4)    A plea of *nolo contendere*.

(5)    A plea of guilty with a recommendation of sentencing leniency by the prosecutor.

(6)    A plea of guilty with an understanding that the prosecutor will take no position on sentencing, will take a position on sentencing only if the judge asks for one, will join in defense counsel's recommendation, or will recommend to the judge or corrections authorities that the defendant

---

[173] *See* United States v. Margala, 662 F.2d 622 (9th Cir. 1982) (defendant properly ordered to forfeit retirement benefits acquired during the course of his business with the corporation which he was convicted of defrauding).

[174] If permitted in the jurisdiction, the prosecutor might agree to allow the defendant to plead to a charge which is not technically included in the original indictment. *But see* Grayer v. State, 519 So.2d 438 (Miss. 1988) (under Mississippi law, a defendant may not enter a plea of guilty to a crime that is not charged in the indictment or is not a lesser included offense of the crime charged).

serve his sentence at a particular institution.

(7) A plea of guilty with the understanding that the prosecutor will intercede on the defendant's behalf with probation or parole officials.

(8) A plea of guilty in exchange for the dismissal of, reduction of, or promise not to bring charges against a third person.[175]

(9) An amendment to the charge to reduce the defendant's sentencing exposure.

(10) An agreement by the prosecutor not to bring further charges against the defendant.

(11) An agreement to a specific sentence, sentencing range, sentencing cap, or that the sentences will run consecutively or concurrently.

(12) An agreement by the prosecutor not to seek habitual or career offender status for sentencing.

(13) An agreement to limit the factual proffer to the court to minimize sentencing exposure.

(14) An agreement by the prosecutor to seek the dismissal or reduction of charges against the defendant pending in other jurisdictions.

(15) An agreement by the prosecutor to make a public announcement to protect the defendant's reputation.[176]

(16) An agreement that the defendant will participate in counseling, rehabilitation, treatment, or a mediation or other dispute resolution program (*See* § 19.12).

(17) An agreement by the defendant to make restitution or pay a fine.

(18) An agreement by the defendant to cooperate by supplying information to the police or testifying against someone else.

(19) An agreement by the defendant to take a polygraph test, which, if passed, results in the dismissal of charges.[177]

(20) An agreement by the defendant to stay away from the victim, or leave the jurisdiction.

(21) An agreement by the defendant to cease and desist from whatever activity brought him to the attention of the authorities.

(22) An agreement by the defendant to stipulate to testimony in another case pending against him.[178]

(23) An agreement by the defendant to waive his right to any appeal,[179] or to waive his right to assert any civil liability.[180]

---

[175] *See, e.g.,* Kent v. United States, 272 F.2d 795 (1st Cir. 1959) (agreement not to prosecute defendant's spouse); Harman v. Mohn, 683 F.2d 834 (4th Cir. 1982); Miles v. Dorsey, 61 F.3d 1459 (10th Cir. 1995). *See also* 50 A.L.R. Fed 829.

[176] *See, e.g.,* State v. Hall, 706 P.2d 1074 (Wash. 1985) (as part of a plea bargain, prosecutor agreed to announce to the media that defendant had no involvement with a certain heroin conspiracy ring as reported by the press).

[177] *See* Annot. Enforceability of Agreement by State Officials to Drop Prosecution If Accused Successfully Passes Polygraph Test, 36 A.L.R.3d 1280.

[178] *See, e.g.,* Couser v. State, 356 A.2d 612 (Md. App. 1976) (prosecutor agreed to dismiss a charge in return for defendant's promise to accept stipulated testimony of a police officer on another charge).

[179] *See* United States v. Ready, 82 F.3d 551 (2d Cir. 1996); United States v. Navarro-Bottello, 912 F.2d 318 (9th Cir. 1992); Commonwealth v. Marsh, 293 A.2d 57 (Pa. 1972). *See generally,* Annot. Waiver of Right to Appeal as Part of Plea Agreement, 89 A.L.R.3d 864; Calhoun, Waiver of Right to Appeal, 23 Hastings Const. L.Q. 127 (1995).

[180] *See* Town of Newton v. Rumery, 480 U.S. 386, 107 S. Ct. 1187, 94 L.Ed.2d 405 (1987).

(24)   An agreement about the disposition of an ancillary civil case, such as forfeiture or tax liability.

In light of the foregoing, some of the most common types of arguments or points of emphasis that are typically advanced by defense counsel include the following:

- Focusing on the weaknesses of the prosecution's case and/or the strengths of the defendant's defenses.
- Pointing out the age of the offense, or the history of non-enforcement of the statute.
- Stressing the defendant's jury appeal or the victim's lack of it.
- Arguing that public sentiment about the case is inconsequential.
- Stressing all mitigating circumstances about the defendant's culpability and why he is deserving of leniency.
- Pointing out the relative lack of harm that occurred from the crime.
- Arguing that the defendant is not as culpable as some other codefendants.
- Arguing that there is a real possibility that the defendant is innocent.
- Highlighting the defendant's salutary background.
- Minimizing the defendant's prior criminal record.
- Pointing out the existence of lesser-included offenses.
- Arguing the appropriateness of pretrial diversion, any available noncriminal disposition, or options of expungement, probation, parole, rehabilitation, community service, or civil dispute resolution.
- Pointing out the special harshness of a particular guilty plea upon the defendant and his family (*e.g.*, loss of employment, license, etc.).
- Arguing that the case is essentially a civil dispute, or point out the defendant's exposure to civil liability.
- Pointing out the defendant's willingness and ability to cooperate with the prosecutor and the police.
- Pointing out the defendant's willingness and ability to make restitution.
- Arguing that the circumstances of the case warrant a departure from the prosecutor's usual plea policies.
- Stressing the defendant's remorse, contrition, and willingness to accept responsibility for his actions.
- Suggesting that the complaining witness has questionable motives and may also be partly responsible.
- Highlighting any police impropriety in the case (*e.g.*, illegal search or seizure), and suggesting the defendant's willingness to forego any potential civil remedies for police improprieties.
- Arguing that a trial may have an adverse impact on certain witnesses.
- Pointing out the judge's likely attitude toward a more lenient disposition of the case.
- Analogizing or distinguishing the instant case from other cases where different plea offers were accepted.

## [8]   Finalizing the Bargain and The Role of the Judge in Bargaining

Once a plea bargain has been agreed upon, it should usually be reduced to writing and signed by all parties except in the simplest of cases. Because plea agreements are essentially contracts between the prosecution and the defendant that may be enforced in the event of a breach (*see* § 19.11), it is desirable to have all of the details of the agreement spelled out, including any contingencies and their possible consequences. The essential elements of a plea agreement include the following:

(1) The specific charges, if any, to which the defendant will plead guilty or *nolo contendere*;

(2) The specific charges the prosecutor will dismiss;

(3) The specific terms of any pretrial diversion (*i.e.*, who will do what, when, where, and how);

(4) Whether the prosecutor will promise not to bring additional charges (*i.e.*, what those charges are, what conduct they relate to, and as of what date);[181]

(5) The specific terms of any binding or non-binding sentencing recommendation to be made by the prosecutor,[182] including how the sentence is to be calculated under what sentencing guidelines;

(6) The specific terms of any probation, parole, fine, restitution, community service, dispute resolution, treatment or rehabilitation, deportation, tax liability, forfeiture, or other consequences, or issues that may be reserved for appeal;

(7) The specific terms under which the defendant will cooperate with the prosecution, including how the sufficiency of that cooperation will be determined and will affect any sentencing recommendation;

(8) Whether the prosecutor will agree not to prosecute others (*e.g.*, a spouse or other relative);

(9) Any stipulations or limitations on the factual basis supporting the plea agreement;

(10) Any agreement that the prosecutor will not call the defendant to testify in any proceeding (*e.g.*, grand jury or trial);

(11) The specific consequences for any breach of the plea agreement; and

(12) A recitation of the right of the defendant to withdraw his plea if the court rejects the plea agreement.[183]

Reducing all the essential terms of the plea agreement to writing is important for four reasons. First, oral side agreements may be more difficult to enforce than written agreements. Second, the judge will usually ask the defendant whether there are any other promises or conditions in connection with the agreement that have not been provided or recited to the court on the record. Third, a written agreement signed by the defendant and his counsel helps to ensure that the defendant enters into the agreement knowingly, intelligently, and voluntarily. And fourth, a written agreement prevents any misunderstandings about the various obligations of the parties.

Under Rule 11(e)(1) of the Federal Rules of Criminal Procedure and the rules of many state jurisdictions,[184] a judge is expressly prohibited from participating

---

[181] *See* ABA Standards, The Prosecution Function, Std 3-3.1(f) ("A prosecutor should not promise not to prosecute for prospective criminal activity, except when such activity is part of an officially supervised investigative and enforcement program.").

[182] *Compare* Fed. R. Crim. P. 11(c)(1)(B) (allowing the prosecution to recommend or not to oppose a particular sentence that will not be binding on the court) *with* Fed. R. Crim. P. 11(c)(1)(C) (allowing an agreement about a specific sentence as being the appropriate disposition).

[183] *See* Fed. R. Crim. P. 11(c)(5) and 11(d).

[184] *See generally*, Annot., Judge's participation in Plea Bargaining Negotiation as Rendewring

directly in plea discussions (*see also* § 19.10[3]). In other jurisdictions, the judge is permitted to participate after the lawyers have reached an agreement.[185] Thus, once a tentative agreement has been reached, the parties may sometimes be permitted to disclose their tentative accord to the judge to find out whether he is inclined to accept it. Moreover, in some jurisdictions, a judge might permit counsel to meet with him informally in chambers or at a bench conference prior to entering the plea to discuss his attitude toward the particular plea proposal.[186]

Since a plea bargain is meaningless unless the judge will accept it, throughout the process of plea bargaining counsel must conduct appropriate research about the presiding judge's likely disposition to the proposed bargain and advise the client accordingly. In this regard, counsel should find out: (1) whether the judge's acceptance of the plea will depend upon his review of a presentence investigation report;[187] (2) whether the judge is willing to depart from any statutory sentencing guidelines;[188] (3) what sentencing parameters the judge is likely to use if no specific sentencing recommendation is made; (4) whether the judge is likely to accept a particular sentencing recommendation; (5) whether the judge is likely to impose a greater sentence if the defendant chooses to go to trial and is convicted; (6) whether the judge is receptive to sentencing alternatives such as probation, community service, dispute resolution, and the like; (7) whether the judge is inclined to impose sentences consecutively or concurrently; and (8) the extent to which the judge is likely to be influenced by public opinion or the media.[189] Depending upon the answers to these questions, counsel might, when possible, seek to have the plea entered before a different judge.[190]

## § 19.10    ENTERING A PLEA UNDER A PLEA AGREEMENT

To enter a valid plea under a plea agreement, it is necessary to understand (1) what types of pleas may be accepted by the court; (2) the procedures that the court must follow in accepting or rejecting a plea of guilty; (3) the procedures that the court must follow in determining whether to accept or reject a plea agreement; and (4) defense counsel's responsibilities to her client and to the court in entering a plea. An understanding of these matters is also essential in formulating an acceptable plea agreement.

---

Accused's Guilty Plea Involuntary, 10 A.L.R. 4th 689; *see also* 56 A.L.R. Fed. 529.

[185] *See* Id. Vermont allows judges to participate directly in plea bargaining. *See* State v. Davis, 584 A.2d 1146 (Vt. 1990).

[186] *See generally*, Schlesinger & Malley, Plea Bargaining and the Judiciary: An Argument for Reform, 30 Drake L. Rev. 581, 595–597 (1980); Note, Guilty Plea Bargaining: Compromise by Prosecutors to Secure Guilty Pleas, 112 U. Pa. L. Rev. 865, 891–907 (1964).

[187] *See* Fed. R. Crim. P. 11(c)(3)(A) (court may defer decision on accepting or rejecting plea agreement until the court has reviewed the presentence report).

[188] *See* Fed. R. Crim. P. 11(b)(1)(M) (the defendant must be advised by the court of its obligation to calculate the applicable sentencing-guideline range, possible departures under the Sentencing Guidelines, and other sentencing factors).

[189] *See* ABA Standards, The Defense Function, Std. 4-8.1(a).

[190] In many state jurisdictions, the prosecutor enjoys virtually complete control over the criminal docket. In such circumstances, defense counsel might convince the prosecutor to agree to schedule the entry of the plea before a particular judge.

## [1]   Types of Pleas

The criminal law recognizes five types of pleas: (1) a plea of not guilty, (2) a "straight" guilty plea, (3) an "*Alford*" plea, (4) a plea of "*nolo contendere,*" and (5) a conditional plea. Each of these types of pleas carries different consequences that are important to understand for plea bargaining and in entering a plea with the court.

### [a]   Plea of Not Guilty

The right to plead not guilty is grounded in the defendant's Fifth and Sixth Amendments rights against self-incrimination, to a trial by jury, and to confront his accusers.[191] A plea of not guilty invokes the presumption of innocence and requires the prosecution to prove all elements of the crime charged beyond a reasonable doubt.[192]

The court must enter a plea of not guilty on behalf of the defendant if he stands mute (*i.e.,* makes no response to the court's inquiry as to how he pleads),[193] otherwise refuses to plead,[194] the court refuses to accept a guilty plea,[195] or if a corporate defendant fails to appear.[196] While some states recognize a plea of "not guilty by reason of insanity," there is no such plea under federal law, and the defense of insanity, like the defense of entrapment, is encompassed within the plea of not guilty.[197]

### [b]   "Straight" Guilty Plea

A "straight" plea of guilty is an unconditional confession of guilt that is tantamount to a conviction.[198] When the defendant enters such a plea, he waives his privilege against self-incrimination, right to trial by jury, right to confront his accusers,[199] all non-jurisdictional defects in the proceedings,[200] and is prohibited from thereafter asserting constitutional challenges to the pretrial proceedings.[201]

---

[191] United States v. Jackson, 390 U.S. 570, 88 S. Ct. 1209, 1216, 20 L. Ed. 2d 138 (1968); Wiley v. Sowders, 647 F.2d 642 (6th Cir. 1981).

[192] Davis v. United States, 160 U.S. 469, 16 S. Ct. 353, 40 L. Ed. 499 (1895); Matthews v. United States, 485 U.S. 58, 108 S. Ct. 883, 90 L. Ed. 2d 54 (1988).

[193] Corbitt v. New Jersey, 439 U.S. 212, 99 S. Ct. 492, 504–505, 58 L. Ed. 2d 466 (1978).

[194] Ruckle v. Warden, Md. Penitentiary, 335 F.2d 336, 338 (4th Cir. 1964).

[195] Lynch v. Overholser, 369 U.S. 705, 82 S. Ct. 1063, 1072, 8 L. Ed. 2d 211 (1962); Fed. R. Crim. P. 11(a).

[196] United States v. Beadon, 49 F.2d 164 (2d Cir. 1931).

[197] Evalt v. United States, 359 F.2d 534 (9th Cir. 1966); Mathews v. United States, 485 U.S. 58, 108 S. Ct. 883, 99 L. Ed. 2d 54 (1988).

[198] Kercheval v. United States, 274 U.S. 220, 47 S. Ct. 582, 71 L. Ed. 1009 (1927); Dickerson v. New Banner Institute, Inc., 460 U.S. 103, 103 S. Ct. 986, 74 L. Ed. 2d 845 (1983).

[199] McCarthy v. United States, 394 U.S. 459, 89 S. Ct. 1166, 1171, 22 L. Ed. 2d 418 (1969).

[200] United States v. Dyer, 136 F.3d 417 (5th Cir. 1998); Walker v. United States, 115 F.3d 603 (8th Cir. 1997); United States v. Markling, 7 F.3d 1309, 1312 (7th Cir. 1993); United States v. Gibson, 835 F.2d 1323, 1324 (10th Cir. 1988).

[201] United States v. Cain, 134 F.3d 1345 (8th Cir. 1998) (defendant's plea of guilty waived any claim of prosecutorial misconduct in the form of pre-indictment delay); Lefkowitz v. Newsome, 420 U.S. 283, 95 S. Ct. 886, 889, 43 L. Ed. 2d 196 (1975); Menna v. New York, 423 U.S. 61, 96 S. Ct. 241, 46 L. Ed. 2d 195 (1975).

Thus, the defendant will be barred from later claiming that the indictment was improper in form,[202] that evidence was obtained against him unlawfully,[203] that he was illegally detained,[204] or that he was denied a speedy trial,[205] except to the extent that any of these matters may show that the plea was not voluntary.[206] However, entering a plea of guilty will not preclude the defendant from thereafter raising constitutional claims related to the power of the government to bring the charges against him.[207] Thus, he will still be permitted to later contend that the indictment or information failed to state an offense,[208] that the statute under which he was charged is unconstitutional,[209] or that the prosecution is barred by double jeopardy to the extent this defect appears on the face of the existing record.[210]

Of course, when a defendant pleads guilty, the plea binds him alone and no other defendant.[211] In a subsequent civil proceeding, the plea may be admitted against the defendant who entered it[212] and thus may have the effect of estopping him from contesting the facts representing the elements of the offense to which he pled guilty.[213] However, a defendant will not be estopped from challenging the forfeiture of property in a subsequent civil case because a plea of guilty does not automatically bind the property as having been used for criminal purposes.[214]

The court has the discretion to decide whether to accept or reject a plea of guilty.[215] In federal practice, Fed. R. Crim. P. 11 sets forth detailed procedures that must be followed by the judge to ensure the voluntariness of the defendant's

[202] Nicholson v. United States, 79 F.2d 387, 389 (8th Cir. 1935); Steffler v. United States, 143 F.2d 772, 774 (7th Cir. 1944).

[203] United States v. Carrasco, 786 F.2d 1452, 1454 n. 2 (9th Cir. 1986); United States v. Johnson, 634 F.2d 385 (8th Cir. 1980).

[204] United States v. Morin, 163 F. Supp. 941 (D. Va. 1958), aff'd, 265 F.2d 241 (3d Cir. 1959).

[205] Thye v. United States, 96 F.3d 635 (2d Cir. 1996); United States v. LoFranco, 818 F.2d 276, (2d Cir. 1987); United States v. Yunis, 723 F.2d 795 (11th Cir. 1984).

[206] See Marrow v. United States, 772 F.2d 525, 529 (9th Cir. 1985); McMann v. Richardson, 397 U.S. 759, 90 S. Ct. 1441, 25 L. Ed. 2d 763 (1970).

[207] United States v. Broce, 488 U.S. 563, 109 S. Ct. 757, 102 L. Ed. 2d 927 (1989); Blackledge v. Perry, 417 U.S. 21, 94 S. Ct. 2098, 2103, 40 L. Ed. 2d 628 (1974).

[208] United States v. Bell, 22 F.3d 274 (11th Cir. 1994); United States v. Ruelas, 106 F.3d 1416 (9th Cir. 1997); United States v. Cooper, 956 F.2d 960 (10th Cir. 1992); United States v. DiFonzo, 603 F.2d 1260 (7th Cir. 1979).

[209] Sodders v. Parratt, 693 F.2d 811 (8th Cir. 1982); Haynes v. United States, 390 U.S. 85, 88 S. Ct. 722, 19 L. Ed. 2d 923 (1968).

[210] United States v. Broce, 488 U.S. 563, 109 S. Ct. 757, 102 L. Ed. 2d 927 (1989); See Menna v. New York, 423 U.S. 61, 96 S. Ct. 241, 46 L. Ed. 2d 195 (1975).

[211] United States v. Palladino, 203 F. Supp. 35 (D. Mass 1962).

[212] United States v. Benson, 640 F.2d 136 (8th Cir. 1981); United States v. Nelson, 574 F.2d 277 (5th Cir. 1978).

[213] Gray v. C.I.R., 708 F.2d 243 (6th Cir. 1983); Larios-Mendez v. Immigration and Naturalization Service, 579 F.2d 144 (9th Cir. 1979); United States v. Eagle Beef Cloth Co., 235 F. Supp. 491 (D. N.Y. 1964).

[214] See United States v. $2,223.40, 157 F. Supp. 300 (D. N.Y. 1957). But see United States v. $31,697.59 Cash, 665 F.2d 903 (9th Cir. 1982) (in a forfeiture proceeding, defendants were collaterally estopped by their guilty pleas from litigating matters disposed of on those pleas).

[215] Lynch v. Overholser, 369 U.S. 705, 82 S. Ct. 1063, 1072, 8 L. Ed. 2d 211 (1962); Santobello v. New York, 404 U.S. 257, 92 S. Ct. 495, 498, 30 L. Ed. 2d 427 (1971).

plea,[216] and the court must be satisfied that there is a factual basis for the plea.[217] While state courts are not bound by the procedures set forth in Fed. R. Crim. P. 11,[218] those courts are still bound by the constitutional requirement that the plea be entered knowingly, intelligently, and voluntarily.[219]

### [c]    *Alford Plea*

An "*Alford*" plea, named after the United States Supreme Court decision of *North Carolina v. Alford*,[220] is a plea of guilty where the defendant nevertheless maintains his innocence. Notwithstanding the antipathy that federal prosecutors (and many state prosecutors) have toward such pleas,[221] the court has the discretion to accept such a plea[222] upon a "strong" factual showing of guilt.[223] Although no admission of guilt is made, an *Alford* plea carries the same consequences and is subject to the same procedure regarding voluntariness as a "straight" guilty plea. A defendant might choose to enter an *Alford* plea out of the pragmatic reality that the prosecution's evidence is overwhelming,[224] or because his mental state at the time of the offense was so impaired (*e.g.*, through extreme intoxication or drug use) that he cannot truly say that he committed the offense charged.

Some judges disfavor *Alford* pleas inasmuch as the defendant is seeking to benefit from the plea without accepting complete responsibility for the offense to which the plea is entered. That is, a judge who might "reward" a defendant for admitting guilt by imposing a sentence that is even lower than that contemplated by the plea bargain is unlikely to offer the same reward to an *Alford* pleader, particularly one who lacks a mitigating factor such as serious memory or other psychological impairment at the time of the offense. Thus, when a defendant proposes to enter an *Alford* plea, defense counsel should appropriately advise him not only about whether the judge is likely to accept the plea, but also any impact that such a plea might have upon sentencing if it is accepted.

If the defendant wants to enter an *Alford* plea but defense counsel knows that the sentencing judge is not inclined to accept it, two options are available. First, counsel might present the plea and, after it is rejected and if the defendant is found guilty at trial, appeal the rejection of the plea. Second, defense counsel might acquiesce in the defendant's decision to falsely admit his guilt to the court in order

---

[216]   United States v. Rios-Ortiz, 830 F.2d 1067, 1070 (9th Cir. 1987).

[217]   Fed. R. Crim. P. 11(b)(3).

[218]   Hendron v. Cowan, 532 F.2d 108 (6th Cir. 1976); Wade v. Coiner, 468 F.2d 1059 (4th Cir. 1972).

[219]   Boykin v. Alabama, 395 U.S. 238, 89 S. Ct. 1709, 1712, 23 L. Ed. 2d 774 (1969).

[220]   400 U.S. 25, 91 S. Ct. 160, 27 L. Ed. 2d 162 (1970).

[221]   *See* G. Nicholas Herman, Plea Bargaining, § 7:12 (1997).

[222]   *See* United States v. O'Brien, 60 F.2d 1067 (9th Cir. 1979); United States v. Bednarski, 445 F.2d 364 (1st Cir. 1971). It may be an abuse of discretion to refuse an Alford plea for the sole reason that the defendant will not admit guilt. *See* United States v. Gaskins, 485 F.2d 1046 (D.C. Cir. 1973); Kennedy v. Frazier, 357 S.E.2d 43 (W. Va. 1987).

[223]   Brownlow v. Groose, 66 F.3d 997 (8th Cir. 1995); United States v. Alber, 56 F.3d 1106 (9th Cir. 1995); United States v. Punch, 709 F.2d 889, 895 (5th Cir. 1983); Willett v. Georgia, 608 F.2d 538 (5th Cir. 1979); Miller v. State, 617 P.2d 516, 518 n. 5 (Alaska 1980). *But see* United States v. Tunning, 69 F.3d 107 (6th Cir. 1995) (strong evidence of actual guilt is not necessary where defendant protests his innocence).

[224]   *See* Colson v. Smith, 438 F.2d 1075, 1081 n. 5 (5th Cir. 1971).

to secure the judge's acceptance of the guilty plea. The latter situation poses an ethical dilemma.

Many attorneys resolve this dilemma by reasoning that, because an attorney never really knows whether the defendant is guilty, the issue of client prevarication is not implicated. However, using ignorance as a convenient moral position may often be belied by overwhelming evidence of guilt. Thus, some courts have opined that it is unethical for an attorney to withhold a client's assertion of innocence from the court or even stand silent when the defendant misrepresents his guilt.[225] On the other hand, many defense lawyers reject this position in practice,[226] and some scholars have taken the view that it is unethical for a lawyer to contradict her client's false assertion of guilt before the court.[227] To the extent that an attorney's acquiescence or participation in a client's false assertion of guilt raises a serious ethical issue, it has been sensibly pointed out that:

> There is, however, a valid social interest in allowing innocent defendants to plead guilty to obtain the advantage of a plea bargain. The argument about the social utility of allowing an *Alford* plea has even more force in the situation where the defendant will hide his assertion of innocence from the court. No question about the integrity of the criminal justice system can arise if the defendant never publicly takes a contradictory position. The harm to society from the defendant's falsehood is far less than when it occurs at trial.[228]

### [d]   Nolo Contendere Plea

A plea of "*nolo contendere*," meaning "I will not contest it,"[229] is expressly permitted in federal cases "only with the consent of the court [and] after due consideration of the views of the parties and the interest of the public in the effective administration of justice."[230] The plea has been criticized as "a foolish concept,"[231] and is regularly opposed by federal prosecutors except in unusual circumstances.[232]

However, the plea has otherwise been described as a "useful device by which a defendant may admit his liability to punishment without being embarrassed in other proceedings."[233] That is, while a *nolo contendere* plea resembles a "straight" guilty plea in almost every respect, the *nolo* plea may not be used against the

---

[225] Bruce v. United States, 379 F.2d 113, 119 n. 17 (D.C. Cir. 1967); United States v. Rogers, 289 F. Supp. 726 (D. Conn. 1968). *But see* State v. Butler, 576 So.2d 515 (La. 1991).

[226] *See* Kamisar, et al., Modern Criminal Procedure, 1161 (4th ed. 1980).

[227] *See* M. Friedman, Professional Responsibility for the Criminal Defense Lawyer: The Three Hardest Questions, 64 Mich. L. Rev. 1469, 1481 (1966); *See also* Christie & Pye, Presumptions and Assumptions in Criminal Law: Another View, Duke L.J. 919, 929 n. 47 (1970). *See generally* Wolfram, Client Perjury, 50 S. Cal. L. Rev. 809 (1977).

[228] D. Rossman, Criminal Law Advocacy: Guilty Pleas, § 9.03 at 9–39 (1996).

[229] Lott v. United States, 367 U.S. 421, 81 S. Ct. 1563, 1567, 6 L. Ed. 2d 940 (1961).

[230] *See* Fed. R. Crim. P. 11(a)(3).

[231] N.Y.U. Institute on Federal Rules of Criminal Procedure 188 (1946) (comments of Judge Learned Hand).

[232] *See* G. Nicholas Herman, Plea Bargaining § 7:12 (1997).

[233] United States v. Pannell, 178 F.2d 98, 100 (3d Cir. 1949).

defendant as an admission in a subsequent civil suit for the same act,[234] and the defendant is not estopped from later denying the facts on which the criminal charge was based.[235] Thus, the primary utility of this plea for the defendant is that it insulates him from automatic civil liability for the same or related wrong.[236]

Except for the foregoing effect, a *nolo contendere* plea operates just like a straight guilty plea. It is tantamount to an admission of guilt for purposes of the criminal case;[237] the defendant is subject to the same punishment as may be imposed on a plea of guilty;[238] nonjurisdictional defects in the proceeding are waived;[239] but the defendant may still raise on appeal defects going to the power of the government to bring the charges against him, such as the constitutionality of the statute under which the charges were brought, or the sufficiency of the indictment or information.[240] Similarly, the procedures prescribed in federal cases for accepting,[241] rejecting,[242] determining the voluntariness of,[243] and factual basis for[244] a guilty plea apply to *nolo contendere* pleas as well.

When the court is called upon to decide whether to accept a plea of *nolo contendere*, the overall test is whether the plea would be in the public interest.[245] In this regard, the federal courts have variously considered the nature and severity of the offense, the size of the defendant (when a corporation), the impact on the economy, the deterrent effect of an admission or finding of guilt, the views of the government, the prior criminal history of the defendant, and the potential for saving the time and expense of a protracted trial.[246]

---

[234] Bell v. Commissioner, 320 F.2d 953 (8th Cir. 1963); Duffy v. Cuyler, 581 F.2d 1059 (3d Cir. 1978); Ranke v. United States, 873 F.2d 1033, 1037 n. 7 (7th Cir. 1989). Some states limit the circumstances under which the plea may not be received as an admission of guilt in a subsequent civil case. *See, e.g.,* Cal. Penal Code § 1016(3) (specifying that such a plea may not be received as an admission only in cases "other than those punishable as felonies.").

[235] Tempo Trucking & Transfer Corp. v. Dickson, 405 F. Supp. 506, (D. N.Y. 1975); United States v. Bagliore, 182 F. Supp. 714, 715 (E.D. N.Y. 1960).

[236] United States v. Graham, 325 F.2d 922 (6th Cir. 1963); City of Burbank v. General Electric Co., 329 F.2d 825, 831–36 (9th Cir. 1964).

[237] Hudson v. United States, 272 U.S. 451, 47 S. Ct. 127, 129, 71 L. Ed. 347 (1926).

[238] Blohm v. C.I.R., 994 F.2d 1542 (11th Cir. 1993); Bell v. Commissioner, 320 F.2d 953 (8th Cir. 1963).

[239] United States v. Freed, 688 F.2d 24, 25 (6th Cir. 1982); Johnson v. Estelle, 704 F.2d 232 (5th Cir. 1983); United Brotherhood of Carpenters & Joiners of America v. United States, 330 U.S. 395, 67 S. Ct. 775, 784, 91 L. Ed. 973 (1947).

[240] United States v. Bessemer & L.E.R. Co., 717 F.2d 593 (D.C. Cir. 1983); United Brotherhood of Carpenters & Joiners of America v. United States, 330 U.S. 395, 67 S. Ct. 775, 784 n. 26, 91 L. Ed. 973 (1947); United States v. Heller, 579 F.2d 990 (6th Cir. 1978).

[241] Fed. R. Crim. P. 11(c); United States v. Brogan, 519 F.2d 29 (6th Cir. 1975).

[242] *See* Fed. R. Crim. P. 11(c); United States v. Brogan, 519 F.2d 29 (6th Cir. 1975).

[243] *See* Fed. R. Crim. P. 11(b)(2).

[244] *See* Fed. R. Crim. P. 11(b)(3).

[245] *See* Fed. R. Crim. P. 11(a)(3).

[246] United States v. H & M Inc., 565 F. Supp. 1 (D. Pa. 1982); United States v. American Bakeries Co., 284 F. Supp. 871 (W. D. Mich. 1968); United States v. Yonkers Contracting Co., 689 F. Supp. 339 (S.D. N.Y. 1988); United States v. Dynalectric Co., 674 F. Supp. 240 (W.D. Ky. 1987).

## *[e]*    ***Conditional Plea***

Under federal law, Fed. R. Crim. P. 11(a)(2) provides that "[w]ith the approval of the court and the consent of the government, a defendant may enter a conditional plea of guilty or *nolo contendere*, reserving in writing the right, on appeal from the judgment, to review of the adverse determination of any specified pretrial motion." If the defendant prevails on appeal, he must be permitted to withdraw his plea.[247] The purpose of a conditional plea is to enable a defendant to preserve specific pretrial issues for appeal without having to go through a trial in a case where acquittal appears unlikely unless the defendant prevails on the pretrial motion.[248]

A defendant need not be advised by the court about the option of entering a conditional plea,[249] and he has no absolute right to enter such a plea.[250] Even with the government's assent to the plea, a condition which is a prerequisite to entering it, the court has complete discretion to accept or reject the plea, and rejection often occurs if the court is not satisfied that the decision on appeal will dispose of the case.[251] The requirement that the plea be in writing is designed to ensure that the plea is entered with the acquiescence of the government, prevent post-plea claims by the defendant that the plea should be deemed conditional merely because it occurred after certain pretrial motions, and to enable the court to verify that the issues specifically reserved for appeal are material to the disposition of the case.[252] However, the government may expressly waive the writing requirement.[253] Issues not *specifically* reserved for presentation on appeal are waived.[254]

Some states do not permit conditional pleas,[255] and others limit appeals from such pleas to certain issues such as search and seizure claims.[256] As an alternative to a conditional plea, a defendant might, as a shortcut to trial, stipulate to the facts sufficient to prove all elements of the charge and preserve his right to appeal a pretrial ruling.[257]

---

[247] Fed. R. Crim. P. 11(a)(2).

[248] United States v. Yasak, 884 F.2d 996 (7th Cir. 1989); United States v. Carrasco, 786 F.2d 1452 (9th Cir. 1986).

[249] United States v. Daniel, 866 F.2d 749, (5th Cir. 1989); United States v. Fisher, 772 F.2d 371 (7th Cir. 1985).

[250] Id.; United States v. Davis, 900 F.2d 1524 (10th Cir. 1990).

[251] United States v. Robinson, 20 F.3d 270 (7th Cir. 1994); United States v. Yasak, 884 F.2d 996 (7th Cir. 1989).

[252] United States v. Carrasco, 786 F.2d 1452 (9th Cir. 1986).

[253] United States v. Yasak, 884 F.2d 996 (7th Cir. 1989).

[254] United States v. Alexander, 761 F.2d 1294 (9th Cir. 1985); United States v. Simmons, 763 F.2d 529 (2d Cir. 1985); United States v. Ryan, 894 F.2d 355 (10th Cir. 1990).

[255] *See, e.g.,* State v. Faber, 343 N.W.2d 659 (Minn. 1984); Mooney v. State, 615 S.W.2d 776 (Tex. Crim. 1981).

[256] *See* State v. Madera, 503 A.2d 136 (Conn. 1985); *But see* State v. Keegan, 457 A.2d 1205 (N.J. Super. 1983).

[257] *See* United States v. Robertson, 698 F.2d 703 (5th Cir. 1983); State v. Johnson, 705 P.2d 773 (Wash. 1985).

## [2]    General Procedures on Entering a Plea

In federal court, when a defendant enters a plea of guilty whether as a "straight" guilty plea, plea of *nolo contendere, Alford* plea, conditional plea, or any of the foregoing pursuant to a plea agreement Fed. R. Crim. P. 11 sets forth procedural and substantive requirements to be followed by the judge to ensure that the plea is knowingly, intelligently, and voluntarily made, and that there is a factual basis for the plea.[258] Rule 11 is addressed to three core concerns: the plea must be free from coercion; the defendant must understand the nature of the charges against him; and the defendant must understand the consequences of his plea.[259]

Thus, in federal cases, the requirements of Rule 11 should be strictly adhered to,[260] and an utter failure to comply with them will ordinarily result in reversal of the conviction and permit the defendant to plead anew.[261] Lesser violations of the Rule that do not affect substantial rights of the defendant will be disregarded as harmless error.[262] While state courts are not required to follow the literal terms of Rule 11, state judges are constitutionally required to ensure, on the record, that the defendant's plea was entered knowingly, intelligently, and voluntarily.[263]

The verbatim proceedings at which the plea is entered must be on the record.[264]

Fed. R. Crim. P. 11(b)(1) provides:

(1)    Advising and Questioning the Defendant. Before the court accepts a plea of guilty or nolo contendere, the defendant may be placed under oath, and the court must address the defendant personally in open court. During this address, the court must inform the defendant of, and determine that the defendant understands, the following:

---

[258] United States v. Bernal, 861 F.2d 434 (5th Cir. 1988); United States v. Ray, 828 F.2d 399 (7th Cir. 1987); United States v. Stitzer, 785 F.2d 1506 (11th Cir. 1986).

[259] United States v. Mosley, 173 F.3d 1318 (11th Cir. 1999); United States v. Muriel, 111 F.3d 975 (1st Cir. 1997); United States v. Zickert, 955 F.2d 665 (11th Cir. 1992); United States v. Bachynsky, 934 F.2d 1349 (5th Cir. 1991); United States v. Buckles, 843 F.2d 469 (11th Cir. 1988).

[260] United States v. Lora, 895 F.2d 878 (2d Cir. 1990); United States v. Reckmeyer, 786 F.2d 1216 (4th Cir. 1986); United States v. DeCicco, 899 F.2d 1531 (7th Cir. 1990).

[261] United States v. Longoria, 113 F.3d 975 (9th Cir. 1997); United States v. Muriel, 111 F.3d 975 (1st Cir. 1997); United States v. Suter, 755 F.2d 523 (7th Cir. 1985); McCarthy v. United States, 394 U.S. 459, 89 S. Ct. 1166, 22 L. Ed. 2d 418 (1969).

[262] Fed. R. Crim. P. 11(h); United States v. Henry, 113 F.3d 37 (5th Cir. 1997); United States v. Watch, 7 F.3d 422 (5th Cir. 1993).

[263] Osborne v. Thompson, 481 F. Supp. 162 (M.D. Tenn. 1979), aff'd, 610 F.2d 461 (6th Cir. 1980); United States v. Newmann, 912 F.2d 1119 (9th Cir. 1990); DeVille v. Whitley, 21 F.3d 654 (5th Cir. 1994). No attempt is made in this Section to canvass the wide-ranging procedures on entering a plea in state practice. While states are free to establish their own procedures for taking guilty pleas, *see* Thornton v. State, 601 S.W.2d 340, 347 (Tex. Crim 1980), most state procedures are similar to the federal requirements.

[264] Fed. R. Crim. P. 11(g). This requirement is necessary to determine compliance with Rule 11, preserve any issues for appellate review, and to prevent the defendant from withdrawing his plea on a whim at a subsequent time. United States v. Young, 927 F.2d 1060 (8th Cir. 1991); United States v. Corbett, 742 F.2d 173 (5th Cir. 1984); United States v. Jaramillo-Suarez, 857 F.2d 1368 (9th Cir. 1988); United States v. Trott, 604 F. Supp. 1045 (D. Del. 1985), aff'd, 779 F.2d 912 (3rd Cir. 1986).

(A)    the government's right, in a prosecution for perjury or false statement, to use against the defendant any statement that the defendant gives under oath;

(B)    the right to plead not guilty, or having already so pleaded, to persist in that plea;

(C)    the right to a jury trial;

(D)    the right to be represented by counsel — and if necessary have the court appoint counsel — at trial and at every other stage of the proceeding;

(E)    the right at trial to confront and cross-examine adverse witnesses, to be protected from compelled self-incrimination, to testify and present evidence, and to compel the attendance of witnesses;

(F)    the defendant's waiver of these trial rights if the court accepts a plea of guilty or nolo contendere;

(G)    the nature of each charge to which the defendant is pleading;

(H)    any maximum possible penalty, including imprisonment, fine, and term of supervised release;

(I)    any mandatory minimum penalty;

(J)    any applicable forfeiture;

(K)    the court's authority to order restitution;

(L)    the court's obligation to impose a special assessment;

(M)    in determining a sentence, the court's obligation to calculate the applicable sentencing-guideline range and to consider that range, possible departures under the Sentencing Guidelines, and other sentencing factors under 18 U.S.C. § 3553(a); and

(N)    the terms of any plea-agreement provision waiving the right to appeal or to collaterally attach the sentence.

In advising the defendant about the foregoing matters, the extent of the court's colloquy with the defendant should be tailored to the complexity of the case, the personal characteristics of the defendant, such as his age, education, intelligence, and alacrity of responses to the court, and whether the defendant is represented by counsel.[265] In no event, however, may the court fail to address the defendant personally as to each of the matters required by Rule 11(b)(1).[266] For purposes of effective assistance of counsel, defense counsel should also cover all of these matters with the defendant.

In federal and state practice, the judge is only required to inform the defendant of the "direct" consequences of his plea (*i.e.*, those listed in Fed. R. Crim. P. 11(c) quoted above), and not so-called "collateral" consequences.[267] "Direct" consequences are those that have a definite, immediate, and largely automatic

---

[265] United States v. Syal, 963 F.2d 900 (6th Cir. 1992); United States v. Maher, 108 F.3d 1513 (2d Cir. 1997); United States v. Stitzer, 785 F.2d 1506 (11th Cir. 1986); United States v. Ray, 828 F.2d 399 (7th Cir. 1987).

[266] *See* United States v. Del Petre, 567 F.2d 928 (9th Cir. 1978); United States v. LeDonne, 21 F.3d 1418 (7th Cir. 1994) (it was permissible for court to allow prosecutor to identify for defendant elements of offense, followed by judge's inquiry of defendant as to whether he understood elements); United States v. Suarez, 155 F.3d 521 (5th Cir. 1998). While there is some conflict in the cases, this also appears to be necessary when the defendant stipulates to facts amounting to a guilty plea. *See* Annot. 53 A.L.R. Fed. 919; *But see* United States v. Lyons, 898 F.2d 210 (1st Cir. 1990); United States v. Stalder, 696 F.2d 59 (8th Cir. 1982).

[267] United States v. Russell, 686 F.2d 35, 38 (D.C. Cir. 1982).

effect on the range of the defendant's punishment,[268] whereas "collateral" consequences are those not related to the length or nature of the sentence imposed.[269] Examples of collateral consequences include the possibility of deportation,[270] parole revocation or eligibility,[271] whether a federal sentence runs concurrently or consecutively to a state sentence,[272] the likelihood of a dishonorable military discharge, the imposition of civil forfeiture, the likelihood of other civil judgments or penalties arising from the plea, the potential for civil commitment proceedings,[273] the possibility of further prosecution,[274] and the possible effect of a guilty plea on a subsequent sentence for another crime.[275]

Along with advising the defendant about and inquiring into the matters specified in Fed. R. Crim. P. 11(b)(1), Fed. R. Crim. P. 11(b)(2) provides that "[b]efore accepting a plea of guilty or nolo contendere, the court must address the defendant personally in open court and determine that the plea is voluntary and did not result from force, threats, or promises (other than promises in a plea agreement)."

The term "voluntary" means willingly, intentionally, without threat of harm or coercion, or promise of favor or leniency.[276] It has never meant the absence of benefits influencing the defendant to plead,[277] and the determination of the voluntariness of the plea does not involve an inquiry into the guilt or innocence of the defendant.[278] The overall test is whether the plea represents a voluntary and intelligent choice among the alternative courses of action available to the defendant.[279] When a minor pleads guilty, parental consent is not required.[280]

---

[268] United States v. Graibe, 946 F.2d 1428 (9th Cir. 1991).

[269] United States v. Romero-Vilca, 850 F.2d 177 (3rd Cir. 1988).

[270] United States v. Olvera, 954 F.2d 788 (2d Cir. 1992).

[271] King v. Dutton, 17 F.3d 151 (6th Cir. 1994).

[272] *But see* United States v. Neely, 38 F.3d 458 (9th Cir. 1994) (because imposition of consecutive sentence is a direct consequence of federal guilty plea, where federal court lacks discretion to order concurrent sentence, federal defendant must be advised of the court's lack of discretion before he can enter a voluntary plea of guilty to a federal charge where State charges are pending); *c.f.,* United States v. Kikuyama, 109 F.3d 536 (9th Cir. 1997) (where court had discretion to impose concurrent or consecutive sentences, court need not warn defendant of the possibility that sentences may run consecutively); United States v. Parkins, 25 F.3d 114 (2d Cir. 1994); United States v. Ospina, 18 F.3d 1332 (6th Cir. 1994).

[273] United States v. United States Currency in Amount of $228,536.00, 895 F.2d 908 (2d Cir. 1990).

[274] United States v. Persico, 774 F.2d 30 (2d Cir. 1985).

[275] Wright v. United States, 624 F.2d 557 (5th Cir. 1980); United States v. Williams, 104 F.3d 213 (8th Cir. 1997) (possibility that guilty plea may be used in subsequent federal proceeding is a collateral consequence).

[276] Yates v. United States, 245 F. Supp. 147 (E.D. Va. 1965).

[277] United States v. Marguez, 909 F.2d 738 (2d Cir. 1990).

[278] United States v. Morin, 265 F.2d 241 (3rd. Cir. 1959).

[279] Parke v. Raley, 506 U.S. 20, 113 S. Ct. 517, 121 L. Ed. 2d 391 (1992); United States v. Rhodes, 913 F.2d 839 (10th Cir. 1990); United States v. Avellino, 136 F.3d 249 (2d Cir. 1998) (if plea resulted from impermissible conduct by government agents, including "Brady" violations, the plea must be reassessed to determine whether, but for the impermissible conduct or violations, the defendant would not have entered the plea); Easter v. Norris, 100 F.3d 523 (8th Cir. 1996); Ivy v. Caspari, 173 F.3d 1136 (8th Cir. 1999).

[280] Ford v. Lockhart, 904 F.2d 458 (8th Cir. 1990).

In determining whether the plea is voluntary, the judge should question the defendant personally and not rely simply on the statements of defense counsel.[281] The court's inquiries need not be framed in the exact language of Rule 11(b)(1); it is sufficient that the judge determines voluntariness based on the record of the entire proceeding.[282] If there is some doubt about voluntariness, the court's inquiry should be more extensive.[283] In addition, the court should evaluate the defendant's competency to plead, the test being whether the defendant has sufficient present ability to consult with his lawyer with a reasonable degree of understanding and has a rational as well as factual understanding of the proceedings against him.[284]

Finally, Fed. R. Crim. P. 11(b)(3) provides that "[b]efore entering a judgment on a guilty plea, the court must determine that there is a factual basis for the plea." This provision does not apply to pleas of *nolo contendere*,[285] or where forfeiture of assets is stipulated in a plea agreement.[286] The purpose of the provision is to make it clear what the defendant admits to, and whether his admissions are factually sufficient to support the crime charged or a lesser offense to the crime charged.[287] It is not necessary that the defendant be in fact guilty.[288]

In determining the factual basis for the plea, while a colloquy between the court and the defendant has been said to be the preferred method,[289] the court may consider all matters of record and need not personally address the defendant if the factual basis is otherwise established.[290] For example, apart from making inquiries of the defendant, the court may rely on representations of counsel,[291] the presentence report,[292] a plea agreement's written description of the essential

---

[281]  Phillips v. United States, 519 F.2d 483 (6th Cir. 1975); United States v. Kerdachi, 756 F.2d 349 (5th Cir. 1985).

[282]  Cochran v. United States, 365 F.2d 310, (6th Cir. 1966); United States v. Ellison, 835 F.2d 687 (7th Cir. 1987).

[283]  United States v. Daniels, 821 F.2d 76 (1st Cir. 1987); Mack v. United States, 635 F.2d 20 (1st Cir. 1980).

[284]  Godinez v. Moran, 509 U.S. 389, 113 S. Ct. 2680, 125 L. Ed. 2d 321 (1993); *See e.g.*, Wilkins v. Bowersox, 145 F.3d 1006 (8th Cir. 1998) (defendant's youth, troubled background, and mental impairment clouded his ability to knowingly, intelligently, and voluntarily enter guilty plea and waiver of presenting mitigating evidence); Miles v. Stainer, 108 F.3d 1109 (9th Cir. 1997); United States v. Lebron, 76 F.3d 29 (1st Cir. 1996) (test for defendant's competency to plead guilty is same test for standing trial-whether defendant understands proceedings against him and has sufficient present ability to consult with his lawyer with reasonable degree of rational understanding).

[285]  United States v. Prince, 533 F.2d 205 (5th Cir. 1976).

[286]  Libretti v. United States, 516 U.S. 29, 116 S. Ct. 356, 133 L. Ed. 2d 271 (1995).

[287]  McCarthy v. United States, 394 U.S. 459, 89 S. Ct. 1166, 22 L. Ed. 2d 418 (1969); Libretti v. United States, 516 U.S. 29, 116 S. Ct. 356, 133 L. Ed. 2d 271 (1995); United States v. Fountain, 777 F.2d 531 (7th Cir. 1985).

[288]  *See* United States v. Hecht, 638 F.2d 651 (3d Cir. 1981).

[289]  United States v. Fountain, 777 F.2d 351 (7th Cir. 1985).

[290]  *See* United States v. Smith, 160 F.3d 117 (2d Cir. 1998); United States v. Musa, 946 F.2d 1297 (7th Cir. 1991); United States v. LeDonne, 21 F.3d 1418 (7th Cir. 1994); United States v. Maher, 108 F.3d 1513 (2d Cir. 1997); United States v. Lumpkins, 845 F.2d 1444 (7th Cir. 1988); United States v. Kriz, 586 F.2d 1178 (8th Cir. 1978); United States v. Pinto, 838 F.2d 1566 (11th Cir. 1988).

[291]  Arango-Alvarez v. United States, 134 F.3d 888 (7th Cir. 1998) (court may find factual basis for guilty plea from anything in the record, including proffer from the government); United States v. Goldberg, 862 F.2d 101 (6th Cir. 1988); United States v. Murphy, 899 F.2d 714 (8th Cir. 1990).

[292]  Howard v. United States, 135 F.3d 506 (7th Cir. 1998); United States v. Graves, 106 F.3d 342 (10th

facts,[293] the testimony of a government, agent or even the indictment itself if the defendant admits the facts testified to or alleged.[294] Usually, the judge will require the government to summarize the evidence in the case and ask the defendant to state whether the summary is correct.[295] Alternatively, the judge might develop the factual basis on the record by having the defendant describe the conduct giving rise to the charge.[296] In a multi-defendant plea hearing, repetition of the factual basis is not required, but the court must make sure that the facts on the record apply to each defendant who pleads.[297]

An evidentiary hearing is not necessary to establish a factual basis,[298] and the guilty plea does not have to be supported by legally admissible evidence.[299] However, if the evidence is not credible[300] or the defendant's admission of guilt is equivocal,[301] acceptance of the plea may constitute constitutional error. Although an *Alford* plea is permitted,[302] there must be a strong factual basis to support it.[303] When the factual basis for any guilty plea is insufficient, the court should refuse to accept the plea, and, depending on the circumstances, proceed with the trial of the case,[304] allow the defendant to withdraw his plea,[305] or set aside the plea and allow the defendant to plead anew.[306]

Under Rule 11 of the Federal Rules of Criminal Procedure, the court may accept a guilty plea and defer a decision on accepting a plea agreement until a later date. It is not necessary that the plea agreement be accepted before the defendant enters a guilty plea. If the court ends up rejecting the plea agreement, the defendant is entitled to withdraw his plea as a matter of right. However, if the

---

Cir. 1997); United States v. Trott, 779 F.2d 912 (3d Cir. 1985).

[293] United States v. Baez, 87 F.3d 805 (6th Cir. 1996).

[294] United States v. Adams, 961 F.2d 505 (5th Cir. 1992); United States v. Martinez-Martinez, 69 F.3d 1215 (1st Cir. 1995); United States v. Isble, 468 F. Supp. 152 (E.D. Tenn. 1979); Montgomery v. United States, 853 F.2d 83 (2d Cir. 1988); United States v. Van Buren, 804 F.2d 688 (6th Cir. 1986); United States v. Cline, 655 F. Supp. 796 (M.D. La. 1987).

[295] United States v. Nash, 29 F.3d 1195 (7th Cir. 1994); United States v. Ford, 363 F.2d 375 (4th Cir. 1966); United States v. Laura, 500 F. Supp. 1347 (E.D. Pa. 1980), aff'd, 667 F.2d 365 (3rd Cir. 1981).

[296] *See* Santobello v. New York, 404 U.S. 257, 92 S. Ct. 495, 30 L. Ed. 2d 427 (1971); United States v. Lovelace, 683 F.2d 248 (7th Cir. 1982).

[297] United States v. Fountain, 777 F.2d 351 (7th Cir. 1985).

[298] United States v. Griffiths, 709 F. Supp. 1036 (D. Utah 1988).

[299] Haring v. Prosise, 462 U.S. 306, 103 S. Ct. 2368, 76 L. Ed. 2d 595 (1983).

[300] *See, e.g.,* United States v. Andrades, 169 F.3d 131 (2d Cir. 1999) (factual basis not established where court did not elicit any information from the parties regarding the offense but merely read bare bones conspiracy charge from indictment and there was no evidence defendant conspired with individuals who were not government agents); United States v. Severino, 800 F.2d 42 (2d Cir. 1986).

[301] United States v. Cano-Guel, 167 F.3d 900 (5th Cir. 1999); United States v. Young, 45 F.3d 1405 (10th Cir. 1995); United States v. Hecht, 638 F.2d 651 (3d Cir. 1981).

[302] North Carolina v. Alford, 400 U.S. 25, 91 S. Ct. 160, 27 L. Ed. 2d 162 (1970).

[303] *See* Brownlow v. Goose, 66 F.3d 997 (8th Cir. 1995); United States v. Punch, 709 F.2d 889 (5th Cir. 1983); United States v. Griffiths, 709 F. Supp. 1036 (D. Utah 1988). *But see* United States v. Tunning, 69 F.3d 107 (6th Cir. 1995).

[304] United States v. Severino, 800 F.2d 42 (2d Cir. 1986); United States v. Brown, 481 F.2d 1035 (8th Cir. 1973).

[305] United States v. White, 483 F.2d 71 (5th Cir. 1973).

[306] United States v. Fountain, 777 F.2d 351 (7th Cir. 1985); United States v. Briggs, 920 F.2d 287 (5th Cir. 1991).

defendant seeks to withdraw his guilty plea after it has been entered but before the court has accepted the plea agreement, he can only do so upon a showing of a "fair and just reason."[307]

## [3]    Entering the Plea Under a Plea Agreement

When the defendant enters a guilty plea pursuant to a plea agreement-whether "straight" plea, *Alford* plea, plea of *nolo contendere*, or conditional plea-all of the requirements discussed in § 19.10[2] are applicable regarding the judge's role in advising the defendant and determining the voluntariness of and factual basis for the plea. In addition, for federal cases, Fed. R. Crim. P. 11(c) sets forth certain procedures in connection with the entry of a guilty plea pursuant to a plea agreement. State courts are free to fashion their own procedures in this regard, and many of them parallel the requirements of Rule 11(c).

Fed. R. Crim. P. 11(c)(1) provides:

(1)    In General. An attorney for the government and the defendant's attorney, or the defendant when proceeding pro se, may discuss and reach a plea agreement. The court must not participate in these discussions. If the defendant pleads guilty or nolo contendere to either a charged offense or a lesser or related offense, the plea agreement may specify that an attorney for the government will:

(A)    not bring, or will move to dismiss, other charges;

(B)    recommend, or agree not to oppose the defendant's request, that a particular sentence or sentencing range is appropriate or that a particular provision of the Sentencing Guidelines, or policy statement, or sentencing factor does or does not apply (such a recommendation or request does not bind the court); or

(C)    agree that a specific sentence or sentencing range is the appropriate disposition of the case, or that a particular provision of the Sentencing Guidelines, or policy statement, or sentencing factor does or does not apply (such a recommendation or request binds the court once the court accepts the plea agreement).

The foregoing types of agreements, commonly referred to as "Type A," "Type B," and "Type C" agreements,[308] are neither mutually exclusive[309] nor exhaustive.[310] For example, if a defendant faces multiple charges, an agreement may be reached for one type of agreement for one charge and another for other charges.[311] Similarly, any number of conditions might be attached to the agreement, and these will be enforceable so long as they are not added after the defendant has pled guilty.[312] However, regardless of the existence of an agreement

---

[307]    Fed. R. Crim. P. 32(e). United States v. Hyde, 520 U.S. 670, 117 S. Ct. 1630, 137 L.Ed2d 935 (1997).

[308]    United States v. Thompson, 680 F.2d 1145, 1153 (7th Cir. 1982); State ex rel. Forbes v. Kaufman, 404 S.E.2d 763, 766 (W. Va. 1991).

[309]    United States v. Carrigan, 778 F.2d 1454 (10th Cir. 1985).

[310]    *See* United States v. Bean, 564 F.2d 700 (5th Cir. 1977).

[311]    Advisory Committee Note to the 1979 amendment of Rule 11(e)(2).

[312]    *See* United States v. Burruezo, 704 F.2d 33 (2d Cir. 1983); United States v. Garcia, 698 F.2d 31 (1st Cir. 1983). A plea agreement may even include a waiver by the defendant of his statutory right to

between the defendant and the government, the judge is never required to accept a plea agreement presented to her.[313] As a practical matter, given that approximately 90% of all criminal cases in the federal system result in guilty pleas,[314] this ultimate power of the judge to prohibit plea agreements altogether is not exercised.

Federal judges are flatly prohibited from participating in any plea discussions with a view toward reaching an agreement.[315] The reasons for this are to obviate the risk of coercing the defendant to accept the plea agreement, to protect the integrity of the judicial process, and to preserve the impartiality of the judge after the plea agreement has been reached.[316] A defendant who has pled guilty after a judge has impermissibly participated in plea discussions[317] should be allowed to replead without having to show that actual prejudice resulted from the judge's participation.[318] However, it is sometimes said that a judge is not prohibited from commenting on a plea proposal after the plea agreement is disclosed in open court;[319] and she is otherwise permitted to inquire into the terms of the agreement,[320] ascertain the defendant's understanding of the agreement,[321] and explain to the defendant the implications of the proposed bargain.[322]

The court's varying responsibilities regarding Type A, Type B, and Type C agreements are set out in Fed. R. Crim. P. 11(c)(2)–(5) as follows:

(2)    Disclosing a Plea Agreement. The parties must disclose the plea agreement in open court when the plea is offered, unless the court for good cause allows the parties to disclose the plea agreement in camera.

---

appeal his sentence so long as the waiver is knowing and voluntary. United States v. Bushert, 997 F.2d 1343 (11th Cir. 1993); United States v. Rivera, 971 F.2d 876 (2d Cir. 1992); *See generally*, Annot. 89 A.L.R.3d 864.

[313] United States v. Gamboa, 166 F.3d 1327 (11th Cir. 1999) (guilty plea to charge of using communication facility in committing drug trafficking offense properly rejected as not adequately reflecting seriousness of drug offense defendant had committed); United States v. Sheperd, 102 F.3d 558 (D.C. Cir. 1996); United States v. Jackson, 563 F.2d 1145 (4th Cir. 1977); State v. DeClue, 805 S.W.2d 253 (Mo. App. 1991).

[314] USSG Ch. 1, Pt. A, subpt. 4(c).

[315] *See generally*, Annot. 56 A.L.R. Fed 529; United States v. Washington, 109 F.3d 459 (8th Cir. 1997); United States v. Werker, 535 F.2d 198 (2d Cir. 1976); United States v. Bruce, 976 F.2d 552 (9th Cir. 1992). This rule is not mandated by the federal constitution and does not apply to state judges. United States v. Adams, 634 F.2d 830 (5th Cir. 1981); Damiano v. Gaughan, 592 F. Supp. 1222, (D. Mass. 1984), aff'd, 770 F.2d 1 (1st Cir. 1985). Vermont, for example, permits judges to actively participate in plea bargaining. *See* State v. Davis, 584 A.2d 1146 (Vt. 1990).

[316] United States v. Bruce, 976 F.2d 552 (9th Cir. 1992).

[317] *See, e.g.,* United States v. Casallas, 59 F.3d 1173 (11th Cir. 1995); United States v. Crowell, 60 F.3d 199 (5th Cir. 1995); United States v. Miles, 10 F.3d 1135 (5th Cir. 1993); United States v. Corbitt, 996 F.2d 1132 (11th Cir. 1993); United States v. Anderson, 993 F.2d 1453 (9th Cir. 1993).

[318] United States v. Diaz, 138 F.3d 1359 (11th Cir. 1998); United States v. Casales, 59 F.3d 1173 (11th Cir. 1995); United States v. Garfield, 987 F.2d 1424 (9th Cir. 1993); United States v. Adams, 634 F.2d 830 (5th Cir. 1981); United States v. Bruce, 976 F.2d 552 (9th Cir. 1992).

[319] *See* United States v. Woods, 775 F.2d 82 (3d Cir. 1985). *But see* United States v. Kraus, 137 F.3d 447 (7th Cir. 1998) (remarks of district court which suggest what will satisfy court as an acceptable agreement are impermissible).

[320] United States v. Arellanes, 767 F.2d 1353 (9th Cir. 1985).

[321] United States v. Kerdachi, 756 F.2d 349 (5th Cir. 1985).

[322] United States v. Morris, 827 F.2d 1348 (9th Cir. 1987).

(3)    Judicial Consideration of a Plea Agreement.

   (A)    To the extent the plea agreement is of the type specified in Rule 11(c)(1)(A) or (C) the court may accept the agreement, reject it, or defer a decision until the court has reviewed the presentence report.

   (B)    To the extent the plea agreement is of the type specified in Rule 11(c)(1)(B), the court must advise the defendant that the defendant has no right to withdraw the plea if the court does not follow the recommendation or request.

(4)    Accepting a Plea Agreement. If the court accepts the plea agreement, it must inform the defendant that to the extent the plea agreement is of the type specified in Rule 11(c)(1)(A) or (C), the agreed disposition will be included in the judgment.

(5)    Rejecting a Plea Agreement. If the court rejects a plea agreement containing provisions of the type specified in Rule 11(c)(1)(A) or (C), the court must do the following on the record and in open court (or, for good cause, in camera):

   (A)    inform the parties that the court rejects the plea agreement;

   (B)    advise the defendant personally that the court is not required to follow the plea agreement and give the defendant an opportunity to withdraw the plea; and

   (C)    advise the defendant personally that if the plea is not withdrawn, the court may dispose of the case less favorably toward the defendant than the plea agreement contemplated.

The purposes of an on-the-record disclosure of the plea agreement[323] are to discourage secret plea bargaining that may adversely affect the public interest in the effective administration of justice, protect the defendant's rights under the agreement, and insulate the prosecution from spurious claims of breach of promise.[324] Where a Type A agreement is involved (*i.e.*, the government promises that in exchange for a plea of guilty or *nolo contendere* to a charged offense or to a lesser or related offense the government will dismiss the other charges), or where a Type C agreement is involved (*i.e.*, the parties agree that a specific sentence is the appropriate disposition of the case), the court may either accept[325] or reject[326] the agreement, and may defer a decision until the court has had an opportunity to consider the presentence report. However, if the court rejects

---

[323]    All of the details of the agreement must be disclosed, along with the reason for the agreement; and it is insufficient to merely disclose those aspects of the agreement which the parties consider important. United States v. Gallington, 488 F.2d 637 (8th Cir. 1973); Baker v. United States, 782 F.2d 85 (6th Cir. 1986).

[324]    State v. Van Egdom, 292 N.W.2d 586 (S. Dakota 1980); United States v. Griffin, 462 F. Supp. 928, 932 (D. Ark. 1978).

[325]    If the parties agree to a specific sentence, the court may accept or reject the whole but may not accept the plea and then impose a sentence greater than that agreed upon, United States v. Herrera, 640 F.2d 958 (9th Cir. 1981), or a sentence less than that agreed upon, United States v. Semler, 883 F.2d 832 (9th Cir. 1989), United States v. Cunavelis, 969 F.2d 1419 (2d Cir. 1992).

[326]    The trial court may refuse to accept the agreement simply because he believes that the bargain will result in too light a sentence under the circumstances. United States v. Ocanas, 628 F.2d 353 (5th Cir. 1980).

either of these types of agreements,[327] it must advise the defendant personally that the court is not bound by the agreement, and the defendant must be given the opportunity to withdraw his plea[328] with the admonition that if he persists in his plea, the disposition of the case may be less favorable to him than that contemplated by the plea agreement.[329] Some courts have stated that, even though the judge has broad discretion in refusing to accept a plea agreement, she must articulate on the record a sound reason for rejecting the agreement.[330] If the court rejects either a Type A or Type C bargain, neither the government nor the defendant can appeal the rejection until after the defendant has been convicted and sentenced.[331]

Under the "Policy Statements" of the *U.S. Sentencing Guidelines*, in the case of a Type A plea agreement that includes the dismissal of any charges or an agreement not to pursue potential charges, it is said that the court may accept the agreement if it is determined "that the remaining charges adequately reflect the seriousness of the actual offense behavior and that accepting the agreement will not undermine the statutory purposes of sentencing or the sentencing guidelines."[332] However, a Type A agreement cannot prevent the conduct underlying the dismissed charge from being considered as "Relevant Conduct" in connection with the count(s) of which the defendant is convicted.[333] In the case of a Type C agreement that includes a specific sentence, the *Guidelines* policy statement says that the court may accept such an agreement if the agreed sentence is within the applicable guideline range, or the agreed sentence departs from the applicable guideline range for justifiable reasons.[334]

If the court accepts a Type A or Type C plea agreement, the court must inform the defendant that it will embody in the judgment and sentence the disposition provided for in the agreement. The reasons for accepting the agreement should be

---

[327] *See generally,* Annot., 60 A.L.R. Fed 621. Once rejected, both parties are released from their obligations under the agreement and may even adopt strategies or positions inconsistent with their previously agreed upon positions. United States v. McGovern, 822 F.2d 739 (8th Cir. 1987); United States v. CFW Construction Co., 583 F. Supp. 197 (D. S.C. 1984).

[328] USSG § 6B1.3.

[329] *See generally,* Annot. What Constitutes "Rejection" of Plea Agreement Under Rule 11(e)(4) of the Federal Rules of Criminal Procedure, Allowing Withdrawal of Plea if Court Rejects Agreement, 60 A.L.R. Fed 621.

[330] United States v. Maddox, 48 F.3d 555 (D.C. Cir. 1995) (trial judge must provide reasoned exercise of discretion to justify rejecting guilty plea which has been agreed to between prosecution and defense); United States v. Robertson, 45 F.3d 1423 (10th Cir. 1995); United States v. Moore, 916 F.2d 1131 (6th Cir. 1990); United States v. Delegal, 678 F.2d 47 (7th Cir. 1982); *contra,* United States v. Moore, 637 F.2d 1194 (8th Cir. 1981).

[331] United States v. Carrigan, 778 F.2d 1454 (10th Cir. 1985).

[332] USSG § 6B1.2(a). *See, e.g.,* United States v. Gamboa, 166 F.3d 1327 (11th Cir. 1999) (charges to which defendant pled guilty did not adequately reflect the seriousness of the actual ofense behavior).

[333] *Id.* Most courts adhere to this view. *See, e.g.,* United States v. McGee, 7 F.3d 1496 (10th Cir. 1993); United States v. Robinson, 14 F.3d 1200 (7th Cir. 1994); United States v. Williams, 10 F.3d 910 (1st Cir. 1993). On the other hand, the courts are divided about whether conduct for dismissed counts may be used in granting an upward departure. *See, e.g.,* United States v. Ashburn, 38 F.3d 803 (5th Cir. 1994) (upward departure may be based on dismissed counts); United States v. Fine, 975 F.2d 596 (9th Cir. 1992) (upward departure may not be based on dismissed counts).

[334] USSG § 6B1.2(c).

set forth on the record.[335] The court's decision to reject any one of these types of agreements will only be reversed in the unusual situation where the rejection is so arbitrary or capricious as to amount to a gross abuse of discretion.[336]

When a Type B agreement is proposed (*i.e.*, the government promises only to make a sentencing recommendation, or agrees not to oppose the defendant's sentencing request), there is nothing for the court to "accept" or "reject" under Fed. R. Crim. P. 11(e)(3) or (4). Under the *U.S. Sentencing Guidelines*, it is said that the court may approve of the recommendation or request if the court is satisfied that the recommended sentence is within the applicable guideline range, or the recommended sentence departs from the guideline range for justifiable reasons.[337] In order that the defendant understands the nonbinding effect of the recommendation or request, Fed. R. Crim. P. 11(e)(2) requires the court to advise the defendant who has entered into a Type B agreement that if the court does not accept the recommendation or request the defendant nevertheless has no right to withdraw his plea.[338] This does not mean, however, that the court may not exercise its discretion to allow the defendant to withdraw his plea in any event.

If the court accepts a Type A or Type C plea agreement, or if there is a Type B agreement that binds only the government and does not require approval of the court, the agreement must be fully carried out.[339] This is so whether the promise resulting from the plea discussions was made directly or indirectly,[340] and the agreement may be enforced even though it was not reduced to writing.[341]

Whether the plea agreement is a Type A, B, or C agreement, it may be accompanied by a written stipulation of facts relevant to sentencing.[342] These stipulations are generally binding on the parties.[343] Under the *U.S. Sentencing Guidelines* policy statement about stipulations, it is said that:

> (a) . . . Except to the extent that a party may be privileged not to disclose certain information, stipulations shall:
>
> > (1) set forth the relevant facts and circumstances of the actual offense conduct and offender characteristics;

---

[335] United States v. Gallington, 488 F.2d 637 (8th Cir. 1973).

[336] United States v. Ocanas, 628 F.2d 353 (5th Cir. 1980); United States v. Bean, 564 F.2d 700 (5th Cir. 1977); United States v. Robertson, 45 F.3d 1423 (10th Cir. 1995) (abuse of discretion found where plea agreement was rejected because the court would not be able to schedule any other case for the time when defendant's case was to be tried); United States v. Miller, 722 F.2d 562 (9th Cir. 1993) (abuse of discretion found where court implemented a categorical rule refusing to accept any plea agreements that left standing only one count in a multi-count indictment).

[337] USSG § 6B1.2(b).

[338] USSG § 6B1.1(b). The failure to comply with this requirement under Fed. R. Crim. P. 11(e)(2) may constitute grounds for vacating the sentence and allowing the defendant to withdraw his plea. United States v. Zickert, 955 F.2d 665 (11th Cir. 1992); United States v. Chan, 97 F.3d 1582 (9th Cir. 1996).

[339] United States v. Bowler, 585 F.2d 851 (7th Cir. 1981); United States v. Blackwell, 694 F.2d 1325 (D.C. Cir. 1982); Allen v. Hadden, 536 F. Supp. 586 (D. Colo. 1982).

[340] United States v. Avery, 621 F.2d 214 (5th Cir. 1980).

[341] Reducing the agreement to writing, while not required by Fed. R. Crim. P. 11, is of course preferable. *See* United States v. Hilton, 772 F.2d 783 (11th Cir. 1985).

[342] USSG § 6B1.4.

[343] *See* United States v. Jefferies, 908 F.2d 1520 (11th Cir. 1990); United States v. Valencia, 985 F.2d 758 (5th Cir. 1993); United States v. Boatner, 966 F.2d 1575 (11th Cir. 1992).

(2) not contain misleading facts; and

(3) set forth with meaningful specificity the reasons why the sentencing range resulting from the proposed agreement is appropriate.

(b) To the extent that the parties disagree about any facts relevant to sentencing, the stipulation shall identify the facts that are in dispute.

(c) A district court may, by local rule identify categories of cases for which the parties are authorized to make the required stipulation orally, on the record, at the time the plea agreement is offered.

(d) The court is not bound by the stipulation, but may with the aid of the presentence report, determine the facts relevant to sentencing.[344]

The foregoing makes clear that although the parties may be bound by their stipulations, the court is not.[345] This is the view taken by most courts, and thus the judge may, for example, adopt the facts in the presentence report in lieu of those stipulated by the parties.[346]

Finally, Fed. R. Crim. P. 11(f) expressly incorporates Federal Rule of Evidence 410 relating to the general admissibility of pleas, plea discussions, and related statements. Fed. R. Evid. 410 provides:

Except as otherwise provided in this rule, evidence of the following is not, in any civil or criminal proceeding, admissible against the defendant who made the plea or was a participant in the plea discussions:

(1) a plea of guilty which was later withdrawn;

(2) a plea of nolo contendere;

(3) any statement made in the course of any proceedings under Rule 11 of the Federal Rules of Criminal Procedure or comparably state procedure regarding either of the foregoing pleas; or

(4) any statement made in the course of plea discussions with an attorney for the prosecuting authority which do not result in a plea of guilty or which result in a plea of guilty later withdrawn.

However, such a statement is admissible (i) in any proceeding wherein another statement made in the course of the same plea or plea discussions has been introduced and the statement ought in fairness be considered contemporaneously with it, or (ii) in a criminal proceeding for perjury or false statement if the statement was made by the defendant

---

[344] USSG § 6B1.4.

[345] *See* United States v. Mankiewicz, 122 F.3d 399 (7th Cir. 1997) (although factual stipulations of the parties are to be given great weight in the absence of significant evidence in the record to the contrary, stipulations as to the law do not absolve the district court from reaching its own view of what the law requires in imposing sentence).

[346] *See, e.g.,* United States v. Williams, 919 F.2d 1451 (10th Cir. 1990); United States v. Mason, 961 F.2d 1460 (9th Cir. 1992); United States v. Russell, 913 F.2d 1288 (8th Cir. 1990); United States v. Woods, 907 F.2d 1540 (5th Cir. 1990). *But see* United States v. Mandel, 905 F.2d 970 (6th Cir. 1990) (in a plea agreement for a specific sentence, court could not depart from that sentence where the parties had stipulated that any departure would constitute a breach of the agreement); United States v. Shields, 44 F.3d 673 (8th Cir. 1995) (refusing to accept the parties' stipulations may undermine the trust defendants place in agreements they make with prosecutors).

under oath, on the record and in the presence of counsel.

Although it has been held that the prosecution cannot use, either directly or indirectly, statements made by a defendant after receiving a grant of immunity as a lead to other evidence,[347] a defendant may execute a voluntary waiver of immunity from the impeachment use of his plea negotiation statements.[348] Thus, as a logical extension of this rule, it would appear that nothing would prevent the government from requiring defendants as a condition of negotiations to agree in advance that, if they breach the plea agreement by not pleading guilty, their statements may be used by the government in its case-in-chief as well as for impeachment purposes.

## [4]    Checklist for Entering the Defendant's Plea and Advising the Client

In light of the foregoing discussion of plea-taking procedure when a plea bargain is involved, defense counsel should consider the following checklist in preparing for the guilty plea hearing in federal court and in advising the client:

(1) Be prepared to advise the court of the specific terms of the plea agreement (or provide a copy of the written agreement to the court).

(2) Be prepared to advise the court of any stipulations between the parties (or provide a copy of any written stipulations to the court).

(3) Review all of the terms of the plea agreement with the defendant to ensure that he understands:

(a) all of its terms and voluntarily assents to it;

(b) that if the plea agreement contains a nonbinding recommendation about sentencing, the court may reject the recommendation without permitting him to withdraw his plea, and impose a more severe sentence than he may anticipate; and

(c) that if the plea agreement involves the dismissal of charges or an agreement about a specific sentence, the court may reject the agreement, provide him with an opportunity to withdraw his plea, and impose a more severe sentence than he anticipated.

(4) Review the indictment or information with the defendant to ensure that he understands:

(a) all charges in the case and the elements of proof for each charge;

(b) that by pleading guilty to a felony he will lose the rights to vote, hold public office, serve on a jury, and possess a firearm;

(c) the maximum possible penalty and any mandatory minimum penalty;

(d) the effect of any drug quantity involved or other aggravating factors or prior offenses that may affect the maximum and any mandatory minimum sentence;

---

[347] Kastigar v. United States, 406 U.S. 441, 92 S. Ct. 1653, 32 L. Ed. 2d 212 (1972).

[348] United States v. Mezzanatto, 513 U.S. 196, 115 S. Ct. 797, 130 L. Ed. 2d 697 (1995).

(e) the duration of any authorized or mandatory term of supervised release, and the consequences for violating any conditions of supervised release;

(f) the unavailability of probation (if applicable);

(g) the possible forfeiture of property (if applicable);

(h) that notice of the conviction must be provided to the victims (if applicable);

(i) that he must pay a special assessment fee; and

(j) that he may be ordered to pay restitution.

(5) Advise the defendant that the court will place him under oath, that subject to the penalty of perjury he will be asked certain questions such as his full name, age, education, and whether he has recently been treated for any mental illness or addiction to drugs, or whether he is currently under the influence of any drugs, alcohol, or medication of any kind.

(6) Advise the defendant of the operation of the Sentencing Guidelines to ensure that he understands:

(a) all ramifications of the Guidelines in his case and an estimate of the applicable Guidelines range;

(b) that parole has been abolished;

(c) the specific sentence to be imposed (if the plea agreement specifies one);

(d) that if the plea agreement does not specify a specific sentence, the court will determine the Guideline sentence after reviewing the presentence report and hearing any objections by counsel to the report;

(e) that the court may, in certain circumstances, depart upward or downward from the Guidelines range, and may impose a sentence that is less or more severe than the sentence called for by the Guidelines;

(f) that, in certain circumstances, he and the government may appeal the sentence imposed; and

(g) that (if applicable) he has chosen to waive the right to appeal his sentence.

(7) Advise the defendant that by pleading guilty he waives the rights of:

(a) trial by jury;

(b) presumption of innocence and privilege against self-incrimination;

(c) proof of guilt beyond a reasonable doubt;

(d) assistance of counsel at trial;

(e) confronting and cross-examining witnesses; and

(f) issuance of subpoenas or compulsory process to compel the attendance of witnesses for his defense.

(8) Prepare the defendant for the possibility that the court may ask him questions about his involvement in the offense and/or whether he agrees with the government's summary of the evidence.

(9) Advise the defendant that:

(a) he will be asked to give information in connection with the preparation of the presentence report and that defense counsel will be present to advise him in that regard;

(b) he and defense counsel will have an opportunity to make any objections to the report and to speak at the sentencing hearing; and

(c) if he is released pending sentencing, his failure to appear at the scheduled time for sentencing is a crime for which he could be imprisoned.

In most jurisdictions, the role of defense counsel at the guilty plea hearing is relatively passive. The judge usually conducts the colloquy,[349] and defense counsel's primary role is to watch out for any defects in the process and bring them to the attention of the court in order to preserve any error for appeal.[350] For example, defense counsel should ensure that the record accurately reflects all terms of the plea agreement[351] and make an appropriate objection if the defendant does not receive all of the benefits of the agreement.[352]

Defense counsel's advocacy is most important when the judge indicates that he may not accept the plea or the agreement. In this situation, counsel must be prepared to argue the propriety and desirability of the agreement much like making a sentencing argument. In addition, it may be necessary for defense counsel to argue the factual basis for the plea or to counter or supplement, as necessary, the factual basis provided by the prosecutor.

## § 19.11    ENFORCING THE PLEA BARGAIN

A plea agreement is vacuous if it is unenforceable. To negotiate a valid bargain and enforce it upon breach, it is necessary to understand (1) the constitutional grounds for enforcing a plea agreement and what remedies are available; (2) what bargains will extend to or bind third persons, including the judge; (3) how the terms of the bargain will be construed; (4) the extent to which the prosecutor and defendant are obligated to perform the bargain in particular circumstances; and (5) the procedure to be followed in enforcing or abrogating a bargain.

---

[349] In some jurisdictions, the judge may delegate the colloquy to defense counsel. *See* Commonwealth v. Colantoni, 488 N.E.2d 3394 (Mass. 1986).

[350] *See* Robinson v. State, 806 P.2d 1128 (Okla. Crim. 1991); People v. Lopez, 525 N.E.2d 5 (N.Y. 1988).

[351] *See* State v. Rutherford, 693 P.2d 1112 (Idaho 1985).

[352] The federal courts are split about whether a breach of the plea agreement can be raised at first instance on appeal. *Cf., e.g.,* United States v. Pryor, 957 F.2d 478 (7th Cir. 1992) and United States v. Flores-Payon, 942 F.2d 556 (9th Cir. 1991) (claim cannot be raised for the first time on appeal) with United States v. Hand, 913 F.2d 854 (10th Cir. 1990) and United States v. Benson, 836 F.2d 1133 (8th Cir. 1988) (claim can be raised for the first time on appeal or under the plain error doctrine).

## [1]    Constitutional Grounds and Remedies for Enforcement

The United States Supreme Court has broadly said, "when a plea rests in any significant degree on a promise or agreement of the prosecutor, so that it can be said to be part of the inducement or consideration, such promise must be fulfilled."[353] However, this due process right of fair dealing by the prosecution is generally not triggered until the defendant actually enters his plea before a judge in reliance on the prosecutor's promise, and if the prosecutor withdraws the plea offer beforehand, the defendant may not usually obtain relief.[354] However, a number of courts have held that even if the defendant has not entered a guilty plea in reliance on a bargain before the prosecution reneges on the agreement, the bargain will be enforceable if the defendant waived his Fifth Amendment privilege against self-incrimination by cooperating with the prosecution under some promise of immunity.[355]

On the other hand, because a plea bargain is, standing alone, without constitutional significance,[356] in the absence of a breach by the prosecutor after the defendant has entered his plea or after he was induced to waive his Fifth Amendment right against self-incrimination in reliance upon the bargain, a defendant will be hard pressed to find a *constitutional* basis for persuading a court to require the prosecutor to honor the terms of her bargain.[357] This has led some courts to enforce the prosecutor's promise in other circumstances of detrimental reliance, as where the defendant waived a statutory right[358] or provided cooperation at some considerable risk to his own safety.[359] Still other courts have required the prosecution to uphold its end of the bargain to promote public confidence in the administration of justice, irrespective of whether the defendant relied to his detriment on the agreement.[360]

When an enforceable plea agreement has been breached by the prosecution, the court and not the defendant chooses the remedy.[361] Generally, the preferred remedy is specific performance.[362] Thus, if the breach involved the failure of the

---

[353] Santobello v. New York, 404 U.S. 257, 262, 92 S. Ct. 495, 499, 30 L. Ed. 2d 427 (1971).

[354] Mabry v. Johnson, 467 U.S. 504, 104 S. Ct. 2543, 81 L. Ed. 2d 437 (1984).

[355] *See, e.g.,* United States v. Harvey, 848 F.2d 1547 (11th Cir. 1988) (breach of oral promise of transactional immunity for information supplied by defendant); United States v. Worthey, 736 F.2d 1429 (10th Cir. 1984) (breach by government after defendant testified before grand jury); People v. Fanger, 748 P.2d 1332 (Colo. App. 1987) (breach after defendant testified at trial for the prosecution).

[356] Mabry v. Johnson, 467 U.S. 504, 104 S. Ct. 2543, 2546, 81 L. Ed. 2d 437 (1984).

[357] *See, e.g.,* People v. Navarroli, 521 N.E.2d 891 (Ill. 1988) (defendant's cooperation in working as an undercover agent gave rise to no constitutional right that the prosecutor abide by the terms of the plea agreement).

[358] *E.g.,* People v. MacRander, 756 P.2d 356 (Colo. 1988) (defendant waived right to a preliminary hearing).

[359] Doe v. District Attorney for Plymouth Dist., 564 N.E.2d 588 (Mass. App. 1991); Ex parte Sides, 501 So.2d 1262 (Ala. 1986); *see* Commonwealth v. Porreca, 567 A.2d 1044 (Pa. Super. 1989).

[360] *See, e.g.,* Commonwealth v. Reyes, 764 S.W.2d 62 (Ky. 1989); *see also* Ex parte Yarber, 437 So.2d 1330 (Ala. 1983).

[361] *See* United States v. Kurkculer, 918 F.2d 295 (1st Cir. 1990); United States v. McGovern, 822 F.2d 739 (8th Cir. 1987).

[362] Margalli-Olvera v. I.N.S., 43 F.3d 345 (8th Cir. 1994); United States v. Jeffries, 908 F.2d 1520 (11th Cir. 1990); United States v. Van Thournout, 100 F.3d 590 (8th Cir. 1996); United States v. Kurkculer, 918 F.2d 295 (1st Cir. 1990); People v. Mancheno, 654 P.2d 211 (Cal. 1982); Westen & Westin,

prosecutor to take a particular position at sentencing, the appropriate remedy would be to resentence the defendant,[363] usually in front of a different judge.[364] If the prosecutor breached an agreement to dismiss particular charges, specific performance would require that those charges be dismissed.[365] Alternatively, the court may permit the defendant to withdraw his plea. The court is given broad discretion in deciding whether to order specific performance or allow the defendant to withdraw his plea.[366]

Sometimes, specific performance or allowing the defendant to withdraw his plea will be unfair to the defendant. For example, neither of these remedies would be meaningful if the prosecutor has reneged on a sentencing recommendation and the defendant has already served a sentence longer than the one the prosecutor would have recommended had she not breached the agreement. In this situation, it would be hollow to order specific performance or allow the defendant to withdraw his plea and risk receiving a longer sentence after conviction at trial. Thus, a court might order that the defendant be resentenced so that he can be released without serving additional time.[367]

In determining the most appropriate remedy, the court should take into account the wishes of the defendant, the nature of the breach, the public interest, and the prejudice to the defendant and the prosecution.[368] Just as a particular remedy may prejudice the defendant, notwithstanding the prosecution's breach, the court will usually avoid a remedy that will unduly prejudice the prosecution. For example, if allowing the defendant to withdraw his plea would effectively make it impossible for the prosecution to try the defendant due to the loss of evidence over a lengthy period of time, specific performance may be the more appropriate remedy rather than permitting the defendant to withdraw his plea.[369] Similarly, if specific performance to prevent the defendant from being prosecuted on specific charges would effectively preclude the prosecutor from legitimately trying the defendant

---

A Constitutional Law of Remedies for Broken Plea Bargains, 66 Cal. L. Rev. 471, 519 nn.166–67 (1978).

[363] *See, e.g.,* United States v. Canada, 960 F.2d 263 (1st Cir. 1992); United States v. Hayes, 946 F.2d 230 (3d Cir. 1991); United States v. Rewis, 969 F.2d 985 (11th Cir. 1992); United States v. Geandinetti, 564 F.2d 723 (5th Cir. 1977); United States v. Brown, 500 F.2d 375 (4th Cir. 1974).

[364] *See, e.g.,* United States v. Goldfaden, 959 F.2d 1324 (5th Cir. 1992); *cf.,* United States v. Torkington, 874 F.2d 1441 (11th Cir. 1989) (whether the original judge should resentence the defendant depends on whether he can disregard his previous views and findings, whether reassignment would be appropriate to preserve the appearance of impartiality, and whether reassignment would be unduly inefficient).

[365] *See., e.g.,* United States v. Lieber, 473 F. Supp. 884 (E.D.N.Y. 1979); United States v. Burns, 990 F.2d 1426 (4th Cir. 1991).

[366] United States v. Barresse, 115 F.3d 610 (8th Cir. 1997); Kingsley v. United States, 968 F.2d 109 (1st Cir. 1992); United States v. Bohn, 959 F.2d 389 (2d Cir. 1992); United States v. Boatner, 966 F.2d 1575 (11th Cir. 1992).

[367] *See* United States v. Garcia, 698 F.2d 31 (1st Cir. 1983); Correale v. United States, 479 F.2d 944 (1st Cir. 1973); *See also* United States v. De la Fuente, 8 F.3d 1333 (9th Cir. 1993) (resentencing was appropriate remedy where government breached plea agreement by failing to move for a sentence below mandatory minimum due to defendant's substantial assistance).

[368] United States v. Walker, 927 F.2d 389 (8th Cir. 1991). *See* State v. Miller, 756 P.2d 122 (Wash. 1988) (emphasizing the remedy desired by the defendant).

[369] *See* People v. Tindle, 460 N.E.2d 1354 (N.Y. 1984). *But see* United States v. Bohn, 959 F.2d 389 (2d Cir. 1992) (holding that the government waived this ground for prejudice by breaching the agreement).

on other charges, specific performance will not be required.[370] Assuming that specific performance is inappropriate, if the defendant refuses to withdraw his plea after being given the opportunity to do so, the refusal will usually waive any other remedy on appeal.[371]

Finally, the vast majority of courts will not award the defendant specific performance if he relies on an agreement breached by the prosecution that contains a benefit that is beyond the power of the law to deliver or violates public policy. For example, except in limited circumstances,[372] an agreement that restricts the type of information that the court may consider in sentencing contravenes public policy and is unenforceable.[373] Also, a plea agreement that calls for a sentence not authorized by law,[374] limits the right of the defendant to testify at the trial of a confederate,[375] was procured by the defendant by fraud, misrepresentation,[376] or a threat of violence,[377] or that purports to bind a party who is beyond the power of the court will not be enforced through specific performance. In such cases, usually the appropriate remedy is to allow the defendant to withdraw his plea,[378] but some courts will reformulate the agreement[379] or nevertheless grant specific performance if vacating the plea will unduly prejudice the defendant.[380]

---

[370] *See* United States v. McGovern, 822 F.2d 739 (8th Cir. 1987).

[371] *See* United States v. Billington, 844 F.2d 445 (7th Cir. 1988); United States v. Holman, 728 F.2d 809 (6th Cir. 1984); United States v. Mack, 655 F.2d 843 (8th Cir. 1981).

[372] Under USSG § 1B1.8, the defendant may agree to cooperate with the government by provid ing information about the unlawful activities of others in exchange for the government's promise that any self-incriminating information provided by the defendant will be kept confidential and not be used by the court in determining the applicable Guidelines range.

[373] *See* United States v. Billington, 844 F.2d 445 (7th Cir. 1988); United States v. Jureidini, 846 F.2d 964 (4th Cir. 1988); United States v. Cook, 668 F.2d 317, 320 n. 4 (7th Cir. 1982); United States v. Avery, 589 F.2d 906, 909 (5th Cir. 1979); State v. McQuay, 452 N.W.2d 377 (Wis. 1990). However, the Eleventh Circuit has held that it will nevertheless enforce such agreements by specific performance. United States v. Boatner, 966 F.2d 1575 (11th Cir. 1992); United States v. Nelson, 837 F.2d 1519 (11th Cir. 1988); United States v. Tobon-Hernandez, 845 F.2d 277 (11th Cir. 1988).

[374] *See* Chae v. People, 780 P.2d 481 (Colo. 1989); Correale v. United States, 479 F.2d 944, 947 (1st Cir. 1973).

[375] *See* United States v. Blackwell, 694 F.2d 1325 (D.C. Cir. 1982); Bhagwat v. State, 658 A.2d 244 (Md. 1995).

[376] *See* State v. Hall, 645 P.2d 1143 (Wash. App. 1982); Lyons v. Goldstein, 47 N.E.2d 425 (1943). However, if the defendant was not responsible for the fraud or misrepresentation, the agreement may be enforced by specific performance. United States v. Kurkculer, 918 F.2d 295 (1st Cir. 1990); United States v. Partida-Parra, 859 F.2d 629 (9th Cir. 1988); United States v. Blackwell, 649 F.2d 1325 (D.C. Cir. 1982); State v. Schaupp, 757 P.2d 970 (Wash. 1988).

[377] *See* United States v. McBride, 571 F. Supp. 596 (S.D. Tex. 1983), aff'd, 915 F.2d 1596 (5th Cir. 1990); United States v. West, 607 F.2d 300 (9th Cir. 1979); United States v. Bridgeman, 523 F.2d 1099 (D.C. Cir. 1975).

[378] *See, e.g.,* State v. Sanders, 628 A.2d 209 (Md. 1993); State v. Burkhart, 566 S.W.2d 871 (Tenn. 1978).

[379] *See, e.g.,* Correale v. United States, 479 F.2d 944 (1st Cir. 1973); Commonwealth v. Zuber, 353 A.2d 441 (1976).

[380] *See, e.g.,* Palermo v. Warden of Green Haven State Prison, 545 F.2d 286 (2d Cir. 1976); State v. Miller, 756 P.2d 122 (Wash. 1988); In re Williams, 583 P.2d 1262 (Wash. App. 1978).

## [2]    Bargains Benefiting or Binding Third Persons

Generally, where a third-party defendant relies upon a benefit in a plea agreement entered into between another defendant and the prosecution, the third-party defendant will be entitled to have the agreement enforced.[381] Similarly, just as a plea agreement may benefit a defendant other than the one who entered into it, the agreement may burden a prosecutor who was not directly a party to the bargain. Thus, on the theory that the "left hand must be informed of what the right one is doing," the bargain of a particular prosecutor will be binding on other prosecutors in the same office regardless of whether the latter knew about the agreement.[382] Moreover, a defendant may be able to obtain specific performance of a promise made by a law enforcement agent,[383] unless the agent did nothing to suggest that she had actual authority to make the promise or the defendant otherwise knew that approval by the prosecutor was necessary.[384]

Whether a bargain made by one prosecutorial office will bind another of the same sovereign in the same jurisdiction will depend on the specific terms of the agreement. For example, if the agreement expressly limits the prosecutor's obligations to the office making the agreement, the bargain has no effect elsewhere.[385] On the other hand, if the agreement explicitly states that it is binding elsewhere and that the prosecutor making the agreement has the authorization to enter into the extraterritorial agreement, it will be enforceable against another prosecutorial office.[386] The only limitation on this rule is that a prosecutor in one sovereign has no authority to bind a non-consenting prosecutor in another sovereign, as where a state prosecutor purports to bind a federal prosecutor who did not assent to the agreement.[387]

When the agreement is unclear about its extraterritorial reach, as where it generally provides that the defendant will not be prosecuted for other violations of law arising out of the offenses charged in the indictment or the investigation giving

---

[381] *See* United States v. D.K.G. Appaloosas, Inc., 630 F. Supp. 1540 (E.D. Tex. 1986) (third-party beneficiary was entitled to enforce agreement regarding property immune from forfeiture); United States v. C.F.W. Construction Co., 583 F. Supp. 197 (D. S.C.), aff'd, 749 F.2d 33 (4th Cir. 1984). *But see* State v. Dibley, 691 P.2d 209 (Wash. Ct. App. 1984) (denying standing to third party raising question about breach of agreement).

[382] Santobello v. New York, 404 U.S. 257, 92 S. Ct. 495, 499, 30 L. Ed. 2d 427 (1971).

[383] *See* United States v. Carrillo, 709 F.2d 35 (9th Cir. 1983); United States v. Rodman, 519 F.2d 1058 (1st Cir. 1975); In re Doe, 410 F. Supp. 1163 (E.D. Mich. 1976).

[384] *See* United States v. Kettering, 861 F.2d 675 (1st Cir. 1988); United States v. Lombardozzi, 467 F.2d 160 (2d Cir. 1972); United States v. Weiss, 599 F.2d 730 (5th Cir. 1979); Commonwealth v. Stipetich, 652 A.2d 1294 (Pa. 1995).

[385] *See* United States v. Ingram, 979 F.2d 1179 (7th Cir. 1992).

[386] *See* United States v. DeMichael, 692 F.2d 1059 (7th Cir. 1982).

[387] *See* United States v. McIntosh, 612 F.2d 835 (4th Cir. 1979); United States v. Cordova-Perez, 65 F.3d 1552 (9th Cir. 1995); United States v. One Parcel of Real Estate Located at 25 Sandra Court, 135 F.3d 462 (7th Cir. 1998) (consent of federal government, or at least that of state officer acting as an agent for federal government, is necessary to bind United States to the terms of a state's plea agreement); Thomas v. I.N.S., 35 F.3d 1332 (9th Cir. 1994) (to bind a prosecutor of another sovereign, the prosecutor making the agreement must have actual, not merely apparent authority). *See also* United States v. Barone, 781 F. Supp. 1072 (E.D. Pa. 1991) (even though federal court could not enjoin a state prosecution that defendant claimed was barred by a promise made by a federal prosecutor, court would direct the federal prosecutor and FBI to give no further assistance to state authorities in their prosecution of the defendant).

rise to those charges, the courts are split about the effect of a purported promise made by a prosecutor of a sovereign in one jurisdiction upon a prosecutor of the same sovereign in another jurisdiction. Some courts resolve the ambiguity in favor of the defendant on the principle that the prosecutor bears a greater degree of responsibility for drafting clear agreements than the defendant,[388] but other courts have held that the extraterritorial restriction on prosecution must be explicit.[389] Still other courts resolve the ambiguity by looking behind the agreement and to what may be reasonably inferred from the negotiations between the parties or from their statements at the plea colloquy.[390]

When a prosecutor makes a promise purporting to provide the defendant with a benefit within the control of another office of the executive branch, the promise will be enforced not only if the prosecutor had actual authority, but if implied authority can be inferred from custom or other circumstances of routine practice or policy.[391] In this way, a number of cases have upheld a prosecutor's promise binding the Internal Revenue Service,[392] Immigration and Naturalization Service,[393] Parole Commission,[394] State Department,[395] and even the office of the Executive itself.[396] On the other hand, as a general rule, where the prosecutor promises to recommend a particular sentence, the promise does not extend to the probation office, which is charged with presenting to the court all facts relevant to sentencing.[397]

As mentioned in § 19.10[3], a judge is never required to accept a plea agreement regardless of its terms.[398] However, if the court accepts the agreement, the judge is implicitly obligated to take those steps necessary to allow the prosecutor to fulfill her end of the bargain.[399] Thus, where the judge accepts an agreement obligating the prosecutor to recommend a particular sentence, the court must provide the prosecutor with an opportunity to make and explain the recommendation.[400] Similarly, if the judge accepts a specific sentence embodied in a plea agreement,

---

[388] *See, e.g.,* United States v. Harvey, 791 F.2d 294 (4th Cir. 1986).

[389] *See, e.g.,* United States v. Annabi, 771 F.2d 670 (2d Cir. 1985) (per curiam).

[390] *See* United States v. Robison, 924 F.2d 612 (6th Cir. 1991); United States v. Russo, 801 F.2d 624 (2d Cir. 1986); United States v. Abbamonte, 759 F.2d 1065 (2d Cir. 1985).

[391] *See* Thomas v. I.N.S., 35 F.3d 1332 (9th Cir. 1994); United States v. Rourke, 74 F.3d 802 (7th Cir. 1996) (Court could look to extrinsic evidence to interpret "government" in plea agreement that extended to other governmental agencies apart from the Department of Justice).

[392] *See* United States v. Lieber, 473 F. Supp. 884 (E.D. N.Y. 1979).

[393] *See* Margalli-Olvera v. I.N.S., 43 F.3d 345 (8th Cir. 1995); Thomas v. I.N.S., 35 F.3d 1332 (9th Cir. 1994).

[394] *See* Allen v. Hadden, 536 F. Supp. 586 (D. Colo. 1982); Palermo v. Warden of Green Haven State Prison, 545 F.2d 286 (2d Cir. 1976). *But see* Augustine v. Brewer, 821 F.2d 365 (7th Cir. 1987).

[395] *See* In re Geisser, 627 F.2d 745 (5th Cir. 1980).

[396] *See* Smith v. Blackburn, 785 F.2d 545 (5th Cir. 1986).

[397] *See* State v. McQuay, 452 N.W.2d 377 (Wis. 1990). *But see* Thomas v. State, 593 So.2d 219 (Fla. 1992) (probation officer may not recommend sentence greater than the one the prosecutor agreed to recommend); Lee v. State, 501 So.2d 591 (Fla. 1987) (presentence report that included a recommendation by the police for incarceration violated prosecutor's agreement to recommend probation).

[398] United States v. Jackson, 563 F.2d 1145 (4th Cir. 1977); State v. DeClue, 805 S.W.2d 252 (Mo. App. 1991).

[399] *See* United States v. Yesil, 991 F.2d 1527 (11th Cir. 1992).

[400] *See* State v. Peterson, 651 P.2d 211 (Wash. 1982).

the defendant may not receive a sentence that is either harsher[401] or more lenient[402] than that specified by the parties.

The judge's obligation to give effect to a plea agreement she has already accepted is less clear when, at the time of sentencing, she is provided information that causes her to believe that the disposition proposed in the plea agreement is inappropriate. As one approach to this situation, the judge may modify the terms of the agreement to bring it in line with the new information she has received.[403] Alternatively, while some courts have held that a judge may not reject an agreement involving a specific sentence bargain after she has previously accepted it,[404] most take the view that after reviewing the presentence report the judge has the inherent power to reject a previously accepted bargain even if she did not expressly condition her earlier acceptance of the agreement on a review of the report.[405] However, whenever a judge alters the terms of the bargain or rescinds her previous acceptance of a bargain, the defendant should be given an opportunity to withdraw his plea.[406] The right to withdraw the plea also exists if the judge rescinds a sentence promise that she made directly to the defendant.[407]

## [3]    Construing the Terms of the Bargain

When the defendant contends that he is entitled to relief due to the prosecutor's breach of a plea agreement, the defendant bears the burden of proving the agreement and the breach by the preponderance of the evidence.[408] Usually, the easiest way to meet this burden is to rely on a written agreement, whether in the form of a formal document or a letter by counsel confirming the terms of an oral agreement. Although not required in federal practice, some jurisdictions require that a plea agreement be in writing; and virtually all jurisdictions, including the

---

[401] *See, e.g.,* State v. Mares, 888 P.2d 930 (N.M. 1994); Connecticut State v. Reid, 526 A.2d 528 (Conn. 1987).

[402] United States v. Mukai, 26 F.3d 953 (9th Cir. 1994); United States v. Semler, 883 F.2d 832 (9th Cir. 1989). *But see* United States v. Johnson, 979 F.2d 396 (6th Cir. 1992) (prosecutor may waive objection to more lenient sentence if he fails to object to defense argument that court impose a more lenient sentence). *Cf.* People v. Siebert, 537 N.W.2d 891 (Mich. 1995) (if court rejects specific sentence in plea agreement and imposes a more lenient sentence, prosecutor should be given the opportunity to withdraw from the bargain) with State v. Warren, 558 A.2d 1312 (N.J. 1989) (prosecutor may not withdraw from plea agreement if judge imposes a more lenient sentence).

[403] *See* United States v. Runck, 601 F.2d 698 (8th Cir. 1979).

[404] *See, e.g.,* United States v. Olesen, 920 F.2d 538 (8th Cir. 1990). *See also* Reffett v. State, 571 N.E.2d 1227 (Ind. 1991).

[405] *See, e.g.,* United States v. Foy, 28 F.3d 464 (5th Cir.), cert. denied, 115 S. Ct. 610 (1994); United States v. Kemper, 908 F.2d 33 (6th Cir. 1990); People v. Dulin, 332 N.W.2d 492 (Mich. App. 1983); Myers v. Frazier, 319 S.E.2d 782 (W. Va. 1984).

[406] *See* State v. Sanders, 628 A.2d 209 (Md. 1993); Ex parte Otinger, 493 So.2d 1362 (Ala. 1986). But see Percival v. State, 745 P.2d 557 (Wyo. 1987) (judge did not have to give defendant the opportunity to withdraw his plea when the court rejected only a part of the agreement).

[407] *See* People v. Dixon, 303 N.W.2d 32 (Mich. App. 1980); *but see* People v. Dulin, 332 N.W.2d 492 (Mich. App. 1983) (criticizing Dixon). *See also* Acosta v. Turner, 666 F.2d 949 (5th Cir. 1982) (holding that defendant is entitled to specific performance of an agreement with the judge concerning the procedure for determining defendant's competency to stand trial).

[408] *See* United States v. LaTray, 739 F. Supp. 88 (N.D. N.Y. 1990), aff'd, 935 F.2d 1277 (2d Cir. 1991).

federal courts, otherwise require that all terms of the agreement be disclosed to the judge on the record at the time the defendant enters his plea.[409]

Generally, a court will refuse to enforce any terms of an agreement that were not disclosed on the record.[410] However, if the defendant later claims that due to fraud, mistake, or duress he did not reveal all terms of the agreement to the court, he may be afforded a hearing to establish the existence of an off-the-record promise if he is specific in his allegations about it and the circumstances under which it was made.[411]

In construing the terms of an agreement and the parties' obligations under it, the courts generally employ traditional contract principles.[412] Thus, the courts will sometimes invoke rules such as the prohibition on the use of parole evidence to contradict the terms of an unambiguous agreement,[413] and the canon of construction that the various provisions of an agreement should be construed as a whole.[414] However, because of the unique nature of plea agreements, a promise that might be unenforceable in a commercial contract may nevertheless be enforced when contained in a plea bargain. For example, while a promise to return stolen property will be insufficient to constitute adequate consideration for a binding commercial contract, such a promise by the defendant in a plea agreement will not permit the prosecution to avoid its obligations under the bargain.[415] Similarly, while a promise to perform a duty imposed by law is invalid consideration for a commercial contract, the defendant's waiver of his privilege against self incrimination by providing information to the prosecution will be sufficient to bind the prosecution to its end of the plea bargain.[416]

Moreover, because plea agreements involve waivers of constitutional rights and implicate the supervisory role of the courts in the proper administration of justice, courts frequently depart from private contract principles when constitutional or

---

[409] *See, e.g.,* Fed. R. Crim. P. 11(c)(2).

[410] Baker v. United States, 781 F.2d 85 (6th Cir. 1986); Siegel v. New York, 691 F.2d 620 (2d Cir. 1982); People v. Selikoff, 318 N.E.2d 784 (N.Y. 1974); Benjamin S. v. Kuriansky, 432 N.E.2d 777 (N.Y. 1982); McCoy v. State, 599 So.2d 645 (Fla. 1992) (where plea agreement did not explicitly state that defendant was obligated to testify truthfully, the court will not vacate the plea or sentence if the defendant testified untruthfully).

[411] *See* Blackledge v. Allison, 431 U.S. 63, 97 S. Ct. 1621, 52 L. Ed. 2d 136 (1977); Perry v. United States, 31 F.3d 1341 (6th Cir. 1994); Davis v. Butler, 825 F.2d 892 (5th Cir. 1987); State v. Lamas, 666 P.2d 94 (Ariz. App. 1983), vacated on other grounds, 694 P.2d 1178 (Ariz. 1985).

[412] United States v. Schilling, 142 F.3d 388 (7th Cir. 1998); United States v. Bunner, 134 F.3d 1000 (10th Cir. 1998); United States v. Jones, 58 F.3d 688 (D.C. Cir. 1995); Carnine v. United States, 974 F.2d 924 (7th Cir. 1992); United States v. Fentress, 792 F.2d 461 (4th Cir. 1986); United States v. Britt, 917 F.2d 353 (8th Cir. 1990); United States v. Krasn, 614 F.2d 1229 (9th Cir. 1980).

[413] *See, e.g.,* United States v. Floyd, 1 F.3d 867 (9th Cir. 1993); United States v. Ajugwo, 82 F.3d 925 (9th Cir. 1996); United States v. Ballis, 28 F.3d 1399 (5th Cir. 1994); United States v. Ingram, 979 F.2d 1179 (7th Cir. 1992); Baker v. United States, 781 F.2d 85 (6th Cir. 1986). *But see* United States v. Garcia, 956 F.2d 41 (4th Cir. 1992) (government could not rely on parole evidence rule to avoid obligation not expressly contained in a plea agreement where the failure to state the obligation was plainly inadvertent).

[414] *See, e.g.,* United States v. Ataya, 864 F.2d 1324 (7th Cir. 1988).

[415] *See* Palermo v. Warden of Green Haven State Prison, 545 F.2d 286 (2d Cir. 1976); United States v. Bowler, 585 F.2d 851 (7th Cir. 1978).

[416] *See* United States v. McBride, 571 F. Supp. 596 (S.D. Tex. 1983), aff'd, 915 F.2d 1596 (5th Cir. 1990).

supervisory concerns dictate the application of other rules of construction or remedies that would be more appropriate in the plea bargain context.[417] This is particularly true in connection with the conduct and obligations of the prosecutor because of concerns for "[t]he honor of the government, public confidence in the fair administration of justice, and the efficient administration of justice in a federal scheme of government."[418]

Thus, for example, because prosecutors typically have more experience in drafting plea agreements, an ambiguity in a plea agreement will often be construed against the prosecution[419] and in a way that upholds the defendant's reasonable interpretation about the promises made in the agreement.[420] In addition, to encourage fair dealing by the prosecutor, where the literal language of the plea agreement leaves the defendant with no practical benefit, some courts will adopt an expanded interpretation of the bargain that gives the defendant the benefit he thought he was obtaining but which was not expressly stated in the agreement.[421]

Generally, however, the courts will not imply a term or obligation into a plea agreement that was not expressly stated. This rule of literal construction has been applied to both the defendant and the prosecution where, for example, the agreement contained a provision waiving the defendant's constitutional right of appeal or the government's statutory right to appeal specific issues,[422] or where the agreement set out the government's position at sentencing.[423]

---

[417] *See, e.g.,* United States v. Ingram, 979 F.2d 1179 (7th Cir. 1992); Staten v. Neal, 880 F.2d 962 (7th Cir. 1989); United States v. Harvey, 791 F.2d 294 (4th Cir. 1986); United States v. Lieber, 473 F. Supp. 884 (E.D. N.Y. 1979).

[418] United States v. Cooper, 70 F.3d 563 (10th Cir. 1995); United States v. Carter, 454 F.2d 426, 428 (4th Cir. 1972) (en banc).

[419] *See, e.g.,* United States v. Phillips, 174 F.3d 1047 (9th Cir. 1999); United States v. Ingram, 979 F.2d 1179 (7th Cir. 1992); United States v. Giorgi, 840 F.2d 1022 (1st Cir. 1988); United States v. Harvey, 791 F.2d 294 (4th Cir. 1986); United States v. Hall, 730 F. Supp. 6646 (M.D. Pa. 1990). *But see* State v. Mares, 888 P.2d 930 (N.M. 1994) (a plea agreement should only be construed in favor of the defendant when the ambiguity cannot be resolved by a review of the relevant direct and extrinsic evidence).

[420] *See, e.g.,* United States v. Bogusz, 43 F.3d 82 (3d Cir. 1994); United States v. Shorteeth, 887 F.2d 253 (10th Cir. 1989); United States v. Harvey, 791 F.2d 294 (4th Cir. 1986); People v. MacRander, 756 P.2d 356 (Colo. 1988).

[421] *See, e.g.,* United States v. De la Fuente, 8 F.3d 1333 (9th Cir. 1993) (construing an agreement that the government "recommend to the sentencing court that defendant be sentenced to the minimum sentence of incarceration required by the sentencing guidelines" as requiring the government to move for a downward departure below the mandatory minimum sentence); United States v. Garcia, 698 F.2d 31 (1st Cir. 1983) (construing government's promise that it "may" recommend probation as requiring such recommendation if the defendant fulfilled his obligation to provide cooperation); State v. Hayes, 423 So.2d 1111 (La. 1982) (prohibiting prosecutor from filing a new charge alleging that defendant was a habitual offender so as not to render meaningless prosecutor's promise that defendant would only receive a four-year sentence).

[422] *See, e.g.,* United States v. Pruitt, 32 F.3d 431 (9th Cir. 1994) (plea agreement does not waive right to bring federal habeas corpus motion unless agreement does so expressly); United States v. Pacheco-Osuna, 23 F.3d 269 (9th Cir. 1994) (government did not waive right to appeal downward departure in plea agreement).

[423] *See, e.g.,* United States v. Benjamin, 138 F.3d 1069 (6th Cir. 1998) (government was obligated to move for downward departure based on substantial assistance where plea agreement stated that government "will" move for such a departure); United States v. Isaac, 141 F.3d 477 (3d Cir. 1998) (plea agreement granting government "sole discretion" to make motion for downward departure for substantial assistance is not reviewable absent a showing of bad faith upon the government); United States v. Forney, 9 F.3d 1492 (11th Cir. 1993) (government not obligated to move for downward

## [4]  The Prosecutor's Performance of the Bargain

The prosecutor is required to perform all material obligations of a plea agreement,[424] and this is so even if the defendant does not benefit from the performance in any practical way. For example, if the agreement obligates the prosecutor to recommend a particular sentence, she must actually make that recommendation in open court even if the judge already knows about the recommendation.[425] However, the defendant will not be afforded a remedy if the prosecutor fails to perform an obligation that is clearly peripheral to the overall benefit the defendant expected to receive, particularly where the obligation did not significantly induce the guilty plea and the defendant was not prejudiced in any way by the prosecutor's failure to perform.[426]

If the prosecutor agrees to recommend a particular sentence, she is not only prohibited from recommending a harsher one,[427] but she may not indicate to the court[428] or the probation officer[429] that she does not believe in the recommendation so as to imply that it should not be accepted. This does not mean that the prosecutor is obligated to express some overt "enthusiasm" for the recommendation.[430] No breach occurs so long as the prosecutor makes the recommendation and she does nothing to affirmatively undercut the recommendation. However, an agreement that obligates the prosecutor to recommend a specific sentence or downward departure from the applicable sentencing range must be explicit.[431] Thus, for example, if the agreement merely gives the prosecutor discretion to recommend a downward departure, the

---

departure based on defendant's substantial assistance where plea agreement merely stated that government would "consider" such a motion); United States v. Nyhuis, 8 F.3d 731 (11th Cir. 1993) (plea agreement barring further charges involving distribution of marijuana did not preclude additional charges involving distribution of cocaine).

[424] Santobello v. New York, 404 U.S. 257, 92 S. Ct. 495, 499, 30 L. Ed. 2d 427 (1971).

[425] *See* United States v. Myers, 32 F.3d 411 (9th Cir. 1994); United States v. Peglera, 33 F.3d 412 (4th Cir. 1994).

[426] *See* Callas v. United States, 578 F. Supp. 1390 (S.D. N.Y. 1984); United States v. Pollard, 959 F.2d 1011 (D.C. Cir. 1992); State v. Bangert, 389 N.W.2d 12 (Wis. 1986).

[427] *See* United States v. Hawley, 93 F.3d 682 (10th Cir. 1996) (government breached agreement not to oppose reduction in defendant's offense level and by making remarks at sentencing advocating enhancement of offense level); State v. Carpenter, 358 A.2d 676 (R.I. 1976).

[428] United States v. Lawlor, 168 F.3d 633 (2d Cir. 1999); United States v. Grimm, 170 F.3d 760 (7th Cir. 1999); United States v. Brown, 500 F.2d 375 (4th Cir. 1974); State v. Poole, 394 N.W.2d 909 (Wis. 1986); Kluttz v. Warden, 669 P.2d 244 (Nev. 1983).

[429] *See* State v. Harlow, 346 S.E.2d 350 (W. Va. 1986). *But see* United States v. Stemm, 847 F.2d 636 (10th Cir. 1988).

[430] *See* United States v. Benchimol, 471 U.S. 453, 105 S. Ct. 2103, 85 L. Ed. 2d 462 (1984).

[431] *See, e.g.,* United States v. Smith, 140 F.3d 1325 (10th Cir. 1998) (where plea agreement did not expressly require government allocution in favor of sentencing recommendation, government did not breach agreement by failing to argue in support of certain sentence adjustments and it was sufficient that the government merely made the court aware of the sentencing recommendation included in the presentence report); United States v. Mitchell, 136 F.3d 1192 (8th Cir. 1998) (unambiguous and unconditional promise to file downward departure motion is binding on the government; and, if promise was part of inducement for the plea, its breach will entitle defendant to specific performance or to withdraw plea); United States v. Benjamin, 138 F.3d 1069 (6th Cir. 1998) (plea agreement that government "will" move for downward departure based on substantial assistance obligated government to make such a motion).

prosecutor's decision not to make such a recommendation will not be disturbed unless the decision was made in bad faith or without any rational basis.[432]

If the prosecutor promises to make no sentence recommendation, she may not, for example, tell the judge that the victim and the arresting officer want the defendant to receive the maximum sentence.[433] However, this will not preclude the prosecutor from allowing the victim or others to address the court and urge a harsher sentence,[434] from opposing a defendant's motion to reduce the sentence he received,[435] or from later opposing the defendant's release on parole.[436] Similarly, a prosecutor's promise to remain silent about a sentence recommendation will prohibit her from affirmatively volunteering adverse information to the probation officer,[437] but not prohibit her from passively allowing the probation officer to review the prosecutor's files in preparing the presentence report.[438] On the other hand, if the promise to make no sentence recommendation reserves a right to the prosecutor to provide the court with all relevant information at sentencing, the prosecutor may call and examine witnesses,[439] provide relevant facts and correct misinformation,[440] and elaborate on the consequences of the defendant's crime and any rationale for appropriate sentencing.[441]

Agreements that require the prosecutor to either reveal or withhold certain information from the court will be carefully construed. For example, a prosecutor's promise to inform the court about the defendant's cooperation does not, without more, obligate the prosecutor to recommend a more lenient sentence.[442] If the plea agreement expressly provides that the defendant is not obligated to provide cooperation, a prosecutor who files a sentencing memorandum emphasizing the defendant's failure to cooperate will be deemed to have breached the agreement.[443] With respect to a prosecutor's promise to withhold certain information from the court, in most circumstances such an agreement will be held to violate public policy as limiting the judge's ability to make a fully informed sentencing decision.[444]

---

[432] *See* United States v. Khan, 920 F.2d 1100 (2d Cir. 1990); United States v. Nelson, 717 F. Supp. 682 (D. Minn. 1989).

[433] *See* Commonwealth v. Martinez, 539 A.2d 399 (Pa. Super. 1988).

[434] *See* Ryan v. State, 479 N.E.2d 517 (Ind. 1985).

[435] *See* Brooks v. United States, 708 F.2d 1280 (7th Cir. 1983); United States v. Ligori, 658 F.2d 130 (3d Cir. 1981); United States v. Mooney, 654 F.2d 482 (7th Cir. 1981). *Cf.*, United States v. Carbone, 739 F.2d 45 (2d Cir. 1984) (the prosecutor must, however, remain silent until the sentence is final).

[436] *See* United States v. Clark, 781 F.2d 730 (9th Cir. 1986).

[437] *See* United States v. Cook, 668 F.2d 317 (7th Cir. 1982).

[438] *See* United States v. Baylin, 696 F.2d 1030 (4th Cir. 1982).

[439] *See* In re Meunier, 491 A.2d 1019 (Vt. 1985).

[440] *See* United States v. Hand, 913 F.2d 854 (10th Cir. 1990); United States v. Block, 660 F.2d 1086 (5th Cir. 1981).

[441] *See* United States v. Diamond, 706 F.2d 105 (2d Cir. 1983).

[442] *See* United States v. Coleman, 895 F.2d 501 (8th Cir. 1990).

[443] *See* United States v. Rewis, 969 F.2d 985 (11th Cir. 1992).

[444] *See* United States v. Fagge, 101 F.3d 232 (2d Cir. 1996) (plea agreement to keep sentencing court ignorant of pertinent information is unenforceable); United States v. Reckmeyer, 786 F.2d 1216 (4th Cir. 1986). However, under USSG § 1B1.8, a promise by the prosecutor that any self-incriminating information provided by a cooperating defendant about the unlawful activities of others will be kept confidential is enforceable. *See* United States v. Shorteeth, 887 F.2d 253 (8th Cir. 1990).

Agreements granting the defendant immunity from future prosecution in exchange for pleading guilty to a pending charge are sometimes more broadly construed. For example, it has been held that such an agreement prohibits the prosecution from instituting a forfeiture action based on the defendant's conduct for which he pled guilty,[445] or from assisting another jurisdiction in bringing additional charges.[446] Prosecutors thus often insist that the agreement limit the restriction on bringing future charges to those known to the prosecutor at the time of the plea. In this regard, some courts differ about whether the agreement will prohibit the prosecutor from bringing additional charges for conduct that she actually knew at the time of the plea or also for conduct she should have known based on the facts to which she had access at the time of the plea.[447]

Once the defendant has pled guilty in reliance on the plea bargain, the prosecutor may not renege on the agreement simply because she has had a change in heart or another prosecutor in the same office disagrees with the bargain.[448] In addition, in the absence of fraud by the defendant, a prosecutor may not rescind her end of the bargain due to a unilateral mistake on her part[449] or a mutual mistake of the parties as otherwise might be permitted in private contract law.[450] This is true even if the mistake stems from a mistake about the law[451] or the discovery of new facts concerning the gravity of the defendant's conduct.[452] On the other hand, if the defendant defrauds the prosecutor,[453] escapes from custody prior to sentencing,[454] or is convicted of another crime after the prosecutor promises to recommend a particular disposition,[455] most courts will permit the prosecutor to abrogate the bargain.

---

[445] *See* United States v. Hall, 730 F. Supp. 646 (M.D. Pa. 1990).

[446] *See* United States v. Barone, 781 F. Supp. 1072 (E. D. Pa. 1991).

[447] *Cf.,* United States v. Sutton, 794 F.2d 1415 (9th Cir. 1986) (taking the more narrow view) with State v. Earl, 497 A.2d 28 (1985) (taking the broader view).

[448] *See, e.g.,* United States v. Lieber, 473 F. Supp. 884 (E.D. N.Y. 1979); State v. Lordan, 363 A.2d 201 (N.H. 1976).

[449] *See, e.g.,* United States v. Partida-Parra, 859 F.2d 629 (9th Cir. 1988); Perkins v. Court of Appeals, 738 S.W.2d 276 (Tex. Crim. App. 1987); Ex parte Cassady v. State, 486 S.2d 453 (Ala. 1986); Epperson v. State, 530 N.E.2d 743 (Ind. App. 1988).

[450] *See, e.g.,* United States v. Atkinson, 979 F.2d 1219 (7th Cir. 1992). The defendant also may not rescind his end of the bargain on this ground. *See* United States v. Oliveros-Orosco, 942 F.2d 644 (9th Cir. 1991); United States v. Zweber, 913 F.2d 705 (9th Cir. 1990). *But see* State v. Dezeler, 427 N.W.2d 231 (Minn. 1988) (permitting defendant to withdraw his plea where both parties miscalculated defendant's criminal history score).

[451] *See* United States v. Hallam, 472 F.2d 168 (9th Cir. 1973); Kisloff v. Covington, 539 N.E.2d 565 (N.Y. 1989).

[452] *See, e.g.,* State v. Thomas, 294 A.2d 57 (N.J. 1972); Perkins v. Court of Appeals, 738 S.W.2d 276 (Tex. Crim. App. 1987).

[453] *See* United States v. Partida-Parra, 859 F.2d 629 (9th Cir. 1988).

[454] *See, e.g.,* People v. Garvin, 406 N.W.2d 469 (Mich. App. 1987); State v. Yates, 533 P.2d 846 (Wash. App. 1975).

[455] *See* State v. Richmond, 896 P.2d 1112 (Kan. App. 1995); In re A.R.E.G., 543 N.E.2d 589 (Ill. App. 1989); State v. Windom, 485 N.W.2d 832 (Wis. 1992); State v. Pascall, 358 N.E.2d 1368 (Ohio App. 1972).

## [5]    The Defendant's Performance of the Bargain

Generally, if the defendant fails to perform his end of the plea bargain, the prosecution cannot be compelled to perform its end of the bargain.[456] This is particularly so if the unfulfilled obligation of the defendant constitutes a material and substantial part of the entire agreement.[457] Moreover, the mere fact that the defendant's breach was caused by a good-faith mistake,[458] or resulted from circumstances beyond his control such as the court's rejection of his plea,[459] will not excuse the breach and prevent the prosecutor from abrogating the agreement. For example, a prosecutor may rescind an agreement breached by the defendant even where the defendant acted under a good-faith belief that he was in compliance with the agreement, and despite the defendant's offer to cure the breach at a time when the prosecutor could easily have mitigated any prejudice resulting from the breach.[460]

However, in some circumstances, the courts have excused the defendant's breach and at least permitted him to withdraw his plea. For example, it has been held that where the defendant failed to fully cooperate with the government, he was nevertheless entitled to withdraw his plea under an agreement that promised he would receive a specific sentence.[461] Under the "unclean hands" doctrine, the prosecution may not mislead the defendant into breaching an agreement and then seek to be released from its terms.[462] In addition, under an equal protection analysis, a defendant may still be entitled to the benefits of an agreement if he cannot fulfill an obligation to pay restitution due to indigency.[463] In any event, if the plea agreement itself contains a provision that deals with the consequences of the defendant's breach, the prosecutor will usually be permitted to insist upon the remedy provided in the agreement.[464]

---

[456] *See* United States v. Gonzalez-Sanchez, 825 F.2d 572 (1st Cir. 1987); United States v. Reardon, 787 F.2d 512 (10th Cir. 1986); United States v. Donahey, 529 F.2d 831 (5th Cir. 1976); State v. Hovind, 431 N.W.2d 366 (Iowa 1988); People v. Curdgel, 634 N.E.2d 199 (N.Y. 1994).

[457] *See* United States v. Finch, 964 F.2d 571 (6th Cir. 1992); United States v. Ataya, 864 F.2d 1324 (7th Cir. 1988); State v. Rivest, 316 N.W.2d 395 (Wis. 1982); People v. McCormick, 859 P.2d 846 (Colo. 1993).

[458] *See* Stokes v. Armontrout, 851 F.2d 1085 (8th Cir. 1988).

[459] *See* United States v. McGovern, 822 F.2d 739 (8th Cir. 1987). *See also* United States v. Spiropoulos, 976 F.2d 155 (3d Cir. 1992) (defendant was unable to provide substantial assistance because target of government investigation died).

[460] *See* Ricketts v. Adamson, 438 U.S. 1, 107 S. Ct. 2680, 97 L. Ed. 2d 1 (1987).

[461] *See* United States v. Fernandez, 960 F.2d 771 (9th Cir. 1991). *See also* Innes v. Dalsheim, 864 F.2d 974 (2d Cir. 1988) (where defendant breached agreement by being arrested prior to sentencing, he must still be allowed to withdraw his plea where the agreement called for the imposition of concurrent sentences).

[462] *See* United States v. San Pedro, 781 F. Supp. 761 (S.D. Fla. 1991) (where the government deliberately left the defendant unclear about whether the agreement's promise of immunity applied to his grand jury testimony, the government could not abrogate the agreement when the defendant testified falsely).

[463] *See* McGee v. City of Oklahoma City, 761 P.2d 863 (Okl. Cr. App. 1988) (requiring that the court establish a reasonable payment schedule for an indigent defendant to pay restitution before withholding from him the benefit of a plea bargain).

[464] *See* United States v. Fitch, 964 F.2d 571 (6th Cir. 1992).

## [6]    Procedure for Enforcing or Abrogating the Bargain

If the prosecution breaches the plea agreement, whether at the guilty plea hearing or at sentencing, defense counsel should make an immediate objection or otherwise file a motion requesting that the court enforce the agreement or permit the defendant to withdraw his plea. If it is necessary for the court to determine whether a breach has occurred, as where there is a dispute about the interpretation of a provision in the agreement, counsel should request a hearing to present documentary evidence about the plea negotiations[465] or even testimony from the prosecutor[466] or defense counsel. Preferably, the hearing should be held in the court where the plea agreement was accepted, even if the breach occurred in a different jurisdiction.[467]

The courts are divided about whether a defendant waives the right to raise the breach of an agreement on appeal when no objection to the breach was made in the trial court.[468] Where waiver has been found, either by the defendant[469] or the prosecutor,[470] the courts reason that the parties should have made their objections before the trial judge who was in the best position to resolve the dispute about the alleged breach and provide an appropriate remedy. However, even in jurisdictions that will find a waiver, a defendant may still be able to raise the breach on post-conviction relief in the trial court if he can show that he did not knowingly waive his objection to the breach.[471]

A defendant must be given access to any appropriate procedure that would permit him to appropriately obtain the benefits due him under a plea agreement. For example, if the government honors its promise to file a motion under Fed. R. Crim. P. 35 requesting a post-sentence reduction in the defendant's sentence in exchange for his cooperation, the trial judge must hold a hearing on the motion.[472] Similarly, if the defendant faces subsequent charges which he contends are barred by an earlier plea agreement, he should be afforded a hearing on his contention before the judge who will preside at the forthcoming trial.[473] Ordinarily, if the judge disagrees with the defendant's claim that a breach has occurred, the defendant is not entitled to an interlocutory appeal.[474] However, an immediate

---

[465] *See, e.g.,* United States v. Hall, 730 F. Supp. 646 (M.D. Pa. 1990).

[466] *See, e.g.,* United States v. Ataya, 864 F.2d 1324 (7th Cir. 1988); United States v. Giorgi, 840 F.2d 1022 (1st Cir. 1988); United States v. Fields, 766 F.2d 1161 (7th Cir. 1985).

[467] *See, e.g.,* United States v. Harvey, 791 F.2d 294 (4th Cir. 1986); United States v. D.K.G. Appaloosas, Inc., 630 F. Supp. 1540 (E.D. Tex. 1986).

[468] For cases finding waiver, *see, e.g.,* United States v. Pryor, 957 F.2d 478 (7th Cir. 1992); United States v. Flores-Payon, 942 F.2d 556 (9th Cir. 1991); United States v. Jeffries, 908 F.2d 1520 (11th Cir. 1990); United States v. Argentine, 814 F.2d 783 (1st Cir. 1987); State v. Georgeoff, 788 P.2d 1185 (Ariz. 1990); In re A.R.E.G., 543 N.E.2d 589 (Ill. App. 1989). For cases holding that a breach may be raised for the first time on appeal, *see, e.g.,* United States v. Hand, 913 F.2d 854, 856 n.2 (10th Cir. 1990); United States v. Baylin, 696 F.2d 1030 (4th Cir. 1982); United States v. Moscahlaidis, 868 F.2d 1357 (3d Cir. 1989); Paradiso v. United States, 689 F.2d 28 (2d Cir. 1982); United States v. Benson, 836 F.2d 1133 (8th Cir. 1988); State v. Marshall, 899 P.2d 1068 (Kan. App. 1995).

[469] *See* United States v. Argentine, 814 F.2d 783 (1st Cir. 1987).

[470] *See* United States v. Johnson, 979 F.2d 396 (6th Cir. 1992).

[471] *See* State v. Georgeoff, 788 P.2d 1185 (Ariz. 1990).

[472] *See* United States v. Hernandez, 34 F.3d 998 (11th Cir. 1994).

[473] *See* United States v. Thompson, 814 F.2d 1472 (10th Cir. 1986).

[474] *See* United States v. Brizendine, 659 F.2d 215 (D.C. Cir. 1981).

appeal may lie if the defendant's claim of breach is intertwined with a claim of double jeopardy,[475] and some jurisdictions will permit a defendant to obtain a writ of mandamus ordering the judge to comply with a plea agreement that has already been accepted.[476]

If the prosecutor contends that the defendant breached the plea agreement, judicial approval will ordinarily be required before the prosecutor will be permitted to abrogate her end of the bargain.[477] The prosecution must establish by the preponderance of the evidence[478] not only that a breach occurred, but that it was material and substantial.[479] The same burden of proof rests on the defendant if he claims that the prosecution was the breaching party.[480]

## § 19.12　MEDIATION IN CRIMINAL CASES

A number of jurisdictions have established programs to mediate disputes in certain criminal cases such as those involving non-violent crimes, juvenile crime, gang violence, writing bad checks, property crimes, and sometimes domestic violence.[481] These programs typically bring together the complainant and the accused, along with a trained mediator, in an effort to resolve the dispute and prevent its reoccurrence. When used in lieu of prosecution, these programs are thought to be advantageous in expeditiously resolving complaints, facilitating restitution, and in streamlining congested court dockets by disposing of cases that are otherwise frequently dismissed because of the complaining witness's reluctance to subject the offender to the criminal process. Sometimes post-conviction mediation is available in lieu of incarceration or as part of the defendant's sentencing and rehabilitation.

Some commentators are critical of publicly supported mediation in criminal cases on the ground that such mediation does not adequately take into account the retributive and deterrent functions of criminal prosecution. This criticism is most acute with respect to mediation of domestic violence cases,[482] and a number of jurisdictions have enacted statutes specifically prohibiting prosecutors and judges

---

[475] *See* United States v. Persico, 774 F.2d 30 (2d Cir. 1985). *But see* United States v. Thompson, 814 F.2d 1472 (10th Cir. 1986).

[476] *See, e.g.,* Perkins v. Court of Appeals, 738 S.W.2d 276 (Tex. Crim. App. 1987).

[477] *See* United States v. Ataya, 864 F.2d 1324 (7th Cir. 1988); State v. Rivest, 316 N.W.2d 395 (Wis. 1982).

[478] United States v. Verrusio, 803 F.2d 885 (7th Cir. 1986).

[479] United States v. Fitch, 964 F.2d 571 (6th Cir. 1992).

[480] *See* United States v. LaTray, 739 F. Supp. 88 (N.D. N.Y. 1990), aff'd, 935 F.2d 1277 (2d Cir. 1991).

[481] *See generally,* Nancy H. Rogers & Craig A. McEwen, Mediation: Law, Policy & Practice, § 12:04 (1994); Cottam, Mediation and Young People: A Look at How Far We've Come, 29 Creighton L. Rev. 1517 (1996); Joseph, Victim-Offender Mediation: What Social & Political Factors Will Affect Its Development?, 11 Ohio St. L. J. on Disp. Res. 207 (1996); Woolpert, Victim-Offender Reconciliation Programs, in Community Mediation: A Handbook for Practitioners and Researchers (Duffy, Grosch, & Olczak eds. 1991).

[482] *See* Lerman, Mediation of Wife Abuse Cases: The Adverse Impact of Informal Dispute Resolution on Women, 7 Harv. Women's L. J. 57 (1984); Woods, Mediation: A Backlash to Women's Progress on Family Law Issues, 19 Clearinghouse Rev. 431 (1985); Rogers & Salem, A Student's Guide to Mediation and the Law, 211–222 (1987); Ending Mandatory Divorce Mediation for Battered Women, 15 Harv. Women's L. J. 272 (1992).

from referring domestic abuse cases to mediation.[483] Other states authorize mediation of criminal cases more broadly and do not specifically exempt domestic violence cases.[484]

The availability of mediation in certain types of criminal cases is, of course, important in plea bargaining as an alternative to traditional criminal prosecution and punishment. After the defendant is charged, defense counsel might propose to the prosecutor that the defendant and complainant participate in a mediation program in return for a dismissal of the charges, or propose that mediation form all or part of the disposition of the case upon the defendant's plea of guilty or *nolo contendere*. Because the availability of mediation programs and the types of cases in which they may be employed vary significantly, counsel must be thoroughly familiar with the programs available in the relevant jurisdiction, any statutory limitations on the use of those programs, and the prosecutor's policies about them in plea bargaining.

---

[483] *See* Nancy H. Rogers & Craig A. McEwen, Mediation: Law, Policy & Practice, § 12:04 (1994).

[484] *See* Id. *See also generally,* Developments in the Law: Legal Responses to Domestic Violence, 106 Harv. L. Rev. 1498 (1993); Bethel & Singer, Mediation: A New Remedy for Cases of Domestic Violence, 7 Vt. L. Rev. 15 (1982).

# Appendix A

## NEGOTIATION & MEDIATION ROLE PLAYS

### SYNOPSIS

**Note on Dates:** YR-0 means the present year; YR-1 means last year; YR-2 means the year before last, etc.

**Note to Mediators:** If you are asked to serve as a mediator in a case, see the "General Suggestions To Mediators For How To Mediate A Case" in Appendix B.

Your professor will provide you with any confidential facts for the role you are assigned to play in a particular case.

## (1)   Bloch & McDonald (Premarital Agreement)

Henry Bloch and Jane McDonald plan to marry February 1, YR∓1. They have been dating for four years. Henry is three-fourth's owner of Cape Fear Textiles and Jane has been his secretary for the last four years. Henry has been married before and wishes to have a premarital agreement prepared so that he is protected in case the marriage ends. Jane has agreed to sign the agreement so long as she agrees with its contents. Jane has never been married before and currently lives with her elderly mother.

The State of Jefferson has adopted the provisions of the Uniform Premarital Act given below. The parties seek to negotiate a premarital agreement.

### § 1   Definitions.

As used in this Act:

(1)   "Premarital agreement" means an agreement between prospective spouses made in contemplation of marriage and to be effective upon marriage.

(2)   "Property" means an interest, present or future, legal or equitable, vested or contingent, in real or personal property, including income and earnings.

## § 2   Formalities.

A premarital agreement must be in writing and signed by both parties. It is enforceable without consideration.

## § 3   Content.

(a)   Parties to a premarital agreement may contract with respect to:

(1)   the rights and obligations of each of the parties in any of the property of either or both of them whenever and wherever acquired or located;

(2)   the right to buy, sell, use, transfer, exchange, abandon, lease, consume, expend, assign, create a security interest in, mortgage, encumber, dispose of, or otherwise manage and control property;

(3)   the disposition of property upon separation, marital dissolution, death, or the occurrence or nonoccurrence of any other event;

(4)   the modification or elimination of spousal support;

(5)   the making of a will, trust, or other arrangement to carry out the provisions of the agreement;

(6)   the ownership rights in and disposition of the death benefit from a life insurance policy;

(7)   the choice of law governing the construction of the agreement; and

(8)   any other matter, including their personal rights and obligations, not in violation of public policy or a statute imposing a criminal penalty.

(b)   The right of a child to support may not be adversely affected by a premarital agreement.

## § 4   Amendment, Revocation.

After marriage, a premarital agreement may be amended or revoked only by a written agreement signed by the parties. The amended agreement or the revocation is enforceable without consideration.

## § 5   Enforcement.

(a)   A premarital agreement is not enforceable if the party against whom enforcement is sought proves that:

(1)   that party did not execute the agreement voluntarily; or

(2)   the agreement was unconscionable when it was executed and, before execution of the agreement, that party:

(i)   was not provided a fair and reasonable disclosure of the property or financial obligations of the other party;

(ii)   did not voluntarily and expressly waive, in writing, any right to disclosure of the property or financial obligations of the other party beyond the disclosure provided; and

  (iii) did not have, or reasonably could not have had, an adequate knowledge of the property or financial obligations of the other party.

 (b) If a provision of a premarital agreement modifies or eliminates spousal support and that modification or elimination causes one party to the agreement to be eligible for support under a program of public assistance at the time of separation or marital dissolution, a Court, notwithstanding the terms of the agreement, may require the other party to provide support to the extent necessary to avoid that eligibility.

 (c) An issue of unconscionability of a premarital agreement shall be decided by the court as a matter of law.

---

## (2) <u>Bloch v. Bloch</u>
## (Separation Agreement)

Henry and Jane Bloch, who consulted you about a premarital agreement ten years ago (*see* (1) Block & McDonald — Premarital Agreement) have run into hard times, and are anticipating a separation. When Henry and Jane first contemplated marriage, they asked you to draft a Premarital Agreement. However, because things were going so well and they had stars in their eyes, they decided they didn't need one. They never signed a Premarital Agreement. They have been married ten years. (Assume they married on February 1, YR-10.)

When Henry and Jane first consulted you about the Premarital Agreement eleven years ago, Henry owned three-fourths of Cape Fear Textiles. Henry bought out his sister-in-law's one-quarter interest in Cape Fear Textiles on March 1, YR-10. Jane was Henry's secretary at Cape Fear Textiles at the time of their marriage.

Jane and Henry have never been able to conceive a child, but they adopted one child, Katherine (Kathy) McDonald Bloch, who was born on January 1, YR-8. A final Order of Adoption was entered on September 1, YR-8.

After Kathy came to live with them, Jane stopped working as Henry's secretary at Cape Fear Textiles. At first she planned to return to work after six months. However, Jane found that it was too hard to leave Kathy with a babysitter. Henry agreed that Jane should try staying home from work. His business had picked up, and he was able to pay another secretary a good salary.

Both of Henry's children from his first marriage, Daniel and John Bloch, are now adults. On March 1, YR-2, Henry transferred one-third interest in Cape Fear Textiles to Daniel and one third to John. Henry continues to own one-third of Cape Fear Textiles.

Henry continues to pay alimony of $1000 a month to his first wife. Although old alimony orders continue in force in our state of Jefferson, the Jefferson legislature has enacted a new statute to replace alimony. It is called Post-Separation Support. Because it is a new statute, there is no case law interpreting it. The statute is provided below.

Henry and Jane's joint tax return for YR-1 shows Henry's gross salary from Cape Fear Textiles was $75,000 and Jane's income from her inheritance from her father was $20,000. Henry and Jane also have $25,000 in a money market account.

The State of Jefferson has adopted child support guidelines, which a court uses to determine how much should be paid in child support by a non-custodial parent to the custodial parent. Jefferson's guidelines are based on the "Income Shares Model," in which each parent's income is added to the income of the other parent and then adjusted for health insurance obligations and work related childcare costs. The amount of the child support obligation is then derived from a chart showing the amount of child support the child support enforcement agency has determined will be necessary for the number of children in the family with parents whose adjusted combined income is of a certain amount. That child support obligation is then divided between the two parents based on the percentage of the total income each earns.

Based on Jefferson's child support guidelines, and based on the parties' reported income for YR-1 and the fact that Henry currently pays $300 a month for health insurance for the family ($100 per person), Henry would be expected to pay $676 in child support if Jane has custody of Kathy for more than 243 days per year. Jane would be expected to pay $260 to Henry if he has custody of Kathy for more than 243 days per year. However, a judge may deviate from these amounts for "good cause." Some Jefferson judges have deviated from the guidelines if the non-custodial parent has an outstanding spousal support order. The amount of the deviation is within the judge's discretion. Judges may also deviate from the guideline amount for other "good cause." Under the Jefferson child support guidelines, child support terminates when the child reaches eighteen years of age. However, the parties may extend support beyond that age in their Separation Agreement.

If the parties work out a child support agreement and do not litigate the issue, they of course can agree to any child support amount for any length of time. However, a court will not enforce an agreement that is not in the child's best interest. If the parties include child support in their Separation Agreement and ask the court to incorporate the agreement into their divorce decree, the agreement will be a court order enforceable by contempt. The judge who has been asked to incorporate the separation agreement into the divorce decree has the authority to reject the child support amount reached by the parties if he determines that it is not in the best interests of the child. He can then substitute the state guideline amount into the child support portion of the agreement.

The State of Jefferson has also adopted Equitable Distribution. The relevant statute regarding equitable distribution is also given below. The parties seek to negotiate a comprehensive separation agreement.

## SPOUSAL SUPPORT AT DIVORCE

### § 50-16.1A  Definitions.

As used in this Chapter, unless the context clearly requires otherwise, the following definitions apply:

(1) "Dependent spouse" means a spouse, whether husband or wife, who is actually substantially dependent upon the other spouse for his or her maintenance and support or is substantially in need of maintenance and support from the other spouse.

(2) "Marital misconduct" means any of the following acts that occur during the marriage and prior to or on the date of separation:

(i) Illicit sexual behavior. For the purpose of this section, illicit sexual behavior means acts of sexual or deviate sexual intercourse, deviate sexual acts, voluntarily engaged in by a spouse with someone other than the other spouse;

(ii) Involuntary separation of the spouses in consequence of a criminal act committed prior to the proceeding in which alimony is sought;

(iii) Abandonment of the other spouse;

(iv) Malicious turning out-of-doors of the other spouse;

(v) Cruel or barbarous treatment endangering the life of the other spouse;

(vi) Indignities rendering the condition of the other spouse intolerable and life burdensome;

(vii) Reckless spending of the income of either party, or the destruction, waste, diversion, or concealment of assets;

(viii) Excessive use of alcohol or drugs so as to render the condition of the other spouse intolerable and life burdensome;

(ix) Willful failure to provide necessary subsistence according to one's means and condition so as to render the condition of the other spouse intolerable and life burdensome.

(3) "Post-separation support" means spousal support to be paid until the earlier of either the date specified in the order of post-separation support, or an order awarding or denying alimony. Post-separation support may be ordered in an action for divorce, whether absolute or from bed and board, for annulment, or for alimony without divorce.

(4) "Supporting spouse" means a spouse, whether husband or wife, upon whom the other spouse is actually substantially dependent for maintenance and support or from whom such spouse is substantially in need of maintenance and support.

## § 50-16.2A  Post-separation support.

(a) In an action brought pursuant to this Chapter, either party may move for post-separation support. The verified pleading, verified motion, or affidavit of the moving party shall set forth the factual basis for the relief requested.

(b) In ordering post-separation support, the court shall base its award on the financial needs of the parties, considering the parties accustomed standard of living, the present employment income and other recurring earnings of each party from any source, their income-earning abilities, the separate and marital debt service obligations, those expenses reasonably necessary to support each of the parties, and each party's respective legal obligations to support any other persons.

(c) Except when subsection (d) of this section applies, a dependent spouse is entitled to an award of post-separation support if, based on consideration of the factors specified in subsection (b) of this section, the court finds that the resources of the dependent spouse are not adequate to meet his or her reasonable needs and the supporting spouse has the ability to pay.

(d)   At a hearing on post-separation support, the judge shall consider marital misconduct by the dependent spouse occurring prior to or on the date of separation in deciding whether to award post-separation support and in deciding the amount of post-separation support. When the judge considers these acts by the dependent spouse, the judge shall also consider any marital misconduct by the supporting spouse in deciding whether to award post-separation support and in deciding the amount of post-separation support.

(e)   Nothing herein shall prevent a court from considering incidents of post date-of-separation marital misconduct as corroborating evidence supporting other evidence that marital misconduct occurred during the marriage and prior to the date of separation.

## PROPERTY DIVISION AT DIVORCE

### § 50-20   Distribution by court of marital property upon divorce.

(a)   Upon application of a party, the court shall determine what is the marital property and shall provide for an equitable distribution of the martial property between the parties in accordance with the provisions of this section.

(b)   For purposes of this section:

(1)   "Marital property" means all real and personal property acquired by either spouse or both spouses during the course of the marriage and before the date of the separation of the parties, and presently owned, except property determined to be separate property in accordance with subdivision (2) of this subsection. Marital property includes all vested and non-vested pension, retirement, and other deferred compensation rights, and vested and non-vested military pensions eligible under the federal Uniformed Services Former Spouses' Protection Act. It is presumed that all property acquired after the date of marriage and before the date of separation is marital property except property which is separate property under subdivision (2) of this subsection. This presumption may be rebutted by the greater weight of the evidence.

(2)   "Separate property" means all real and personal property acquired by a spouse before marriage or acquired by a spouse by bequest, devise, descent, or gift during the course of marriage. However, property acquired by gift from the other spouse during the course of the marriage shall be considered separate property only if such an intention is stated in the conveyance. Property acquired in exchange for separate property shall remain separate property regardless of whether the title is in the name of the husband or wife or both and shall not be considered to be marital property unless a contrary intention is expressly stated in the conveyance. The increase in value of separate property and the income derived from separate property shall be considered separate property. All professional licenses and business licenses which would terminate on transfer shall be considered separate property.

(3)   "Distributive award" means payments that are payable either in a lump sum or over a period of time in fixed amount, but shall not include alimony payments or other similar payments for support and maintenance

which are treated as ordinary income to the recipient under the Internal Revenue Code.

(c)   The difficulty of evaluating any component asset or any interest in a business, corporation or profession, and the economic desirability of retaining such asset or interest, intact and free from any claim or interference by the other party;

(d)   Before, during or after marriage the parties may by written agreement, duly executed and acknowledged, or by a written agreement valid in the jurisdiction where executed, provide for distribution of the marital property in a manner deemed by the parties to be equitable and the agreement shall be binding on the parties.

(e)   Subject to the presumption of subsection (c) of this section that an equal division is equitable, it shall be presumed in every action that an in-kind distribution of marital or divisible property is equitable. This presumption may be rebutted by the greater weight of the evidence, or by evidence that the property is a closely held business entity or is otherwise not susceptible of division in-kind. In any action in which the presumption is rebutted, the court in lieu of an in-kind distribution shall provide for a distributive award in order to achieve equity between the parties. The court may provide for a distributive award to facilitate, effectuate or supplement a distribution of marital or divisible property. The court may provide that any distributive award payable over a period of time be secured by a lien on specific property.

(f)   Unless good cause is shown that there should not be an interim distribution, the court may, at any time after an action for equitable distribution has been filed and prior to the final judgment of equitable distribution, enter orders declaring what is separate property and may also enter orders dividing part of the marital property, or debt, or marital debt between the parties. The partial distribution may provide for a distributive award and may also provide for a distribution of marital property and marital debt. Any such orders entered shall be taken into consideration at trial and proper credit given.

(g)   In any order for the distribution of property made pursuant to this section, the court shall make written findings of fact that support the determination that the marital property has been equitably divided.

-------

## (3)   Daye v. City of Rexford
## (Employment Discrimination)

On July 31, YR-2, at approximately 1:30 a.m., Marsha Woods, who worked as a cleaning lady for a small office complex, was walking home from work in the City of Rexford, State of Rexford. As she walked by the unfenced parking lot of the Rexford Police Department, she saw two males who had somehow managed to break into one of the police cars parked in the lot and who were rummaging through the contents of the car. The lighting in the parking lot was poor and it was difficult for her to see the two men. However, she heard one of them, who was African-American and later identified as Max Stimpson, refer to the other as "Joey." Although she wasn't at all positive, she thought that "Joey" (who was white) looked like "Joey Smith" who some months ago had worked one night with her and her co-workers cleaning the office complex.

Upon seeing what the two men were doing, she hurried across the street and called 911 from a phone booth. The police operator told her that officers would be dispatched to the scene right away, and asked her to stay in the phone booth until the officers arrived.

Within two minutes, Officers Blake Bowes and Donald Crews arrived in their squad car. Upon seeing the officers, the two suspects ran. Officer Crews gave chase on foot and tackled Stimpson on the street about 25 yards away from where Ms. Woods remained in the phone booth. According to Ms. Woods, she saw Officer Crews beat Stimpson four times with a flashlight while Stimpson was on the ground and was not offering any resistance. Officer Crews, who is white, claims that he subdued Stimpson with the flashlight by hitting him with it two times because Stimpson was struggling and resisting arrest. "Joey," who had also run when the officers arrived, was never caught.

Officer Bowes interviewed Ms. Woods about what she had seen in the parking lot and from the phone booth. In his police report, Bowes wrote that Ms. Woods had described the suspect called "Joey" as being "white; blue eyes; dark hair; about medium height & build; and 25-30 years old." The report noted that Ms. Woods thought the suspect "looked like one, Joey Smith, but witness couldn't see suspect very well."

Stimpson, who was bleeding from his head and face from the flashlight blows, was arrested for "resisting arrest" and "felony breaking and entering into a police vehicle." Officer Crews took Stimpson in handcuffs to the local hospital to be treated. However, when the handcuffs were removed at the hospital and Stimpson was being treated by a physician's assistant, Stimpson somehow managed to escape through a fire-door exit and has not been apprehended since.

On August 3, YR-2, the case was turned over to Detective Kyle Daye, the only African-American detective in the Rexford Police Department and one of four African-Americans on the force out of a total of 40 officers. Daye is 38 years old and has been with the police department for ten years. He began as a patrol officer, and worked his way up to the rank of detective which he has held since January, YR-3. Like other detectives on the force, Daye's primary job is to investigate unsolved felony cases.

When Daye was assigned the instant case to apprehend Stimpson and "Joey," he was well aware of the significant media criticism that had been brought against the police department for its failure to adequately secure the unfenced parking lot area at the police station, and its failure to prevent the escape of Stimpson. The Chief of Police, Harold Burns, expressly told Daye to "solve this case quickly and at all costs."

On August 4, YR-2, Daye reviewed Bowes' report and interviewed Ms. Woods. She told him the same things she had told Bowes about what she saw in the parking lot and how Crews subdued Stimpson. The next day, Daye presented Ms. Woods' account of what she saw in the parking lot to the local magistrate, Richard Larson, and obtained a warrant for the arrest of a defendant (who was named in the warrant as "Joey Smith") for felony breaking and entering into a police vehicle. The warrant was a standard, pre-printed form that contained designated spaces to enter the defendant's address, telephone number, race, sex, date of birth, age, social security number, drivers license number and State, and name of defendant's employer. As a matter of proper practice, an officer who swears out an arrest warrant will include as much of this information on the warrant as is known to the officer. However, none of the foregoing information was filled in on the warrant when it was signed and issued by Magistrate Larson on August 5, YR-2. Magistrate Larson, who was 72 years old at the time, is now deceased.

On August 6, YR-2, Daye contacted Ms. Woods' employer who told him that a "Joey Smith" had worked only one night for the cleaning company some months ago, and that the only information the company had on Smith was that his last known address was 1211 Mineral Springs Drive in Rexford City. Daye went to that address, but no "Joey Smith" was living there and the current residents said they knew nothing about a "Joey Smith."

On August 7, YR-2, Daye asked Assistant Detective, Fran Payton, to provide him with a computer printout of all the "Joey Smith's" in the State of Rexford's drivers license data bank. The printout listed six persons under the name of "Joey Smith," one of which was a "Joey Lee Smith," born March 7, YR-29, with an address at 1211 Mineral Springs Drive, Rexford City. Payton is white and is the only female officer on the Rexford City Police force. She had no formal responsibilities in connection with Daye's investigation.

On August 8, YR-2, Daye ran a criminal record check on "Joey Lee Smith," which showed that this individual had two convictions for misdemeanor larceny in the State of Rexford in the past five years. Thus concluding that "Joey Lee Smith" was the proper suspect in the case, on August 8 Daye wrote in the address of 1211 Mineral Springs Drive onto the arrest warrant that had been issued by Magistrate Larson on August 5, YR-2. Daye says that when Magistrate Larson had signed the warrant, Daye had told Larson that Daye would add to the warrant the proper address for "Joey Smith" when Daye ascertained it, and that Larson said, "Ok." Daye made no other additions or changes to the warrant.

On August 9, YR-2, Daye took the computer printout from the State of Rexford's drivers license data bank to Assistant Detective Payton and told her to enter the name of "Joey Lee Smith, DOB 3/7/YR-29" into the National Crime Information Center (NCIC) database as being wanted on a Rexford City warrant for felony breaking and entering into a police vehicle. This NCIC computer database contains the names of and other pertinent information on all persons in the country for whom there are outstanding arrest warrants, and all police departments throughout the country can access the database. Payton, however, emphatically says that Daye told her to enter the name of "Joey Allen Smith, DOB 3/7/YR-39" (who was one of the other six names listed on the State of Rexford's drivers license data bank printout) into the NCIC database; and this was the name that she entered into that database.

After entering "Joey Allen Smith, DOB 3/7/YR-39 . . . wanted on Rexford City warrant for Felony B & E of a Police Vehicle" into the NCIC computer database, Payton handed Daye a hard copy of the computer entry, which Daye admits he did not review but simply put in his file. There is nothing in the Rexford City Police Department Officers Manual that either expressly required Payton to give Daye a hard copy of the NCIC database entry or expressly required Daye to review it for accuracy.

On September 1, YR-1, the "Joey Allen Smith" who had been entered into the NCIC database was in the Town of Tarville, some 150 miles from the City of Rexford. When he went to the local Department of Motor Vehicle's Drivers License Office to renew his driver's license, the DMV officer checked the NCIC database and saw that Mr. Smith was wanted on the unserved felony warrant for breaking and entering into a police vehicle. Accordingly, the Tarville police promptly arrested Mr. Smith and took him into custody, where he remained in jail for 48 hours until the Tarville Chief of Police and the City of Rexford Chief of Police (Harold Burns) figured out the mistaken entry into the NCIC database and that Mr. Smith was in fact not the proper suspect wanted on the warrant.

Mr. Joey Allen Smith is a prominent citizen and certified public accountant in the small Town of Tarville. He is married, has two young children, and has no criminal record. His arrest received extensive coverage in the local media.

On September 4, YR-1, The Rexford City Manager, pursuant to the recommendation of Chief Burns, placed Daye on temporary suspension without pay as permitted by the City's Personnel Policy. This suspension lasted until October 5, YR-1 when, after Burns had completed an investigation, the City Manager decided to demote Daye to Patrol Officer. As a detective, Daye was making $48,000 per year; but effective October 5, YR-1, his demotion resulted in his making $36,000 per year. Although Chief Burns also investigated Payton's involvement in what had happened, she was not suspended or disciplined in any way. There was extensive media coverage in the City of Rexford about Daye's demotion and the mistaken arrest of Joey Allen Smith.

The parties agree that the City Manager followed all proper procedural due process requirements under the Personnel Policy in disciplining Daye. However, Daye's attorney has advised counsel for the City that Daye intends to pursue a claim against the City for race discrimination in violation of Title VII of the Federal Civil Rights Act, but is willing to try to resolve the matter before initiating procedures under Title VII. Daye's attorney contends that there were no grounds for disciplining Daye at all. And, to the extent there were any valid grounds for disciplining Daye, he was the victim of disparate treatment because Payton, who is white and who Daye contends was solely responsible for entering the wrong "Joey Smith" into the NCIC database, was not disciplined at all.

Counsel for the City of Rexford has advised Daye's lawyer that the City Manager's decision was based on Chief Burns' opinion (1) that Daye had no "probable cause" under the Fourth Amendment to the U.S. Constitution and State law to support a warrant for the arrest of anyone in the case (*i.e.*, that Daye had no reasonably trustworthy information that would lead an officer of reasonable caution to believe that Joey Lee Smith committed the breaking and entering of the police vehicle); (2) that the arrest warrant did not "particularly describe" the person to be arrested as required by the Fourth Amendment and State law; (3) that Payton was not disciplined because it could not be conclusively determined which "Joey Smith" Daye told Payton to enter into the NCIC database, and Payton otherwise had no responsibilities in the investigation of Daye's case; and (4) that Daye nevertheless should have reviewed the hard copy of the NCIC computer entry given him by Payton to ensure the accuracy of the information entered into the database. However, counsel for the City of Rexford is also agreeable to exploring a resolution of Daye's race discrimination claims without litigation.

The parties are in agreement about the basic legal principles pertaining to proof and damages in a Title VII case. Title VII prohibits discrimination (*i.e.*, treating individuals differently) in connection with employment based on race, color, sex, national origin, and religion. The burden of persuasion in such a case remains throughout on the plaintiff. The plaintiff must first establish a prima facie case that he was disciplined when another employee of a different race should have been disciplined and was not. The defendant then bears the burden of production to show some specific and legitimate non-discriminatory reason for the employment action.

The plaintiff must then show that the defendant's reason for the employment action was either (a) false or (b) a mere pretext for discrimination (*i.e.*, that the defendant's proffered reason was not the true reason for the employment action but was, at least in part, motivated by discriminatory animus). A showing of *either* of these things is, by itself, sufficient to permit a jury to infer that the employment action was motivated by discriminatory animus. The State of Rexford allows the plaintiff to prevail in so-called "mixed motive" cases, where the employment action was motivated by both lawful and unlawful considerations. A prevailing plaintiff is entitled to backpay; reinstatement to former position; if reinstatement is not practical or available, to "front pay" (*i.e.* lost wages likely to be incurred until the employee obtains new employment at a wage that is comparable to what he was previously earning); damages for emotional distress and medical expenses for such distress upon a showing of "some specific discernible injury to the plaintiff's emotional state;" and reasonable attorney's fees and litigation expenses.

---

## (4) French v. Goff
## (Automobile Personal Injury)

Counsel for Sandy French has sent the following settlement brochure letter to the adjuster for Pat Goff's automobile liability insurance carrier:

Ms. Rose A. Braves
Claim Specialist
Auto Mutual Insurance Co.

| Re: | My Client: | Sandy French |
|---|---|---|
| | Your Insured: | Pat Goff |
| | Your Claim No. | 33-1795-262 |
| | Date of Accident: | August 11, YR-2 |

Dear Ms. Braves:

As you know, I represent Ms. Sandy French in connection with the personal injuries she sustained in an automobile accident on August 11, YR-2 when your insured's car rear-ended Ms. French's van on Weaver Dairy Road. This letter and its enclosures are provided for settlement discussions only. After you have had the opportunity to review this claim, I look forward to hearing from you and hope we can resolve this matter without the necessity of litigation.

LIABILITY

On August 11, YR-2, at approximately 10:30 a.m., Ms. French was driving south on Weaver Dairy Road, a two-lane road in rural, Orange County. She had not driven this road before and was on her way to the town of Pittsborough. The speed limit on Weaver Dairy is 55 m.p.h.

Pittsborough Road intersects Weaver Dairy approximately five miles from the Orange County and Caswell County line. As Ms. French was driving south on Weaver Dairy, she realized that she had inadvertently passed the turn-off from Weaver Dairy to Pittsborough Road. Accordingly, she pulled over to the right-hand, paved shoulder of Weaver Dairy; and, after seeing no cars behind her or any traveling north in the opposite lane of Weaver Dairy, she executed a three-point turn or U-turn to travel north on Weaver Dairy and back towards the intersection of Weaver Dairy and Pittsborough Road.

Approximately one-tenth of a mile south of the point where Ms. French executed her U-turn on Weaver Dairy, there is a moderately sharp curve in the road. (The speed limit for the curve is 45 m.p.h.) Mr. Goff, who was traveling north on Weaver Dairy, rounded that curve at a high rate of speed, and crashed into the rear of Ms. French's van just as she had completed her U-turn and was about to proceed north on Weaver Dairy. The police officer who investigated the accident gave no citation to either driver, apparently because he was unable to determine fault in the accident. (*See* Accident Report enclosed).

It is our contention that your insured was negligent in that he was driving in excess of the speed limit, was otherwise driving at a speed that was in excess of what was reasonable when rounding the curve on Weaver Dairy, or failed to properly reduce his speed to avoid the collision. As you know, this State recognizes the doctrine of "comparative negligence" whereby, in any action to recover damages for personal injury, the contributory negligence of the claimant does not bar recovery, but the amount of damages otherwise recoverable will be diminished in the proportion which the contributory negligence of the claimant bears to the negligent conduct which caused the damages. The doctrine of last clear chance is not recognized in our jurisdiction. Of course, we contend that Ms. French was not contributorily negligent in causing the accident; but, if she was, her damages are merely to be reduced by the extent of any such negligence.

## MEDICAL TREATMENT

The following summarizes Ms. French's medical treatment with verbatim excerpts from the pertinent records. (*See* enclosed medical records).

### Orange County Emergency Medical Services

8/11/YR-2:      Taken by ambulance to Rolland Hospital. Patient was spinally immobilized. Patient had neck pain, and lower outside left leg pain. Has trouble remembering events of motor vehicle accident, either events leading up to the accident or after the accident.

### Rolland Hospital Emergency Room:

8/11/YR-2:      Pain at base of neck. Soreness above left ankle. Pain in shoulder blades, wincing with pain. C-spine films show possible ligamentous injury. Advised to take warm soaks and showers. Given analgesics, Ibuprofen 800 mg.

### Midtown Family Medicine:

9/4/YR-2      Persistent stiffness in lower back, especially after sitting for long periods of time. Also, pain in left calf, and pain in dorsiflexion of left ankle. Diagnosis of flexion extension injury; low back; contusion left leg. Physical therapy recommended.

<u>Comprehensive Physical Therapy Center</u>:

9/8/YR-2 to      (Patient had 14 physical therapy sessions to treat left
2/24/YR-1        foot pain, and thoracic and lumbar back pain.)

<u>Midtown Family Medicine</u>:

9/25/YR-2        Occasional pain and stiffness above the left iliac crest.
                 Still some limitation of dorsiflexion in ankle. Advised to
                 continue physical therapy.

<u>Midtown Family Medicine</u>:

2/12/YR-1        Patient has persistent back pain from MVA 6 months
                 ago. Pain is poorly localized, felt diffusely in upper and
                 lower back, dull in quality and most bothersome at
                 night. Diagnosis of back pain and referred to Spine
                 Center for further therapy.

<u>Spine Center</u>:

2/13/YR-1        Patient seen over ten times over a twelve week period
to 4/9/YR-1      for evaluation and treatment. Diagnosis of cervical de-
                 rangement, and lumbar derangement. (Report of 4/9/
                 YR-1 states resolved cervical and lumbar
                 derangement).

<u>Norville Chiropractic Center</u>:

2/16/YR-1        (Patient underwent 14 therapy sessions, consisting of
to 4/13/         electrical muscle stimulation, manipulation, and
YR-1             ultrasound.)

<u>Midtown Family Medicine</u>:

10/28/YR-1       Patient's back pain has resolved, but she has continued
                 to have discomfort in her left foot and ankle that be-
                 comes aggravated with activity as well as decreased
                 dorsiflexion in the left ankle . . . . It is my impression
                 that the persistent symptoms are related to the initial
                 accident on 8/11/YR-2. If she continues to have persis-
                 tent pain, I believe she will need further evaluation
                 with left foot and ankle x-rays and would strongly rec-
                 ommend further evaluation by an orthopedist.

<u>SPECIAL DAMAGES</u>

<u>A. Medical Expenses</u>

Orange County EMS                                    $ 400
Rolland Hospital                                     $1,500

| Midtown Family Medicine | $ 400 |
| Spine Center | $1,000 |
| Comprehensive PT Center | $1,400 |
| Norville Chiropractic Center | $1,300 |
| Total Medical Bills: | $6,000 |

### B. Lost Income

Ms. French is self-employed as the sole instructor in "French's Aerobic Dance & Fitness Studio," which she has owned and operated for the past eight years. She is married, and her husband is a lieutenant in the Oxford Police Department. At the time of the collision, she was 38 years old.

From August 12, YR-2 to September 12, YR-2, she was forced to cancel all of her aerobics classes. These are group classes with approximately 10 students in each group. She has two group classes a day (one hour each session) four days a week. Each student pays a $20 fee per one-hour session. Thus, in the four weeks from August 12 to September 12, YR-2, Ms. French's gross lost income totaled $6,400 (*i.e.*, 10 students per group/session × 2 groups/sessions per day = 20 students per day × $20 per student = $400 per day × 4 days per week = $1,600 per week × 4 weeks = $6,400). In addition, from September 13, YR-2 to October 28, YR-1, she missed an additional 30 one-hour sessions for gross income lost of $6,000 (*i.e.*, 10 students per session × $20 per student = $200 per session × 30 sessions = $6,000). Total lost income: $12,400

TOTAL SPECIAL DAMAGES = $18,400

The foregoing shows that Ms. French's course of treatment spanned a period of eight months. Although her cervical and lumbar problems have resolved, she still continues to have periodic pain in her left ankle.

I am authorized to extend an offer to settle this case for $40,000. Again, I look forward to hearing from you after you have had an opportunity to review this claim.

Sincerely,
Counsel for Ms. French

---

### (5)  Hillsborough v. Hughes
### (Condemnation Case on Appeal)

On April 25, YR-3, the Town of Hillsborough filed a lawsuit condemning 79.767 acres of land owned by George Hughes for the purpose of building a reservoir for the Town's future water supply. The case was tried before a jury which, on December 30, YR-1, rendered a verdict for $323,073 as just compensation for the taking. On December 31, YR-1, the trial court entered a final Judgment in accordance with the jury verdict and, as authorized by statute, taxed an additional $9,500 against the Town for Hughes' expenses for expert witnesses and other costs. The Town has timely filed a notice of appeal to the State Court of Appeals, but the parties are interested in exploring a settlement of the case to avoid the delay and expense of an appeal and a possible retrial of the case.

The property condemned by the Town consisted of 79.767 acres of a 93.112-acre tract of vacant, undeveloped land located in rural, Cedar Grove Township. Hughes retained 13.345 acres of the entire tract after the taking. Where, as in this case, less than the entire tract is condemned, the applicable measure of just compensation is the greater of (a) the fair market value of the tract taken (the 79.767 acres), or (b) the difference between the fair market value of the entire tract (the 93.112 acres) and the fair market value of the remainder retained by the landowner (the 13.345 acres). Fair market value must be established as of the time of the taking which is the date of the filing of the condemnation action — in this case, April 25, YR-3. The jury's verdict of just compensation in the instant case represented the difference between the fair market value of the entire tract and the fair market value of the remainder.

At trial, Hughes called Charles Moody as an expert in real estate and timber appraisal. Moody testified that, at the time of the taking, the fair market value of the entire tract (93.112 acres) was $358,500, the fair market value of the parcel taken (79.767 acres) was $307,120, and the fair market value of the remainder (13.345 acres) was $33,500. In arriving at his opinion about the value of the entire tract and parcel taken, he employed a three-step analysis.

First, based on twelve comparable sales, he concluded that the average fair market value of properties similar to the Hughes' property was $2,500 per acre. These comparable sales included properties that had timber, and he assumed that the highest and best use of the Hughes' property was for residential development. Second, based on a "Forest Inventory Data Summary Appraisal Report" dated June 21 and September 25, YR-4 that he had received from a timber expert, Richard Bernard, Moody estimated that the separate value of the timber on the entire tract and parcel taken was $1,350 per acre and that an astute seller could obtain this per acre amount by selling the timber before putting the property on the market for sale. Third, he then added the separate $1,350 per acre timber value — a calculation that he characterized as "a lump sum adjustment for the timber contribution value" — to arrive at $3,850 per acre which, in turn, he multiplied by the 93.112 acres of the entire tract for a total value of $358,500 (rounded), and by the 79.767 acres of the parcel taken for a total value of $307,120 (rounded).

Stated another way, as he explained on cross-examination, Moody's $358,500 (rounded) total fair market value for the entire tract was calculated as the sum of $232,780 based on the average per acre price of the twelve comparable sales ($2500 per acre × 93.112 acres) and $125,701 based on the average per acre timber value ($1,350 per acre timber value × 93.112 acres). Similarly, the $307,120 (rounded) total value for the parcel taken was calculated as the sum of $199,418 ($2,500 per acre × 79.767 acres) and $107,685 ($1,350 per acre timber value × 79.767 acres). Because Moody did not attribute any merchantable timber value to the 13.345-acre remainder, he based its fair market value of $33,500 (rounded) solely on $2,500 per acre figure derived from his twelve comparable sales.

Hughes also called Richard Bernard, an expert in timber valuation, to testify about his June 21 and September 25, YR-4 appraisals of the timber on the Hughes' property that were relied upon by Moody. Bernard testified that, as of June, YR-4, the clear-cut value of the timber was $98,500, and as of September, YR-4, the clear-cut value was $160,000. If only a "selective cut" were done (i.e., only 51 trees per acre were removed and 70 trees per acre remained), the value of the timber on the 79.767 acres taken was $131,360 in YR-4. Bernard admitted that his valuations, inasmuch as they were made in YR-4, were not based on the time of the taking of April 25, YR-3, and none of his valuations were "to a reasonable degree of professional certainty or probability."

The trial judge overruled the Town's timely objections to all of the foregoing testimony by Moody and Bernard.

The Town's expert appraiser, Frank Leatherman, drew upon twenty-four comparable sales to appraise the Hughes' property. His opinion about the per acre fair market value was similar to the $2,500 per acre "base" value used by Moody, except that Leatherman valued the property as a whole and did not add on a separate, additional amount for the timber on the property. Leatherman concluded that the fair market value of the entire tract was $232,780 ($2,500 per acre × 93.112 acres), the fair market value of the parcel taken was $183,464 ($2,300 per acre × 79.767 acres), and the fair market value of the remainder was $49,376 ($3,700 per acre × 13.345 acres).

Notwithstanding the trial court's decision to admit the testimony of Moody and Bernard, the Court ultimately provided the jury with a legally correct jury instruction proposed by the Town as follows:

> The testimony suggests the existence of a certain amount of timber on the Hughes property on the date of the taking, and that this timber had some value. In determining the fair market value of the property, you may take into consideration all the factors you conclude affected the fair market value of this property on the date of the taking consistent with my other instructions. If you are persuaded that the existence of the timber on this property affected the market value, you may take this into consideration in your determination of the fair market value of the property. However, you may not add to the fair market value of this property the sales value of the timber that might have been or could have been removed from the property.

The jury's verdict of $323,073 was within $2000 of Moody's just compensation calculation of $325,000 (i.e., $358,500 for the entire tract less $33,500 for the remainder). In contrast, the verdict was $139,609 greater than Leatherman's just compensation calculation. His just compensation calculation was $183,464 for the tract taken, which is greater than his calculation of the difference between the value of the entire tract and the value of the remainder at $183,404 (i.e., $232,780 for the entire tract less $49,376 for the remainder).

On appeal, the Town would contend that Moody's and Bernard's testimony about the separate value of the timber on Hughes' property violated the so-called "unit rule" of valuation, which thus far has not been addressed in any appellate decision in the instant jurisdiction but has been recognized in the majority of other jurisdictions. Under this rule, in a condemnation case, an expert may not testify to the fair market value of timber or any other substance or commodity on the land and then add that value to the fair market value of the land itself as additional compensation for the taking. That is, the land must be valued as a whole, and not as the sum total of the values of different components or features of the land. Numerous cases in other jurisdictions have held that the admission of testimony that violates the rule constitutes reversible error and mandates a new trial. Moreover, Bernard's valuation of the timber was neither based on the time of the taking nor based on "a reasonable degree of professional certainty" as is required by the rules of evidence.

The Town contends that had Moody (and Bernard) not been permitted to testify to the separate value of the timber on the property in arriving at the property's value, Moody's ultimate just compensation calculation would have been based on $2,500 per acre. This would have established a value for the tract taken at $199,418 ($2,500 × 79.767 acres), a value for the entire tract at $232,780 ($2,500 × 93.112), and a value for the remainder at $33,362 ($2,500 × 13.345). Just compensation would then have been $199,418, or only about $16,000 more than Leatherman's just compensation calculation of $183,464.

On the other hand, Hughes would argue on appeal that (1) the unit rule of valuation has not been recognized in the instant jurisdiction; (2) even if the State Court of Appeals were to recognize that rule, Moody's consideration of the value of the timber on the property was limited to merely making an upward "adjustment" to the value of Hughes' property in light of the fact that it contained merchantable timber and therefore was more valuable than any of the twelve comparable sales Moody relied upon; (3) even though Bernard's appraisals of the timber were conducted in YR-4 and were not to "a reasonable degree of professional certainty," his testimony was not in admissible *per se* and the judge had broad discretion to admit it and allow the jury to accord it whatever weight the jury chose to give it; and (4) even if the trial judge erred in admitting Moody's and Bernard's testimony about the separate value of the timber, the error was harmless and thus "probably did not influence the verdict" under the applicable harmless error standard in light of the correct jury instruction that the judge gave to the jury about the extent to which the value of the timber could be considered in determining the fair market value of the property for just compensation purposes.

(Other general legal considerations about condemnation cases are found at § 11.10 of the main text.)

———

## (6) Joseph v. Peters
## (Medical Malpractice)

Matthew Joseph, 23 years old, filed a medical malpractice action against his podiatric physician, Dr. Andrew Peters, alleging medical negligence and an additional cause of action for battery. Prior to treatment, Joseph was an avid amateur triathlete who showed considerable promise in his sport. As a triathlete, he competed in events that combine swimming, bicycling, and running.

Joseph sought medical care from Dr. Peters on two occasions for treatment of acute pain at the insertion of the achilles tendon on the back of the right heel. Initial conservative treatment prescribed by Dr. Peters provided Joseph little, if any, relief. Treatment at Joseph's second office visit consisted of a steroid injection adjacent to the tendon insertion at the back of Joseph's right heel, and the application of an ambulatory, below the knee, fiberglass cast.

Feeling better one week after this treatment, Joseph removed the cast at home in order to resume his triathlon-training program. During the first training session after removing the cast, Joseph sustained a rupture of the achilles tendon that required surgical repair and several months of physical therapy and rehabilitation. Despite the surgery and subsequent physical therapy, Joseph continues to experience pain and limitation in his right leg. Physicians that have recently evaluated Joseph agree that he has a 15% permanent disability of the right leg and, as such, he will be unable to competitively compete in future triathlons.

Injection of steroid near the achilles tendon is a controversial treatment. In his complaint, Joseph seeks $20,000 for the cost of surgery and therapy following tendon rupture, $10,000 for lost income, $400,000 for past, present and future pain and suffering, and $250,000 in punitive damages. Dr. Peters' medical malpractice limits are $1,000,000.

---

### (7)　Kegnim v. Drake
### (Automobile Personal Injury)

Paul Kegnim, 28 years old, and Mary Kegnim, 26 years old, were married shortly after they graduated from high school. Both are intelligent but pursued no further schooling after high school. They have no children and live in a modest apartment. Throughout their marriage, they have made just enough money to make ends meet.

On June 1 YR-4, at dusk, Mary was driving Paul home from his work in their old pick-up truck. As Mary was driving north on Highway 54 (a two-lane road) and came upon the intersection of Highway 54 and Elm Street, she saw two cars that had apparently been involved in an accident and were partially blocking the intersection. She slowed her truck and, as the light at the intersection was green for the cars traveling on Highway 54, began to slowly turn to the right with the intention of going around the two cars in the intersection and continuing to proceed north on Highway 54. However, just as she turned to the right, her pick-up truck was struck from behind at approximately 15 m.p.h. by a sport utility vehicle owned and operated by Don Drake who was driving home on Highway 54 after work. The rear brake lights and turn-signal lights on Mary's truck were not working at the time, but these defects do not constitute negligence *per se* in the applicable jurisdiction. The impact broke the tailgate on Mary's truck and moderately damaged the front bumper on Don's vehicle.

Mary, Paul, and Don were all wearing their seatbelts. Although each of them was somewhat "shaken up" at the time of impact, none of them sought medical treatment that evening. The police officer who investigated the accident issued a citation to Mary for "improper vehicle equipment" for the non-working rear brake lights and turn-signal lights, and a citation to Don for "failure to reduce speed to avoid an accident" when he failed to slow down and rear-ended Mary's truck. Mary and Don paid off the fines for these traffic violations without having to make any court appearance.

Since YR-8, and continuing through the time of the accident, Paul was employed in the maintenance department at a local manufacturing plant, where he had health insurance for himself and his wife that essentially covered all medical bills except for chiropractic bills and nonprescription medications. He also had a life insurance policy through his employer that would pay Mary $150,000 upon his death. Paul's gross salary in YR-4 was $36,000 per year. Mary was not working at the time of the accident, but she had periodically worked as a cashier in a grocery store and had been actively looking for a full-time job as a cashier at which she could earn about $24,000 gross per year.

In YR-6, Paul had a kidney transplant. As a result, he has monthly checkups and takes medications to prevent kidney rejection at a total cost of $200 per month. These checkups and the monthly medical expenses are ongoing. Mary's only relevant medical history is that she severely dislocated her left knee about one year before the accident. She underwent physical therapy for that knee injury and says that, just before the automobile accident, her knee was "basically back to normal."

On the morning after the accident, Mary and Paul went to Rex Hospital because both were experiencing significant soreness. In addition, Mary's left knee was aching to the point that it was difficult for her to walk. Both were initially diagnosed with "cervical lumbar strain and sprain" and referred to physical therapy. Mary's medical record from Rex Hospital on the day after the accident also noted that she had pain in her left knee.

Thereafter, from June 1, YR-4 to the end of YR-1, Mary and Paul received extensive and fairly regular medical treatment from a variety of health-care providers. Both are still currently receiving periodic treatment, but medical records and bills after the end of YR-1 have not yet been obtained. A summary of the existing medical bills for Mary and Paul are as follows:

| Health-care Provider | Mary | Paul |
|---|---|---|
| Rex Hospital | $6,000 | $7,500 |
| Orient Acupuncture Clinic | $400 | $400 |
| Dix Hospital | $700 | $1,500 |
| Tri-County Orthopedics, P.A. | $500 | $800 |
| Physical Therapy, Inc. | $2,000 | $3,000 |
| Rogers Chiropractic | $2,200 | $2,200 |
| | $11,800 | $15,400 |

Mary's medical reports variously describe her as having anxiety; depression; muscle tension; muscle spasms of her back, shoulder, and neck; muscle strain; myofacial pain; chronic fatigue; chronic back syndrome; long-term headaches; left arm pain; and chronic left knee pain. Dr. Wu at Rex Hospital has given her a 5% permanent partial impairment rating to her back, and Dr. Jones at Dix Hospital has given her a 20% permanent partial impairment rating to her left knee. All x-rays and MRI tests were negative. Both doctors have also diagnosed Mary as suffering from "fibromyalgia" — a condition represented by chronic pains, spasms, stiffness, and fatigue in the back, neck, shoulder region, arms, hands, knees, hips, legs, and feet, also accompanied by anxiety, headaches, and sleep disturbance. One of Dr. Jones' medical reports expressly states that all of Mary's medical problems are directly attributable to the trauma of the automobile accident.

Paul's medical reports variously describe him as having chronic back pain; myofacial pain syndrome; muscle spasms in the back and neck; rib pain; shoulder pain; swelling and pain in the left ankle; constant aching; limited spinal mobility; and significant lumbar facet pain. Drs. Wu and Jones have also diagnosed Paul with "fibromylagia related to auto accident and not in any way related to kidney transplant or renal disease." One of Dr. Jones' medical reports states that "I feel the patient is 100% disabled from his occupation due to accident, and this is permanent." All x-rays were negative, but an MRI showed "minimal disc protrusion central and slightly to the left, T8–9 and T9–10 level."

Paul worked half time for one week after the accident, and he took off the remaining three weeks in June YR-4 by using up his accumulated vacation and sick-leave time. He had hoped that he could return to full-time work on July 1, YR-4, but his persistent neck and back pain prevented him from doing so.

Consequently, he was placed on temporary leave from his work (without pay) from July 1, YR-4 to the end of December, YR-4, and ultimately was terminated from his job effective January 1, YR-3. By March 1, YR-3, Paul's health insurance coverage had lapsed and his life insurance policy was cancelled because he was unable to afford the monthly payments. Since that time, he and Mary have had no health insurance and he has had no life insurance. Mary has not worked since the accident. From April 1, YR-3 to the present, Mary and Paul have been living on monthly social security disability payments.

On May 1, YR-1, Mary and Paul filed a personal injury action against Don. Don's answer to the Complaint denied any negligence on his part and alleged that Mary was contributorily negligent. (The applicable jurisdiction is a "pure contributory negligence" state, which means that contributory negligence on the part of a claimant — however slight — bars any recovery for the claimant as a matter of law). In addition, Don filed a counterclaim against Mary, alleging that her negligence in the accident proximately caused him to incur medical expenses in the amount of $200 and pain and suffering.

Mary, Paul, and Don have each been deposed, and the parties have engaged in other discovery. Don has received a copy of all of Mary's and Paul's medical records and bills through the end of YR-1, along with pertinent lost-wages information regarding Paul. Mary and Paul have received a synopsis of a report from Dr. Joel Smith who Don intends to call as a medical expert at trial. In this report, Dr. Smith opines that after reviewing the medical reports and bills for Mary and Paul: (1) Mary was not injured in the accident except for minor aches and pains that should have resolved within one week and for which reasonable medical expenses should not have exceeded $500; (2) Paul sustained only a relatively minor whiplash injury for which reasonable medical expenses should not have exceeded $2,000; and (3) fibromyalgia is essentially a fictitious medical condition which, to the extent it exists at all, exists "only in a patient's mind."

Discovery also revealed that Don had one doctor's visit on the day after the accident for which he paid $200, and his whiplash injury resolved in a few days. Don incurred no lost wages through his full-time employment as an Emergency Medical Technician and ambulance driver. His automobile liability insurance policy limits are $50,000 for each person, and $100,000 total for each accident. He has no personal assets to pay a judgment in excess of $100,000. The same automobile liability insurance carrier insures Mary, Paul, and Don. Property damage is not an issue.

----

## (8) <u>Lowe v. Interstate Feed Cooperative, Inc.</u> (Wrongful Employment Discharge)

Les Lowe is now 29 years old. After completing high school at age 18, he took a job with Interstate Feed Cooperative, Inc., where he worked until he was terminated on January 14, YR-1. By all accounts, he was a "satisfactory" employee throughout his approximately 10 years of employment with Interstate Feed.

Interstate Feed is a manufacturer and supplier of feed and fertilizer for commercial farmers. It has approximately 30 plants throughout the country, including the plant where Lowe worked in the State of Caldonia. As a "Coopera-tive," the company is owned by the thousands of commercial farmers nationwide who regularly buy their feed and fertilizer from it. The company is run by a Board of Directors which is elected by the farmers, and none of the employees of the company (except for the Chairman of the Board of Directors) is under a written contract of employment for a specified term. That is, all employees of the company are "employees at will" — which means that they may be terminated with or without cause and at any time, except that no employee may be terminated in violation of certain public policies declared by the State of Caldonia.

In Caldonia, it is a violation of public policy for any employer to discharge or terminate any employee in retaliation for that employee's testimony at a judicial or quasi-judicial proceeding, such as a proceeding to determine whether another worker who is terminated from his job or otherwise leaves his job is entitled to State unemployment benefits. For example, even in the case of an "at will" employee, if an employer fires such an employee in retaliation for his testimony against the employer at a Caldonia Employment Security Commission (ESC) hearing to determine whether another employee of the employer is entitled to unemployment benefits, the employee who is terminated in retaliation for his testimony is accorded a cause of action for "wrongful discharge." Under this cause of action (1) the employee claiming wrongful discharge bears the burden of proving that his testimony at the Employment Security Commission hearing was "a substantial factor" in the employer's decision to terminate him; (2) the employer bears the burden of proving (as a complete defense) that the employer would have terminated the employee even if the employee had not testified at the hearing; and (3) only if the jury finds in favor of the employee on both issues (1) and (2), may the jury award to the employee "actual damages" he sustained (i.e., that amount of money necessary to place him in the same economic position in which he would have been had the wrongful discharge not occurred).

When Lowe first began working for Interstate Feed, he worked in the Feed Manufacturing Department of the plant. In September of YR-3, he was transferred to a newly created department called the Feed Bin Repair (FBR) Department in which he held the title of Supervisor. This Department, which did not exist at any other plants owned by Interstate Feed, was an experimental project. Employees in the FBR Department installed, maintained, and repaired large metal feed bins at no cost to farmers who purchased the bins from Interstate Feed to store feed for their livestock. According to Lowe, Russ Reese who was the Plant Manager for Interstate Feed in Caldonia in YR-3, told Lowe that if the project was unsuccessful, Lowe would be transferred back to the Feed Manufacturing Department.

In January of YR-2, Gary Huttle, who had not previously worked at the Caldonia Plant, replaced Reese as the Plant's new manager. At that time there were, in addition to Lowe, two other employees in the FBR Department. These employees were Thad Archer (an elderly gentleman who essentially did odd jobs in the Department and was not actively engaged in the rigorous labor involved in installing and repairing feed bins), and Henry Sowler. On at least three occasions between January and November, YR-2, Huttle told all three employees that the FBR Department would have to be shut down if it did not become profitable.

In late November, YR-2, Randy Barker, a long-time employee in the Feed Manufacturing Department at the plant, tendered his resignation from Interstate Feed. Shortly thereafter, he filed a claim for unemployment benefits with the Caldonia ESC. To be eligible for unemployment benefits, Barker had to prove to the ESC that he did not voluntarily resign, but was essentially forced to resign due to unfair or intolerable working conditions imposed upon him by Interstate Feed.

In connection with his hearing before the ESC, Barker subpoenaed Lowe and two other employees at the Plant, Wayne Dolely and Tom Teeter, to testify on Barker's behalf. Barker's hearing with the ESC was scheduled for January 7, YR-1. The day before (January 6, YR-1), Huttle summoned Lowe to Huttle's office and said to Lowe in a brief, private conversation: "Don't let Randy Barker get you into any trouble." Lowe interpreted this remark as an effort on Huttle's part to induce Lowe to ignore the subpoena and not attend the hearing, or otherwise to testify in favor of Interstate Feed at the hearing. However, Lowe said nothing to Huttle or anyone else about Lowe's interpretation of Huttle's remark, and Lowe simply left Huttle's office after the remark was made.

The next day (January 7, YR-1), Lowe, along with Dolely and Teeter, showed up at the ESC hearing as commanded by Barker's subpoena. Lowe testified that Barker was a "first-rate employee," and that in Lowe's opinion Barker was forced to resign because Huttle imposed various excessive and unreasonable working conditions and demands upon Barker. Lowe left the hearing immediately after his testimony and did not hear the testimony of any other witnesses. The other witnesses who testified were Dolely, Teeter, and Huttle. At the conclusion of the hearing, the ESC Judge ruled that Barker was ineligible for unemployment benefits because he had voluntarily resigned and had not carried his burden of proof to show that Interstate Feed had essentially forced him to resign.

On January 10, YR-1, Henry Sowler abruptly resigned from the FBR Department. On January 14, YR-1, Huttle told Lowe and Thad Archer that in light of Sowler's resignation and the lack of profitability of the FBR Department, "higher management" at Interstate Feed had decided to close down the Department, and both Lowe's and Archer's jobs would be terminated effective the next day (January 15, YR-1). Lowe asked Huttle whether Lowe could be transferred back to the Feed Manufacturing Department (as Reese had promised), but Huttle told Lowe that there were no other current openings at the Plant. Lowe and Archer were given two-weeks severance pay. Archer did not ask for any transfer and decided to retire.

On March 15, YR-1, Lowe filed an administrative complaint with the Caldonia Department of Labor's Workplace Retaliatory Discrimination Division (WRDD), alleging that he was wrongfully discharged by Interstate Feed in retaliation for his testimony for Barker at the ESC hearing. The WRDD conducted an investigation but took no action in the case in light of Interstate Feed's claim that Lowe's job was terminated when the FBR Department was closed down for lack of profitability. On November 1, YR-1, as required by statute, the WRDD issued Lowe a "right to sue letter" which permitted him to file, if he wished, a lawsuit against Interstate Feed for wrongful discharge. This "right to sue letter" neither expressly nor impliedly indicated any opinion by the WRDD about the merits of Lowe's claim.

On December 1, YR-1, Lowe's attorney wrote to counsel for Interstate Feed, offering to discuss the possibility of resolving the case without litigation. The letter pointed out that (1) at the time Lowe was terminated, he was making $48,000 gross per year with Interstate Feed; (2) from January 15, YR-1 to the end of March, YR-1, Lowe had no income (other than the two-weeks severance pay which totaled approximately $2,000); (3) from April 1, YR-1 to the end of September, YR-1, Lowe received unemployment benefits of $1000 per month; and (4) since October 1, YR-1, Lowe has been working for a construction company at an approximate gross salary of $2,000 per month. The letter included appropriate documentation verifying these factual assertions.

## (9) **Mann v. Parsons University Medical Center** (Nursing malpractice)

Amy Mann is a 76-year-old widow of modest means. She is a retired elementary school teacher and spends most of her time engaged in various civic and charitable organizations.

Parsons University Medical Center is a renowned medical research institution at Parsons University. Nearly all of the medical research conducted at the Center is federally funded through grants given out by the National Institutes of Health (NIH). As a condition to receiving federal grants from NIH, the Center must comply with various safety and reporting procedures established by the Office for Protection from Research Risks (OPRR) of NIH. The purpose of these safety and reporting procedures is to ensure that persons who participate in clinical research trials are not negligently exposed to dangers that may harm them. Participants in clinical research trials at the Center are either patients at the Center's Hospital or volunteers who are paid a modest fee for participating in a research study.

On July 2, YR-2, Ms. Mann volunteered to participate in a research study conducted by the Mental Health Clinical Research Section for Late Life Depression at Parsons University Medical Center. She was not a patient at the Center and was in excellent physical and mental health. On the same day, in connection with the study, she underwent an MRI, which she had never had before. A young nurse inserted earplugs into Ms. Mann's ears; and even though Ms. Mann told the nurse that the ear plugs were not blocking out any sound, the nurse took no steps to ensure that the plugs were properly inserted to protect against the noise from the MRI. The MRI lasted one hour.

During the MRI, Ms. Mann experienced extreme noise from the machine, but she assumed that the procedure was safe. Within hours after the procedure, she began experiencing a continuous high-pitched ringing and humming sound in her ears, a symptom she had never experienced before. During the next few days, the ringing did not go away, and she therefore reported her symptoms and what had happened to Mr. Bobby Barnes, the research-study coordinator. Mr. Barnes told her that he had been concerned about the competence of the nurse on several occasions, and Ms. Mann later learned that Ms. Simone Poole, another volunteer in the study, had also complained to Barnes that the nurse apparently did not know how to properly insert the earplugs.

On July 9, YR-2, Ms. Mann consulted Drs. Steve Gatch and Harold Tofler at Tryon Hospital. They diagnosed her with "tinnitus secondary to noise exposure during [the] MRI at Parsons Medical Center." (Tinnitus is a persistent ringing, whistling, or humming sound in the ears). Follow-up examinations by Dr. Wendell York on July 24, YR-2 and Dr. Harold Pointer on September 21, YR-2 revealed that her tinnitus had not improved.

In March, YR-1, Ms. Mann consulted three physicians to obtain a final diagnosis and prognosis about her chronic tinnitus. Dr. Paula Mosley, Dr. Wendell York, and Dr. Carrie Jones all now confirm that her tinnitus is permanent. Each of them is of the opinion that the cause of Ms. Mann's condition stems solely from the MRI she received at the Center when she was provided inadequate hearing protection during the procedure.

Ms. Mann's medical bills total $900.00. According to standard mortality statistics, Ms. Mann has a remaining life expectancy of 10.6 years. The Center paid her a total of $100 for the four hours during which she participated in the clinical study.

---

## (10)  Martel v. Simba
## (Unfair Debt Collection)

This case involves a dispute between the Martel family and the Simba Rental Corporation. Although no complaint has been filed yet, the attorneys for the opposing sides have already discussed the case and are familiar with each other's positions.

On July 9, YR-2, Cindy and Mark Martel went to Simba Rental to rent a television. They signed one of Simba's standard "rental with option to buy" contracts for a 19" color T.V. The contract required weekly payments of $16.00 for 78 weeks. If the Martels wanted to purchase this T.V. at the end of the rental period, they could do so for a final payment of $55.00. Thus, total payments to purchase were $1,303.00. The contract had a blank for Simba to fill in the "cash price," but this was not completed. The T.V. the Martels acquired from Simba regularly costs about $350.00 at national retail stores. At furniture stores that cater to low-income customers who purchase by installment sales contracts, similar sets frequently cost about $600.00.

Things proceeded smoothly for almost a year, during which the Martels made a total of 50 payments at $16.00 each. Then, Simba did not receive two $16.00 payments from the Martels. Simba sent out one of its employees, Richard Johnson, to confer with the Martels. Johnson, who is 6'5" tall and weighs 240 lbs., went to the Martels' home on a Monday afternoon. Mr. Martel was not home. Ms. Martel, who is 5 feet tall and weighs 100 lbs., told Johnson that she was sure her husband had sent the payments, but if he hadn't they would send them at once.

On Thursday, after the mail revealed no payment from the Martels, Johnson went back to the Martels' home. What exactly happened then is in dispute, but everyone agrees that Johnson entered the house and took the T.V.

Ms. Martel says that on the Monday afternoon when Johnson first went to the Martels' home, Johnson told her that if the Martels didn't pay, he would be back to take the television. She told him that her husband left for work at 3:00 p.m., and that if Johnson came back he would have to come before 3:00 p.m. so he could talk to her husband. She said Johnson ended the conversation by repeating that if he had to come back, he wouldn't leave without the T.V. She says Johnson came back to her house after 3:00 p.m. on Thursday. She was there with her three year old son and a neighbor's child. Johnson knocked on the door, and her son went to the door and told her who was there. She says that the knocking then continued for at least five minutes before she opened the door and told Johnson to leave. He refused to leave. She closed the door and he started banging on the door again. Finally, she opened the door a little to tell him to leave. She then backed away from the door because she thought he was going to push her out of the way. She kept telling him to leave. He came in and unplugged the television and took it with him.

Ms. Martel was so upset that she called her husband to come home from work. When Mr. Martel got home, he discovered that the door had come away from the hinges in two places. The Martels called the police. The investigating officer, after talking to the Martels, went to the Simba office to talk to Johnson.

Johnson told the officer that when Johnson went to the Martels' house on Thursday, he knocked on the door just two or three times before a child came to the door. When a minute passed with nothing else happening, he knocked once more, waited, then knocked steadily for three or four minutes. When Ms. Martel finally opened the door, he told her that he had to take the T.V. She told him to come back when her husband was home, but he told her he couldn't wait. After a few minutes of discussion in this vein, she stepped away from the door, leaving it open. Johnson took this to mean that it was okay with her for him to enter. He went in, she again told him to leave, and he picked up the T.V. and left.

The police officer arrested Johnson and charged him with misdemeanor trespass, felony larceny, and misdemeanor malicious destruction of property. A criminal trespass is the entering upon the premises of another by one who knows that he is not authorized to do so, as where he enters in defiance of an order not to enter the premises. Felony larceny is the trespassory taking and carrying away of the personal property of another (where the property has a fair market value in excess of $1,000) with the intent to permanently deprive the possessor of the property. The offense occurs so long as the trespassory taking of the personal property is from the *possession* of another; ownership is not the key. The charges have come up for trial on three occasions but have been postponed each time at the defendant's request.

The Martels are considering suing for:

1) Intentional infliction of emotional distress
2) Damage to their door
3) Trespass
4) Unfair debt collection
5) Violation of Chapter 25A of the Retail Installment Sales Act (RISA).

The elements of the tort of intentional infliction of emotional distress are (1) extreme and outrageous conduct, (2) which is intended to cause and does cause (3) severe emotional distress. The term "severe emotional distress" means "any emotional or nervous disorder such as, for example, neurosis, psychosis, chronic depression, phobia, or any other type of severe and disabling emotional or mental condition which may be generally recognized and diagnosed by professionals trained to do so."

Unfair Debt Collection: If the Martels can show that in collecting the debt Mr. Johnson "used or threatened to use violence or any illegal means to cause harm to the person, reputation or property of any person" in violation of the Unfair Debt Collection Act, they would be entitled to (1) an automatic civil penalty of $2,000, (2) actual damages (*e.g.*, for damage to the door), (3) compensatory damages (*e.g.* for any intentional infliction of emotional distress), (4) at least nominal damages (*e.g.*, for any trespass), and (5) reasonable attorney's fees.

Violation of Chapter 25A of the Retail Installment Sales Act (RISA): If the contract between Simba and the Martels is found to be a "consumer credit sale" contract as opposed to a mere "rental" contract, RISA would apply to the contract. *See* General Statute Sec. 25A-2 below. Under the Retail Installment Sales Act (RISA), "[t]he finance charge for a consumer credit installment sales contract may not exceed: (1) Twenty-four percent (24%) per annum where the amount financed is less than one thousand five hundred dollars ($1,500)." In this case, if RISA applies, the "amount financed" for the Martels' television set would be $600.00 given that, at stores that cater to low-income customers who purchase by installment sales contracts, similar sets cost approximately $600.00. According to interest tables, if the contract is in fact a "consumer credit sale" of a television, and the cost of the item was $600.00, the finance charge for 18 months was well over the 24% permitted under the statute. That is, a 24% finance charge on a $600.00 item for 18 months is $120.38, but the Martels were paying a finance charge of $648.00 (i.e., $16.00 × 78 weeks = $1,248 ($1248-$600 = $648). The statutory penalty permitted for a violation of the Retail Installment Sales Act is given in Section 25A-44 below. As stated earlier, the Martels have made a total of 50 payments of $16.00 each.

### § 25A-2   "Consumer credit sale" defined.

A "consumer credit sale" is a sale of goods or services in which:

(1)   The seller is one who in the ordinary course of business regularly extends or arranges for the extension of consumer credit, or offers to extend or arrange for the extension of such credit,

(2)   The buyer is a natural person,

(3)   The goods or services are purchased primarily for a personal, family, household or agricultural purpose,

(4)   Either the debt representing the price of the goods or services is payable in installments or a finance charge is imposed, and

(5)   The amount financed does not exceed twenty-five thousand dollars ($25,000).

"Sale" includes but is not limited to any contract in the form of a bailment or lease if the bailee or lessee contracts to pay as compensation for use a sum substantially equivalent to or in excess of the aggregate value of the goods and services involved, and it is agreed that the bailee or lessee will become, or for no other or for a nominal consideration, has the option to become, the owner of the goods and services upon compliance with his obligations under such contract.

### § 25A-44   Remedies and penalties.

The following remedies shall apply to consumer credit sales:

(1) In the event that a consumer credit sale contract requires the payment of a finance charge not more than two times in excess of that permitted by this Chapter, the seller or an assignee of the seller shall not be permitted to recover any finance charge under that contract and, in addition, the seller shall be liable to the buyer in an amount that is two times the amount of any finance charge that has been received by the seller, plus reasonable attorney's fees incurred by the buyer as determined by the court. However, if the requirement of an excess charge results from an accidental or good faith error, the seller shall be liable only for the amount by which the finance charge exceeds the rates permitted by this Chapter.

(2) In the event that a consumer credit sale contract requires the payment of a finance charge more than two times that permitted by this Chapter, the contract shall be void. The buyer may, at his option, retain

without any liability any goods delivered under such a contract and the seller or an assignee of the rights shall not be entitled to recover anything under such contract.

(3) Any buyer injured by any violation of this Act may bring an action for recovery of damages, including reasonable attorney's fees.

---

## (11)  Monolith v. Sat-Lith[1]
## (Breach of Covenant Not to Compete)

Monolith, Inc. is a New York-based corporation with headquarters in White Plains, New York. Monolith is engaged in the manufacture, sale, and servicing of sophisticated, high technology lithographic/printing equipment, including computer-controlled laser printing for books, newspapers and magazines. C. Icon started the company in YR-30. It became a publicly held corporation in YR-20, but Icon has remained as President and CEO. Monolith has shown phenomenal growth since YR-20 and now has assets exceeding $750 million.

B. Clubb, a Texan, joined Monolith as an assistant design engineer in Monolith's RTP (Research Triangle Park, North Carolina) office in YR-25. Clubb demonstrated outstanding design expertise and an adroit ability to learn the finest details about the printing and lithographic business. Clubb designed Monolith's new plant that opened in Mebane, North Carolina in YR-19 and was made plant manager.

In YR-15, Monolith's research staff produced a technological breakthrough that permitted the use of long-distance phone lines that allowed point-source lithography printing from any location in the country. The process is unique and has a number of speed and cost benefits that promised to move Monolith to the forefront of U.S. companies in the field. Projections were that the new technology might eventually be responsible for more than fifty-percent of Monolith's profits. However, the process needed further development and application before it could bear fruit.

In YR-13, Clubb moved back to Texas to a new Monolith plant where the still-secret process could be further developed, tested, and marketed. Icon considered the project his/her personal project and Monolith has spent millions of dollars on the research and development of technology, marketing, and materials that will allow efficient trouble shooting and maintenance of production equipment.

However, Clubb recently tendered his/her resignation and gave Monolith two weeks notice. In a phone call to Icon, Clubb said s/he had just started an independent lithographic/printing company, Sat-Lith, that will use a newly developed process that relies on satellites rather than long-distance phone lines. Clubb developed the idea for the satellite technology after meeting N. Mallott, a design engineer. Clubb expressed regrets to Icon over leaving Monolith but said that s/he felt constrained at Monolith, particularly over Icon's commitment to the phone line technology. Clubb told Icon that s/he believed satellites are the technology of the future and that once the process is fully developed it will propel Sat-Lith to the front of the field.

---

[1] This role play was developed by Professors Neil Vidmar and Diane Dimont of Duke Law School and Professor David Cohen of the University of Texas (Austin) School of Law, and is reproduced in this book with their permission.

Icon became very angry during the conversation and threatened Clubb with a lawsuit. Icon reminded Clubb that Clubb's contract of employment with Monolith contained a "non- competition" clause, a covenant forbidding Clubb to utilize the proprietary materials of Monolith gained through employment with Monolith and forbidding employment with a competing business for two years after termination of employment with Monolith. Angry words on the part of both Clubb and Icon were exchanged before Clubb hung up.

Icon then learned through an informant that about six-weeks ago, Clubb made copies of what Clubb claims are "personal papers", including training and service manuals, technical specifications, and design and marketing materials. In fact, all of the materials came from Monolith's files. An independent company copied fifteen boxes of files of original documents. The originals were returned to the Texas Monolith plant. The copies were shipped to the Sat-Lith office outside Houston. Upon learning this information, Icon placed a call to Clubb and threatened a legal injunction to make Clubb return the copies.

Both Icon and Clubb have retained legal counsel on the matter but no lawsuit has been filed. Sat-Lith's attorney, Auston, called Monolith's attorney, Wrangle, to see if the dispute can be settled without a lawsuit. Icon reluctantly agreed. A meeting has been set up between Icon and Clubb.

The relevant parts of the Contract of Employment signed by Clubb in YR-12 (after s/he had re-established domicile in Texas) are as follows:

(1) Whereas, Employee, in consideration of the agreements herein contained and the compensation to be paid to Employee, expressly agrees that Employee will not, for a period of twenty-four (24) months after termination of employment hereunder for any reason whatsoever, directly or indirectly as Employer, Employee, Stockholder or in any other capacity whatsoever, solicit, serve or cater to or engage in, assist, be interested in or be connected with any other form of corporation in the same or similar business of Employer soliciting, serving or catering to any of the customers served by Employee or by any other employee of Employer during the term of Employee's employment.

(2) Employee's employment is subject to termination at any time by Employer Monolith, Inc.

(3) Employee . . . expressly agrees upon employment to maintain as confidential and proprietary all material — service manuals, diagrams, schematics, and other compilations — specifically designated as confidential and proprietary. Upon termination of employment with Monolith, Employee expressly agrees to return to Monolith all property then in Employee's possession . . . [and] not retain any copies or reproductions of materials entrusted to Employee during period of employment.

(4) New York law shall govern the interpretation and enforcement of this contract.

[The contract also included provisions giving Clubb a promotion and raise in salary].

Decisions in the following cases are relevant to consider: Travel Masters, Inc., et. al. v. Star Tours, Inc., 827 S.W.2d 830 (Tex. 1991); Picker International, Inc. v.

Blanton, 756 F. Supp 971 (D. 1990); Desantis, et. al. v. Wackenhut Corp., 793 S.W.2d 670 (Tex. 1990); Light v. Centel Cellular Co. of Texas, 883 S.W.2d 642 (Tex. 1994).

---

## (12)   Seaver v. Excellent Pet Foods Co.[2]
## (Breach of Distributorship Agreement)

Excellent Pet Foods Co. is a privately owned company run by its owner and president, Bill Clowson from its headquarters in Atlanta, Georgia. The company manufactures pet foods for dogs, cats, fish, birds, and other domestic animals. It sells its dog food under the brand name Happy Pet.

Excellent has been successfully selling its Happy Pet dog foods throughout the southeastern United States for many years. Happy Pet is distributed directly by the Company through a series of regional and district warehouses.

Happy Pet is a premium dog food whose price tends toward the higher end of the range of dog food prices. Competition for shelf space in the dog food business is fierce. As a product, Happy Pet differentiates itself from its competitors on the basis that its ingredients and formula provide a dog food that is more easily digested, especially good for dogs with food allergies, and breeds that tend to have flatulence. Happy Pet dog foods include specially blended foods for puppies, adults, and older dogs, as well as dogs with sensitive skin.

Bill has decided to expand sales of Happy Pet north into all of the United States east of the Mississippi River. He has no capital to finance the expansion, so he intends to break with company tradition and policy and use independent local dealers to distribute his dog food. Excellent has hired Jim Anderson as its new marketing director to head up this expansion. Jim's principle experience is with companies that distribute their products through independent dealers.

Bob Seaver was a salesman/truck driver for the distributor of another dog food. This distributor operates from Wheeling, West Virginia in a large territory that includes southeastern Ohio, northern West Virginia, and eastern Pennsylvania. Bob lives in Columbus, Ohio and runs the route that includes Columbus and southeastern Ohio. He has broken down his distribution area into driving routes so that he can call customers and solicit their orders in the afternoon and deliver the dog food the next day. It takes him two weeks to go through his entire route.

Bob is also required to travel on weekends to dog shows and present his employer's dog food at a booth. Bob is familiar with Happy Pet because Excellent also has a booth at dog shows in West Virginia where Happy Pet is distributed. Excellent's contacts have suggested to Jim that Bob is an intelligent, ambitious, hard working young man who might be interested in setting up his own pet food distributorship with the right product and some backing. Jim has visited a dog show and arranged to meet Bob.

After several meetings, Jim proposed that Bob become the distributor of Happy Pet for all of southern Ohio, including Columbus, Dayton, Cincinnati, and Marietta. Bob had asked for a territory that included all of Ohio, including the populous industrial cities of Toledo, Cleveland, and Youngstown. Bob argues that Ohio is

---

[2] This role play was developed by Richard J. Snider, Esq., and is reproduced in this book with his permission.

crisscrossed east and west by Interstates 90, 80, and 70 and north and south by Interstates 71, 75, and 77, making it possible to service the entire state from a single, central location in Columbus.

Jim tells Bob that Excellent has no current plans to expand into northern Ohio for at least the next year. Jim says that if Bob does well in southern Ohio during that time, Excellent may expand his territory to include northern Ohio. These statements are repeated and expanded in a series of letters and meetings between Jim and Bob, and later, in a more general way, at a meeting with Bill Clowson in Atlanta where Jim, Bob, and Bill shake hands on an agreement.

Bob agrees to set up a warehouse in Columbus, Ohio at his own expense from which he will he will distribute Happy Pet in a territory that includes all of Ohio south of Interstate 70 including Columbus. Bob organizes a corporation called Happy Pets of Ohio, Inc. Then, he leases a building and outfits it with proper shelving and materials handling equipment, including a leased forklift truck. Bob also leases a delivery truck. Excellent agrees to supply Bob with its dog food products and to provide a line of credit of $50,000 for the purchase of Happy Pet dog food, personally guaranteed by Bob and his wife. The line of credit is to be reduced $10,000 every six months, beginning one year after the commencement of the agreement.

A month after Bob has quit his job, opened his warehouse, and received his first truckload of dog food, the attached distributorship agreement arrives in the mail. The agreement makes no mention of Bob's option or right of first refusal to expand his territory into northern Ohio. When Bob asks about this, Jim tells Bob that Excellent's attorneys will not permit him to make a forward promise like that, but he reassures Bob that they have a handshake agreement on these terms. Jim reminds Bob that the entire plan was discussed and affirmed with Bill at headquarters just a few weeks ago, and therefore the very highest authority, the owner of the company, approved the deal. Jim tells Bob that he and Bill were roommates in college and have been friends for more than 10 years and that Jim knows that Bill is a man of his word who can be trusted to keep his promises. Jim also says that it would hurt Excellent's entire expansion plan if the company got a reputation for not honoring its commitments. Jim offers to put Bob in touch with other distributors who will tell him how well the company has treated them.

Bob is not sophisticated in these matters and, after what his lawyer charged him to set up his corporation, he decides he cannot afford, after all his other start up expenses, to ask his attorney to look over the distributorship agreement. In addition, he has already quit his job and personally committed himself on the warehouse lease, the fork lift lease, the truck lease, and $50,000 worth of dog food which he has no way to pay for except from the sales of dog food. He decides he has no choice but to sign the agreement without any changes.

Bob's distributorship initially does well. Almost all his old customers whom he knew from his route in southeastern Ohio with the other company agree to try his product. Their initial purchases give him strong cash flow. Encouraged, he hires an experienced salesman-driver from another dog food distributor already driving a route in southwestern Ohio to develop that part of Bob's territory. The new salesman/driver is also able to persuade most of his former customers to carry Happy Pet and again, there are strong initial sales. Bob gives up his route and hires a driver for it so that he can devote all his time to the office.

After the first blush, however, the business begins to deteriorate. Happy Pet sells poorly out of the retail stores. Bob's customers complain that it is an unknown brand and is overpriced. They suggest the company should advertise more and reduce its price. Some of his customers do not reorder, telling Bob that they have limited space to display dog food products and can only carry those that turnover rapidly.

Other customers complain that the new driver does not rotate the product when he makes his deliveries — *i.e.*, by failing to put the new delivery on the bottom and the older product on the top. They also say that sometimes he is a day or two late getting the delivery to the store. In addition, when Bob asks his driver about the sales display materials from Excellent that Bob gave him to use in the stores, Bob learns his driver has not set them up.

Excellent is also not satisfied. Jim keeps pushing Bob to increase sales. When Jim sends an agent to examine Bob's operation and territory, the agent returns with reports that there are complaints from retailers about stale food and late deliveries. Bob answers that this is a temporary problem related to the driver and will be solved as soon as he fires the driver and trains a new one. The agent also reports that he cannot find in the retail stores the sales materials the company has asked Bob to use, including sales brochures and free sample packs. Bob answers that he has already distributed all the literature and samples the company gave him when he started and that he cannot afford to buy more. Bob complains that no one in Ohio knows the product and asks the company to do some advertising. The company says it has been selling its product well without major advertising for years in its original territory and thinks Bob needs to be a better salesman, or better yet, that he should hire an additional salesman to develop his territory.

To improve his cash flow, Bob begins selling Happy Pet in some cities north of I-70 and outside his territory. Also, to make his sales appear as though they are increasing and to reduce the price he has to pay Excellent for dog food, Bob begins to sell Happy Pet to Happy Pet dealers in West Virginia and Kentucky. As a new dealer, Bob gets a special price. Also, his discount increases based on the volume he sells. The dealers outside Bob's territory get his special price and he keeps the volume discount. All of this, however, proves insufficient because the basic problem is that Happy Pet is a gourmet premium dog food that sells low volumes at high prices. Consequently, Bob begins to distribute another, more modestly priced dog food in his territory without saying anything to Excellent.

Bob's troubles reach a crisis at the end of his first year when Bob is not able to make the first $10,000 repayment on the line of credit note. In fact, Bob has been unable to pay for his deliveries for several weeks, and now owes Excellent more than $100,000, including the original sum borrowed. At about the same time, Bob learns at a dog show that Excellent has set up a separate distributorship in northern Ohio that includes some cities where Bob has distribution. Worse, he learns that this dealer thinks its territory also includes Columbus, Ohio, and that it has been offering Happy Pet there at a price lower than Bob's.

Twenty-two months into the 36-month distributorship agreement, Bob receives a certified letter from Excellent terminating his distributorship immediately, without notice. At a dog show the next weekend, he learns that Excellent has awarded his southern Ohio territory to the new, northern Ohio distributor. In addition, he learns the new Happy Pet distributor in his territory is the salesman/

driver who formerly worked for Bob. Worse, it becomes apparent to Bob as he travels his territory that his former salesman/driver must have a copy of Bob's customer list. A secretary overhears him express his concern in a telephone conversation, and then she tells Bob that she saw the driver copying the route books (which show the name of the customer, the decision making buyer at that retailer, and their history of purchases, as well as other proprietary trade information).

Bob consults his attorney. He feels that Excellent breached the distributorship agreement by not providing him adequate support, particularly advertising support. He also thinks Excellent's sales goals were unreasonable causing him to expand too rapidly. He is also upset that the northern Ohio territory was set up without first offering it to him as Excellent had agreed. He is especially angry that Excellent hired his former driver to run the new territory and that his former driver seems to have stolen copies of his route books.

Excellent, of course, says that it had every right to terminate the agreement. Bob was performing poorly, his payment history was laughable, he was distributing outside his territory and he was distributing a competing brand of dog food. That the new dealer is Bob's former driver is mere happenstance. The information he used to contact the stores could be found in any phone book.

Bob's lawyer suggests that both parties attempt to resolve their conflict before starting any litigation. Excellent's lawyer agrees.

The Agreement to distribute Happy Pet dog food that was entered into between Excellent Pet Foods and Bob Seaver for his Company, Happy Pets of Ohio, Inc. was as follows:

### AGREEMENT TO DISTRIBUTE HAPPY PET DOG FOOD

THIS AGREEMENT is made at Atlanta, Georgia this 10th day of November, YR-2, by and between Excellent Pet Foods Company of Atlanta Georgia, a Georgia corporation hereinafter referred to as "Seller," and Happy Pets of Ohio, Inc. of Columbus, Ohio, an Ohio corporation hereinafter referred to as "Dealer."

WHEREAS, Seller is in the business of manufacturing and marketing branded pet foods; and Seller desires to grant a distributorship for the sale of Seller's brand of Happy Pet dog food to Dealer and Dealer desires to operate a business to distribute Happy Pet dog food.

NOW, THEREFORE, in consideration of the mutual promises and covenants contained in this Agreement, the parties agree as follows:

1. Appointment: Seller hereby appoints Dealer as the sole and exclusive distributor for the sale of Seller's branded dog food products at wholesale.

2. Territory: The exclusive distributorship shall cover the following territory, to wit: all of that part of the State of Ohio south of Interstate 70 including all of the territory within the city limits of Columbus, Ohio.

Dealer agrees that Dealer will not sell any of Seller's dog food products in any other Territory without the prior written consent of Seller or the exclusive distributor in whose Territory the sale is contemplated.

Seller agrees to notify, in writing, all other distributors of its dog food products that Dealer has the sole and exclusive right to sell such products at wholesale in the

Territory.

3. Price: All purchase orders by Dealer shall be on forms furnished by Seller. Seller agrees to exert Seller's best efforts to supply Dealer's needs in the regular course of its business within three (3) days of its receipt of any order. All orders will be shipped freight prepaid to Dealer's business address by the most economical system of transportation selected by Seller.

The purchase price of the goods shall be established by the Seller. The price list currently in force is attached to this Agreement. Seller will give Dealer ten (10) day's advance notice in writing of a change of purchase price.

Dealer shall pay Seller net cash within thirty (30) days from receipt of Seller's invoice or shall be entitled to a five percent (5%) discount for payment within ten (10) days from receipt of Seller's invoice.

Dealer may return any products that are defective within fourteen (14) days of delivery thereof, and Seller shall replace all such defective products at Seller's expense with Dealer's next order.

4. Dealer Representations: Dealer covenants, warrants, and agrees:

Dealer is a corporation duly formed and in good standing in the State of Ohio.

Dealer will use its best efforts to market and sell at wholesale the branded dog food products covered by this Agreement in the territory specified during the term of this Agreement.

Dealer will maintain an inventory of the products at all times adequate to satisfy, for a period of ten (10) days, the demand therefore in the territory covered by this Agreement.

Dealer shall use such advertising material as Seller may, at Seller's option, require and will promote Seller's product in any manner Seller shall deem necessary.

Dealer will not sell products of a similar nature manufactured by the competitors of Seller within the territory or in any place within one hundred (100) miles of the outside boundary of the territory at any time during the term of this Agreement, or for a period of two (2) years after the termination of this Agreement, regardless of the cause of termination.

Dealer shall not at any time, except in performing the responsibilities of this Agreement, divulge, or use for the purposes of Distributor, any confidential or business information relating to the business affairs of Seller.

5. Seller Representations: Seller covenants, warrants, and agrees:

Seller is a corporation duly formed and in good standing in the State of Georgia.

Seller has not granted and will not grant, without prior written consent of Dealer, to any person, entity, or organization, the right to sell or market the products covered by this Agreement in the Territory covered by this Agreement and will not itself or by its employees or agents make any such sales.

Dealer shall have the right to use and, unless otherwise instructed by Seller, shall use the trade name Happy Pet, for the term of this Agreement. Dealer shall obtain necessary licenses, registrations with appropriate governmental authorities, and a telephone listing under the trade name in the territory assigned to Dealer. The trade name registrations including telephone numbers will automatically become the property of, and revert to, Seller on termination of this Agreement.

6. Training and Assistance: Seller shall furnish to Dealer, at Seller's expense, such assistance and instruction as Seller deems necessary or appropriate to assist Dealer in developing its business including not less than six (6) days of field training each year.

Dealer shall agree, and shall cause any associate, to participate in all training programs, seminars, and field training provided by Seller.

Seller shall furnish Dealer without cost all promotional and advertising materials and supplies set forth in the list attached to this Agreement.

Dealer shall obtain prior written approval from Seller of any advertising copy, promotional material, or other written or printed material used by Dealer in promoting sales of Seller's goods and not provided by Seller.

7. Term: The term of this Agreement shall be for three (3) years beginning on the date first written above and subject to the following:

Provided Dealer is not in default in this Agreement, Dealer may elect, by written notice to Seller at least sixty (60) days prior to the end of the original term of this Agreement, to extend this Agreement for one (1) additional year on the same terms and conditions including this right of renewal.

If Dealer is in default in any payment to Seller for a period of thirty (30) days after demand for payment from Seller or if Dealer defaults in performing any of the other terms, conditions, or promises of this Agreement, and continues in default for a period of thirty (30) days after written notice thereof, Seller shall have the right at the expiration of the ten (10) days notice of default, to terminate this Agreement upon giving written notice of the termination at the expiration of the notice period.

On the termination of this Agreement for any reason, Seller shall have the option to repurchase the products then in the possession of Dealer, and available for sale, at prices originally billed to Dealer plus actual freight on the shipment of them to Dealer, and with deductions from monies due or to become due to Marketing Agent under this Agreement. As to any of Marketing Agents products not repurchased by it within ten (10) days of such termination, Dealer shall have the right to dispose of such products in the regular course of its business.

Dealer shall have no right after termination of this Agreement to use the name Happy Pet or any similar name that may confuse or tend to confuse the general public.

8. Miscellaneous: All notices under this Agreement shall be in writing and shall be deemed to have been duly given on the date of service, if served personally on the party to whom notice is to be given.

Any and all claims or controversy that may be attributed to the contractual agreement and are not resolved by mutual agreement of the parties, including breach of agreement, will be settled by arbitration according with established rules utilizing the American Arbitration Association, and then judgment may be entered in a court of law.

If any legal action or other proceeding is brought for the enforcement of this Agreement, or because of an alleged dispute, breach, default, or misrepresentation in connection with any of the provisions of this Agreement, the successful or prevailing party or parties shall be entitled to recover reasonable attorney fees and other costs incurred in that action or proceeding, in addition to any other relief to which it may be entitled.

This Agreement constitutes the entire Agreement between the parties pertaining to the subject matter contained in it and supersedes all prior and contemporaneous agreements, representations, and understandings of the parties. No supplement, modification, or amendment of this Agreement shall be binding unless executed in writing by all the parties to this Agreement. No waiver of any of the provisions of this Agreement shall be deemed or shall constitute a waiver of any other provision, whether or not similar, nor shall any waiver constitute a continuing waiver. No waiver shall be binding unless executed in writing by the party making the waiver.

This Agreement shall be binding on and shall inure to the benefit of the successors and assigns of the parties to this Agreement.

This Agreement shall be governed and construed according to the laws of the State of Georgia.

IN WITNESS WHEREOF, the parties have executed this Agreement at the place and on the date first above written.

----

## (13)  Solomon Clinic v. Carr
## (Breach of Employment Contract)

The dispute between the parties is represented by the following pleadings:

| | |
|---|---|
| STATE OF NORTH CAROLINA<br>COUNTY OF DURHAM<br>SOLOMON CLINIC, P.A.,<br>            Plaintiff,<br>       v.<br>MOREY J. CARR, M.D.<br>            Defendant. | IN THE GENERAL COURT OF JUSTICE<br>SUPERIOR COURT DIVISION<br>YR-0 CVS 00871<br>COMPLAINT |

Plaintiff, Solomon Clinic, P.A., through its attorney, complains of the Defendant, Morey J. Carr, M.D., as follows:

### PARTIES
1. Plaintiff Solomon Clinic, P.A. ("Solomon Clinic") is a North Carolina Professional Corporation organized under the laws of the State of North Carolina. Solomon Clinic's principal place of business is in Durham, North Carolina.
2. Defendant, Morey J. Carr, M.D. ("Dr. Carr"), is a resident and citizen of the State of North Carolina, residing in Chapel Hill, North Carolina.

### JURISDICTION AND VENUE
3. Jurisdiction and venue are proper in this Court pursuant to N.C. Gen. Stat. § 1-75.4(5).

## FACTUAL ALLEGATIONS

4. In YR-2, Solomon Clinic and Dr. Carr began negotiations for Dr. Carr to work as a plastic surgeon for Solomon Clinic.

5. As a result of these negotiations, on August 29, YR-2, Dr. Carr entered into a written Employment Agreement ("Agreement") with Solomon Clinic to provide plastic surgery services.

6. Dr. Carr signed the Agreement and agreed to abide by its terms. The Agreement was effective on October 1, YR-2.

7. Among other things, the Agreement sets forth the amount and method of calculating Dr. Carr's compensation. The Agreement provides that Dr. Carr shall receive monthly advances based on her estimated net income, which the Agreement defines as income collected, less direct and indirect expenses and necessary tax withholdings. Any overages or shortages to the estimate are to be reconciled at the fiscal year's end. In pertinent part, the Agreement states the following:

> 3(a) The compensation for Employee [Dr. Carr] shall be determined by a formula based on gross fees collected by Corporation [Solomon Clinic] resulting from professional services personally provided by or attributable to Employee less Corporation's direct and indirect overhead and other costs of rendering such services . . . . Employee acknowledges that the determination of direct and indirect overhead and other costs among all physicians employed by Corporation requires some judgment and discretion on the part of the Corporation's Board of Directors and its management, and further may be changed or amended from time to time by the Board. All determinations regarding fees, costs and allocations of overhead expenses shall be made by Corporation in accordance with the compensation formula established by Corporation's Board of Directors for physician employees, and all such determinations shall be final and conclusive.

8. The Agreement further describes the calculation and payment of earned compensation at the close of Solomon Clinic's fiscal year, including the offset of advances. In pertinent part, the Agreement provides:

> 3(b) The amount of the monthly advances against compensation shall be subject to review and adjustment at the end of each fiscal year by Corporation, and at other times during the term hereof with the mutual agreement of Employee and Corporation. . . . In the event that Employee has received advances against compensation in excess of the earned compensation (said difference being hereinafter referred to as a "Negative Balance"), then such Negative Balance shall be reimbursed by Employee to Corporation within 30 days following the notification to Employee by the Corporation of the Negative Balance . . . .

> Anything contained herein to the contrary notwithstanding, in the event that Employee's employment with the Corporation shall at any time terminate for any reason, the Employee shall reimburse to the Corporation the Negative Balance within 30 days following the notification to Employee by Corporation of the Negative Balance.

9. The Agreement also provides that Solomon Clinic has the right, notwithstanding anything contrary contained in the Agreement and at any time during the term of the Agreement, to reduce the amount of monthly advances should it reasonably appear to Solomon Clinic or its management that Dr. Carr would have a significant

Negative Balance due to low productivity or collections if the current rate of monthly advances continued.

10. On August 3, YR-1, Dr. Carr notified Solomon Clinic that she would not be renewing her Employment Agreement upon its expiration on September 30, YR-1.

11. As provided under the terms of the Agreement, Solomon Clinic withheld Dr. Carr's August, YR-1 monthly advance due to a significant Negative Balance amounting to $132,367.00.

12. In a letter dated September 22, YR-1, Dr. Carr informed Solomon Clinic that she protested the withholding of her wages and further disputed any amount due and owing to Solomon Clinic under the Agreement.

13. According to the Agreement, however, Dr. Carr agreed that, upon termination of the Agreement for any reason, she would be obligated to reimburse to Solomon Clinic the Negative Balance within 30 days following notification to her by Solomon Clinic of her Negative Balance.

14. On October 4,YR-1, Solomon Clinic notified Dr. Carr in writing that her Negative Balance of $132,367.00 was due and owing. Dr. Carr, however, has not paid the Negative Balance of $132,367.00.

15. In addition, Dr. Carr agreed under the terms of the Agreement to refrain from practicing plastic surgery for a period of two years after September 30, YR-1 and within a 35 mile radius of and Solomon Clinic medical office (which offices are in Chapel Hill and Durham, North Carolina) after termination of her employment with Solomon Clinic for any reason.

16. Upon information and belief, Dr. Carr currently practices plastic surgery at the Surgery Institute of North Carolina located in Cary, North Carolina, which Institute is within a 35 mile radius of the Solomon Clinic offices located in Chapel Hill and Durham, North Carolina.

## COUNT ONE — BREACH OF EMPLOYMENT AGREEMENT

17. Dr. Carr entered into a valid employment agreement with Solomon Clinic.

18. Solomon Clinic has demanded payment from Dr. Carr for her Negative Balance as provided under the terms of the Agreement, and the Clinic has performed all conditions precedent to Dr. Carr's performance of the Agreement.

19. Dr. Carr has failed and continues to refuse to repay to Solomon Clinic her Negative Balance as provided under the terms and conditions of the Agreement.

20. Dr. Carr has violated and continues to violate the express terms of the Agreement by practicing plastic surgery within two years after September 30, YR-1 and within a 35 mile radius of Solomon Clinic's two offices.

21. Dr. Carr has therefore breached the express terms and conditions of the Agreement.

22. As a direct and proximate result of Dr. Carr's breach of the Agreement, Solomon Clinic has incurred monetary damages in the amount of $132,367.00.

23. Solomon Clinic and Dr. Carr entered into a valid written Employment Agreement containing a valid and enforceable restrictive covenant, wherein Dr. Carr, for reasonable consideration, agreed not to practice plastic surgery within two years and a 35 mile radius of any Solomon Clinic office following the termination of the Agreement.

24. Solomon Clinic will likely be successful on the merits of its claim against Dr. Carr for breach of the restrictive covenant contained in her Employment Agreement with Solomon Clinic.

25. Further, there is the likelihood that Solomon Clinic will sustain irreparable loss, and its rights will be violated unless a preliminary injunction is issued.

26. No adequate remedy exists at law to compensate Solomon Clinic for Dr. Carr's violation of the restrictive covenant contained in the Employment Agreement, therefore entitling Solomon Clinic to a permanent injunction.

WHEREFORE, the Plaintiff prays for relief as follows:

1. That pursuant to Rule 65 of the North Carolina Rules of Civil Procedure and N.C. Gen. Stat. § 1-485, Dr. Carr be preliminary and permanently enjoined from working for the Surgery Institute of North Carolina or any other plastic surgery practice for a two year period and within a 35 mile radius from any office of Solomon Clinic;

2. That Solomon Clinic recover from Dr. Carr damages in the amount of $132,367.00, plus interest;

3. That Solomon Clinic recover compensatory damages from Dr. Carr in an amount that includes, but is not limited to, damage for lost patients and reputation and other losses Solomon Clinic has incurred and will incur by reason of the breach of the restrictive covenant contained in her Employment Agreement, as shall be determined by the trier of fact; and

4. That a trial by jury be had on all issues triable.

| | |
|---|---|
| STATE OF NORTH CAROLINA<br>COUNTY OF DURHAM<br>SOLOMON CLINIC, P.A.,<br>Plaintiff,<br>v.<br>MOREY J. CARR, M.D.<br>Defendant. | IN THE GENERAL COURT OF JUSTICE<br>SUPERIOR COURT DIVISION<br>YR-0 CVS 00871<br>ANSWER & COUNTERCLAIMS |

Defendant, Morey J. Carr, M.D., through her attorney, answers Plaintiff's Complaint as follows:

1. Defendant admits the allegations in Paragraphs 1 through 10, 12 through 16, and 19 of Plaintiff's Complaint.

2. Defendant denies the allegations in Paragraphs 11, 17, 18, and 20 through 26 of Plaintiff's complaint.

### FIRST DEFENSE AND COUNTERCLAIM
### FOR BREACH OF EMPLOYMENT AGREEMENT

3. Defendant incorporates by reference all the admissions and denials in Paragraphs 1 and 2 above as if fully set forth herein.

4. Plaintiff and Defendant entered into an Employment Agreement on August 29, YR-2, which was effective on October 1, YR-2.

5. Pursuant to the Employment Agreement at Paragraph 3 (a), Plaintiff's Board of Directors was required to establish a compensation formula.

6. Pursuant to the Employment Agreement at Paragraph 6, Plaintiff was required to "furnish [Defendant] with an office, stenographic services, medical supplies and equipment and such other supplies, equipment, facilities, and services suitable to [Defendant's] position and adequate for the performance of [Defendant's] duties."

7. From October 1, YR-2 through September 30, YR-1, Plaintiff breached the Employment Agreement in that:

(a) Plaintiff's Board of Directors did not have or establish a compensation formula as required by Paragraph 3 (a) of the Employment Agreement, but rather based compensation on ad hoc decisions of accounting department employees who from time to time consulted individual members of the Practice when a question arose about compensation.

(b) Plaintiff did not provide facilities and services adequate for the performance of Defendant's duties as called for in Paragraph 6 of the Employment Agreement, in that, among other things, Plaintiff provided unsuitable support personnel, inadequate management services, failed to collect Defendant's billings, and otherwise generally failed to operate the business of the medical practice in an efficient, reasonable, and competent manner adequate for the performance of Defendant's responsibilities.

8. As a consequence of these breaches of contract, Defendant was and is not obligated to pay Plaintiff for any "Negative Balance" as that term is defined in Paragraph 3 (b) of the Employment Agreement, and Defendant is entitled to recover damages from Plaintiff in the amount of Defendant's gross fees properly collected by Plaintiff less Defendant's share of direct and indirect costs properly allocated to Defendant by Plaintiff, which damages are to be calculated by the trier of fact.

## SECOND DEFENSE AND COUNTERCLAIM
## FOR FRAUDULENT MISREPRESENTATION
## AND CONCEALMENT OF MATERIAL FACTS

9. Defendant incorporates by reference all the admissions and denials set forth in Paragraphs 1 and 2 above as if fully set forth herein.

10. Preceding the making of the Employment Agreement and as an inducement for Defendant to make the Agreement, Ms. Clara Adkins, Administrator and Executive Vice President of Plaintiff's corporation and an agent, servant, employee, and officer of Plaintiff, negligently and/or intentionally made certain positive assertions and representations of material past or existing facts, which representations were recklessly or falsely made when Ms. Adkins made them and Ms. Adkins knew or should have known that such representations were false, intending that Defendant would rely on such representations, which Defendant did rely upon to her injury and detriment.

11. Preceding the making of the Employment Agreement and as an inducement for Defendant to make the Agreement, Ms. Clara Adkins negligently and/or intentionally concealed material past or existing facts, of which concealed facts Ms. Adkins had or should have had knowledge and which Ms. Adkins failed to fully disclose when there was a duty to disclose, and which were recklessly or falsely concealed when Ms. Adkins knew or should have known that such concealed facts were material to Defendant's making a decision to enter into the Employment Agreement, intending that Defendant would rely on the absence of disclosure, which Defendant did rely upon to her injury and detriment.

12. The misrepresentations of Ms. Adkins referred to in Paragraph 10 included but were not limited to statements that:

(a) Plastic surgeons in the Chapel Hill-Durham area customarily earn $250,000 to $350,000 per year and Defendant could expect to earn at least that amount within a reasonable time, and that Defendant would be one of the highest earning physicians in the practice.

(b) Defendant could expect to have a Negative Balance after the first 3 months of the term of the Employment Agreement but none at the end of the first year of the term of the Employment Agreement, excepting only special equipment purchases made by Defendant, which purchases Defendant could control.

(c) Plaintiff would manage all business aspects of the practice and would "pamper" Defendant by providing her with a receptionist whose primary responsibility would be to schedule Defendant's appointments, and by providing her a new office with new carpet, wallpaper, and furnishings.

(d) Defendant would have the benefit of offices in both Durham and Chapel Hill, and Plaintiff's other physician employees would provide internal patient referrals to Defendant which would be a "tremendous benefit" to Defendant.

(e) Plaintiff would "team up" Defendant with Dr. Joel Smith, a general surgeon in the Practice, and promote the team as a "breast reconstruction specialty" of the Practice.

(f) Plaintiff was "a very [financially] strong entity" capable of "carrying" Defendant until her practice was established.

(g) Plaintiff would make a "tremendous financial investment" in Defendant's practice, and Plaintiff would promote Defendant's practice by spending at least $5,000 on advertising and organizing seminars.

(h) The plastic surgeon previously employed by Plaintiff has done "very, very well [financially]."

13. On information and belief, the material facts referred to in Paragraph 11 that were concealed from Defendant and about which Defendant made inquiry but did not receive a truthful response included but were not limited to:

(a) That most doctors newly hired during the several years preceding Defendant's employment had Negative Balances after the first and often after the second and third years of employment.

(b) That the plastic surgeon previously employed by the practice had not done well financially, had left the practice under a cloud, and was in YR-2 engaged in litigation over his Negative Balance with the Plaintiff.

14. By reason of the foregoing, Defendant is entitled to void and set aside the Employment Agreement and to receive damages in an amount equal to the fair market value of her services to Plaintiff during her employment, which amount is to be determined by the trier of fact.

## THIRD DEFENSE AND COUNTERCLAIM
## TO VOID COVENANT NOT TO COMPETE

15. Defendant incorporates by reference all the admissions and denials in Paragraphs 1 and 2 above as if fully set forth herein.

16. This court has jurisdiction over this counterclaim pursuant to N. C. Gen. Stat. § 1-253 et. seq. and North Carolina Rules of Civil Procedure, Rule 57.

17. The Employment Agreement contains at Paragraph 22 a restrictive covenant prohibiting Defendant from practicing plastic surgery for two years within 35 miles of any medical office operated by Plaintiff, and Defendant is and has been practicing plastic surgery in Cary, North Carolina (which is within 35 miles of Plaintiff's offices) since the time of the termination of the Employment Agreement on September 30, YR-1.

18. This covenant is unreasonable as a matter of law as to scope, time and territory, and violates public policy by creating a risk of substantial harm to the public because of the public interest in the choice of selecting a plastic surgeon, the shortage of plastic surgeons in the restricted area, the potential impact of Plaintiff establishing a monopoly on plastic surgery services in the area, and the need for the availability of a plastic surgeon at all times for emergencies.

## FOURTH DEFENSE AND COUNTERCLAIM FOR VIOLATIONS FOR THE N.C. WAGE AND HOUR ACT
### N.C. GEN. STAT. § 95-25.1 et. seq.

19. Defendant incorporates by reference all the admissions and denials in Paragraphs 1 and 2 above as if fully set forth herein.

20. Defendant was a salaried employee of Plaintiff earning $10,000 per month, payable in arrears on the first business day of the month following the month worked.

21. Defendant worked the entire month of August, YR-1.

22. On and after September 1, YR-1, Plaintiff, wrongfully and without prior notice, withheld and refused to pay Defendant her wages for the month of August YR-1 in violation of N.C. Gen. Stat. § 95-25.6.

23. Defendant worked the entire month of September YR-1, and terminated her employment on September 30, YR-1.

24. On and after October 1, YR-1, Plaintiff wrongfully withheld and refused to pay Defendant her wages for the month of September YR-1 in violation of N. C. Gen. Stat.§ 95-25.7.

25. Plaintiff withheld Defendant's wages for the months of August and September YR-1 without proper authorization as provided in N.C. Gen. Stat. § 95-25.8.

26. By reason of the foregoing, Defendant is entitled to her wages in the amount of $10,000 each for the months of August and September, YR-1; and for damages as provided by N.C. Gen. Stat. § 95-25.22 in an amount equal to the wrongfully withheld wages, plus costs and attorneys fees — all as authorized by that Statute.

## FIFTH DEFENSE AND COUNTERCLAIM FOR VIOLATIONS OF THE N.C. UNFAIR AND DECEPTIVE
### TRADE PRACTICES ACT N.C. GEN. STAT. § 75-1.1 et. seq.

27. Defendant incorporates by reference all the admissions and denials in Paragraphs 1 and 2 above as if fully set forth herein.

28. Alternatively, the Employment Agreement between Plaintiff and Defendant constituted a joint venture between the parties and did not constitute an employer-employee relationship.

29. Plaintiff's fraudulent misrepresentations and concealment of material facts described in the Second Defense and Counterclaim for Fraudulent Misrepresentation and Concealment of Material Facts constituted unfair and deceptive acts and/or practices in or affecting commerce in North Carolina in violation of N.C. Gen. Stat. § 75-1.1 et seq.

30. Plaintiff's wrongful acts were intentional and undertaken for the purpose of deceiving Defendant and had a natural tendency to deceive and injure Defendant.

31. Plaintiff's wrongful conduct proximately damaged Defendant in that Plaintiff's acts deprived Defendant of her earnings and what she would have earned as a plastic surgeon but for the joint venture between the parties.

32. By reason of the foregoing, Defendant is entitled to recover actual damages to be determined by the trier of fact, plus treble the actual damages, plus costs and attorney's fees — all as provided by the Unfair and Deceptive Trade Practices Act.

WHEREFORE, Defendant prays the court as follows:

1. That this cause be tried by jury as to all issues triable before a jury;

2. That this court enter a declaratory judgment voiding the restrictive covenant or covenant not to complete in the Employment Agreement;

3. That Plaintiff have and recover nothing from Defendant and that the Employment Agreement be declared void and set aside;

4. That Defendant have and recover of Plaintiff damages for breach of contract as proved at trial and that the same be set off against any damages awarded to Plaintiff;

5. That the Employment Agreement be voided and set aside and Defendant have and recover the reasonable value of her services to the Plaintiff in an amount proved at trial;

6. That Defendant have and recover wages in the amount of $20,000 and damages in an amount equal to the amount of wages awarded plus costs and attorney fees as provided by statute, and that the same be set off against any damages awarded to Plaintiff; and

7. That Defendant have and recover actual damages for unfair and deceptive trade practices, that such damages be trebled, and that Defendant recover costs and attorney fees as provided by statute, and that the same be setoff against any damages awarded to Plaintiff.

––––––––––

Solomon Clinic timely filed a Reply to Dr. Carr's Answer & Counterclaims. That Reply admitted Paragraphs 4, 5, 6, 16, 17, 20, 21, and 23 of Carr's Answer & Counterclaims, and denied all of the other allegations.

The parties agree that none of the claims in the Complaint or in the Answer & Counterclaims are subject to dismissal for failure to state a claim upon which relief may be granted. They further agree that all claims are triable by jury, except that the issues of (1) the validity of the restrictive covenant (or covenant not to compete) contained in the Employment Agreement and (2) whether there has been a violation of the North Carolina Wage and Hour Act are solely matters of law to be decided by the Judge. Finally, the parties agree that each side has properly pled the correct measure of damages for the various claims.

————————

# Appendix B

## GENERAL SUGGESTIONS TO MEDIATORS FOR HOW TO MEDIATE A CASE

Because this book does not focus on how to mediate a case, which is otherwise covered in a "mediation" or "alternative dispute resolution" course, provided below are some general, step-by-step suggestions about how to conduct mediation if you are called upon to serve as the mediator in any of the cases contained in Appendix A. These suggestions should be read in connection with the discussion in Chapter 16 about what mediators do.

## [I]  Introductions and the Mediator's Introductory Remarks

At the outset of the mediation, in a joint session attended by all participants, introduce yourself as the mediator, and then have all participants introduce themselves to one another if they have not already done so.

After these personal introductions, you should make some brief (no longer than ten minutes) introductory remarks to all participants that describe your role as mediator and the overall mediation process. The following is an example of such opening remarks (after the personal introductions):

> The lawyers here are no doubt familiar with the mediation process, and they may have already explained to you a bit about what we will be doing. However, for those of you who have never participated in mediation before, I would like to take a few minutes to share with you my role and generally how the process works.
>
> Let me emphasize at the outset that I am completely neutral and impartial in this case. I have no first-hand knowledge about its facts or circumstances, [but I have read the pre-mediation materials that each side has provided to me]. My role in this mediation is to try to assist you in reaching a possible agreement. My role is to facilitate — not to dictate a solution or to serve as a judge in the case. In this process, you own the problem, the means for solving it, and any agreement you might reach.
>
> It is important to know that the mediation process is confidential. With very few exceptions, whatever is said or done here remains confidential, and cannot later be used by one side against the other in litigation. In addition, when one side shares information with me that they specifically instruct me to keep confidential, I am prohibited from revealing that information to the other side. Also, I am prohibited from revealing anything that goes on in this mediation to anyone outside of this room, unless all parties give me permission to do so or unless required by law. You should also know that, even though I am a lawyer, when I am serving as your mediator I am ethically prohibited from giving any legal advice.
>
> The format of what we will be doing consists of two phases: first, this initial joint session (and perhaps another joint session, if that might be useful); and second, private caucusing. In this initial joint session, I will give each side an opportunity to share whatever they would like to say about the

case, either through an opening statement by counsel or a statement made by counsel and his/her client. I may ask some clarifying questions after each opening statement or after we have heard all opening statements. At the conclusion of the opening statements, each side might also wish to ask some clarifying questions of the other. In this way, we can bring to the table at the outset as much non-confidential information as you might wish to share with one another.

In the second phase, the private caucuses, I will meet privately with each side. It is likely I will hold multiple private meetings with each side. These private sessions are often useful to clarify information, and to discuss your underlying interests, feelings, objectives, possible solutions to the dispute, and particular proposals that might resolve the case. It is during these private sessions that you might wish to share with me confidential information. Even though I am prohibited from disclosing confidential information to the other side without your permission, knowing such information often helps me better understand your particular interests and needs, and may lead to more mutually satisfactory proposals to resolve the case.

Please understand that the private caucuses might take some time, and the amount of time I spend caucusing with any one side does not mean that I favor one side over another. During the private caucuses, I might ask a number of questions and even play "the devil's advocate," so to speak — all in an effort to better understand your side of the controversy, and to help you evaluate whether your negotiating positions are realistic. Again, it is not my purpose to be judgmental or to dictate a solution to your case. But experience has shown that if ample time and patience are devoted to fully exploring all aspects of the controversy from the perspectives of both sides, the prospects for a mutually satisfactory settlement are greatly enhanced.

Finally, if a settlement is reached in the case, we will reconvene in a joint session at which I will detail the terms of the settlement, and we will agree upon any technical arrangements for executing the settlement. If, after giving this mediation process a fair chance to work, it appears that no agreement can be reached, it is my duty to declare an impasse. If that happens, that does not mean you might not resolve this case later on. Indeed, parties more often than not end up resolving their disputes by agreement even after an initial mediation was unsuccessful.

Before we begin, do any of you have any questions about my role or the mediation process?

## [II]   <u>The Parties' Opening Statements</u>

After making your introductory remarks, give each side an opportunity to make an opening statement. As a matter of common practice, usually the claimant is called upon first to make an opening statement. Unless it is absolutely necessary, it is usually undesirable to interrupt any side during their opening statement. If you need some clarification about the facts or have other questions about the circumstances of the case (*e.g.*, the status of any prior settlement discussions or the status of the litigation), ask about these matters either after each opening statement or after you have heard the opening statements of both sides.

After the parties have finished their opening statements, you may wish to give them the opportunity to ask clarifying questions of one another. Don't allow this to turn into an inquisition or cross-examination. The limited purpose of this opportunity is to allow the parties to exchange relevant information that they feel comfortable sharing in a joint session.

Sometimes, particularly when the parties deliberately take a non-adversarial and noncompetitive approach to the mediation, both sides may begin discussing or even negotiating the case during the initial joint session. If this happens, and for so long as it remains productive, there is no need to end the joint session and begin private caucusing. However, in most situations, you will find it appropriate to begin private caucusing shortly after the parties have completed their opening statements.

## [III]  **Private Caucusing**

In the vast majority of cases, mediators hold the first private caucus with the claimant. Then, after holding a private caucus with the opposing party, private caucusing continues with private meetings alternating between one side and the other for the remainder of the mediation. Sometimes, although rarely, you may find it useful to interrupt caucusing and bring the parties back together in another joint session. For example, this might be appropriate if the parties express a desire to reconvene in a joint session, or if exchanging certain information or discussing a particular proposal would be more efficient in a joint meeting.

Generally, you should use your private caucuses with each side to:

(a)   Ask questions to clarify the facts or obtain additional relevant information;

(b)   Ask about the parties' underlying interests or needs (*e.g.*, emotional, psychological, economic, physical, or social);

(c)   Listen to the parties without interruption, and allow them to vent if necessary;

(d)   Find out about the parties' primary, secondary, and incidental objectives, and the reasons for them;

(e)   Identify the issues;

(f)   Understand how the parties evaluate the case legally and factually, and what assumptions underlie those evaluations;

(g)   Explore potential solutions or proposals (both non-monetary and monetary);

(h)   Discourage the parties from disclosing their bottom lines (resistance points) to you until late in the mediation process after a number of proposals or offers, and counteroffers have first been fully considered;

(i)   Probe the reasons supporting particular proposals, offers, and counteroffers;

(j)   Discuss the risks, costs, and alternatives to not reaching an agreement;

(k)   Help the parties understand one another's points of view;

(l)   Play "the devil's advocate" or otherwise help the parties to evaluate whether their negotiating positions are realistic;

(m)   Clarify what information is to be kept confidential from the other side;

(n)   Make sure you understand the extent of the parties' authority to make or accept an offer or proposal;

(o)   Communicate to the parties the various proposals, offers, and counteroffers you are asked to communicate and, as appropriate, the reasons underlying them;

(p)    Suggest alternative potential solutions, if appropriate;

(q)    Give the clients and their attorneys ample opportunity to confer alone if they wish;

(r)    Engage in appropriate mediator tactics and techniques to facilitate a possible settlement (*see, e.g.*, Sec. 16.07 in main text).

## [IV]    Concluding the Mediation

If an agreement is reached, bring the parties back into a joint session. Then, carefully detail all terms of the agreement, and ask each side to confirm their understanding of those terms. Be sure to ask whether there are any other matters that need to be included in the agreement. Once all terms are understood, make sure the parties understand the steps that will be taken to effectuate the final agreement (*e.g.*, appropriate arrangements for preparing and executing settlement documents).

If the parties have not reached a settlement, it is usually desirable to bring them back into a joint session at which you might briefly summarize any points of agreement that have been reached by them. In addition, you might indicate that you would be willing to resume the mediation at some later time if the parties desire. Finally, you should thank the parties for their efforts, and express your hope that they might still reach a mutually satisfactory agreement at some future date.

# Appendix C

## PLEA BARGAINING ROLE PLAYS

### SYNOPSIS

---

__Note on Dates:__ YR-O means the present year; YR-1 means last year; YR-2 means the year before last, etc.

Your professor will provide you with the confidential facts for the role you are assigned to play in a particular case.

## (1)  __State v. Able__
## (Embezzlement)

On December 15, YR-1, the grand jury for Caswell County indicted Jona Able on three separate counts of embezzling a total of $15,000 from the Holy Congregational Church. He was arrested on December 30, YR-1 and released from custody on a $30,000 secured bond pending trial. Because numerous prominent citizens in the County are members of the Church, the charges against Able have been the subject of widespread publicity.

Able is 31 years old, single, and a self-employed certified public accountant. His parents are long-time members of the Church, and his father is a well-known orthopedic surgeon who has consistently donated large sums of money to the Church. Able grew up in the Church, and in the past had been a member of the choir and an alter boy. In college, he was a National Merit Scholar, and he has an MBA degree. By all accounts, he is known as intelligent, energetic, caring, and fun loving. The charges against him are a great shock to his family, friends, and the members of the Church. He has no prior criminal record.

The investigation that led to the charges against Able began in early October, YR-1, shortly after Able announced to the Church that he was going to take a solo biking trip across the country for the next six months. Because Able had been donating his services to the Church as a part-time bookkeeper (a position he had held without pay for over five years), the Church had to find a temporary replacement for him to handle the bookkeeping. Accordingly, the Church hired Mary Miles, another long-standing member of the congregation, to attend to the Church's books during Able's leave of absence.

In the first week of October, YR-1, Miles discovered some suspicious discrepancies in the Church's books. She reported this to the head pastor who, in turn, notified the police. Thereafter, an investigation conducted by various law enforcement agencies uncovered evidence that on September 4, September 20, and September 24 YR-1, Able had forged the pastor's signature on three of the Church's checking-account checks, had made each check payable to himself, and had deposited each check into his personal bank account. Each of the checks was written for $5,000.

Under the law in the applicable jurisdiction, each separate act by Able of depositing a forged check into his personal bank account constituted a separate offense of embezzlement. The Caswell County Prosecutor publicly announced that "the investigation is still ongoing and there may be further indictments against Mr. Able."

Embezzlement is a Class G felony. Under the jurisdiction's sentencing law, the court must include in the judgment of conviction (regardless of whether the conviction is by jury verdict or pursuant to a guilty plea) a specific term of imprisonment for each count in the indictment for which the defendant is convicted. However, the court may order that the prison terms run concurrently or consecutively, and may order an appropriate fine. In addition, the court may suspend any active prison term, in whole or in part, if the defendant complies with specified conditions of probation, which may include essentially any conditions or restrictions of any kind that the court deems appropriate (such as community service, house arrest with electronic monitoring, counseling, etc.). If probation is imposed in lieu of requiring the defendant to serve an active prison term, the court may require the defendant to serve the prison term set out in the judgment if he violates any of the conditions of probation during the probationary period set by the court.

In connection with the statutory mandate that the court include in the judgment of conviction a specific term of imprisonment on each count for which the defendant has been convicted (even if the court suspends the entire sentence of imprisonment by placing the defendant on probation), the court must select the term of imprisonment from one of three ranges of sentences: the "aggravated range," the "mitigated range," or the "presumptive range." That is, based on the evidence, other reliable information, and the stipulations of the parties presented at the sentencing hearing, the court must determine all aggravating and mitigating factors present in the case, with the prosecutor bearing the burden of proof by a preponderance of the evidence on any aggravating factors, and the defendant bearing the burden of proof by a preponderance of the evidence on any mitigating factors. If the court finds that aggravating factors are present and are sufficient to outweigh any mitigating factors, it may impose a sentence permitted by the "aggravated range"; and if the court finds that mitigating factors are present and are sufficient to outweigh any aggravating factors, it may impose a sentence permitted by the "mitigated range." (The court may consider any aggravating or mitigating factors that it deems reasonably related to the purposes of sentencing, and it must make specific, on-the-record findings of fact as to any aggravating or mitigating factors found.) If there are no aggravating or mitigating factors, or the aggravating and mitigating factors that are present do not outweigh one another, the court must impose a sentence permitted by the "presumptive range."

For each Class G felony, where the defendant has no prior criminal history, the statutorily authorized "aggravated range" is 13 to 16 months imprisonment; the "mitigated range" is 8 to 10 months; and the "presumptive range" is 10–13 months. Thus, for example, if the court chooses to sentence the defendant in the "presumptive range," it has the discretion to impose a term of imprisonment that is for either 10, 12, or 13 months. If the court sentences a defendant on three embezzlement counts for 12 months on each count, the defendant would serve 3 years in prison if the sentences were ordered to run consecutively and were not suspended subject to the defendant's compliance with specified conditions of probation.

The Prosecutor and Able's defense counsel have agreed to discuss a possible disposition of the case.

---

## (2)  State v. Devlin
## (Potential Capital Murder)

Last Thursday, YR-0, around mid morning, Debbie Falk and Sarah Steele, two college students at a small liberal arts college in Helena City, State of Helena, were taking a walk in the campus arboretum. David Devlin, another college student, who a number of students and professors say had been "acting very strangely" in the past few months, held up the two women at gun point and took them in his pick-up truck to a secluded area near Helena Lake. There, he released Sarah unharmed and drove off with Debbie still in the truck.

It took Sarah nearly an hour to reach the main road and find a telephone to call the police. After the police picked up Sarah and interviewed her, they obtained an arrest warrant on Devlin for second-degree kidnapping. Sarah told the police that when she was in the pick-up truck, Devlin was "terrorizing" her and Debbie with the gun by waiving it in their faces, was "wild-eyed and seemed to be foaming about the mouth," and kept saying that he was "going to kill Debbie."

The police immediately issued an "all points bulletin" on Devlin, and began a massive search to find Devlin and Debbie. The District Attorney for Helena County was notified, and she arranged for the State Bureau of Investigation to join in the search.

By early Thursday evening, the police had thoroughly searched the area within a ten-mile radius of the location where Devlin had released Sarah, but he and Debbie were nowhere to be found. Major TV stations carried news of the search and, by Friday morning, major newspapers throughout the State were reporting the story. This extensive media coverage was occasioned by the fact that Debbie was a gold-medal contender on the U.S. Olympic swim team. The search was expanded statewide, and authorities in the contiguous States of Selena and Norlina were put on alert.

On Friday morning, the District Attorney met with various officials from the college and Devlin's parents who all reported that in recent months Devlin had been exhibiting signs of progressively severe psychological disorders, but that he had been placed on certain medications which, it was hoped, would control his mental instability. The principal psychologist who had been treating Devlin opined that if Devlin did not take his medications, there was an appreciable risk that he might seriously harm or even kill Debbie. Devlin was 19 years old and had no criminal record.

Also on Friday morning, the District Attorney met with Debbie's parents. They were in shock, and they made it clear to the District Attorney that they didn't care about the outcome of any criminal case against Devlin so long as Debbie was found.

The massive search continued over the weekend, and the FBI was called into the case. With each day's passing, speculation has grown that Debbie might be dead. Finally, late yesterday afternoon (Monday, YR-0), a highway patrolman arrested

Devlin for driving drunk in his pick-up truck on a rural road in the northern part of the State of Norlina. Devlin was taken into custody in Norlina City and held without bond when the authorities there discovered he was wanted on the State of Helena felony kidnapping charge.

Upon being taken into custody in Norlina City, Devlin telephoned defense counsel in Helena City who immediately chartered a private plane and flew to Norlina. At 8:00 p.m. yesterday, defense counsel arrived at the jail where Devlin was being held. Just before seeing Devlin, defense counsel called the District Attorney in Helena City from the Norlina jail, and it was decided that she would immediately leave for Norlina City to be available to talk with defense counsel after he had conferred with his client.

After this telephone call to the District Attorney, defense counsel was permitted to meet with Devlin alone in a private room for as long as counsel wanted. The District Attorney from Helena City arrived at the jail in Norlina City shortly after 10:00 p.m.

It is now 12:30 a.m. in the morning (Tuesday, YR-0), and defense counsel has just come out from his meeting with Devlin, which has been going on for the past four hours. Defense counsel and the District Attorney are ready to sit down to talk.

In the State of Helena, "any person who shall unlawfully confine, restrain, or remove from one place to another, any other person 16 years of age or over without the consent of such person . . . shall be guilty of kidnapping if such confinement, restraint or removal is for the purpose of . . . doing serious bodily harm to or terrorizing the person so confined, restrained or removed or any other person." If the person kidnapped either was not released by the defendant in a safe place or had been seriously injured or sexually assaulted, the offense is kidnapping in the first degree and is punishable as a Class C felony, which carries a maximum term of imprisonment of 8 years for a defendant who has no prior criminal record. If the person kidnapped was released in a safe place by the defendant and had not been seriously injured or sexually assaulted, the offense is kidnapping in the second degree and is punishable as a Class E felony, which carries a maximum term of imprisonment of 3 years for a defendant who has no prior criminal record.

First-degree murder in the State of Helena is a Class A felony, punishable by death or life imprisonment without parole. The offense is defined as "a murder which is perpetrated by means of . . . imprisonment, starving, torture, or by any other kind of willful, deliberate, and premeditated killing, or which is committed in the perpetration or attempted perpetration of any . . . rape or sex offense, kidnapping, or other felony committed or attempted with the use of a deadly weapon." Any other kind of murder is murder in the second degree and is punishable as a Class B2 felony, which carries a maximum term of imprisonment of 20 years for a defendant who has no prior criminal record.

Upon a conviction or plea of guilty to first-degree murder, the court must hold a separate jury proceeding to determine punishment, and the proceeding is conducted essentially like a trial. The sentencing jury hears evidence from the State and the defendant, and is required to consider certain aggravating and mitigating circumstances to determine whether the defendant should be sentenced to death or life imprisonment without parole. The jury's decision on sentencing must be unanimous, and if the jury cannot unanimously agree, then the defendant must be sentenced to life imprisonment without parole. Among the statutory aggravating circumstances that the jury is permitted to consider are: "(1) that the murder was committed while the defendant was engaged in the commission of or attempt to commit any rape or sex offense . . . or kidnapping; (2) that the murder was especially heinous, atrocious, or cruel; and (3) that the defendant knowingly created a great risk of death to more than one person by means of a weapon which would normally be hazardous to the lives of more than one person." Among the unlimited mitigating circumstances that the jury may be consider are: "(1) that the defendant has no significant history of prior criminal activity; (2) that the murder was committed while the defendant was under the influence of mental or emotional disturbance; (3) that the capacity of the defendant to appreciate the criminality of his conduct or to conform his conduct to the requirements of the law was impaired; (4) the age of the defendant at the time of the crime; and (5) any other circumstance arising from the evidence which the jury deems to have mitigating value."

The State of Helena recognizes the defense of insanity, which, if proven by the defendant by a preponderance of the evidence, entitles the defendant to a verdict of not guilty by reason of insanity. Upon such a verdict, the defendant is committed to a mental facility from which he cannot be released until he shows by clear and convincing evidence that he would no longer create a substantial risk of bodily injury to another person due to a present mental disease or defect. The jurisdiction uses the so-called "M'Naghten test" of insanity. Under this test, "a person is insane if, at the time of his act, he was laboring under such a defect of reason, arising from a disease of the mind, that he (1) did not know the nature and quality of the act that he was doing; or (2) if he did know it, he did not know that what he was doing was wrong in the sense that, at the time of doing the act, he did not know the difference between right and wrong."

---

## (3)  State v. Tate
## (Child Sex Offense)

Morey Maze is the Director of the Bladen County Department of Social Services, which has a statutory responsibility to conduct initial investigations of potential child sex offense or child abuse cases. Maze has written the following DSS Report from her notes:

### DSS Report Re: Walter E. Tate (1/6/YR-0)

On 12/29/YR-1, I interviewed Melissa R. Tate of 611 Oakwood Lane, Clarkesville, who had come to DSS because of concern for her 11 year-old daughter, Clara. Melissa is 31 years old, a schoolteacher at Clarkesville Elementary, and was formerly married to Ronald S. Baker whom she divorced on 11/5/YR-2. Clara was born of that marriage. Baker contributes child support and has regular visitation with Clara.

Melissa married Walter E. Tate this past Xmas day. She has taken his last name, and had dated him for 8 months before the marriage. Walter is 36 years old, and teaches at Summerville Elementary School where he has taught since YR-10. He was living with Melissa at 611 Oakwood Lane until she told him to move out of the house on 12/28/YR-1 due to the events described below. Walter is now temporarily staying at his parents' house at 109 Bristol Drive, Summerville. Melissa and Walter have not spoken since 12/28. She says she wants no contact with him until all matters are resolved.

Melissa says that, on the evening of 12/27/YR-1, Walter went to bed alone. She later joined him in bed. They had no sexual relations that night, and she says that they otherwise have a "fairly normal" sex life. When she went to bed, Walter was asleep as far as she could tell. She "doesn't know for a fact" whether Walter woke up at any time during the night.

Melissa says that, around midnight, Clara came into her bedroom. Clara said she had a bad dream, and then crawled into bed between Melissa and Walter. After a while, Clara crawled out of the bed and went back to her bedroom. Sometime later, Clara came back and crawled into bed between Melissa and Walter again. Then, after another while, Clara went back to her bedroom once more where she remained for the rest of the night. Melissa recalls all of this vaguely, being "half-asleep the whole time." Melissa cannot remember any other occasion when Clara got into Melissa's bed when Walter was sleeping in the same bed with Melissa.

During the next morning, 12/28/YR-1, Clara acted "strangely shy, withdrawn, tearful, not talkative." There was no school that day. In the early afternoon, Melissa pressed Clara about what was wrong. Eventually, Clara told Melissa, "Walt rubbed me and stuff under my underwear last night; and then I felt his finger in me [pointing to her vaginal area]." Melissa says she got Clara to clarify that the "rubbing and stuff" occurred during the first time Clara got into Melissa's bed during the night, and that Clara felt Walter's finger in her during the second time she had gotten into Melissa's bed that night.

Later in the afternoon of 12/28, Melissa told Walter what Clara had said. Walter "blew up, got irate, said it was garbage, denied everything, and threw a fit." Melissa then told Walter to get out of the house. Walter packed up some things, said he was going to his parents' house, and left. Melissa told him she didn't want to see or hear from him "until all of this is over."

Melissa says she "doesn't think Walter is the type" who would do any harm to Clara. But, she says Walter had told her sometime in the summer of YR-1 that he once, "a long time ago," was accused of "fondling" a 10-year-old girl at Summerville Elementary, but he said the entire story was "garbage" and that nothing came of it. It is in light of this previous event, combined now with Clara's story, that Melissa decided to come to DSS today. (The prior event referred to by Melissa was apparently reported to this DSS office on 2/4/YR-1 under File No. 2-4-1-0012 by a school counselor at Summerville Elementary, but the file shows there was no follow-up because the girl left the school shortly after the event when her parents moved away to Yanceville and didn't want to talk with DSS).

I interviewed Clara on 12/30/YR-1 with Melissa's permission. The interview was conducted alone with Clara and was videotaped by a hidden camera on the back wall of the room. After small talk about Xmas presents, ice-skating lessons, and school, I asked Clara about the night of 12/27/YR-1. Clara didn't want to talk about it. Finally, she said she "had a bad dream . . . went to Mama's bed . . . Walt put his hand in my underpants . . . rubbed me and stuff . . . I got scared and went to my room . . . went to Mama's bed again later . . . then Walt, he put his finger down here . . . felt his finger in me down here [pointing to vaginal area]." Clara was quiet and tearful when saying this. When asked about her relationship with Walter, she just said, "He's ok." When asked about her relationship with her father, she just said, "He's funny." The interview lasted about 40 minutes. (See videotape).

On the afternoon of 12/30/YR-1, Melissa took Clara to her pediatrician, Dr. Sandra Jones, in Clarkesville. The physical exam showed no evidence of physical trauma.

On 1/2/YR-0, I phoned Walter at his parents' house, after having told Melissa that I would do so. Walter did not know Melissa had gone to DSS. He told me he wasn't going to talk; he said, "everything is garbage;" and he said, "I'm going to sue you if DSS does anything."

Also on 1/2/YR-0, I had a brief phone conversation with Melissa. I suggested she consider having Clara see a child psychologist. I recommended Lisa Popkin in Clarkesville. Melissa said she would think about it. I told Melissa we would probably send a DSS report to the County Prosecutor's Office.

On 1/3/YR-0, DSS had a staff conference on the case. As a result of the conference, DSS recommends that this case be transferred to the County Prosecutor for possible grand jury consideration.

*  *  *  *  *

*  *  *

On January 2, YR-0, shortly after receiving the phone call from Morey Maze of DSS, Walter Tate contacted the same defense lawyer he had hired when Tate had been accused of fondling the 10-year-old girl at Summerville Elementary School in February, YR-1. On January 4, YR-0, defense counsel contacted DSS about the status of its investigation regarding Clara, and was told that the matter had been referred to the County Prosecutor's Office. Defense counsel subsequently contacted the Prosecutor who has now provided counsel with a copy of Morey Maze's DSS Report. The Prosecutor has told defense counsel that she is considering referring the case to the grand jury, but is willing to meet with defense counsel before taking any further action in the case.

In the applicable jurisdiction, the crime of "taking indecent liberties with a child" prohibits any person "being 16 years of age or more and at least five years older than the child in question, [from] willfully taking or attempting to take any immoral, improper, or indecent liberties with any child of either sex under the age of 16 years for the purpose of arousing or gratifying sexual desire." Not knowing the age of the child is no defense. The crime is not unconstitutional for vagueness and is a Class F felony. A defendant convicted of the crime (whether by jury or pursuant to a guilty plea) must serve a mandatory-minimum active sentence of no less than 6 months before he may be placed on probation. The maximum sentence for the crime is 2 years for a first-time offender with no prior convictions. (The acts that Clara alleges Tate committed upon her fall within the acts prohibited by this crime).

The crime of "first-degree sexual offense" in the jurisdiction prohibits any person from "engaging in a sexual act with a victim who is a child under the age of 13 years." "Sexual act" is defined as "the insertion of any part of a person's body, other than the male sex organ, into another person's . . . vagina." This is a Class B1 felony, which carries a mandatory-minimum active sentence of 2 years before the defendant may be placed on probation, and the maximum sentence for the crime is 15 years for a first-time offender with no prior convictions. This is a "strict liability crime" and thus no mistake of fact about the age of the victim may be asserted as a defense.

Finally, the jurisdiction has the crime of "assault on a child under age 13" which, consistent with the common-law definition of assault and battery, (1) prohibits any person from willfully attempting to inflict any injury upon a child under the age of 13 so as to give the child reason to fear or expect immediate bodily harm, or (2) prohibits any person from intentional and wrongful or offensive physical contact with a child under the age of 13 without the child's consent. This is a Class 2 misdemeanor, carrying a maximum sentence of 30 days imprisonment. A defendant convicted of this crime may receive probation without serving any jail time. This is also a strict liability crime, so that any claim by the defendant that he made a mistake about the victim's age is not a defense.

The jurisdiction recognizes the defense of "unconsciousness," which may negate the actus reus of all of the foregoing crimes. That is, for a defendant to be held criminally responsible for any of the acts prohibited by the foregoing crimes, the commission of those acts must have been "voluntary." Thus, if the defendant committed any of the prohibited acts in a state of unconsciousness, as where he was asleep at the time, the requisite proof of the actus reus would not be satisfied because it cannot be said that acts committed by a defendant when he was asleep were committed voluntarily.

The State Supreme Court has held that all three crimes are separate offenses for double jeopardy purposes, and thus a defendant may be convicted and sentenced on each of those offenses for conduct arising out of the same facts. The court is given broad discretion in sentencing, including the discretion to impose sentences concurrently or consecutively, so long as any applicable mandatory-minimum active sentence is imposed and the sentence does not exceed the statutory maximum authorized for the particular crime.

A defendant convicted of either "taking indecent liberties with a child" or "first-degree sexual offense" is required to be registered (for a period of ten years from the date of conviction or plea of guilty) with the sheriff in the county where the defendant resides. This registration includes the name, address, description, and photograph of the defendant, and the crimes for which he has been convicted. This registration is a public record that is included in the Statewide Police Information Network, and may otherwise be accessed over the Internet by anyone throughout the country.

# INDEX

[References are to pages.]

## A

**ABDICATION**
Negotiation technique, . . . 179

**ACTIVE LISTENING**
Interviewing client, . . . 33
Non-verbal clues, attentiveness to, . . . 33
Structuring of story by client, attentiveness to, . . . 34

**ADJOURNMENT**
Negotiation tactic, . . . 179

**ADMISSIONS, REQUESTS FOR**
Negotiating during litigation and, . . . 290

**ADVERSARIAL MODEL**
Advantages, . . . 161
Bargaining leverage, differences in, . . . 155
Competitive style and, . . . 158
Compromise stage, . . . 150
Cooperative style and, . . . 158
Defined, . . . 150
Disadvantages, . . . 161
Face-to-face negotiations (*See* FACE-TO-FACE NEGOTIATIONS)
Factors affecting utility of, . . . 153
Future dealings between parties or negotiators, . . . 155
Nature of dispute or problem, . . . 154
Other side's negotiating approach, . . . 154
Pressures to reach agreement, . . . 155
Resistance points, establishing, . . . 150, 199, 227, 231
Stages of negotiation, . . . 150
Target point, establishing, . . . 150, 199, 227, 231
Generally, . . . 151

**AGGRESSIVENESS**
Negotiating technique, . . . 179

**ANGER**
Negotiating technique, . . . 179

**ANNUITIES**
Structured settlements, . . . 358

**ANSWER**
Negotiating during litigation and filing, . . . 287

**ANTHROPOLOGY**
Negotiating, anthropological approaches to, . . . 139

**ANXIETY**
Inhibitors of communication, . . . 37

**ATTORNEY-CLIENT PRIVILEGE.** *See* PRIVILEGED COMMUNICATIONS

**ATTORNEY'S FEES**
Contingent fees (*See* CONTINGENT FEES)
Ethical considerations, . . . 27, 117
Fixed amount, . . . 117
General retainer, . . . 117

**ATTORNEY'S FEES**—Cont.
Hourly rate, . . . 117
Initial meeting with client, establishing fees during, . . . 27
Judgment, making offer of; treatment of attorney's fees, . . . 291
Rate of fee, . . . 117
Retainer fee, . . . 117
Telephone conferences, charging client for, . . . 28

**AUTHORITY TO NEGOTIATE**
Lack of or limited, . . . 186

## B

**BIAS AND PREJUDICE**
Inhibitors of communication, prejudices as, . . . 37

**BLAMING**
Negotiating technique, . . . 180

**BLOCKING TECHNIQUES**
Negotiations, . . . 182

**BLUFFING**
Negotiating technique, . . . 180

**BRACKETING**
Negotiating tactic, . . . 185

**BR'ER RABBIT**
Negotiating technique, . . . 180

## C

**CAUCUS**
Negotiation tactic, . . . 179

**CIVIL LITIGATION, NEGOTIATION DURING.**
*See* NEGOTIATING DURING LITIGATION

**CLIENT-CENTERED MODEL**
Decision-making model, . . . 11, 14

**CLOSED QUESTIONS**
Interviewing client
    Funnel technique, . . . 45
    Generally, . . . 42

**COALITION**
Negotiating tactic, . . . 181
Plea bargaining tactic, . . . 425

**"COLLABORATIVE LAW" AGREEMENTS**
Civil litigation, negotiations during, . . . 296

**COLLABORATIVE MODEL**
Decision-making model, . . . 13, 14

**COMMUNICATE, DUTY TO**
Ethical considerations, . . . 96

**COMPANY POLICY EXCUSE**
Negotiating tactic, . . . 181

**COMPETENT REPRESENTATION**
Ethical considerations, . . . 95

I-1

[References are to pages.]

[References are to pages.]

## J

## L

## M

[References are to pages.]

[References are to pages.]